# INTRODUCTION TO PERSONALITY

**Second Edition**

## HOLT, RINEHART AND WINSTON

New York  Chicago  San Francisco  Atlanta
Dallas  Montreal  Toronto  London  Sydney

# INTRODUCTION TO
## PERSONALITY

### SECOND EDITION

## Walter Mischel
STANFORD UNIVERSITY

**Library of Congress Cataloging in Publication Data**

Mischel, Walter.
    Introduction to personality.

    Bibliography: p. 515
    Includes indexes.
    1. Personality.   I. Title.
BF698.M555 1976     155.2     75-11626
**ISBN 0-03-089537-5**

Cover Art: From *Santa Monica, 1973* by Sam Francis. Grateful acknowledgment is made to the artist for permission to reproduce his work.

Grateful acknowledgment is made for photographs from the following sources:

Aureon Institute, p. 277
Authenticated News International, pp. 114, 510
Ilona Baldassano, p. 403
Jon Brenneis from *Scientific American*, p. 477
L. Courteville—Agence TOP, p. 47
Russell Dian, p. 341
Benedict J. Fernandez, p. 376
Bob Fletcher, p. 474
Rapho Guillimette, p. 354
Steve Hurwitz, pp. 127, 470
Iris Kleinman, p. 90
Hank Kranzler, pp. 82, 300
Tony Pacheco, Authenticated News International, p. 219
Carl Purcell, National Education Association, p. 77
Sal Rovetto, p. 160
Arthur Singer, p. 249
Rick Smolan, pp. 77, 106, 189, 252, 501
Suzanne Szasz, pp. 193, 314
Vista, pp. 35, 423
Fred Weiss, pp. 15, 49, 67, 293, 331

For permission to reprint from copyright material, the author is indebted to the
    following:

Aldus Books. Table 3-4. From *Man and His Symbols* by Carl G. Jung. Copyright
    1964 Aldus Books.

(continued p. 575)

*To my parents*

# PREFACE
## to First Edition

This book is an introduction to major approaches, methods, and findings in the field of personality. It presents an overview of basic theories, strategies, issues, and conclusions in the psychological study of personality.

Traditionally, students have been introduced to personality psychology by reading about the ideas of major theorists. Theoretical orientations to personality study, in my view, are a necessary beginning but not an end in themselves. To offer a theoretical overview and historical perspective this book begins with a survey of the basic concepts and assumptions that major approaches share, and the fundamental differences between them.

But to go beyond an exposition of the alternative conceptions of personality proposed by different theorists, to move beyond views of man-in-general, also requires attention to tactics. The transition from abstractions concerning the possible nature of human beings to specific investigations of individuals is, after all, a chief difference between philosophy and psychology. Therefore this book surveys the distinctive tactics for personality study associated with each of the theoretical orientations discussed. A study of the methods that these orientations provide to assess people, and an overview of the results that come from these assessments, in turn should inform us about the strengths and weaknesses of the theories that guide the assessments.

It has long been fashionable to call personality psychology a young field and to profess how little we know about the mysteries of man. While no one can quarrel with modesty, in fact the field is quickly getting older and, fortunately, apologies for its youth and ignorance are becoming less necessary. Indeed, studies that clarify the value and limits of our theories are accumulating rapidly. In recent years empirical findings have been pouring in from many sources as more researchers are studying socially relevant behaviors, gradually illuminating the nature of personality processes and the causes of social behavior. It therefore is becoming possible now to introduce students of personality not only to the hypotheses of authorities but also to some of the findings and conclusions (albeit tentative) that are emerging. This book therefore includes an integration of research on various core topics of the field (such as identification, frustration-aggression, anxiety, defense, self-concepts— to name but a few). These topics are presented not as a catalogue of facts but in the hope of increasing the student's understanding of complex human behavior so that he may learn about its substantive nature and not merely about theoretical speculations. Wherever possible research findings, in turn, are related to the relevant theoretical orientations and methods, as well as to specific case examples, so that their implications for understanding basic issues become evident.

While some theories of personality address themselves to different phenomena and thus may co-exist and even be complementary, other positions are essentially incompatible. Perhaps the most lucid confrontations between theories, and the most dramatic tests of their utility, have come from studies of personality development and change, and of deviance and therapeutic behavior modification. In the context of the growth and modification of personality the theoretical problems of the field become especially meaningful and vivid, and the student can more easily see their implications. Consequently the text also includes some coverage of content often relegated to the fields of socialization and abnormal personality but only when the issues and findings influence basic conceptions of personality.

The four parts of this book are presented in a sequence that I hope will provide a coherent, integrated survey of the field. At the same time, the presentation was deliberately designed to permit the instructor great flexibility in selecting material for the specific objectives of his course. For example, the present progression from personality theories in Part I to personality assessment in Part II can be altered easily. Rather than reading all the theories in Part I first and then studying their associated assessment strategies in Part II the student can be assigned any one theoretical orientation and its relevant strategies as a single unit before he progresses to the next orientation and its methods. To maximize flexibility the parts and chapters were written to serve as self-contained units that can be assigned in almost any pattern, depending on the instructor's goals and the background of the students. For example, while theory-oriented introductions to personality might focus on Parts I and II, more research-oriented and advanced courses might put greater emphasis on the content of Parts III and IV. The accompanying *Instructor's Manual* provides objective and discussion questions to facilitate such a flexible use of the text.

It is a pleasure to acknowledge my debt to the many people who helped with constructive comments and careful readings of manuscript drafts. Some of the most valuable criticisms came from Gerald Davison, Rogers Elliott, Joan Grusec, Perry London, Peter Madison, Paul Mussen, Toni Raskoff, David Rosenhan, Carla Senders, and Jack Shaffer. The Instructor's Manual and the subject index for the text were meticulously prepared by Toni Raskoff, who also served as my most helpful assistant throughout this project. I am grateful to Darlene Lapham who performed the work of many secretaries and transformed endless yellow scraps into typed manuscript. My daughter Judith assisted with clerical work. My wife Harriet contributed to many aspects of the writing and, except for her own modesty, would be credited as the text's co-author.

*Walter Mischel*
*Stanford, California*

# PREFACE
## to Second Edition

In addition to taking account of the many new developments in the area, the second edition of *Introduction to Personality* includes some significant organizational changes. These changes are intended to increase the effectiveness and coherence of the presentation while retaining the basic structure of the first edition.

Part 1 still presents an overview of the theoretical conceptions provided by each of the major approaches to personality. Part 2, however, has been expanded substantially to survey more broadly the important applications associated with each theoretical approach. In the first edition, Part 2 was limited to the assessment strategies of each approach while the topics of deviance and personality change were relegated to a separate section at the end of the book (Part 4). The current edition, instead, integrates material on adaptation (the "healthy, fully functioning personality"), deviance, and personality change into Part 2 insofar as it fits with other applications of each of the theoretical approaches with which it is associated. Materials central to personality psychology from Part 4 of the first edition have been incorporated into Part 2 wherever relevant and Part 4 no longer exists as a separate section. This reorganization is intended to integrate more closely the links between theoretical conceptions of personality and their important applications, while avoiding overlap with abnormal psychology courses.

Part 3 (Personality Development and Basic Processes) continues to offer a systematic overview of major current research issues and findings. Changes throughout Part 3 reflect the vigorous growth of research in the field, including new developments in such topics as genetic antecedents, sex bias and sex-role stereotypes, aggression and televised violence, self-control (including biofeedback and moral behavior), and attribution theory. There also has been a flood of theoretical and empirical developments dealing with the role of the environment, the analysis of situations, the conceptualization of individual differences, and the interaction of the person with specific conditions. The growth of interest in these topics has been so great that a completely new chapter has been added to treat them in detail (Chapter 21, The Interaction of Person and Situation). In that chapter I also try to be explicit about my own theoretical preferences so that readers interested in the author's orientation can identify it easily.

The sequence of chapters can be adapted readily to emphasize even more the specific links between each theoretical approach and the research most relevant to it. For example, the following chapter sequences group the conceptions and applications of each theoretical approach with research closely connected to it:

|  | APPROACHES | | | |
| --- | --- | --- | --- | --- |
|  | TRAIT | PSYCHODYNAMIC | BEHAVIORAL | PHENOMENOLOGICAL |
| Conceptions | 2 | 3, 4 | 4, 5 | 6 |
| Applications | 7, 8 | 9 | 10, 11 | 12 |
| Research | 14, 15, 17, 20 | 15, 16, 17, 18, 19 | 13, 15, 16, 19 | 19, 20 |

The introduction (1) and the final chapter (21) cut across issues relevant to all the approaches. Of course, each of the research chapters also has some bearing on all the approaches, making conceptual overlap inevitable in Part 3, and permitting alternative groupings of that material.

*Readings in Personality* (edited by Harriet N. Mischel and Walter Mischel, published by Holt, Rinehart and Winston) provides readings from original sources in a sequence that parallels the present text's organization. The text is also supplemented by a new *Instructor's Manual* for the second edition, developed by Professor James Calhoun.

Preparation of the second edition was greatly helped by the thoughtful, detailed comments of many reviewers. Especially useful were the analyses of the manuscript by James Calhoun, Kent Houston, Robert Kaplan, James D. Laird, Alan Marlatt, Paul Mussen, and Susan Pepper. Susan Arbuckle prepared the index with diligence and care. The publisher's staff did much to facilitate the production of the work; Deborah Doty and Elyce Misher were consistently attentive and deeply involved in the manuscript's transformation into book form.

My wife Harriet remains a major force behind the book. She contributed continuously and significantly at every point in the work's development, from the first general conception of the organization to the last specific summary point.

*Walter Mischel*
*Stanford, California*

# CONTENTS

# INTRODUCTION
## TO
# PERSONALITY

**Second Edition**

# CHAPTER 1
# INTRODUCTION

## WHAT IS PERSONALITY?

Most thoughtful people have asked the question, "What is personality?" but few agree on an answer. The term "personality" has many definitions, but no single meaning is accepted universally.

### MANY DEFINITIONS—LITTLE CONSENSUS

In popular usage, personality is often equated with social adroitness and effectiveness. In this usage, personality is the ability to elicit positive reactions from other people in one's typical dealings with them. For example, we may speak of someone as having "a lot of personality" or a "popular personality," and advertisements for glamour courses promise to give those who enroll "more personality."

Less superficially, personality may be taken to be an individual's most striking or dominant characteristics. In that sense a person may be said to be a "shy personality" or a "neurotic personality," meaning that his most dominant attribute appears to be shyness or neurosis.

More formal definitions of personality by psychologists also show little consensus. Influential personality theorists tell us that personality is:

> . . . the dynamic organization within the individual of those psychophysical systems that determine his characteristic behavior and thought (Allport, 1961, p. 28).
> . . . a person's unique pattern of traits (Guilford, 1959, p. 5).
> . . . the most adequate conceptualization of a person's behavior in all its detail (McClelland, 1951, p. 69).

As these examples imply, there may be as many different meanings of the term personality as there are theorists who have tried to define it. Nevertheless, a common theme runs throughout most definitions of personality: "personality" usually refers to the distinctive patterns of behavior (including thoughts and emotions) that characterize each individual's adaptation to the situations of his or her life. Each theorist uses the particular concepts and language of his theory to carve a more specific formulation of personality. These different views of personality will become increasingly clear as we examine the concepts and findings of personality psychologists throughout this book.

## PERSONALITY AS A FIELD OF PSYCHOLOGY

Within the discipline of psychology, personality is a field of study rather than a particular aspect of the individual. No other area of psychology claims to cover as much territory as the field of personality does. Indeed personality study overlaps extensively with neighboring areas. The field of personality is at the crossroads of most areas of psychology: it is the point of convergence between the study of human development and change, of abnormality and deviance as well as of competence and fulfillment, of emotions and thought, of learning, and of social relations. The breadth of the field is not surprising because for many psychologists the object of personality study has been nothing less than the total person. Given such an ambitious goal, the student cannot expect to find simple definitions of what personality study includes.

## THE STUDY OF PERSONALITY

To study the "total individual" or the "whole person" may be a worthy goal, but it is a practical impossibility. To progress beyond recognizing and admiring the complexity of man, the researcher must select things about people that he can study. In practice, personality study deals with many aspects of the complex behavior of individuals. The term "behavior" is used broadly; it includes emotions and covert mental activities, such as thoughts or "cognitions," as well as overt actions.

Traditionally, personality study has been devoted to generating theories about human nature and individuality, and about the causes and meaning of important psychological differences among individuals. In this effort, many personality psychologists have tried to find the most enduring and stable human attributes. Much attention has also been given to measuring complex human behavior as objectively as possible and to discovering useful methods for studying individuals. In addition, personality psychologists study how people develop and change, as well as how they remain stable throughout the course of life.

## AN EXAMPLE

Consider these two cases: Wilson and Robinson both are college freshmen taking a large introductory course in economics. Their instructor returns the midterm examination in class, and Wilson and Robinson both receive a D grade. Right after class, Wilson goes up to the instructor. He seems distressed and upset: he perspires profusely as he talks, his hands tremble slightly, he speaks slowly and softly, almost whispering. His face is flushed and he appears to be on the verge of tears. He apologizes for his "poor performance" and seems to accuse himself bitterly. "I really have no good excuse—it was so stupid of me—I just don't know how I could have done such a sloppy job." He spends most of the rest of the day alone in his dormitory, cuts his classes, and writes a long entry in his diary.

Robinson, on the other hand, rushes out of the lecture room at the end of class and quickly starts to joke loudly with his girlfriend about the economics course. He makes fun of the course, comments acidly about the instructor's lecture and seems to pay little attention to his grade as he walks briskly to his next class. In that class (English composition) Robinson participates more actively than usual and makes a few excellent comments that surprise his teacher.

This example illustrates what everyone knows: different people "respond" differently to similar events. Both students received a D; yet each reacted differently to the experience. Why? How consistent are these differences? Would Wilson and Robinson show similar differences in their response to a D in physical education? Would each respond similarly if he were fired from his part-time job? Would Wilson also be apologetic and self-effacing if he received a personal rebuff from a close friend? Will Robinson treat a poor grade the same way when he is a senior? What do the observed differences in the reactions of the two students to their grade imply about their other characteristics? That is, on the basis of what we know about them already, can we predict accurately other differences between them? For example, do these men also differ in their academic aspirations and in their past achievements and failures? Do they generally show different degrees of anxiety about tests? What might have caused such differences between them? How are such differences maintained, and how might they be changed? What else must we know about each man to predict what he will do next? Personality psychologists ask questions of this sort.

To grasp the range and nature of the events encompassed by the field of personality, we must examine what psychologists of personality do professionally, and that is the purpose of this book. In this effort we will survey major *personality theories*, focusing on their basic *conceptions* in Part 1 and on their *applications* for assessment and change in Part 2. Then we will examine research on *personality development and basic processes* (Part 3) to present an overview of what is known about the determinants and nature of personality.

## PERSONALITY THEORIES: CONCEPTIONS

Some personality psychologists are most concerned with theory and generate ideas about the causes and nature of "personality." Each theorist conceptualizes personality somewhat differently. Obviously, Sigmund Freud's view of personality, which emphasized unconscious motives, is very different from the formulations of an early behaviorist like John Watson, who stressed learned habits. Indeed the concepts employed by such widely differing theories may have almost nothing in common.

Some personality theorists believe that human behaviors have their roots in unconscious motives whose true nature is outside the individual's awareness and whose sources lie deeply buried in his distant past. Others focus on the current conditions of the individual's life and on his present relationships and experiences. While some theorists search for signs of wishes, attitudes, and character traits that are not directly observable, others attend to the person's overt actions—the things he visibly does—and seek to sample them as directly and precisely as possible.

A few of the many theoretical alternatives for conceptualizing the same behavior are shown in Figure 1-1. The same behavior—Jane's becoming tense in response to an exam scheduled for tomorrow—is open to diverse interpretations about the reasons underlying her upset. Is Jane's reaction a sign of her more generalized fearfulness? Is it a symptom of an underlying problem provoked or symbolized in some complex way by the exam? Is it part of a learned pattern of exam

**Figure 1-1** EXAMPLES OF ALTERNATIVE CONCEPTUALIZATIONS ABOUT THE MECHANISMS (REASONS) UNDERLYING THE SAME BEHAVIOR

| SITUATION | CONCEPTIONS ABOUT POSSIBLE UNDERLYING MECHANISMS | RESPONSE |
|---|---|---|
| Jane is at her desk preparing for an exam tomorrow. | Jane is a generally fearful person with diffuse anxieties. Jane really fears "success" and unconsciously wants to fail. Jane has learned to fear exams and has poor study habits. Jane's upset reflects her identity crisis about herself as a person. | Jane becomes increasingly tense and cannot study effectively. |

fears and poor habits for studying? Is it related to more basic conflicts and insecurities about herself?

The conceptualizations one generates about the meaning of behavior are more than idle games: they guide the ways we think about ourselves and the solutions we seek in efforts to better our lives. For example, if Jane's tension reflects unconscious conflicts about academic success and a fear that success would undermine her "femininity" (Horner, 1972), it might help her to seek better insights into her own motives. In contrast, if Jane's behavior reflects poor study skills, it might be better for her to learn ways of reducing exam-related tensions (e.g., by learning to relax) while also mastering more effective ways of studying.

Students are easily puzzled by a field in which different theorists may fail to agree even about the meaning of the same behavior. It may help, however, to recognize that lack of agreement in this instance merely means that the same events can be construed in many different ways. The events are tangible and real enough: nature goes on "minding its own business"; the events of life keep on happening no matter how people understand them. People behave and "do things" continuously, but the meaning of those actions and the reasons for them may be conceptualized from many vantage points and for many purposes.

In Part 1 of this book we will examine some of the major theoretical orientations to personality. We will survey some of the main ideas developed to describe and understand psychological differences among people, and we will consider the concepts that are central to diverse views of human nature. The range of these concepts is great. Included are ideas about our most basic human characteristics, about the motives and attitudes that may underlie actions, about the chief crises of life, about the conditions of experience that mold human values, beliefs, and choices, and about the processes and concepts through which people try to understand themselves and to make sense of the world.

When a theorist is developing his ideas, he often tries to extend them as far as possible. He attempts to explore their ramifications and their implications about as many facets of life as possible. He tests the limits of his ideas by probing their relevance for diverse areas. Such a stretching of concepts can be extremely fruitful for the builder of theories because it helps him to generalize and to see how far his ideas may apply. Thus the theorist may try to make his ideas about the "unconscious" or the "self" or "early experience" or "conditioning" serve to explain a host of different human phenomena. He may use one or two favorite concepts to deal with everything from love to hate, from birth trauma to fears about death, from deep disturbance to great achievement. While such an extension of ideas may help the theorist, the perceptive student must always ask, "Does it fit?" and "How does he know?" and "What would we have to do to discover whether he is right or wrong?" and "What are the consequences of thinking about it that way?"

Such an analytical, skeptical attitude is the essence of the scientific approach. It is a necessary attitude if we want to go beyond learning what different men say about human nature and personality to *testing ideas* so that we can discriminate between those that have no support and those that are worthy of further study, and so that we can develop better concepts whenever possible.

## PERSONALITY THEORIES: APPLICATIONS

To convert personality theories from speculations about man into ideas that can be studied scientifically, we must be able to put them into *testable* terms. It is basic to science that any position advanced, any conceptualization, must be potentially testable. This is what differentiates science from the simple assertion of opinions or beliefs. Perhaps the most distinctive feature of modern personality study as a science has been its concern with putting ideas into testable form and studying them empirically.

The process of converting personality study into a scientific discipline is beset by many hazards. Attitudes toward the systematic and scientific study of personality often are ambivalent. On the one hand, it seems fascinating to try to gain insight into the causes of one's own behavior and the genesis of one's own personality. But at the same time we may resist actually achieving such an understanding and seeing ourselves objectively. Many scholars feel that it does violence to man's complexity and "humanness" to study and "objectify" him in the framework of science. Instead, they suggest that perhaps the most perceptive and provoking studies of personality are found in great literary creations, such as the characters of a Dickens or a Dostoyevsky novel.

No one perceives himself in an entirely objective way. Thus while it may be fashionable to say in public that human behavior, like that of other organisms, is "lawfully determined," privately the laws of nature may seem to be operating on everyone except oneself. Subjectively, while other people's behavior may be seen as controlled by "variables" or "conditions," one's own important thoughts, feelings, dreams, and actions may seem to defy such control and to resist objective assessment.

Even within the field of personality psychology, there is a certain amount of resistance to "objectifying" personality. For every personality psychologist who believes that man must be studied under carefully controlled experimental conditions, there is another who believes that man can be understood only by investigating him under "naturalistic," lifelike conditions. While some personality psychologists commit themselves to quantitative, statistical techniques for gathering information from large groups, others rely on intuition and subjective judgments based on lengthy personal experience with a few individuals. While some urge us to concentrate on man's "peak experiences"—his moments of personal, spiritual, or religious climax and fulfillment—others prefer to systematically study simpler behaviors under conditions that permit a clearer analysis of causation—for example, the responses of a young child to specific instructions under the closely controlled conditions of a testing room in his school.

Different experts favor different techniques of investigation, but all of them generally share a conviction that ultimately theoretical ideas about personality and human behavior must be tested and applied. To test theoretical ideas, it is necessary to turn from theories to methods and applications. Therefore in Part 2 we will consider methods of personality study and assessment. We will describe the main methods of assessing persons favored by each theoretical approach and examine their relevance for understanding the individual. It will become evident that personality assessment does not just supply assessments of persons: it also assesses the ideas of the assessor—or more precisely, of the theory he follows. That is, efforts to measure and analyze behavior supply information not only about the people who are measured but also about the meaning of the tests and ideas used in the measurement process. What we learn about ten children from their answers to an intelligence test, for example, tells us something about the test and the concept of "intelligence," as well as something about the children.

Personality theories also may be applied to help improve the psychological qualities of our lives. Even people whose problems are not sufficiently severe to seek help from professionals still search for ways to live their lives more fully and satisfyingly. But what constitutes a "fuller," "more satisfying" life? Given the diversity and complexity of human strengths and problems, it seems evident that simple notions of psychological adequacy in terms of "good adjustment" or "sound personality" are hopelessly naive. More adequate definitions of "adaptation" and "abnormality," of "mental health" and "deviance," hinge on the personality theory that guides one. The theoretical conceptions in Part 1 provide distinctive notions about the nature of psychological adequacy and deviance. Each also dictates the strategies chosen to try to change troublesome (problematic) behaviors and to encourage more adequate, constructive alternatives.

Many personality psychologists are concerned about practical questions regarding the prediction and modification of behavior. They tend to concentrate on a search for useful techniques to deal with human problems and to foster more advantageous patterns of growth. In addition to having enormous practical and social importance, attempts to understand and change behaviors provide one of the sharpest testing grounds for ideas about personality. Insights gained in this manner are being applied in further efforts to help people. These efforts include different forms of psychotherapy, various special learning programs, and changes in the psychological environment to permit people to develop their full potential. Research on these topics informs us about the usefulness and implications of different ideas about personality change. The concepts and methods relevant to adaptation, deviance, and personality change are discussed at many points in Part 2.

## PERSONALITY DEVELOPMENT AND BASIC PROCESSES

The field of personality is moving away from global theorizing about the nature of man. While still pursuing theory, most personality psychologists now try to cast their questions in a form that permits them to be studied empirically. By going beyond abstract speculation and studying people empirically, they hope to discover the conditions that determine complex behavior and important differences among individuals. Much contemporary personality research therefore focuses on the role of specific social experiences and environmental events in personality development. Part 3 considers personality development and discusses research on the basic processes determining complex human behavior. Research in personality has investigated an almost unlimited range of topics.

For example, how does an individual gradually become a psychological "male" or "female"? That is, how does a person acquire a psychological sexual identity, a sense of being masculine or feminine, and the attitudes and behavioral patterns that differentiate him or her from the opposite sex? What are the effects of changing beliefs about male and female roles in society?

One pattern that regularly seems to characterize males more than females is "aggression." But what determines aggression? Is it an instinctual, natural response to strong frustration, or a socially acquired pattern? If, for example, man has an aggressive "killer instinct," would it help to provide socially acceptable "outlets" for aggression? Does watching aggression (for example, in ancient days in the Roman Colosseum or now on television and in movies and theaters) reduce the viewer's later tendency to be aggressive—or does it increase it? Given the pervasiveness of aggression and violence within individual lives and throughout society, the meaning of aggression and its potential control are topics of crucial social importance.

One of aggression's closest competitors for attention and study is "anxiety." Indeed it has become a truism that we live in an "age of anxiety" and that much of the time when man is not fighting he is worrying. How does anxiety develop, and what are its consequences for individuals who have it in different degrees? How do people cope with psychological pain and anxiety? In addition to fighting with others, the individual often seems to fight with himself and to become conflicted and anxious in the process. Different researchers have conceptualized such internal conflicts in different ways, for example by suggesting "unconscious defenses." If so, against what do people "defend," and how do they do it?

How does the individual develop from the helplessness and dependency of the newborn to the competence and mastery of the adequate, mature adult who manages to control himself and his environment to a considerable extent? In addition to engaging in all sorts of actions, people also generate concepts and theories about themselves. They evaluate their own actions, develop expectations about their own strengths and weaknesses, and, just like the scientist who studies them, try to understand and assess themselves. How does the individual develop concepts about himself, and how does he become a regulator and assessor of his own behavior? Indeed, how may the individual become a theorist about the meaning of his own personality and life? And how do the qualities of the person interact with those of the environment in which he or she lives to determine behavior?

# SUMMARY

1. To psychologists, personality is a field of study rather than a particular aspect of people. Personality psychology is a field of great breadth, overlapping the neighboring areas of human development, creativity and abnormality, emotions, cognition, learning, and social relations. This book is an introduction to the field of personality. It surveys personality theories and their applications, as well as personality development and basic processes.

2. Traditionally, much attention has been devoted to generating theories about human nature and individual differences. Personality theories differ in their degree of emphasis on the past and the present, the conscious and the unconscious, the directly observable and the relatively unobservable. The essence of a scientific approach to personality is to test various ideas, to evaluate the evidence supporting them, and to seek better ones. It is this potential testability of personality theory that differentiates a science of personality from the simple assertion of opinions or beliefs.

3. Major personality theories have important applications for assessment and personality change. They provide strategies for seeking information about people and for changing behavior in constructive ways. The widespread existence of psychological problems makes the search for effective strategies to improve the quality of life especially important. The successes achieved by these applications reflect on the value (and limitations) of the personality theories that guide them.

4. Contemporary personality research investigates the effects of experiences and events on personality and studies the nature and meaning of important psychological differences among individuals. Examples of the topics investigated include sexual identity, the determinants of aggression, the nature and causes of anxiety, the development of competence and mastery, the concepts and theories that people develop about themselves, and the interaction of the individual with the environment.

Part 1 provides an overview of major theoretical conceptions for the study of personality. The theoretical approach discussed in Chapter 2 emphasizes comparisons between persons with respect to their main psychological characteristics. A second approach to personality is most deeply rooted in the ideas of Freud (Chapter 3). Its origins are in the psychiatric clinic and the intensive study of disturbed people. Quite different is the approach that grows out of the experimental tradition in psychology (Chapters 4 and 5). The experimentalist is most concerned with isolating important cause-and-effect relations in the objective analysis of behavior by experimental methods. Especially in recent years, the ideas and procedures used by the experimentalist have shown increasing relevance for the study of people and for personality change. The final chapter of Part 1 (Chapter 6) discusses efforts to study the individual's ways of looking at the world. Here, the focus is on how people see or construe themselves and others, on how the individual comes to know himself and his world, rather than on his attributes and the causes of his actions.

# PART 1

# 1

# PERSONALITY THEORIES
# Conceptions

Part 1 introduces the reader to the central conceptions associated with each of these major personality theories and presents a broad overview of their central ideas as quickly and succinctly as possible. In later sections (Part 2) we will return to these basic conceptions and will elaborate each of them by examining their applications and consequences in greater detail and depth. The reader should be alert to the fact that the presentation of theories in Part 1 thus provides only a first glimpse, outlining the basic concepts of major personality theories; their specific applications for personality assessment and for personality change are presented in Part 2. Since the impact and value of personality theories to a large extent depend on their contributions to understanding and helping individuals, the richness—and limitations—of each position will not be entirely evident (and should not be judged with any finality) until the reader has studied its applications as well as its basic concepts.

# CHAPTER 2

# TRAIT THEORIES Conceptions

One of the most enduring approaches to personality seeks to label and classify people according to their psychological characteristics. Since the beginnings of language men have tried to describe each other by grouping the enormous differences among people into categories. This chapter discusses efforts to study personality by classifying individual differences into basic types and traits.

## TYPES AND TRAITS

In their early phases most sciences are concerned with *naming* things and *classifying* them into groups or categories in an orderly fashion. Such taxonomies are seen, for example, in the biological classification of living things into genera and species. In daily life people also categorize themselves on almost endless dimensions. Some of these involve overt attributes—for example, sex, race, nationality, occupation—while others require indirect inferences about hypothesized attributes—such as temperament, character, motives, attitudes.

## TYPES

Some categorizations sort individuals into discrete categories or *types*. In the ancient theory of temperaments, for example, the Greek physician Hippocrates assigned persons to one of four types of temperament: *choleric* (irritable), *melancholic* (depressed), *sanguine* (optimistic), and *phlegmatic* (calm, listless). In accord with the biology of his time (about 400 B.C.), Hippocrates attributed each temperament to a predominance of one of the bodily humors; yellow bile, black bile, blood, and phlegm. A choleric temperament was caused by an excess of yellow bile; a depressive temperament reflected the predominance of black bile; the sanguine person had too much blood; and phlegmatic people suffered from an excess of phlegm.

Other typologies have searched for constitutional types, seeking associations between physique and indices of temperament. Such groupings in terms of body build have considerable popular appeal, as seen in the prevalence of stereotypes linking the body to the psyche: fat people are "jolly" and "lazy," thin people are "morose" and "sensitive," and so on.

Formal classifications of the possible links between personality and somatic type were developed by the German psychiatrist Kretschmer and more recently by an American physician, William H. Sheldon. Sheldon's classification has received most attention. In 1942 he suggested three dimensions of physique, and their corresponding temperaments. These are summarized in Figure 2-1.

As Figure 2-1 suggests, the endomorphic individual is obese, the mesomorph has an athletic build, and the ectomorph is tall, thin and stoop-shouldered. Rather

Figure 2-1  SHELDON'S PHYSIQUE DIMENSIONS AND THEIR ASSOCIATED TEMPERAMENTS

| PHYSIQUE | TEMPERAMENT |
|---|---|
| *Endomorphic* (soft and round, overdeveloped digestive viscera) | *Viscerotonic* (relaxed, loves to eat, sociable) |
| *Mesomorphic* (muscular, rectangular, strong) | *Somatotonic* (energetic, assertive, courageous) |
| *Ectomorphic* (long, fragile, large brain and sensitive nervous system) | *Cerebrotonic* (restrained, fearful, introvertive, artistic) |

than dividing people into three distinct types, Sheldon considered every individual's status on each dimension. He developed a seven-point rating system for measuring somatotypes. For example, a 7-3-1 would be high on endomorphy, moderate on mesomorphy, and low on ectomorphy, presumably with corresponding levels of the associated temperaments. Sheldon's typology thus was quite sophisticated, especially by comparison with earlier formulations.

Sheldon's ideas about the association between body build and temperament are supported to some extent when untrained people rate the personality characteristics of others. In part these findings may reflect the fact that stereotyped ideas about the characteristics of fat, athletic, and skinny people are shared by the raters. For example, if raters think most fat people are "jolly" and thin people "sensitive," they may base their judgments of the individuals they rate on these stereotypes rather than on observed behavior. Thus they may rate a fat person as jolly, no matter how he behaves. Studies of behavior that avoid such stereotypes generally provide less evidence for the value of this system (e.g., Tyler, 1956).

Other typologies have grouped people into purely psychological categories. The Swiss psychiatrist Carl Jung, for example, considered all people either predominantly "introverts" or "extraverts." The introvert tends to withdraw into himself, especially when faced by emotional conflict and stress. He prefers to be alone, is shy, avoids people. In contrast, the extravert responds to stress by trying to lose himself among others. He tends to be in an occupation that lets him deal directly with many people—such as sales or promotional work—and he is likely to be conventional, outgoing and sociable.

Jung's introversion-extraversion typology has continued to intrigue psychologists and has been extensively researched for many years. The results suggest that people differ in the degree to which they are introverted and extraverted rather

Are there links between physique and personality?

than fitting into one or the other category exclusively. Most other hypothesized psychological typologies also turn out to involve a *continuum* of individual differences rather than discrete types.

## LIMITATIONS OF TYPOLOGIES

Typologies are appealing because of their simplicity, but it is their simplicity that limits their value. Generally an individual's behaviors are so complex, diverse, and variable that he cannot be sorted usefully into a simplistic category or slot. While some human characteristics may be usefully typed (e.g., blood type, sex) and while human conditions sometimes may be typed (imprisoned or free, hospitalized or out-patient), it seems inconceivable to find a useful typology for pigeonholing the total individual into one of a few personality categories.

## TRAITS VERSUS TYPES

Typologies usually assume discrete, discontinuous categories (like male *or* female). Traits, however, are continuous dimensions on which individual differences may be arranged quantitatively in terms of the *amount* of the characteristic the individual has (like degrees of intelligence). In fact, psychological measurements usually indicate a continuous dimension of individual differences in the degree of the measured attribute, with most people displaying an intermediate amount (Figure 2-2).

Many psychologists who use a trait approach investigate such personality dimensions as aggressiveness, dependency, and the striving to achieve high standards of excellence. Great differences have been found among people in the degree to which they show such dispositions.

Figure 2-2  OBTAINED DISTRIBUTION FOR INDIVIDUAL DIFFERENCES

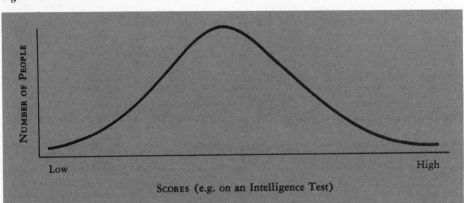

One continuous dimension (from low to high) is usually found.

**Figure 2-3**   INDIVIDUAL DIFFERENCES IN RESPONSE TO THE SAME STIMULUS

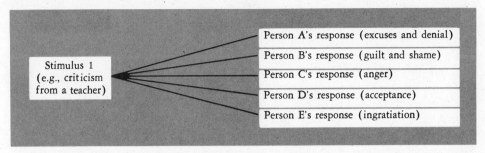

The trait approach emphasizes consistent differences among people in their response to the same stimulus.

The trait approach begins with the common-sense observation that individuals often differ greatly and consistently in their responses to the same psychological situation or stimulus. That is, when different people are confronted with the same event—the same social encounter, the same test question, the same frightening experience—each individual tends to react in a somewhat different way. The basic idea that no two people react identically to the same stimulus is shown schematically in Figure 2-3. Moreover, in everday life most of us are impressed with the distinctive *consistency* of one individual's responses over a wide variety of stimulus situations: we expect an "aggressive" person to differ consistently from others in his responses to many stimuli.

In its simplest meaning, the term "trait" refers to consistent differences between the behavior or characteristics of two or more people. Thus, "a trait is any distinguishable, relatively enduring way in which one individual varies from another" (Guilford, 1959, p. 6.).

To understand the reasons for individual differences some early theorists also invoked the "trait" as an explanation: in their view the trait was the property within the person that accounted for his unique but relatively stable reactions to stimuli. Thus the trait became a construct to explain behavior—a hypothesized reason for enduring individual differences. Many spokesmen for the trait position have theorized extensively about these hypothesized dispositions. Before examining their formal views, however, we should consider how traits are used informally by people in daily life. Indeed every person is a trait theorist, in the sense that he generates ideas about his own dispositions and the characteristics of other people.

## TRAIT ATTRIBUTIONS

When people describe each other psychologically in daily life, they spontaneously use dispositional or trait terms. We all characterize each other (and ourselves) with such terms as aggressive, dependent, fearful, introverted, anxious, submissive—the list is almost endless. We see a person behaving in a particular way—for example, sitting at his desk for an hour yawning—and attribute a trait to him—"unmotivated" or "lazy" or "bored" or "dull."

These simple trait attributions are often adequate to "explain" events for many everyday purposes in common-sense psychology (Heider, 1958; Kelley, 1973). In these common-sense explanations, traits are invoked not just as descriptions of what people do but also as the causes of their behavior. Thus in everyday practice traits may be used first simply as adjectives describing behavior ("He behaves in a lazy way"), but the description is soon generalized from the behavior to the person ("He *is* lazy") and then abstracted to "He has a lazy disposition" or "He is unmotivated." These descriptions pose no problems as long as their basis is recalled—he is construed as behaving in a lazy way and no more. A hazard in trait attribution is that we easily forget that nothing is explained if the state *we* have attributed to the person from his behavior ("He has a trait of laziness") is now invoked as the *cause* of the behavior from which it was inferred. We then quickly emerge with the tautology, "He behaves in a lazy way because he has a lazy disposition," or because he is "unmotivated."

The trait approach to formal personality study begins with the common-sense conviction that personality can be described with trait terms, but it extends and refines those descriptions by arriving at them quantitatively and systematically. Efforts to explain individual differences by formal trait theories entail some of the same problems that arise when traits are offered as causes by the layman. However, numerous safeguards have been developed to try to control some of these difficulties (see Chapter 8).

## *GORDON ALLPORT*

One of the most outstanding trait psychologists was Gordon Allport, whose conceptions of traits have had an important influence for more than 30 years. In Allport's theory, traits have a very real and vital existence: they are the ultimate realities of psychological organization. Allport favored a biophysical conception that

> does not hold that every trait-name necessarily implies a trait; but rather that behind all confusion of terms, behind the disagreement of judges, and apart from errors and failures of empirical observation, there are none the less *bona fide* mental structures in each personality that account for the consistency of its behavior (1937, p. 289).

According to Allport, traits are determining tendencies or predispositions to respond. These dispositions serve to integrate what would otherwise be dissimilar stimuli and responses. In other words, a trait is

> a generalized and focalized neuropsychic system (peculiar to the individual) with the capacity to render many stimuli functionally equivalent, and to ini-

tiate and guide consistent (equivalent) forms of adaptive and expressive behavior (1937, p. 295).

Allport implied that traits are not linked to a small number of specific stimuli or responses, but are relatively *general* and enduring: by uniting responses to numerous stimuli, they produce fairly broad consistencies in behavior, as schematized in Figure 2-4.

Allport was convinced that some people have dispositions that pervade most aspects of their behavior. He called these highly generalized dispositions *cardinal* traits. For example, if a man's whole life seems to be organized around goal achievement and the attainment of excellence, then achievement might be his cardinal trait. Less pervasive but still quite generalized dispositions are *central* traits, and Allport thought that many people are broadly influenced by central traits. Finally, more specific, narrow traits are called *secondary* dispositions or "attitudes."

Allport believed that the individual's pattern of dispositions or "personality structure" determines his behavior. This emphasis on structure rather than environment or stimulus conditions is seen in his colorful phrase, "The same fire that melts the butter hardens the egg" (1937, p. 102). Allport was an ardent spokesman for the importance of individual differences: no two people are completely alike, and hence no two people respond identically to the same event. Each person's behavior is determined by his particular trait structure.

According to Allport, traits never occur in any two people in exactly the same way: they operate in *unique* ways in each person. This conviction was consistent with his emphasis on the individuality and uniqueness of each personality. To the extent that any trait is unique within a person rather than common among many people, it cannot be studied by making comparisons among people. Consequently Allport urged the thorough study of individuals through intensive and long-term case studies. He also believed, however, that because of shared experiences and common cultural influence, most persons tend to develop some *roughly* common kinds of traits: they can be compared on these common dispositions.

Many of Allport's theories were most relevant to the phenomenological approach (see Chapter 6) and to the in-depth study of lives rather than to the quan-

**Figure 2-4**  AN EXAMPLE OF A TRAIT AS THE UNIFIER OF STIMULI AND RESPONSES

titative study of groups. He contributed to trait theory, but he was critical of many of the statistical methods and quantitative research strategies favored by other trait theorists.

## R. B. CATTELL

Raymond B. Cattell (e.g., 1950, 1965) has been another important proponent of trait theory. For Cattell the trait is also the basic unit of study; it is a "mental structure," inferred from behavior, and a fundamental construct that accounts for behavioral regularity or consistency. Like Allport, Cattell distinguished between *common traits*, which are possessed by all people, and *unique traits*, which occur only in a particular person and cannot be found in another in exactly the same form.

Cattell also distinguished *surface traits* from *source traits* (see Table 2-1 for selected examples). Surface traits are clusters of overt or manifest trait elements (responses) that seem to go together. Source traits are the underlying variables that are the causal entities determining the surface manifestations. In research, trait elements (in the form of test responses or scores) are intercorrelated statistically until collections of elements that correlate positively in all possible combinations are discovered. This procedure, according to Cattell, yields surface traits.

For Cattell source traits can be identified only by means of the mathematical technique of factor analysis (discussed further in Chapter 8). Using this technique, the investigator tries to estimate the factors or dimensions that appear to underlie surface variations in behavior. According to Cattell, the basic aim in research and assessment should be identification of source traits. In his view, these traits are divided between those that reflect environmental conditions (*environmental-mold traits*) and those that reflect constitutional factors (*constitutional traits*). Moreover, source traits may either be *general* (those affecting behavior in many different situations) or *specific*. Specific source traits are particularized sources of personality reaction that operate in one situation only, and Cattell pays little attention to them.

---

**TABLE 2-1   Surface Traits and Source Traits Studied by Cattell**

| | |
|---|---|
| Examples of Surface Traits:<br>(Cattell, 1950) | Integrity, altruism—dishonesty,<br>   undependability<br>Disciplined thoughtfulness—foolishness<br>Thrift, tidiness, obstinacy—lability,<br>   curiosity, intuition |
| Examples of Source Traits:<br>(Cattell, 1965) | Ego strength—emotionality and<br>   neuroticism<br>Dominance—submissiveness |

NOTE: These are selected and abbreviated examples from much longer lists.

---

Cattell uses three kinds of data to discover general source traits: *life records,* in which everyday behavior situations are observed and rated; *self-ratings;* and *objective tests,* in which the person is observed in situations that are specifically designed to elicit responses from which behavior in other situations can be predicted. The data from all three sources are subjected to factor analysis. In his own work, Cattell shows a preference for factor analysis of life-record data based on many behavior ratings for large samples of persons. Some 14 or 15 clusters of intercorrelations or source traits have been reported from such investigations, but only six have been found repeatedly (Vernon, 1964).

In Cattell's system, traits may also be grouped into classes or modalities on the basis of how they are expressed. Those that are relevant to the individual's being "set into action" with respect to some goal are called *dynamic traits,* whereas those concerned with his effectiveness in gaining the goal are *ability traits.* Traits concerned with energy or emotional reactivity are named *temperament traits.* Cattell has speculated extensively about the relationships between various traits and the development of personality (1965).

## H. J. EYSENCK

The extensive researches of the English psychologist Hans Eysenck have complemented the work of the American trait theorists, and supplemented it in many important ways. Eysenck (1961) has extended the search for personality dimensions to the area of abnormal behavior, studying such traits as *neuroticism.* He also has investigated *introversion-extraversion* as a dimensional trait (although Carl Jung originally proposed "introvert" and "extravert" as personality *types*). Eysenck and his associates have pursued an elaborate and sophisticated statistical methodology in their search for the dimensions needed for an adequate conceptualization of personality structure. In addition to providing a set of descriptive dimensions, Eysenck and his colleagues have studied the associations between people's status on these dimensions and their scores on a variety of other personality and intellectual measures.

Eysenck emphasized that his dimension of introversion-extraversion is based entirely on research and "must stand and fall by empirical confirmation" (Eysenck & Rachman, 1965, p. 19). In his words:

> The typical extravert is sociable, likes parties, has many friends, needs to have people to talk to, and does not like reading or studying by himself. He craves excitement, takes chances, often sticks his neck out, acts on the spur of the moment, and is generally an impulsive individual. He is fond of practical jokes, always has a ready answer, and generally likes change; he is carefree, easygoing, optimistic, and "likes to laugh and be merry." He prefers to keep moving and doing things, tends to be aggressive and loses his temper quickly; altogether his feelings are not kept under tight control, and he is not always a reliable person.

The typical introvert is a quiet, retiring sort of person, introspective, fond of books rather than people; he is reserved and distant except to intimate friends. He tends to plan ahead, "looks before he leaps," and mistrusts the impulse of the moment. He does not like excitement, takes matters of everyday life with proper seriousness, and likes a well-ordered mode of life. He keeps his feelings under close control, seldom behaves in an aggressive manner, and does not lose his temper easily. He is reliable, somewhat pessimistic and places great value on ethical standards.

Eysenck and his colleagues recognized that these descriptions may sound almost like caricatures because they portray "perfect" extraverts and introverts while in fact most people are mixtures who fall in the middle rather than at the extremes of the dimensions (see Figure 2-5). As Figure 2-5 shows, Eysenck suggested that the second major dimension of personality is *emotional stability* or *neuroticism*. This dimension describes at one end people who tend to be moody, touchy, anxious, restless and so on. At the other extreme are people who are characterized by such terms as stable, calm, carefree, even-tempered, and reliable. As Eysenck stressed, the ultimate value of these dimensions will depend on the research support they receive.

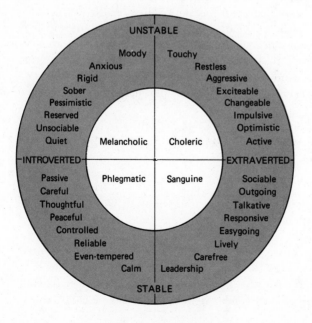

**Figure 2-5**   DIMENSIONS OF PERSONALITY

The inner ring shows the "four temperaments" of Hippocrates; the outer ring shows the results of modern factor analytic studies of the intercorrelations between traits by Eysenck and others (Eysenck & Rachman, 1965).

## COMMON FEATURES OF TRAIT THEORIES

Now consider the principal common characteristics of trait approaches.

### GENERALITY OF TRAITS

Trait theorists often disagree about the specific content and structure of the basic traits needed to describe personality, but their general conceptions have much similarity. They all use the trait to account for consistencies in an individual's behavior and to explain why persons respond differently to the same stimulus. They view traits as dispositions that determine such behaviors. Each differentiates between relatively superficial traits (e.g., Cattell's surface traits) and more basic, underlying traits (e.g., Cattell's source traits). Each recognizes that traits vary in breadth or generality, Allport perhaps placing the strongest emphasis on the relative generality of traits across many situations. Each theorist also admits trait fluctuations, or changes in a person's position with respect to a disposition. At the same time, each is committed to a search for relatively broad, stable traits.

### SEARCH FOR BASIC TRAITS

If it is assumed that behavior is mainly determined by broad traits that manifest themselves stably across many conditions, then it is understandable that personality psychologists should search for these dispositions and pay less attention to other variables. Guided by the assumption that highly generalized dispositions exist, a main objective of trait psychology has been to identify the individual's position on one or more dimensions (e.g., neuroticism, extraversion) by comparing him with other persons tested under comparable, standardized conditions. If it is believed that positions on these dimensions are relatively stable across testing situations and over long time periods, then the main emphasis in the study of personality becomes the development of reliable instruments that can accurately tap the person's underlying traits. This has been the predominant concern of traditional trait approaches. Less attention has been paid to the effects of environmental conditions on traits and behavior.

### INFERRING TRAITS FROM BEHAVIORAL SIGNS

In the search for dispositions one always *infers* traits from the individual's behavior—for example, from what he says about himself on a questionnaire. The person's responses or behaviors are taken as *indicators* of his underlying traits. The trait approach to personality is a "sign" approach in the sense that there is no interest in the test behavior itself. That is, test responses are of value not in their own right but only as *signs* of the traits that underlie them; test behavior is always used as a sign of nontest behavior (Loevinger, 1957). The trait psychologist is not interested in answers on an inventory or IBM score sheet for their own sake, but only in a subject's responses to a test as reliable cues or signs of his dispositions. It is therefore essential to demonstrate the relation between test behaviors and the traits they purportedly represent. We will consider relevant efforts of this sort in detail later (Chapter 8).

## QUANTITATIVE METHODS

A main feature of the trait approach has been its quantitative methodology. This methodology is "psychometric" in the sense that it attempts to measure individual differences. The psychometric approach to individual differences tries to infer the underlying trait structure of individuals. Psychometricians study persons and groups on trait dimensions by comparing their quantitative scores on tests. To do this reliably the preferred research strategy is to sample many subjects, to compare large groups under uniform testing conditions, and to devise sophisticated statistical techniques in the search for basic traits (Chapters 7 and 8).

## TRAIT DIMENSIONS AND INDIVIDUAL DIFFERENCES

After many years of searching, trait theorists still disagree as to which trait dimensions are the basic units of personality. Some suggest as many as sixteen basic traits; others as few as two or three. Table 2-2 gives the five trait dimensions that were studied in one research program. For each dimension, it shows the adjectives describing the two ends of each rating scale it includes. In spite of disagreement about basic dimensions, there is usually some overlap in the findings of different trait theorists. Probably the two dimensions found most consistently involve extraversion-introversion and adjustment and integration as opposed to disorganization and anxiety (e.g., Vernon, 1964).

Many contemporary trait researchers remain committed to identifying "the most important individual differences in mankind" (Goldberg, 1973, p. 1). Their effort rests on the assumption that the most significant individual differences—those that are most important in daily human relationships—become encoded into the natural language of the culture as single-word trait terms. Using a variety of methods (discussed in Chapters 7 and 8) they try to identify basic trait terms in the language and to categorize them into comprehensive groupings. This classification task is an enormous one, given that thousands of trait terms (over 18,000 in one count) are found in English. The hope underlying this great effort is that the ultimate development of better theories of personality (and better methods of personality assessment) will be helped by having at hand an extensive, well-organized vocabulary for describing human attributes in trait terms.

**TABLE 2-2   Some Trait Dimensions and Their Components**

| TRAIT DIMENSION | DESCRIPTIVE COMPONENTS[a] |
|---|---|
| I. Extraversion or Surgency | Talkative—Silent<br>Frank, Open—Secretive<br>Adventurous—Cautious<br>Sociable—Reclusive |
| II. Agreeableness | Good-natured—Irritable<br>Not Jealous—Jealous<br>Mild, Gentle—Headstrong<br>Cooperative—Negativistic |
| III. Conscientiousness | Fussy, Tidy—Careless<br>Responsible—Undependable<br>Scrupulous—Unscrupulous<br>Persevering—Quitting, Fickle |
| IV. Emotional Stability | Poised—Nervous, Tense<br>Calm—Anxious<br>Composed—Excitable<br>Not Hypochondriacal—<br>    Hypochondriacal |
| V. Culture | Artistically Sensitive—<br>    Artistically Insensitive<br>Intellectual—Unreflective, Narrow<br>Polished, Refined—Crude, Boorish<br>Imaginative—Simple, Direct |

Adapted from Norman (1963).
[a] Adjectives describing the two ends of the scales that comprise the dimension.

Research in the trait tradition does not only describe individual differences. It also examines the relationships between an individual's position on many personality dimensions and his behavior in other situations. For example, a group of school children may be tested for their intellectual abilities and also given questionnaires concerning beliefs and attitudes. In addition they may be asked to rate their own attributes on several scales, and they may be rated on a set of characteristics by their teachers and their peers. The results are examined statistically to discover the associations or correlations among all of the obtained indications of behavior. When very many associations emerge from this procedure it often helps to simplify them by means of further statistical techniques. The findings of trait research help to illuminate the organization or structure of personality and indicate what kinds of behaviors are most likely to occur together. The results help us to answer questions like these: Do aggressive children become aggressive adults? Are adolescent boys who are aggressive at home likely to be aggressive at school? Is aggressiveness related to intelligence? What relations exist between aggressiveness, dependency, and anxiety?

## INTERACTION OF TRAITS AND SITUATIONS

In recent years trait theorists have increasingly recognized that an adequate approach to the study of traits must also deal seriously with how the qualities of the person and the situation influence each other—that is, their "interaction" (e.g., Bowers, 1973; Endler, 1973; Mischel, 1973a). To study such interaction one must examine the ways in which the manifestations of a person's traits depend on his psychological situation at the moment. For example, rather than exhibit anxiety everywhere, an individual may be anxious only under some set of relatively narrow circumstances, such as test-taking in math, but not under many other conditions (e.g., Endler, 1973). Moreover, his anxiety may express itself in some ways (such as subjective feelings of fear and upset) but not in others (for example, there may be no physical changes, such as increased perspiration or heart rate). The implications of these specific interactions for contemporary trait theory are profound, as will become evident when the applications of trait approaches are discussed in Part 2, and when we consider the topic of interaction in detail (Chapter 21).

## SUMMARY

1. Since earliest times people have labeled and classified each other according to their psychological characteristics. *Typologies* classify people into discrete categories. Among others, Hippocrates, Sheldon, and Jung have proposed typologies of personality, but the very simplicity that makes these typologies appealing also limits their value. An individual personality cannot be fitted neatly into one category or another.

2. *Traits* are continuous dimensions on which individual differences may be arranged quantitatively in accord with the amount of an attribute that the individual has.

3. In everyday life people habitually use trait terms. They employ these terms not just to describe what people do but also to explain their behavior. We have not really explained anything, however, if after attributing a trait to a person on the basis of his behavior, we later invoke that trait as the cause of the very behavior from which we inferred it.

4. Trait theorists conceptualize traits as underlying properties, qualities, or processes that exist in persons. Traits also are constructs to account for

observed behavioral consistencies within persons and for the enduring and stable behavioral differences among them in their responses to similar stimuli (situations).

5. For Allport, traits are the ultimate realities of psychological organization. They are the mental structures that account for consistency in behavior. In his view, traits are predispositions to respond, and they serve to integrate what would otherwise be dissimilar stimuli and responses. Traits are relatively general and enduring, although they may range in generality from highly generalized *cardinal* through *central* to *secondary* traits or more specific "attitudes." An individual's "personality structure" is his pattern of dispositions or traits. Allport emphasized this structure, rather than the environment or stimulus conditions, in his analysis of human behavior. He stressed individual differences and the uniqueness of each person. Although he recognized some roughly common traits on which individuals can be compared, he urged the intensive study of the individual. He disapproved of many of the statistical methods and quantitative research strategies favored by other trait theorists.

6. Cattell distinguished between *surface* traits and *source* traits. Surface traits are identified by statistical correlations; source traits, by factor analysis. Through factor analysis Cattell tried to estimate the basic dimensions or factors underlying surface variations in behavior. Extensions of trait theory have been provided by Eysenck, who emphasizes the dimensions of introversion–extraversion and emotional stability (neuroticism).

7. In spite of their many differences, most trait theorists share the following theoretical assumptions and strategies:

   a. Traits are assumed to be general underlying dispositions that account for consistencies in behavior.
   b. Some traits are considered to be relatively superficial and specific; others that are more basic and widely generalized are assumed to produce consistencies across many situations.
   c. The predominant objective is the identification of underlying broad dispositions. Emphasis is on the measurement of an individual's position on one or more dimensions by means of objective instruments or tests administered under standard conditions.
   d. A person's tested or sampled behaviors (including what he says about himself) are viewed as signs of his underlying traits.
   e. To search for basic traits a psychometric strategy is used which samples and compares large groups of subjects quantitatively under uniform conditions.

8. There is still disagreement about which traits are the basic units of personality, but the search continues. There is also increasing recognition that the qualities of the person interact with those of the situation(s) in which he or she functions.

# CHAPTER 3

# PSYCHODYNAMIC THEORIES Conceptions

Quantification, large samples of subjects, and objective measurements are the characteristics of the psychometric search for personality traits. Other psychologists (like Allport) have felt for many years that emphasis on the quantitative study of large groups of people slights the qualitative, intense study of the individual. Rather than relying on numbers and tests to describe people in terms of discrete traits, many personality psychologists, beginning in the early 1930s, hoped to achieve better insights by another route. Perhaps by studying the whole individual in depth, guided by clinical intuition and by informal techniques like the interview, one could achieve generally valid insights into human nature and could generate useful statements about individuals. There have been several different formulations in this general movement, but the most influential force has been Sigmund Freud's psychodynamic theory and its variations.

Most trait psychologists tried to map the structure of personality by discovering the stable psychological dimensions on which people could be compared. They emphasized the relatively enduring qualities of personality and the conscious content of the mind, as revealed by direct self-report and introspection. A completely different approach was developed almost single-handedly by the Viennese physician, Sigmund Freud. During his lifetime (1856–1939) Freud invented psychoanalysis, reshaped the field of psychology, and influenced many later developments in all the social sciences and in Western concepts of human nature.

Working as a physician treating disturbed persons in Vienna at the turn of the century, Freud startled the neo-Victorian world by formulating a theory that upset many prevalent assumptions about human nature. Rather than seeing consciousness as the core of the mind, Freud compared personality to an iceberg: only the surface tips show themselves overtly. Rather than viewing man as a supremely rational being, he construed him as driven by impulses and striving to satisfy deep and lasting sexual and aggressive urgings. Rather than relying on people's reports about themselves as accurate self-representations, he interpreted verbalizations and overt behavior as highly indirect, disguised, symbolic representations of unconscious underlying forces.

In the course of more than 40 years of active writing and clinical research Freud developed a theory of personality, a method of treatment for personality disturbances, and an extensive body of clinical observations based on his therapeutic experiences and his analyses of himself. The following sections summarize some of the main points of Freud's theoretical position. It should be evident that what follows is a summary of a theory, not of a collection of facts. The evaluation of that theory is a separate task, and one that is undertaken in the many later parts of this book that assess relevant research evidence.

Freud developed both his theory and his psychoanalytic treatment on the basis of extensive clinical observation of neurotic persons. It was with the problems of hysteria that Freud began his observations of the neurotic process. He noted certain sensory anesthesias and motor paralyses that seemed to have no neurological origin but rather to express a way of defending against unacceptable unconscious wishes. For example, a soldier who cannot admit his fear of facing battle develops a motor paralysis without a neurological basis. The fundamental feature of hysteria, according to Freud, is the presence of massive repression and the development of a symptom pattern that indirectly or symbolically expresses the repressed needs and wishes. On the basis of careful clinical observations Freud gradually generated his theory of personality, continuously modifying his ideas in the light of his accumulating clinical experiences.

## PSYCHIC STRUCTURE

According to Freud (1933) personality has a three-part structure: id, ego, and superego. Although the three parts interact intimately, each has its own characteristics.

## THE ID

The id is the mental province or agency containing everything inherited, especially the instincts. It is the basis of personality, the energy source for the whole system, and the foundation from which the ego and superego later become differentiated. The id, according to Freud, is the innermost core of personality, and it is closely linked to biological processes.

Increases in energy generated by internal or external stimulation produce tension and discomfort that the id cannot tolerate. The id seeks immediate tension reduction. This tendency toward immediate tension reduction is called the *pleasure principle,* and the id obeys it, seeking immediate satisfaction of instinctual wishes and impulses, regardless of rational or logical considerations.

Freud (1940) believed the impulses of the id to be chiefly sexual and aggressive instincts. He classified these impulses or instincts into the categories of "life" or sexual instincts and "death" or aggressive instincts. The psychological representations of these instincts are wishes, and they often are irrational and unconscious.

To discharge tension the id forms an internal image or hallucination of the desired object. The hungry infant, for example, may conjure up an internal representation of the mother's breast. The resulting image is considered a wish fulfillment, similar to the attempted wish fulfillment that Freud believed characterized normal dreams and the hallucinations of psychotics. "Primary process thinking" was Freud's term for such direct, reality-ignoring attempts to satisfy needs irrationally. Because mental images by themselves cannot reduce tension, a "secondary process" develops in the form of the ego.

## THE EGO

The ego is a direct outgrowth of the id. Freud described its origin this way:

> Under the influence of the real external world around us, one portion of the id has undergone a special development. From what was originally a cortical layer, equipped with the organs for receiving stimuli and with arrangements for acting as a protective shield against stimuli, a special organization has arisen which henceforward acts as an intermediary between the id and the external world. To this region of our mind we have given the name of *ego* (Freud, 1933, p. 2).

The ego is in direct contact with the external world. It is governed by considerations of safety, and its task is preservation of the organism. The ego wages its battle for survival against both the external world and the internal instinctual demands of the id. In this task it has to continuously differentiate between the mental representations of wish-fulfilling images and the actual perceptual characteristics of the outer world of reality. In its search for food or sexual release, for example, it must locate the appropriate tension-reducing objects in the environment so that tension reduction can actually occur. That is, it must go from image to object, and find satisfaction for id impulses while simultaneously preserving itself.

The ego's function is governed by the *reality principle*, which requires it to test reality and to delay discharge of tension until the appropriate object and environmental conditions are found. The ego operates by means of a "secondary process" that involves realistic, logical thinking and planning through the use of the higher or cognitive mental processes. That is, while the id seeks immediate tension reduction by such primary process means as wish-fulfilling imagery and direct gratification of sexual and aggressive impulses, the ego, like an executive, mediates between the id and the world, testing reality and making decisions about various courses of available action. For example, it delays impulses for immediate sexual gratification until the environmental conditions are appropriate.

## THE SUPEREGO

Here is a glimpse of Freud's view of the development of the third mental structure, the superego:

> The long period of childhood, during which the growing human being lives in dependence on his parents, leaves behind it as a precipitate the formation in his ego of a special agency in which this parental influence is prolonged. It has received the name of *superego*. In so far as this superego is differentiated from the ego or is opposed to it, it constitutes a third power which the ego must take into account (Freud, 1933, p. 2).

Thus the superego is the agency that internalizes the parental influence. It represents the morals and standards of society that have become part of the internal world of the individual in the course of the development of his personality. The superego is the conscience, the judge of right and wrong, of good and bad, in accord with the internalized standards of the parents and thus, indirectly, of society. It represents the ideal. Whereas the id seeks pleasure and the ego tests reality, the superego seeks perfection. The superego, for Freud, involved the internalization of parental control in the form of self-control. For example, the individual with a well-developed superego refrains from "bad" or "evil" temptations, such as stealing when hungry or killing when angry, even when there are no external constraints (in the form of police or other people) to stop him. The hypothesized mechanisms in this process, and the research relevant to it, are crucial for understanding personality development; they will be discussed in detail in later chapters.

# PERSONALITY DYNAMICS

According to Freud (1915), the three parts of the psychic structure—id, ego, and superego—are in perpetual conflict. The dynamics of personality involve a continuous interaction and clash between id impulses seeking release and inhibitions or restraining forces against them—an interplay between driving forces or urgings and inhibitory constraining forces. These urges or impulses and counterforces propel or motivate personality.

## CONFLICT

The quest for immediate satisfaction of impulses reflects man's hedonistic nature: people are motivated to avoid pain and to achieve immediate tension reduction. This drive for immediate satisfaction of instinctual demands leads to an early and enduring clash between the individual and the environment. Conflict develops to the degree that the environment and its representatives in the form of other persons, notably the parents in childhood, exercise censorial and controlling functions that punish or impede immediate impulse expression.

The person in time comes to incorporate the societal code by which he is raised, largely through a process of internalizing parental characteristics. Thus in Freud's view perpetual warfare and conflict exist between man and environment. Insofar as societal values become "internalized" as part of the person, this warfare is waged internally between the components of personality and it produces anxiety.

## ANXIETY

Freud (1933) distinguished three kinds of anxiety. In *neurotic anxiety* the person fears that his instincts will get out of control and cause him to behave in ways that will be punished. In *moral anxiety* the person feels conscience-stricken or guilty about unacceptable things that he feels he has done or even contemplates. Both neurotic and moral anxiety are derivatives of *reality anxiety*, the fear of real dangers in the external world.

The sequence of events in reality anxiety (or "objective anxiety") is simple: a danger exists in the external world, the person perceives it, and his perception evokes anxiety. This sequence may be summarized as:

$$\text{external danger} \rightarrow \text{perception of danger} \rightarrow \text{reality anxiety}$$

Anxiety is a state of painful tension and, as with other tensions, the organism seeks to reduce it. When anxiety cannot be handled effectively by realistic methods, the organism may resort to unrealistic *defenses*. Elaborate defenses are developed to avoid anxiety and to come to terms with the instinctual impulses seeking release as they conflict with the barriers of the external world and with internalized inhibitions. These defenses serve as disguises through which man hides his motives and conflicts from himself as well as from others.

## MECHANISMS OF DEFENSE

Psychodynamic theorists emphasize that when threat becomes especially serious it may lead to intense and widespread inhibitions. In the psychodynamic view, such defensive inhibition is desperate and primitive. It is a massive, generalized inhibitory reaction rather than a specific response to the particular danger. This *denial* defense is called forth when the person can neither escape nor attack the threat. If the panic is sufficient, the only possible alternative may be to deny it. Outright denial may be possible for the young child because he is not yet upset by violating the demands of reality testing. When the child becomes cognitively too mature to deny objective facts in the interests of defense, denial becomes a less plausible alternative and he may resort to repression.

In psychodynamic theory *repression* usually refers to a particular type of denial: "the forgetting, or ejection from consciousness, of memories of threat, and especially the ejection from awareness of impulses in oneself that might have objectionable consequences" (White, 1964, p. 214).

Repression was one of the initial concepts in Freud's theory and became one of its cornerstones. Material in the unconscious that is relatively inaccessible to conscious awareness is said to be in a state of repression. The ego may become aware that the expression of a particular instinctual demand would be dangerous, and the demand must therefore be suppressed, removed, made powerless. Repression is thus a defense mechanism of the ego.

Freud (1920) believed that the mechanisms of denial and repression were the most fundamental or primitive defenses and played a part in other defenses. Indeed he thought that other defenses started with a massive inhibition of an impulse, which was followed by various elaborations.

In *projection* the person's own unacceptable impulses are inhibited and the source of the anxiety is attributed to another person. For example, one's own temptations toward homosexuality are attributed to a friend. Projection presumably gives relief because it reduces neurotic or moral anxiety. In this way, the unacceptable impulse to be homosexual, in this example, can be expressed indirectly, under the guise of the person's defending himself against his "queer" friends, while avoiding the anxiety that would be generated by admitting homosexual wishes.

Replacement in consciousness of an anxiety-producing impulse by its opposite is another defense; it is termed *reaction formation*. For example, frightened by her own sexual impulses, a woman may become the outspoken leader of a "ban the filth" vigilante group that vigorously censors books and movies it construes to be obscene. Through projection and reaction formation the id impulse is expressed, but in a disguise that makes it acceptable to the ego.

Another defensive mechanism is *intellectualization* or the tendency to transform emotional conflicts into abstract, quasi-intellectual terms. One example is the rationalization of feelings by making excuses. Thus, a man who has unconscious, deeply hostile impulses toward his wife might invent elaborate excuses that serve to disrupt and even terminate their relations without admitting his true feelings. He might create many spurious reasons to stay away from home and persistently disappoint and hurt his wife. He might invoke "pressures at the office," "a hectic schedule," "worrying about inflation and politics," and "fatigue" as excuses for ignoring, avoiding, and frustrating his wife.

*Sublimation*, according to Freud, is an ego defense that is particularly significant in the development of culture. It consists of a displacement or redirection of impulses from an object (or target) that is sexual to one that is social in character. For example, if in the course of her normal development masturbation becomes too threatening to the young girl, she may sublimate (or transform) her impulses into a socially acceptable form, such as horseback riding and other athletic endeavors.

## PSYCHIC ENERGY

Thus the essence of Freudian personality dynamics is the transformation of motives: the basic impulses persist and press for discharge, but the objects at which they are directed and the manner in which they are expressed are transformed

Freud believed unconscious impulses may be transformed and expressed in many different socially acceptable ways.

**Figure 3-1**  THE PSYCHODYNAMIC TRANSFORMATION OF MOTIVES: EXAMPLES OF DISPLACEMENT IN THE FORM OF SUBLIMATION

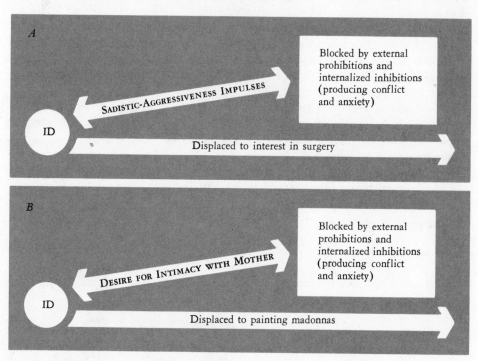

(1917). Freud thought that these transformations involved a finite amount of energy that was contained in the person. This energy or *libido* is "cathected" (attached) onto aspects of the internal and external environment. The energy available to the organism may be continuously transformed and cathected, or focused, onto different objects, but the total amount of energy is conserved and stable. Freud's energy system thus was consistent with the hydraulic models of nineteenth century physics. The id was seen as a kind of dynamo, and the total psyche was viewed as a closed system motivated to maintain equilibrium: any forces that were built up required discharge. The discharge could be indirect. Cathexes (the investments of instinctual impulses in objects) could be *displaced* from one object to another, for instance from one's mother to other women, or more remotely, from the genitals, for example, to phallic symbols.

Some of these transformations or displacements are schematized in Figure 3-1. For example, if sadistic aggressive impulses are too threatening to self-acceptance, they might be transformed into a more socially sanctioned form, such as an interest in surgery. Likewise, sexual wishes toward the mother might be displaced into a career of painting madonnas, as some Freudians think happened among certain Renaissance painters. Freud (1909) himself suggested such dynamics in the case of Leonardo Da Vinci.

In sum, psychodynamics involve a continuous conflict between id impulses seeking discharge and defenses designed to transform these wishes into an acceptable form for the person. In the course of these transformations psychic energy is exchanged and cathected onto different objects.

## NEUROTIC ANXIETY AND SIGNS OF CONFLICT

Sometimes the defenses that disguise basic motives may become inadequate, as in pathological conditions, but even under the usual circumstances of everyday life the defenses are occasionally penetrated and the person betrays himself (Freud, 1960). Such betrayals of underlying motives are manifested most readily when defenses are relaxed, as in dream life during sleep or in jokes and slips of the tongue. The defense process involves distortion and displacement; private meanings develop as objects and events become symbols representing things quite different from themselves. It is believed that these meanings are partially revealed by behavioral "signs" or symptoms that may symbolize or indirectly represent disguised wishes and unconscious conflicts. For example, phobias such as the fear of snakes may reflect basic sexual conflicts; in this case, the feared snake has symbolic meaning.

It is now possible to consider the Freudian conception of how neurotic anxiety may develop. The sequence here (depicted in Figure 3-2) begins with the child's aggressive or sexual impulses that seek direct release. These expressions or efforts at discharge may be strongly punished and blocked by extreme external dangers or threats (e.g., intense parental punishment such as withdrawal of love) and hence lead to objective anxiety. The child may become especially afraid that his impulses will lead to loss of parental love: in time, therefore, he may come to fear his own impulses. Because this state is painful, he tries to repress his impulses (or defend against them with other mechanisms). If the ego is weak, the repression is only partly successful and the instinctual impulses persist. Unless expressed in some acceptable form, these impulses become increasingly "pent up," gradually building up to the point where they become hard to repress. Consequently there may be a

Figure 3-2   SEQUENCE IN FREUDIAN CONCEPTION OF NEUROTIC ANXIETY

Internal Sexual and Aggressive Impulses    External Punishment and Danger    Objective Anxiety

Neurotic Anxiety    Emergence of Derivatives of Impulses    Partial Breakdown of Repression    Repression of Impulses partial breakdown of repression, and components or derivatives of the impulses may break through, producing some neurotic anxiety. Anxiety, in this view, functions as a danger signal warning the individual that repressed impulses are starting to break through the defenses. Rather than emerging directly however, the person's unacceptable impulses or motives express themselves indirectly and symbolically in disguised or transformed ways.

Freud felt that the symbolic meaning of behavior was expressed with particular clarity in neurotic acts such as compulsions and obsessions. He cited the case of a girl who compulsively rinsed out her washbasin many times after washing. Freud thought that the significance of this ceremonial was expressed in the proverb, "Don't throw away dirty water until you have clean." He interpreted the girl's action as a warning to her sister, to whom she was very close, "not to separate from her unsatisfactory husband until she had established a relationship with a better man" (Freud, 1959, vol. 2, p. 28).

Another patient was able to sit only in a particular chair and could leave it only with much difficulty. In Freud's analysis of her problem, the chair symbolized the husband to whom she remained faithful. Freud saw the symbolic meaning of her compulsion in her sentence, "It is so hard to part from anything (chair or husband) in which one has once settled oneself" (Freud, 1959, vol. 2, p. 29). Thus the important object of conflict—the husband—was transformed into a trivial one—the chair. Freud cited these and many similar cases as evidence for the view that neurotic behaviors express unconscious motives and ideas symbolically and that the acts themselves have a defensive function in the dynamics of personality.

The clinician's task, then, is to decipher the unconscious meaning of the patient's behavior, and to discover the conflicts and dynamics that might underlie his seemingly irrational behavior patterns. To illustrate, Table 3-1 shows some hypothesized equivalences between certain symptoms and psychodynamic states. Equiva-

**TABLE 3-1   Possible Meanings of Some Behavioral Signs According to Freudian Theory**

| BEHAVIORAL SIGN | POSSIBLE UNDERLYING MEANING |
|---|---|
| Fear of snakes | Sexual conflicts concerning genitals |
| Compulsive cleanliness | Reaction against anal impulses |
| Obsessive thought "My mother is drowning." | Imperfectly repressed hostility toward mother |
| Paranoid jealousy | Homosexual wishes |
| Preoccupation with money | Problems around toilet training |
| Crusading against obscenity | Reaction formation against own unacceptable wishes |

lences like these are hypothesized by skilled, psychoanalytically oriented clinicians, using methods like those discussed in Chapter 9.

## THE ORIGINS OF NEUROSES

In Freud's view, serious problems, such as the neuroses, and the roots of the symptoms that characterize them, begin in early childhood:

> . . . It seems that neuroses are acquired only in early childhood (up to the age of six), even though their symptoms may not make their appearance till much later. The childhood neurosis may become manifest for a short time or may even be overlooked. In every case the later neurotic illness links up with the prelude in childhood.
>
> . . . There is no difficulty in accounting for this aetiological preference for the first period of childhood. The neuroses are, as we know, disorders of the ego; and it is not to be wondered at if the ego, so long as it is feeble, immature and incapable of resistance, fails to deal with tasks which it could cope with later on with the utmost ease. In these circumstances instinctual demands from within, no less than excitations from the external world, operate as 'traumas', particularly if they are met halfway by certain innate dispositions (Freud, 1933, pp. 41–42).

Although, as these quotations indicate, neuroses were seen as the products of early childhood traumas plus innate dispositions, even the behavior of less disturbed persons was believed to reflect expressions of underlying unconscious motives and conflicts. These manifestations could be seen in the "psychopathology of everyday life"—the occurrence of meaningful but common unconscious expressions, as discussed next.

## THE PSYCHOPATHOLOGY OF EVERYDAY LIFE

Some of Freud's most fascinating—and controversial—ideas involved the elaboration of possible hidden meanings that might underlie such common occurrences as slips of the tongue, errors in writing, jokes, and dreams. In Freud's (1901, 1920) view, "mistakes" may be unconsciously motivated by impulses that the individual is reluctant to express directly or openly. To show that mistakes may really be motivated by underlying wishes, Freud pointed out many instances in which even the attempt to "correct" the error appears to betray a hidden, unacceptable meaning. In one case, for example, a dignitary introduced a general as "this battle-scared veteran" and tried to "correct" his mistake by saying "bottle-scarred veteran." Examples of other seemingly innocuous manifestations, the latent (unconscious) wishes inferred to motivate them, and the underlying transformations, are summarized in Table 3-2.

**TABLE 3-2**    **Examples of Behavioral Manifestations Motivated by Unconscious Wishes**

| MANIFESTATION | LATENT (UNCONSCIOUS) WISH | TRANSFORMATION INVOLVED |
|---|---|---|
| slip of tongue: May I "insort" (instead of escort) you. | to insult | condensation: (insult + escort = "insort") |
| slip of tongue: "Gentlemen, I declare a quorum present and herewith declare the session *closed.*" | to close the meeting | association of opposites (open = closed) |
| dream of disappointment in quality of theater tickets, as result of having gotten them too soon. | I married too soon; I could have gotten a better husband by waiting | symbolism (getting tickets too soon = marrying too soon) |
| dream of breaking an arm | desire to break marriage vows | conversion into visual imagery (breaking vows = breaking an arm) |

Freud (1920).

# PSYCHOSEXUAL STAGES AND PERSONALITY DEVELOPMENT

Freud (1933) organized his theory of personality development around psychosexual stages. Body pleasure, Freud believed, is focused successively on different zones (mouth, anus, genitals) in the course of development. The oral, anal, and phallic stages unfold during the first five years of life. A quiet or repressive latency period of about five or six years follows these three stages. In adolescence the pregenital impulses are activated again at puberty. If they are successfully utilized, the individual reaches the mature or genital stage.

The pleasure derived from the oral, anal, and genital zones is related to one general source: the "libido" or energy of the sexual instincts. In each psychosexual stage the libido is focused on the pleasure-giving ("erogenous") zone that characterizes that stage and that provides unique potentialities for gratification or frustration. According to the theory, the person's experiences at each stage—oral, anal, phallic, and genital—leave a characteristic imprint that influences his future development.

The special experiences (vicissitudes) encountered by sexual impulses at any of the early psychosexual stages, either in the form of overindulgence or deprivation, may produce "fixation." Fixation is an arrest in sexual impulses at an early stage of psychosexual development; it may lead to a character structure built around the unresolved difficulties of that period.

## THE ORAL STAGE

The dependent person is said to be fixated at the *oral stage*, which occurs at a time when the infant is totally dependent upon others for satisfaction of his needs. The oral stage characterizes the first year of life. According to Freud, it is divided into two periods: (1) sucking; (2) biting and chewing. Later character traits develop from these earliest modes of oral pleasure. More specifically, oral incorporation (as in sucking and taking in milk in the first oral period) becomes the prototype of such pleasures as those gained from the acquisition of knowledge or possessions. The gullible person (who is "easily taken in") is fixated at the oral, incorporative level of personality. The sarcastic, bitingly argumentative person is fixated at the second oral period—the sadistic level associated with biting and chewing.

## THE ANAL STAGE

During the anal stage (in the second year of life) toilet training is initiated, giving the child his first experience with imposed control of an instinctual impulse. The way in which this training is conducted affects later traits and values. Internal conflicts about withholding and retentiveness may arise in a person who has remained preoccupied with unresolved problems of the anal phase. The expressive character (cruel, destructive, tempestuous, and disorderly), according to the theory, results from fixation in the early anal phase, in which pleasure is localized in the expulsion of feces. This fixation may result from extreme repressive measures on the part of the mother (or other person) in toilet training. Pleasure is located in the retention of feces later in the anal phase. A person fixated at this level would show character traits of obstinacy and stinginess, precision and orderliness.

## THE PHALLIC STAGE

Next the phallic stage, characterized by masturbatory stimulation and the observation of the anatomical distinction between the sexes, sets the scene for the "Oedipus complex." According to Freud, the Oedipus complex, though modified and repressed after the age of five, remains a vital force in later personality. Both boys and girls love their mother as the satisfier of their basic needs and resent their father as a rival for their mother's affections. In addition, the boy fears castration by the father as retribution for his incestuous desires for his mother and his death wish toward his father. Castration fear is reinforced by the child's conception of the female as a castrated male and often by direct threats of castration accompanying discouragement of the boy's masturbation. Castration anxiety, in the boy, results in the repression of his sexual desire for his mother and in hostility toward his father. Gradually, to reduce the anxiety of possible castration by the father, the boy tries to become like him or to "identify" with him.

Identification with the father in turn helps the boy gain some vicarious satisfaction of his sexual impulses toward his mother. In this last phase of the Oedipus complex of the male, the superego reaches its final development as the internalized standards of parents and society: the opposition to incest and aggression becomes part of the child's own value system.

In the female, penis envy, resulting from the discovery that she lacks the more desirable male organ, is the impetus for the exchange of her original love object—the mother—for a new object, the father. Unlike the boy's Oedipus complex, which is repressed through fear, the girl—having nothing to lose—persists in her sexual desire for her father. This desire does, naturally, undergo some modification because of realistic barriers.

A latency period, characterized by reduced overt sexuality, follows at the end of the phallic stage. Memories of infantile sexuality are repressed and socially forbidden sexual activity is forgotten.

## THE GENITAL STAGE

The love objects of the pregenital period are essentially selfish or "narcissistic": that is, others are loved only because they provide additional forms of body pleasure to the child. Some of this narcissism eventually becomes channeled into genuine "object choices" or love relations, and the adolescent begins to love others for altruistic reasons. In the well-socialized adult the experiences of the oral, anal, and phallic stages have become fused and synthesized with genital impulses. This final phase of maturity is called the genital stage, and in it the individual is capable of genuine love and adult sexual satisfactions.

## FIXATION AND REGRESSION

The concepts of "fixation" and "regression" are closely connected with Freud's conceptualization of psychosexual stages of development. As previously noted, fixation means that a sexual impulse is arrested at an early stage. Regression is reversion to an earlier stage, the return of the libido to its former halting places in development. Fixation and regression are interdependent, for the stronger the fixations in the course of development, the more easily the individual regresses to them when he meets later difficulties. Fixation is caused by too great an intensity of the inevitable conflict at each stage of psychosexual development. The excessive stress may be due to severe deprivation or to overindulgence of the libido at a particular stage, or to inconsistent alternations between indulgence and deprivation.

In sum, the psychodynamics of personality are intimately related to the individual's mode of coping with problems encountered at each stage of psychosexual development. The result is reflected in the nature of character formation, symptoms, defense mechanisms, and relations with other people. When the individual's resolution of central problems at any stage of development is especially inadequate, later stress may cause him to regress to that earlier stage and to display behavior typical of that less mature period.

## FREUDIAN IDENTIFICATION THEORY

Many aspects of Freud's theory of psychosexual stages have been modified and even rejected in recent years. Some of his closely related concepts regarding identification, however, have continued to be influential.

Early personality development occurs in the setting of the family. In that context Freud strongly emphasized the child's attachment to the mother and the rivalry between son and father for her attentions (the "Oedipus situation") as the early occasion for the expression, restraint, and conversion of impulses. But he also saw the relations between child and parent as the bases for identification with, or internalization of, the standards of the parent. This identification process Freud attributed to two mechanisms that operate during psychosexual development.

"Anaclitic identification" is based on the intense dependency of a child on his mother, beginning early in the course of the infant's development. Because of the helplessness of the infant, his dependency upon his caretaker is profound. Identification for girls is based mainly on this early love or dependency relation with the mother. In anaclitic identification the child must first have developed a dependent love relationship with his caretaker (usually the mother). Later, when the mother begins to withdraw some of her nurturant attention, the child tries to recapture her by imitating and reproducing her in actions and fantasy. The extensive research that has been devoted to this mechanism is discussed in later chapters.

For boys dependency or "anaclitic" identification with the mother is supplemented later by "identification with the aggressor." The "aggressor" is the father during the Oedipal phase of development. Identification with the aggressor is motivated by fear of harm and castration by the punitive father in retribution for the son's fantasies and his libidinal wishes toward the mother. Freud described the situation vividly:

> . . . When a boy (from the age of two or three) has entered the phallic phase of his libidinal development, is feeling pleasurable sensations in his sexual organ and has learnt to procure these at will by manual stimulation, he becomes his mother's lover. He wishes to possess her physically in such ways as he has divined from his observations and intuitions about sexual life, and he tries to seduce her by showing her the male organ which he is proud to own. In a word, his early awakened masculinity seeks to take his father's place with her; his father has hitherto in any case been an envied model to the boy, owing to the physical strength he perceives in him and the authority with which he finds him clothed. His father now becomes a rival who stands in his way and whom he would like to get rid of (Freud, 1933, p. 46).

The hostile feelings that the boy experiences in the Oedipal situation engender great anxiety in him; he desires the mother but fears castration from the father. To defend against the resulting anxiety he resolves the Oedipal dilemma, repressing his aggressive wishes against his father and trying to become more like him. It is as though the boy believes that if he *"is"* the father he cannot be hurt by him. Identification with the aggressor requires that the boy have a strong (but ambivalent) relation with the father, in which his love for him is mixed with hostility because the father possesses the mother and interferes with the son's libidinal urges. Freud thought that, as a result of this additional process of identification with the aggressor, boys develop a stricter superego.

## NEO-FREUDIAN PSYCHOANALYTIC DEVELOPMENTS

In the years since Freud, a number of psychoanalytic theorists have proposed modifications in Freud's original theory. Most of these positions rest on humanistic conceptions of man forged out of the theorist's personal experiences with patients in psychotherapy and presenting his own conception of human nature. Many of these writings have helped to elaborate psychoanalytic concepts and to extend them in new directions.

### CARL JUNG

Carl Jung, an admirer and onetime associate of Freud, broke with his colleague and developed his own theory of psychoanalysis and his own method of psychotherapy. His approach became known as *analytical psychology*. Although it retains Freud's unconscious processes, it posits a *collective unconscious*—a transpersonal, inherited foundation of personality. The contents of the collective unconscious are *"archetypes"* or "primordial images." Unlike the personal unconscious, whose contents were once conscious but have been forgotten or repressed, the contents of the collective unconscious have never been in consciousness and therefore are not individually acquired; they owe their existence exclusively to heredity. Examples of archetypes (primordial images) include God, the young potent hero, the wise old man, rebirth (resurrection), Earth Mother, the Fairy Godmother, the hostile brethren, to list a few from a long collection found popularly in human legends and literature.

In Jung's view, the psyche included not only a conscious side but also a covert or *"shadow"* aspect that is unconscious. The process of personal growth involves an unfolding of this shadow and its gradual integration with the rest of the personality into a meaningful, coherent life pattern. The personality includes in everyone both a masculine, assertive aspect (the *"animus"*), and a feminine, soft, passive aspect (the *"anima"*). While both sexes have both animus and anima, in males the animus tends to be more fully expressed but the anima remains more in the "shadow," while in females the anima dominates and the animus is relatively unexpressed.

**TABLE 3-3   Jung's Four Ways of Experiencing the World**

| WAYS OF EXPERIENCING | CHARACTERISTICS |
| --- | --- |
| Sensing | Knowing through sensory systems |
| Intuition | Quick guessing about what underlies sensory inputs |
| Feeling | Focus on the emotional aspects of experience—its beauty or ugliness, pleasantness or unpleasantness |
| Thinking | Abstract thought, reasoning |

Jung described four basic ways of experiencing (contacting) the world: *sensing, intuition, feeling,* and *thinking,* summarized in Table 3-3. According to Jung, people differ consistently in the degree to which they emphasize each way of experiencing. One person, for example, might typically prefer intuitive leaps with little abstract thought, while another might know the world mostly through his senses with little use of either intuition or reason. In addition, recall that Jung was the one who had suggested a polarity of *extraversion-introversion* (as noted in the previous chapter). Like the four ways of experiencing, these two attitudes of extraversion-introversion are divided so that one is dominant in the conscious life while the other influences the unconscious side of the personality.

Jung broadened the concept of psychic energy. He did not exclude the sexual instinct of Freudian theory but thought it was only one among many instincts. Jung placed great emphasis on the directed aim or purposiveness of personality development. He believed that goal-directed behavior cannot be given an exclusively causal or historical explanation. For Jung the meaning of behavior may become fully intelligible only in terms of its end-products or final effects; we need to understand man not only in terms of his past but also in the light of his purposes and goal strivings.

Jung, like Freud, emphasized symbolic meanings. He believed, for example, that "abnormal behaviors" are expressions of the unconscious mind; some examples of these expressions are shown in Table 3-4, and they reveal clear overlap with Freud's thinking. Also like Freud, Jung thought that abnormal behaviors were merely one way in which the contents of the unconscious may reveal themselves. More often, he felt, they are expressed in dreams.

Jung went beyond Freud, however, in his increasing fascination with dreams as unconscious expressions of great interest in their own right. (He believed that this contrasts with their use merely as starting points for saying whatever comes to mind, i.e., "free associations," discussed in Chapter 9.) As Jung put it: ". . . I came increasingly to disagree with free association as Freud first employed it; I wanted to keep as close as possible to the dream itself, and to exclude all the irrelevant ideas and associations that it might evoke" (Jung, 1964, p. 28).

In the same direction, Jung became intrigued by the unconscious for its own sake. He viewed the unconscious not just as the source of instincts but as a vital,

**TABLE 3-4   Examples of Unconscious Symbolic Meanings
Believed To Underlie Abnormal Behavior ("Symptoms")
According to Jung**

| BEHAVIOR | UNDERLYING MEANING |
| --- | --- |
| Asthma attack | "She can't breathe the atmosphere at home" |
| Vomiting | "He can't digest—(some unpleasant fact)" |
| Spasm and inability to swallow | "He can't swallow it" |
| Leg paralysis | "She can't go on any longer" |

Jung (1964).

rich part of everyone's life, more significant than the conscious world, full of symbols communicated through dreams. The focus of Jungian psychology became the study of man's relation to his unconscious; its method taught the individual to become increasingly receptive to his own dreams, and to let his unconscious serve as a guide for how to live.

Jung's conception of personality is complex, more a set of observations than a coherent theory. His observations often dwelled on the multiple, contradictory forces in life: "I see in all that happens the play of opposites" (1963, p. 235). Yet he also was one of the first to conceptualize a *self* that actively strives for oneness and unity. Jung saw the self (the striving for wholeness) as an archetype that is expressed in many ways. The expressions of the striving for wholeness include the *mandala* (a magic circle archetype shown in Figure 3-3), and various religious and transcendental experiences. He devoted much of his life to the study of these expressions in primitive societies, alchemy, mythology, dreams, and symbols. To achieve unity and wholeness man must become increasingly aware of the wisdom available in his personal and collective unconscious and must learn to live in harmony with it.

## ERICH FROMM

Fromm's (1941, 1947) psychology represents an expansion of fundamental Freudian concepts to man as a member of society. Freud saw personality development as a reaction to satisfactions and frustrations of physiological drives. In contrast, for Fromm man is primarily a social being to be understood in terms of his relation to others. According to Fromm, individual psychology is fundamentally social psychology. In addition to the biological factors, man has psychological qualities, such as tendencies to grow, develop, and realize potentialities, that result in a desire for freedom and a striving for justice and truth. Thus human nature has a force of its own that influences the evolution of the social processes.

The difference between Freud's biological orientation and Fromm's social ori-

**Figure 3-3  A MANDALA**

entation is illustrated by Fromm's explanation of character traits. Fromm criticized Freud's idea that fixation of libido at certain erogenous (pleasure-giving) zones is the cause of later character traits. According to Fromm, character traits develop from experiences with others. Psychosexual problems and attitudes are rooted in the whole of the character structure. They are expressions in the language of the body of an attitude toward the world that is essentially socially conditioned. According to Freud, cultural phenomena are the result of societal suppressions of instinctual drives. For Fromm, ideologies and culture in general are based on the social character, which is molded by the mode of existence of a given society. In turn, the dominant character traits become productive forces shaping the social process.

Another major point of departure from Freud is Fromm's belief that ideals like truth, justice, and freedom can be genuine strivings and not simply rationalizations of baser motives. Freud's psychology is a psychology of instinctual drives that defines pleasure in terms of tension reduction. Fromm's psychology tries to make a place for positive attributes, such as tenderness and the human ability to love, and implies that these human needs have a force of their own. He believes that character is not the result of passive adaptation to social conditions but of a dynamic adaptation on the basis of elements that are either biologically inherent in human nature or have become inherent as the result of historic evolution.

## ERIK ERIKSON

The psychoanalyst Erik Erikson (1963) has proposed stages of development that call attention to problems of social adaptation (Table 3-5). As the child grows up he faces a wider range of human relationships. The solution of the specific problems at each of eight *psychosocial* stages (rather than psychosexual stages) determines how adequate a person he will become. Erikson's focus on psychosocial development reflects the growing neo-Freudian emphasis on broad social and cultural forces, rather than instinctual drives alone.

At each stage of development Erikson hypothesizes a psychosocial "crisis" that arises from the person's efforts to solve the problems facing him at that stage. For

**TABLE 3-5   Erikson's Stages of Psychosocial Development**

| STAGE AND AGE | PSYCHOSOCIAL CRISIS | OPTIMAL OUTCOME |
| --- | --- | --- |
| I. Oral-sensory (1st year of life) | Trust vs. Mistrust | Basic trust and optimism |
| II. Muscular-anal (2nd year) | Autonomy vs. Shame, doubt | Sense of control over oneself and the environment |
| III. Locomotor-genital (3rd through 5th year) | Initiative vs. Guilt | Goal-directedness and purpose |
| IV. Latency (6th year to start of puberty) | Industry vs. Inferiority | Competence |
| V. Puberty and Adolescence | Identity vs. Role Confusion | Reintegration of past with present and future goals, fidelity |
| VI. Early Adulthood | Intimacy vs. Isolation | Commitment, sharing, closeness and love |
| VII. Young and Middle Adult | Generativity vs. Self-absorption | Production and concern with the world and future generations |
| VIII. Mature Adult | Integrity vs. Despair | Perspective, satisfaction with one's past life, wisdom |

Based on Erikson (1963) and modified from original.

example, in the first stage of life (the "oral sensory" stage of the first year) the crisis involves "trust versus mistrust." Erikson hypothesizes that at this stage the child's relation to his mother forms his basic attitudes about "getting" and "giving." If the crisis is properly resolved, the experiences at this stage lay the foundation for later trust, drive, and hope.

A notable innovation of Erikson's stages is that they extend beyond infancy to include crises of adolescence and adulthood. He sees development as a process that extends throughout life, rather than being entirely determined in the early years. In this developmental process, "ego identity" is the central point of organization.

> The integration . . . of ego identity is . . . more than the sum of the childhood identifications. It is the accrued experience of the ego's ability to integrate all identifications with the vicissitudes of the libido, with the aptitudes developed out of endowment, and with the opportunities offered in social roles (Erikson, 1963, p. 261).

The underlying assumptions of his view of development are:

> (1) that the human personality in principle develops according to steps predetermined in the growing person's readiness to be driven toward, to be aware of, and to interact with, a widening social radius; and (2) that society, in principle, tends to be so constituted as to meet and invite this succession of potentialities for interaction and attempts to safeguard and to encourage the proper rate and the proper sequence of their enfolding (Erikson, 1963, p. 270).

Erikson's stages go much beyond childhood and include the psychosocial crises of the adult.

Erikson's ideas have become popular in many parts of our culture, and his thoughts concerning the "identity crises" of adolescence are discussed widely. Indeed the phrase "identity crisis" has become a part of common parlance. Both provocative and literate, most of Erikson's ideas have had more impact on broad concepts of human nature and on the general intellectual culture than on specific scientific formulations. Erikson believes that every young person must generate for himself some "central perspective and direction" that gives him a meaningful sense of unity and purpose, and that integrates the remnants of his childhood with the expectations and hopes of adulthood (Erikson, 1968). This sense of identity involves a synthesis of how the person has come to see himself and his awareness of what the important other people in his life expect him to be.

## OTHER NEO-FREUDIAN ANALYSTS

In many respects the formulations of Fromm and Erikson are representative of the contributions of numerous other "neo-Freudians," such as Alfred Adler, Harry Stack Sullivan, Karen Horney and David Rapaport. Generally these neo-Freudians advocate more concern with "ego processes" and "reality testing" and less attention to the role of instincts, libidinal energy, and distinct psychosexual developmental stages.

For Freud the id and the instincts were the dominant aspects of the total personality. The ego was subservient to the id's instinctual wishes, even in healthy personalities. More recent theorists identified with the psychoanalytic tradition have put more emphasis on social variables shaping personality and have emphasized less the role of instincts and genetically determined maturation. These neo-Freudians or "ego psychologists" assert a "conflict-free sphere" of the ego (Hartmann, Kris & Loewenstein, 1947; Rapaport, 1951). In their view, the ego has its own sources of energy and follows a course of development independent of the id and the instincts. That is, some portion of ego functioning is not determined by the attempt to avoid conflict between the id and the demands of society.

One of these neo-Freudians, Harry Stack Sullivan, most explicitly emphasizes the crucial importance of interpersonal processes and human relations for the development of personality. He conceptualizes psychiatry as a form of *social* psychology. For Sullivan the individual can be understood only in his relations to the significant people in his life. A somewhat similar emphasis characterizes the writings of Alfred Adler, who focuses on the person's total "life style" and his "social interest," thus also viewing man as a social being. These theorists, just like Jung, Fromm, and Erikson, have influenced general views about man and personality and broad attitudes toward psychotherapy; they have not generated specific testable hypotheses for research. Most of them are or were practicing psychotherapists and humanistic writers rather than experimental researchers and scientists. Their contribution, therefore, may prove to have more impact on the history of ideas than on the field of psychology as a formal area of science.

# IMPLICATIONS AND OVERVIEW

It is not simple—and probably impossible—to capture the essence of the Freudian approach and its derivatives so that their main implications for current personality psychology can be understood. However, the risk of oversimplification should not deter us from seeking a broader perspective. The following sections dwell on some especially noteworthy points, without attempting to be complete.

## MOTIVATIONAL DETERMINISM

Freudian psychoanalytic theory offers a motivationally determined view of behavior. The causal chain can be complex and indirect, with the events in one area or system of the personality exerting their effects on another, but every behavior, no matter how subtle or trivial, has its ultimate motivational cause within the person's dynamics. Much of the process of psychoanalytic assessment and therapy is a search for such underlying causes. A psychodynamic explanation of behavior consists of a delineation of the motives that produced it. The focus is not on behavior but on the motivational roots that it presumably serves and reflects.

Freudians tend to equate the deterministic nature of events with *motivational* determinism. They believe that all behavior, even the seemingly most absurd or trivial, is motivated and functionally significant for the organism's intrapsychic adaptation. They may view any behavioral manifestation as a sign of basic, pervasive, and highly generalized but largely unconscious forces. The most important motives for an individual's behavior are primarily unconscious. Man thus may be victimized by his own hidden motives, and he perceives these motives only through the distortions of defensive maneuvers enacted within himself in ways only dimly known to him. The basic psychodynamics of the person are established early in life during the stages of psychosexual development. The role of subsequent experiences is determined by the motivational patterns established in early childhood.

## IMAGE OF MAN

Freud constructed a compelling image of what a person might be, erecting a sweeping and novel theoretical system of man's relationship to himself and to his world. Freud saw the person as struggling with himself and the world, blocked by anxieties, conflicted, and plagued by his own unacceptable wishes and unconscious secrets. This picture of man has captivated the imagination of many laymen as well as clinicians, and consequently has had an enormous impact on philosophical as well as psychological conceptions of human nature. In Freud's view man is not the unemotional, rational being that Victorian society thought he was. Instead, he is torn by unconscious conflicts and wishes whose vicissitudes push him in seemingly puzzling ways.

Freud's emphasis on unconscious impulses as the most basic determinants of behavior is seen in an analogy in which the relation of the id and the ego is likened to that between a horse and its rider:

> . . . The horse provides the locomotive energy, and the rider has the prerogative of determining the goal and of guiding the movements of his powerful mount towards it. But all too often in the relations between the ego and the id we find a picture of the less ideal situation in which the rider is obliged to guide his horse in the direction in which it itself wants to go (Freud, 1933, p. 108).

Thus in Freud's psychology the id is stubborn and strong and frequently the ego cannot really control it effectively.

Freud believed that environmental sources of excitation were less important than inborn instincts in the dynamics of personality. He thought that external stimuli make fewer demands and in any event, can always be avoided, whereas one's own impulses and needs cannot be escaped. Consequently he made instinctual impulses and their vicissitudes the core of personality functioning.

Such grand theoretical systems, whether in pre-Christian Greece or post-Victorian Vienna, have dramatic intellectual functions, regardless of their ultimate scientific standing. They supply man with a new language to describe himself and to bring some sense and structure to his often disordered experiences. Constructions like the "id" are ways of conceptualizing complex aspects of experience. It is essential to remember, however, that such constructions are just that: conceptualizations about experience and not revelations of fact. Their usefulness must be demonstrated: in their research harvest, in the fruitfulness of the predictions that can be derived from them, and in their convenience for psychotherapy. Later chapters will examine some of the relevant evidence.

The impact of Freud's theory on society and on philosophy, as well as on the social sciences, is almost universally hailed as profound; its significance is frequently compared with the contributions of Darwin. Freud's contributions have been widely acknowledged, and they need no new praises here. The evidence relevant to Freud's theory as a scientific psychological system, however, has been questioned persistently.

Although Freud attempted to create a general psychology of man, his main systematic impressions were of thinking and feeling processes of conflict-ridden persons caught up in drastic personal crises. Moreover, Freud observed these tortured individuals only under extremely artificial conditions: lying on a couch during the psychotherapy hour in an environment deliberately made as asocial as possible. This drastically restricted observational base helped to foster a theory that is almost entirely a theory of intrapsychic anxiety and conflict and that pays little attention to the social environment and to the interpersonal context of behavior.

Furthermore, Freud tried to construct a theory of development at a time in history when few adequate concepts about learning were available in social science. Without having at hand a suitable set of learning concepts and terms for personality development, Freud relied on his own preference for a "body language": he preferred to say "oral" rather than "dependent," "anal" rather than "compulsive," "genital" rather than "mature." Freud's body language, while picturesque, unfortunately has made his theory difficult to integrate with scientific psychology. As we will see in the next chapter, some attempts have been made to translate Freud's ideas into different terms.

## TESTABILITY OF FREUD'S IDEAS

One of the main criticisms is that Freud's theory is hard to test. That is true in part because his constructs are ambiguous and hard to quantify. The terms often are loose and metaphoric and convey different meanings in different contexts. Clear, observable referents for them are rarely specified. Just what observations are required to conclude, for example, that an individual is fixated at the anal stage? Under what conditions may we conclude that he *is not* fixated at that stage? How can the extent or amount of his fixation be assessed? Likewise, is the college student radical who commits himself to fight the "establishment" really "intellectualizing" his emotional conflicts with "authority figures" (like his father) and his "Oedipal problems," or is he truly motivated to undo political evils? What would he have to do to show that he is motivated by his professed idealism rather than by unconscious conflicts? Often the answers to questions like these depend on the clinical judgments of trained experts. It therefore becomes essential to study how closely experts really do agree with each other and how well they can support their opinions with evidence (Chapter 9).

According to many critics some aspects of Freud's theory consist of little more than labels or categories for grouping data. Such labels (for example, the "death wish") cannot be tested and cannot be assessed by any methodology. Bluntly, some of these concepts do not offer the possibility of ever being disconfirmed by research. One danger here is that the psychologist may be beguiled into believing that these labels increase his explanatory powers when, instead, they merely lead him to after-the-fact sweeping generalities. Sometimes it is easy to interpret truisms as if they were insights.

In spite of these problems, many attempts have been made to clarify Freudian constructs, especially those dealing with defense mechanisms and conflict, and to submit them to experimental study (e.g., Blum, 1953; Hilgard, 1952; Holmes & Schallow, 1969; Masserman, 1952; Sears, 1943, 1944). Research has been plentiful and hundreds of investigators have produced a voluminous literature. Freud's followers have extended many of his concepts, emphasizing ego processes and social variables more than their mentor did and deemphasizing hereditary and instinctual forces. Some of the research that they have influenced is discussed in later chapters.

## PSYCHODYNAMIC THEORY AND TRAIT THEORY

Finally, and surprisingly, the psychodynamic approach to personality shares some basic assumptions with trait theory. As we have seen, psychodynamic theories assume that people develop a stable, basic, core personality that exerts itself pervasively, albeit indirectly and in disguised forms. Thus both trait theory and the psychodynamic approach assume the existence of enduring predispositions that determine behaviors across diverse situations. Again like trait theory, these hypothesized underlying predispositions or psychodynamics are inferred from behavioral signs.

The psychodynamic strategy of this inferential process, however, is radically different from the procedure favored by most trait theorists. Most trait research has been guided by a measurement model in which trait indicators are *directly* and *additively* related to the inferred underlying trait (Loevinger, 1957). For example, the more submissive behavior the person displays, the stronger the underlying trait of submissiveness. In contrast, psychodynamic theory posits highly *indirect*, nonadditive relations between behavior and hypothesized underlying states. For example, submissive behavior may be interpreted as a sign of underlying aggression, or of passivity-hostility conflicts, or of resistance disguising some other, more threatening characterological problems.

If one accepts these psychodynamic beliefs, it follows that great attention should be paid to clinical inferences and tests designed to reveal the individual's "underlying personality" and his dynamics from indirect behavioral signs. The methods and problems associated with these psychodynamically oriented clinical procedures are explored in later chapters.

## APPLICATIONS OF FREUD'S IDEAS

This chapter has merely sketched the outline of psychodynamic conceptions. The applications of these ideas for the assessment and treatment of persons probably have been more extensive than those of any other psychological theory. Consequently an adequate view of the meaning and implications of psychodynamic theory, and of its current status, cannot be achieved until these applications are examined in Part 2.

## SUMMARY

1. The most influential psychodynamic theory has been that of Sigmund Freud. Freud's theory and method of treating personality disturbances were based on extensive clinical observation of neurotic persons and on self-analysis.

2. In Freud's view, the id, ego, and superego form the tripartite structure of the personality. The *id* is the primary, instinctual core. It obeys the

"pleasure principle," seeking immediate gratification of impulses. The *ego* mediates between the instinctual demands of the id and the outer world of reality. Its energy is derived from the id, and it operates by means of "secondary processes": logical thinking and rational planning. The ego functions to test reality, localizing the appropriate objects for gratification in the environment so that tension reduction can occur. The *superego* represents the internalized moral standards of the society, achieved through the internalization of parental control and characteristics in the course of socialization.

3. Personality dynamics involve a perpetual conflict between the id, ego, and superego. This conflict is accompanied by continuous transformations of the finite amount of energy or "libido" contained in the person. The basic conflict is between the person's instinctual impulses and learned inhibitions and anxieties regarding their expression. The major determinants of man's behavior are unconscious and irrational: individuals are driven by persistent, illogical demands from within.

4. Man's hedonistic desire for immediate gratification of his sexual and aggressive instincts puts him in conflict with his environment. The conflict becomes internal when the person has incorporated the prohibitions of the culture in which he has been raised.

5. This struggle between impulse and inhibition produces anxiety. Defenses may be used by the ego when it is unable to handle anxiety effectively. Transformed by these defenses, the person's unacceptable impulses and unconscious motives express themselves indirectly or symbolically in disguised forms.

6. Freud's theory of personality development posits a series of psychosexual stages: oral, anal, phallic, and genital, so named for the erogenous zone which characterizes each. Later personality traits develop according to the individual's experience at each of these stages of maturation.

7. "Anaclitic identification" and "identification with the aggressor" are two Freudian identification mechanisms. The first is based on the intense dependency of a child on his mother. The second, identification with the aggressor, is based on the boy's fear of potential castration by his father in retribution for his incestuous desires for his mother.

8. In general, the psychoanalytic followers of Freud have deemphasized the role of instincts and psychosexual stages and have concerned themselves more with the social milieu and the ego. Their conception of human nature has been less deterministic, less drive oriented, and more humanistic.

9. One especially striking departure from Freud is the psychology of Jung. Jung emphasized the unconscious and its symbolic and mystical expressions. He focused on dreams and on man's need to achieve unity through greater awareness of his collective and personal unconscious.

10. Freud's theory and image of man have had a profound impact, but it has proved difficult to test many of his ideas scientifically.

# CHAPTER 4

# PSYCHODYNAMIC BEHAVIOR THEORY Conceptions

This chapter introduces some of the basic concepts of *behavioral* approaches to personality. Several distinct types of behavior theory have been developed over the years. They often bear similar labels, but in fact they are very different from each other. What unites them is a common emphasis on learning experiences as the main determinants of personality and a commitment to a rigorous methodology for studying behavior experimentally.

While they are often intrigued by the insights of Freud and his followers, behaviorally oriented psychologists are primarily dedicated to the scientific, rigorous study of psychology. They have devoted themselves to the development of an experimental methodology through which precise and reliable research might be possible. Heavily influenced by strategies in other natural sciences, early workers in this field began with careful study of lower animals in highly controlled laboratory situations. While some were fascinated by Freud's bold speculations about the mind, most were skeptical about his informal clinical methods. Rather than probe the dreams and free associations of neurotic patients or theorize broadly about human nature and society, these researchers sought a system that would be objectively testable, preferably by laboratory techniques.

Psychologists in this tradition focused on the basic processes of learning through which an organism in interaction with its environment acquires and performs a repertoire of responses. They studied the learning mechanisms through which certain events—"stimuli"—become associated with particular behaviors or responses. Like all scientific theorists, their objective was to understand causes—in this case, learning or the ways in which stimuli become associated with responses.

## DOLLARD AND MILLER

In this chapter we will concentrate on one type of behavior theory: the version developed in the late 1940s by John Dollard and Neal Miller at Yale University. We will call their orientation "psychodynamic behavior theory" because it is a major effort to integrate some of the fundamental ideas of Freudian psychodynamic theory with the concepts, language, and methods of experimental laboratory research on behavior and learning.

### PRIMARY NEEDS AND LEARNING

The newborn infant begins his life with a set of *innate* or *primary* biological needs, such as the need for food and water, oxygen, and warmth. Satisfaction of these needs to some minimal degree is essential for the organism's survival. But although these needs are innate, the behaviors required to satisfy them involve learning.

For example, sucking is an innate response that is readily elicited in the newborn when a nipple stimulates his mouth. But although the sucking response itself may be innate, its efficiency increases with practice. Thus even the seemingly elementary response patterns required to satisfy primary needs depend on learning processes for their efficient execution. The most casual observation of other cultures quickly reveals that there are almost endless ways to fulfill even such primary needs as hunger and thirst. Through learning great variability develops in the ways in which needs are fulfilled. Consider, for example, food preferences: the gourmet dishes of one culture may be the causes of nausea in another. The same learned variability seen in food preferences also is found in standards of shelter, clothing, aesthetics, and values when one compares different cultures.

Most human behaviors involve goals and incentives whose relations to innate needs are extremely remote. People seem to strive for such exceedingly diverse goals as money, status, power, love, charity, competence, mastery, creativity, self-realization, and so on. These and many more strivings have been characterized and classified as human motives. Neal Miller and John Dollard have deeply explored the learning processes through which such motives may evolve from primary needs.

Starting with the basic assumption that behavior is learned, Dollard and Miller (1950) have constructed a learning theory to explain the wide range of behavior involved in normal personality, neurosis, and psychotherapy. In their view, the four important factors in the learning process are drive (motivation), cue (stimulus), response (act or thought), and reinforcement (reward). In its simplest form, their idea is that

> in order to learn one must want something, notice something, do something, and get something (Miller & Dollard, 1941, p. 2).

These four events correspond respectively to "drive," "cue," "response," and "reward." Learning, in their view, is the process through which a particular response and a cue stimulus become connected.

Think of an animal in the psychologist's laboratory. Motivated by the *drive* of hunger, the animal engages in diffuse activity. At one point he happens to see a lever (*cue*). His *response*, at first accidental, is to press the lever, and this action releases food into his cup. The animal eats the food at once, thereby reducing the tension of his hunger drive (*reward* or *reinforcement*). Now in the future when he is hungry, he is more likely to press the lever again: the association between the cue stimulus (the lever) and the response (pressing it) has been strengthened. On subsequent trials the hungry animal will press the lever sooner. Let us consider each of the four components of learning separately.

## DRIVE

According to Dollard and Miller (1950), any strong stimuli (internal or external) may impel action and thus serve as drives. The stronger the stimulus the greater its drive function. A mild stimulus (such as the faint sound of a distant horn) does not motivate behavior as much as a strong stimulus (the blare of the horn near one's ear). Examples of strong stimuli are hunger pangs and pain-inducing noise—they motivate behavior. While any stimulus may become strong enough to act as a drive, certain classes of stimuli (such as hunger, thirst, fatigue, pain, and sex) are the primary basis for most motivation. These stimuli are "primary" or innate drives. The strength of the primary drives varies with the conditions of deprivation: the greater the deprivation, the stronger the drive.

Often the operation of primary drives is not easy to observe directly. Society generally protects its members from the unpleasant force of strong primary drives by providing for their reduction before they become overwhelming. In instances when this is not true—for example, conditions of prolonged famine in India— psychologists usually are not present to study behavior systematically. Moreover, social inhibitions—for example, in the area of sex—may further prevent the direct or complete public expression of primary drives. Consequently, much visible behavior is motivated by already altered "secondary" or learned drives. It is these transformed motives that are most evident under conditions of modern society and that are important in civilized human behavior.

According to Dollard and Miller, these learned drives are acquired on the basis of the primary (unlearned, innate) drives and are elaborations of them. The acquisition of fear as a learned drive has been studied carefully. (Some of the specific mechanisms of such learning are discussed in detail in the next chapter.) A fear is learned if it occurs in response to previously neutral cues (e.g., a white room). A learned fear is also a drive in the sense that it motivates behavior (e.g., escape from the room) and its reduction is reinforcing.

In one study, rats were exposed to electric shock in a white compartment and were permitted to escape to a black compartment where there was no shock (Miller, 1948). Eventually the rats responded with fear to the white compartment alone (that is, without shock). Even when the shock (primary drive stimulus) was no longer present, the animals learned new responses, such as pressing a lever or turning a wheel, in order to escape from the harmless white compartment. In common sense terms, they behaved as if they were afraid of an objectively harmless stimulus. The motivation for this new learning lies, according to Miller and Dollard, in the reduction of the learned fear of the white compartment. Thus fear is conceptualized as both a learned response and a learned drive, and its reduction is considered to be a reinforcement.

Dollard and Miller's emphasis on drives, both "primary" and "secondary," is reminiscent of the Freudian emphasis on motives and impulses as the forces underlying behavior. While Freud's conceptualization stresses instinctual wishes, however, Dollard and Miller's makes room for many learned motives, whose roots are in primary drives.

## CUE

"The drive impels a person to respond. Cues determine when he will respond, where he will respond and which response he will make" (Dollard & Miller, 1950, p. 32). The lunch bell, for example, functions as a cue for the hungry schoolchild to put away his books and get his lunchbox. Cues may be auditory, visual, olfactory, and so on. They may vary in intensity, and various combinations of stimuli may function as cues. Changes, differences, and the direction and size of differences may be more distinctive cues than is an isolated stimulus. For example, a person may not know the absolute length of an unmarked line but yet be able to tell which of two lines is the longer.

In Dollard and Miller's formulation a very intense stimulus may become a drive. A stimulus thus may serve as both a drive and a cue, motivating behavior and directing it as well.

## RESPONSE

Before a response to a cue can be rewarded and learned, it must of course occur. Dollard and Miller suggest ranking the organism's responses according to their probability of occurrence. They call this order the "initial hierarchy." Learning changes the order of responses in the hierarchy. An initially weak response, if properly rewarded, may come to occupy the dominant position. The new hierarchy produced by learning is termed the "resultant hierarchy." With learning and development, the hierarchy of responses becomes linked to language, and it is heavily influenced by the culture in which social learning has occurred.

## REINFORCEMENT

A reinforcement is a specific event that strengthens the tendency for a response to be repeated. A reduction in the strength of a drive reinforces any immediately preceding response. In other words, drive reduction serves as a reinforcement (or reward). This is true for both primary and secondary, or acquired, drives. The reduction or avoidance of painful stimulation, and of learned fears or anxieties associated with pain and punishment, also may function as a reinforcement. We saw earlier that rats seemed to work hard to escape from the white, fear-inducing compartment (Miller, 1948).

Miller and Dollard's concept of reinforcement as drive reducing or tension reducing has some similarity to Freud's "pleasure principle." Both concepts view need states as states of high tension and construe the reduction of tension, and the attainment of equilibrium, as the organism's goals.

Reinforcement is essential to the maintenance of a habit as well as to its learning. *Extinction* is the gradual elimination of a tendency to perform a response; it occurs when that response is repeated without reinforcement. The time required to extinguish a habit depends on the habit's initial strength and on the conditions of the extinction situation. Conditions of weak drive, effortful responses, short time between extinction trials, and strong alternative responses influence extinction.

According to Dollard and Miller, extinction merely inhibits the old habit; it does not destroy it. If new responses performed during extinction are rewarded, they may be strengthened to the point where they supersede the old habit. For example, if a child is praised and rewarded for independent, autonomous play but consistently nonrewarded (extinguished) when he dependently seeks help, the independent pattern will become predominant over the dependent one.

More recently Miller (1963) has speculated about possible alternatives to his drive-reduction concept of reinforcement learning. His hypothesis of an alternative to drive reduction includes the tentative assumption of "activating" or "go" mechanisms in the brain. These "go" mechanisms, Miller conjectured, could be activated in a variety of ways (such as by thinking), not merely by the reduction of drives or noxious stimulation.

## CONFLICT

An individual may experience conflict when he wants to pursue two or more goals that are mutually exclusive. For example, a person may want to spend the evening with a friend but thinks he should prepare for an examination facing him the next morning; or she may want to express her anger at her parents but also does not want to hurt them. When an individual must choose among incompatible alternatives, he or she may undergo conflict.

Neal Miller's (1959) conceptualization of conflict, which is influenced by Lewin (1935), hypothesizes *approach* and *avoidance* tendencies. For example, in an "approach-approach" conflict the person is torn, at least momentarily, between two desirable goals. Conversely, people often face "avoidance-avoidance" conflicts between two undesirable alternatives: to study tediously for a dull subject or flunk the examination, for example. The individual may wish to avoid both of these aversive events, but each time he starts to move away from his desk he reminds himself how awful it would be to fail the test.

Some of the most difficult conflicts involve goals or incentives that are both positive and negative in valence. These are the goals toward which we have "mixed feelings" or ambivalent attitudes. For example, we may want the pleasure of a gourmet treat but not the calories, or we may desire the fun of a vacation spree but not the expense, or we may love certain aspects of a parent but hate him in other respects.

Recall that approach-avoidance conflicts had a predominant place in Freud's hypotheses regarding intrapsychic clashes—for example, between id impulses and inhibitory anxieties. Just as conflict is central to Freud's conception of personality dynamics, so it is the core of Dollard and Miller's theory. But whereas Freud developed his ideas about conflict from inferences regarding id-ego-superego clashes in his neurotic patients, Dollard and Miller tested their ideas in careful experiments with rats.

Miller's original theory of conflict was based on a number of animal experiments (e.g., Brown, 1942, 1948; Miller, 1959). In one study, for example, hungry rats learned how to run down an alley to get food at a distinctive point in the maze. To generate "ambivalence" (approach-avoidance tendencies), the rats were given a quick electric shock while they were eating. To test the resulting conflict, the rats were later placed again at the start of the alley. The hungry rat now started toward the food but halted and hesitated before reaching it. The distance from the food at which he stopped could be changed by manipulating either the amount of his hunger or the strength of the electric shock.

Dollard and Miller applied the concept of *goal gradients* to analyze conflict. Goal gradients are changes in response strength as a function of distance from the goal object. To assess the strength of approach and avoidance tendencies at different points from the goal, a harness apparatus was devised to measure a rat's pull toward a positive reinforcement (food) or away from a negative reinforcement (shock).

The light harness enabled the experimenter to restrain the rat for a moment along the route to the goal and measure (in grams) the strength of the animal's pull on the harness at each test point (Brown, 1948). The rats pulled harder when they were restrained nearer the goal than when they were restrained farther away from it. This finding is evidenced by the slope of the approach gradient (shown in Figure 4-1) connecting the near test point and the far test point.

**Figure 4-1** APPROACH AND AVOIDANCE GRADIENTS

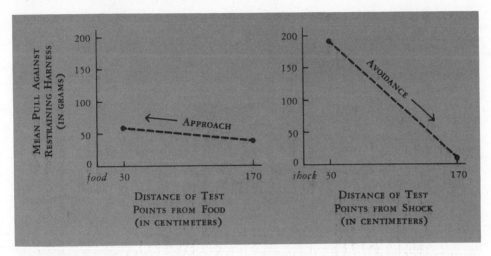

Adapted from Brown (1948).

Similar procedures were used with rats who received an electric shock at the end of the alley. When these animals were later placed at the same point in the alley where they had been shocked before (but now with no shock), they ran away from the spot. Moreover, the nearer the rats were to that spot when tested in the restraining harness, the harder they generally pulled to get away (Figure 4-1). The steeper slope of the avoidance gradient (when compared to the approach gradient) is especially noteworthy.

On the basis of these and similar studies, Dollard and Miller conceptualized conflict in learning terms, according to the following principles:

1. The tendency to approach a goal (the gradient of approach) becomes stronger the nearer the individual is to the goal.

2. The tendency to avoid a negative stimulus (the gradient of avoidance) becomes stronger the nearer the individual is to the stimulus.

3. The gradient of avoidance is steeper than the gradient of approach. (That is, the strength of the avoidance tendency increases more quickly with nearness than does the tendency to approach.)

4. An increase in the drive associated with either approach or avoidance raises the general level of that gradient.

In sum, the drive-conflict model posits the simultaneous existence of drive-like forces (approach tendencies) and of inhibitory forces (avoidance tendencies). Predictions about behavior in an approach-avoidance conflict involve inferences about the strength of the approach tendencies and of the inhibiting forces, the resulting behavior being a function of their net effect. Within this general framework of drive-conflict theory, many formulations have been advanced that are similar to the intrapsychic conflicts between id impulses and ego defenses that are crucial in Freud's theory.

## NEUROTIC CONFLICT

Like Freud, Dollard and Miller conceptualize conflict and anxiety as the core ingredients of neurotic behavior. In Freud's formulation, neurotic conflict involves a clash between id impulses seeking expression and internalized inhibitions that censor and restrain the expression of those impulses in accord with the culture's taboos. Dollard and Miller state the same basic ideas in the language of learning theory.

In Dollard and Miller's view of neurosis, strong fear (anxiety) is a learned drive that motivates a conflict concerning "goal responses" for other strong drives, such as sex or aggression. Specifically, when the neurotic person begins to approach goals that might reduce such drives as sex or aggression, strong fear is elicited in him. Such fear may be elicited by thoughts relevant to the drive goals, as well as by any overt approach attempts. For example, sexual wishes or hostile feelings toward a parent may be frightening; hence a conflict ensues between the wishes and the fear triggered by their expression. These inhibitory fearful responses further prevent drive reduction, so that the blocked drives (such as sex and aggression) continue to "build up" to a higher level. The person is thus trapped in an unbearable conflict between his frustrated, pent-up drives and the fear connected with approach responses relevant to their release.

The neurotic person in this dilemma may be stimulated simultaneously by the frustrated drives and by the fear that they evoke. The high drive state connected with this conflict produces "misery" and interferes with clear thinking, discrimination, and effective problem solving. The "symptoms" shown by the neurotic arise from the build up of the drives and of the fear that inhibits their release.

## ANXIETY AND REPRESSION

Like Freud, Dollard and Miller accept unconscious factors as critically important determinants of behavior, and, again like Freud, they give anxiety (or learned fear) a central place in dynamics. In their view, repression involves the learned response of *not-thinking* of something and it is motivated by the secondary drive of fear. That is, due to past experiences certain thoughts may have come to arouse fear as a result of their associations with pain or punishment. By not thinking these thoughts, the fear stimuli are reduced and the response (of not-thinking) is further reinforced. Eventually "not-thinking" (inhibiting, stopping, repressing) becomes anticipatory, in the sense that the individual avoids particular thoughts before they can lead to painful outcomes. This formulation is similar to Freud's idea that repression is the result of anxiety and functions to reduce the anxiety caused when unacceptable material starts to emerge from the unconscious to the conscious.

Dollard and Miller's account thus serves as a clear translation of the psychodynamic formulation of anxiety, repression, and defense into the terms of reinforcement learning theory. Defenses and symptoms (e.g., phobias, hysterical blindness) are reinforced by the immediate reduction of the fear drive. While the temporary effect of the symptom is drive reduction and momentary relief, its long-range effects may be debilitating. For example, a phobic symptom may prevent a person from working effectively and hence create new dilemmas, fear, guilt, and other conditions of high drive conflict.

## IMPLICATIONS

As was noted in the last chapter, Freud constructed a theory of development without the benefit of learning concepts. He adopted a body language and invented new terms like "fixation" that made it difficult to coordinate his theory with experimental psychology. Dollard and Miller demonstrated that this coordination could be achieved. They drew on laboratory research with animals to devise a personality theory in learning terms that closely paralleled, and in many respects translated, Freudian theory. The psychodynamic emphasis on motives, on unconscious processes, on internal conflicts and defenses, such as repression, remained largely unchanged. Many psychologists found Freud's basic ideas more congenial and easier to adopt when they were put into the language of learning and experimental psychology. Consequently these concepts stimulated much research.

Many analyses of the individual's socialization into his culture have been guided by the motivational formulations of Miller and Dollard. In accord with their theory, inhibition training by socialization agents may produce conflicts between approach tendencies and avoidance tendencies, just as in Freud's view the child experiences conflict between his impulses and his anxiety regarding the consequences of expressing those impulses. Examples of this model are found in the analysis of motivational conflicts resulting from toilet training and from the socialization of sexual impulses (e.g., Mussen, Conger & Kagan, 1974). In recent years there have been many theoretical extensions (and criticisms, e.g., Maher, 1966) of conflict theory, with applications to diverse phenomena (e.g., Renner, 1964, 1967). Epstein (1962, 1967) has moved conceptually toward a more general theory of human conflict and anxiety.

Other psychologists have been troubled because the research by Miller and his colleagues is based mainly on animal studies. Indeed, this fact has earned it some of its greatest criticism. Careful investigation carried out with a lower species, such as the rat, whose behavior is far removed from human problems, may not hold up when extrapolations are made to people. Many critics have objected that human social behavior is of a fundamentally different nature than the behavior of animals in the laboratory and therefore requires a different methodology.

Some critics found the rodent a philosophically and aesthetically unappealing model for man and rejected animal analogies for human personality. They were repelled by the analogies between rat and person and believed that in the transition from the clinic to the laboratory some of the most exciting features of Freud's view of man were lost.

Of course the real test of a position is not its appeal to friends and critics, but the research and conceptual advances that it produces. Dollard and Miller's psychodynamic behavior theory cannot be evaluated in these respects until we have examined the relevant evidence, which is presented in later chapters.

## BEYOND PRIMARY DRIVES

One of the most influential aspects of Dollard and Miller's theory is its emphasis on drives and motivation. The concept of learned motivation has been especially provocative because it implies a way of understanding the genesis of human social behavior from biological roots. Inspired by Dollard and Miller, but seeking to go beyond animal experiments and primary drives, many personality theorists have tried to discover higher-order motives for complex human behavior.

### HIGHER-ORDER APPROACH MOTIVES

Most animal experiments on motivation have dealt with such primary physiological drives as hunger, thirst, or sex. Because these drives all involve specific physiological changes in the organism (e.g., increased salivation), considerable agreement can be reached about their nature, at least in laboratory studies with animals. Students of personality and human motivation, however, have been more interested in drives, goal strivings, and motives that have no specific physiological correlates. Even casual observation reveals the great variety of human actions and the diverse events that may serve as goals, incentives, or reinforcers: for example, babies seem to be "reinforced" by watching rattles, children by play with blocks, adolescents by recognition from each other, business executives by "success," and college teachers by endless talk. Motivational theorists try to group the main needs and motives that may be the forces driving people to engage in widely different behavior patterns.

In recent years many theorists have hypothesized different motives with unspecified physiological correlates. Examples of these "higher-order" motives include the person's need for activity and his needs to explore, manipulate, and investigate the environment (Berlyne, 1966; Nunnally & Lemond, 1973). Many other motives also have been suggested as possible learned derivatives of these more basic ones. Moreover, while some theorists, in accord with Dollard and Miller's original formulation, consider all motives to be derived from their association with the reduction of primary (innate) physiological drives, others have suggested additional "intrinsic" (unlearned) motives that are not derived from specific physiological drives.

There is no final agreement about how to conceptualize motives, and different theoreticians emphasize different human needs. Motives that have received research attention in recent years include achievement, activity, affiliation, competence, consistency, curiosity, dependency, exploratory behavior, identity, informa-

**TABLE 4-1   Some Human Needs According to Murray (1938)**

Abasement (to comply and accept punishment)
Achievement (to strive to reach goals quickly and well)
Affiliation (to form friendships)
Aggression (to hurt another)
Autonomy (to strive for independence)
Counteraction (to overcome defeat)
Deference (to serve gladly)
Defendance (to defend and justify oneself)
Dominance (to control or influence others)
Exhibition (to excite, shock, self-dramatize)
Harmavoidance (to avoid injury, pain, sickness, death)
Infavoidance (to avoid humiliation)

These examples are the first dozen needs from a much longer alphabetical list.

tion, social approval, and stimulation. Some theoreticians have hypothesized even more differentiated needs. Henry Murray's (1938) classification includes 28 different "psychogenic" (nonphysiological) needs; examples are shown in Table 4-1.

## COMPETENCE MOTIVATION

Robert White (1959) has suggested that many of the hypothesized higher-order motives, such as play, curiosity, and adventure seeking, may be subsumed under a more fundamental desire for competence or effective functioning and mastery. White further suggests that such a competence or "effectance" motive may be intrinsic and that many activities (like play) may be enjoyed for their own sake, whether or not they reduce or satisfy primary drives. White has discussed the nature of effective or competent coping with the environment as seen in such common activities as walking, exploring and crawling, and language. He comments that the behavior that is effective in all these efforts "is directed, selective, and persistent, and it is continued not only because it serves primary drives, which indeed it cannot serve until it is almost perfected, but because it satisfies an intrinsic need to deal with the environment" (White, 1959, p. 319).

Competence or "effectance" motivation thus implies a desire to achieve mastery of a task simply for its own sake. The particular tasks to be mastered may be virtually infinite—any response pattern is potentially perfectable, whether it is tightrope walking, building towers with toy blocks, flower arranging, or scientific theory building. The satisfaction of doing such tasks competently, White believes, does not depend merely on their link to primary drive reduction or on praise and approval elicited from others: the effectance motive is intrinsic.

White's view that a higher-order motive, such as effectance or competence, is independent of primary drives, such as hunger and sex, differs from the original formulations of Dollard and Miller and of Freud. As we saw, Dollard and Miller try to conceptualize all motives as learned derivatives of physiological drives, and Freud construed libidinal energy and sexual and aggressive instincts as the basis of

Competence motivation refers to the desire to achieve mastery.

human strivings. The actual origins of hypothesized higher-order motives like competence are hard (if not impossible) to trace definitively. Regardless of their roots, it has become clear, however, that many different types of gratification can serve as goals and incentives that people may pursue passionately and that appear to have little relation to primary drives.

## SUMMARY

1. Dollard and Miller's behavior theory represents a fusion of psychoanalytic concepts with the more objective language and methods of laboratory

studies of animal learning. Their theory emphasizes drive, cue, response, and reinforcement as the basic components of learning. *Drives* are strong stimuli that impel action. Primary or innate drives (such as hunger, pain, sex) are the basis of motivation. Many other drives or motives may be learned from their association with primary drive reduction. *Cues* direct behavior, determining when, where, and how the *response* (behavior) will occur. A *reinforcement* is any specific event that strengthens the likelihood of a response. Reinforcement is essential to the learning and to the maintenance of a response. Events that reduce a drive serve as reinforcements.

2. Dollard and Miller translate such Freudian dynamic concepts as internal conflict and repression into the terms of learning theory. They interpret conflict in terms of the simultaneous existence of approach and avoidance tendencies. Their theory suggests that the strength of these drive-like forces depends on the organism's distance from the goal object, and that behavior is a function of the net effect of approach and avoidance tendencies. Moreover, Dollard and Miller construed repression as a learned response of "not-thinking" that reduces the learned drive of fear.

3. Many personality theorists, influenced by Miller and Dollard, have hypothesized and studied a variety of human motives in an attempt to analyze approach-avoidance conflicts in socialization, choice behavior, and other areas of human relations. Some of these motives have been conceptualized as learned derivatives of primary drives, in accord with Dollard and Miller's original formulation.

4. Some motivational theorists have gone beyond Dollard and Miller's initial drive-reduction ideas to posit the existence of intrinsic motives (e.g., curiosity, achievement, affiliation, identity, stimulation, and social approval) that are motivating in their own right, do not depend on the reduction of primary drives like hunger and sex, and do not have specific physiological correlates.

5. Robert White proposes competence or "effectance" motivation, which is a fundamental desire to achieve mastery of a task for its own sake. He hypothesizes that the effectance motive is independent of primary drives such as hunger and sex and suggests that many of the hypothesized higher-order motives (play, curiosity, adventure seeking) can be subsumed under this intrinsic need to deal with the environment. Regardless of whether motives are intrinsic or learned derivatives of primary drives, it is evident that people may strive for many goals that seem to bear little relation to primary drives.

# CHAPTER 5

# SOCIAL BEHAVIOR THEORIES Conceptions

This chapter discusses more recent behavioral approaches for understanding the phenomena of personality. It will be seen that these conceptions share with Dollard and Miller's psychodynamic behavior theory a belief in the importance of learning for personality development. In many other respects, however, the positions discussed in this chapter depart sharply from the ideas that guided Dollard and Miller. Several varieties of behavior theory have been formulated in recent years, and many of them have developed in distinctly new directions. Among the most influential conceptions have been the ideas of B. F. Skinner, Julian B. Rotter, and Albert Bandura.

## B. F. SKINNER'S RADICAL BEHAVIORISM

Although he is also a learning theorist, B. F. Skinner's (1953, 1974) approach is radically different from Dollard and Miller's. Skinner differs fundamentally from these theorists in his concern with *behavior* rather than with dispositions and motives, and in his unwillingness to infer learned drives or any other internal motivational forces and traits.

## REJECTION OF INFERRED MOTIVES
## AND DYNAMICS

We saw in the last chapter that many human motives have been hypothesized and that there is no firm consensus about the most basic ones. Theories concerning motivation have helped to reveal the variety and complexity of human strivings, and also have contributed to the development of research about their causes (Part 3). In most research on motives investigators have been inspired by the model of experimental research on biological drives in animals. In animal studies of motivation, the hypothesized need of the animal (his hunger or sex drive, for example) has been linked clearly to observable conditions manipulated in the laboratory. For example, the strength of the hunger drive may be inferred in part from the amount of time that the animal has been deprived of food. When a dog has not been fed for two days, we may safely say that his hunger drive is high. In such cases references to drives and motives involve no serious ambiguity. Likewise, some careful investigations of hypothesized higher-order motives in people have specified clearly the objective conditions that define the motive (e.g., McClelland *et al.*, 1953).

Less rigorous applications of motivational theory to personality, however, may use motives loosely (for example as "wishes" and "desires"), and their value as explanations of behavior is open to serious question. The tendency to invoke motives as explanations of why people behave as they do is understandable, because that is how we "explain" behavior in common sense terms. To explain why a child spent an unusual amount of time cleaning and grooming himself neatly, we easily might say "because he had strong cleanliness needs" or "because he had a compulsive desire for order." Such hypotheses about motives may sound like explanations, but they tell us little unless the motive is defined objectively and unless the causes of the motive itself are established. What makes the child have "cleanliness needs"? What determines his "compulsive desires"? Why does he "wish" to be clean?

B. F. Skinner and his associates have criticized many concepts regarding human needs as being no more than motivational labels attached to human activities. Thus orderly behavior may be attributed to a motive for orderliness, submissive behavior to submissiveness needs, exploratory behavior to the need to explore, and so on. To avoid this circularity and to untangle explaining from naming, behaviorally oriented psychologists like Skinner prefer to analyze behaviors in terms of the observable events and conditions that seem to vary with them. Hence they refrain from positing specific motivations. Rather than hypothesize the needs that may propel a particular activity, they try to discover the events that strengthen its future likelihood and that maintain or change it. Thus they search for the conditions that regulate the behavior rather than hypothesize need states inside the person as motives that drive him.

In Skinner's view, psychology is the science of behavior: inferences about un-observable inner states and motives are not adequate explanations, and they add nothing to a scientific account of the conditions controlling behavior. For Skinner "motivation" is simply the result of depriving or satiating an organism of some substance such as water or food for a given period of time. Thus a "drive" is just a convenient way of referring to the observable effects of such deprivation or satia-tion. Likewise, Skinner avoids any inferences about internal "conflicts" (e.g., among approach and avoidance tendencies), preferring an experimental analysis of the ac-tual stimulus conditions that control the particular behavior.

## BASIC STRATEGY

Skinner's work is based on the premise that a genuine science of human be-havior is not only possible but desirable. In his view, science should try to predict and determine experimentally (i.e., "control") the behavior of the individual orga-nism. The cause-and-effect relationships in behavior become the laws of behavioral science (Skinner, 1974).

Skinner proposes a "functional analysis" of the organism as a behaving system. Such an analysis tries to link the organism's behavior to the precise conditions that control or determine it. Skinner's approach therefore concentrates on the observ-able covariations between "independent variables" (stimulus events) and "depend-ent variables" (response patterns). The variables in a functional analysis, according to Skinner, must be external, observable, and described in physical and quantitative terms.

Insofar as relevant variables can be brought under the control of experimental manipulation, Skinner contends that the laboratory offers the best chance of obtain-ing a scientific analysis of behavior. Furthermore, the experimental study of behav-ior has much to gain from dealing with the behavior of animals below the complex human level. Science, Skinner points out, advances from the simple to the complex and is constantly concerned with whether the processes and laws discovered at one stage are adequate for the next.

## CLASSICAL CONDITIONING AND
## CONDITIONED REINFORCERS

Like most other experimental psychologists, Skinner recognized the impor-tance of the type of "classical" or "respondent" conditioning initially discovered by Pavlov. To understand Skinner's own contributions, we must consider first the na-ture of classical conditioning.

The essence of this phenomenon lies in the experiment in which a dish of food is presented often to a food-deprived (hungry) organism. In time, the empty dish alone will elicit a primary or unconditioned response—salivation. To some extent the empty dish thus becomes a conditioned reinforcer by virtue of its close associ-ation with the unconditioned reinforcing stimulus (food). Another example of a conditioned reinforcer is seen if a light is turned on each time food is given to a hungry animal. The light eventually becomes a conditioned reinforcer, and it may be used to some extent just as food is used to influence behavior.

Several rules govern the acquisition of conditioned reinforcers. The more often the conditioned stimulus (light in our last example) is paired with the unconditioned stimulus (food), the more reinforcing it becomes. There must not be too great a time interval between the two events (the light and the food). Finally the reinforcing power of the conditioned stimulus may be lost rapidly if it is never again associated with the unconditioned stimulus.

Conditioning principles have been extended to explain many complex social phenomena. Some studies of interpersonal attraction conceptualize the development of affections in conditioning terms (e.g., Byrne, 1969; Lott & Lott, 1968). These studies suggest that the evaluation of people and objects may be a function of the proportion of positive reinforcements associated with them (Griffitt & Guay, 1969). For example, your affection toward a friend may be related to the degree to which he has been associated with gratifications for you.

In addition to attractions and positive feelings, fears often are experienced in personality development. Considering that the child's world is full of potential dangers to him, the prevalence of fears in childhood is not surprising, although their variety is sometimes startling. Even a casual inquiry into the fears of a three-year-old, for example, reveals how diverse his anxieties may be. Some of these, like fear of "robbers" and of "monsters," seem understandable. Others require more empathy for the different world of the small child: his fear of being flushed down the toilet and drowning, or his fear of being sucked into the vacuum cleaner. While such fears may seem amusing to the adult, they may be traumatic to the child.

Many stimuli are intrinsically dangerous to the developing child, and these painful stimuli (like hot stoves) are rapidly identified. But how do initially neutral stimuli acquire the power to evoke fearful and anxious emotional responses? According to learning theorists, laboratory research on aversive classical conditioning helps us to understand how anxiety develops in response to objectively non-threatening events. Specifically, the individual may become afraid of intrinsically neutral things as a result of their close association with noxious or painful stimulation.

In *aversive* classical conditioning, the unconditioned stimulus is a pain-producing event. For example, if you see a light and experience an electric shock together for several trials, the light alone can come to evoke components of your emotional pain reaction to the shock. Neutral stimuli that are associated contiguously (close together in time) with an aversive unconditioned stimulus then become aversive conditioned stimuli capable of eliciting fear and avoidance responses. Thus through positive and aversive classical conditioning intense emotional reactions may be acquired to previously neutral stimuli. The classical conditioning design is schematized in Figure 5-1.

The case of Albert illustrates classically conditioned responses and their generalization (Watson & Raynor, 1920). A severe rat phobia was induced in Albert, a

**Figure 5-1**   CLASSICAL CONDITIONING (AVERSIVE)

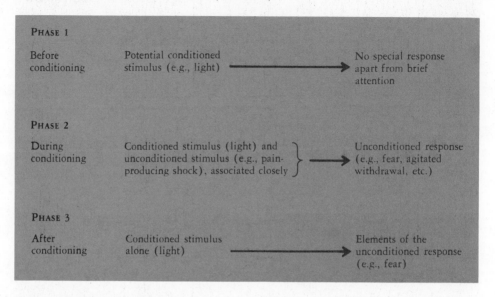

In classical conditioning, as a result of close association with an unconditioned stimulus (e.g., shock), a previously neutral event (e.g., light) may become a conditioned stimulus capable of eliciting an unconditioned response (e.g., fear).

young child, who had not been afraid of rats before, by simply pairing the presentation of a white rat with aversive stimulation. Just as Albert reached for the animal, a loud, fear-producing noise was made, and contiguous presentations of rat and aversive noise were repeated several times. Albert developed an intense fear reaction to the rat. His fear also generalized: when he was later presented with a wide range of new furry stimuli, including cotton, fur coats, human hair, wool, and other animals, he displayed a phobic reaction to them, although they themselves had not been paired with noise. It will be seen that this is a human example of the kind of learning manifested when rats who had been shocked in a white compartment responded fearfully to the compartment itself (Miller, 1948).

An especially dramatic demonstration of aversive (or "traumatic") conditioning was conducted with adult volunteers (Campbell, Sanderson & Laverty, 1964). The unconditioned stimulus was extraordinarily traumatic: a temporary interruption of breathing, induced by the drug Scoline, which produces momentary motor paralysis without impairing consciousness. While producing no permanent harm, the drug temporarily generated in most volunteers a horrible terror and the feeling that they were dying. The conditioned stimulus was a neutral tone. On the basis of a single pairing (of tone with drug effects), a long-lasting, conditioned fear response to the neutral tone was generated in the subjects. This fear reaction was evidenced by marked changes in such emotional indicators as heart rate, muscle tension, and respiration. Moreover, this traumatic, conditioned emotional reaction was highly resistant to extinction; it persisted intensely despite many repeated extinction trials.

Results of this type have been interpreted as evidence that the neurotic emotional reactions found in phobias may reflect conditioning rather than unconscious wishes and intrapsychic conflicts (e.g., Bandura, 1969). The implications for both the theory and the treatment of disturbed behavior may be profound, as later chapters discuss.

Demonstrations like those reported in the foregoing studies are understandably rare because of the possible hazards to the volunteers. They serve, however, not just as academic demonstrations but provide a basis for the development of more effective therapeutic techniques. If the principles through which traumatic reactions are acquired can be understood, it should be possible to apply the same principles for therapeutic purposes.

## OPERANT CONDITIONING AND RESPONSE CONSEQUENCES

Skinner incorporated into his position many concepts regarding classical conditioning, but he concentrated on another aspect of learning. According to Skinner (1953), most human social behaviors involve freely emitted response patterns or "operants." The term "operant" implies an active organism that "operates" upon its world, changing the environment and being changed by it. The outcomes of these operant response patterns modify the likelihood that similar responses will occur in the future. That is, operant behavior is determined by its consequences. If the outcomes or consequences of the response are favorable or reinforcing, then the operant will be more likely to be emitted again in future similar situations. Contrary to some widespread misconceptions, "reinforcers" or favorable outcomes are not restricted to such primitive rewards as food pellets or sexual satisfactions. Almost any events may serve as reinforcers, including such cognitive gratifications as information (Jones, 1966) or the achievement of competence.

On the other hand, if the consequences of the responses are not favorable (not reinforcing), then the operant is less likely to occur in the future. For example, if a mother responds with attention and warm concern to her child's whining and clinging dependency, the chances increase that he will show similar dependency in the future. But if she systematically ignores the dependency and leaves it unrewarded, its future likelihood decreases.

Most of Skinner's research on learning has concentrated on the role of rewards or reinforcement as determinants of behavior change. The usual methods in these studies has been to set up conditions in which an organism may freely perform or emit responses ("operants"). The experimenter preselects a particular response class (e.g., personal pronouns in interview talk, lever pressing in a study with rats). He then makes the delivery of a reinforcer contingent (dependent) on the subject's emitting the selected operant response. For example, he makes praiseful comments like "good" only when the interviewee uses such personal pronouns as "I" or "me." Or he may make food delivery to the animal contingent on the bar-pressing

**Figure 5-2** OPERANT CONDITIONING

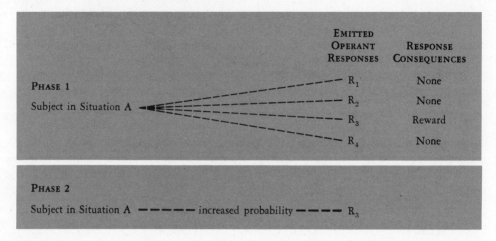

In any situation a subject emits many operant responses: if an operant is immediately followed by a reward (reinforcement) he will be more likely to emit it again in a similar situation.

response. The process, called "operant conditioning," is shown graphically in Figure 5-2.

As will be discussed in later chapters, studies have shown repeatedly that alterations in response consequences (the outcomes to which the behavior leads) may change a wide range of behaviors, from psychotic talk, delinquency, and neurotic sexual aberrations to social interactions in nursery school. Most of these studies have tried to modify therapeutically such problematic behaviors as severe fears. They also have shown that individual behavior can be accurately predicted from knowledge of the environment in which the subject is to be observed. A child's dependent behavior at home, for example, may be predicted from knowledge of the mother's willingness to reinforce dependency (e.g., Bijou, 1965). Likewise, assessments of the adequacy of a person's adjustment may be most accurate when they are based on knowledge of the environmental conditions in his life (Mischel, 1968).

## DISCRIMINATION

The stimuli that signal the time or place when an operant will have favorable consequences are called *discriminative stimuli*. Changes in discriminative stimuli lead to changes in behavior. Without discriminative stimuli we would not know the outcomes to which different behaviors would be likely to lead. We quickly learn to drive a car through green traffic lights but not through red ones, to talk to people who smile and not to those who seem uninviting, to shout exuberantly at football games but not during church sermons. Life without environmental cues regarding the probable consequence of behavior would be absurdly chaotic.

"Generalized reinforcers" often are subtle and involve complex human relationships.

## CONDITIONED GENERALIZED REINFORCERS

As noted before, neutral stimuli may acquire value and become conditioned reinforcers when they become associated with other stimuli that already have reinforcing powers and emotion-arousing properties. Conditioned reinforcers become *generalized* when they are paired with more than one primary reinforcer. A good example of a conditioned generalized reinforcer is money because it can provide so many different primary gratifications (food, shelter, comfort, medical help, and alleviation of pain). Gradually generalized reinforcers may become quite potent even when the primary reinforcers upon which they were initially based do not accompany them any more. Some people, for example, seem to learn to love money for its own sake and work to amass "paper profits" that they never trade in for primary rewards.

Some generalized reinforcers are obvious—like money—but others are subtle and involve complex social relationships. Attention and social approval from people who are likely to supply reinforcement—such as the mother, a loved one or a teacher—often is an especially strong generalized reinforcer. Such behaviors as showing off and pretending to be ill, for example, often may inadvertently be reinforced by people who attend to them and who react with interest, approval, or concern.

Because outcomes like attention and affection are not physical objects but features of other people's behavior, they tend to be difficult to define and to recognize clearly—both by the psychologist who tries to study them and by the person who is controlled by them. When we are not sure whether another significant person is being attentive or affectionate to us, our behavior will not be consistently reinforced by him. Under these conditions of inconsistent or intermittent reinforcement, behaviors may become highly perseverative, as seen in the frustrated lover's struggles for signs of affection or the insecure child's unremitting pursuit of attention.

## SUPERSTITIONS AND IRRATIONALITY

The relationship between the occurrence of an operant response and the reinforcement that follows it is often causal. For example, turn the door knob and the door opens, the outcome reinforcing the action. Consequently in the future we are likely to turn door knobs to enter and leave rooms, and our behavior at the door seems rational. Often, however, the response-reinforcement relationship may be quite accidental, and then bizarre and seemingly superstitious behavior may be produced. For example, a primitive tribe may persist in offering human sacrifices to the gods to end severe droughts because occasionally a sacrifice has been followed by rain.

The genesis of superstition, according to Skinner, may be demonstrated by giving a pigeon a bit of food at regular intervals—say every 15 seconds—regardless of what he is doing. Skinner (1953, p. 85) describes the strange rituals that may be conditioned in this way:

> When food is first given, the pigeon will be behaving in some way—if only standing still—and conditioning will take place. It is then more probable that the same behavior will be in progress when food is given again. If this proves to be the case, the "operant" will be further strengthened. If not, some other behavior will be strengthened. Eventually a given bit of behavior reaches a frequency at which it is often reinforced. It then becomes a permanent part of the repertoire of the bird, even though the food has been given by a clock which is unrelated to the bird's behavior. Conspicuous responses which have been established in this way include turning sharply to one side, hopping from one foot to the other and back, bowing and scraping, turning around, strutting, and raising the head. The topography of the behavior may continue to drift with further reinforcements, since slight modifications in the form of response may coincide with the receipt of food.

It may seem amusing to watch pigeons generate elaborate superstitious rituals and bizarre behaviors as a result of accidental reinforcement contingencies. It is tragic, however, if people inadvertently become bizarre and develop neurotic symptom syndromes in fundamentally similar ways. According to many Skinnerians, there is much overlap between the ways in which pigeons become victimized by the vicissitudes of reinforcement and the manner in which people may become twisted by the response-reinforcement arrangements in their lives. These ideas have been widely applied in both analyses and modifications of human problems (Chapters 10 and 11).

## SUMMARY

In sum, B. F. Skinner differs both from psychodynamic theorists and from Miller and Dollard in his renunciation of motivational and dispositional constructs. Instead of trying to infer motives and conflicts, Skinnerians devote themselves to the experimental analysis of the observable conditions controlling behavior.

The learning formulations of Skinner and other "neobehaviorists" have stimulated a great deal of systematic research on the effects of reinforcement, the patterning of reinforcement, and the phenomena of generalization and discrimination in learning. Many of these studies help to clarify the ways in which patterns of behavior develop and change; they will be discussed in later chapters that deal with socialization and behavior change.

# SOCIAL LEARNING AND SOCIAL BEHAVIOR THEORY

The behavior theories discussed so far emphasize the role of reinforcement or reward in learning. The importance given to reinforcement is understandable for at least two reasons. First, reinforcement and incentives have been shown repeatedly to be powerful influences in learning and in choice of behavior in many different settings. For example, as economists have long recognized, the pay-offs yielded by various alternatives are important determinants of choices in financial and business decisions. There also have been ample demonstrations that the consequences to which response patterns lead are critical determinants of psychological behaviors. Second, until recently most research on learning has studied animals rather than people, and with animals direct reinforcement was thought to be the main learning mechanism.

In more recent work with complex human and interpersonal behavior the possibility of *social* learning without any apparent direct reinforcement is being recognized. Now the concepts and principles of learning have been developed and extended to interpersonal phenomena, and have been taken out of the animal laboratory and applied to diverse human domains. These extensions include clinical psychology (e.g., Rotter, 1954; Rotter, Chance, & Phares, 1972; Ullmann & Krasner, 1969; Wolpe, 1958); personality development (e.g., Bandura & Walters, 1963); personality assessment and structure (e.g., Mischel, 1968, 1973a); and behavior change (Bandura, 1969; Eysenck & Rachman, 1965; Krasner & Ullmann, 1973). Moreover, many of the original learning concepts have been liberalized and integrated with ideas and findings from other areas (Chapter 6).

## EXPECTANCIES AND VALUES

J. B. Rotter's (1954, 1972) social learning formulation introduces a more cognitive element to personality-oriented learning theories. He emphasizes the individual's subjective expectations about future outcomes and the subjective value of reinforcements in the person's psychological situation. In Rotter's theory, the probability that a particular pattern of behavior will occur depends on the individual's expectancies concerning the outcomes to which his behavior will lead and the perceived values of those outcomes. For example, whether a child behaves dependently or self-assertively with his teacher depends on his expectations regarding the probable consequences (e.g., attention, disapproval, affection) of either behavior and the value to him of those consequences.

Prediction in Rotter's approach requires estimating the individual's relevant expectancies and values in the psychological choice situations that confront him. The person's subjective expectancies regarding probable outcomes reflect his past learning experiences in similar situations. That is, expectations are a function of the person's direct past reinforcement. Likewise, the subjective values of outcomes are a function of prior learning. Specific expectancies, in Rotter's formulation, are easily modifiable by even seemingly minor alterations in the individual's situation. "Generalized expectancies" are assumed to be more consistent and stable across situations. Thus generalized expectancies are more like traits, although they are construed as learned expectations.

## THE IMPORTANCE OF AWARENESS IN LEARNING

A cognitive orientation in learning theory was also encouraged by the finding that learning is vastly enhanced when the learner is aware of the contingencies and rules governing the consequences to which his responses will lead (Bandura, 1969). Under many conditions the person's private expectations and hypotheses about what is happening to him may affect his actions much more than does the objective reality of the rules and reinforcements that actually govern the outcomes of his behaviors. Thus awareness of the relevant rules and contingencies greatly facilitates learning.

Consider, for example, an operant conditioning situation in which the experimenter gave social reinforcement (saying "Mmm-hmm") to college students when they said human nouns (e.g., "girl") in a word-naming task. Not surprisingly, subjects who became aware of the contingency for reinforcement (i.e., guessed correctly that social reinforcement from the experimenter depended on their saying human nouns) greatly increased their output of human nouns (De Nike, 1964). Those who remained unaware of the contingency did as poorly as subjects in a control group, who were reinforced randomly for 10 percent of their responses (see Figure 5-3, Part A). Most interesting, the students showed no appreciable improvement in their performance until they correctly discerned the contingency for reinforcement; as soon as they became aware of the contingency they gave dramatically more human noun responses (Figure 5-3, B).

**Figure 5-3**   AWARENESS AND VERBAL CONDITIONING

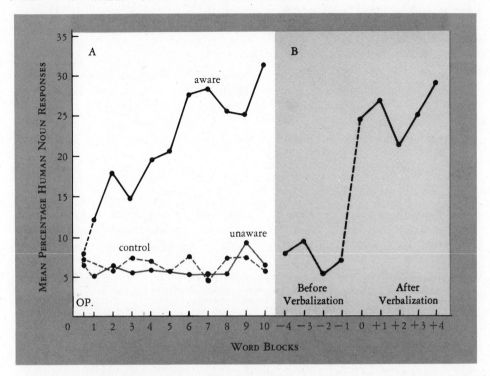

A, Mean percentage of human noun responses given by the aware, unaware, and control groups on each word block during the conditioning task. B, Mean percentage of human noun responses given by subjects in the aware group before and after they verbalized the reinforcement contingency correctly. (Adapted by Spielberger & De Nike, 1966, from De Nike, 1964.)

It appears from other research, however, that some learning in humans can occur without awareness (Martin, Hawryluk & Guse, 1974). This fact really should not be surprising considering that lower organisms with dubious capacities for cognitive symbolization and awareness—such as the cockroach and the earthworm—also manage to learn and can be conditioned.

## *RULES AND SYMBOLIC PROCESSES*

Learning is also improved substantially by instructions and rules. Rules help us to link discrete bits of information and powerfully affect our ability to learn and remember those materials (e.g., Anderson & Bower, 1973). In socialization, if the rules governing reinforcement are verbalized, children can more readily learn the standards that they are supposed to adopt (e.g., Aronfreed, 1966). When children are informed that particular performance patterns are good and that others are unsatisfactory, they adopt the appropriate standards more easily than when there are no clear verbal rules (Liebert & Allen, 1967). Thus in child-rearing it helps not only to reward appropriate behavior but also to specify the relevant rule. In addition to praising kind behaviors, for example, the parent might describe what exactly is being rewarded, as, "That's good: I like it when you are nice and gentle with your baby sister."

Symbolic and cognitive processes also may be crucial in classical conditioning. Suppose, for example, that a person has been conditioned in an experiment to fear a light because it is repeatedly paired with electric shock. Now if the experimenter tells him that the light (the conditioned stimulus) will not be connected again with the electric shock, his emotional reactions to the conditioned stimulus can quickly extinguish (Bandura, 1969). On later trials he can see the light without becoming aroused.

## OBSERVATIONAL LEARNING

Observational learning refers to learning without any direct rewards or reinforcement (e.g., Bandura, 1969, 1971). People learn by observing other persons and events and not merely from the direct consequences of what they themselves do.

---

**Children learn adult roles partly through observation and imitation.**

---

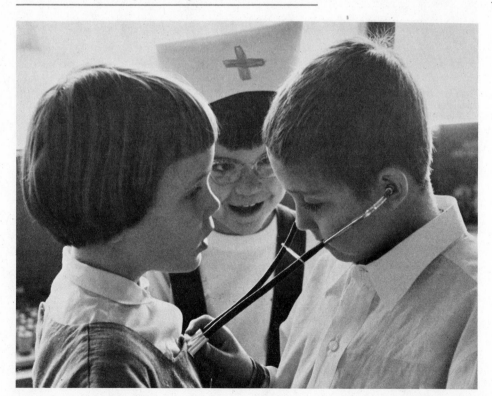

What you know and how you behave depends on what you see and hear and not just on what you get.

Sometimes learning without direct reinforcement is called "cognitive," sometimes "vicarious," and sometimes "observational" or "modeling." All these terms refer to an individual's acquisition of new knowledge and potential behavior through observation without receiving any direct external reinforcement for his own acts or without even making the observed response. Observational learning may occur when people watch what others ("models") do, or when they attend to the physical environment, to events, and to symbols such as words and pictures. Much human learning depends on perceptual-cognitive processes (like selective, focused attention) and on observation of the social and physical environment rather than on direct reinforcement for the individual's own actions. The acquisition of new behavior through observation is especially evident in the learning of language and of complex rules (e.g., Zimmerman & Rosenthal, 1974). We learn about "right" and "wrong," for example, by watching others as well as by acting ourselves.

## DISTINCTION BETWEEN ACQUISITION AND PERFORMANCE

No individual does all the things he has learned and can do. Obviously there are discrepancies between what a person has learned or knows and can do, and what he actually does in particular situations. For example, most adolescent girls know how to throw stones, fight, and steal. But even among girls who have acquired these skills to the same extent, there are striking individual differences in the degree to which they choose to perform them. Likewise, although most people in our culture know how to rob or murder, only some actually commit such crimes. There are major discrepancies between what a person is able to do in any given situation and what he or she actually does. Therefore it is useful to distinguish between the learning or acquisition of behaviors and their performance.

Learning or the acquisition of novel responses is regulated by sensory and cognitive processes. It may be facilitated by incentives and reinforcements, but it is not dependent upon them (e.g., Bandura, 1971). That is, what a person *can* do depends on what he *knows* and on the skills, information, rules, and response patterns he has acquired or learned. These learned behaviors are acquired through observation and cognitive processes and not just through conditioning and direct reinforcement. Learning thus depends on the learner's attention to the task, and on how well he "codes" (organizes, represents) and rehearses the information from his senses (e.g., Bandura & Jeffery, 1973).

Incentives and reinforcement, however, are important determinants of response selection in *performance*. A person's choice of what to do in any given situation—of which response to select from among the enormous number of potential behaviors he is capable of enacting—depends on motivational variables and incentives. The behavior he selects depends on the outcomes he expects the different behavioral acts to elicit.

A person may not perform a particular behavior because he never learned it initially. On the other hand, the response pattern may be potentially available to him, but it is not elicited by the particular stimulus and reward conditions. That is, his response may be inhibited; the incentive conditions in the situation may not be strong enough to elicit it. When a more potent incentive is introduced the response may be produced readily.

## EFFECTS OF OBSERVING OTHER PEOPLE'S OUTCOMES

Your expectations regarding the probable consequences of particular behaviors depend not only on the outcomes you have received for what you did in similar situations, but also on the consequences you have observed other people obtain. Watching the outcomes that other people receive may provide valuable information about the consequences that you probably will get for similar behavior.

When a person observes that other people ("models") obtain positive reinforcing consequences for a response pattern, he tends to act more readily in similar ways. For instance, if a child sees other children receive encouragement and praise for, let us say, aggressiveness at play, his own tendency to behave aggressively in similar situations will increase. Conversely, when social models are punished for their behavior, observers tend to become more inhibited about displaying similar behavior.

A study of imitation illustrates the effects of observing the consequences of other people's behavior. In this study children watched a film of an adult who displayed novel aggressive responses, such as hitting and kicking a Bobo doll (Bandura, 1965). The consequences produced by the adult's aggressive behavior were deliberately varied. In one condition the film sequence showed the adult's aggressive behavior punished; in a second it was rewarded; and in a third it had no consequences. When tested after the film, children who had observed aggressive behaviors punished imitated them less than those who had seen aggressiveness rewarded or ignored. Table 5-1 summarizes the general pattern obtained in research on this topic.

Did the differences in performance found by Bandura (1965) mirror differences in learning? Posttests revealed that when the children were offered attractive incen-

**TABLE 5-1   Effects of Modeling and Observed Consequences**

| OBSERVER SEES | PROBABILITY THAT OBSERVER WILL LATER PERFORM MODEL'S BEHAVIOR |
|---|---|
| No model | Lowest |
| Model's behavior punished | Low |
| Model's behavior without consequence | Higher |
| Model's behavior rewarded | Highest |

tives to reproduce the model's responses, the differences between the conditions were erased. It seems that the children in all conditions had *learned* the model's behavior equally well; the observation of different consequences, however, had inhibited or facilitated their later *performance* of the behavior.

In sum, it is not necessary to enact particular behaviors in order to learn their consequences: vicarious as well as direct consequences of performances affect subsequent behavior. For example, a bank clerk does not have to be arrested for stealing from the safe to learn some of the consequences of such behavior. Information that alters the person's anticipations of the probable outcomes to which a behavior will lead should also change the probability that he will engage in the behavior— although it may not affect his ability to execute the behavior.

Vicarious experiences also may lead to strong conditioned emotional reactions (Berger, 1962). In one experiment, adults repeatedly observed the sounding of a buzzer paired with fear responses feigned by another adult. Gradually the observers themselves developed conditioned fear responses to the sound of the buzzer alone (Bandura & Rosenthal, 1966). Consider also the development of strong fears of dogs or snakes. Even someone who was never harmed by an animal may come to fear it intensely after observing the emotional upset of other people when they are confronted with the animal.

## CONSISTENCY AND DISCRIMINATIVENESS IN PERSONALITY

Social learning theory influences ideas about the nature of personality traits. Recall that trait theories hypothesize broad dispositions and cross-situational consistencies as the basic units of personality (Chapter 2). In contrast, social behavior theory suggests that a person will behave consistently across situations only to the extent that similar behavior leads, or is expected to lead, to similar consequences across those conditions (Mischel, 1968). According to the learning principles of stimulus generalization and discrimination, behaviors become widely generalized only when they are reinforced uniformly across many stimulus conditions. Most social behaviors are not uniformly rewarded across different settings or situations. For example, while physical aggression is encouraged among boys sparring in the gym, it is not supported when the boys aggress toward their fathers or their younger siblings. Consequently sharp discriminations develop, the individual becoming aggressive in one context and not in the other (Bandura, 1973).

Guided by the idea that behavior depends on its probable outcomes, many behavior theorists emphasize "behavioral specificity" rather than trait consistency across conditions that entail different discriminative stimuli. On the other hand, if responses are uniformly rewarded across diverse conditions, "generalization" occurs, and the person will show similar behaviors across many situations. For example, a boy whose father reinforces him for physical aggressiveness everywhere might become aggressive pervasively and fight with his siblings as well as with his friends in many settings at home and at school. Thus, depending on stimulus conditions, the same person might show a trait like aggressiveness across several contexts or he might be highly discriminative and behave one way in some settings but quite differently in others.

Consider a woman who seems hostile and fiercely independent some of the time but passive, dependent, and feminine on other occasions. What is she really like? Which one of these two patterns reflects the woman that she really is? Is one pattern in the service of the other, or might both be in the service of a third motive? Must she be a really aggressive person with a facade of passivity—or is she a warm, passive-dependent woman with a surface defense of aggressiveness? Social behavior theory suggests that it is possible for her to be *all* of these—a hostile, fiercely independent, passive, dependent, feminine, aggressive, warm person all in one (Mischel, 1969). Of course which of these she is at any particular moment would not be random and capricious; it would depend on discriminative stimuli— who she is with, when, how, and much, much more. But each of these aspects of her self may be a quite genuine and real aspect of her total being.

## AN ALTERNATIVE TO MOTIVATIONAL VICISSITUDES

Psychodynamic theorizing assumes a set of basic personality motives and dispositions that endure, although their overt response forms may change. That is, basic motives persist although their behavioral manifestations are transformed defensively. In that view, for example, a child of 12 years may substitute excessive obedience to a parent for his earlier phobic reaction as a way of reducing anxiety over parental rejection (Kagan, 1969). This model is analogous to the closed hydraulic system in physics in which a gallon of water is converted to steam and recondensed to liquid: the form of the water may be transformed, but its basic nature is conserved. Such a Freudian-derived personality model is widely shared by many personality psychologists.

In the opinion of social learning theorists, however, this model is inappropriate and has led to some tragic mistakes in clinical treatment and diagnosis for 50 years (e.g., Bandura, 1969; Mischel, 1968, 1969; Peterson, 1968). They suggest that seemingly diverse behaviors do not necessarily reflect a uniform underlying motivational pattern. Instead they view behaviors as relatively discrete and controlled by relatively independent causes and maintaining conditions.

In accord with the psychodynamic view, if a child shows attachment and dependency in some contexts but not in others, one would begin a search to separate the defensive facade from the basic motivation underlying it. But in the social behavior view, seeming inconsistencies, rather than serve one underlying motive, actually may be under the control of relatively separate causal variables. The two behavior patterns may not reflect a "symptom" or facade in the service of a motive but rather may reflect discrimination learning in the service of the total organism. Similarly, social learning theory suggests that while a child's fears sometimes may be in the service of an underlying motive, they are more likely to involve an organized but relatively independent response system that is evoked and maintained by its own set of regulating conditions.

This distinction between theoretical positions leads to quite different interpretations regarding the causes of personality problems. The case of "Pearson Brack," an American airman, offers one example (Grinker & Spiegel, 1945, pp. 197–207; Mischel, 1968).

Pearson Brack was a bombardier in the Tunisian theater of operations during World War II. During Brack's ninth mission his airplane was severely damaged by flak. It suddenly jolted and rolled, and then began to dive. The pilot regained control of the plane just in time to avoid crashing. During the plane's fall, however, Brack was hurled violently against the bombsight and was seriously injured. After his return from this mission he was hospitalized for a month and then, seemingly recovered, was returned to flight duty. On his next two missions, the tenth and eleventh, he fainted, and gradually his problem was brought to the attention of a psychodynamically oriented psychiatrist. Direct observation revealed that Brack's tendency to faint seemed specifically linked to being at an altitude of about 10,000 feet.

After intensive interviews, the psychiatrist concluded that Brack's fainting was connected to deep, underlying anxieties rooted in his childhood experiences. Brack was viewed as a basically immature person with long-standing insecurity who had inadequately identified with his father. The near-fatal plane incident was seen as essentially trivial, except in so far as it precipitated anxiety in an already insecure and immature individual.

In contrast, a social behavior analysis of the same case (Mischel, 1968) emphasized the severe emotional trauma that might have been conditioned to altitude cues during the mishap. That is, if Brack's injury occurred at about 10,000 feet, then any altitude cues present at that time might have become conditioned stimuli capable of eliciting a traumatic reaction (such as fainting). In that case, every time Brack later re-experienced cues connected with the accident (such as being in a plane at a comparable altitude), he would again become emotionally debilitated.

From the viewpoint of social behavior theory, the relevant causes of Brack's problem were the current conditions that seemed to control its occurrence, in this instance altitude cues that may have been associated with the trauma. But from the perspective of psychodynamic theory, the causes were Brack's inferred underlying anxiety and its antecedents in childhood. Consequently the psychiatrist searched for the hypothesized roots of the problem in the form of repressed underlying anxieties. After excluding organic damage, the psychiatrist hypothesized that the fainting reflected deep underlying anxiety, symptomatic of Brack's brittle personality structure. He interpreted Brack's fainting as a surface sign of basic fear and anxiety and of dynamics that could only be comprehended in the light of childhood traumas and identifications.

Who was right? Was Brack's fainting predisposed by an inadequate identification, or a conditioned traumatic reaction, or a little bit of both, or neither? At this juncture there is no way of answering these questions definitively. But be clear

about this point: regardless of who is correct, the psychodynamic and social learning views are fundamentally different. Evidence relevant to these two positions will
be considered often in later pages.

## FOCUS ON CURRENT SOCIAL BEHAVIOR

The social behavior view has many implications for the study of persons. Social behavior assessments do not describe the individual in generalized trait terms,
sort him into type categories, or infer his conflicts and motives (Mischel, 1968).
Instead they sample what the individual does now in relation to the conditions in
which he does it. In this sense, behavioral assessment involves an exploration of the
unique or "idiographic" aspects of the single person by analyzing how he changes
in response to changes in stimulus conditions (Chapter 10). In the case of bombardier Brack, for example, behavioral assessments would entail studying changes
in his emotional response to airplanes as a result of changing and re-arranging altitude cues or other stimuli that seemed to affect his fainting problem most potently.

In sum, psychodynamic theories distinguish between overt or "symptomatic"
behaviors and their basic or underlying psychic causes. These causes are believed
to be enduring motives and their defensive transformations established early in the
course of the individual's psychosexual development. Consequently psychodynamic
theories look for the motivational roots of personality in childhood. In contrast,
social behavior analyses seek the current causes of the person's behavior. Social
learning approaches to personality thus pay less attention to motivational and dispositional constructs and instead look more at the individual's behavior, and at the
functional relations between what he does and the psychological conditions of his
life.

What people do, of course, includes much more than motor acts. Far more
than rats and other lower organisms that have been favorite subjects in experiments, humans do exceedingly complex and varied things, and they do them in
their heads and guts as well as with their hands and feet. But to understand these
complex activities, social behavior theorists suggest that it might be wiser to spend

**Figure 5-4**   THE SOCIAL BEHAVIOR APPROACH EMPHASIZES THAT THE SAME PERSON BE-
HAVES DIFFERENTLY IN RESPONSE TO VARIOUS PSYCHOLOGICAL SITUATIONS
(STIMULI)

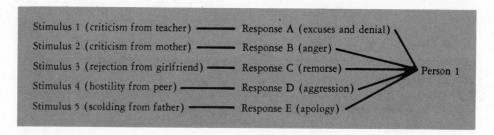

more time looking at what people are doing rather than try to infer the global motives and traits propelling them.

Recall that trait theories emphasize differences *between* people in their response to the same stimulus. In contrast, social behavior theories emphasize differences in the behavior of the *same* person as a result of even slight changes in conditions. This emphasis on the role of the stimulus in the regulation of the individual's behavior is indicated in Figure 5-4. Social behavior analyses try to discover the impact or meaning of particular stimulus conditions in the person's life by observing how changes in those conditions alter what he thinks and does.

## COGNITION AND BEHAVIOR

In recent years psychologists have become very much interested in "cognition." Cognition is a term with many meanings, but most simply it means processing of information (e.g., Neisser, 1967) as in thinking, and in the mental representation and manipulation of events. Cognition is involved in processes like selective attention, information gathering, and motivated or goal-directed thinking (problem solving).

Psychologists who are concerned with cognition emphasize that a comprehensive approach to personality and social behavior needs to consider the person's "representational" or "coding" processes. That is, they want to understand the *mediation* that occurs inside the person between the stimuli that impinge on him and the overt responses that he emits (e.g., Baldwin, 1969). Cognitive orientations are discussed elsewhere in this book, but they overlap with contemporary social learning formulations to the extent that current social learning views include considerations of symbolic activities (as in observational learning, e.g., Bandura, 1971) and seek to study the individual's interpretation of events and experiences (e.g., Mischel, 1973a). Social learning theories thus take account of mediation; they do not view stimuli as impinging on an empty organism that automatically emits a set of specific fixed acts. Explicit recognition of the links between cognition and learning is found in a "cognitive social learning" approach to personality presented in Chapter 21.

It is widely recognized that the impact a stimulus has on an individual depends on many factors. For example, unless the stimulus is noticed, obviously it will not influence the person. Likewise, the impact the stimulus has depends not just on its objective physical characteristics but also on how it is presented, including any instructions, labels, and contextual cues that serve to change its usual meaning. If you watch a murder scene knowing it is part of a rehearsal for a play obviously you will react differently than if you think a real murder is being committed. A bottle of clear liquid labeled "poison" is very different from the same bottle without the label. It would be naive to restrict the definition of a stimulus sequence to its gross physical properties. In any given situation, behavior is influenced by the total stimulus complex rather than by any single, context-free stimulus acting in isolation.

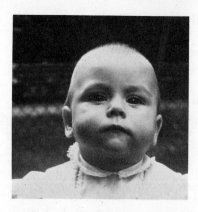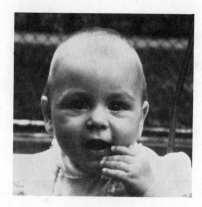

Even the young child processes information actively and is not an empty organism.

Many psychologists strongly emphasize the importance of the individual's interpretation or "cognitive appraisal" of the situation. They call attention to the *meaning* of the stimulus. Behaviorally oriented psychologists recognize this point but usually go a step further, believing that their task must include isolating the exact variables that determine what a stimulus may mean in a particular context, so that they can identify the conditions that control meaning.

In recent years most psychologists have recognized the importance of cognition and information for many aspects of complex behavior. Information and instructions may powerfully affect human learning processes and performance. For example, directions on how to reach one's destination in a new city obviously are more effective than trial and error gropings. Similarly, informational feedback about past performance and instructions about the present situation and about contingencies that will arise in the future critically affect the individual's behavior.

We already noted the effects that occur when people watch the behavior of live or filmed models directly. Important social and interpersonal behavior can also be modified by symbolic and cognitive processes that do not depend upon actual observation of a model's behavior. For example, individuals may alter their attitudes after either reading or hearing about the relevant behavior of others (e.g., Bandura & Mischel, 1965; Duncker, 1938). Often these symbolically produced effects are strikingly potent and may significantly alter such personality-relevant behaviors as self-control patterns, aggressiveness, and achievement strivings (Mischel, 1968). Although the underlying mechanisms are still unclear, new information conveyed through language and symbols can dramatically change the meaning of stimuli and reinforcers.

## THE ACTIVE ORGANISM

An emphasis on the role of stimulus conditions is easily misinterpreted as implying a passive view of man—an image of an organism that is empty except for some psychological glue that cements or bonds a bundle of responses automatically to impinging external stimuli. It is true that behavioral analyses attend to the exact covariations between changing conditions and the individual's changing behavior. But while alterations in conditions may come to regulate the individual's behavior, it is the person—not the stimulus or the situation—that is alive and that does the acting. Responses reside only in organisms, not in stimuli or conditions. Current behavior theories concentrate on stimuli in an attempt to understand and to change the person, hopefully for the better (Chapter 11).

Social learning approaches are recognizing that the individual is not a passive bundle of responses. Men have long learning histories and long memories, and much of what has happened to them gets internalized and affects all their current responses and future expectations. A man interprets himself and his behavior—he evaluates, judges, and regulates his own performance. In addition to being rewarded and punished by the external environment, people learn to monitor and evaluate their own behavior and to reward and punish themselves, thus modifying their own behavior and influencing their environment (Bandura, 1971; Mischel, 1973a, 1974). The principles that govern whether an individual rewards or condemns his own behavior have been given much attention in recent theorizing on social learning. The conditions that control the choice of self-administered rewards and punishments, and their relevance for the maintenance and modification of behavior, will be discussed in later chapters.

## SUMMARY

In sum, according to social learning or social behavior theories, direct and vicarious learning experiences determine the potential behaviors available to the individual. The person's choice among these behavioral alternatives depends on the probable consequences (reinforcements) to which each alternative is most likely to lead in that particular situation (e.g., Rotter, 1954). Expectancies about these probable consequences depend on direct and vicarious past experiences in similar situations.

Even subtle changes in the situation may alter expectancies about the probable consequences of behavior. Therefore behavior is often specific for a situation, and the individual shows great discrimination in what he does.

Social behavior theories seek to analyze the conditions that covary with changes in what people do. The focus therefore is on current behavior change in response to stimulus changes, rather than on inferences about global dispositions. But while the focus is on what the person is doing now, the behaviors studied include self-regulatory and self-control patterns, and the things the individual does privately and covertly. Similarly, while the emphasis is on the "stimulus" or situation, the stimulus often is exceedingly complex—including, for example, instructions and information about other people's behavior.

## OVERVIEW AND IMPLICATIONS

We have surveyed a great deal of information in this chapter. It is time to pause and seek some perspective on the main ideas and implications of the positions that have been discussed here and in the previous chapter.

### THE VARIETIES OF BEHAVIOR THEORIES

Early efforts to apply concepts from learning theories to problems of personality relied heavily on "stimulus-response" formulations that had emerged from laboratory research on simple learning with lower animals. The most important concepts in these formulations were direct reinforcement (in the form of rewards and punishments for the animal's behaviors); primary and learned drives (the satisfaction of which was believed to have reinforcing effects); and conflict in situations like those mirrored in the approach-avoidance paradigms of Miller and Dollard. More recent social learning formulations have focused on observational and cognitive processes in the learning of complex social and interpersonal behaviors. The term "learning theory" or "behavior theory" is often applied to all these positions, sometimes producing confusion because the positions have many fundamental dissimilarities. It is therefore important to distinguish between early "stimulus-response" models that focused on reinforcement and minimized cognitive processes, psychodynamic behavior theories that were based on Freud, and contemporary social learning theories that do not share those emphases.

### TRADITIONAL BEHAVIOR THEORIES

Some of the earliest behavioristic formulations shared many of the basic assumptions of trait theory in the sense that they construed personality as a system of broad and relatively stable dispositions. Their term for these dispositions was "habits" rather than "traits," but they accepted some of the assumptions of trait theory. In particular, they believed that habits are generalized response dispositions with stable, consistent properties. Like most behavior theories, these early conceptualizations stressed that habits are learned (e.g., Watson, 1925). Extensions of these behavioral formulations have attempted to fuse the concepts of psychodynamic theory with principles and terms emerging from animal research in laboratory studies of learning. Indeed, Dollard and Miller have devised, as we saw in Chapter 4, a psychodynamic behavior theory that tries to integrate psychoanalytic ideas with the more objective language and methodology of experimental animal research.

### SKINNER'S RADICAL BEHAVIORISM

In an extremely different vein, other workers, stimulated most notably by B. F. Skinner, have focused on the empirical and experimental analysis of behavior. They avoid inferences about unobservable motives and states in the organism and dwell instead on the observable conditions that seem to control or cause behavior in clearly defined situations. These radically behavioristic views differ sharply from Dollard and Miller's focus on motives and psychic conflicts.

## SOCIAL LEARNING AND SOCIAL BEHAVIOR THEORIES

Most recently, a number of theorists have attempted to make learning and behavior theories more "social" and less Freudian. They prefer to study complex social learning rather than simpler animal responding. Some inevitable confusion is introduced by the fact that the same term, "social learning theory," has been used by such diverse theorists as Dollard and Miller, Rotter, and Bandura. We are using the terms "social behavior" and "social learning" theories for approaches that focus on observed social behavior rather than on inferred motives (e.g., Bandura, 1969; Bandura & Walters, 1963; Mischel, 1968; Rotter, 1954). Social behavior theories actually draw on a wide range of phenomena and principles. Although they are committed to the understanding and analysis of behavior from the perspective of learning theory, they have tried to develop an adequately comprehensive, yet rigorous, approach to personality.

Influenced heavily by Skinner, most social behavior approaches emphasize what an organism *does* rather than make inferences about the attributes it *has* (Mischel, 1968). Social behavior analyses of human problems involve descriptions of the covariation between environmental conditions and what the person does, but they avoid inferences about the meaning of the behavior as a sign of some generalized trait or underlying motive. The focus is on what the organism is doing at the present moment rather than on the global dispositions, dynamics, or motives that it may possess or on the individual's inferred (but unobserved) history.

Most current social learning theories do not limit themselves to simple reinforcement principles. Although it is sometimes believed that contemporary social learning formulations neglect cognitive processes, in fact they rely heavily on them in their account of the development of all complex social behaviors.

## FOCUS ON BEHAVIOR VERSUS MOTIVES

Most modern behavioral approaches (beginning with Skinner's) try to handle the phenomena to which Freud and Miller and Dollard addressed themselves—but do so without invoking motivational constructs requiring inferences about hypothesized conflicts and needs.

Consider the problem of behavioral inconsistency. If one assumes that people have highly generalized traits and motives (as do trait and dynamic theories), then seemingly discrepant behaviors from one individual need special interpretations. Having judged a man to be basically hostile and impulsive, for example, how does one handle new evidence that he is also friendly and controlled? Both a Freudian and a Miller and Dollard analysis of such a person would search for underlying impulses and defenses or counter forces erected against them. The individual's discrepant behaviors might be signs of his underlying conflicts. His occasional "friendliness" and "controlled" behavior might be interpreted as a facade, or as a sign of unconscious efforts to defend against fundamental aggressive impulses, or as manifestations of an approach-avoidance conflict.

A contemporary social learning analysis (e.g., Mischel, 1968, 1969) approaches the same phenomenon quite differently. It focuses on subtle discrimination training throughout socialization. Rather than call upon special defensive mechanisms to mediate between hypothesized motives and supposedly discrepant surface behaviors, it views the diverse behaviors themselves as the predictable products of socialization processes, in which discrimination has a central role. If in the course of the individual's development "aggressiveness" and "impulsiveness" are modeled, expected, and rewarded in some situations but "friendliness" and "control" are learned and encouraged in other situations, then he will display both kinds of behavior, depending on just where he is and the particular conditions. Defense mechanisms, conflicts, displacement, or other underlying processes are not invoked to account for these seeming inconsistencies because the diverse behaviors are seen as the products of discrimination rather than as the signs of underlying conflict. The theoretical position you take on this issue has critical implications for your approach to most other phenomena of personality. Because of its importance, evidence relevant to this issue will be discussed often in later chapters.

## THE COMPLEXITY OF SOCIAL LEARNING

Most contemporary social behavior theories recognize that people may generate patterns of behavior in complex ways; they do not simply and automatically emit discrete conditioned responses in relation to specific evoking stimuli. The complexity of the "rule systems" that may regulate how persons generate behavior may be seen best in language learning. The child's acquisition of the grammatical system of his language is an extraordinary accomplishment whose mechanisms still are not understood fully (e.g., Chomsky, 1965). It is also widely agreed that how the individual interprets and perceives internal and external stimuli influences how he ultimately reacts to them. While early "stimulus-response" theories often left a void between the stimulus and the response, more current learning approaches recognize that the organism is an alive, active processor and storehouse of information rather than a thoughtless, unfeeling automaton. Research and theorizing, however, investigate what the person is *doing* (including what he is doing in his head) rather than try to infer the global motives, dispositions, or traits that he *has*.

While behavior theories emphasize learning they recognize that the structure and capacities of the organism limit what it can learn and do. Granted that learning is crucially important, within every species and every individual there are structurally imposed limits on potential behavior, as for example, in the limits of human memory (e.g., Miller, 1956). Behavioral learning theories have to recognize that response capacities are restricted by the capacities and characteristics of the organism.

Although current behavior theories acknowledge the existence of internal states and processes, they emphasize that these internal events can only be studied through their behavioral referents and manifestations—such as self-reports or physiological measures of emotionality. Social learning approaches, like all other objective approaches, therefore have to rely on behavior as the basis of their observations.

## WHERE IS THE PERSON IN BEHAVIOR THEORY?

Many critics appreciate the contributions of behavioral approaches for applied purposes (Part 2) but fault them vehemently for excessive attention to the "stimulus" or "situation" (e.g., Adinolfi, 1971; Alker, 1972; Bowers, 1973). They view this overemphasis as part of a "situationism in psychology" that erroneously minimizes the importance of dispositional or intrapsychic determinants such as traits (Bowers, 1973). In this vein, Carlson (1971) wonders "where is the person?" in current behaviorally oriented psychology and implies that a focus on the momentary situational determinants of behavior may lead one to lose the person in personality psychology.

There tends to be agreement that an adequate approach to personality must deal both with the person and the situation, focusing on their interaction rather than on either one in isolation (e.g., Endler, 1973; Mischel, 1973a; Moos, 1974). It is much less clear how such interaction should be conceptualized and studied, as will become apparent in Parts 2 and 3 of this book. The controversies are complex, the implications are profound, and there is little agreement on how to resolve the basic issues. An attempt to conceptualize some of the many problems of person-situation interaction is offered in the final chapter of this book.

## SUMMARY

1. B. F. Skinner's approach differs from that of Dollard and Miller (and from psychodynamic views) in refusing to infer drives or other internal motivational forces or traits. In Skinner's position, empirical analysis of the stimulus conditions controlling behavior replaces inferences about internal conflicts and underlying motives. Skinner's conceptualization leads to the analysis of behavior in terms of conditioning processes.

2. In classical conditioning, a potent and a neutral stimulus event have been paired together so that eventually the previously neutral event alone evokes portions of the same response that the potent one did initially. Classical conditioning principles have been extended to explain some complex social phenomena and neurotic or abnormal behaviors such as irrational fears.

3. Operant conditioning refers to behavior changes produced by reinforcement or reward for responses. Information and attention, as well as food and sexual gratification, are among the numerous outcomes that can serve as reinforcers and increase the probability of a particular behavior in operant conditioning.

4. Contemporary social learning theories (also called "social behavior theories") recognize that the human being is a complex and active interpreter of the world around him. Nevertheless, they focus on what the person is *doing* rather than on his underlying dispositions. They seek to understand the stimulus conditions influencing behavior.

5. J. B. Rotter introduced the notion of *expectancy* to personality-oriented learning theories. An individual's expectancies about the consequences of his behavior and the value to him of those consequences determine his choices. These expectancies and values are learned from past reinforcement.

6. Recent social learning theories emphasize observational learning. Complex and important potential behavior can be acquired without external reinforcement to the learner. Observational learning without direct reinforcement may account for the learning of many novel responses. Outcomes, incentives, and reinforcements are important, however, as determinants of what the person does in a particular situation, that is, which response he selects from the repertoire of alternatives available to him.

7. Social learning theory does not posit the existence of broad traits or dispositions. Instead, it views both consistency and discriminativeness in behavior as dependent on the conditions of learning and the cues in the situation.

8. Social behavior analyses study the covarying changes of conditions and behavior. Both the conditions and the behaviors may be exceedingly complex; they may involve much more than simple physical stimulus attributes. An especially important aspect of personality involves the person's reactions to himself and his self-regulation of outcomes that do not depend simply on the external environment.

9. Social behavior theory searches for causes in the current conditions that demonstrably control the person's present behaviors. This emphasis contrasts with traditional dynamic theories, which infer the person's motives, conflicts, and dispositions from behavioral "signs" and which construe his behaviors as being in the service of underlying motives and their dynamic transformations.

10. The focus of social behavior theory is on what the person is doing in the "here and now" rather than on reconstructions of his psychic history. There is a refusal to hypothesize drives, forces, motives, and other broad dispositions as explanations, and an emphasis on the individual's potential for change. Although often labeled "behavioristic," these features are not unique to a behavioral position. Surprisingly, they just as fully fit most of the existentially oriented and "phenomenological" positions, which will be discussed in the next chapter.

# CHAPTER 6

# PHENOMENOLOGICAL THEORIES Conceptions

This chapter presents an overview of several theories that deal with the "self" and with the person's subjective, internal experiences and personal concepts. There are many complexities and nuances in the diverse versions of the orientation to personality presented in this chapter. In spite of these variations, however, a few fundamental themes emerge as its chief characteristics.

For purposes of abbreviation and simplicity, we will call the orientation depicted in this chapter "phenomenological," although some of the positions encompassed here have been given other labels, such as "self" theories, "construct" theories, "humanistic" theories, "cognitive" theories, and "existential" theories. Most phenomenological theories are distinctive both in the concepts they reject and in the ones they emphasize. They tend to reject most of the dynamic and motivational concepts of psychoanalytic theories and motivational learning theories (Miller & Dollard) and also most of the assumptions of trait theories.

The rejection, or at least the minimization of motivational explanations, is accompanied by an emphasis on the person's immediate experiences and on his current relationships, perceptions, and encounters. The person thus is viewed as an experiencing being, rather than as a "personality structure" or as a syndrome of "psychodynamics" produced by his motivational history and long-term dispositions. The focus of this orientation tends to be on the individual's subjective experience, his personal view of the world and of himself, and his private concepts. Most of the approaches discussed in this chapter also stress man's positive strivings and his tendencies toward growth and self-actualization.

Most of the theories presented here are concerned broadly with cognition—with how man comes to know and understand his world and himself. An interest in cognition implies attention to the internal or mental processes through which the individual "codes" and categorizes information. Influenced by the Swiss psychologist Jean Piaget, cognitive theories call attention to man's "mental structures," and to the active ways in which the mind generates meaning and experience. Ulric Neisser, for example, puts it this way (1967, p. 3): "Whether beautiful or ugly or just conveniently at hand, the world of experience is produced by the man who experiences it." That statement, of course, does not imply that there is no "real" world of objects—houses, mountains, people, tables, books—and it does not suggest that the "environment" is a fiction that does not affect our private experience. The cognitive position stresses, however, that "we have no direct immediate access to the world, nor to any of its properties. . . . Whatever we know about reality has been *mediated*, not only by the organs of sense but by complex systems which interpret and reinterpret sensory information" (Neisser, 1967, p. 3).

Many studies on the mechanisms involved in cognition, and on the "stimulus as coded" (Lawrence, 1959), are being conducted in fields that bear only indirectly on personality, such as memory research and perception (e.g., Bower, 1969). Nevertheless, as a general orientation the cognitive approach has major importance for the study of persons.

Some personality psychologists concerned with cognition have tried to understand how the individual perceives, thinks, interprets, and experiences his world; that is, they have tried to grasp the individual's point of view. Their focus is on stimuli as they are interpreted, on events as they are represented cognitively inside the beholder, on persons and events of life as seen by the perceiver. In sum, they are most interested in the person's experience as *he* perceives and categorizes it—his phenomenology. Ideally, they would like to look at the world through the "subject's" eyes and to stand in his shoes, to *be* him long enough to experience a bit of what he experiences. This phenomenological stance is the main concern of the present chapter.

## SOURCES OF THE PHENOMENOLOGICAL APPROACH

The orientation presented in this chapter has numerous sources. For example, among the many early theorists who were fascinated with the self were William

James, George H. Mead, and John Dewey. Another early theorist concerned with the self was Carl Jung. As early as the start of the century, Jung called attention to the organism's strivings for self-realization and integration, and the existence of creative processes that go beyond the basic instincts of Freudian psychology. Also important were Gestalt psychology and existential philosophy. Given all these contributors, it becomes a bit arbitrary to select a few for detailed exposition. Hence, the ideas that are presented next should be considered merely representative and far from exhaustive.

## ALLPORT'S CONTRIBUTION

We saw in Chapter 2 that Gordon Allport recognized the existence of some common traits that all people might share in varying degrees. Some of his other ideas are most relevant to a phenomenological approach, however, and fit best in the present chapter. Allport emphasizes the *uniqueness* of the individual and of the integrated patterns that distinguish each person. He also notes the *lack of motivational continuity* during the individual's life and criticizes the Freudian emphasis on the enduring role of sexual and aggressive motives.

According to Allport, behavior is motivated originally by instincts, but later it may be capable of sustaining itself indefinitely without biological reinforcement. Allport sees most normal adult motives as no longer having a functional relation to their historical roots. "Motives are contemporary. . . . Whatever drives must drive now. . . . The character of motives alters so radically from infancy to maturity that we may speak of adult motives as *supplanting* the motives of infancy" (1940, p. 545). This idea has been called "functional autonomy" to indicate that a habit, say practicing the violin at a certain hour each day, need not be tied to any basic motive of infancy. The extent to which an individual's motives are autonomous is a measure of his maturity, according to Allport.

Allport thus stresses the contemporaneity of motives (1961). In his view, the past is not important unless it can be shown to be dynamically active in the present. He believes that historical facts about a person's past, while helping to reveal the total course of the individual's life, do not adequately explain the person's conduct today. In his words, "Past motives explain nothing unless they are also present motives" (1961, p. 220).

While fully recognizing the unity of growth in personality development, Allport emphasizes that later motives do not necessarily depend on earlier ones. Although the life of a plant is continuous with that of its seed, the seed no longer feeds and sustains the mature plant. In human terms, while a musician may have been spurred to mastery of his instrument through the need to overcome inferiority feelings, his later love of music is functionally autonomous from its origins.

Allport was also one of the strongest advocates of the self as a key feature of personality. To avoid a homunculus or manikin-in-the-mind conception of self or ego, he has coined the term *proprium*. In his view, the propriate functions of the personality include bodily sense, self-identity, self-esteem, self-extension, rational thinking, self-image, propriate striving, and knowing. The proprium contains the root of the consistency that characterizes attitudes, goals, and values. This proprium is not innate (a newborn does not have a self); it develops in time.

In addition to de-emphasizing the person's early motivations and his distant past, Allport focuses on the individual's currently perceived experiences, his phenomenological self, and his unique pattern of adaptation. He also favors a *wholistic* view of man as an integrated, bio-social organism, rather than as a bundle of traits and motives.

## LEWIN'S FIELD THEORY

Still another important post-Freudian influence came from field theories (e.g., Lewin, 1936). These positions construed behavior as determined by the person's psychological life space—by the events that exist in his total psychological situation at the moment—rather than by past events or enduring, situation-free dispositions. The most elegant formulation of this position was Kurt Lewin's "field theory."

The field concept of physics culminating in Einstein's theory of relativity was the inspiration for Kurt Lewin's theory of personality. Einstein's concept of "fields of force" had an expression in the Gestalt movement of psychology, which asserts that each part of a whole is dependent upon every other part. The Gestaltists applied the notion of a field of interrelated components primarily to perception. They proposed that the way in which an object is perceived depends upon the total context or configuration of its surroundings. What is perceived depends on the *relationships* among components of a perceptual field, rather than on the fixed characteristics of the individual components.

Lewin proposed the application of field theory to all branches of psychology. Field theory for him was a set of concepts that facilitate the translation of phenomenological experience. In his view, such conceptualizing was the psychologist's primary task as a scientist.

Lewin defined *life space* as the totality of facts that determine the behavior (B) of an individual at a certain moment. The life space includes the person (P) and the psychological environment (E), as depicted in Figure 6-1. Thus behavior is a function of the person and his environment, as expressed in the formula $B = f(P, E)$.

Lewin also discussed the question of the temporal relationship of an event and the conditions that produce it. Generally this question concerns whether past events only, or future events also, can cause change. Ordinary cause, based on the notion of causation in classical physics, assumes that something past is the cause of present events. Teleological theories assume that future events influence present events. Lewin's thesis is that neither past nor future, by definition, exists at the present moment and therefore neither can have an effect at the present. Past events have a position in the historical causal chains whose interweavings create the present situation, but only those events that are functioning in the present situ-

Figure 6-1   LEWIN'S LIFE SPACE

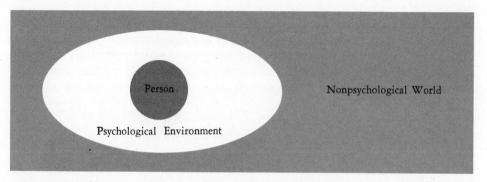

The life space contains the person in his psychological environment, which is delineated by a boundary (the ellipse) from the non-psychological world.

ation need to be taken account of. Such events are, by definition, current or momentary. In other words, only present facts can cause present behavior.

In representing the life space, Lewin therefore took into account only that which is contemporary. He termed this the principle of *contemporaneity* (Lewin, 1936). This does not mean the field theorists are not interested in historical problems or in the effects of previous experience. As Lewin (1951) pointed out, field theorists have been instrumental in enlarging the temporal scope of the psychological experiment to include situations that contain a history that is systematically created throughout hours or weeks. For example, college students in an experiment might be given repeated failure experiences (on a series of achievement tasks) during several sessions. The effects of these experiences on the students' subsequent aspirations and expectancies for success might then be measured.

The boundaries between the person and the psychological environment and between the life space and the physical world are *permeable*, that is capable of mutual influence. That makes prediction difficult because one cannot be sure beforehand when and what facts will permeate a boundary and influence a fact from another region. Lewin asserts that the psychologist might therefore concentrate on describing and explaining the concrete psychological situation in terms of field theory rather than attempt prediction.

Lewin (1935) rejected the notion of constant, entity-like personality characteristics such as unchanging traits. As a result of dynamic forces, psychological reality is always changing. The environment of the individual does not serve merely to facilitate tendencies that are permanently established in the person's nature (1936). Habits are not frozen associations, but rather the result of forces in the organism and its life space.

Lewin was similarly dissatisfied with the usual concept of needs. In descriptions of psychological reality, Lewin said, the needs that are producing effects in the momentary situation are the only ones that have to be represented. A need in

Lewin's theory corresponds to a tension system of the inner-person region. Lewin was also interested in reward and punishment. Instead of the hedonistic formulations of early learning theorists, Lewin construed rewards as devices for controlling behavior in momentary situations by causing changes in the psychological environment and in the tension systems of the person.

For Lewin, behavior and development are functions of the same structural and dynamic factors. Both are a function of the person and the psychological environment. In general, with increasing maturity there is greater differentiation of the person and the psychological environment.

Lewin's field theory had a major impact on experimental social psychology. His students extended his ideas and pursued them through ingenious experiments designed to alter the subject's life space—by altering his perception about himself, about other people, about events. The effects of these alterations on attitudes, aspirations, task persistence, and other indices were then examined carefully. Until recently Lewin's influence on personality psychology has been less extensive. There is now, however, an increasing recognition of the importance of the psychological situation in studies of traits and motives (e.g., Mischel, 1973a).

## PHENOMENOLOGY AND EXISTENTIALISM

The writings of Snygg and Combs (1949) also stressed the phenomenological features of the field; they influenced psychologists interested in the subject's awareness and private experiences. More recently, Carl Rogers and George A. Kelly have developed positions in which private experiences, subjective perceptions, and the self all have an important part.

Somewhat similar themes emphasizing the role of higher-order "positive" motives—growth, fulfillment, and the self and its actualization—have been developed by Abraham Maslow and others. According to Maslow, for example, man is innately good. Growth motivation moves the individual through hierarchically ordered degrees of health to ultimate self-actualization. "Every person is, in part, his own project, and makes himself" (Maslow, 1965, p. 308). Behavior is seen as goal directed, striving, purposeful, and motivated by higher actualization needs rather than by primary biological drives alone. (Some of Maslow's specific work is discussed in Chapter 12, pp. 258–288.)

The ideas of most of these theorists have much in common with the existential philosophical position developed by such European thinkers and writers as Kierkegaard, Sartre, and Camus. The key features of their orientation are expressed by Rollo May, a proponent of existential psychology. Thinking about a patient of his in psychotherapy, May recognizes that he has available all sorts of information about her, such as hypotheses from her Rorschach and diagnoses from her neurologist. He then comments (1961, p. 26):

But if, as I sit here, I am chiefly thinking of these *whys* and *hows* of the way the problem came about, I will have grasped everything *except the most important thing of all, the existing person.* Indeed, I will have grasped every-thing except the only real source of data I have, namely, this experiencing human being, this person now emerging, becoming, "building world," as the existential psychologists put it, immediately in this room with me.

As May's remarks indicate, the emphasis of existentialists is on phenomenologi-cal experience, on the "here and now" rather than on etiology or distant historical causes in the person's early childhood. Furthermore, the view of man preferred by theorists in the existential orientation sees him as capable of choice and respon-sibility rather than as the victim of unconscious forces or of habits.

The Swiss existential psychiatrist Binswanger commented that Freudian theory pictured man not yet as man in the full sense, but only as a creature buffeted about by life. Binswanger believes that for man to be fully himself—that is, to be truly realized or actualized as a human being—he must "look fate in the face." In his view, the fact that human life is determined by forces and conditions is only one side of the truth. The other side is that we ourselves "determine these forces as our fate" (cited in May, 1961, p. 252). Thus in the phenomenological and exis-tential orientation, man is seen as a being whose actualization requires much more than the fulfillment of biological needs and of sexual and aggressive instincts.

To understand some of the main features of the phenomenological orientation more closely, we shall consider the ideas of one of its most articulate proponents, Carl Rogers, in the next section.

## CARL ROGERS' SELF THEORY

### UNIQUE EXPERIENCE

Rogers' phenomenological theory of personality emphasizes the uniquely expe-rienced reality of the person. Rogers regards behavior as the result of immediate perceptual events as they actually are experienced by the individual. Because no one else, no matter how hard he tries, can completely assume another person's "in-ternal frame of reference," the person himself has the greatest potential for aware-ness of what reality is for him. In other words, each man potentially is the world's best expert on himself and has the best information about himself.

In Rogers' view, "behavior is basically the goal-directed attempt of the orga-nism to satisfy its needs as experienced, in the field as perceived" (1951, p. 491). The emphasis is on the person's perceptions as the determinants of his actions: how one sees and interprets events determines how one reacts to them.

### SELF-ACTUALIZATION

Like most phenomenologists, Rogers advocates abandoning specific motiva-tional constructs and views the organism as functioning as an organized whole. He maintains that "there is one central source of energy in the human organism; that it is a function of the whole organism rather than some portion of it; and that it is perhaps best conceptualized as a tendency toward fulfillment, toward actualization, toward the maintenance and enhancement of the organism" (1963, p. 6). Thus the inherent tendency of the organism is to actualize itself. "Motivation" then becomes not a special construct but an overall characteristic of simply being alive.

In line with his essentially positive view of human nature, Rogers asserts that emotions are beneficial to adjustment. Instead of stressing the disruptive effects of anxiety, Rogers believes that "emotion accompanies and in general facilitates . . . goal-directed behavior, . . . the intensity of the emotion being related to the perceived significance of the behavior for the maintenance and enhancement of the organism" (1951, p. 493).

The organism in the course of actualizing itself engages in a valuing process. Experiences that are perceived as enhancing it are valued positively (and approached). Experiences that are perceived as negating enhancement or maintenance of the organism are valued negatively (and avoided). "The organism has one basic tendency and striving—to actualize, maintain, and enhance the experiencing organism" (Rogers, 1951, p. 487).

## THE SELF

The self is a central concept for Rogers—indeed, his theory is often referred to as a self theory of personality. The self or self-concept (the two terms are equivalent for Rogers) is an "organized, consistent, conceptual gestalt composed of perceptions of the characteristics of the 'I' or 'me' and the perceptions of the relationships of the 'I' or 'me' to others and to various aspects of life, together with the values attached to these perceptions" (Rogers, 1959, p. 200). As a result of interaction with the environment, a portion of the perceptual field gradually becomes differentiated into the self. This perceived self (self-concept) influences perception and behavior. That is, the interpretation of the self—as strong or weak, for example—affects how one perceives the rest of one's world.

The experiences of the self become invested with values. These values are the result of direct experience with the environment, or they may be introjected or taken over from others. For example, a young child finds it organismically enjoyable to relieve himself whenever he experiences physiological tension in the bowel or bladder. However, he may sometimes also experience parental words and actions indicating that such behavior is bad, and that he is not lovable when he does this. A conflict then develops that may result in distortion and denial of experience. That is, the parental attitudes may be experienced as if they were based on the evidence of the child's own experience. In this example, the satisfaction of defecating may start to be experienced as bad even though a more accurate symbolization would be that it is often experienced as organismically satisfying. Rogers goes on to suggest that in bowel training, denial or distortion of experience may be avoided if the parent is able genuinely to accept the child's feelings and at the same time accepts his or her own feelings.

## CONSISTENCY AND POSITIVE REGARD

Rogers proposes two systems—the self (self-concept) and the organism—that may be in opposition or in harmony. When these systems are in opposition and incongruence, the result is maladjustment, for then the self becomes rigidly organized, losing contact with actual organismic experience and fraught with tensions. Perception is selective, the primary criterion being the consistency of an experience with the self-concept. The self-concept thus serves as a frame of reference for evaluating and monitoring the actual experiences of the organism. Unconscious denial of experience that is inconsistent with the concept of self is, Rogers believes, what the Freudians have tried to explain by the mechanism of repression. Experiences that are inconsistent with the self may be perceived as threats, and the more threat there is the more rigid and defensive the self structure becomes to maintain itself. At the same time, the self-concept becomes less congruent with organismic reality and loses contact with the actual experiences of the organism.

Rogers (1959) assumes a universal need for positive regard, which develops as the awareness of the self emerges. This need leads the person to desire acceptance and love from the important people in his life. Sometimes they may accept him conditionally (i.e. depending on his specific behavior), or they may accept him in his own right and give him unconditional regard. The person needs positive regard not only from others but also from his self. The need for self-regard develops out of self-experiences associated with the satisfaction or frustration of the need for positive regard. If a person experiences only unconditional positive regard, his self-regard also would be unconditional. In that case the needs for positive regard and self-regard would never be at variance with "organismic evaluation." Such a state would represent genuine psychological adjustment and full functioning.

Rogers assumes a universal need for positive regard.

Most people do not achieve such ideal adjustment. Often a self-experience is avoided or sought only because it is less (or more) worthy of self-regard. For example, a child may experience anger toward his mother but avoids accepting that feeling because he wants to be a "good boy." When that happens, Rogers speaks of the individual's having acquired a "condition of worth." Experiences that are in accord with the individual's conditions of worth tend to be perceived accurately in awareness, but experiences that violate the conditions of worth may be denied to awareness and distorted grossly. When there is a significant amount of incongruence between the individual's self-concept and his evaluation of an experience, then defenses may become unable to work successfully. For example, if a young man persistently experiences himself as painfully dissatisfied and "unhappy" in his efforts at schoolwork, but views himself as having to "succeed at college" in order to be an adequate person, he may experience great strain in his defensive efforts.

Rogers' theory, like Freud's, posits that accurate awareness of experiences may be threatening to the self and therefore may be prevented. Anxiety in Rogers' theory might be interpreted as the tension exhibited by the organized concept of the self when it senses (without full awareness, i.e. by "subceptions") that the recognition or symbolization of certain experiences would be destructive of its organization (1951). If a person's concept of the self has been built around his "masculinity," for example, experiences that might imply that he has some homosexual tendencies would threaten him severely. Anxiety thus involves a basic threat to the self, and defenses are erected to avoid it.

"Client-centered" (Rogerian) therapy seeks to bring about the harmonious interaction of the self and the organism and to facilitate a greater congruence between the conceptual structure of the self and the phenomenal field of experience. The warm and unconditionally accepting attitude of the counselor hopefully enables the client to perceive and examine experiences that are inconsistent with his current self-structure. The client can then revise his self-structure to permit it to assimilate these inconsistent experiences. According to Rogers, the client gradually reorganizes his self-concept to bring it into line with the reality of organismic experience: "He will *be*, in more unified fashion, what he organismically *is*, and this seems to be the essence of therapy" (1955, p. 269). In recent years Rogers has moved beyond individual client-centered therapy to form and lead many encounter groups intended to encourage psychological growth (see Chapter 12).

## ROGERS' PERSPECTIVE ON HIS OWN WORK

Looking back at the almost 50 years of his contributions to psychology, Rogers (1974) tried to pinpoint the essence of his approach. In his view, his most fundamental idea was that:

> . . . the individual has within himself vast resources for self-understanding, for altering his self-concept, his attitudes, and his self-directed behavior—and that these resources can be tapped if only a definable climate of facilitative psychological attitudes can be provided (Rogers, 1974, p. 116).

Such a climate for growth requires an atmosphere in which feelings can be confronted, expressed, and accepted fully and freely. His continued emphasis on man's potential freedom, the hallmark of a humanistic orientation, remains unchanged:

> My experience in therapy and in groups makes it impossible for me to deny the reality and significance of human choice. To me it is not an illusion that man is to some degree the architect of himself . . . for me the humanistic approach is the only possible one. It is for each person, however, to follow the pathway—behavioristic or humanistic—that he finds most congenial (Rogers, 1974, p. 119).

In the same humanistic vein he decries modern technology and calls for autonomy and self-exploration:

> Our culture, increasingly based on the conquest of nature and the control of man, is in decline. Emerging through the ruins is the new person, highly aware, self-directing, an explorer of inner, perhaps more than outer, space, scornful of the conformity of institutions and the dogma of authority. He does not believe in being behaviorally shaped, or in shaping the behavior of others. He is most assuredly humanistic rather than technological. In my judgment he has a high probability of survival (Rogers, 1974, p. 119).

*In sum*, Rogers' theory highlights many of the chief points of the phenomenological and humanistic approach to personality. It emphasizes the person's perceived reality, his subjective experiences, his organismic striving for actualization, his potential for growth and freedom. It rejects or deemphasizes specific biological drives, and focuses on the experienced self rather than on historical causes or stable trait structures. A unique feature of Rogers' position is his emphasis on unconditional acceptance as a requisite for self-regard. Other theorists have emphasized different aspects of experience in their formulations. One of the most influential of these positions is George Kelly's theory, which is discussed in the next section.

## GEORGE KELLY'S PSYCHOLOGY OF PERSONAL CONSTRUCTS

As students of general semantics often point out, "The map is not the terrain." Yet the two are often confused. Psychologically it is equally true that our constructs and abstractions about behavior are not the same as the behaviors that are being categorized. In addition to acting as motivated organisms, people also are perceivers and construers of behavior, and they generate abstractions about themselves and others. These hypotheses and constructions have long intrigued psychologists interested in subjective states, in phenomenology, and in the experience of the self.

## THE SUBJECT'S CONSTRUCTS

In the psychodynamic approach, the motive is the chief unit, unconscious conflicts are the processes of greatest interest, and the clinical judge is the favored instrument. Kelly's (1955) personal construct theory, in contrast, seeks to illuminate the person's own categories rather than the hypotheses of the psychologist. Its main units are the person's constructs—the way he categorizes his own experiences. Rather than seeing man as victimized by his impulses and defenses, this position views him as an active, ever-changing creator of hypotheses and a player of multiple roles.

According to Kelly, trait psychology tries to find the subject's place on the *theorist's* personality dimension. "Personal construct theory" instead tries to see how the subject aligns events on *his own* dimensions. It is Kelly's hope to discover the nature of the subject's construct dimensions rather than to locate his position on the dimensions of the psychologist's theory.

## MAN-THE-SCIENTIST

The psychology of personal constructs explores the subjective maps that people generate in coping with the psychological terrain of their lives. Kelly emphasizes that, just like the scientist who studies him, the human subject also construes or abstracts behavior, categorizing, interpreting, labeling, and judging himself and his world. The individuals assessed by psychologists are themselves assessors who evaluate and construe their own behavior; they even assess the personality psychologists who try to assess them. Constructions and hypotheses about behavior are formulated by all persons regardless of their formal degrees and credentials as scientists. According to Kelly it is these constructions, and not merely simple physical responses, that must be studied in an adequate approach to personality. Categorizing behavior is equally evident when a psychotic patient describes his personal, private ideas in therapy and when a scientist discusses his favorite constructs and theories at a professional meeting. Both men represent the environment internally and express their representations and private experiences in their psychological constructions. Personal constructions, and not objective behavior descriptions on clear dimensions, confront the personality psychologist.

Kelly notes that most psychological scientists view themselves as motivated to achieve cognitive clarity and to understand phenomena, including their own lives. Yet the subjects of their theories, unlike the theorists themselves, are seen as unaware victims of psychic forces and traits that they can neither understand nor control. Kelly tries to remove this discrepancy between the theorist and the subject and to treat all men as if they were scientists.

Just like the scientist, the subject generates constructs and hypotheses with which he tries to anticipate and control events in his life. Therefore to understand the subject, one has to understand his constructs or private personality theory. To study an individual's constructs one has to find behavioral examples or "referents" for them. We cannot know what another person means when he says, "I have too much ego," or "I am not a friendly person," or "I may be falling in love," unless he gives us behavioral examples. Examples (referents) are required whether the construct is personal, for example the way a patient construes himself "as a man," or theoretical, as when a psychologist talks about "introversion" or "ego defenses." Constructs can become known only through behavior.

## CONSTRUCTIVE ALTERNATIVISM

The same events can be alternatively categorized. While man may not always be able to change events, he can always construe them differently. That is what Kelly meant by "constructive alternativism." To illustrate, consider this event: a boy drops his mother's favorite vase. What does it mean? The event is simply that the vase has been broken. Yet ask the child's psychoanalyst and he may point to the boy's unconscious hostility; ask the mother and she tells you how "mean" he is; his father says he is "spoiled"; the child's teacher may see the event as evidence of the child's "laziness" and chronic "clumsiness"; grandmother calls it just an "accident"; and the child himself may construe the event as reflecting his "stupidity." While the event cannot be undone—the vase is broken—its interpretation is open to alternative constructions, and these may lead to different courses of action.

Kelly's theory began with this fundamental postulate: "A person's processes are psychologically channelized by the ways in which he anticipates events" (Kelly, 1955, p. 46). Phrased differently, this postulate means that a person's activities are guided (stabilized, channelized) by the constructs (ways) he uses to predict (anticipate) events. This postulate shares with other phenomenological theories an emphasis on the person's subjective view, but it is more specific in its focus on how the individual predicts or anticipates events. The postulate is further elaborated by a set of formal corollaries. Although the details of the theory need not concern us here, several of the main ideas require comment.

Kelly is concerned with the *convenience* of constructs rather than with their absolute truth. Rather than try to assess whether a particular construct is true, Kelly attends to its convenience or utility for the construer. For example, rather than try to assess whether or not a client is "really a latent homosexual" or "really going crazy," he tries to discover the implications for the client's life of construing himself in that way. If the construction is not convenient, then the task is to find a better alternative—that is, one that predicts better and leads to better outcomes. Just as a psychologist may get stuck with an inadequate theory, so his subjects also may impale themselves on their constructions and construe themselves into a dilemma. Individuals may torture themselves into believing that "I am not worthy enough" or "I am not successful enough," as if these verdicts were matters of undisputable fact rather than constructions and hypotheses about behavior. The job of psychotherapy is to provide the conditions in which personal constructs can be elaborated, tested for their implications, and, if necessary, modified. Just like the scientist, the subject needs the chance to test his constructs and to validate or invalidate them, progressively modifying them in the light of his new experience.

### *ROLES*

Another idea that merits special attention is Kelly's emphasis on roles and role enactments. Rather than seeing man as the possessor of fairly stable, broadly generalized traits, Kelly saw him as capable of enacting many different roles and of engaging in continuous change. A role, for Kelly, is an attempt to see another person through the other's glasses—that is, to look at a person through *his* constructs—and to structure one's actions in that light. To enact a role requires that behavior be guided by perception of the other person's viewpoint. Thus to "role play" your mother, for example, you would have to try to see things (including yourself) as she does, "through her eyes," and to act in light of those perceptions. You would try to behave as if you really were your mother. Kelly used the technique of role playing extensively as a therapeutic procedure designed to help persons gain new perspectives and to generate more convenient ways of living.

### *MAN IS WHAT HE MAKES OF HIMSELF*

Like other phenomenologists, Kelly rejects the idea of specific motives. His view of human nature focuses on how man construes himself and on what he does in the light of those constructs. Kelly (like Rogers) believes that no special concepts are required to understand why man is motivated and active: every person is motivated "for no other reason than that he is alive" (Kelly, 1958, p. 49). For Kelly the concept of motivation "can appear only as a redundancy" (1958, p. 50).

He believes, like many existentialists, that man *is* what he *does* and comes to know his nature by seeing what he is doing. Starting from his clinical experiences with troubled college students in Fort Hays, Kansas, where he taught for many years, Kelly independently reached a position that overlaps remarkably with the views of such European existential philosophers as Sartre (1956). In Sartre's (1956) existentialist conception, "existence precedes essence": there is no human nature— man simply *is*, and he is nothing else but what he "makes of himself."

## FEELING AND FULFILLMENT

Kelly believes that his theory, though it focuses on the person's constructs, is not purely concerned with cognitive and intellectual functions. Constructs he says, often are not verbal, and they may involve highly emotional phenomena. Nevertheless some critics find that his view of man-the-scientist neglects man as an emotional being. Since Kelly's work many phenomenologically oriented psychologists have become increasingly committed to the affective, nonverbal components of experience. This search for feeling is seen in numerous recent psychological movements, both within psychology as a formal discipline and in the larger social scene.

The concern with feelings, the sense of being "out of touch" and isolated from emotional experiences, is illustrated poignantly in these excerpts from a troubled college student's letter:

Long ago I lost touch with my body—my brain became separated from my body, and started commanding it. My body turned into just a machine for transporting my brain around from place to place to talk unfeelingly and analytically with other detached brains. I was glad it was a big and efficient machine—but I thought it was the inferior part of me, and that my brain should be in charge and call the tune for my feelings, letting the "positive" ones out and keeping the "negative" ones safely tucked in. . . .

But now I feel lost in that head, out of phase with people—and somehow I want to reach them and my own guts—to know what I really feel, and stop all these precious intellectual games—to really live and not just to exist—So what do I do now?

The idea expressed by this distressed student is shared by many others who want "to make contact" emotionally both with themselves and with other people.

## EXPANDING CONSCIOUSNESS

Probably the most dramatic and controversial manifestation of this trend to achieve deeper feeling was the effort to expand consciousness and emotional experiences by means of psychedelic drugs. Initially drugs such as psilocybin and LSD were advocated most energetically by Timothy Leary and Richard Alpert when they were psychologists at Harvard in 1961 and 1962. In the 1960's the "mind-expanding" movement through drug-induced "trips" or psychic "voyages" gained many enthusiastic participants. Although drawing heavily on Freudian dynamic psychology for its interpretations, this movement had a different purpose from that espoused by most neo-analytic followers of Freud. The neo-analysts emphasized "ego psychology" and the impulse-free (or "conflict-free") spheres of the ego and of rational control processes. Many advocates of consciousness expansion, instead, seemed to seek a return of the "primacy of the id"—a focus on feeling and fantasy, on "primary processes" rather than on logic and rational thought. This effort to capture pure feeling, to experience more closely one's bodily states, to escape from "ego" and "superego" and societal constraints, and to live fully in the "here and now," was seen most vividly in the "hippie" movement and the "drug culture" of the 1960's. We shall consider these experiences again in later sections (Chapter 12).

Such drugs as LSD undoubtedly produce major alterations in subjective experience, including the intensification of feelings (e.g., Leary, Litwin & Metzner, 1963), but enthusiasm for them was soon tempered by the recognition that they entail serious risks. While the much less controversial drug, marijuana, has received increasing acceptance, there also has been a trend to search for greater awareness without the aid of any drugs.

## AWAY FROM ALIENATION

Several routes to increasing awareness have relied on psychological experiences rather than on drugs. These efforts include meditation (Ornstein, 1972), encounter groups, and "marathons" of the type developed at the Esalen Institute in Big Sur, California (Schutz, 1967). While meditative techniques have been based mainly on Oriental religious sources (Ornstein & Naranjo, 1971), the encounter or "sensitivity training" movement has drawn on various role-play and psychodrama techniques, on existential philosophy, and on Freudian dynamic psychology. The resulting syntheses are seen in the ideas of the "Gestalt therapy" of Fritz Perls (1969), in the efforts to expand human awareness and to achieve "joy" and true communication (e.g., Schutz, 1967), and in the pursuit of "peak experiences" and "self-actualization" (e.g., Maslow, 1971). Because the implications of these positions are most relevant for psychotherapy and personality change they will be discussed in that context in later sections (Chapter 12).

## TOWARD FULFILLMENT: MASLOW'S SELF-ACTUALIZING PERSON

One of the most influential spokesmen for the importance of becoming "in touch" with one's true feelings and fulfilling oneself totally was Abraham Maslow (1968, 1971). Maslow's theory overlaps considerably with that of Rogers. But Maslow was an especially emphatic advocate of man's vast positive potential for growth and fulfillment. The striving toward actualization of this potential is a basic quality of being human:

> Man demonstrates *in his own nature* a pressure toward fuller and fuller Being, more and more perfect actualization of his humanness in exactly the same naturalistic, scientific sense that an acorn may be said to be "pressing toward" being an oak tree, or that a tiger can be observed to "push toward" being tigerish, or a horse toward being equine. . . . (Maslow, 1968, p. 160).

Maslow's commitment was to study "optimal man" and to discover the qualities of those people who seemed to be closest to realizing all their potentialities. In his view, man has higher "growth needs"—needs to self-actualize and fulfill himself—that emerge when more primitive needs (physiological needs, safety needs, needs for belongingness and self-esteem) are satisfied. Maslow wanted to focus on the qualities of feeling and experience that seem to distinguish self-actualizing, fully functioning people. Therefore, he searched for the attributes that seemed to mark such people as Beethoven, Einstein, Jefferson, Lincoln, Walt Whitman, as well as some of the individuals he knew personally and admired most. These positive qualities are elaborated as part of the humanistic view of the "healthy personality" in Chapter 12.

Self-actualization may be seen not only as a human need and as a quality of certain people, but also as a subjective experience that many of us may have, even if only momentarily, at some points in life. Maslow called this special state a "peak experience"; a temporary experience of fulfillment and joy in which the person loses self-centeredness and (in varying degrees of intensity) feels a nonstriving happiness, a moment of perfection. Words that may be used to describe this

In a "peak experience" the person may achieve
a moment of fulfillment and joy.

state include "aliveness," "beauty," "ecstasy," "effortlessness," "uniqueness," and "wholeness." Such peak experiences have been reported in many contexts, including the esthetic appreciation of nature and beauty, worship, intimate relationships with others, and creative activities.

## CRITICAL IMPLICATIONS

Many personality psychologists welcome the emphasis on the person's cognitions, feelings, and personal interpretations of experience stressed by the theories discussed in this chapter. Indeed this concern with how the individual construes events and sees himself and his world has been a most influential force, and it has generated a great deal of research. The resulting contributions are widely acknowledged. On the other hand, there have been some sharp criticisms.

The existential belief that "man is what he makes of himself" and what he conceives himself to be is extremely appealing to many people. It also raises some key issues. First, psychologists committed to a deterministic view of science have to ask what are the *causes* that govern what man makes of himself and conceives himself to be—how do individual men come to make themselves and conceive themselves in particular ways? While philosophers may put the springs of action and cognition into the will (as Sartre does), the scientifically oriented psychologist seeks the variables that account for the phenomena of being and will itself. While able to accept in part the idea that the individual is what he makes of himself, the psychologist as a scientist has to go further and search for the conditions that make him, including those conditions that influence (or make) his self-conceptions.

114

The existential idea that man is "in possession of himself," rather than possessed by a human nature, and that he is what he makes of himself, has profound implications for the study of personality. Instead of a search for where the individual stands with regard to the assessor's dimensions, the assessor's task becomes the elaboration of what the individual is making of himself. To the extent that the assessor seeks a full account, however, he also must search for the causes of that existence. This last step is where most psychologists concerned with observable causes part company with the existentialist. It is also the point at which many psychologists have chosen for themselves a humanistic existentialism rather than a deterministic psychology.

## ARE COGNITIONS THE CAUSES OF BEHAVIOR?

In spite of the obvious importance of personal constructs and other cognitions, one cannot assume that they are the main causes of the person's behavior. Verbal constructs and cognitions do not always cause or even influence nonverbal behavior and the things we do. The relations between personal concepts and other behaviors often are quite indirect and remote. Currently there is relatively little evidence that changes in personal constructs—or in opinions, beliefs, or values—necessarily produce important behavior changes (Festinger, 1964). Often cognitive and value changes may *follow* as a function of particular behavioral performances, rather than serve as the causes for these performances (e.g., Bem, 1972; Festinger, 1957). That is, constructs and cognitions may be realigned to make them consistent with behavior and may be used to justify that behavior. The issues and evidence on this topic are discussed in later chapters.

## INCOMPLETE EXPLANATIONS

Perhaps the most fundamental criticism of cognitive and phenomenological explanations is that they are incomplete and do not provide a sufficiently detailed and comprehensive analysis of the causes controlling behavior. In Kelly's theory, for example, personal constructs are viewed as key determinants of behavior, but what determines the constructs that a person has? Offering the construct as a cause of the observed behavior may be an example of an unfinished causal explanation. Such unfinished analyses are found whenever mental states, perceptions, cognitions, feelings, motives, or similar constructs are offered as explanations of behavior while the determinants of the mental states themselves are ignored. Skinner (1964, p. 93) has called this the use of "mental way stations" for unfinished causal sequences and says:

A disturbance in behavior is not explained by relating it to felt anxiety until the anxiety has in turn been explained. An action is not explained by attributing it to expectations until the expectations have in turn been accounted for.

In his view, a comprehensive analysis must include the conditions or *variables* that control the behavior of interest and not merely the hypothetical intervening mental steps.

Phenomenological positions have been criticized for removing the perceiver or "construer" from the causal chain—and hence removing him from scientific study. This feature—problematic for researchers interested in discovering the causes of human behavior—may also be one of its attractions for humanistically oriented psychologists.

Some phenomenological theorists have accused their behaviorally oriented critics of treating man as an "empty organism," a machine-like automaton devoid of thought and feeling, a merely reflexive creature. In spite of many heated debates and widespread misconceptions, few psychologists really suggest that man's internal processes and mental activities should be ignored or excluded in psychological studies. As Skinner has noted, even advocates of a rigorous behavioral position believe that:

> No entity or process which has any useful explanatory force is to be rejected on the ground that it is subjective or mental. The data which have made it important must, however, be studied and formulated in effective ways (Skinner, 1964, p. 96).

The issue thus is not the existence of mental activity and its importance, but rather the most useful and interesting strategies for discovering more about how the brain works and generates observable "outputs."

## IS THE SELF A "DOER"?

Phenomenological accounts of the self in personality have been criticized most strongly for being descriptive rather than explanatory (see Brewster Smith's 1950 discussion). In his analysis, Smith has noted the importance of distinguishing between two different meanings of the self. One meaning of the self is as the *doer* of behavior. That meaning refers to the diverse processes that comprise the individual's personality. The self as doer is simply a summary term for these processes. The second meaning is the *self-as-object*. This definition refers to the person's concepts and attitudes about himself.

Smith argues that this distinction between the self-as-doer or process, and the phenomenal construct of the self—that is, the self-as-object perceived by the individual—has been confused by phenomenologists. He notes that Rogers, for example, talks about the self this way:

> When the self is free from any threat of attack or likelihood of attack, then it is possible for the self to consider these hitherto rejected perceptions, to make new differentiations, and to reintegrate the self in such a way as to include them (Rogers, 1947, p. 365).

Smith questions these feats of the self, commenting on the confusion between the self as a causal agent and the self as an experienced phenomenon:

> Can a phenomenal self consider perceptions and reintegrate itself . . . , or is this rather double-talk resulting from the attempt to make one good concept do the work of two? (Smith, 1950, p. 520).

Thus Smith faulted self theorists for endowing the self-as-object (which is a concept that the individual has about himself) with all sorts of causal powers, such as the ability to evaluate itself, guard itself, and change itself.

## SOCIAL BEHAVIOR THEORY, EXISTENTIALISM AND PHENOMENOLOGY

Psychological theories sometimes have unexpected similarities. In the last chapter we saw that social behavior theory involves a focus on what the person is doing in the here and now, rather than on reconstructions of his psychic history, and a reluctance to hypothesize drives, forces, motives, and other psychic dispositions as explanations. This chapter has shown that all these features, surprisingly, are not unique to a behavioral position. They just as fully seem to describe the platform of some existentially oriented and phenomenological psychologists. This conceptual union may be unexpected. Yet the behavioral focus on what the person is doing, rather than on his attributes or motives, fits the existential doctrine exquisitely. As Sartre put it, "existence precedes essence." He meant by that phrase that

> man first of all exists, encounters himself, surges up in the world—and defines himself afterwards. If man as the existentialist sees him is not definable, it is because to begin with he is nothing. He will not be anything until later, and then he will be what he makes of himself. Thus, there is no human nature. . . . Man simply is (Sartre, 1965, p. 28).

Thus a renunciation of preconceptions about motives, traits, and the content of human nature is hardly unique to Skinnerians and other contemporary behaviorists. George Kelly meant something similar when he said, "I am what I do," and urged that to know what one is one must look at what one does. Substantive constructs about universal human "essences," about specific dynamics, agencies of the mind, fundamental complexes and conflicts, sexual and aggressive drives or other basic motives as foundations of later development—all these and similar constructs about the nature of personality are as rejected by existentialism as they are by current social behavior theories. Similarly, both positions insist that it is impossible to conceptualize man apart from the context or environment in which he exists.

The possible conceptual compatibility between modern social behavior theory and the existential-phenomenological orientation seems to hinge on several common qualities. Both share a focus on the here and now, a reluctance to posit specific motivational and trait constructs, an emphasis on what the person is doing—on "where he is at"—rather than on the constructs of the psychologist who studies him, a disinterest in distant historical reconstruction, and a concern with new action possibilities for the individual. These commonalities are impressive.

While the overlap between the behavioral and existential-phenomenological orientation seems intriguing, the magnitude of their union should not be exaggerated. First, is attention to the subject's *phenomenology* really compatible with a behavior approach? Skinner's focus on observable behavior has emphasized the simplest sort of physical responses, such as movements, in order to obtain the most precise possible response measures. It would be difficult to see how subjective experience can be studied in such terms. In more recent extensions, however, social learning theorists stress that it would be absurd to try to define out of existence the concepts, perceptions, and experiences of the people we are studying (Mischel, 1968, 1973a). Indeed these phenomena can be studied like any other complex behaviors—if appropriate observable events are found as referents for them. There have been many suggestions for doing that, for example in the work of George Kelly and others (reviewed in Mischel, 1968).

The social behavior and existentialist positions do suffer from one critical incompatibility. The existentialist takes the philosophical position that man, the individual, is responsible, and he attributes to man the ultimate causes of his behavior. In Sartre's phrase, man "is what he wills to be" (1956, p. 291). Though the behaviorist may share Sartre's desire to put "every man in possession of himself," rather than allow him to be possessed by psychic forces, a behavioral analysis of causation cannot begin with the person's will as the fundamental cause of what he does, nor can it end with his constructs as a final explanation of his behavior.

George Kelly (personal communication, 1965) once emphasized his belief that personal constructs are the basic units and that it is personal constructs, rather than stimuli, that determine behavior. He recalled vividly from his Navy experience during World War II how very differently he related to the same officer on different occasions depending on how, at the time, he construed that officer. He remembered that the captain seemed different to him in an informal role, chatting with his jacket off, from the way he seemed when he wore his officer's coat. You see, Kelly said, it is not the stimulus—the captain—but how I construed him that channelized my reactions to him.

But a social behavior theorist would find this story an excellent example, not of "construct control," but of "stimulus control": with his four stripes on, you see the captain one way; without his four stripes, you see him differently. To understand the construct change, in the behavioral view, you have to include in your understanding how those four stripes came to control it.

The phenomenological and behavioral positions differ in their focus of attention: the former seeks to know and understand the subject's experience; the behaviorally oriented psychologist wants to clarify the conditions that control the subject's ultimate behavior, including the events that control his constructs, cognitions, and feelings.

A behavioral approach insists on specific causal analyses that precisely link what the individual does and construes to the conditions in which he does it. Without becoming embroiled here in philosophical complexities, we can say that existential positions seem to stop sooner in their causal analyses, making man the ultimate cause of what he does. Similarly phenomenological positions put the causes of behavior in the perceptions and constructs of the individual. In behavioral analyses, as Skinner has emphasized, one needs to consider not only how an individual's perceptions and concepts affect his behavior, but also what are the observable causes and the controlling conditions governing the perceptions and concepts themselves. The humanistically oriented existentialist may want to remove the individual from the causal chain and to make man the prime cause of his own behaviors; the behaviorally oriented psychologist seeks to put man in nature's causal chain and to delineate the conditions that determine what he does and therefore what he is.

Is a reasonable synthesis of phenomenological psychology and social learning theory possible? Perhaps. Such a synthesis would require the ability to view man both as an active construer who perceives, interprets, and influences his environment and himself and as a creature in nature, continuously responsive to the conditions of his life (as discussed further in Chapter 21).

## SUMMARY

1. The diverse theories discussed in this chapter all reject specific motivational and dynamic concepts. Instead they focus on the immediate perceived experience and concepts of the individual, and on his striving toward growth and self-actualization.

2. Allport's theory of personality stresses the functional autonomy of motives and argues that motives that are functioning currently in the mature individual may be independent of their historical roots. He gives central importance to the phenomenological or perceived self.

3. Lewin's field theory introduces the notion of life space and the importance of the psychological environment. His theory stresses the immediate relationships between person and environment and elements in the environment, rather than dealing with these as absolute entities. Contemporaneity is an important feature of this viewpoint. Lewin was dissatisfied with the usual concepts of traits and needs and saw behavior and development as functions of dynamic changes in the psychological environment and in the tension systems of the person.

4. Many of the positions discussed in this chapter have in common an interest in subjective experience and a positive view of human nature. Man is seen as purposeful and striving toward self-fulfillment, not simply as

driven by unconscious forces and motivated by the necessity to satisfy his biological needs.

5. Carl Rogers' theory is illustrative of the central characteristics of the phenomenological approach to personality. The emphasis is on the person's unique experienced reality. In this theory the *self* (self-concept) is a conscious perception of self-as-object. This self-concept develops as the result of direct experience with the environment and may also incorporate the perceptions of others. The experienced self in turn influences perception and behavior. Maladjustment occurs when the sense of self and a person's perceptions and experiences are in opposition and disharmony.

6. George Kelly's theory stresses the necessity of understanding the individual's own dimensions, categories, and hypotheses rather than viewing him in terms of the psychologist's constructs. It also emphasizes the convenience of the person's hypotheses and constructs for dealing with experience. Role play may help the person to select and practice more satisfactory, convenient modes of construing his world in alternative ways.

7. Psychedelic drugs, meditation, and encounter groups have been favored by recent movements that emphasize nonverbal, emotional components of experience and existence. Some of these approaches seek to explore and expand consciousness and awareness through a variety of techniques aimed at escape from the "reality-oriented ego" into the realm of pure feeling and enhanced sensitivity. Others search for fulfillment through self-actualization and "peak experiences," as Maslow emphasized.

8. The phenomenological emphasis has made many contributions. Nevertheless, it also has been criticized. A focus on the person's subjective perceptions and cognitions does not necessarily uncover the causes of his behavior. Indeed the relations between cognition and behavior may be highly complex. Moreover, sometimes self theorists seem to confuse the self as an experienced phenomenon and as an agent determining behavior. Finally, explanations that do not look beyond the individual to the stimulus conditions causing his phenomenal experiences may be criticized as incomplete accounts.

9. Current behavior theories share some common features with phenomenological approaches. In the phenomenological approach of Kelly, for example, we know a man by what we see him doing. Curiously, a similar statement could come from contemporary behavior theorists. Another often unexpected similarity between the social behavior approach and the phenomenological orientation is that both favor concentrating on the "here and now" situation rather than on inferences about the person's past.

10. Lest the reader erroneously exaggerate the closeness between the empiricism of such behaviorists as Skinner and the phenomenology of the existentially oriented, it should be stressed that there are fundamental differences between them. A chief difference between current social behavior views and the views discussed in this chapter has to do with the heavy emphasis that cognitive formulations place on the *causal role* of cognitions and self-concepts as pervasive determinants of the behaviors comprising personality. The question is not the existence of such cognitions and self-concepts, but, rather, their adequacy as explanations of the complex phenomena of personality.

In this part of the book we will examine some of the main applications for assessment and personality change associated with each of the orientations discussed in the preceding pages. Each of the theoretical conceptions surveyed in Part 1 has led to distinctive methods for studying persons and for attempting to produce constructive personality change. These applications have been quite diverse, and the reader will be introduced to assessment techniques ranging from questionnaires to projective tests and behavior sampling, and to therapeutic approaches that extend from psychodynamic psychotherapy to behavior modification and encounter groups.

Each of the main applications will be discussed in the context of the orientation and assumptions most relevant to it. The findings, issues, and problems from these applications in turn can shed light on the relevant theoretical conceptions.

The theories adopted by personality psychologists are not rigid entities but broad guidelines that change as knowledge and concepts change. Therefore orientations often overlap, and methods may merge and borrow from theoretical and technical neighbors. Nevertheless there also are real differences. To highlight some of the critical differences among approaches in concrete terms, each will be applied to an analysis of the same person—"Gary W." As psychologists, how should we construe Gary? What is he "really" like? How can we get to know and understand him better?

Each orientation supplies its own answers to these questions. It will be seen that the concepts and methods of each orientation add distinctive information about Gary. Sometimes the new information may seem consistent with the old; sometimes it may seem to conflict with it; sometimes it may reflect the complexity of Gary's personality; and sometimes it may illuminate the strengths and weaknesses of current psychological ideas and techniques.

Each theoretical approach also has influenced conceptions of the meaning of personality "adaptation" (adjustment) and "deviance." Definitions of adaptation depend on the personality theory to which one adheres. Each of the main theoretical approaches to personality discussed in Part 1 has its own view of what constitutes "ideal adjustment" and "maladjustment." Recall, for example, the Freudian emphasis on recognition of unconscious impulses, and Rogers' concern with self-actualization and congruity. Clearly, each theorist would interpret adequacy and deviance in terms of his guiding constructs about personality. The theoretical orientation you adopt thus guides how you evaluate people and how you assess the adequacy or inappropriateness of their behavior, as Part 2 will show.

Theories of personality can be evaluated at least partly according to their relevance and efficacy for the modification of human behavior. Personality changes occur throughout life, but usually it is impossible to study them systematically. Hence their exact nature remains unclear. In most research situations the conditions that can be studied tend to be of momentary duration and little strength. Ethical concerns as well as practical limitations prevent psychologists from generating really powerful and enduring changes in the laboratory. Instead, the major changes of life unfold under the chaotic, uncontrolled conditions of the real world, and we glimpse only fragments of this process. An important exception is the therapeutic setting in which individuals seek help for problems that plague them. In the context of research on therapy and personality change, therefore, psychological principles for the modification of human behavior can receive their definitive test. The results should inform us not merely about the efficacy of particular techniques but also more broadly about the nature of personality and the conditions under which it may change—for good or for ill.

While some approaches (particularly trait theories) have had a great deal of impact on personality assessment, they have had little influence on strategies for personality change. Conversely, other positions (especially behavioral approaches) have had the greatest impact on procedures for generating change, and still others (psychodynamic and phenomenological approaches) have influenced both personality assessment and personality change to a large degree.

The next two chapters, 7 and 8, consider applications most relevant to trait theories. Specifically, Chapter 7 gives a brief history of trait measurement, describes some trait instruments and strategies, and gives examples of their applications. Chapter 8 provides a more general discussion and evaluation of basic issues relevant to the uses of the trait approach. Chapter 9 deals with applications guided mainly by psychodynamic theories. Chapters 10 and 11 consider the chief methods of behavioral theories for personality assessment and behavior modification respectively; and Chapter 12 explores the applications of the phenomenological orientation.

As the reader progresses through Part 2, it will become increasingly evident that an adequate understanding and appraisal of personality theories depends on knowing more than what each theorist asserted; it requires the closest attention to the applications that his conceptions have generated and to the problems, issues, failures, and successes that those applications reveal.

# CHAPTER 7

# TRAIT THEORIES
## Applications (I)

This chapter examines some of the major applications of trait theories. It begins by looking at the history of the trait approach to measurement and then illustrates some of the main methods and tactics that have grown from those roots. It also considers some of the problems that have arisen in those applications and some of the new research directions designed to clarify the nature of personality.

Probably the most important impact of the trait approach has been its methodology: it has provided basic concepts and measures to assess individual differences and to test hypotheses about personality. The most appealing feature of this methodology is that it permits a quantitative, orderly study of individual differences in an area that always before had defied measurement.

Late in the nineteenth century trait psychologists recognized the hazards of basing impressions of people on informal, subjective judgments about them. Consequently they tried to go beyond casual impressions by devising more formal tests. In this way they hoped to develop objective procedures for measuring important individual differences. For these trait theorists any attempt to study personality without tests would be as naive as a biological science without microscopes. Since the end of the nineteenth century there have been continuous systematic efforts to study personality traits quantitatively by means of tests. This movement, often called the *psychometric trait approach,* has been one of the main forces in the study of personality; its roots extend far into the past and its implications for an understanding of personality are profound.

## THE BEGINNINGS OF THE PSYCHOMETRIC APPROACH

Psychometric testing started in the psychological laboratories during the last decades of the nineteenth century. Sir Francis Galton was administering tests in his London laboratory as early as 1882, in an effort to establish an inventory of human abilities. In his studies of human inheritance, he included measures of sensory acuity, reaction time, and strength of movement. His aim was to measure the resemblance between large numbers of related and unrelated persons. Galton also devised a questionnaire that was an important forerunner of those developed in later years.

James McKeen Cattell was an American psychologist who had a major role in the development of psychological testing. In 1890 Cattell suggested a standard series of tests for the study of mental processes. These tests were typical of the kind appearing at that time. They included measures of strength of grip, rate of arm movement, amount of pressure needed to produce pain on the forehead, reaction time for sound, and speed of color naming.

Tests of reading, judgment, and memory were also being used with some schoolchildren toward the end of the last century. A first attempt to evaluate test scores systematically is found in a study by T. L. Bolton that appeared in 1892. Bolton analyzed data from about 1500 schoolchildren, comparing their memory spans with their teachers' estimates of their "intellectual acuteness," and found little correspondence. A 1901 monograph likewise reported disappointing results: the relationships found between Cattell's various tests at Columbia College and students' academic standing were negligible (Wissler, 1901).

The simple, specific, sensorimotor measures popular in the laboratories at the end of the nineteenth century were important forerunners of later tests. But the tests favored during this period were primarily laboratory-bound techniques for comparing individual differences on single measures rather than on organized scales. It was the development of intelligence testing in the early twentieth century that made "psychometrics" a special and prominent field in its own right (Watson, 1959).

Intelligence testing grew out of efforts to separate
retarded children into special programs.

## INTELLIGENCE TESTING

Intelligence testing evolved in response to practical demands, primarily the
need to separate the "uneducable" or severely retarded children into special
schools that could provide a simplified curriculum. In the 1890s, Alfred Binet, a
Frenchman and a physician by training, began to try to measure intelligence. He
wanted to discover how "bright" and "dull" children differ and began empirically,
without any clear preconceptions about the nature of their difference. Binet and
his associates believed that available tests lacked measures of complex processes
and overemphasized sensory tasks. It was their hope that individual differences in
ability would be reflected better in more complex tasks. Accordingly they proposed
a series of tests including measures of aesthetic appreciation, attention, comprehen-
sion, imagination, memory, mental imagery, moral feelings, muscular force, force of
will, motor ability, suggestibility, and visual discrimination.

Ultimately, Binet's scales successfully differentiated children with respect to
scholastic standing. Reactions to the Binet scales were enthusiastic because they
seemed to fill the urgent need for a practical way to study mental processes without depending on an individual's introspective reports. The test supplied a single
overall score that offered a general and simple summary of mental status. This
summary score permitted ready comparisons between individuals in terms of their
level of mental development. The Binet scales were revised and extended several
times, most notably by Lewis M. Terman of Stanford University in 1916. Terman's
revision produced the now classic Stanford-Binet, which became a popular standard for all later work on mental ability testing.

Virtually all of the developments in mental and personality testing have been
influenced more or less directly by Binet's original work. Following the pioneering
work of Binet, an extremely influential series of intelligence scales that are still
very popular was developed by David Wechsler. These scales assess the individual's
standing in relation to large numbers of other people of the same age, and thus
have considerable practical value. The person's general intelligence quotient or

Figure 7-1   ITEMS SIMILAR TO THOSE ON STANDARD INTELLIGENCE TESTS (SUCH AS THE WECHSLER INTELLIGENCE SCALE)

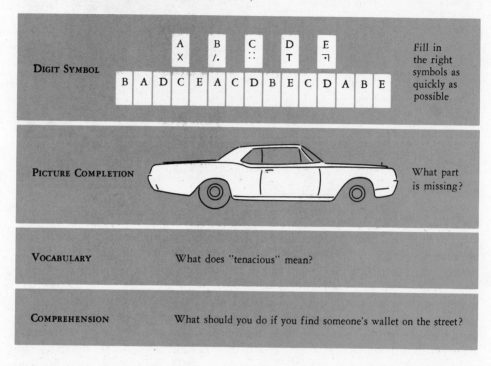

"IQ" score summarizes his "full-scale" or total test achievement. His standing on the main subcomponents of the test also is computed. Items similar to those found on such IQ scales are presented in Figure 7-1.

## EARLY PERSONALITY MEASUREMENT

Early questionnaires and inventories to measure individual differences in personality arose in the wake of the successful measurement of intelligence and flourished especially during the 1920s and 1930s. Interest in self-description or self-report as a method of personality assessment was stimulated by an inventory devised during the First World War (Watson, 1959). This was Woodworth's *Personal Data Sheet,* later known as the *Psychoneurotic Inventory,* and it was aimed at detecting soldiers who would be likely to break down under wartime stress. Because it was highly impractical to give individual psychiatric interviews to recruits, Woodworth listed the kinds of symptoms psychiatrists would probably ask about in interviews and condensed them into a paper-and-pencil questionnaire of more than one hundred items. Examples are: "Do you wet your bed at night?" "Do you day-dream frequently?" The respondent must answer "yes" or "no" to each question, and the tally of his answers is his final score. Soldiers who gave many affirmative responses were followed up with individual interviews. This method was valuable as a grossly condensed, simplified, and economic alternative to interviewing all subjects individually. Often questionnaires are still employed as substitutes for interviews.

The Woodworth questionnaire was not used extensively, but it was a forerunner of the many other self-report devices that flourished in the next two decades. These self-report devices compared people usually with respect to a single summary score, which served as an index of their "overall level of adjustment," just as single scores or mental quotients were developed to describe the level of "general intelligence." In addition to efforts to assess adjustment and psychiatric status, attempts to measure individuals on various personality dimensions soon became extremely popular.

# THE NATURE OF TRAIT TESTS

The psychometric approach to the study of personality relies on tests intended to tap personality traits. These traits or dispositions are assumed to be quantifiable and scalable. As J. P. Guilford, a leading spokesman for the psychometric trait position, said:

> By [scalability] we mean that a trait is a certain quality or attribute, and different individuals have different degrees of it. . . . If individuals differ in a trait by having higher or lower degrees of it, we can represent the trait by means of a single straight line. . . . Individual trait positions may be represented by points on the line (Guilford, 1959, pp. 64–65).

## SCORING TRAITS

Thus traits like aggressiveness or introversion, or submissiveness or masculinity, for example, may be conceived as quantifiable attributes similar to physical dimensions. It is assumed that individuals differ from each other more or less enduringly in the degree (or amount) to which they possess each of these attributes. It is also assumed that at least some traits are *common* in the population. Measurement usually proceeds with respect to one trait at a time. On the basis of his test results, each individual is assigned a point position on a single trait scale. It is generally assumed that most traits are scalable in some way and can be described quantitatively. Given these assumptions, the challenge for psychometricians is to find the appropriate measurement operations for important personality traits (Guilford, 1959).

To illustrate, Figure 7-2 depicts a hypothetical profile of test scores for one person on eight trait scales. The profile suggests that this man's scores were highest on the "submissiveness" test, lowest on the "aggressiveness" test, and intermediate on the other measures.

**Figure 7-2**  ONE PERSON'S HYPOTHETICAL TEST PROFILE ON EIGHT TRAIT SCALES

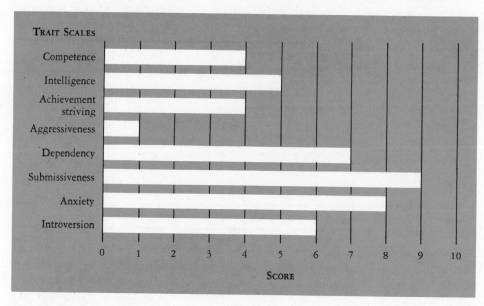

But what do these scores mean? Just how high or low is this person on each of these attributes? The scores have little meaning unless they can be compared with norms or with the scores of other people who took the same tests. Trait psychologists compare the scores of different people on one measure at a time, as Figure 7-3 illustrates. The figure shows a hypothetical distribution of scores for 230 people on a dependency scale.

**Figure 7-3**  NUMBER OF PEOPLE AT EACH SCORE LEVEL ON A DEPENDENCY TEST

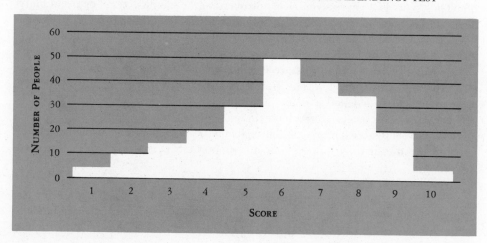

A comparison of the dependency score from Figure 7-2 with the data in Figure 7-3 suggests that on this measure the subject's score (7) was the same as that of 40 of the 230 tested people, that only 60 people scored higher, and that 130 scored lower than he did.

The meaning of these comparisons depends, of course, on many considerations, such as the appropriateness of the comparison sample. For example, how many of the 230 people were much older or younger than the subject, or came from utterly different backgrounds, or were of the opposite sex? Most important, the meaning of the scores depends on the nature and quality of the test.

## STRUCTURED SELF-REPORTS AND RATINGS

Data about persons can be obtained from three sources: the person himself may report or rate (judge) aspects of himself; other people may judge him; or his performance may be elicited and observed directly.

Psychometric inferences about traits usually have been based on self-reports. The term "self-report" refers to any statements a person makes about himself; "structured" self-reports are statements in the form of restricted reactions to items. On structured self-report tests the respondent must react to sets of questions or items with one of a limited number of prescribed choices (e.g., "yes," "no," "strongly agree," "frequently," "don't know"). Examples are shown in Figure 7-4. These items contrast with open-ended or unstructured tests (like the projective devices in Chapter 9), on which the subject may supply his own reactions freely. The distinction between "structured" and "unstructured" or "open-ended" tests is a matter of degree only. The extent to which a test is structured depends on the items and the instructions to the subject: less structured techniques allow greater variation in response.

Many formats have been devised for eliciting trait ratings (see Figure 7-4). On some scales, for example, the subject may be told that "7" indicates that the item is completely applicable to himself and "1" indicates complete nonapplicability, and that he should check the point on the continuum that describes his own reaction. On scales like this, subjects are asked to express the extent of their aggreement or disagreement with the particular item or to rate themselves with respect to the particular descriptions supplied. They may also be asked to judge the attributes of other people they know, for example, their peers at work or in school, or members of their family.

## OBJECTIVITY OF MEASUREMENT

In their approach to testing, trait-oriented psychologists (as well as those of many other theoretical persuasions) emphasize "objectivity." "Objectivity" in the study of personality is the condition that exists when every observer (or "judge") who sees a particular sample of behavior (e.g., a test answer sheet) draws the same conclusions from it. Objectivity depends on the entire testing procedure, including

**Figure 7-4  EXAMPLES OF DIFFERENT TYPES OF STRUCTURED TEST ITEMS**

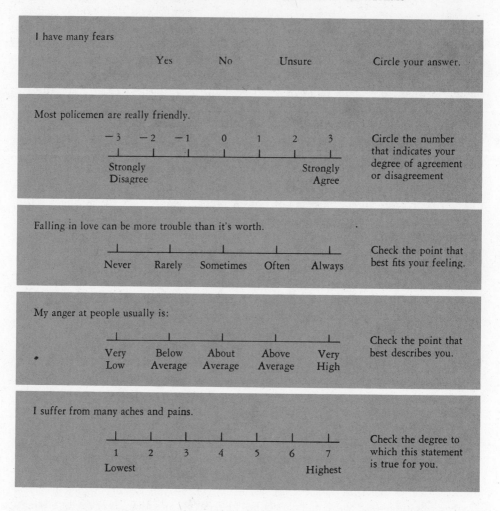

the interaction between the examiner and the subject, the instructions and test items, the available response choices, and the scoring and interpretation procedures. Anything that enhances the uniformity of the testing conditions to which different subjects are exposed increases the objectivity of a test. Objectivity is also furthered by standardized (uniform) test materials, instructions, answer sheets, and scoring procedures. Effective standardization requires uniformity in other conditions that could affect test performance. Depending on what is being measured, these conditions may include the time of administration, the physical conditions under which measurement occurs, the sex of the examiner, and so on. The psychometrician thus attempts to make the stimulus material as uniform as possible by giving every subject the same standardized test and directions.

A lack of objectivity increases the risk of bias and unfairness, as when a test is given to some people by a "friendly" examiner in a comfortable, relaxed setting but to others by a "cold" examiner in a noisy, crowded room. Likewise, objectivity is reduced, and fair comparisons among people are prevented, if the test questions are changed on different occasions or scored differently depending on the prejudices of the tester or other momentary whims.

No matter how careful the attempt to maintain objectivity may be, it is beset with problems. In practice it has become increasingly evident that scores on any personality trait test are affected by all sorts of variables that are irrelevant to the trait the test is trying to measure. For example, even such gross examiner and subject characteristics as sex, as well as such subtler attributes as friendliness, may affect scores (Masling, 1960; Mischel, 1968). Other irrelevant characteristics of the respondent, such as his manner, may significantly affect the examiner's evaluation of the test results. There are many possible sources for bias. More attractive or appealing persons, for example, may be scored more liberally, even when scoring is relatively objective and standardized, as it is on intelligence tests (Masling, 1959).

In spite of some early hopes to the contrary, no psychological test provides anything remotely analogous to a mental X-ray. A test merely yields a sample of behavior under particular eliciting conditions. The observed behavior is always elicited in a context—in a psychological situation. No matter how carefully standardized, the test is never able to eliminate or "control out" all determinants other than the trait of interest. The consistency and meaning of what is being sampled therefore must be demonstrated and cannot be assumed no matter how uniform the eliciting conditions may be for all subjects.

## CORRELATIONS

The specific techniques for assessing the consistency and meaning of test behavior are considered later (Chapter 8). At this point it suffices to note that most applications of trait psychology involve a search for *correlations* among tests. Such correlations simply examine the degree of association (relation) between the scores achieved by a group of individuals on one set of measures with their scores on another set. For example, do people who score high on Test 1 also tend to score higher on Test 2, and do those who score low on Test 1 also score low on Test 2? To the degree that the relative position of individuals remains consistent across the measures, high correlations are obtained; conversely, when relative positions change easily, correlations decrease, indicating that responses to the two tests are not as closely related. When correlations among tests are high, responses on one test can be used to predict responses on the other; e.g., if you succeed on 1 you are likely to succeed on 2. When correlations are low, one cannot predict performance (relative position) on one test from knowing scores on the other test.

## THE CASE OF GARY W.

So far we have been considering tests in general, ignoring the individual person. A focus on methods can seem barren unless we pause periodically to apply those methods to the individual. Therefore we now turn to "Gary W."

Gary W. is not an unusual person, except in the sense that every individual is unique. He is presented here as a "case" example of an essentially normal human being whose characteristics and history are neither dramatically bizarre nor especially exciting. Often case histories serve to illustrate rare and even esoteric qualities—the strange sex criminal, the twisted neurotic, the "split personality." Our purpose in considering Gary, however, is not to display odd and curious bits of abnormality, not to shock and titillate, but rather to concretize and make more real the methods and ideas created to deal with personality. Lest our concepts and techniques become excessively abstract, we must apply them to the data of daily life and examine their relevance—and occasionally their irrelevance—for understanding the particular individual (and not just man-in-general). For this reason we have selected "Gary" as an "ordinary" person, one among hundreds of millions, but still, like all individuals, unique enough to surprise us occasionally, complex enough to defy pat explanations, troubled enough to encounter problems, and human enough to be confused about himself, at least some of the time, and to confuse even more often those who try to understand him.

As we proceed, new information regarding Gary W. will be made available so that the contributions of different kinds of personality data can be evaluated more competently. In addition, as the applications of different theoretical approaches to personality are discussed, Gary will be conceptualized from the perspective of each of them. Thus in later chapters Gary will be construed from the perspectives of the major frameworks available for studying personality.

At this point the information about Gary will be limited to a few demographic facts that introduce him and his background, impressions of his personality obtained from a friend, and some psychometric data about him guided by the methods and concepts of the trait approach.

### GARY W.: DEMOGRAPHIC FACTS

Gary W. was born in Boston 25 years ago. He comes from an old New England family of moderate means. His father is a businessman. Both parents are alive, and currently in the midst of divorcing. Gary has an older and now married brother who is a successful physician.

After attending a private boarding school as an adolescent, Gary went to Hilson college. His record was good but not outstanding. On tests of intellectual ability (the Wechsler Adult Intelligence Scale) Gary's scores indicated he was of superior intelligence. Upon graduation he entered the Navy and received an officer's commission. He served for three years, part of the time stationed around Southeast Asia, and then returned to seek a Master's Degree in business. Currently he is in graduate school and still unmarried. Here is what one of his friends says about him.

*Impressions of Gary W. by a Fellow Graduate Student:*

From the moment I first met Gary, one year ago, he seemed likable enough, but he always seemed preoccupied. His personality had a forced quality, as though he were trying to be something he wasn't. Central to his personality is his over-concern with himself. It's not conceit, but rather continual self-observation and self-criticism. In personal relationships he seems always to be trying to figure out what the other person expects of him and seems to have no personality of his own. He can be friendly and outgoing with a shy, self-conscious person. He often displays a cynical humor and arbitrary bossiness bordering on personal insult, which seems to be his only method of feeling at ease. Feeling at ease seems to mean dominating the relationship as completely as possible. If he encounters someone more capable than he is, Gary tends to draw back within himself, too afraid of being shown up by the other person to develop any kind of close relationship. Gary is something of a "loner." He has few close friends, since his relationships are based on domination (or fear of being dominated) rather than companionship. Gary is very conscious of social standards, grades, any measure of superiority. If he doesn't reach the mark, he feels he is a failure, but even if he does he seems not to be satisfied. An ironic feature of his personality is that though he seems to seek attention, he is uncomfortable once he gets it. When speaking to a group of people, he becomes extremely nervous, and, at times, so confused that he cannot continue, and starts falling apart. He wants to succeed. He is ambitious and able, and very persistent. He seems really driven to do well.

So far we know relatively little about Gary. The impression his friend gives us, while interesting, may be of dubious value: we know neither its accuracy nor its meaning. Then how can we proceed further and find out more about Gary? From the viewpoint of trait theory, we want quantitative information that reliably reveals Gary's status on important dispositions. One major step in that direction is provided by Gary's scores on psychometric tests. So that these data can be properly understood, they will be introduced in the context of our discussion of some major trait measures. Examples of these measures, and issues generated by them, are given next.

## PSYCHOMETRIC SCALES: EXAMPLES
## AND PROBLEMS

Most trait-oriented research has tried to study important attributes through questionnaires. Psychometric trait assessment usually is based on lengthy scales that require many responses. Typically these scales require the individual to report his *general* reaction to broad and hypothetical situations, rather than his specific responses to a few concrete real choices. The most thoroughly studied questionnaire is the Minnesota Multiphasic Personality Inventory (MMPI), and it has become the basis for investigating many personality traits and types.

### THE MMPI

The MMPI best exemplifies most features of the psychometric approach. This widely used, influential test contains a set of self-report scales that initially were devised to classify mental patients into types on many psychiatric dimensions (Hathaway & McKinley, 1942, 1943). In format, the MMPI comprises 550 printed statements to which one may answer "true," "false," or "cannot say" (undecided). The items range over diverse topics and differ widely in style. They inquire into attitudes, emotional reactions, psychiatric symptoms, the subject's past and other content, with items similar to these:

Sometimes I think I may kill myself.
My greatest troubles are inside myself.
I certainly have little self-assurance.
I wish I were not so awkward.
I am shy.

Psychometric self-report tests such as the MMPI are called "psychometric," "objective," and "standardized." All these adjectives correctly describe the printed stimulus material, the scoring procedure, and the administration. The stimulus materials are objective and standardized or reproducible in the sense that they usually are presented as printed items on questionnaires, inventories, or rating scales. Likewise, the scoring procedure is objective because the respondent has to react to each question or item with one of a limited number of prescribed or "structured" choices by selecting, for example, from printed answers like "yes," "no," "strongly agree," "frequently," "don't know."

Both the questions and the instructions on psychometric tests, however, usually require the respondent to extrapolate extensively from behavior; to go far beyond direct behavior observation; and to supply subjective inferences about the psychological meaning of behavior. While the stimulus questions are standardized, that is, printed and therefore always the same on each occasion, their exact referents often are unclear. For example, the test asks questions like "Are you shy?" or "Do you worry a lot?" or "Is it really wise to trust other people?" Such ambiguous items require the respondent to interpret behavior and to provide inferences about psychological attributes. Hence, he must construe and evaluate behavior, and generalize about it, rather than describe particular behaviors in particular contexts on clear dimensions.

One really cannot expect that people would be either willing or able to reveal themselves accurately in response to such items. Such an expectation would be especially unreasonable when the respondents are emotionally upset, disturbed, or aware that their answers may be used to make important decisions about them and their future. Recognizing these problems (e.g., Meehl, 1945), researchers have tried to establish the meaning of particular answer patterns on the test empirically by research.

The investigator starts with a pool of items and administers them to a group known to differ on an external criterion or measure (for example, males versus females, or hospitalized versus nonhospitalized people). Ideally, the test scales are constructed so that ultimately only those items are retained that best discriminate among people who differ on the selected external criteria. For example, if an item such as "I cry easily" tends to be answered affirmatively by people who have been hospitalized for psychiatric problems, but not by those who have no history of psychiatric hospitalization, the item would be retained on a "maladjustment" scale. Gradually the meaning of the scales becomes defined by their associations with other measures or information. The procedures have to be repeated or replicated, to assure that only the relatively stable associations between configurations of test behavior and criterion information are retained.

For example, the MMPI scales are administered to many groups of subjects, such as college students, medical personnel, and nonpsychiatric patients, as well as psychiatric patients who have been independently diagnosed as having symptoms of some type of schizophrenia. The items then are examined to determine the ones on which there are significant differences between the answers of particular diagnostic groups as compared to "normals." In this manner it becomes possible gradually to devise scales that discriminate among different groups of people.

MMPI items have been sorted into ten basic scales named Hypochondriasis (Hs), Depression (D), Hysteria (Hy), Psychopathic deviate (Pd), Masculinity-femininity (Mf), Paranoia (Pa), Psychasthenia (Pt), Schizophrenia (Sc), Hypomania (Ma), and Social introversion (Si). It would be incorrect, however, to think that these scales tap the entities whose names they bear. Instead, these labels serve as abbreviations for scales whose meanings are defined by their extensive correlations (associations) with other indices (e.g., psychiatrist's ratings of adjustment, scores on other personality questionnaires). These correlations have been amassed during several decades of vigorous research with the MMPI scales.

In addition to the ten basic scales, three "control" scales have been devised. The L or Lie scale was intended to measure the tendency to falsify about oneself by "faking good." High scores on this scale indicate that the individual has endorsed many items that suggest he does unlikely things such as daily reading all the newspaper editorials or never telling a lie. The K scale, the second control, was intended to indicate defensiveness in the form of a tendency to present oneself in a more socially desirable way. The F scale, the third control, sought to tap the intrusive effects of answering the items carelessly and confusedly, as indicated by describing oneself as having rare and improbable characteristics.

The results of an individual's MMPI answers (or the summary of a group's average responses) may be recorded in the form of a "profile." Such a profile for our case, Gary W., is illustrated in Figure 7-5. Gary's position on each scale is summarized in terms of converted or T scores. These scores readily provide quantitative comparisons against norms, a T score of 50 being the average score for the particular normative reference group. In recent years sophisticated procedures have been developed to discriminate people with extreme scores for many different diagnostic and selection purposes. Collections of MMPI profiles have been "coded" in different ways and catalogued in "handbooks" or "atlases" which may be conveniently used to compare a single individual's profile to similar profiles and information collected in many cases (Marks & Seeman, 1963; Gilberstadt & Duker, 1965).

Gary's MMPI profile fits most closely a 2-8/8-2 code in the atlas developed by Marks and Seeman (1963, p. 137). We can see what types of information the atlas provides for individuals whose average MMPI profiles are most similar to Gary's. The atlas tells us that people with this type of profile are most often described with characteristics like these:

> Keeps his distance and avoids close relations with people; tends to fear emotional involvement with others; manifests his psychic conflicts with somatic

**Figure 7-5**  GARY'S MMPI PROFILE

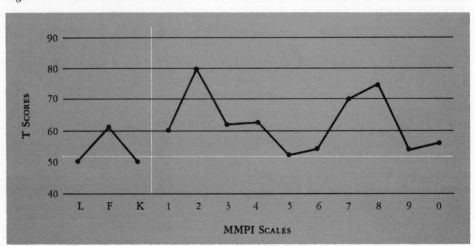

Similar to Atlas Code Type 2-8/8-2, Marks and Seeman (1963).

symptoms, tends to be resentful, shows obsessive thinking, feels tense, jumpy, and high-strung.

The atlas also provides much other normative or "average" information found previously for people with Gary's profile. These data are a helpful first approximation. How well they really fit Gary and how closely they match other data about him is still an open question. On first impression, some of the atlas statements seem at least somewhat consistent with the impressions given by Gary's fellow graduate student, who also judged him to be "shy" and a "loner." On the other hand, the same student rated Gary as high in ambition, aspiration level, and "drive." These ratings seem to contradict parts of the atlas information. Specifically, the 2-8/8-2 atlas code lists high aspirations and ambitiousness as characteristics that are *least* descriptive of people with his profile. Who is right? Is Gary's friend inaccurate, or does this part of the atlas simply not fit Gary? To achieve further understanding of Gary, we would need much more information about him.

Research on the MMPI continues at the rate of about a hundred studies a year. In addition, the MMPI has become the model for dozens of other personality questionnaires. Many investigators drew on the large pool of MMPI items to create special personality scales (e.g., dealing with anxiety), whose meaning they studied empirically. Popular descendants of the MMPI include the California Psychological Inventory (CPI) and the Taylor Manifest Anxiety Scale (MAS).

## THE CALIFORNIA F SCALE

MMPI scales and atlases have some practical value in personality assessment and clinical work. Many psychologists, however, are most interested in the search for theoretically important personality traits, and have tried to use a variety of personality questionnaires for that purpose. One of the most popular and extensively researched of these self-report measures is the California *F* Scale (Adorno et al., 1950). This measure was intended to assess authoritarian attitudes. It contains a set of items like these:

> The most important thing to teach children is absolute obedience to their parents.
> Any good leader should be strict with people under him in order to gain their respect.
> Prison is too good for sex criminals. They should be publicly whipped or worse.
> There are two kinds of people in the world: the weak and the strong.
> No decent man can respect a woman who has had sex relations before marriage.

Strong agreement with items like these results in a high *F* Scale, or "authoritarianism," score.

Gary's score on the *F* Scale was slightly below average when compared to other college students. What does that imply about him? As with all scales, the meaning of high or low scores on this measure depends on the network of associations that have been found for the test in research.

An enormous set of correlations has emerged from more than a hundred studies that have related *F* Scale scores to other variables. Correlations have been found with such diverse variables as intelligence, family ideology, prejudice, anxiety, voting behavior, military reenlistment intent, and cooperation in psychological experiments (Titus & Hollander, 1957), and even reactions to the U.S.-Soviet space race (Mischel & Schopler, 1959).

For example, in one study among college students with high scores on the California *F* Scale (suggesting strong ideological conservatism), 76 percent stated they perferred the Republican Party, whereas 65 percent of those low on the *F* Scale preferred the Democratic Party (Leventhal, Jacobs & Kurdirka, 1964). The relationships between *F* Scale scores and stated voting behavior indicated that students with high *F* Scale scores tended to choose the more conservative political candidate.

The *F* Scale is most strongly correlated with other paper-and-pencil measures, but not as closely associated with nonquestionnaire measures of interpersonal behaviors (Titus & Hollander, 1957). Correlations between the *F* Scale and other questionnaires sampling attitudes (e.g., toward minority groups) sometimes reach impressive magnitude. The relationships obtained between the *F* Scale and nonquestionnaire measures, on the other hand, tend to be much lower in magnitude. Scores on the *F* Scale also tend to be highly correlated with education, more highly educated people tending to respond in a much less authoritarian fashion.

## MASCULINITY-FEMININITY

Another trait dimension that has received much attention psychometrically is "masculinity-femininity." Inferences about masculinity or femininity in research have relied mainly on people's verbal reports about their sex-role attributes, attitudes, interests, values, and preferences, or on ratings made by their parents or peers. On the paper-and-pencil Terman-Miles masculinity-femininity (M-F) test, for example, adolescents and adults are asked to report their interests, emotional attitudes, and so on (Terman & Miles, 1936). The Gough Femininity Scale likewise is a paper-and-pencil inventory that asks for self-descriptions in a two-choice format (Gough, 1952).

Other tests have avoided asking the subject to characterize his own traits and instead require him to indicate the kinds of toys, games, and activities he would prefer. All of these measures ask the subject to indicate his preferences for stereotypically masculine or feminine objects or activities. On the IT Scale, for example, the child is presented with a drawing of "IT," an ambiguous child-figure, and asked to choose what IT would like in a series of objects or picture cards associated with either masculine or feminine sex roles (for example, cowboy guns or dress-up dolls). The resulting scores are intended to reflect the child's degree of masculinity-femininity in his sex-role preferences (Brown, 1957).

Masculinity-femininity measures traditionally have been constructed empirically so that on each item the response scored "masculine" is the one that is endorsed by most males while the one scored "feminine" is the one favored verbally by the majority of females. Any individual's masculinity-femininity score therefore serves as an index of how closely his self-reports, self-descriptions, and preferences correspond with those of the majority in his sex. Similarly, when an observer rates the attributes of others on a masculinity-femininity dimension, the score is intended to reflect that rater's judgment of how closely the ratee matches the attributes supposedly displayed by most males or females. (More recent approaches and issues in the study of sex roles are discussed in Chapters 14 and 15.) Gary's scores on a traditional masculinity-femininity self-report inventory placed him within the average range for male college students.

## THE PROBLEM OF RESPONSE SETS

The interpretation of psychometric self-report scales like the foregoing may be complicated by "response sets." Response sets are certain special response tendencies in people's answers to test questions. Such "sets" have to be understood in order to interpret self-reports and ratings properly. One of the most studied response sets is the tendency to endorse socially undesirable items.

Differences among people in their willingness to express complaints and to describe themselves openly in socially undesirable terms may substantially influence their answers to self-report inventories (e.g., Edwards, 1957, 1959, 1961). On psychiatric scales like the MMPI, scores indicating maladjustment and negative traits (like depression, paranoia, hypochondriasis) depend on the respondent's willingness to endorse socially undesirable statements. His scores on these scales will be high if he confesses such things as irregular bowel habits and bodily ills and eccentric or bizarre and socially taboo thoughts and acts. His profile may therefore reflect the degree to which he endorses socially undesirable items rather than other traits.

It is difficult to evaluate the social desirability interpretation of self-report scores on psychiatric inventories. Even a true self-report of real problematic or idiosyncratic behavior would require endorsing socially undesirable items (Block, 1965). For example, Gary's scores on an anxiety questionnaire might be elevated because he tends to describe himself in socially undesirable terms, or because he is accurately describing some of his real troubles and fears.

Apart from its problems as a response set, social desirability has also been researched extensively as a personality characteristic or motive. Crowne and Marlowe (1964) conducted some thorough studies of the motive to seek social approval. As part of their studies they constructed a measure of social desirability (SD) and assessed how groups of persons who differed in SD behaved in a number of experimental situations. In general, results suggested that people who were high on the Marlowe-Crowne SD scale, when compared to those with low scores, tended to be more cautious, conventional, and persuasible. Thus the same variable that complicates test interpretations may also be a meaningful dimension for substantive personality research.

Another response set is agreement or "acquiescence," which is the tendency to agree with statements, especially ambiguous attitude statements, irrespective of their specific content. On self-report questionnaires like the California F Scale, or the MMPI, the total scores are a direct function of how often the respondent agrees with, or says "yes" to, the items. This is because questions are worded so that agreement increases the trait score. The more often the person answers "yes" on the California F Scale, for example, the higher his "authoritarian" score will be. Therefore it is difficult to distinguish the role of scale content from the effect of a tendency for subjects to say "yes" to items regardless of their content.

Yes-saying or acquiescence to *any* opinionated or doctrinaire generalizations about social issues, regardless of specific content, according to some interpretations may greatly influence answers on the California F Scale (Bass, 1955). Messick and Jackson (1961) likewise believe that acquiescence response sets have critical effects on inventories of the true-false or agree-disagree type such as the MMPI. They believe that the factors found on such tests may primarily reflect response style rather than specific item content (Jackson & Messick, 1958).

To correct for the role of agreement response sets, some investigators have tried to rephrase the items to reverse their meaning and to have both favorable and unfavorable versions for each item . The wording of many inventory items, however, is difficult to reverse. Chapman and Campbell (1957) discuss the problems of trying to reverse an F Scale item like "the wild sex life of the old Greeks and Romans was tame compared to some of the goings-on in this country, even in places where people might least expect it." As they put it:

> How is this item to be reversed? One could say "the sex life that goes on even in places where one least today expects it is nothing compared to the wild sex life of the Greeks and Romans." Thus reversed, the item would still seem to appeal to the prurient moralizing that the initial item sought to tap (Chapman & Campbell, 1957, p. 129).

Several analyses have questioned the importance of agreement response sets on self-report devices (e.g., Block, 1965; Norman, 1966; Rorer, 1965). They argue that tendencies to agree with items regardless of their content may play a fairly trivial role. Block (1965), for example, showed that the basic factor structure of the MMPI did not change even when only scales balanced to eliminate the role of agreement response sets were employed. Nevertheless, it has now become a standard practice to try to avoid response sets in scale construction by attempting to balance the number of items keyed true and false (Wiggins, 1973).

As was illustrated in the Crowne and Marlowe studies of SD, there also have been some efforts to view individual differences in response sets as reflecting stable, trait-like "stylistic" consistencies, rather than as measurement errors that require correction. These response styles, in turn, have been conceptualized as traits and their correlations with other personality indices have been sought. Thus one researcher's methodological troubles may be another's personality dimension.

## OVERLAP AMONG MEASURES?

In addition to response sets, self-report trait tests often share another problem. High correlations among paper-and-pencil inventories may partly reflect the fact that inventory constructors often borrow items from earlier inventories. Different tests actually may contain similar items presented in similar formats. For example, Eysenck's (1952) measure for inferring neuroticism and extraversion-introversion contains such questions as: Are your feelings easily hurt? Are you rather shy? Do you find it difficult to get into conversation with strangers? Are you troubled with feelings of inferiority? Very similar items occur on such other tests as the MMPI. Even within the subscales of a single test, items may overlap considerably. Shure and Rogers (1965) noted that the basic scales of the MMPI consist of items that overlap 69 percent, on the average, with items on one or more other scales of the test.

Campbell and Fiske (1959) analyzed many of the correlations among personality measures reported in the literature. They found that much commonality was attributable to similarity or overlap between the methods employed to elicit responses. In other words, correlations among measures intended to tap different traits often are largely due to similarities between sampling methods (Campbell, 1960; Campbell & Fiske, 1959). If, for example, three questionnaires are used to measure "dependency," the correlations obtained among them may be more attributable to similarity in the questionnaires than to the trait consistency they intend to elicit. If different methods were employed (e.g., a questionnaire, a peer rating, and a behavior observation), the correlations would be substantially lower. On the basis of a review of relevant studies, Campbell and Fiske (1959) concluded that the effect of method is usually greater than the effect of the trait measured. Applied to our case, this means that we have to be sure that the patterns of traits attributed to Gary do not merely reflect overlap among the questionnaires he has answered.

Moreover, we would want to know if Gary's trait would test out identically if it were measured by a technique that is not a questionnaire. To be most confident of his level of authoritarianism, for example, we would want to see what he *does* with authority figures behaviorally as well as what he *says* about authority on questionnaires. To have faith that he is a "loner," fears emotional involvement, and is anxious, we would want to measure each of these attributes in several ways, not just by questionnaires. Otherwise, how could we be sure that the impression we get of him reflects more than his manner of talking about himself on inventories?

## RELATIONS WITH INTELLIGENCE

It is also important to examine the correlations found between personality tests and measures of intelligence. Consider, for example, the relations among measures of personality and performance in a small group. Mann (1959) reviewed and surveyed the voluminous research on this topic in the years from 1900 to 1957. The personality variables in his survey included adjustment, extraversion-introversion, dominance, masculinity-femininity, and interpersonal sensitivity. He also measured intelligence. The behavior of the people in groups served as the performance criteria. These behaviors were scored on leadership, popularity, activity rate, conformity, and other dimensions. From the hundreds of correlations obtained it was concluded that "the best predictor of an individual's performance in groups is intelligence" (p. 264).

Mann's results are not atypical. Many personality measures are substantially correlated with tests of intelligence. Intelligence has been found to correlate negatively with authoritarianism and prejudice, and positively with certain measures of honesty and indices of impulse control, creativity, and so on. The magnitude of these correlations is quite variable, but not infrequently it is as large as the associations between the personality test and the other external referents that serve to define it (e.g., Getzels & Jackson, 1962). The correlations obtained among personality indices therefore may depend partly on relations between the personality measures and intelligence. Intelligence may play an especially important role in self-report inventories and other paper-and-pencil personality questionnaires that intend to assess maladaptive behavior (Mischel, 1968).

In light of these facts, Campbell and Fiske (1959) have rightly urged that investigations of all traits should include correlations between the ostensible trait and measures of intelligence. If a personality trait covaries (correlates) largely with intelligence, to invoke it as a new disposition is of little value.

## SUMMARY

1. Mental testing at the turn of the century was the forerunner of later developments in the psychometric approach to personality. The intelligence test developed by Binet early in the twentieth century profoundly influenced the history of psychometric mental and personality testing.

2. In the psychometric approach to personality, the aim is to measure an individual with respect to one or more single traits, such as aggressiveness or introversion. In order to measure objectively, the psychometrician attempts to create *standardized* self-report questionnaires and rating scales that will yield results that can be *reproduced* easily by independent observers.

3. Gary W. is introduced to elucidate the applications of the trait approach. His case will also be subjected to the methods of other theoretical approaches in subsequent chapters.

4. The MMPI is one of the most widely used personality tests. It contains a set of self-report scales whose meanings are defined empirically by their correlations with other test indices and with behaviors displayed by the person in other situations. MMPI "atlases" provide descriptive information for various average test profiles or code types.

5. The California *F* Scale and the various masculinity-femininity scales are typical of the pencil-and-paper questionnaires used to study important attributes in the psychometric trait approach.

6. Attention has been called to response "sets," which may affect the meaning of self-reports and ratings. Among these sets are the willingness to endorse socially undesirable statements, and the tendency to agree (or disagree) with ambiguous statements regardless of their content. Many researchers consider response sets as interferences that may cause errors in psychometric tests. Others see them as indicative of personality traits, such as the disposition to behave in socially desirable ways.

7. Similarity and overlap of measurement methods often contribute to the correlations found among traits. To demonstrate that a distinctive trait is being tapped, it is helpful to study it by at least two different methods.

8. It is also necessary to demonstrate that a new trait test measures a trait that is not already measured by another test. Intelligence measures are frequently substantially correlated with personality tests. Therefore it is important to demonstrate that any new personality test is not mainly redundant with IQ tests.

# CHAPTER

## *8*

# TRAIT
# THEORIES
## Applications (II)

Applications of the trait approach to personality are discussed further in this chapter. We move now beyond specific tests and strategies generated by the trait approach to consider more general issues that must be understood in order to achieve a perspective on trait theories, their applications, their problems, and their value.

## FROM TEST RESPONSES TO TRAIT FACTORS

How can one go from test responses to the traits that they reflect? As noted before (Chapter 2), trait theorists are interested mainly in discovering basic traits, not just in comparing people's test scores. In their search for "underlying traits" they begin with test responses, usually in the form of self-ratings or ratings by others. But the range of possible trait ratings is as large as the number of trait names available in the language. A casual glance at any dictionary makes it plain that when people try to describe personality in trait terms, an almost endless set of names is available to them. A systematic search for all "trait names" in a standard English dictionary produced some 18,000 terms (Allport & Odbert, 1936). In a later effort Cattell (1947, 1957) selected from this list 4504 terms that Allport (1937, p. 366) had characterized as real traits of personality.

## SIMPLIFYING TEST RESULTS

Trait terms that number in the thousands—even the 550 responses of the MMPI—are unmanageable as descriptive units, especially in attempts to evaluate many people and to characterize the patternings of their behavior. Consider, for example, the mass of data yielded by the 550 MMPI responses from each of a hundred persons.

To extract order parsimoniously from such a stack of facts investigators searching for underlying traits try to group responses into more basic clusters of units that are correlated with each other but independent of the other responses. For this purpose many trait psychologists (e.g., Cattell, 1965) have turned to factor analysis, a mathematical procedure that helps to sort test responses into relatively homogeneous clusters.

## DOES FACTOR ANALYSIS DISCOVER
## BASIC TRAITS?

Factor analysis does not necessarily reveal the basic traits of persons. The results depend on the tests and the subjects selected by the researcher, and on the details of his procedures and decisions. Factor analysis is a very useful tool for reducing a large set of correlated measures to fewer unrelated dimensions. As such, it can be a powerful aid to psychological research by clarifying what response patterns go together. Suppose, for example, that 50 students have answered 10 personality questionnaires, each of which contains 100 questions. A factor analysis of this mass of information can show which parts of the test performances go together (i.e., are closely correlated with each other yet uncorrelated with other parts).

But as Overall (1964) has noted, factor analysis cannot establish which characteristics of persons or things being measured are "real" or "primary." The factors obtained are simply names given to the correlations found among the particular measures. In other words, factor analysis yields a greatly simplified patterning of the test data put into it; but it cannot go beyond the limitations of the original tests and it depends on many decisions by the investigator (e.g., in the type of factor analysis he conducts). Consequently, while the factor analytic search for underlying "source traits" (Chapter 2) favored by such trait theorists as Cattell (1965) may yield mathematically pure factors, their psychological meaningfulness and relevance for the person's actual behavior cannot be assumed or taken for granted; they must be demonstrated.

## ARE TRAITS IN THE RATED PERSON OR IN THE RATER?

Both the approach and the problems of trying to discover traits through factor analysis of ratings are illustrated in a series of extensive and sophisticated factor-analytic studies (Norman, 1961, 1963; Tupes & Christal, 1958, 1961). These studies investigated the factors obtained for diverse samples of subjects rated by their peers on rating scales. The scales themselves originated from a condensed version of the thousands of trait names originally identified by Allport and Odbert's search for trait names in the dictionary. After much research 20 scales were selected and many judges were asked to rate other people on them. The results were carefully factor-analyzed.

The same set of five relatively independent factors appeared consistently across several studies. This exciting finding led to the conclusion that a "highly stable structure of personal characteristics has been identified" (Norman, 1963, p. 581). The five factors (summarized in Table 2-2) were extraversion, agreeableness, conscientiousness, emotional stability, and culture.

It seemed reasonable to conclude from these results that a stable, five-factor structure of personality exists. The findings came from many different samples of subjects and raters; the data included ratings based on interpersonal observations up to three years in length; and, most important, the agreement found between factors across samples was excellent (Norman, 1963). The conclusion that these data revealed a consistent, stable, generalized, five-factor personality structure rested on the basic assumption that the "obtained structure reflected the organization of these attributes in the ratees" (Passini & Norman, 1966, p. 44).

In fact, this assumption was not justified. Surprisingly the factor structure that emerged when total strangers were rated was very similar to the five-factor structure obtained from ratings of people the raters knew well (Passini & Norman, 1966). In this study judges rated fellow college students whom they did not know. The judges' contacts with the ratees in the rating situation were made by being in the same room with them for less than 15 minutes, and there was no opportunity for verbal communication. The rating task was made credible by asking the raters to judge the subjects as "you would imagine" them to be. The authors pointed out that the raters could not possibly have known the ratee's attributes on dimensions like "sociable-reclusive," "cooperative-negativistic," or "responsible-undependable." The results nevertheless yielded factors extremely similar to the five factors found from ratings by close acquaintances in the earlier studies. As the authors noted, the main information available to the raters "was whatever they carried in their heads"!

## TRAIT RATINGS AND STEREOTYPES

Thus the factors identified by trait ratings may reflect the social stereotypes and concepts of the judges rather than the trait organization of the rated persons. Mulaik (1964), for example, conducted three separate factor-analytic studies, using many trait-rating scales, to determine the degree to which the method reveals the subject's personality factors as opposed to the rater's conceptual factors. The judges in one study rated real persons on the scales, including family members, close acquaintances, and themselves. In a second study they rated stereotypes like "Suburban Housewife," "Mental Patient," and "Air Force General." The raters in the third study rated the "meaning" of 20 trait words. An index of factor similarity revealed much similarity between the factors found for ratings of real persons and those found for ratings of stereotypes and words. On the basis of these and many similar results the investigator concluded that personality factors that emerge from ratings may reflect the raters' conceptual categories rather than the traits of the subjects being judged. Some of the many issues raised by these findings will be explored further in later chapters.

In spite of these problems, the descriptions of people obtained from different raters in different contexts often do agree with each other. For example, ratings of a student by his peers may match to a considerable degree independent behavior ratings by other observers. Thus, agreement was found between peer nominations on clearly described dimensions of aggressive and dependent behavior and separate behavior ratings of actual aggressive and dependent behavior (Winder & Wiggins, 1964). Subjects were first classified into high, intermediate, and low groups on aggression and dependency on the basis of their peer reputations. Separate behavior ratings made later indicated that the three groups differed from each other significantly in the amount of aggression and dependency they displayed overtly in an experimental situation. Similarly, college students who were preselected as extremely high or low in aggressiveness (on the basis of ratings by their peers) also tended to be rated in similar ways by independent judges who observed their interaction (Gormly & Edelberg, 1974).

In sum, people obviously do not perceive an empty world. There are congruences between a rater's trait constructs and the traits of people he rates (e.g., Norman, 1966, 1969; Lay & Jackson, 1969), but these relationships tend to be much more complex than a naive trait psychology of "common sense" would suggest (Mischel, 1968).

In light of all these problems it becomes understandable that different investigators may arrive at somewhat different schemas of trait organization. Nevertheless, a few basic trait dimensions seem to be found over and over again. Introversion-extraversion, adjustment, and some variation of potency ("strong-weak") and adequacy ("good-bad") are often included. It is difficult to know the extent to which these factors reflect the conceptual dimensions shared by observers or the attributes of subjects. Probably they reflect both to some extent, and perhaps the two are almost impossible to separate clearly.

## EVALUATING TRAIT TESTS

To evaluate trait approaches and their applications requires that we evaluate the trait tests on which they rely. In recent years there has been a loud public outcry against the widespread use of trait tests in schools, business, and government. Critics both inside and outside the psychological profession have raised grave questions about the ethics, as well as the value, of many personality assessment practices that are most central to the trait approach. Neither the questions nor the answers are simple.

## ETHICAL CONCERNS

There have been strong objections to judging people's personalities with tests. Much of the public outrage has centered on the fear that tests are invasions of privacy, that they force people to answer questions that may be used to discriminate against them. Understandably people are reluctant to have testers pry into their lives and extract information that may contribute to negative decisions about them. The problem is even more keen if the tests are of dubious validity.

Proper evaluation of the ethics of personality assessment and rational assessment of the testing procedures are matters of great social importance. The public and its legal representatives (in Congress, for example) have been handicapped by widespread ignorance of the tests and the techniques underlying their development. The ethical and social problems involved in the multimillion dollar personality-testing business are formidable indeed. The scope of the problem is indicated by the publication of literally thousands of personality tests, many of which are widely used throughout our society. Given the magnitude of the problem and the public's confusion about personality testing, it is especially important to consider in some depth the main problems that arise in attempts to interpret what personality tests really do and really don't permit us to say about individuals. We now have a considerable amount of data about Gary W., for example, but we are still very uncertain about how to evaluate it. How sure can we be of the impressions we have? How wise or hazardous would it be to base important decisions on this information?

The rest of this chapter will consider only problems relevant to the interpretation of objective personality trait tests. In later chapters, the discussion will be extended to many other techniques for evaluating personality. As we have seen, trait-oriented research usually has assessed differences between people on paper-and-pencil inventories and questionnaires. Many problems arise in efforts to clarify the meaning of the answers. Notice that almost all the psychometric information we have about Gary is based on what he *says* about himself. His MMPI profile, his California *F* Scale, his masculinity-femininity score, all rest on self-reports on questionnaires. Since we want to know more about Gary than how he answers questionnaires, it is crucial to establish what his scores do and do not imply about him.

## ON BEING DUPED BY TESTS

In daily life people function like trait psychologists to the extent that they infer personality dispositions from behavioral cues. Often these impressions are formed quickly and are based on minimal information. The taxi driver who claims he can spot the main qualities of his rider's personality in 10 minutes is a common example. Usually such snap diagnoses are not taken seriously and are dismissed easily as cliches. When a personality description is offered by a more creditable diagnostician it tends to be accepted much more readily even if it is equally wrong. College students in one study were administered personality tests and then were all given written personality interpretations (Ulrich, Stachnik, & Stainton, 1963). Although the interpretations were supposedly based on their psychological test results, in fact each of the 57 students obtained the same report, illustrated by the following excerpts (p. 832):

> You have a strong need for other people to like you and for them to admire you. . . . Your sexual adjustment has presented some problems for you. . . . Disciplined and controlled on the outside, you tend to be worrisome and insecure inside. . . . Some of your aspirations tend to be pretty unrealistic.

The vast majority of the students indicated the reports captured their personalities excellently. Of the 57 students, 53 rated the report either excellent or good, only three giving it an average rating, one calling it poor, and none very poor. Their overall enthusiasm was also reflected in spontaneous comments of great praise. For example, "I agree with almost all of your statements and think they answer the problems I may have." Or, "On the nose! Very good. I wish you had said more, but what you did mention was all true without a doubt. I wish you could go further into this personality sometime." Other students indicated they felt they had been helped substantially by the interpretations.

The ease with which these students were duped about their own personality is not at all atypical; it reflects less their gullibility than the intrinsic hazards of personality impressions and everyday trait descriptions. When personality impressions are stated in broad terms they are difficult to disconfirm. The individual may readily add extra meaning to cliches and adopt them with great confidence even when they turn out to be untrue (or untestable). Thus the naive person may attribute profound significance to the vague comments provided by palmists and newspaper astrologers and may accept as personal revelations "insights" that could fit almost anyone.

It is therefore extremely important for psychologists to provide real support and evidence for their statements about personality and to make their statements in a form that is testable. You should approach the matters of "reliability" and "validity" in personality study (defined and discussed next) not as mere textbook terms to be memorized and not used: instead, try to see these concepts as guides for establishing the value of psychologists' claims about the nature of personality.

## RELIABILITY

A number of techniques are available for estimating the consistency or "reliability" of personality observations or measures. When the same test is given to the same group of people on two occasions, a retest correlation or "coefficient of stability" is obtained. This measure provides an index of *temporal reliability*. Generally, the longer the time interval, the lower the coefficient of stability. If there is only a short interval between test and retest, the two occasions are not entirely independent. For example, if subjects remember some of their initial responses, the correlation is strengthened.

Other reliability estimates are more concerned with the consistency with which different parts or alternate forms of a test measure behavior. The correlation between parts of a single form gives an index of *internal consistency*. Consistency may also be measured by the intercorrelation of scores on *alternate forms* of a test administered to the same set of subjects. The alternate-form method is especially valuable for assessing the effects of an intervening procedure, such as psychotherapy or special training, on test performance, because it avoids the contaminating effects of administering the same form twice.

If subjective judgment enters into scoring decisions, a special kind of reliability check is needed. This check is called *interscorer agreement* or consistency, and it is the degree to which different scorers or judges arrive at the same statements about the same test data. For example, if three judges try to infer personality traits from subjects' interview behavior and dream reports, it would be necessary to establish the degree to which the three assessors reach the same conclusions. As noted before, interscorer agreement is easiest to achieve when scoring is objective, as on highly structured tests (for example, when all answers are given as either "yes" or "no").

## VALIDITY

Someone's self-report on a 10-item questionnaire provides his *stated* reactions to the items under the specific testing conditions. Thus if a person reports that he is "very friendly," that is what he *says* about himself on the test. To know more than that, one needs validity research to establish the meaning and implications of the test answers. The various types of validity research are summarized in Table 8-1.

*Content* or *face validity* is the demonstration that the items on a test adequately represent a defined broader *class* of behavior. For example, judges would have to agree that the different items on a "friendliness" questionnaire all in fact seem to deal with the class or topic of friendliness. In practice, content validity often is assumed rather than demonstrated. Even if the content validity of the items is shown acceptably, it cannot be assumed that the answers provide an index of the individual's "true" trait position. We do not know whether or not the person who says he is friendly, for example, is really friendly. A self-description is a self-description, a description by another person is another person's description, and the relationships between such data and other nontest events have to be demonstrated.

To go beyond description of the sampled behavior, one has to determine the relationship between it and scores on other measures that serve as referents or

**TABLE 8-1    Strategies and Purposes in Psychometric Personality Test Construction**

| TYPE OF VALIDATION | GENERAL PROCEDURE | USE OF TEST RESPONSES |
|---|---|---|
| 1. Content | Demonstration that test content is representative of a broader class | Self-description |
| 2. Criterion<br>  a. concurrent | Correlation between test scores and other presently available data | Substitute for less convenient sample with known correlation to criterion |
|   b. predictive | Correlation between test scores and later status on a criterion | Selection, placement, and other diagnostic and classificatory decisions; discrimination between groups |
| 3. Construct | Invention of theory regarding what accounts for obtained test scores; empirical demonstration of theory, using diverse strategies | Inference about personality attributes; personality description in terms of psychological constructs; refinement of theory |

standards, thus providing *criterion validity*. For example, psychiatrists' ratings about progress in therapy, teachers' ratings of school performance, the subject's behavior on another test, his self-report on another occasion, may be selected as criteria. In our discussion of the MMPI in the last chapter we noted several examples of "criterion validity research," although we did not call it by that name. Recall, for instance, the correlations between score patterns and such external information about the respondents as their history of psychiatric hospitalization. Criterion validity may be established by a correlation among concurrently available data (such as current test score and present psychiatric diagnosis). Criterion validity also can be predictive if it comes from correlations between a measure and data collected at a later time, for example, pretherapy diagnosis and adjustment ratings after a year of psychotherapy. Correlations may be looked for between data that seem to have a strong surface similarity in content, such as a child's arithmetic performance on an IQ test and his future success in an arithmetic course. Or they may be sought between measures whose contents appear quite dissimilar, such as a patient's drawings and a psychiatric diagnosis.

Tests based on criterion validity may be used for various practical purposes, depending on their specific validation procedures. Obviously a test may have concurrent validity and still be unable to predict future behavior. Likewise, a test may have predictive validity without concurrent validity if, for example, it can predict suicide five years before a patient kills himself but relates to no other measure at the time of administration.

Personality psychologists guided by trait theory usually want to infer and describe a person's dispositions from his test responses. *Construct* or *trait validation* is the effort to elaborate the inferred traits determining test behavior (Campbell, 1960). The concept of "construct validity" was introduced by trait psychologists for problems in which the assessor accepts

> no existing measure as a definitive criterion of the quality with which he is concerned. Here the traits or qualities underlying test performance are of central importance (American Psychological Association, 1966, pp. 13–14).

The chief characteristic of construct validation is the simultaneous validation of the test and of the trait construct. The investigator interested in the traits supposedly accounting for personality test responses must generate a concept or theory about the underlying dispositions or traits that he believes determine responses on his test. He then can employ a variety of methods to establish a network of relationships intended to illuminate what is related to his concept about the underlying disposition and what is not.

Traditionally, construct validity involves the following steps. The investigator begins with a hunch about a dimension on which individual differences can be compared, for example, "submissiveness." He might regard submissiveness as a "tendency to yield to the will and suggestions of others" (Sarason, 1966, p. 127). To study this tendency he devises a measure of submissiveness. He has no one definite criterion, however, and instead may use diverse behavioral samples as indices of the subject's underlying trait of submissiveness. He then proceeds to formulate and test hypotheses about how submissiveness, as displayed on his tests, does and does not relate to other behaviors in particular situations. On the basis of his findings he progressively revises and refines his construct. Thus construct validation involves testing and revising hypotheses about relations by examining the empirical associations among responses evoked in different situations.

Construct validation is distinguished from other strategies on the grounds that in construct validity the investigator's construct is not fully *equivalent* to any *one* behavioral measure or criterion. The investigator may not be at all sure about the particular criteria that are most appropriate for the construct. Construct validation thus is simply hypothesis testing and theory building with imperfect and incomplete operations and with many referents for the investigator's emerging concept.

## CONSTRUCT VALIDITY: AN EXAMPLE

Textbook accounts of trait methodology generally describe it distantly, with abstractions, discussing such concepts as reliability and validity, as in the preceding pages. In actual practice most researchers begin much more concretely, with a hunch or a direct observation, and try to follow their lead within a broad methodological framework. This much more tangible, step-by-step discovery process may be illustrated by studies of delay of gratification as a personality construct.

It is commonly believed that people differ in their preference or tolerance for delayed gratification. It has often been noted that young children find it hard to wait for delayed rewards. Clinically, the inability to postpone gratification for the sake of delayed rewards is generally considered an important factor in immaturity, maladjustment, and "psychopathy." Mowrer and Ullmann (1945), for example, thought the inability to tolerate delay of reinforcement was a critical factor in the development of criminal behavior. Surprisingly, in spite of the important role of delay of reward in many personality theories, little systematic research had been devoted to the topic before the series of studies described next.

## DEVISING A MEASURE

As a first step, the actual reward preferences of children in a Trinidadian village were assessed (Mischel, 1958). Additional information was also collected about each child in an effort to establish relationships between reward preferences and other characteristics. The subjects of the first study were boys and girls between the ages of 7 and 9, in the elementary section of a rural Trinidad school. In pre-experimental sessions two rewards or "reinforcements" of use for the experimental situation had to be selected. For this purpose, in a pre-test a smaller sample of boys and girls from the same age group, but taken from another rural Trinidadian school, were seen in individual sessions. In these meetings their preferences for various specific reinforcements were elicited. As a result, two reinforcements (both candy, but varying markedly in size, price, and packaging,—i.e., a 1-cent and a 10-cent candy) were chosen.

In the main study, at the village school itself, the children's task was to fill out a simple questionnaire. All the youngsters were sufficiently literate for this, as the questionnaire simply asked each child to indicate his ethnic group, age, socio-economic·status, and presence or absence of the father within the household. After the subjects completed the questionnaire, the experimenter displayed the two kinds of reinforcements and said: "I would like to give each of you a piece of candy, but I don't have enough of these (indicating the larger, more preferred reinforcement) with me today. So you can either get this one (indicating the smaller, less preferred reinforcement) right now, today, or, if you want to, you can wait for this one (indicating), which I will bring back next Wednesday [one week later]." The fact that getting the smaller candy immediately precluded getting the larger one the following week, and vice versa, was stressed. The children were asked to indicate their choice on their questionnaires.

## FINDING A NETWORK OF CORRELATIONS

The data were analyzed statistically to assess any relations between preference for either of the reinforcements and other measures. For example, is a child's tendency to delay gratification also a sign of his maturity? The relationship between

**TABLE 8-2   Percent Choosing Immediate or Delayed Reward
at Each Age**

| CHOICE | AGE | | |
|---|---|---|---|
| | 7 | 8 | 9 |
| Immediate reward | 81% | 48% | 20% |
| Delayed reward | 19% | 52% | 80% |

Adapted from Mischel (1958).

age and reward preference is found in Table 8-2, which shows the percentage of children in each age group choosing immediate versus delayed rewards (Mischel, 1958). A larger proportion of children chose to delay gratification at the older age levels. This finding fits the common view that increasing maturity brings an increasing ability to delay gratification. Since the finding has now been replicated several times, one may feel more confident about its accuracy (e.g., Melikian, 1959; Mischel & Metzner, 1962).

It is also widely believed that lower-class youngsters tend to be more impulsive than those from higher socioeconomic backgrounds. Comparison of the "high" versus "low" socioeconomic groups on reward preferences, however, did not yield a significant difference. The lack of relationship here could not be considered definitive, however, because the measure of socioeconomic level employed was extremely crude (type of housing). A failure to find an association among variables in this instance leaves one unsure whether the measures were inadequate or whether the relationship really did not exist.

To further develop the construct validity of preference for immediate, smaller rewards, as opposed to delayed, larger rewards, its relations to other variables, such as social responsibility, were explored next (Mischel, 1961b). It was hypothesized that youngsters who prefer immediate, smaller rewards would show less social responsibility than those who tend to choose larger, delayed rewards. This prediction was based on the belief that in a choice situation people select to wait for delayed more valuable rewards to the degree that they expect the more attractive reward actually to materialize. Such expectations require subjects to have faith that the promise-maker will keep his promise. The children, in other words, must trust that the agent who promises delayed gratifications will really supply them. Such trust or willingness to postpone immediate smaller gratification probably is also a basic ingredient of social responsibility; therefore ability to delay gratification should be positively related to social responsibility scores and negatively related to delinquent or criminal behavior.

Social responsibility was measured by answers to a carefully constructed and independently validated self-report questionnaire—the Social Responsibility Scale—as well as by the behavioral criterion of known delinquency. The Social Responsibility Scale has been found to correlate substantially with other measures of personal and social adjustment; it was designed to "discriminate children who have, with their peers, a reputation for responsibility as contrasted with children who have little reputation for responsibility" (Harris, 1957, p. 326). Harris' theory of responsibility, to which the items in the scale are related, conceptualizes responsibility "as a composite of attitude elements reflecting behavior classifiable as reliable, accountable, loyal, or doing an effective job" (Harris, 1957, p. 322).

The subjects were Trinidadian children. Some came from a large elementary government school on the outskirts of the capital city. Another sample came from a boys' "industrial school" that, in reality, is a reform school for committed juvenile delinquents; it also is on the outskirts of the capital. Just as in the initial study, an actual behavior choice that elicited preference for either immediate, smaller rewards or delayed, larger rewards was used at each school, and the Social Responsibility Scale was administered to each group. In addition, at the industrial school two items were added to obtain a preliminary test of the consistency with which subjects prefer immediate or delayed rewards. They were: "I would rather get ten dollars right now than have to wait a whole month and get thirty dollars then," and "I would rather wait to get a much larger gift much later rather than get a smaller one now."

The results showed, as was predicted, that a significantly larger proportion of delinquents chose immediate, smaller rewards. Moreover, and also as expected, among the delinquent children, those who preferred the delayed, larger reward had significantly higher social responsibility scores. Where three measures of reward preference had been used, the reliability or consistency of such preferences (Table 8-3) could be examined. The results showed a significant, but far from perfect, association among the responses on the three measures. Because these measures had much in common in their phrasing and were all obtained within the same testing situation, the data provided only a limited first step in the appraisal of the consistency of such reinforcement preferences within people.

**TABLE 8-3    Consistency of Preference for Immediate or Delayed Rewards: Relation of Childrens' Actual Choice to Their Questionnaire Preferences**

| ACTUAL CHOICE | QUESTIONNAIRE PREFERENCES | | |
| --- | --- | --- | --- |
| | CONSISTENTLY IMMEDIATE | CONSISTENTLY DELAYED | INCONSISTENT |
| Immediate, smaller candy | 12 | 4 | 15 |
| Delayed, larger candy | 4 | 19 | 16 |

NOTE: Each number represents a child: e.g., 12 children who consistently said they preferred immediate reward on the questionnaire also chose an immediate, smaller (rather than a delayed, larger) candy.

Adapted from Mischel (1961b).

## EXTENDING THE CONSTRUCT

In light of the overall encouraging results obtained in these studies with a simple index or delay-of-reward, later studies pursued the topic further and more systematically. More items were added to the measure of reward preferences, and the extended procedure was administered in various cultural settings in different parts of the world to further explore the meaning of the results obtained by discovering their correlates. Simultaneously the test items themselves were progressively revised, and the internal consistency and reliability features of the test were examined more systematically.

Gradually the program of research obtained significant correlations between preference for delayed, larger reinforcement or immediate, smaller gratifications and many other theoretically relevant behaviors, so that it provided an extensive network of construct validity. For example, children who chose to wait for rewards tended to have higher social responsibility, to cheat less, and to yield to temptation more slowly (Mischel & Gilligan, 1964). They also tended to be more concerned about achievement (Mischel, 1961b) and to be somewhat brighter (Mischel & Metzner, 1962) than children who chose immediate gratifications, although these relationships were not very strong. Preference for delayed rewards not only increases with age and differs radically across cultures, but also varies predictably as a function of certain rearing conditions in the home (Mischel, 1966b). Preferences for delayed rewards in choice situations are unrelated, however, to the standards children set for rewarding their own behavior (Mischel & Masters, 1966), and to their choice between immediate and delayed unavoidable punishments of different magnitudes (Mischel & Grusec, 1967). Other studies have investigated delay behavior experimentally and have systematically explored many of the conditions that control it. In this fashion a continuously expanding network of construct validity may be gradually established and progressively revised (e.g., Klineberg, 1968; Shybut, 1968; Gallimore, Weiss & Finney, 1974; Mischel, 1974). A fundamentally similar strategy has guided explorations of the construct validity of numerous traits.

## THE ROLE OF SITUATIONS AND INTERACTIONS

A main goal of trait psychology has been to discover the individual's position on one or more personality dimensions by comparing him with other persons tested under similar conditions. It was assumed that an individual's position on these dimensions would be relatively stable across testing situations and over lengthy time periods, if the test was sufficiently reliable. Therefore the main focus in trait psychology was on the development of reliable instruments administered under standard conditions. Such instruments were thought to tap accurately the person's presumably stable, highly generalized traits.

## SPECIFICITY IN TRAITS: DISCRIMINATIVE BEHAVIOR

The early psychometricians tended to follow the example of simple physical measurement, hoping that the measurement of traits would be basically similar to such measurements as table length with rulers, or temperature with thermometers. They unquestioningly assumed that broad trait structures exist and lead people to behave consistently. Consequently, they did not pay much attention to the role of environmental variables as determinants of behavior. Instead, they concentrated on standardization of measurement conditions in the hope that broad traits would emerge.

In more recent years a great deal of research has shown that performances on trait measures are affected by a variety of stimulus conditions, and can be modified by numerous environmental changes (Masling, 1960; Mischel, 1974; Peterson, 1968; Vernon, 1964). Most important, it has been found that normal people tend to show considerable variability in their behavior even across seemingly similar conditions. A person may be dependent with his wife, for example, but not with his boss, and even his dependency at home may be highly specific, varying as a result of slight situational alterations, such as subtle changes in his wife's reactions to him, or the presence of other family members. Thus behavior may be much more situation-specific and discriminative than early trait theorists had thought.

Studies of individual differences on common trait dimensions have produced many networks of correlations. These associations tend to be large and enduring when people rate themselves or others with broad trait terms (e.g., Block, 1971). For example, on questionnaires, people may describe their traits consistently (e.g., E. L. Kelly, 1955). When ongoing behavior in specific situations is sampled objectively by different, independent measures, however, the association generally tends to be quite modest. Thus while people often show consistency on questionnaires and ratings, these data tend to have limited value for predicting their actual behavior in specific situations.

The correlational research on delay of gratification discussed in the last section is fairly representative of correlational research done on other personality dimensions. As we saw, some supporting validity data were easily obtained. The networks of relationships from such research extend far and wide and provide ample evidence that people's behavior has some consistency, that it is not totally situation-specific. What a person does in one setting is not independent of what he does in other settings, and it is, of course, related to what he did before and to what he will probably do again. In general, however, correlational work on voluntary delay of reward and on other personality dispositions suggests that the strength of the associations generally tends to be too low for confident predictions about behavior in the individual case.

Therefore we have to be most cautious about generalizing from an individual's test behavior to his personality and behavior outside the test. For example, we cannot safely conclude that Gary's lack of authoritarianism on the California *F* Scale precludes his behaving in highly arbitrary, "authoritarian" ways under certain life conditions. Perhaps, then, his friend was right when he noted that Gary could be "arbitrary" and "bossy," with an insulting, cynical humor. The same friend also described Gary as "friendly and outgoing"—but only when he is "with a shy, self-conscious person." As these examples indicate, Gary's authoritarianism, his friendliness or hostility, and other key features of his behavior, are not situation-free attributes: they depend on many modifying conditions and hence are relatively specific. Likewise, the fact that Gary's self-reported sex-role interests and attitudes gave him an "average" score on the masculinity-femininity dimension in no way precludes his having diverse sexual problems that are not "average." For example, while his interests may be stereotypically masculine to an average degree, he still may be plagued by idiosyncratic sexual conflicts and may be suffering from relatively unique behavioral problems in his actual sexual relations.

"Behavioral specificity," or the dependence of behavior on specific situational conditions, has been discovered regularly on character traits like rigidity, or social conformity, or honesty, or aggression, or on most other nonintellective personality dimensions (Mischel, 1968; Peterson, 1968; Vernon, 1964). Specificity tends to be high, for example, among the components of traits like dependency, or self-control, or attitudes toward authority—although trait theorists originally believed these to be highly generalized dispositions. Results of this kind present a basic problem for approaches to personality that assume the existence of relatively situation-free, broad dispositions.

What a person does depends in part on the situation.

The phrase "personality coefficient" has been coined to describe the modest correlation (usually between .20 and .30) typically found in personality research linking responses on questionnaires to other behavior (Mischel, 1968). Such correlations are too small to have value for most individual assessment purposes other than gross screening decisions. For example, Gary's MMPI profile might be useful as a preliminary screening device to help decide whether or not he might need further testing before being selected for a "sensitive" government job. It would be of more limited value, however, in predicting specific important things about his behavior as an individual.

The evaluation of all data on trait consistency depends of course on the standards selected to evaluate them. A modest consistency coefficient (of about .30, for example) can be taken as evidence either of the relative specificity of the particular behaviors or of the presence of some cross-situational generality (Burton, 1963). Furthermore, one has to infer dispositions from imperfect behavioral measurements that involve errors. Nevertheless, it is gradually being recognized that behavioral fluctuations reflect more than imperfections in measuring instruments (Loevinger, 1957). Each individual may be consistent in his own behavior on some traits (e.g., Bem & Allen, 1974). But on many traits most of us show only limited consistency across situations (Mischel, 1973a). The utility of describing everyone in broad trait terms (e.g., "impulsive," "dependent") is therefore being questioned deeply. Indeed, it has to be challenged (Peterson, 1968), and it raises many complex issues (discussed in Chapter 21).

## USES AND MISUSES OF TRAITS

Obviously behavior is not completely situation-specific. We do not have to start with a blank mind in every new situation; we have memories, we generalize from past to future, and our earlier experiences influence our present behavior. Overall "average" differences between individuals can be construed easily and used to discriminate among them for many purposes. Knowing how your friend behaved before can help you predict how he probably will act again in similar situations. The impact of any situation or stimulus depends on the person who experiences it, and different people differ greatly in how they cope with most stimulus conditions. It is a truism that one person's favorite "stimulus" may be the stuff of another's nightmares and that in the same "stimulus situation" one individual may react with aggression, another with love, a third with indifference. The evidence does not imply that different people will not act differently with some consistency in particular classes of situations; it does suggest that the particular classes of conditions tend to be much narrower than traditional trait theories have assumed, and for purposes of important individual decision-making require highly individualized assessments of what the specific situations mean to the person.

To apply these abstract points more concretely, it might help to think again about Gary. It is certainly possible to form some generalizations about his seemingly major qualities, strengths, and problems. Such generalizations help us to differentiate Gary from other people, and to compare him with them. We learned, for example, that the MMPI indicated Gary tended to be interpersonally distant, to avoid close relations with people, and to fear emotional involvement. Such characterizations may help one to gain a quick overall impression of Gary. But in order to predict what Gary will do in specific situations, or to make decisions about him (as in therapy or vocational counseling), it would be necessary to conduct a much more individually oriented study that considers the specific qualities of Gary as they relate to the specific situations of interest in his life. Just when does Gary become more—or less—"interpersonally distant"? Under what conditions does he *not* avoid close relations with people? When does his tendency to "fear emotional involvement" increase? When does it decrease? The analysis and prediction of specific behavior requires that we ask specific questions like these to link behavior to conditions rather than to paint personality portraits with more general characterizations.

The utility of inferring broad traits depends on the particular purpose for which the inference is made. Although inferences about global traits may have limited value for the practical prediction of a person's specific future behavior in specific situations, or for the design of specific treatment programs to help him, sometimes they have value for the person himself—for example, when he must abstract attributes to answer such everyday questions as: "Is your friend reliable?"; "What kind of person is my sister?"; "Might this person be a good roommate?"; or "What are *you* like?" Inferences about broad traits also may have value for such purposes as gross initial screening decisions (as in personnel selection), studying average differences between groups of individuals in personality research (Block, 1971), or the layman's everyday perception of persons (e.g., Mischel, Jeffery & Patterson, 1974; Schneider, 1973). Finally, while comparisons *between* people in large, unselected groups on most common traits suggest that discriminativeness tends to be the rule, for some people a considerable degree of consistency can be demonstrated, at least on some dimensions some of the time (Chapter 21).

## THE INTERACTION OF DISPOSITIONS AND CONDITIONS

Some studies have tried to analyze the role of situations and of conditions as well as the role of dispositions. Sophisticated trait research has started to take situations and "stimulus conditions" into account seriously (e.g., Argyle & Little, 1972; Endler, 1973; Moos, 1974). Knowledge of individual differences alone often tells us little unless it is combined with information about the conditions and situational variables that influence the behavior of interest. Conversely, the effects of conditions depend on the individuals in them. Research results consistently suggest that the interaction of individual differences and particular conditions tends to be most important.

Consider, for example, Moos's (1968) studies of self-reported reactions by staff and psychiatric patients to various settings in the hospital. The findings were based on ratings in nine settings with regard to a dimension of "sociable, friendly, peaceful" versus "unsociable, hostile, angry" behavior. These results revealed, first, that different individuals reacted differently to the settings. Second, a given person might be high on the dimension in the morning but not at lunch, high with another patient but not when with a nurse, low in small group therapy, moderate in industrial therapy, but high in individual therapy, etc. An entirely different pattern might characterize the next person.

We might be able to predict many of the things Gary will do simply by knowing something about the situation in which he will be: at school in an economics course Gary is likely to behave very differently than he does on a date with his girlfriend at a football game. On the other hand, our predictions in each case probably would be best if we considered Gary's relevant qualities as an individual—his academic interests and skills, his attitudes toward girls, his past behavior on dates at football games—as well as the situation when we try to predict his behavior in each setting. In other words, we may predict best if we know what each situation means to the individual, and consider the unique interaction of the person and the setting, rather than concentrating either on the situation itself or on the individual in an environmental and social vacuum.

## MODERATOR VARIABLES

Wallach (1962) and Kogan and Wallach (1964) have noted that many "moderator variables" may influence the correlations found in trait research. That is, the relations between any two variables often depend on several other variables. For instance, correlations between measures of risk-taking and impulsivity may be found for males but not for females; they may even be negative for one sex but positive for the other. Similarly, relations between two measures might be positive for children with low IQ but negative for highly intelligent children, or they might occur under "relaxed" testing conditions but not under "anxious" conditions. The concept of moderator variables was introduced to trait theory to refer to the fact that the effects of any particular disposition generally are "moderated" by or dependent upon many other conditions and variables. Such variables as the subject's age, his sex, his IQ, the experimenter's sex, and the characteristics of the situation all are common moderators of test behavior.

## THE ASSESSMENT OF SETTINGS

One trend in recent studies has been to describe settings or "ecological" variables rather than dispositions. This approach is seen best in the work of Barker and his associates, which emphasizes detailed description of the environments in which children behave (e.g., Barker & Wright, 1951; Barker, 1968). In a basically similar vein, other researchers have made an effort to sample carefully some of the specific characteristics of different social settings and to systematically analyze the nature of situations (e.g., Moos & Insel, 1974; Ittelson et al, 1974; Price, 1974). These and other workers have been analyzing the characteristics of the environment, rather than searching only for the traits of the subject, and have been exploring the specific interactions of the person and the environment in ways discussed in Chapter 21.

# ADAPTATION, DEVIANCE, AND CHANGE

By now it should be plain that the major applications of the trait approach have been tests and measurement procedures for studying individual differences. Trait theories emphasize the stability of human qualities, not their change and potential modification. It should not be surprising that trait-oriented approaches to human adaptation and to "abnormal" behavior also have searched for a taxonomy for classifying troubled persons according to their stable, enduring traits. Examples are the vigorous efforts to characterize individuals on dimensions such as "emotional stability versus neuroticism" (Eysenck & Rachman, 1965). Likewise, the classical typologies of "mental illness" are based on the assumption that problematic behaviors reflect underlying, consistent dispositions and that people with psychological problems can be classified reliably into different types. The most influential of these classifications remains the psychiatric diagnostic system originally devised more than 50 years ago by Emil Kraepelin, but frequently revised since then (e.g., Davison & Neale, 1974).

In sum, the trait approach has led to a long search for a taxonomy of deviance that would classify people into different categories on the basis of the abnormal "signs" (trait indicators) displayed in their behavior.

## TAXONOMIES OF DEVIANCE

With taxonomies of deviance, as with all classification schemes, a crucial question is how well experts can reach agreement. Clinicians (e.g., psychiatrists) can achieve fair and even good agreement when they classify people into a few major psychiatric categories like "neurotic" versus "psychotic." They agree much less, however, when they attempt more subtle classifications into specific subcategories such as type of neurosis or psychosis (e.g., Ash, 1949; Schmidt & Fonda, 1956; Sandifer et al., 1964).

Zigler and Phillips (1961) studied the frequency of 35 psychiatric symptoms among hundreds of mental hospital patients who had been diagnosed into four major categories (psychoneurotic, schizophrenic, manic-depressive, and character disorder; see Table 8-4). The 35 symptoms (such as depressed, withdrawn, irresponsible behavior, lying) are drawn from descriptions of patients by the doctor at admission (Phillips & Rabinovitch, 1958). Of the 35 symptoms, 30 or more were found in the diagnosed manic-depressives, in the character disorder group, and in both the neurotic and schizophrenic groups. Thus persons who are given different psychiatric disease labels actually may display highly overlapping behaviors.

**TABLE 8-4   Percentage of Individuals in Total Sample and in Each Diagnostic Category Manifesting Each Symptom**

| SYMPTOM[a] | TOTAL HOSPITAL (N = 793) | MANIC-DEPRESSIVE (N = 75) | PSYCHO-NEUROTIC (N = 152) | CHARACTER DISORDER (N = 279) | SCHIZOPHRENIC (N = 287) |
|---|---|---|---|---|---|
| Depressed | 38 | 64 | 58 | 31 | 28 |
| Hallucinations | 19 | 11 | 4 | 12 | 35 |
| Emotional outburst | 14 | 17 | 12 | 18 | 9 |
| Self-depreciation | 12 | 16 | 16 | 8 | 13 |
| Bizarre ideas | 9 | 11 | 1 | 2 | 20 |
| Headaches | 6 | 7 | 10 | 4 | 5 |
| Mood swings | 5 | 9 | 5 | 4 | 4 |
| Lying | 3 | 0 | 1 | 7 | 0 |
| Depersonalization | 3 | 4 | 1 | 0 | 6 |

[a] Every fourth symptom is shown from a total list of 35. Adapted from Zigler and Phillips (1961).

Zigler and Phillips' (1961, p. 73) overall results indicated that "membership in a particular diagnostic group conveys only minimal information" about the individual's behavior. Their findings probably also reflect the fact that the behavior of troubled individuals, just like the behavior of those who function more effectively, changes across situations and over time. It is as difficult to pigeonhole people into psychiatric diagnoses as it is to categorize them according to normal types and traits.

More recent studies, using the revised version of the standard psychiatric diagnostic system for schizophrenia, also conclude that it is an inadequate classification and does not provide a satisfactory nomenclature (Blashfield, 1973).

The weaknesses of the diagnostic system have been illustrated dramatically by studies in which normal persons sought admission to psychiatric hospitals (Rosenhan, 1973). They found that perfectly "sane" individuals (including professionals and graduate students in the "mental health" fields) are consistently treated by the hospital staff as if they were insane as soon as they are admitted and placed in the role of "mental patients." Having been labeled "psychotic," the pseudo-patients continued to be treated as insane even when their behavior was totally rational and "normal." The results demonstrated vividly the perils of "being sane in insane places"; the "patients" were judged by where they were rather than by their own behavior.

Recognizing the many problems, but challenged by them, trait-oriented psychologists continue to search for better typologies of adaptation and deviance based mainly on factor analyses of a variety of rating scales (e.g., Lorr et al., 1965; Wiggins, 1973). Other researchers focus on differences in the adjustment history and prognosis (probable recovery) of different subgroups of psychiatric patients (e.g., Farina, 1972; Phillips, 1953).

## *THE GENETIC AND BIOCHEMICAL APPROACH*

Trait theories tend to imply that at least some basic personality traits are likely to have both a genetic and a biochemical source. The search for a genetic component in personality traits is seen in Eysenck's (1967) work on introversion-extraversion, and in research on schizophrenia and other patterns of severe disorder (e.g., Gottesman, 1963, 1966; Gottesman & Shields, 1969; Rosenthal, 1971; Snyder, et al., 1974). At present, there are some important, highly suggestive leads about genetic bases of certain psychological individual differences (some of which are discussed in Chapter 13). Conclusions, however, still seem a long way from being either exact or final. Similarly, the search for biochemical (organic) conditions associated with particular personality patterns (especially patterns that are severely deviant) continues actively. But for most forms of social and interpersonal deviance no organic causes have been found and the majority of these problems are considered nonorganic or "functional" in origin. While recognizing the potential importance of genetic and biochemical research for complex human behavior, other psychologists search for ways in which the psychological environment can be harnessed effectively to improve the quality of human adaptation now (e.g., Chapter 11).

## SUMMARY

1. Factor analysis is a mathematical procedure that sorts test responses into homogeneous clusters. It is a useful procedure for simplifying data but it does not automatically reveal basic traits. For example, the personality factors identified from ratings of personalities may partly reflect the rater's conceptual categories.

2. Trait research tends to focus on correlations among what people say on paper-and-pencil inventories and questionnaires. The interpretation of these questionnaire findings poses some special problems, because what a person says about his attributes does not necessarily reflect accurately either his traits or the things that he does outside the test. Self-reports thus may or may not be closely related to other indices of the person's nontest behavior.

3. No matter how carefully the psychometrician designs and standardizes his procedures, the psychological situation affects responses on personality tests. Therefore the consistency (*reliability*) and meaning (*validity*) of a personality test has to be demonstrated by research.

4. According to trait theory, an individual's test behaviors are signs from which his underlying dispositions may be inferred. *Criterion validation*

assesses the relationship between the obtained sample and other criterion data, either concurrently or predictively. *Construct validation* tries to elaborate the inferred traits determining test behavior. The researcher guided by the construct "anxiety," for example, must demonstrate through studies how his measures and results illuminate the meaning of his construct.

5. Studies on delay of gratification as a personality dimension illustrate the way in which construct validity research proceeds from direct observation and hunches, through standardization of a measure and demonstrations of reliability and validity on a step-by-step basis.

6. Although early trait theorists assumed the existence of relatively broad traits, research suggests that what people do depends on numerous moderating conditions. Evidence for the existence of broad traits has been questioned severely.

7. Complex interactions among dispositional and situational variables influence behavior. The relationship between any two variables—a child's dependency and his school achievements, for example—may be moderated by many other variables, such as his age, IQ, anxiety, the type of task, and the conditions of testing.

8. Recent studies of dispositions have tried to analyze the role of situations and of conditions as well as of individual differences. Other researchers are focusing on settings and the environment, rather than on the dispositions of the individual.

9. The trait approach has been applied to a search for a taxonomy of deviance. Such a taxonomy classifies people into various types, as in psychiatric diagnosis, on the basis of their abnormal behaviors. Taxonomies of deviance tend to have limited reliability because of the variability of the behaviors displayed by individuals within most categories. The trait approach also continues to stimulate research into the possible genetic and biochemical bases of both normal and abnormal personality traits.

# CHAPTER 9

# PSYCHODYNAMIC THEORIES Applications

## GLOBAL PSYCHODYNAMIC ORIENTATION

An exciting feature of Freudian psychology was that it promised a methodology for at last studying personality in proper depth and for treating complex human problems with the sophistication they deserved. Chapter 3 conveyed some of the main concepts that guide the psychodynamic study of personality. In accord with these concepts, psychodynamically oriented psychologists try to induce the person to reveal his unconscious processes, conflicts, and dynamics. In this approach, the objective is to unravel disguises and defenses, to decipher the symbolic meanings of behaviors, to uncover unconscious motives, and to identify the "underlying causes" of the person's behavior.

Psychodynamic theorists clearly recognized the inconsistencies among a person's overt behaviors across seemingly similar situations. Thus the "behavioral specificity" found in trait measures and discussed in the last chapter was no surprise to many of them. They felt, however, that the observed inconsistencies in the individual's behavior could be understood as merely superficial diversities that masked the fundamentally consistent, underlying motives that actually drove him enduringly. Recall in this regard Freud's focus on the vicissitudes of impulses. According to psychodynamic theory, the basic motives persist and press for discharge across diverse settings, but their overt manifestations or "symptoms" are transformed defensively. Hence the task is to find the person's fundamental motives and enduring dynamics behind the defensive facade and surface distortions of his overt behavior.

## MINIMIZING THE SITUATION

To achieve these aims the psychodynamically oriented psychologist tries to eliminate situational interferences so that external determinants of behavior can be minimized and defenses bypassed. It was hoped that generalized dynamic patterns would, under ambiguous conditions, penetrate the person's facade and reveal themselves. Therefore techniques were developed in which cues in the situation are kept deliberately vague and unclear. These beliefs about the importance of stimulus ambiguity guide the conduct of the assessment interview and of all other data collection. Instead of asking detailed and structured questions, psychodynamic inquiries tend to be "open-ended" probes that leave the respondent's task unclear so that his underlying motives and dynamics can emerge.

Psychodynamic assessment tends to emphasize global personality descriptions and reconstructions of the person's history. These historical reconstructions deal with the ways in which the person handled his sexual and aggressive impulses during his childhood struggles with problems characteristic of each of the pregenital psychosexual stages. Clues are also sought about traumatic experiences, central defenses, and basic character traits. The following excerpts are taken from a psychodynamic report written about our "Gary W." and based on interviews and special test situations that will be discussed later in this chapter. The report not only provides new information about Gary, but also illustrates some of the features of a clinical psychodynamic case conceptualization guided by Freudian theory.

*An Example: Excerpts from Freudian Conceptualization of Gary W.*

Oedipal themes abound in the case of Gary W., although he has grown a long way toward resolving them. W. emotionally describes his feeling that his father was his "severest critic" and that he is his mother's favorite. He says that he no longer sees adults as all-knowing, and he refers to his father as mellowed and "out of it." He reports warmth and affection for his mother, although these feelings are mixed.

In his own sibling relationships, Gary seems to have displaced much of his rivalry with his father onto his older brother. W. describes great outbursts of anger vented on Charles with obvious intent to injure. He compares Charles with their father and says that the two are alike in many respects. He is on better terms with Charles since the latter was in a car crash in which he got pretty smashed up. (This in some respects parallels his present hostile condescension, rather than competitive hostility, toward the father since the latter has proved himself a failure in business).

A recent revival of the Oedipal situation occurred when Gary's girl friend left him for his roommate. She may well have symbolized his mother to him more than is usual: she is older, was married before, and has a child from the previous marriage. After he confessed his love to his girl, she told him that she had been seeing his roommate. W. felt humiliated and "wounded in my vanity" because these events went on "behind my back." His feelings are reminiscent of the chagrin felt by the little boy when he realizes his father's role vis-a-vis his mother. W. attempted to resolve his anger by recognizing that he was not in a position financially to marry her whereas his roommate was. His apparent satisfaction that his roommate after all has not married her, and that they may have broken up, also is consistent with the conceptualization that this relationship was filled with Oedipal themes.

The incomplete resolution of the Oedipal conflict is further evident in W.'s fear of injury and physical illness, in the depression which has followed a motorcycle accident (castration anxiety)— and in the distinction he makes between girl friends ("good girls") and sex objects ("fast girls"). Incomplete identification with his father, whether a cause or a result of this unresolved situation, is apparent. His search for a strong male figure is evident in his reactions to the headmaster and teacher at boarding school, described respectively as "a very definite, determined sort of person" and "not the sort of man you could push around." He is quite openly disparaging of his father, albeit on intellectual grounds. (This tends to be W.'s typical style.)

According to Gary, his mother sees sex as something bad and nasty. This report, as well as his suggestion that his mother's frigidity has undermined his father's masculinity, may represent wishes that his mother may not be responsive to his father. He himself may regard sexuality ambivalently—his sexual experiences seem to involve much parental rebellion and he keeps his sex objects separate from his affections. When he speaks about sex he talks crudely of "making it."

Gary's anxiety in social situations in general, and his fear of public speaking in particular, are further indices of his basic insecurity and his brittle defenses. He is concerned that he will be found lacking. The underlying castration anxiety is expressed symbolically in his comment that when he stands up to speak in public, he is afraid "the audience is ready to chop my head off," and when there is a possibility of debate, that he will be "caught with my pants down."

Gary shows some concern about homosexuality. He mentions it spontaneously when talking about friendship, and his descriptions of living in close proximity with other males include tension, friction, and annoyance. This anxiety is illustrated in his uncomfortable relationship to his present roommate. His first two responses to cards on the Rorschach are also interesting in this connection. Laughter accompanies the statement that two figures are "grinding their bottoms." The perception of animals rather than human figures further serves as a defense to reduce his anxiety. Paranoid tendencies appear in both the fantasy and interview material (e.g., seeing "eyes" on the Rorschach) and suggest some projection of the homosexual conflict.

The battle being waged between impulses, reality, and conscience are evidenced by Gary's concern with control and his obsessive-compulsive traits. W. makes a tenuous distinction between passion and reason, rejecting the former and clinging to the latter. He extends this distinction to interpersonal relations, drawing a line between "companionship" and "love." He reports an inability to empathize and form good object-relations. An example of repression of affect is W.'s difficulty in expressing anger. In this area, as in others, he tends to intellectualize as a way to systematize and control anxiety. His problems in expressing anger may also be reflected in his speech difficulties and in his verbal blocks, especially in public and social situations.

Instinctual elements arise to disturb the tenuous control gained by secondary processes. He complains that he sometimes gets drunk when he should be accomplishing things. He says he admires people with enough self-discipline not to drink, smoke, and sleep late. He speaks of trying to force himself not to do the things he knows are bad for him and interfere with his long-range objectives.

The need to control is also apparent in his performance and behavior on many of the psychological tests, where his approach is analytic rather than imaginative, and his expressive movements tight and controlled. (His attention to detail and his constant intellectualization of real feeling on the Rorschach, his hobby of insect study, and his admission that often "trivialities" bother him for a long time add up to a picture of restriction and repression in the service of anxiety reduction.) There is an anal retentive aspect of this need to control, which comes out rather clearly in his interaction with the assessor when he says testily, "Didn't you show that to me already—are you trying to squeeze more out of me. . . ." A further compulsive trait is W.'s frequent counting, and the way he rigidly breaks his ability self-ratings down into component parts, and strives to ensure complete accuracy and coverage of whatever he is discussing about himself.

The need for control may circle back to castration anxiety. The two themes come together in W.'s fear of physical injury and in his fear of losing his brain capacity. The culmination of these two fears occurred when W.'s motorcycle failed him, and he is still preoccupied with this incident. He relates these fears more directly to the Oedipal conflict when, in the phrase association test, he links anger at his brother with fear of losing his "marbles."

Note that the focus in this report is on hypothesized underlying dynamics. It is implicitly assumed that sexual and aggressive motives and unconscious conflicts exert fairly pervasive effects on many behaviors. Statements about behavior tend to be relatively global and undifferentiated. The emphasis is on unacceptable impulses and defenses for coping with the anxiety they arouse. There is also an attempt to link current sexual and aggressive problems to relations with the parents and to Oedipal problems in early childhood.

If this report is valid it offers a whole new perspective on Gary, and provides a way of seeing meaning and unity throughout his diverse behaviors. For example, his relations with his brother and with women became part of his larger efforts to cope with Oedipal problems. Indeed, a main attraction of psychodynamic theory is that it offers a systematic, unified view of the individual. Rather than seeing the person as a conglomerate of discrete traits, it views him as an integrated, dynamic creature: when his underlying core personality is revealed, his seemingly diverse, discrepant behaviors become meaningful, and all fit into the total whole. It becomes easy to see why such an elegant conceptual system is attractive. But the key question that has to be answered by scientifically oriented students is: Does the system have validity? Do psychodynamic reports of the kind made about Gary provide accurate and useful insights?

## RELYING ON THE CLINICIAN

Psychodynamic assessments rely primarily on the intuitions of the personality assessor. While the interpretation of responses on psychometric tests is objective and straightforward, the interpretation of clinical data is usually highly subjective and dependent more on the clinician than on his tests. The rules for relating behavioral signs to unconscious meanings and dynamics are largely implicit, and the constructs themselves tend to be difficult to specify. Consequently, the psychoanalytically oriented assessor has to depend mainly on clinical judgments, although the reliability and utility of his interpretations can be evaluated objectively.

The merits of such clinical assessments depend on the evidence supporting the techniques upon which the personality psychologist relies in generating his inferences, and on the value of clinical judgment itself. Because psychodynamic theories rest on the belief that the core of personality is revealed by highly indirect behavioral signs, evidence for the value of these indirect signs of personality is most important. This chapter reviews some of the main clinical methods that have been studied in the search for valuable signs of personality. Probably the most important of these methods are the projective techniques.

## PROJECTIVE TECHNIQUES

Free association and the analysis of dreams are the methods of personality study that stem most directly from Freud's work. In free association, the person is instructed to give his thoughts complete freedom and to report daydreams, feelings, and images no matter how incoherent, illogical, or meaningless they might seem to him. This technique may be employed either with a minimum of prompting or by offering brief phrases as a stimulus to encourage associations.

Freud believed that dreams were similar to the patients' free associations. He thought the dream was an expression of the most primitive workings and contents of the mind, the "primary process." Dreams were interpreted as fulfilling a wish or discharging tension by inducing an image of the desired goal. Through the interpretation of dreams, Freud felt that he was penetrating into the unconscious.

## INTEGRATING PSYCHODYNAMIC CONCEPTS AND PSYCHOMETRIC METHODS

Free association and dream analysis, while remaining the basic tools of orthodox psychoanalytic therapy, have had only indirect impacts for the personality assessments conducted by psychologists. Both techniques have been used for research purposes and as parts of larger projects for the intensive assessment of individuals. They have not, however, been widely adopted in personality study, probably because they are considered too time consuming and are believed to require extensive contact with the subject to establish a comfortable atmosphere free of initial inhibitions before they can be used profitably. Most personality psychologists currently believe it is uneconomical to devote much time to gathering dream data and free-association material. Reports of dreams are sometimes elicited in the course of clinical interviewing, and client's dreams are extensively described and interpreted in the psychoanalytic literature.

In the principal techniques of classical psychoanalysis, the depth interview and free association, the assessment conditions are the opposite of standardization and objectivity. The emphasis is on clinical intuition and personal experience to weave interpretations that the clinician believes fit the particular person. In these "depth" studies, psychodynamics are inferred in accord with the general principles of psychoanalytic theory. These clinical studies by psychoanalysts typically are based on relatively informal direct clinical observations of individual clients during psychoanalysis. Unfortunately these analyses often tend to be reported so loosely that their research value is dubious (Janis, 1958).

While intrigued by psychodynamic theory, many clinically oriented personality psychologists also have been influenced in their approach by psychometric testing, with its long tradition of concern with reliability and objective measurement. As we have seen, the minimal requirement of psychometric testing is that methods must be sufficiently formal to permit standardized administration and to allow research about the reliability and validity of the quantitative results. Through projective tests, many psychologists wished to combine at least some of the quantitative features of psychometric testing with the insights they hoped to achieve from clinical judgments about psychodynamics. Probably the two most influential projective techniques have been the Rorschach and the Thematic Apperception Test.

## THE RORSCHACH

The Rorschach is one of the most popular projective tests. Developed by the psychiatrist Herman Rorschach in 1921, the Rorschach test consists of a series of complex, bilaterally symmetrical inkblots on 10 separate cards (Figure 9-1). Some of the blots are black and white, and some colored. The subject is instructed to look at the inkblots one at a time and to say everything that the inkblot could resemble or look like. The examiner then generally conducts an inquiry into the details of the subject's interpretation of the blot, or what stimulus characteristics led to the percept.

*Gary's Reactions to Two of the Rorschach Inkblot Cards:*

*Response:*

> This looks like two dogs, head-to-foot (laughs), licking each other.
> That's about it, that's all.

*Inquiry answers (to the question "What about the inkblot made you think of two dogs?"):*

> They're sort of fuzzy . . . kinda shapeless. It was the dark skin and the furry effect that made me think of it.

*Response:*

> Didn't we have this one already?
> This could be an ogre laughing—his head thrown back and he's laughing, his eyes and mouth wide open.
> These over here look like insects, tsetse flies in fact, with tiny, tiny legs, and small, delicate and rather beautiful wings.
> That's it, that's enough.

*Inquiry answers:*

> It's the shaggyness and the hugeness, the massiveness of the shape.
> The wings over here, head here.

The subject's responses may be scored in terms of location (the place on the card that the response refers to) and such determinants as the physical aspects of the blot (e.g., shape, color, shading, or an expression of movement) that suggested the response. The originality of the responses, the content, and other characteristics

**Figure 9-1**  INKBLOT SIMILAR TO THOSE IN THE RORSCHACH TEST

**Figure 9-2**  PICTURE SIMILAR TO THOSE ON THE TAT

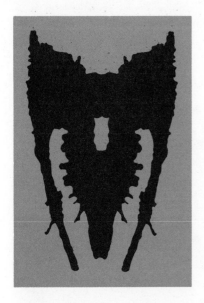

also may be coded. The frequency of various responses may be counted and then used in interpretation. The interpreter may seek to relate these scores to aspects of the subject's personality, such as his creative capacity, maturity, contact with reality, emotional control, and anxiety. A more recent inkblot test, similar to the Rorschach but with a more objective, standardized procedure, is the Holtzman inkblot technique (1961).

## THE THEMATIC APPERCEPTION TEST (TAT)

The Thematic Apperception Test or TAT was developed by Morgan and Murray in the Harvard Psychological Clinic research program during the 1930s. The test consists of a series of pictures and one blank card (see Figure 9-2). Somewhat different sets of pictures are available for young males (under 14), young females, adult males, and adult females. The cards are presented one at a time.

The subject usually is told that it is a story-telling test and that he is to make up as dramatic or interesting a story as he can for each picture. He is instructed to tell what has led up to the event shown in the picture, to describe what is happening at the moment, what the characters are feeling and thinking, and then to give the outcome. He is encouraged to give free reign to his imagination and to say whatever comes to mind. Typically, the length of time that elapses before the subject begins telling the story and the total time he takes for each story are recorded.

As suggested by the name of the test, it is expected that the subject will interpret an ambiguous stimulus according to his individual readiness to perceive in a certain way ("apperception"). Furthermore, the themes that recur in these imaginative productions are thought to have basic significance. Special scoring keys have been designed for use with the TAT (e.g., McClelland et al., 1953; Mussen & Naylor, 1954), or the stories may be used "clinically," the clinician interpreting the themes intuitively in accord with his personality theory.

*Two of Gary's Stories from the TAT*

*Card depicting two men:* Two men have gone on a hunting trip. It is dawn now and the younger one is still sound asleep. The older one is watching over him. Thinking how much he reminds him of when he was young and could sleep no-matter-what. Also, seeing the boy sleeping there makes him long for the son he never had. He's raising his hand about to stroke him on the forehead. I think he'll be too embarrassed to go ahead with it. He'll start a fire and put on some coffee and wait for the younger man to wake up.

*Card depicting young man and older woman:* This depicts a mother-son relationship. The mother is a strong, stalwart person. Her son is hesitating at the doorway. He wants to ask her advice about something but isn't sure whether it's the right thing to do. Maybe he should make up his own mind. I think he'll just come in and have a chat with her. He won't ask her advice but will work things out for himself. Maybe it's a career choice, a girl friend . . . I don't know what, but whatever it is, he'll decide himself. He'll make his own plans, figure out what the consequences will be, and work it out from there.

## CHARACTERISTICS OF PROJECTIVE TECHNIQUES

The main characteristic of projective techniques like the Rorschach and the TAT is the way in which the testing situation is usually structured so that the task is *ambiguous*. Typically, there are also attempts to *disguise the purpose* of the test (e.g., Bell, 1948), and the person is given *freedom to respond* in any way that he likes.

In projective testing the assessor confronts the subject with ambiguous stimuli and asks ambiguous questions. For example, he asks, "What might this be?" "What could this remind you of?" (while showing an inkblot) or he says, "Create the most imaginative story that you can [showing a picture], including what the people are thinking and feeling, what led up to this situation, and how it all comes out." Or he reads words and asks the subject to "say the first thing that comes to mind."

**Figure 9-3** SOME DIFFERENCES BETWEEN AN OBJECTIVE PERFORMANCE TEST AND A PROJECTIVE TEST

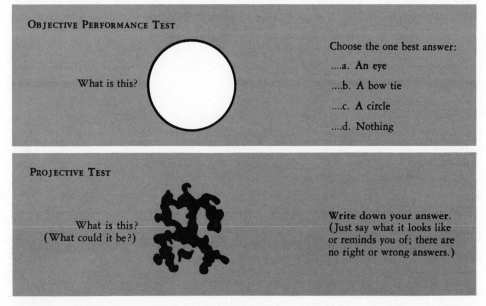

OBJECTIVE PERFORMANCE TEST

What is this?

Choose the one best answer:

....a. An eye

....b. A bow tie

....c. A circle

....d. Nothing

PROJECTIVE TEST

What is this?
(What could it be?)

Write down your answer.
(Just say what it looks like
or reminds you of; there are
no right or wrong answers.)

In objective performance tests the subject must choose between definite right or wrong answers. In projective tests the stimulus and instructions are ambiguous and the subject has greater freedom to respond in accord with his interpretation of the stimulus.

The same stimulus materials with different instructions could be used non-projectively by asking the person to trace the blots, count the pictures, or spell the words in the association list. Similarly, almost any test item can be used projectively with appropriate instructions. Some stimuli, of course, lend themselves more readily than others to projective use, primarily because they more easily evoke a wide range of responses. Therefore, fairly amorphous stimuli such as inkblots, unclear pictures, barely audible sounds, clay, plastic materials, and paint have been favorites. Some differences between projective techniques and more objective, structured performance tests (such as tests of achievement and ability) are depicted in Figure 9-3.

Projective techniques have been favored by psychoanalytically oriented assessors because they assumed that the "unconscious inner life" is at least partially revealed in responses to the projective test situation. The assumptions underlying projective tests reflect the influences of psychoanalytic theory: the emphasis on the unconsciously motivated nature of behavior, the importance of unconscious material, and the conception that the person has a central, enduring "core" or basic personality organization. This core personality is reflected more or less pervasively in the person's behavior, according to psychodynamic theory. And this core is most readily revealed through free responses in an ambiguous, nonthreatening situation of the kind created by projective tests (MacFarlane & Tuddenham, 1951).

Traditionally, projective techniques are presented to the subject with special pains to disguise their purposes. This practice reflects the belief that projective data reveal unacceptable unconscious aspects of the person. Presumably the person has erected defensive maneuvers and censorship operations that prevent the expression of these impulses unless his defenses are relaxed.

Although the general characteristics and purposes of projective tests are widely agreed upon, there is much uncertainty about the actual nature of the "projection" that occurs in response to these tests. One exceptionally clear discussion of projection is offered by Henry A. Murray (1951), who notes that for Freud projection meant the occurrence of a real delusion or misbelief in which the patient actually believes something about another person that is not true. But projection in the projective test situation is not what Freud meant by the term. On the projective test the subject typically is asked to play a game of "make-believe" and obediently does so, obligingly spinning fantasies that he knows are far from reality. As Murray puts it, the subject is encouraged not to project a delusion, but to *imagine* something, to invent interactions or dramas that he creates in his head as he proceeds on the test. Consequently, Murray stresses, in projective testing we are dealing with *imaginative* projection rather than with Freudian projection. The subject's verbal responses should therefore not be automatically interpreted as if they mirrored his real views of the world and his nontest behavior.

## SCORING AND INTERPRETATION

For many years the field was full of workers eagerly trying to invent projective devices. This search for stimulus materials that would elicit rich data about personality resulted in a proliferation of techniques, many of them lacking serious research support. Summaries of these tests are widely available, and reviews have been numerous (e.g., Anderson & Anderson, 1951; Vernon, 1964; Zubin, Eron & Schumer, 1965).

While it has been relatively simple to invent projective devices, it has been extremely difficult to establish what they measure. The initial aim and hope of projectivists was to create a "situationless" situation in which only the core or central aspects of personality would emerge (Frank, 1939). The data elicited by these techniques, however, instead of providing a royal road to the unconscious, seem to include a heterogeneous mixture of verbal responses, momentary states, bits of autobiography, and so on. Projective response, like most other behavior, is "subject to conscious control and distortion and therefore is not necessarily a reliable or valid reflection of personality" (Holmes, 1974, p. 328).

Just what is projected in response to the stimuli employed by projective devices is unclear and controversial (e.g., Murstein, 1963; Zubin, Eron & Schumer, 1965). Thus the meaning of the person's answers is open to diverse clinical interpretations, depending heavily on the theoretical preferences and subjective judgments of the interpreter.

Scores on projective techniques usually depend extensively on the clinician's judgments about the meaning of the responses as signs of traits or dynamic states in the subject. *Interscorer consistency*, or interscorer reliability, must be demonstrated whenever scoring involves subjective judgments, as often occurs with projective data. Interscorer reliability decreases to the extent that highly subjective interpretations are required by the judge. That is, reliability is likely to be low when judgments depend upon the intuitions of the interpreter. For example, "old man strangling boy on couch" in a TAT story might be categorized as reflecting underlying "psychopathic trends," "defense against repressed homosexuality," or "hostile acting-out," depending on the interpreter's subjective judgments. Many critics have recognized that such interpretation may be markedly influenced by projection on the part of the interpreter himself.

Manuals with explicit instructions for scoring help to increase agreement among judges. Agreement is also increased when judges are trained with examples and sample scoring decisions so that they can learn to make similar judgments. Manuals that are sufficiently detailed and objective to permit good scoring reliability have been developed for scoring achievement needs and other motives, as in the work of Atkinson (1958).

## SCORING TAT THEMES: NEED FOR ACHIEVEMENT

One especially important research application of projective techniques has been developed by David C. McClelland and his colleagues (1953), who scored various fantasy indices on the TAT. Specifically, these researchers studied motives as expressed through TAT stories. The motive of greatest interest to them was the need to achieve ("*n* Ach"), defined as competition with a standard of excellence.

The need to achieve has been studied extensively by scoring the subject's achievement imagery in his stories to TAT cards. If, for example, the person creates stories in which the hero is studying hard for a profession and strives to improve himself, to compete against standards of excellence, and to advance far in his career, the story gets high *n* Ach scores. This technique has become an important way of measuring the motive to achieve. It is notable in part because it is a rare example of a fairly objective use of projective data. While this technique is not employed widely with individual clients in clinical assessment, it has been used often in research.

Although TAT and other projective themes and fantasies are interesting in their own right, their relations to other behaviors tend to be complex and indirect. Thoughts and fantasies as measured through projective and story-telling techniques usually are correlated only marginally with measures of relevant overt behavior. For example, achievement concerns and ideation measured from TAT stories relate only in limited ways to other measures of achievement (such as grades or vocational achievements). The same is true for other content areas, such as the associations between aggression imagery and aggression-relevant overt behavior. These conclusions emerge from an enormously extensive tabulation of the correlations obtained between many kinds of motivational imagery (TAT themes) and behavior ratings reported by Skolnick (1966). Sometimes measures of fantasy and thought were found to be positively related to relevant actions, less often negatively, and most frequently not at all. McClelland (1966), reviewing this survey, noted that while the overall number of significant associations implied some degree of relationship, "the relationship is not close." About 25 percent of the predicted relationships were supported, generally at low magnitudes. Although the correlations tend to be small, many associations have been found between $n$ Ach and other measures.

Applied to the individual case, this means we cannot assume that fantasy themes revealed on projective tests are reflected directly in aspects of the person's nontest behavior. For example, Gary might show relatively little achievement striving on the stories he tells to the TAT; nevertheless, he might feel driven to achieve outstandingly in financial and business activities. Moreover, his achievement orientation in business might not be generalized to other areas. For example, he might show much less concern with achievement in intellectual pursuits and social relations. Although limited in their value for understanding the single case, TAT themes may be used fruitfully to study group differences and broad trends. The results often are provocative and theoretically valuable. McClelland (1961), for example, has found intriguing relations between TAT achievement themes and many economic and social measures of achievement orientation in different cultures.

## VALIDITY RESEARCH ON PROJECTIVE TESTS

For more than three decades psychologists have searched for important information about personality by means of projective tests. Hundreds of studies have been conducted on the validity of these projective techniques. The volume of research has become too great for a complete review even in books devoted to that purpose.

The overall results on the major projective techniques suggest that some significant validity correlations are often found. In clinical applications, however, these associations tend to be difficult to interpret firmly because of many methodological problems (e.g., Cronbach, 1949; Zubin, Eron & Schumer, 1965).

Even when obvious identifying data are removed from the protocol, for example, the subject's comments may provide test-irrelevant clues about his occupation, education, ideational bizarreness, interests, achievements, etc. Knowing that the subject is a doctor, for instance, affects the judge's interpretations by giving him many extra cues about the person, but the interpretations in this case reveal nothing about the specific value of the test as a personality measure. Similarly, the degree of homogeneity of subjects in the sample affects how easily judges can discriminate among them. For instance, judges might reliably discriminate the Rorschach protocols of a dozen graduate students from those of twelve acutely disorganized and hospitalized schizophrenics, but they might find it much harder to differentiate among the students. Moreover, clues like the number of responses in the protocol may be correlated with the respondent's intelligence or verbal fluency and thus serve as a basis for prediction apart from the content of the responses or other protocol features on which the interpretation ostensibly hinges.

Apart from the fact that correlations may be spuriously inflated by methodological inadequacies, they are still generally so low that they limit the utility of projective tests for making good decisions about individuals. That is, when the correlations tend to be very low (for example in the .20 to .40 range or lower), they permit one to say little about the person tested. According to critical reviews, predictions based on personality inferences from projective data generally tend to be less accurate than those more easily available from cheaper and simpler data (Mischel, 1968; Peterson, 1968).

Other researchers, while recognizing the practical limitations of projective testing, continue to be fascinated by the projective situation as a method for studying important personality processes. They construe such tests as the Rorschach as providing a kind of perceptual test or an interview setting. In these situations they seek to study persons clinically or to conduct research on the mechanisms of projection (e.g., Zubin, Eron & Schumer, 1965).

Some clinical psychologists have noted that clinical assessments, in accord with psychodynamic theory, require individualized judgments of the meaning of the person's total pattern of behavior. Therefore they argue, properly, that the total personality configuration must be evaluated. This kind of global personality assessment involves intuitive judgments about the meaning of behavior patterns and their relations. Global assessment requires experienced clinicians guided by theory, as well as by intuition, and draws on many data sources rather than on just one or two tests.

# CLINICAL JUDGMENT

While trait theorists rely on tests to infer personality, dynamic theorists rely on the clinician. Most of the fabric of Freudian dynamic theory depends on the hypotheses and inferences generated by experienced clinicians. Consequently while the methodology of trait theory involves research on tests and dimensions, the methodology of dynamic psychology to a large degree involves research into the efficacy of the clinician and his judgments. Some of the most sophisticated clinical studies were conducted by the "Harvard personologists," as discussed next.

## THE HARVARD PERSONOLOGISTS
## AND GLOBAL ASSESSMENT

Henry A. Murray, Robert W. White, and their many colleagues at the Harvard Psychological Clinic provided a rare model for the intensive clinical study of individual lives. Throughout the 1940s and early in the 1950s this group vigorously devoted itself to the portrayal of persons in depth. The Harvard "personologists" (as these students of personality called themselves) were influenced strongly by the dynamic motivational psychology of Freud, by "biosocial" organismic views that emphasized the wholeness, integration, and adaptiveness of personality, and by Gordon Allport's stress on the uniqueness and individuality of every person. They synthesized these influences into a distinct assessment style that became widely respected although only rarely adopted by other psychologists.

The Harvard group focused on intensive, many-faceted studies of small samples of subjects. In one project (Murray, 1938) Harvard college undergraduates were studied over a period of many years and data were gathered on their personality development and maturation at many points in their lives. The techniques in this general "longitudinal" strategy included administering projective and objective tests of many kinds at different times, gathering extensive biographical data on each person, obtaining his own autobiographical sketches, observing his behavior directly, and conducting elaborate interviews with him. These methods probed ingeniously and thoroughly into many topics and most facets of his life (see Table 9-1). The results often provided rich narrative accounts of life histories, as in Robert White's *Lives in Progress* (1952), which traced several lives over many years.

The assessors in the Harvard clinical studies were experienced psychologists who interpreted their data clinically. Usually a group of several assessors studied each subject, and to share their insights they pooled their overall impressions at a staff conference or "diagnostic council." These councils became a model for clinical practice. In them a case conference was conducted in detail and in depth about each individual. On the basis of the council's discussions, inferences were generated about each subject's personality—his basic needs, motives, conflicts, and dynamics; his central dispositions, attitudes, and values; his main character strengths and liabilities. Each piece of assessment information thus served as a sign of the individual's personality as it was interpreted by the council of assessors.

**TABLE 9-1  Examples of Topics Included in the Study of Lives by the Harvard Personologists**

Personal history (early development, school and college, major experiences)

Family relations and childhood memories (including school relations, reactions to authority)

Sexual development (earliest recollections, first experiences, masturbation)

Present dilemmas (discussion of current problems)

Abilities and interests (physical, mechanical, social, economic, erotic)

Aesthetic preferences (judgments, attitudes, tastes regarding art)

Level of aspiration (goal setting, reactions to success and failure)

Ethical standards (cheating to succeed, resistance to temptation)

Imaginal productivity (reactions to inkblots)

Musical reveries (report of images evoked by phonograph music)

Dramatic productions (constructing a dramatic scene with toys)

Based on Murray (1938).

This clinical strategy is illustrated in one of the important applied projects of the personologists—their effort to select officers for the supersensitive Office of Strategic Services (OSS) during the Second World War. OSS officers in World War II had to perform critical and difficult secret intelligence assignments, often behind enemy lines and under great stress. The personologists obviously could not devote the same lengthy time to studying OSS candidates that they had given to Harvard undergraduates in the relaxed prewar days in Cambridge. Nevertheless, they attempted to use the same general strategy of global clinical assessment. For this purpose, teams of assessors studied small groups of OSS candidates intensively, usually for a few days or a weekend, in special secret retreats or "stations" located in various parts of the country. Many different measures were obtained on each candidate.

One of the most interesting innovations was the situational test. In this procedure subjects were required to perform stressful, life-like tasks under extremely difficult conditions. For example, "The Bridge" task required building a wooden bridge under simulated dangerous field conditions and under high stress and anxiety. But such situational tests were not used to obtain a sample of the subjects' bridge-building skills. Instead, the clinicians made higher-order inferences, based on the behavior observed during the task, about each subject's underlying personality. It was these inferences of unobserved attributes or dispositions, rather than the behavior actually observed in the sampled situation, that entered into the assessment report and that became the bases for clinical predictions. In this fashion, behavior samples and situational tests were transformed into inferences about underlying dispositions.

To illustrate, in the *Assessment of Men* by the OSS staff (1948), the bridge-building situation was used to generate answers to questions like these (p. 326):

> Who took the lead in finally crossing the chasm? And why did he do it? Was it to show his superiority? Why did each of the others fall back from the trip? Did they fear failure? It is obvious that the chief value of this situation was to raise questions about personality dynamics which required an explanation on the basis of the personality trends already explored. If these could not supply a reasonable explanation, then new information had to be sought, new deductions made.

In the situational test, just as on the projective test, the subject's behavior thus was clinically interpreted as a clue revealing his personality. Although behavior is sampled and observed, the observations serve mainly as signs from which to infer the motives that prompted the behaviors.

In the global clinical assessment strategy the assessors form their impressions of the subject on the basis of many data sources: his performance on various projective and objective tests, his autobiography and total personal history, and his reactions to thorough interviews. Several assessors study the same person and each generates his own clinical impressions. Later, at a conference, the assessors discuss and share their interpretations and pool their judgments. Gradually they synthesize

**Figure 9-4**   GLOBAL PSYCHODYNAMIC ASSESSMENT

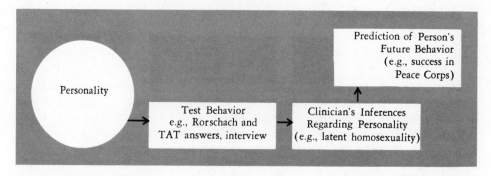

The clinician infers the subject's personality from his test behavior and predicts his future behavior by judging how a person with that personality would probably react to specific future situations.

their impressions and achieve consensus, jointly arriving at a conceptualization of each subject's overall personality structure and dynamics (like the psychodynamic conceptualization of Gary given earlier in this chapter). To predict the person's behavior in a new situation (for example under attack behind enemy lines), they try to infer, from the personality they have hypothesized, how such an individual would probably react to the demands and stresses of that situation. This global assessment model is schematized in Figure 9-4.

## ASSESSING THE CLINICIAN

The explorations of the Harvard personologists made it plain that research on the clinical use of test data actually is inseparable from research on clinical judgment. That is because interpretations about the meaning of test responses as signs of underlying dynamics usually depend on the clinician and his own subjective inferences. In recent years therefore much attention has been devoted to investigations of clinical judgment.

Global judging ability has been evaluated by many different methods (Cline, 1964; Taft, 1955). Perception of emotional expression in photographs, pictures, and movies has sometimes been used in clinical skill research. Clinical judging skills also have been assessed by having judges rate and rank traits, write personality descriptions, match persons with data about them, and predict behavior. Predictions may be about specific behavior, like answers on a personality inventory, or about behavior as general as the person's future occupational success and personality adjustment. Judges have been asked to predict the subject's own responses (e.g., self-ratings, test scores), as well as data about him obtained from observers (e.g., peers, experts). Some of the main results are reviewed next—and they have surprised many people.

## EFFECTS OF CLINICAL TRAINING

To study clinical ability researchers have compared the relative accuracy of judges who had varying degrees of clinical training with those who were untrained. Studies of this kind compare the judgmental accuracy of psychologists, psychiatrists, psychiatric social workers, or other trained clinicians with the judgments of clinically inexperienced groups (e.g., nurses, secretaries, college students). Some studies also investigate the effects of amount of training, usually by comparing the accuracy of judges who have different degrees of clinical experience. The effect of special training programs on subsequent judgmental skill has also been measured.

Crow (1957) studied the effects of clinical training upon global judgmental skill. He placed senior medical students in either an experimental group that received extensive instruction on physician-patient relationships and obtained experience in such relationships through prolonged contacts with patients, or in a control group that remained unexposed to intensive interpersonal training. All students were given tests of interpersonal perception at the beginning, during, and at the conclusion of the training year. On each occasion these tests measured how accurately the judges predicted the self-ratings and actual MMPI test responses of patients whose interview behavior they observed on films.

Unexpectedly, the clinically trained students tended to be *less* accurate than those in the control group. Training led these judges to become much more variable in their estimates (paying more attention to individual differences) than those in the control group. In addition, the trained judges expected less agreement than there was between the patients' self-ratings and their actual test responses. The more the judges tried to take account of individual differences between patients, the less accurate they became. In other words, because of their clinical training, judges became more sensitive and responsive to what they perceived to be individual differences. Consequently they also became less accurate than those who based their predictions on their stereotypes.

On the whole, studies show no clear advantage for trained judges. Psychologists do not score consistently better or worse than nonpsychologists (e.g., secretaries, college students, nurses), and clinical training and experience do not usually improve the accuracy of global judgments (e.g., Danet, 1965; Goldberg, 1959; Kremers, 1960; Luft, 1951). Clinical training and experience may even be somewhat detrimental and may reduce judgmental accuracy, or at least introduce systematic biases, such as a greater emphasis on pathology and less favorable prognoses (e.g., Soskin, 1954, 1959; Taft, 1955). Surprisingly, giving judges accurate feedback information about their predictions does not seem to facilitate their predictive accuracy (Sechrest, Gallimore & Hersch, 1967).

It is possible to criticize much of the laboratory research on accuracy of interpersonal perception and global judgment because it uses artificial situations that do not represent the actual diagnostic problems confronting the practitioner. It may be argued that in practice the clinician is free to base his inferences on his favorite diagnostic technique and is not constricted by the experimenter's techniques. Recognizing these objections, a number of investigators have studied the effects of training on accuracy in common diagnostic tasks typical of those used in the clinic (e.g., Goldberg, 1959). Again, the results tend to be negative and thus consistent with those found from the more artificial laboratory studies (Mischel, 1968).

## COMBINING CLINICAL JUDGES AND TESTS

In their clinical practice, many judges tend to rely on a fairly standard battery of personality tests and techniques for the assessment of most problems. It may therefore be that to obtain good results the clinician has to draw on all these diagnostic aids. This set of procedures usually includes the Rorschach inkblots and often also the TAT and the MMPI. Many clinicians also ask the client to complete a series of unfinished sentences, to draw some pictures, and to participate in a short interview. Responses to all these tests then are interpreted clinically. Researchers have tried to analyze the relative contributions of the different parts of the total procedure as it is used in the clinic.

For example, Kostlan (1954) studied which of the most common data sources and data combinations allow the clinician to make the best personality inferences. He selected four popular sources of clinical information: the social case history, the MMPI, the Rorschach, and an incomplete sentence test (on which the person must finish such sentence stems as "I feel . . ."). Twenty experienced clinical psychologists were the judges, and each was assigned data for five outpatients at a Veterans Administration Psychiatric Clinic. The clinicians worked under each of five conditions. In four conditions *one* of the data sources was missing. For example, the clinician obtained the Rorschach, the sentence completions, and the social history, but not the MMPI. In a fifth condition the clinician saw only a face sheet stating minimal identifying information (age, marital status, occupation, education, and referral source). The judges studied and used the diagnostic data as they would normally, and then indicated their inferences about the patient on a 283-item checklist. To assess the accuracy of these inferences they were compared with those made by a panel of judges who used all four sources of clinical information, and with progress reports from the patients' therapists.

The minimal identifying facts on the fact sheet (age, marital status, etc.) provided inferences that were not surpassed in accuracy by judgments based on any other data source or combination, unless the clinician also had the social case history. Thus only inferences from data that included the social history were more accurate than those from the identifying data alone.

Golden (1964) studied the incremental effects when experienced clinicians combine the Rorschach, TAT, and MMPI tests as opposed to using them singly. He found that neither the reliability nor the validity of clinical inferences increased as a function of the number of tests used, nor were there any differences between tests or pairs of tests. In another study, information from none of the tests used improved predictions beyond the level attained from biographical data alone, and student nurses predicted as well as clinicians when both had only the basic biographical information (Soskin, 1959).

To evaluate clinical inferences properly it is also essential to know their reliability. How well do experienced clinicians reach agreement with each other in the inferences that they derive from standard data sources? A classic study of the reliability of clinical judgments examined the inferences made by expert clinicians from each of five sources (Little & Schneidman, 1959). The sources included the Rorschach, TAT, MMPI, and case histories. Agreement among judges about personality dynamics was only slight. On the whole, the investigators found their results "distressing" (p. 26). No matter how fascinating inferences about personality dynamics may seem intuitively, they cannot be useful when expert judges cannot agree about them.

In a sophisticated study of judgment reliability (Goldberg & Werts, 1966), experienced clinical psychologists independently ranked each of four sets of ten neuropsychiatric patients on one of four traits. The traits were adjustment, ego strength, intelligence, and dependency. These rankings were based on one of four data sources (the MMPI, Rorschach, Wechsler Intelligence Test, or a vocational history). The overall results revealed that "the judgments of one experienced clinician working from one data source bear no relationship to the judgments of another clinician working from another data source" (p. 204), even when the different clinicians are all experienced and are diagnosing the same patient on what is supposed to be the same trait. Essentially similar results have emerged from numerous other investigations. For example, the average clinical interjudge agreement was negligible for inferences from the Rorschach, TAT, and sentence completion protocols (Howard, 1962).

## ARE THERE GOOD JUDGES OF PERSONALITY?

There are large individual differences in accuracy among judges for any judgment task. Is judgmental accuracy strongly consistent across diverse situations so that we can generalize confidently about relatively good or poor judges? One group of studies (Cline, 1964) found some generality in judgmental accuracy. Other studies, however, provided no support for any consistency in the accuracy of clinical judgments (e.g., Crow & Hammond, 1957; Krech, Crutchfield & Ballachey, 1962).

In spite of the overall negative research findings on judgmental accuracy, many clinicians have subjective faith in the utility of their judgments. Is confidence about the validity of inferences related to their empirical accuracy? Oskamp (1965) found that judges became more confident of their judgments as they received more information about a case. However, although self-confidence increased with information, accuracy did not. Moreover, clinicians may confidently agree with each other about the meaning of cues, even when the cues are not valid indicators (e.g., Chapman & Chapman, 1969; Goldberg, 1968).

In sum, studies of clinical inference generally have led to negative conclusions about its predictive validity (e.g., Goldberg, 1959; Holtzman & Sells, 1954; Kelly & Fiske, 1951). Experienced clinicians tend to be no more accurate than inexperienced nonprofessionals like secretaries (Goldberg, 1959; Crow, 1957; Soskin, 1959).

The accuracy of trait inferences is not improved by clinical training; when the judge departs from common stereotypes he may become less accurate (e.g., Crow, 1957; Stelmachers & McHugh, 1964). Moreover, these conclusions generally obtain regardless of the test data on which judges base their interpretations (e.g., Stelmachers & McHugh, 1964). Thus while clinical judgments are often better than random guesses, they usually provide poorer predictions than those available from cheaper and simpler sources like biographical and social case history information, or from the combination of facts by statistical rules (called "actuarial prediction", see Meehl, 1954; Wiggins, 1973).

## ADAPTATION, DEVIANCE, AND CHANGE

Psychodynamic theories have not only had a profound effect on personality assessment, but they have also shaped ideas about adaptation, deviance, and personality change to a degree probably unsurpassed by any other psychological approach.

### THE HEALTHY PERSONALITY

For Freud, a "healthy personality" showed itself in the ability to love and work and required a harmony among id, ego, and superego. Referring to the goal of psychotherapy, Freud used the phrase "Where id was, there shall ego be." He meant that for the healthy personality rational choice and control replace irrational, impulse-driven compulsion. A healthy personality also required "mature" (genital) psychosexual development. In the healthy person, for Freud, genital sexuality replaces earlier forms of psychosexuality. That is, the healthy individual is one who achieves psychosexual maturity, having progressed through the psychosexual stages of development (Chapter 3) without becoming fixated at (or without regressing back to) any early, pregenital stages.

From the psychodynamic perspective, adequate adaptation requires that the individual achieves and accepts sufficient insight into his own unconscious motives. The person who can cope adequately is the one who can face his impulses and conflicts without having to resort to massive unconscious defenses that sap his psychic energy in the service of distorting either his own wishes or reality itself. "Symptoms" represent the return of unsuccessfully repressed materials, reemerging to torture the person in disguised forms; breakdowns represent the inadequacy of defenses to deal with unconscious conflicts and the failure of the ego to achieve sufficient strength to cope with the demands of external reality and the internal pressures of id and super ego as they wage their warfare.

In Freud's words (1940, pp. 62–63):

> . . . The ego has been weakened by the internal conflict; we must come to its aid. The position is like a civil war which can only be decided by the help of an ally from without. The analytical physician and the weakened ego of the

For Freud, a healthy personality requires mature psychosexual development.

patient, basing themselves upon the real external world, are to combine against the enemies, the instinctual demands of the id, and the moral demands of the superego. We form a pact with each other. The patient's sick ego promises us the most candor, promises, that is, to put at our disposal all of the material which his self-perception provides; we, on the other hand, assure him of the strictest discretion and put at his service our experience in interpreting material that has been influenced by the unconscious. Our knowledge shall compensate for his ignorance and shall give his ego once more mastery over the lost provinces of his mental life. This pact constitutes the analytic situation.

## BEHAVIOR AS A SYMPTOM OF PSYCHODYNAMICS

Consistent with psychoanalytic theory, the psychodynamic approach views an individual's problematic behavior as symptomatic (rather than of main interest in its own right) and searches for the possible causes of these symptoms by making inferences about his personality dynamics. For example, an individual who has a

189

bad stutter might be viewed as repressing his hostility, one with asthma as suffering from dependency conflicts, and one with snake fears as victimized by unconscious sexual problems. This focus on the meaning of behavior as a symptom (sign) guides the psychodynamic strategy for understanding both normal and abnormal behavior. Thus the psychodynamically oriented clinician seeks to infer the person's unconscious conflicts, his defense structure, problems in his psychosexual development, and the symbolic meaning and functions of his behavior.

Many features of the traditional psychodynamic approach to adaptation and deviance are illustrated in the Freudian conceptualization of Gary (pp. 169–171). The report refers to Gary's fear of injury, his anxiety in social situations and fear of public speaking, and his problems in forming close relations. Rather than conceptualizing these behaviors as problems in their own right, they are viewed as signs (symptoms) that reflect (often very indirectly) such hypothetical, inferred problems as his "castration anxiety," "need for control," "unresolved Oedipal themes," "brittle defenses," and "basic insecurity."

## PSYCHOANALYTIC PSYCHOTHERAPIES

Most forms of psychotherapy that view problematic behavior as a symptom have tried to achieve change by helping the individual to gain insight, awareness, and self-acceptance. Traditionally, this type of therapy is pursued in the context of a relationship between the client and the clinician that evolves over a lengthy period of time during regular interview meetings. Generally the meetings involve a verbal exchange of about an hour's duration several times weekly in the clinician's office. The major influence on such psychotherapy has been Freud's psychoanalytic therapy. The objective of psychoanalytic therapy is to give the person insight into the unconscious motives and conflicts believed to determine his behavior. Freud maintained that the major aim of psychoanalytic treatment should be to make the person's unconscious become conscious. In the ideally psychoanalyzed person unconscious motives purportedly become largely recognized and conscious. Therefore psychoanalytically oriented treatment tries to increase the person's capacity for insight so that he can recognize his unconscious impulses and their expressions. In addition to getting insight, the person hopefully learns to "accept" his impulses. Such insight, and the conversion of the unconscious to the conscious by removal of repressions and other defenses, is believed to reduce symptoms and to be a prerequisite for durable behavior change.

The focus is on the inferred personality dynamics and unconscious motives rather than on the observed symptoms because of the belief that changes in the overt behavior (or symptoms) will lead to new (and perhaps even worse) behavioral manifestations unless the underlying conflicts and psychic problems are treated (Chapter 3). That is, "symptom change" or behavioral alterations, are believed to be followed by new symptoms, or "symptom substitution," unless the psychic roots are uncovered. For example, in this view, removal of a snake phobia might produce new symptoms unless the unconscious and symbolic meanings of the fear are explored and their dynamic bases changed. Similarly, frigidity in a woman might be seen as a symptom of her basic sexual conflicts. If that is true, then efforts to teach her to enjoy sexual relations would only mask her underlying problems without solving them. In Gary's case, efforts to directly reduce his fear of public speaking, for example, might result in even more severe unconscious blocks such as facial ticks or speech impairment. The psychodynamic conceptualization suggests that help for Gary's fears, or for his interpersonal problems, requires working with him to achieve and accept insights into their emotional origins and unconscious meanings.

From the psychoanalytic viewpoint, insight means more than intellectual or rational recognition of one's unconscious impulses. Psychoanalysts often distinguish intellectual from emotional insight, the latter being considered vital for therapeutic progress and for fully adequate functioning. Emotional insight implies that the person "works through" his problems and comes to understand and accept his impulses fully, not merely in an abstract, detached, rational way.

According to psychoanalytic theory, the greatest barrier to insight is the person's own defensiveness. The potential eruption of unconscious materials generates anxiety, which the individual avoids by developing *resistance* to facing his conflicts and true motives. For example, he may try unconsciously to steer the therapeutic interview away from the issues and feelings that are most problematic for him. In psychoanalysis these resistances are slowly overcome, with the aid of interpretation by the therapist. The person's free associations (saying whatever comes to mind) and the analysis of his dreams are important vehicles for facilitating the release of repressed material and overcoming defensive resistance.

This process of working through and achieving insights is believed to grow out of the intense transference relationship that the client develops with respect to the therapist. Psychodynamic theory suggests that feelings and problems that were experienced initially in relations with the parents or siblings during childhood now are transferred to the relationship with the therapist. Gradually, according to the theory, unconscious resistances and defenses against threatening ideas and feelings are overcome: the client slowly faces, works through, and accepts his unconscious impulses and conflicts. He thus achieves insight and basic change in his personality.

While Freud's ideas have been most influential, many treatment variations and innovations have been introduced by Freudians and other contemporary psychotherapists. The specific style and conduct of the psychotherapeutic interview thus has gone through many changes, and the exact procedures and interpretations that are used depend on the theoretical viewpoint of the particular clinician (e.g., Alexander & French, 1946). To the extent that different psychotherapists adhere to somewhat different concepts about the nature of basic personality dynamics, they are likely to emphasize different interpretations and techniques and to focus on different aspects of the client's behavior.

## LIMITATIONS AND NEW DIRECTIONS
## IN PSYCHOTHERAPIES

Traditional psychodynamic psychotherapies in general have been criticized in recent years on at least three counts.

1. First, the validity and meaning of the client's insights into his unconscious motives and "real underlying feelings" has been questioned. If experienced clinicians cannot reach agreement about the psychodynamic meaning of the client's behavior, and if they adhere to different conceptions of human motivation and personality dynamics, depending on their particular theory, then what do the client's "insights" and "awareness" really mean? The question is particularly troublesome in light of the limited support found for the role of unconscious processes in research on defense mechanisms (Chapter 18). Given these facts, skeptics suggest that the patient's "cure" may largely consist of his conversion to the clinician's belief system (e.g., Bandura, 1969). Thus clients whose therapists are Freudians may acquire Freudian insights; those treated by Jungians gain Jungian insights; those treated by disciples of Fromm achieve insights consistent with his view; and so on. In other words, in treatment the client may learn to conceptualize himself in terms of his clinician's favored theoretical constructs.

This criticism is cogent, but it does not necessarily imply that these reconceptualizations have no value. Consider, for example, a man who has construed himself as "a failure, a queer, stupid and weak." It is plausible that he may benefit from reconceptualizing himself, in part, for example, as "neurotic, conflicted, victimized by a castrating mother, and driven by unconscious guilt." Regardless of their absolute truth value, such reinterpretations may provide the individual with a less aversive and more convenient set of constructs about himself. It would be most important, however, to show that these reconceptualizations also help the person to deal more effectively with his life problems and with the troubles that led him to seek help in the first place.

2. Second, the value of traditional therapeutic activities is seriously questioned by studies on the outcomes that they yield. In 1952 Eysenck's review of treatment outcomes noted that the improvement rate was about 64 percent for patients who received intensive and prolonged psychotherapy. This rate did not exceed the improvement rate (72 percent) for similar patients who were treated only custodially (by confinement in mental hospitals) or by general practitioners. In a follow-up almost 10 years later, Eysenck (1961) found nothing to change the picture. On the contrary, more data indicated that untreated patients did not differ from those who received intensive psychotherapy, both groups showing some improvement.

Eysenck's conclusions are themselves open to severe criticism and are not widely accepted (e.g., Bergin, 1971; Kiesler, 1966; Rosenzweig, 1954). The methodological limitations of most research on treatment outcomes are great, and therefore firm conclusions have been hard to reach; the literature on the outcomes of psychotherapy is extremely difficult to interpret. Nevertheless, while not as dismal as Eysenck implied, most of the results (e.g., Bandura, 1969; Bergin, 1966, 1971) do

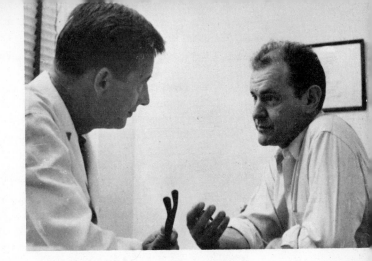

Psychotherapy research must discover *"what* treatment, by *whom,* is most effective for *this* individual with *that* specific problem . . ."

not provide strong evidence in favor of traditional psychotherapy. The research evidence supporting psychoanalytic therapy leads even highly sympathetic reviewers to conclude, "Quantitative research on psychoanalytic therapy presents itself, so far, as an unreliable support for clinical practice" (Luborsky & Spence, 1971, p. 430). Yet many experienced clinicians remain convinced that much of value exists in psychodynamically oriented therapy and believe that future research should be devoted to identifying its most promising components. Regardless of theoretical orientation, there is wide agreement that research must be more specific than it has been, and must be aimed at discovering *"what* treatment, by *whom,* is most effective for *this* individual with *that* specific problem, and under *which* set of circumstances" (Paul, 1967b, p. 111). While traditional psychotherapy taken as a whole may not produce strong overall effects, some people may be significantly helped by it while others may be actively hurt by it. The potential gain or loss would depend on the particular person, problem, and therapist.

3. Finally, assuming that traditional psychotherapies surely do help some people, they still would have only limited value for meeting the enormous psychological problems that our society faces. Indeed only a small percentage of people would qualify for traditional psychotherapy. In regard to psychoanalysis, for example, Freud believed that the good prospective patient should possess a reasonable degree of education and be fairly young; he should be sufficiently distressed by his problems to want to change, but not too distressed because psychoanalytic therapy cannot be conducted with severely confused, depressed, or debilitated persons (Freud, 1959, Vol. 1). Similarly, people with severe fears or obsessions were thought to be poor risks because they had given in to their symptoms completely, thus reducing anxiety and motivation for therapy (Freud, 1959, Vol. 2). Given these limitations and the costs and time required for psychoanalytic treatment, the method would be either inappropriate or unavailable for most troubled people even if it were proved valuable for some. As early as 1918 Freud said:

> You know that the therapeutic effects we can achieve are very inconsiderable in number. We are but a handful of people, and even by working hard each

one of us can deal in a year with only a small number of persons. Against the vast amount of neurotic misery which is in the world, and perhaps need not be, the quantity we can do away with is almost negligible. Besides this, the necessities of our own existence limit our work to the well-to-do classes. . . . At present we can do nothing in the crowded ranks of the people, who suffer exceedingly from neuroses (1959, Vol. 2, p. 401).

Many clinicians have recognized the need for new forms of therapy and behavior change; numerous promising strategies have been developed to meet practical challenges in helping people. These efforts cover such diverse approaches as community mental health programs and preventive counseling in the schools (e.g., Cowen, Gardner, & Zax, 1967), therapy conducted conjointly with the whole family rather than with the individual alone (Satir, 1967), and innovations stimulated by the concepts of existential psychology (e.g., Laing, 1965). Perhaps the most popular new developments are therapeutic groups (discussed in Chapter 12) and behavior therapies (Chapter 11).

## IMPLICATIONS

Confronted with results of the kind reviewed in this chapter, psychologists have reacted in many ways. Some have construed the negative research data on psychodynamically oriented clinical applications as reflecting mainly on specific techniques, judges, or clinicians, or on the limitations of the research strategies (e.g., Wachtel, 1973), but not on the basic assumptions of the psychodynamic approach that guided them. As a result many still use, and rely on, techniques like the Rorschach and the TAT, often employing them more like an interview than a standardized test. They point out that these devices simply provide a set of ambiguous stimuli to which the person reacts; the clinician then bases his assessments in part on his interpretations of the dynamic meanings revealed by the test behavior. Likewise, they continue to practice psychodynamically oriented therapy, noting: "We dare not make changes so we stay with the old model, not because it is necessarily the best, but because we have poor rules for testing it" (Luborsky & Spence, 1971, p. 432). Critics contend, however, that the justifiability of this practice depends upon the evidence supporting the value of clinical inferences and judgments about dispositions and the efficacy of psychodynamic therapy.

### ALTERNATIVE STRATEGIES

Regardless of what the ultimate conclusion may prove to be, many psychologists are beginning to pursue a variety of directions vigorously. In one direction, the clinical judgment process itself is being analyzed (e.g., Bieri et al., 1966; Goldberg, 1968; Wiggins, 1973). Rather than studying the accuracy of the judge, researchers are examining *how* he judges personality and the mechanisms of his inferences. Other investigators have been studying a closely related area: "person perception" and the processes through which people form impressions of each other and of themselves (e.g., Anderson, 1965, 1972). Attention is thus turning to the "information processing" of the human judge and to the cognitive activity of the clinician. Investigations in this vein reveal some of the complexities of the information processing that underlies social judgments in general, and clinical inferences in particular. Computers also may help to simulate human judgment processes and even serve as analogs for personality structure and dynamics. For example, Dr. Kenneth Colby has been designing computer programs that behave like psychoanalysts and is studying how they work. This strategy has made the high-speed computer its ally (e.g., Colby, 1965; Colby & Hilf, 1973; Loehlin, 1968).

Some researchers also have tried to analyze the processes that occur in various types of person-clinician interactions such as the interview in psychotherapy and to discover the essential skills of effective therapists (e.g., Truax & Mitchell, 1971). They suggest that the limitations of the clinician may reflect more on his lack of interpersonal skills than on the personality theory that guides him. Consequently they emphasize the therapist's personality more than his personality theory.

In still another direction, some psychodynamically oriented investigators have turned to research on cognitive processes, emotions, and "ego functions." Their interest has tended to shift away from unconscious motives and impulses to the person's modes of dealing with information—his cognitive styles for handling problems. "Cognitive styles" refer to self-consistent ways of approaching and transforming information, especially through perception, memory, and thought. Influenced by the "ego psychologists," psychodynamic researchers have looked for consistent cognitive and emotional styles that people might habitually employ in coping with the problems of their lives. These researchers are influenced by psychodynamic concepts, but they follow a methodology that does not depend on the clinician and that takes full account of current developments in the study of cognition and information processing (e.g., Singer & Antrobus, 1972). For example, they rely on objective tests of perceptual and cognitive problem-solving (e.g., the speed with which the subject can find a hidden figure embedded in a picture), as in the work of Witkin (1965).

## NEED FOR NEW ASSUMPTIONS?

A final reaction to negative data of the sort discussed in this chapter has questioned not merely psychodynamic methods but also the theoretical assumptions that guide them (e.g., Bandura, 1971; Krasner & Ullmann, 1973; Peterson, 1968). Thus not only the methods are being challenged but also the psychodynamic constructs that led to them and govern their use. These critics have started to pursue completely different routes. Rather than inferring unconscious motives, searching for insights, or seeking generalized dispositions, they are trying to discover the specific conditions that cause important *change* in behavior (for example, as discussed in Chapter 11). They also have urged an approach to persons that focuses on the experimental analysis of their behavior, described in the next chapter.

## SUMMARY

1. Psychodynamically oriented psychologists attempt to study personality in depth and try to eliminate situational interferences in the hope of circumventing defenses and reaching basic dynamics and motives. Guided by psychoanalytic theory, the traditional focus has been on reconstructions of early history, particularly the early handling of sexual and aggressive impulses, and inferences regarding personality in global, dynamic terms.

2. In the psychodynamic approach the Rorschach and the TAT (Thematic Apperception Test) are projective tests that have been especially popular. The Rorschach consists of a series of complex inkblots. The subject says what the inkblots resemble or look like to him. The TAT consists of a series of ambiguous pictures for which subjects are asked to make up a story.

3. The main characteristics of projective techniques are that they are presented as ambiguous tasks for the subject; the purpose of the test is disguised, and the person is free to respond as he wishes. The clinician then may interpret the meaning of the answers in accord with his theory, experience, and intuitions, trying to infer the person's psychodynamics and personality from his responses.

4. The Freudian concept of projection as a defense mechanism should not be confused with projective techniques. Projection for Freud was a real delusion or misbelief on the part of the patient. Projective tests deal with imaginative projection, or "make-believe," which the subject is encouraged to produce on the test.

5. Several procedures have been devised to handle the complex questions of reliability and validity of interpretations made from projective test responses. It is especially important to demonstrate interscorer consistency—the degree to which different judges arrive at the same interpretive statements from the same test data. Manuals with explicit instructions and practice training help increase agreement among judges.

6. The study of achievement motives as expressed through TAT stories has been carefully standardized by means of objective scoring procedures. Research on the need for achievement as expressed in TAT themes has yielded an extensive network of correlations.

7. Research on the clinical uses of projective tests indicates that many methodological problems make it difficult to interpret the results clearly. Most important, the correlations that are found tend to be too low to permit more accurate predictions about individuals than could be made from simpler data.

8. The clinician is a central instrument in psychodynamic assessment. Harvard personologists have provided a model for the intensive clinical study of individuals. Trained assessors collected diverse data on each subject and, in council, made inferences about the individual's personality dynamics.

9. The validity of clinical judgment must be evaluated empirically. Surprisingly but consistently, studies on the effect of clinical training do not show a clear advantage for trained judges in making global judgments. Research also indicates that the information from various clinical tests does not enable the experienced clinician to make more accurate predictions than he could have made from biographical data. Experienced judges may not agree with each other in their inferences about personality dynamics even when they are using the same test data from the same individual.

10. The psychodynamic approach to adaptation and deviance distinguishes between symptom and underlying disorder and seeks such hypothetical causes as internal conflicts, dynamics, and unconscious motives.

11. Influenced by Freud's theory, most traditional approaches to personality change have emphasized insight and awareness and acceptance of unconscious motives and feelings, although there have been many variations in specific techniques and theory. The efficacy of these approaches to personality change has been questioned on both practical and theoretical grounds and there now is a search for useful innovations such as encounter groups.

12. Reactions to criticisms regarding psychodynamic assessment and psychotherapy have been divided. On the one hand, the problems have been judged to reflect inadequacies in specific techniques and research methods. Consequently further attention is being focused on clinical processes and on clarifying person-clinician interactions. Influenced by the "ego psychologists" and new orientations in psychodynamic theory, other researchers have turned to the study of personality and "cognitive styles." Another reaction has been more radical: it has questioned the basic theoretical assumptions that guide psychodynamic applications and has found other ways of conceptualizing, assessing, and modifying behavior.

# CHAPTER 10

# BEHAVIORAL THEORIES
# Applications (I)

Because there have been several distinctly different behavioral approaches to personality (Chapters 4 and 5), it should not be surprising that each of these has led to somewhat different applications. The psychodynamic behavior theory of Miller and Dollard drew mainly on the experimental methods of general psychology, testing its hypotheses in carefully conducted experiments. Psychologists influenced by B. F. Skinner's formulations often began by studying pigeons and other animals in the laboratory. More recently they have applied their ideas to clinical settings and devised assessments and behavior change programs for a wide range of human problems. The assessment and modification of complex behavior in diverse clinical and experimental settings also has been guided by various other social learning theories. This chapter considers the applications of behavioral theories to assessment; the next chapter examines their applications to behavior change.

# CHARACTERISTICS OF SOCIAL
# BEHAVIOR APPLICATIONS

Applications of current social behavior theory focus on selected, carefully defined behaviors and the observable stimulus conditions that seem to covary with them. One tries to observe what the person does, rather than to infer what he has or is. The search is for the stimulus conditions controlling or causing particular behavior patterns; one does not try to interpret the behaviors as indirect signs of the person's underlying motives and dispositions. For this purpose behavioral assessments seek to specify objectively the response patterns of interest, and to identify relevant stimulus conditions.

The common denominator of all behavioral methods is their emphasis on the careful measurement of specific behavior in relation to systematic changes in stimulus conditions. This focus on the covariation between changes in events (the stimulus conditions) and changes in responses (the person's behavior) is a fundamental feature of "stimulus-response" approaches. The emphasis on how changes in stimulus conditions lead to alterations in responses is also a chief characteristic of the experimental method that has been an important model for behavioral approaches.

## BEHAVIOR AS SIGN OR SAMPLE?

The trait and dynamic approaches discussed in previous chapters searched for tests from which to infer dispositions, or depended on clinical judges to interpret the individual's dynamics from his behavior. Investigators who were guided by the assumption that personality traits and dynamics would be very broadly pervasive studied behavior in highly generalized or "typical" contexts, rather than in well-specified situations. Their preference for items dealing with reactions to general rather than specific situations is related to their belief in broad dispositions that cause general and enduring behavioral consistencies across many different situations. In accord with that belief, they have selected items that refer to relatively general, vague, or typical situations, trying to minimize the role of specific stimuli or conditions. The most extreme forms of this preference for ambiguous stimuli are the blurred pictures of the TAT or the inkblots of the Rorschach.

In contrast, behavioral assessments have been guided by a greater emphasis on the role of stimulus conditions as moderators and regulators of behavior. Rather than seeking behavioral signs of the individual's general traits and motives, behavioral approaches have focused on the specific conditions and processes—both "inside" and "outside" the person—that might govern his behavior. For this purpose behaviorally oriented psychologists have followed an experimental strategy in which stimulus conditions are varied so that one can observe systematically any changes in the behavior of interest in relation to the changing conditions.

In one sense, all psychological approaches are based on behavioral observation: check marks on MMPI answer sheets and stories in response to inkblots obviously are behaviors just as much as crying or running or fighting. Moreover, we saw that the dynamic approach also samples such life-like behaviors as bridge-building under stress in the OSS research. The difference between approaches depends on how these behaviors are used. As we saw, in the dynamic orientation the observed behaviors serve as highly indirect *signs* (symptoms) of the dispositions and motives that might underlie them. In contrast, in behavior assessments the observed behavior is treated as a *sample*, and interest is focused on how the specific sampled behavior is affected by alterations in conditions. Behavioral approaches thus seek to directly assess stimulus-response covariations.

## CASE EXAMPLE: CONDITIONS CONTROLLING GARY'S ANXIETY

The general strategy of behavior assessment can be illustrated by once again considering the case of Gary W. An assessment of Gary in the framework of a behavioral orientation obviously would focus on his behavior in relation to stimulus conditions. But what behaviors, and in relation to which conditions? Rather than seeking a portrait of Gary's personality and behavior "in general," or an estimate of his "average" or dominant propensities and attributes, a behavioral perspective dictates a much more specific focus. The particular behavior patterns selected for study depend on the particular problem that requires investigation. In clinical situations, priorities are indicated by the client; in research contexts, they are selected by the investigator.

During his first term of graduate school Gary found himself troubled enough to seek help at the school's counseling center. As part of the behavioral assessment that followed, Gary was asked to list and rank in order of importance the three problems that he found most distressing in himself and that he wanted to change if possible. He listed "feeling anxious and losing my grip" as his greatest problem. To assess the behavioral referents for his felt "anxiety," Gary was asked to specify in more detail just what changes in himself indicated to him that he was or was not anxious and "losing his grip."

He indicated that when he became anxious he felt changes in his heart rate, became tense, perspired, and found it most difficult to speak coherently. Next, to explore the covariation between increases and decreases in this state and changes in stimulus conditions, Gary was asked to keep an hour-by-hour diary sampling most of the waking hours during the daytime for a period of two weeks and indicating the type of activity that occurred during each hour. Discussion with him of this record suggested that anxiety tended to occur primarily in connection with public speaking occasions—specifically, in classroom situations in which he was required to speak before a group. As indicated by the summary shown in Table 10-1, only on one occasion that was not temporally close to public speaking did Gary find himself highly anxious. That occasion turned out to be one in which he was brooding in his room, thinking about his public speaking failures in the classroom.

Having established a seemingly reliable covariation between the occurrence of

**TABLE 10-1    Occurrence of Gary's Self-Reported Anxiety Attacks in Relation to Public Speaking**

| OCCURRENCE OF ANXIETY | HOURS WITH ANXIETY (10) | HOURS WITHOUT ANXIETY (80) |
|---|---|---|
| Within 1 hour of public speaking | 9 (90%) | 0 (0%) |
| No public speaking within 1 hour | 1 (10%) | 80 (100%) |

anxiety and public speaking in the social-evaluative conditions of the classroom, his assessors delineated the specific components of the public speaking situation that led to relatively more and less anxiety. The purpose here was to establish a hierarchy of anxiety-evoking stimuli ranging from the mild to the exceedingly severe. This hierarchy then was used in a treatment designed to gradually desensitize Gary to these fear stimuli by "systematic desensitization" (described in the next chapter).

Note that this behavioral assessment of Gary is quite specific: it is not an effort to characterize his whole personality, to describe "what he is like," or to infer his motives and dynamics. Instead, the assessment restricts itself to some clearly delineated problems and tries to analyze them in objective terms without extrapolating beyond the observed relations. Moreover, the analysis focuses on the *conditions* in which Gary's behavior occurs and on the covariation between those conditions and his problem. Behavior assessment tends to be focused assessment, usually concentrating on those aspects of behavior that can be changed and that require change. Indeed, as will be seen often in this chapter, behavior assessment and behavior change (treatment) are almost inextricably fused.

The foregoing assessment of Gary illustrates one rather crude form of studying stimulus-response covariations. Of course there are many different ways in which these covariations can be sampled. This chapter illustrates some of the main tactics developed for the direct measurement of human behavior within the framework of the social behavior orientation.

## DIRECT BEHAVIOR MEASUREMENT

For many purposes in personality study it is important to sample and observe behavior in carefully structured, life-like or *in vivo* situations. In clinical applications, direct observation may give both client and assessor an opportunity to assess life problems and to select treatment objectives. Direct observation of behavior samples also may be used to assess the relative efficacy of various treatment procedures. Finally, behavior sampling has an important part in experimental research on personality.

The types of data collected in the behavioral approach include situational samples of both nonverbal and verbal behavior, as well as physiological measurements of emotional reactions. In addition, a comprehensive assessment often includes an analysis of effective rewards or reinforcing stimuli in the person's life. Examples of all of these measures are given in the following sections.

## SITUATIONAL BEHAVIOR SAMPLING

Many informal attempts have been made to record people's behavior in ongoing life-like situations. For example, a concealed observer may try to write or dictate an account of the naturalistic behavior that he is watching. This procedure has the disadvantage of requiring the observer to devote part of his attention to the actual recording and thus restricts the attention he can pay to the subject's ongoing behavior. Informal observations often also suffer from lack of precision. Lovaas and his associates (1965b) wanted a comprehensive description that would contain not only the behaviors the subject performed but also the duration and the specific time of onset of each type of behavior. Such detailed information is needed if one wants to determine the covariations among an individual's specific behaviors, or their alterations in relation to various changes in his environment and in the behavior of other people.

Lovaas and his collaborators (1965b) devised an apparatus that consists of a panel of buttons that are depressed by the observer. Each button represents a category of behavior (for example, "talking," "running," "sitting alone") and is attached to an automatic pen-recorder. Whenever a button is depressed, the corresponding pen on the recorder is activated. A continuous record is thus provided.

The observer depresses the button when the subject starts the specific behavior designated by that button and does not release the button until the particular behavior is discontinued. The observer after a little practice can devote his whole attention to watching what the subject is doing and yet record up to twelve different categories of behavior without looking at the button panel. The apparatus permits a record that is precise enough to include duration and the specific time of onset of each behavior. The method can then be applied to discover covariations among the individual's different behaviors and between his behavior and that of other people in the situation.

Even without the aid of such sophisticated apparatus, there have been many attempts to measure important interpersonal and emotional behaviors precisely. Some impressive examples come from assessments of the intensity or magnitude of such emotional behaviors as seemingly irrational fears (phobias).

The strength of diverse avoidance behaviors has been assessed reliably in clinical situations by exposing fearful individuals to series of real or symbolic fear-inducing stimuli. For example, fear of heights was assessed by measuring the distance that the phobic person could climb on a metal fire escape (Lazarus, 1961). The same people were assessed again after receiving therapy to alleviate their fears. In this phase the subjects were invited to ascend eight stories by elevator to a roof garden and to count the passing cars below for two minutes. Claustrophobic behavior—fear of closed spaces—was measured by asking each person to sit in a cubicle containing large French windows opening onto a balcony. The assessor shut the windows and slowly moved a large screen nearer and nearer to the subject, thus gradually constricting his space. Of course each subject was free to open the windows, and thereby to terminate the procedure, whenever he wished, although he was instructed to persevere as long as possible. The measure of claustrophobia was the least distance at which the person could tolerate the screen.

To measure fear and avoidance responses to snakes, fearful volunteer subjects were exposed to snakes in a laboratory (Lang & Lazovik, 1963; Lang, Lazovik & Reynolds, 1965). At first each volunteer was asked simply to look down into a top-less glass case, 15 feet from the entrance to the room, that contained a nonpoison-ous, five-foot black snake. The subject was assured that the snake was harmless and was invited to come as close as he could. If he could come all the way to the case, the experimenter touched the snake and asked the subject to try to do so also. If the subject succeeded, the assessor picked up the snake barehanded and asked the subject to hold it. Each of the increasingly bold approach steps was scored. In addition to measuring approach behavior directly, some studies also asked people to rate their subjective reactions after trying the actual approach behavior (Lang, Lazovik & Reynolds, 1965).

Another study assessed nursery-school children's fear of dogs (Bandura, Grusec & Menlove, 1966). Each child was led into a room containing, in the far corner, a playpen in which a dog was enclosed. The children's approach behavior was scaled objectively according to how near they ventured toward the animal. To get the highest scores the child had to climb into the playpen and sit in it while playing with the dog.

Direct behavior sampling has also been tried extensively in the analysis of psychotic behavior. One study, for instance, employed a time-sampling technique. At regular 30-minute intervals, psychiatric nurses sought out and observed each hospitalized patient for periods of one to three minutes, without directly interacting with him (Ayllon & Haughton, 1964). The behavior observed in each sample was classified for the occurrence of three previously defined behaviors (for example, psychotic talk), and the time-check recordings were used to compute the relative frequency of the various behaviors. This time-sampling technique was supplemented by recordings of all the interactions between patient and nurses (such as each time the patient entered the nursing office). The resulting data served as a basis for designing and evaluating a treatment program.

## VERBAL BEHAVIOR

What a person says—his "verbal behavior"—may be just as important as what he does nonverbally. Most personality assessors, guided by trait and psychodynamic theories, have focused on verbalizations as signs of personality, rather than as descriptions of reactions to stimulus conditions. In social behavior assessment, on the other hand, what the person says is intended to help define the relevant stimuli and the response patterns that they have come to evoke and to specify the covariations between them. For example, a number of self-report techniques have been used to sample specific self-reported fears (Geer, 1965; Lang & Lazovik, 1963; Wolpe & Lang, 1964). These schedules list many items that were found to elicit frequent anxiety in patients. The respondent indicates on scales the degree of disturbance provoked by such items as strangers, bats, ugly people, mice, making mistakes, and looking foolish.

As was illustrated in the assessment of Gary's public speaking anxieties, a daily record may provide another valuable first step in the identification of problem-producing stimuli. Many behaviorally oriented clinicians routinely ask their clients to keep specific records listing the exact conditions under which their anxieties and problems seem to increase or decrease (Wolpe & Lazarus, 1966). The person may be asked to prepare by himself lists of all the stimulus conditions or events that create discomfort, distress, or other painful emotional reactions.

Metcalfe (1956) conducted an analysis of stimulus conditions controlling bronchial asthmatic seizures in a young female patient. The young woman kept a detailed diary during an 85-day period in which she was hospitalized but free to visit outside. She was instructed to record all symptoms related to respiration, particularly "real asthmatic attacks" (involving tightness of the chest, wheezing, and severe respiratory distress). She also was asked to record physical symptoms not related to respiration and all her activities such as games, dancing, occupational therapy, shopping, meetings, and visits.

In this time period asthmatic attacks occurred on 15 of the 85 days. An examination of the temporal relations between her self-reported activities and asthmatic attacks indicated that contacts with her mother appeared to be a main eliciting condition for asthma: 9 of her 15 attacks followed recent contact with her mother. Moreover, 80 percent of her asthma-free days occurred when she had no contact with her mother. No strong relations were found between the occurrence of attacks and other possible sources of stress, such as interviews. Further assessments confirmed that contact with the mother in the home appeared to be the main stimulus for asthmatic episodes. As Metcalfe's case study suggests, verbal reports (in the form of written records) may be helpful in behavior assessment, especially when it is inconvenient and unfeasible to observe the person's daily life patterns directly.

Although often helpful, verbal descriptions are not completely adequate substitutes for direct sampling of life behaviors *in vivo*. Many people (for example, children, disorganized adults, people with language deficiencies) cannot supply accurate descriptions. Moreover, even with articulate individuals, verbal self-reports may not be accurate.

Metcalfe also showed his client words associated with the mother and mother-relevant pictorial stimuli on the TAT and Rorschach. Neither these stimuli nor interview discussions about her mother elicited asthmatic attacks. These results show that responses to verbal or symbolic presentations of stimuli (in interviews and tests) may not be adequate substitutes for assessment of direct reactions to the real events supposedly represented by the symbolic stimuli.

## MEASUREMENT OF BODILY CHANGES

Measures of bodily changes in response to stimulation also provide important information, especially when the stimuli are stressful or arousing. Various indirect measures of bodily reactions during emotional activity have been developed. One of the most convenient methods is the polygraph recording of some of the critical effects produced by the bodily activity involved in the reactions of the autonomic nervous system. The polygraph apparatus contains a series of devices that translate indices of body changes into a visual record by deflecting a pen across a moving paper chart.

One popular component of polygraphic measurement is the *electrocardiogram* (*EKG*). As the heart beats its muscular contractions produce patterns of electrical activity that may be detected by electrodes placed near the heart on the body surface. Figure 10-1 shows a record of heartbeats monitored by the polygraph, the area from one peak to another on the record representing one beat of the heart. An especially useful index of heart activity is based on the *rate* at which the person's heart is beating: it is measured in terms of the time between each beat on the electrocardiogram.

In a basically similar manner, changes in blood volume may be recorded by means of a *plethysmograph*. Other examples of valuable indices include changes in the electrical activity of the skin due to sweating (recorded by a galvanometer and called the *galvanic skin response* or *GSR*), changes in blood pressure, and changes in muscular activity.

Intense emotional arousal is generally accompanied by high levels of "activation" (e.g., Malmo, 1959), shown by increases in the activity of the cerebral cortex, increases in muscle tension and, at the behavioral level, increasingly vigorous activity and excitement. The degree of activation in the cerebral cortex may be inferred from "brain waves" recorded by the electroencephalograph (EEG), as illustrated in the records shown in Figure 10-2. As the EEG patterns in this figure indicate, the frequency, amplitude, and other characteristics of brain waves vary according to the subject's degree of behavioral arousal and excitement.

It is obviously difficult to study bodily changes in life-like situations if one has to keep the subject in a fixed position and hooked up with elaborate wiring to a big machine. While these conditions permit laboratory studies they hinder attempts to sample physiological changes under *in vivo* conditions. A radio link between the electrode and the main apparatus makes it possible to eliminate the usual wires and provides many advantages, permitting the researcher to move the subject outside the confines of the laboratory. This procedure is called *telemetry*. The subject wears a simple miniature radio transmitter, which relays the signals from biological events picked up by electrodes. The transmission is picked up by the distant re-

Figure 10-1 HEART RHYTHM IN AN ELDERLY SUBJECT

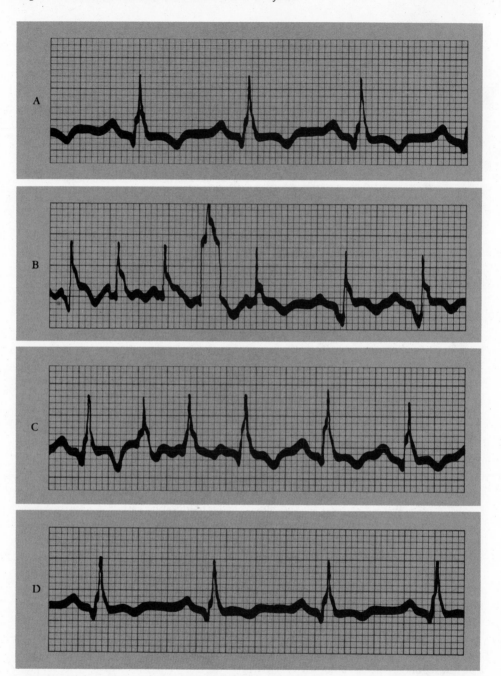

*A*, Normal heart rhythm (control level, rate 80). *B* and *C*, Initial beats show an abnormally irregular heartbeat during extreme emotional arousal. Last two beats show the heart rate has increased to 115. *D*, Following the end of arousal, heart rate returns to control level; abnormal beating is no longer present. (Courtesy of George Prozan, M.D.)

**Figure 10-2**  VARIOUS HUMAN EEG PATTERNS UNDER SEVERAL AROUSAL STATES

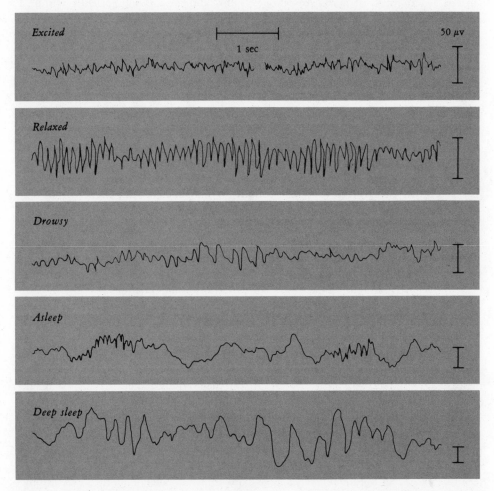

From H. Jasper, in Penfield and Erickson, *Epilepsy and Cerebral Localization*, 1941. Courtesy of Charles C Thomas, Publisher, Springfield, Ill.

cording apparatus, which converts it into the usual pen-and-paper record. Such a system is used routinely to monitor the physiological status of astronauts, for example.

## RELATIONS AMONG MEASURES

The foregoing examples of behavioral measures illustrate the multiplicity of human response systems. People respond verbally, through overt social and inter-personal actions, and covertly through thoughts and feelings, as well as physiologically through changes in bodily activity. The relationships among a person's various reactions, both across response systems and among submeasures within a system, tend to be extremely complex.

Sometimes significant correlations across response systems are found. For example, Geer (1965) administered a fear survey schedule to undergraduates to select a high fear and a low fear group for spider phobia. An equal number of high and low fear subjects were then assigned to experimental and control conditions. In the experimental condition subjects were shown pictures of a spider; in the control condition they saw pictures of a snake. For all subjects measures of autonomic arousal were taken physiologically in the form of GSR responses through finger electrodes. When they were presented with pictures of spiders, people who had reported high spider fear on the inventory showed significantly greater GSRs than did the other subjects. Moreover, this increased autonomic arousal was found only in response to directly relevant fear stimuli. When subjects with high fear of spiders were shown pictures of snakes, their GSR did not increase. The verbal report and the physiological measures were concordant in this case.

On the other hand, behavioral specificity is often found. When one compares across response systems, for example by obtaining verbal self-reports as well as overt behavior samples in the same domain, the different response systems turn out to be only partly similar, or even unrelated, and often independent (Mischel, 1968). In other words, we cannot assume that particular response measures will be closely correlated with other aspects of the person's behavior. For example, in one study the subjects were recruited by a newspaper advertisement inviting them to participate in procedures to help eliminate fear of snakes. In fact, "38 percent of the subjects who had defined themselves as snake phobic proved, much to their surprise, relatively fearless" on a behavioral test that required them to approach and handle a live snake (Bandura, Blanchard & Ritter, 1969, p. 178). The same problems of behavioral specificity (lack of extensive correlations among different aspects of an individual's behavior) discussed in regard to trait and psychodynamic approaches apply equally in the context of behavior assessment. Consequently, whenever possible it is preferable to use diverse tests—for example, overt behavior, self-reports, and direct autonomic measures—both to assess behaviors and to determine the effects of treatments on altering them.

Note again that behavior assessments sample the person's behaviors but usually do not interpret them as possible signs of his traits and motives. That is, behavior assessments do not assume that a person's test behavior will be a sign of his nontest behavior. They do not assume, for example, that his responses to incomplete sentences on a test will relate to his interpersonal behavior at home. Instead, behavior assessments seek to sample the relevant behavior directly—for example, to observe the individual's specific interpersonal behaviors with his family at home. If inferences beyond the sampled behaviors were to be made, all the problems of reliability and validity discussed in earlier chapters would, of course, apply here just as well. In other words, to the extent that one does not directly sample the behaviors of interest, and wants to extrapolate, for example, from what the person does in a laboratory test situation to what he does in real life (or from brain waves to social behavior), one must show the reliability and validity of the measurements just as much as when one wants to generalize from scores on a trait questionnaire to actual behavior.

## MEASURING REWARDS OR REINFORCING STIMULI

So far we have considered the direct measurement of various responses. Behavior assessments, however, analyze not just what the person does (and says and feels), but also the conditions that regulate or determine what he does. For that reason, behavior assessments have to find the rewards or reinforcers that may be influencing a person's behavior. If discovered, these reinforcers also can serve as incentives in therapy programs to help modify behavior in more positive or advantageous directions as discussed in the next chapter. Psychologists who emphasize the role of reinforcement in human behavior have devoted much attention to discovering and measuring effective reinforcers. The individual's actual choices in life-like situations, as well as his verbal preferences or ratings, reveal some of the potent reinforcers that influence him. The reinforcement value of particular stimuli also may be assessed directly by observing their effects on the individual's performance (e.g., Weir, 1965).

Primary reinforcers like food, and generalized conditioned reinforcers such as praise, social approval, and money, are effective for most people. Sometimes, however, it is difficult to find potent reinforcers that it would be feasible to manipulate. In some learning situations with children and with chronic behavior problems it has been especially difficult to find realistic and effective reinforcers. For example, in one programed instruction project, the investigators tried to use social approval and information feedback about test results as reinforcers for their pupils (Birnbrauer, Bijou, Wolf & Kidder, 1965). The investigators soon discovered that right and wrong answers seemed to be one and the same to the children. Indeed often the children did not even look at the answers the teaching programs supplied. Learning academic subjects was of little value to these children, and the researchers had to find better reinforcers. In other situations it has been discovered that such social rewards as praise may have little value with disturbed or delinquent patients (e.g., Atkinson, 1957; Cairns, 1959). Sometimes smiles and praise from the clinician may even lead to anxiety and hostility rather than to the intended beneficial effects.

A main problem in finding reinforcers with disturbed groups (such as hospitalized schizophrenic patients) has been that many of the usual reinforcers prove to be ineffective, especially with people who have spent many years living in the back wards of a mental hospital. Ayllon and Azrin (1965) have shown how effective reinforcers can be discovered for seemingly unmotivated psychotic patients.

**TABLE 10-2   Mean Tokens Exchanged for Various Available Reinforcers (by 8 Patients during 42 Days)**

| REINFORCERS | MEAN TOKENS PAID | NUMBER OF PATIENTS PAYING ANY TOKENS |
|---|---|---|
| Privacy | 1352.25 | 8 |
| Commissary items | 969.62 | 8 |
| Leave from ward | 616.37 | 8 |
| Social interaction with staff | 3.75 | 3 |
| Recreational opportunities | 2.37 | 5 |
| Devotional opportunities | .62 | 3 |

Based on Ayllon and Azrin (1965).

These reinforcers then can serve to motivate the patients to engage in more adaptive behavior. The assessments in these investigations were guided by the principle that any behavior with a high natural frequency of occurrence can serve as a reinforcer for other less likely behaviors (Premack, 1965).

As a first step the patients were observed directly in the ward to discover their most frequent behaviors in situations that permitted them freedom to do what they wished. Throughout the day observers carefully recorded the things the patients did, or tried to do, without pressures from the staff. The frequency of these activities provided an index of their potential values as reinforcers.

Six categories of reinforcers were established on the basis of extensive observation. These categories were: privacy, leave from the ward, social interactions with the staff, devotional opportunities, recreational opportunities, and items from the hospital canteen. "Privacy," for example, included such freedoms as choice of bedroom or of eating group, and getting a personal cabinet, a room-divider screen, or other means of preserving autonomy. "Recreational opportunities" included exclusive use of a radio or television set, attending movies and dances, and similar entertainments.

The patients could obtain each of the reinforcers with a specific number of tokens, and they earned these tokens by participating in such rehabilitative functions as self-care and job training. A sensitive index of the subjective reinforcement value of the available activities is obtained by considering the outcomes for which the patients later chose to exchange most of their tokens. Over 42 days the mean tokens exchanged by eight patients for the available reinforcers are shown in Table 10-2. Note that chances to interact socially with the staff and opportunity for recreation and spiritual devotion are most unpopular. These data on reinforcement value suggest that, with chronic hospitalized patients such as these, therapy programs that rely primarily on social motivations would not fare well, and that such reinforcers as privacy, autonomy, and freedom might be the most effective incentives.

## REINFORCEMENT, REWARDS, OR INCENTIVES?

Students sometimes wonder if "reinforcement" is just jargon for terms like "reward" or "incentive." The terms do overlap in meaning, but some behavior theorists prefer "reinforcement" to "reward" for an important reason. Many events that look as if they should be "rewards" in common sense terms may turn out to have little effect on the behavior of a particular person. Thus such "rewards" as praise and verbal approval may mean nothing to a delinquent teen-ager, just as monetary rewards may have little impact on the behavior of a young child and rewards like "attention from others" may actually be aversive to a schizophrenic patient. Moreover, in some cultures and under some conditions people work hard to be allowed to eat insects, or to whip themselves until they bleed, and have to be restrained physically not to cut and torture themselves. Such painful activities hardly seem to be "rewarding." Consequently, some psychologists prefer the term "reinforcement" for the particular events—whatever they happen to be—that come to strengthen behavior under particular conditions. "Reinforcement" is defined empirically by its effects rather than by its intrinsic qualities. This empirical approach to reinforcement avoids invoking motives and thus deliberately prevents the psychologist from confusing his desires with those of the people he is studying. However, the empirical definition of reinforcement leaves many theoretical questions unanswered.

Moreover, a large number of conditions may influence what events will and will not be effective reinforcers for a particular individual at any given time. These moderating conditions include the person's age, sex, culture, reference group, prior experience—in short, his total developmental and learning history and the details of the particular situation in which he is at the moment. The meaning of any incentive or potential reinforcing stimulus, and hence its impact on the individual, depends on many moderating conditions—such as its context. For example, the value of a reinforcer depends on its *relation* to other stimuli. Suppose, for example, that while you are admiring the attractive treats on display in the window of a food store, a poor old man stumbles by and becomes sick in front of the store window. This sight would at least momentarily affect the subjective value for you of the food on display.

The incentive value or potential reinforcement value of an event (the food in this example) depends on the total context and not just on the item by itself. Ice cream with a cockroach crawling nearby on the table does not have the same value as ice cream in a pleasant setting. It is arbitrary to separate a single stimulus from other important features of the situation, and recent research supports the idea that the relations and contrasts among potential reinforcers influence the impact they have on behavior (e.g., Reynolds, 1961).

In practice we never can know a person's total experiences relevant to any stimulus. Hence it becomes difficult to predict the acquired meaning of specific stimuli for an individual unless we actually sample and observe his behavior directly. Unless we know the meaning of a stimulus for the particular individual his behavior may seem mysterious.

# ASSESSING THE CONDITIONS
# CONTROLLING BEHAVIOR

To assess behavior fully, behavior theorists believe that we have to identify the conditions that control it. But how do we know whether or not a response pattern is really controlled or caused by a particular set of conditions? Behaviorally oriented psychologists test the conditions by introducing a change and observing whether or not it produces the expected modification in behavior. They ask: Does a systematic change in stimulus conditions (a "treatment") in fact change the particular response pattern that it supposedly controls? If we hypothesize that a child's reading problem is caused by poor vision, we would expect appropriate treatment (such as corrective eye glasses or corrective surgery) to be followed by a change in the behavior (that is, an improvement in reading). The same should be true for psychological causes. For example, if we believe that the child's reading difficulty is caused by an emotional problem in his relation to his mother, we should try to show that the appropriate change in that relationship will yield the expected improvement in reading. That is, to understand behavior fully we need to know the conditions that cause it. We can be most confident that we understand those conditions when we can show that a change in them yields the predicted change in the response pattern.

A rigid distinction between behavior assessment and treatment (i.e. behavior change) thus is neither meaningful nor possible. Indeed, some of the most important innovations in behavior assessment have grown out of therapeutic efforts to modify problematic behavior (discussed in the next chapter). A main characteristic of these assessment methods is that they are linked closely to behavior change and cannot really be separated from it.

## FUNCTIONAL ANALYSES

The close connection between behavior assessment and behavior change is most evident in "functional analyses"—that is, analyses of the precise covariations between changes in stimulus conditions and changes in a selected behavior pattern. Such functional analyses are the foundations of behavior assessments, and they are illustrated most clearly in studies that try to change behavior systematically. The basic steps may be seen in a study that was designed to help a girl in nursery school (Allen et al., 1964).

Ann was a bright four-year-old from an upper-middle-class background who increasingly isolated herself from children in her nursery school. At the same time she developed various ingenious techniques to gain prolonged attention from the adults around her. She successfully coerced attention from her teachers, who found her many mental and physical skills highly attractive. Gradually, however, her efforts to maintain adult attention led her to become extremely isolated from other children.

Soon Ann was isolating herself most of the time from other youngsters. This seemed to be happening because most of the attention that adults were giving her was contingent, quite unintentionally, upon behaviors that were incompatible with Ann's relating to other children. Precisely those activities that led Ann away from play with her own peers were being unwittingly reinforced by the attention that her teachers showered on her. The more distressing and problematic Ann's behavior became, the more it elicited interest and close attention from her deeply concerned teachers.

Obviously Ann was slipping into a vicious cycle that had to be interrupted. Consequently a therapeutic plan was formed according to which Ann would no longer receive adult attention for her isolate behavior and her attempts at solitary interactions with adults. At the same time the adults gave her attention only when she played with other children. That is, attention from adults became contingent on her playing with her peers.

As part of the assessment, two observers continuously sampled and recorded Ann's proximity to and interactions with adults and children in school at regular 10-second intervals. The therapeutic plan was instituted after five days of base-line data had been recorded. Now whenever Ann started to interact with children an adult quickly attended to her, rewarding her participation in the group's play activities. Even approximations to social play, such as standing or playing near another child, were followed promptly by attention from a teacher. This attention was designed to further encourage Ann's interactions with other children. For example: "You three girls have a cozy house. Here are some more cups, Ann, for your tea party." Whenever Ann began to leave the group or attempted to make solitary contacts with adults, the teachers stopped attending to her.

Figure 10-3 summarizes the effects of the change in the consequences to Ann for isolate behavior with her peers. Notice that in the base-line period before the new response-reinforcement contingencies were instituted Ann was spending only about 10 percent of her school time interacting with other children and 40 percent with adults. For about half the time she was altogether solitary. As soon as the contingencies were changed and adults attended to Ann only when she was near children, her behavior changed quickly in accord with the new contingencies. When adult-child interactions were no longer followed by attention, they quickly diminished to less than 20 percent. On the first day of this new arrangement (day 6), Ann spent almost 60 percent of her time with peers.

To assess the effects of reinforcement more precisely, the procedures were reversed on days 12 to 16. Adults again rewarded Ann with their attention for interacting with them and disregarded her interactions with children. Under these conditions (the "reversal" days in Figure 10-3), Ann's previous behavior reappeared immediately. In a final shift (beginning on day 17), in which attention from adults again became contingent upon Ann's interacting with children, her contact with peers increased to about 60 percent. After the end of the special reinforcement procedures (day 25), periodic postchecks indicated that Ann's increased play behavior with peers tended to remain fairly stable.

**Figure 10-3**  PERCENTAGES OF TIME SPENT BY ANN IN SOCIAL INTERACTION DURING APPROXIMATELY TWO HOURS OF EACH MORNING SESSION

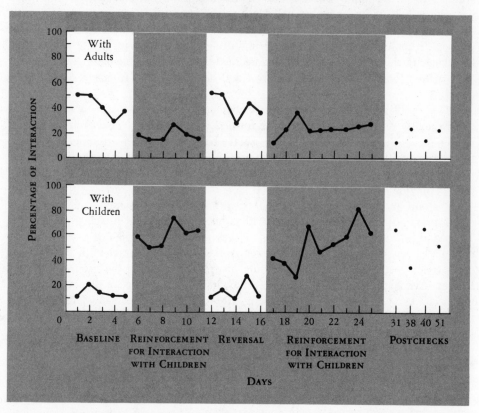

From E. K. Allen, B. Hart, J. S. Buell, F. R. Harris and M. M. Wolf. Effects of social reinforcement on isolate behavior of a nursery school child. *Child Development*, copyright 1964 by the Society for Research in Child Development, Inc., 35, No. 2, 310.

A similar type of functional analysis was conducted by Bijou (1965). In this case, a mother had many problems with her six-year-old son, whom she described as extremely overdemanding. The mother first was oriented to the procedures and data collection techniques of the researchers, and the general assessment strategy was formulated and discussed. The mother and son next were asked to play in a playroom as they normally would at home. After receiving the family's consent, observers monitored and recorded these interactions from an adjacent observation room.

The mother's verbal and nonverbal immediate reactions to each of her child's behaviors were recorded with great care. For example, "excessive demandingness" was defined, in part, as verbal demands by the child to the mother, like "You go there and I'll stay here!" or "No, that's wrong! Do it this way." These behaviors were observed directly in the interaction between mother and child in the play room. After each instance of demanding behavior from the child, the mother's immediate reactions were scored. These data provided information about the maternal behaviors that might be reinforcing and maintaining the child's demandingness with her.

The assessors then tested experimentally whether or not the mother's observed responses to the child's demands were really maintaining his behavior. In this period the mother was counseled to try different reactions to the child's inappropriate behaviors, such as ignoring them totally. She was simultaneously helped to explore experimentally some new reactions to the child's more adaptive, prosocial behaviors (like cooperative play) that would help to strengthen these new behaviors. The subsequent interactions were again observed, assessed, and progressively modified as necessary to increasingly achieve the selected therapeutic goals. Thus personality assessment and behavior change become inextricably fused: the assessments guide the therapeutic program, and the efficacy of the treatment program is in turn continuously assessed.

The same basic designs and concepts have been extended to assess and modify important interpersonal behaviors within the home. In these studies, at the parents' request, the problematic parent-child relationship is observed directly in the home. When distressing interpersonal dilemmas are found, the parent is helped to change his behavior toward the child. These changes are designed, practiced, and assessed in everyday home situations in ways that ultimately lead to a more satisfying relationship (e.g., Hawkins and his colleagues, 1966; Reckers & Lovaas, 1974; Wahler and his collaborators, 1965).

A final example of functional analysis comes from a series of studies (Lovaas, Freitag, Gold & Kassorla, 1965a) assessing the conditions controlling self-destructive behavior in a psychotic nine-year-old girl. This child was extensively and severely self-destructive, tormenting herself violently. Her tragic repertoire included banging her head and arms and pinching and slapping herself repeatedly. Her intensely maladaptive behaviors dated back at least to her third year of life, and currently she engaged in almost no appropriate social activities. Her self-destructive tortures included sticking her head in an electric wall heater, thus setting her hair on fire. She spent much time in repetitive and stereotyped physical self-stimulation, and her interactions with others were minimal.

To explore the possible conditions controlling the child's self-destructiveness, the investigators studied how changes in selected variables affected the child's objectively measured self-destructive behavior. These assessments were made over a period of many sessions. One of the most important parts of the study investigated systematically any changes in the girl's self-destructive behavior following withdrawal of reinforcement (in the form of attention) for previously rewarded behavior.

The assessments revealed that her self-destructiveness seemed to increase most when attention was withdrawn from response patterns for which she previously had been reinforced. Thus the withdrawal of attention (reinforcement) from a previously reinforced response appeared to be the critical stimulus for the girl's self-destructive behavior. In accord with learning theory, the assessors interpreted their results as indicating that in the child's past her self-destructive behavior had led to the reinstatement of attention whenever people had started to withdraw attention from a response pattern they had previously reinforced. Put most simply, this means that whenever her previously reinforced responses began to be unattended by others (extinguished) the girl could consistently reinstate the reinforcement (attention) by hurting herself.

The aversiveness of the pain connected with being burned (or the anxiety connected with warnings about the dangers of fire) serves to deter most children from burning themselves, playing with matches, and injuring themselves. But that is not the whole picture. While hurting oneself is painful, it sometimes may be the only way to obtain such valued outcomes as parental attention. Experimenting with matches and stoves may be dangerous and potentially painful, but it also attracts mother's interest quickly. Thus the same stimulus that supplies pain can also lead to positive consequences and hence may serve to support seemingly bizarre behaviors—such as self-destructive acts. A complete analysis must deal with all the acquired meanings of a stimulus for the individual—not just the normative ones.

A complete analysis also must consider the total relations among stimulus conditions rather than focus on single aspects of reinforcement in isolation. These assessments showed, for example, that this child was highly discriminating in the very particular times and circumstances during which she became self-destructive. For example, massive withdrawal of attention—as when the experimenter withheld attention from an entire session—did not affect her self-destructive behavior. In contrast, the removal of smiles and attention only for previously reinforced responses led to radical changes in her behavior.

The same principles and methods illustrated in this section have been applied to assess a large variety of normal and deviant behaviors in settings that include the home, the school, and the hospital (Goldfried & Sprafkin, 1974).

## EXPERIMENTAL TREATMENTS WITH GROUPS

The preceding section gave examples of the experimental analysis of behavior in the single case. Such analyses are especially valuable in clinical applications. In most clinical situations attention is devoted to a particular individual's problematic behavior, and if he is to be helped, the specific conditions covarying with changes in his problems must be isolated. For most research purposes, however, the majority of personality psychologists prefer to study many people rather than isolated individuals, hoping to obtain more general results. A basic experimental procedure is followed for that purpose. First, the behaviorally oriented personality psychologist selects a problem, choosing the variables whose effects he wants to understand.

In clinical settings the person's difficulties dictate what has to be assessed. In research, however, the problem, and hence the behaviors to be studied, may be dictated by the experimenter's theory and by his interests. If he is interested in the effects of success and failure on cheating, for example, he might want to devise a very competitive achievement situation in which children would be led to think either that they are doing well or that they are failing. He could later observe how these manipulations influenced how much each child cheated in a standardized "temptation" situation in which attainment of a valuable prize required the subject to violate the rules.

Usually the investigator studies the effects of one variable at a time. The essence of the procedure is to select groups of subjects who are comparable in all respects and who receive the same treatments with the critical exception of the one variable the investigator wants to test. For example, in one method adopted in personality research with children, the youngster bowls in a realistic miniature "electronic" bowling alley in which his bowling scores are illuminated automatically on a display panel after each trial. The apparatus is designed so that his "scores" can be programmed by the experimenter in a way that seems realistic though it is actually independent of the child's performance. The scores the child actually receives depend, of course, upon the condition to which he is assigned, so that variables like "success" and "failure" can be systematically manipulated over many trials.

In addition to manipulating performance through feedback, such a method also permits one to study in other, separate experiments, many different social and interpersonal conditions. Examples are the effect of achievements ostensibly obtained by peer or adult models, and the social evaluation processes by which the subject compares his performance with that of others. These and many other variables can be selected, one at a time, and their effects can be assessed.

## AN ILLUSTRATIVE EXPERIMENT

To illustrate more concretely, in one study with the bowling game children were randomly assigned into one of three conditions: "success," "failure," and a "control" condition in which they neither succeeded nor failed. Success and failure were manipulated by supplying the children with different norms for interpreting the relative quality of their bowling achievements, while the actual scores they received were identical (Mischel, Coates & Raskoff, 1968). In the *success* condition, the child was told at the outset, "From our previous testing we've found that boys [girls] of your age should be able to score about 10 on this game; any score above 10 is a very good score, and any score below 10 is a poor score." These children later received "good scores" often during 60 turns on the bowling task. In the *failure* condition, each subject was told that "boys [girls] of your age should be able to score about 30 on this game; any score above 30 is a very good score, and any score below 30 is a poor score." Thus, these youngsters were led to expect that an average of at least 30 was needed to do well, but they actually averaged only 20 and they received "good scores" very rarely during their 60 bowling trials.

In the *control* condition the children did not receive scores for their bowling performance. The score lights never went on, and the game was left unplugged.

Subjects were told, "We haven't set up the scoring part of the game yet; we're still just working on the runway and the ball return mechanism." It was emphasized that no skill was involved, and that the child was bowling only to provide information about how adequately the machine functioned. These children were exposed to the same apparatus and procedures as the others, but without experiencing either success or failure.

Thus children in all groups presumably received comparable treatment except for the success-failure manipulation. The effects of manipulating this one variable on their behavior during and after the game could then be assessed systematically by comparing children in the three groups. For example, one class of subsequent behavior might be the children's estimates of their probable future performance on similar tasks. Or one might see how the children later rewarded their own performance (for example, by helping themselves to freely available candy treats in any amounts they wished to take). Various statistical procedures can then be used to determine whether observed differences between groups are reliable and meaningful. The actual findings from studies of this sort are discussed later (Chapter 19).

Of course, the experimental method is basic to all science and is in no sense restricted to research within the framework of behavioral psychology. Although behaviorally oriented researchers have tended to favor experimental methodology, experimental techniques also are employed extensively in psychodynamic and trait-oriented research and are valuable parts of the methodology of all psychological approaches, as later chapters will show. The experimental method is included in the present chapter, however, because it is the very essence of the social behavior approach to assessment.

## ADAPTATION AND DEVIANCE

Behavioral theories also influence how one thinks about adaptation and deviance, as this section shows.

### EVALUATING THE CONSEQUENCES OF BEHAVIOR, NOT THE PERSON

In the behavioral approach one avoids evaluating the health, adequacy, or abnormality of the person or personality as a whole. Instead, when judgments must be made, they focus on evaluation of the individual's specific behaviors. Behaviors are evaluated on the basis of the kinds of consequences that they produce for the person who generates them and for other people who are affected by them. "Advantageous" (adaptive, constructive) behaviors are those whose consequences are judged to be favorable; conversely, "disadvantageous" (problematic, maladaptive, destructive) behaviors are those that yield negative effects.

Evaluations about the positive or negative consequences of behavior are social and ethical judgments that depend on the values and standards of the community

Behaviors may be evaluated on the basis of the consequences they produce.

that makes them. Advantageous behaviors are those judged to have positive personal and interpersonal consequences (e.g., helping people "feel good," or increasing constructive, creative outcomes) without any aversive impact on others. Behaviors that have negative, life-threatening, destructive consequences, or those that endanger the full potentialities of the person or other people (e.g., debilitating fears, homicidal attempts), would be considered maladaptive.

The behavioral approach also implies a high value for the development of the individual's total competencies and skills so that he or she can maximize opportunities and options. Similarly, the person must be able to discern the important contingencies and rules of reinforcement in his or her life in order to maximize satisfactions and minimize aversive, disadvantageous outcomes. To be able to overcome unfavorable environments and life conditions, a high premium is also put on the development of effective strategies for self-control and for modifying the impact of the environment itself to make it more favorable.

Beyond these generalizations, the behavioral approach to deviance has sharply attacked the traditional "disease" models that view problematic (deviant, disadvantageous) behaviors as symptoms of an underlying mental illness, as discussed next.

## BASES OF "DISEASE MODELS"

Historically, with the growth of modern biology and medicine, disease explanations of abnormal behavior became especially favored. At the turn of this century the discovery and cure of a psychotic disorder stemming from syphilis ("general paresis") greatly reinforced the belief that deviant behavior might be a sign of organic disease. Similarly, more recent findings concerning biochemical and genetic antecedents in certain forms of mental deficiency bolstered the biological approach to psychological problems.

In the biological view, deviant behaviors are construed as symptoms of underlying organic pathology. Different types or patterns of deviant behavior (e.g., delusions, depression) presumably might be linked to different types of pathology (e.g., brain infections, tumors), just as different symptoms of physical disease may be attributed to particular underlying organic causes. As noted previously (Chapter 8), research continues in the search for organic causes of psychological problems, but at present most difficulties in social behavior appear to be "functional" (nonorganic). Nevertheless, the disease view is still widely used as an *analogy* for conceptualizing psychological problems even when no physical disease has been implicated. In this quasi-disease approach the person is seen as a "patient" whose deviant behaviors are considered "symptoms" of his underlying *mental* or emotional pathology comparable to a physical disease like influenza or cancer. The patient's disturbed behavior is not the focus of interest because it is seen as merely symptomatic of his underlying pathology, as was illustrated in the psychodynamic approach to problematic behaviors.

## CRITICISM OF DISEASE MODEL

Behaviorally oriented critics argue that while the disease model may be appropriate for the analysis and treatment of physical illness in medicine, it is not useful for conceptualizing psychological problems (e.g., Bandura, 1969; Krasner & Ullmann, 1973). When there are no identified discrete organic causes (like germs) that can be tied clearly to social behavior, speculations about hypothesized pathology cannot help the troubled person. On the contrary, conceptualizing behavior in terms of diseases whose properties and physiological bases are not established can divert the assessor from the psychological and life conditions that influence the maladaptive behavior. The disease model may also lead to an unfortunate emphasis on psychiatric hospitalization, rather than on new learning experiences in life settings and on social education (e.g., Hobbs, 1966).

Szasz (1960) has been a foremost critic of the "disease approach" to psychological problems. He believes that to speak of "mental illness" as if it were a disease-like sickness is to subscribe to a myth. He contends that the so-called sick person has problems of living and is not a victim of "demons, witches, fate, or mental illness" (Szasz, 1960, p. 118). The term "mental illness" may have had some value initially in that it permitted troubled and unusual individuals to be considered "sick" rather than morally reprehensible. But while shielding the individual from social criticism, the concept of mental illness also divests him of the privileges and human rights that are part of responsibility. Szasz maintains that the hospitalized, legally committed mental patient in fact loses his basic freedoms and is victimized by society rather than by a disease.

Moreover, the widespread practice of construing the whole person as either "sick" or "healthy" is often unjust, because a person may function perfectly well in many aspects of his life and be incompetent or deficient only in some domains. In fact, most "mentally ill" individuals are capable of much adequate and responsible behavior and show impairments that are relatively specific rather than generalized (Fairweather, Sanders, Cressler & Maynard, 1969). Therefore many therapists bemoan the "common tendency to classify people as either sick or well, even though a person's social status *should* primarily be determined by his ability to assume particular rights and duties" (Fairweather et al., 1969, p. 18).

These criticisms of the disease model do not deny the possibility that future research may reveal distinctive pathology, genetic patterns, or brain or hormonal problems correlated with at least some patterns of deviant behavior that now are considered to be of psychological origin. In spite of these reservations, however, the limitations of the disease model for understanding and treating most behavior problems are being increasingly recognized. As Peterson (1968, p. 5), for example, put it: "A child who strangles kittens or spits at his mother does not have a disease although he does have something that somebody judges to be a problem." Beyond these theoretical criticisms, the utility of the psychiatric disease approach depends in part on how well expert judges can agree about the type of mental disease that an individual may have and, as we have seen (Chapter 8), there is little agreement about specific diagnostic classifications.

## DEVIANCE AS PROBLEMATIC BEHAVIOR

An alternative to the disease approach to psychological disturbances is seen in social learning and behavior theories. The essence of this alternative is a focus on the disadvantageous behaviors themselves. Rather than viewing maladaptive patterns as merely symptoms or signs of underlying diseases or dynamics, this view rejects the symptom-disease distinction in all its forms and concentrates on the individual's problematic behaviors. For example, rather than interpreting an individual's fear of snakes as possibly symbolic of unconscious sexual conflicts, the behavior therapist deals with the snake phobia itself and attempts to treat it in its own right. This social behavior view of psychological disorder contends that such terms as "mental illness" and "maladjustment" refer merely to social judgments about what a person *does* rather than to diseases or to sick dispositions that he *has* (Mischel, 1968). Thus in the behavioral approach the focus shifts from hypothesized but unobservable physical or mental disorders in the person to his problematic behaviors. The focus on behavior was illustrated in the assessment of Gary in this chapter. Rather than infer Gary's traits and motives, or try to reconstruct his his-

tory, the troublesome behaviors (e.g., anxiety related to public speaking) were identified so that they could be modified directly.

The social behavior orientation to deviance usually assumes a fundamental *continuity between normal and abnormal behavior* (e.g., Bandura & Walters, 1963;
Kanfer & Phillips, 1970; Ullmann & Krasner, 1969). This orientation, rather than
attributing deviance to distinct pathology or basically different conditions, sees it as
governed by the same laws that might (under other specific circumstances) lead to
adequate or even creative behavior. That is, normal and abnormal behavior are not
viewed as distinctly separate entities; instead, all behavior—regardless of its social
value—is analyzed in the same terms. For example, observational learning processes are basically the same regardless of whether a child's parental models are
criminals or pillars of social virtue: the behaviors the child learns will be different
in these two cases but the learning principles will be the same. Similarly, reinforcement principles presumably are the same regardless of whether incompetent
behaviors or creative ones are reinforced. Thus disadvantageous interpersonal behaviors and deviance may result from inadequate or inappropriate social learning
in regard to any (or all) aspects of personality development (Part 3 of this book).
Examples of disadvantageous behaviors include antisocial reactions to frustration,
excessive avoidance patterns in the face of stress and threat, unduly severe self-
evaluations, and negative self-concepts. Belief in the continuity of normal and abnormal behavior also implies that the same basic strategies may be used to understand and study disadvantageous behaviors and more normative behaviors, as was
evident in the last chapter.

Moreover, the emphasis of the behavioral orientation on the specificity of behavior implies that an individual may engage in deviant or disadvantageous behaviors only under some conditions and not under others. A boy may be hyperaggres-
sive at school but not at home, failing in schoolwork but excelling in sports,
popular with boys but terrified of girls. Gary may be anxious about public speaking
but quite calm when facing sports competitions and even when climbing hazardous
mountain peaks. In the behavioral orientation, therefore, one refrains from characterizing the person as normal or deviant, and concentrates instead on a delineation
of his specific problematic behaviors and the situations in which they occur.

Finally, in the social behavior orientation attention is devoted to the *current*,
immediate causes of behaviors rather than to their historical development in early
childhood. This focus on current causes implies a belief that behavior change techniques can be used to modify problems regardless of their historical beginnings in
the individual's past. Regardless of *why* Gary developed public speaking anxiety,
behavior therapists want to modify the fears that trouble him now.

## SUMMARY

1. Although there are various behavioral approaches to personality, their
methods have in common the careful measurement of behavior in rela-

tion to specific stimulus conditions. Behavioral observation is common to all psychological approaches: it is the use that is made of the data obtained that distinguishes between approaches. In the psychodynamic orientation behaviors serve as indirect *signs* of hypothesized underlying dispositions and motives. Behavioral approaches treat observed behavior as a *sample*, and the focus is on how the specific sample is affected by variations in the stimulus conditions.

2. Analysis of the case of Gary W. illustrates the behavioral assessment of anxiety: rather than attempting to make statements concerning underlying motives and conflicts, the search is for how changes in stimulus conditions produce changes in the response patterns of interest.

3. Ways in which behavior may be measured directly include situational behavior sampling, both verbal and nonverbal, and the physiological measurement of emotional reactions. In behavior sampling, the emphasis is on detailed information concerning the onset, magnitude, and duration of the behaviors of interest and the circumstances of their occurrence. The subject himself may supply this information through various self-report techniques such as daily records, lists of problematic situations, or responses on pre-set survey scales (schedules). Polygraphic measurement of bodily changes includes indices of heart rate, changes in blood volume and blood pressure, changes in muscular activity and in sweat gland activity. Brain waves also provide clues about changes in activity level. Telemetry makes possible the sampling of bodily changes outside the laboratory under real-life conditions.

4. The correlations found among these different response measures often are not very high and tend to be complex.

5. The assessment of the reinforcing value of stimuli may be made from an individual's choices in life-like situations, his verbal preferences and ratings, or the observed effects of various stimuli on his actual behavior. In clinical work it may be especially important to discover rewards that are effective for the individual concerned. Sometimes the usual reinforcers are not effective and new ones must be sought to facilitate therapeutic progress.

6. Functional analyses, the foundations of behavior assessments, are illustrated by studies of single cases. Careful observation of the behavior in question as it naturally occurs suggests what specific conditions maintain this behavior. Then systematic changes are made in those conditions until the problem behavior no longer occurs and more satisfying behaviors are substituted.

7. In research using experimental groups the researcher selects and manipulates a variable. To assess the effects of this variable, he compares groups that receive identical treatments except for the one variable that the experimenter manipulates. Statistical techniques help to determine whether the differences found between the groups as a result of the experimental treatment are reliable and meaningful.

8. Behaviorally oriented approaches to adaptation and deviance propose an alternative to both psychiatric diseases and inferred psychodynamics. They suggest, instead, a focus directly on the behaviors themselves and on what the person does rather than his hypothesized underlying mental diseases or dynamics.

# CHAPTER
# 11
# BEHAVIORAL
# THEORIES
# Applications (II)

The most important applications of behavioral approaches have been their innovations for producing change. Traditional approaches to personality change, as noted in Chapter 9, emphasized insight, awareness, and the acceptance of feelings. In recent years social behavior theories (Chapter 5) have been leading to new methods of behavior change based on specific learning experiences. These learning forms of therapy have three main common features. First, they attempt to modify the problematic behavior itself; therefore they are called "behavior therapies." Second, like the social behavior theories and assessments that guide them, behavior therapies emphasize the individual's current behaviors rather than the historical origins of his problems. Third, most behavior therapists assume that disadvantageous or "deviant" behavior can be understood and changed by the same learning principles that govern normal behavior.

Traditionally it has been customary to sharply distinguish normal personality psychology from the study of abnormal personality and to consider these two topics separately. Recently this distinction is becoming blurred. Behavior therapists are trying to show that they can use the same psychological principles to modify all sorts of human problems, regardless of the specific type of problem or its severity. Indeed they prefer to treat severely disturbed human behaviors—such as longstanding, bizarre difficulties that have been highly resistant to other forms of treatment—to demonstrate the potency of their methods and of the principles that guide them.

Behavior therapies are having an increasingly important impact not only on techniques for treating disturbed people but also on theories about the basic nature of personality and its modification. The methods and findings of behavior therapy are posing major challenges to traditional concepts about normal and abnormal personality and the conditions necessary for personality change in highly disturbed, as well as in more adaptive, people.

## BEHAVIOR THERAPY: BASIC STRATEGIES

In this section we will consider some of the main techniques and findings of behavior therapy based on the concepts of learning theories. Thereafter we shall examine some of the implications for theorizing about personality.

### DESENSITIZATION

Learning principles for therapeutic behavior change have been available for more than 50 years, but until recently they were only rarely applied because most therapists were afraid that "symptom substitution" would occur. It was widely believed that the removal of problematic behaviors would be followed by other symptoms that might be even more severely debilitating than the original ones. Joseph Wolpe, a psychiatrist who became skeptical about psychoanalytic theory, took the risk of attempting direct behavior modification with many of his patients. In 1958 he published a book describing a method of "systematic desensitization" based on the principle of classical conditioning.

Wolpe was impressed by the work of such early learning theorists as Pavlov and believed that neurosis involves maladaptive learned habits, especially anxiety (fear) responses. In neurotic behavior, he hypothesized, anxiety has become the conditioned response to stimuli that are not anxiety-provoking for other people. He reasoned that therapy might help the neurotic individual to inhibit anxiety by *counterconditioning* him to make a competing (antagonistic) response to anxiety-eliciting stimuli. In his words, "If a response antagonistic to anxiety can be made to occur in the presence of anxiety-evoking stimuli so that it is accompanied by a complete or partial suppression of the anxiety responses, the bond between these stimuli and the anxiety response will be weakened" (Wolpe, 1958, p. 71). His attempt to desensitize the individual to anxiety-evoking stimuli includes three steps.

1. *Establishing the anxiety stimulus hierarchy.* First the situations that evoke distressing emotional arousal and avoidance are identified by means of a detailed

assessment usually conducted through interviews. Sometimes a person has many areas of anxiety, such as fear of failure, self-doubts, dating, guilt about sex, and so on. Regardless of how many areas or "themes" there are, each is treated separately. For each theme the person grades or ranks the component stimuli on a hierarchy of severity ranging from the most to the least intensely anxiety-provoking events (see Table 11-1). For example, a person who is terrified of public speaking might consider "reading about speeches while alone in my room" a mildly anxiety-provoking stimulus while "walking up before the audience to present the speech" might create severe anxiety in him (e.g., Paul, 1966). In Gary's case, "the minute before starting a formal speech" was the most anxiety provoking, while "watching a friend practice a speech" and "taking notes in the library for a speech" were only moderately disturbing. As another example, a woman who sought treatment for sexual frigidity indicated that "being kissed on cheeks and forehead" evoked merely mild anxiety but thinking about items like "having intercourse in the nude while sitting on husband's lap" produced the most intense anxiety in her (Lazarus, 1963).

2. *Training the incompatible response* (*relaxation*). After identifying and grading the stimuli that evoke anxiety it is necessary to provide the person with responses that he can use later to inhibit his anxiety. Many responses (such as eating

**TABLE 11-1  Items of Different Severity from Four Anxiety Hierarchies**

| SEVERITY (DEGREE OF ANXIETY) | ANXIETY HIERARCHIES (THEMES) | | | |
| --- | --- | --- | --- | --- |
| | 1 INTERPERSONAL REJECTION | 2 GUILT ABOUT WORK | 3 TEST-TAKING | 4 EXPRESSING ANGER |
| Low | Thinking about calling Mary (a new girl-friend) tonight | Thinking "I still haven't answered all my mail" | Getting the reading list for the course | Watching strangers quarrel in street |
| Intermediate | Asking for a date on the telephone | Taking off an hour for lunch | Studying at my desk the night before the final | My brother shouts at his best friend |
| High | Trying a first kiss | Going to a movie instead of working | Sitting in the examination room waiting for the test to be handed out | Saying "No! I don't want to!" to mother |

These items are examples from much longer hierarchies.

and assertive sexual activity) are incompatible with anxiety. Wolpe therefore prefers to use relaxation responses because they can be taught easily and are always inherently incompatible with anxiety: no one can be relaxed and anxious simultaneously. The therapist helps the client to learn to relax by elaborate instructions that teach him first to tense and then to relax parts of the body (arms, shoulders, neck, head) until gradually he can achieve an almost hypnotic state of total calm and deep muscle relaxation. Most people can learn how to relax within a few sessions. The critical problem is to learn to relax to anxiety-evoking stimuli, and that task is attempted in the next phase.

3. *Associating anxiety stimuli and incompatible responses.* In the critical phase, counterconditioning, the client is helped to relax deeply while he is presented with the *least* anxiety-arousing stimulus from the previously established hierarchy. The stimulus event usually is described verbally or presented symbolically (in a picture) while the client is deeply relaxed and calm. As the therapist says the words for the item the client tries to generate the most vivid image of it that he can form in his imagination. As soon as he can concentrate his thoughts on this item while remaining calm, the next, more severe item from the hierarchy is introduced until, step by step, the entire hierarchy is mastered.

If at any point in the procedure the client experiences a decrease in his relaxed state (becoming anxious) while presented with an anxiety stimulus, he signals the therapist. He is promptly instructed to discontinue his image of the stimulus until he regains calmness. After he is fully relaxed again, he is presented a somewhat less severe item from the hierarchy so that he can concentrate on it without anxiety. When he has done that successfully he is ready to advance to the next item in his anxiety hierarchy and the step-by-step progress up the list can be resumed.

In sum, the desensitization (counterconditioning) procedure attempts to make responses strongly antagonistic to anxiety (such as relaxation) occur in the presence of mildly anxiety-evoking stimuli, so that the incompatible response will at least partially prevent the anxiety response. Thus the association between the aversive stimulus and anxiety becomes reduced, while the association of the stimulus with the relaxation reaction becomes strengthened (e.g., Guthrie, 1935; Wolpe, 1958).

Desensitization has been used to modify diverse avoidance patterns and "neurotic" behaviors as well as specific fears. Wolpe (1963), for example, treated an adolescent boy who had a severe hand-washing compulsion. This boy often spent up to three-quarters of an hour in an elaborate ritual of cleaning his genitals after urination and then devoted up to two hours to washing his hands. Wolpe noted that the youngster's washing rituals were always precipitated by urination. Consequently, the boy was desensitized to stimulus hierarchies that dealt with urine and urination. Wolpe reported excellent and rapid progress under this regime. When urination no longer provoked anxiety, the boy abandoned his cleanliness ritual.

Clinical reports of successful desensitization may be encouraging, but they do not provide definitive proof that the clinical procedure, rather than other factors in the client's life, was responsible for the observed improvement. More conclusive evidence has come from controlled experiments. The findings from these studies generally indicate that desensitization is a valuable method for modifying phobias and reducing anxiety (e.g., Davison, 1968; Lang, Lazovik & Reynolds, 1965).

One careful experiment, for example, studied the efficacy of desensitization for treating intense public-speaking anxieties (Paul, 1966). Students who had severe anxieties about speaking in public were assigned to one of four conditions. In one group they received Wolpe's desensitization treatment, learning to relax to progressively more threatening imagined situations connected with public speaking. Students in a second condition received brief traditional, insight-oriented psychotherapy from an expert clinician. In a third condition the students served as control subjects, obtaining only placebo "tranquilizers" and bogus training allegedly designed to help them "handle stress". Thus these subjects were given attention but received no specific treatment. In each of the above conditions the students had five contact hours over a six-week period for their treatments, so that all were given the same amount of time. A fourth group was used as a no-treatment control, taking a pre- and post-treatment assessment battery of tests but receiving no special treatment.

Before and after treatment all students were assessed by tests, ratings, and behavior observations. Public-speaking anxiety was measured through self-report, physiologically and behaviorally (by observations of actual public-speaking behavior under stress). As Figure 11-1 indicates, systematic desensitization was consistently the best treatment. Brief insight-oriented psychotherapy did not differ from attention-placebo, although people in both these conditions obtained greater anxiety reduction (on some measures) than did the untreated controls. On the physiological measures, only the desensitization group showed a significant reduction in anxiety when compared to the no-treatment controls. A follow-up on the test battery six weeks later, and another one two years later, found that improvement was maintained (Paul, 1966, 1967). There were no indications of "symptom substitution." On the contrary, students who had received the counterconditioning treatment in addition to becoming desensitized to public-speaking anxiety, also improved in overall college grades when compared to students in the other conditions (Paul & Shannon, 1966).

## OBSERVATIONAL LEARNING

Fears and other strong emotional reactions may be modified through observational learning. In one study, groups of preschool children who were intensely afraid of dogs observed a fearless peer model playing with one. The brave model displayed progressively bolder approach behavior to the dog while the fearful children watched from a safe distance (Bandura, Grusec & Menlove, 1967). Over a series of eight brief sessions the model progressed from briefly petting the animal through the bars while the dog was locked in a playpen to ultimately joining him

**Figure 11-1**  MEAN REDUCTION IN ANXIETY (FROM PRETEST TO POSTTEST) IN EACH OF THREE MEASURES

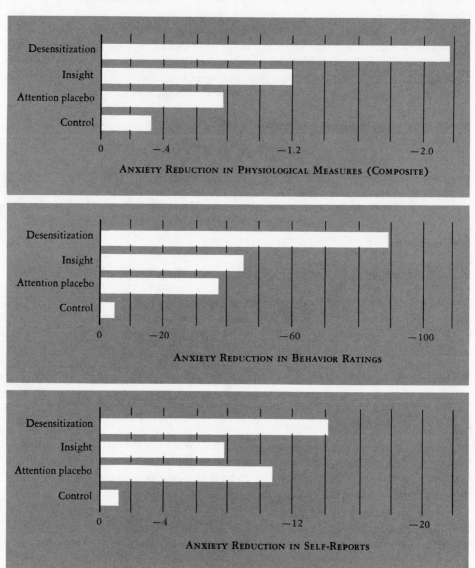

Adapted from Paul (1966).

inside the playpen. In this last phase the child model played joyfully with the dog, hugging and feeding the animal wieners and milk from a baby bottle. Children who had watched the model showed much greater approach behavior to dogs when compared later to their peers in control groups.

In behavior therapy, snake fears have received much attention because of the symbolic sexual significance attributed to them by psychoanalytic theory (Brill, 1949). If such phobias are symbolic of an underlying psychodynamic problem (as is postulated by psychoanalytic theory), then a genuine cure of the phobia cannot be achieved without first modifying the unconscious conflicts supposedly symbolized by the phobic symptom. Many behavior therapists have tried to eliminate these phobias directly without any exploration of their possible unconscious meanings and historical etiology to see whether or not they can obtain enduring improvement (e.g., Lang & Lazovick, 1963). The success of such direct methods would contradict predictions of psychoanalytic theorists and would be of considerable theoretical and practical significance.

In a comprehensive experiment Bandura, Blanchard, and Ritter (1969) studied how various treatment combinations affect severe fear of snakes in adult volunteers. These intensely phobic subjects were assigned randomly to groups that received either systematic desensitization, symbolic modeling in the form of a film, or live modeling with guided participation. In addition, some were assigned to a nontreated control group. The systematic desensitization treatment was the standard Wolpe procedure. In the symbolic modeling treatment, subjects observed a film of children, adolescents, and adults engaging in progressively more threatening contact with a snake. This film began by showing the fearless models handling plastic snakes and progressed through scenes in which the models touched and held a large king snake and let it crawl freely over them (Figure 11-2). Subjects in this treatment were also taught to relax throughout the period of exposure. Moreover, they were able to regulate the film presentation so that if they became anxious they could stop the film and reverse it back to an earlier, less threatening point until they were able to reinduce relaxation and gradually master the next scene.

Finally, in the "live modeling with guided participation group" the fearful subjects first safely observed live models interacting boldly with the snake behind an observation window. Then the model handled the snake fearlessly in front of the subject and gradually led the subject into touching, stroking, and then holding the snake's midsection, first with gloved and then bare hands, as he continued to hold the snake firmly by the head and tail. Progress throughout was paced according to the individual subject's apprehensiveness and proceeded step by step, calmly, until each one was able to perform by himself all the tasks with the snake.

Before and after completion of their respective treatments, the volunteers in all groups were tested for the strength of their fear and avoidance of snakes. They also completed an extensive fear inventory. Some of the main results are shown in Figures 11-3 and 11-4. Of the three methods, modeling with guided participation was most powerful; it produced virtually complete removal of phobic behavior in every subject.

Figure 11-2  PHOTOGRAPHS OF CHILDREN AND ADULTS MODELING PROGRESSIVELY BOLDER INTERACTIONS WITH A KING SNAKE

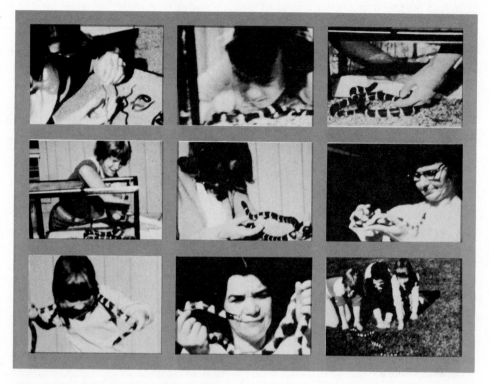

From Bandura, Blanchard, and Ritter (1969).

## CONDITIONED AVERSION

So far we have discussed how stimuli that evoke negative emotional reactions (such as anxiety) can be neutralized. While some people suffer because they have learned to react negatively to certain stimuli, others are plagued because they become pleasurably aroused by stimuli that most people in the culture find neutral or even aversive. One example of this problem is homosexual attraction; another is fetishistic behavior, in which the person may become sexually excited by such objects as undergarments. In these cases, things that are neutral or even disgusting for most people have acquired the power to produce pleasurable emotional arousal. While such reactions may provide the person with some immediate pleasure, they often are severely disadvantageous in their long-term consequences for him. They may, for example, provoke severe guilt and negative self-reactions, as well as scorn and punishment from others, and therefore treatment is needed if the person desires change.

A positively valued stimulus may be neutralized by counterconditioning if it is presented contiguously with stimuli that evoke extremely unpleasant reactions. Gradually, as a result of repeated pairings, the previously positive stimulus acquires some of the aversive emotional properties evoked by the noxious events with which it has been associated.

Consider, for example, helping a man who wants to rid himself of homosexual feelings. In conditioned aversion treatment he might be exposed repeatedly to mildly pleasurable homoerotic stimuli (such as photos of attractive men) paired with intensely negative reactions such as drug-induced nausea or pain from self-administered electric shock. Gradually the homoerotic stimuli should become neutralized or even aversive (e.g., Feldman, 1966).

One young man developed an intense attraction to girdles and became anxious unless he wore one throughout the day (Clark, 1963). His unusual fetish had many debilitating effects on other aspects of his life. For example, his relations with his wife suffered severely because he compulsively wore her undergarments; he also was unable to work without his fetishes. A careful assessment revealed that some of

**Figure 11-3**  EFFECTS OF MODELING AND DESENSITIZATIONS ON THE DEVELOPMENT OF APPROACH RESPONSES TO PREVIOUSLY FEARED STIMULI

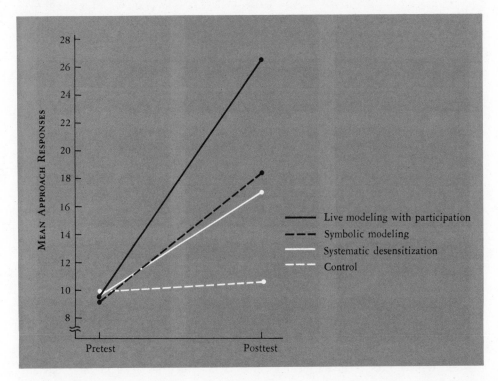

Mean number of approach responses performed by subjects before and after receiving their respective treatments. (From Bandura, Blanchard, & Ritter, 1969.)

Figure 11-4   REDUCTION IN FEAR LEVELS AFTER MODELING AND DESENSITIZATION
TREATMENTS

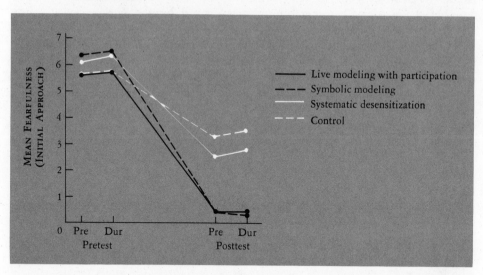

Mean level of fear arousal associated with approach responses that subjects performed before treatment
and the fear levels reported in the post treatment period for the same subset of approach responses.
(*Pre* refers to the intensity of fear subjects experienced when each snake approach response was described to them, and *Dur* signifies the fear level they reported while actually performing the corresponding behavior. From Bandura, Blanchard, & Ritter, 1969.)

the main fetishistic objects that aroused him included stockings and girdles as well
as photos of girdle wearers. To obtain help, the client voluntarily hospitalized himself. During a period of one week, drug-induced nausea was repeatedly paired with
presentations of the fetishistic objects. He was encouraged to wear the undergarments and to contemplate fetishistic pictures while he became increasingly sick
from the medication. As his nausea developed, he also listened to a recording that
he had made earlier on which he had described his fetishistic pleasures in elaborate
detail. These treatments occurred about twice daily. Follow-up tests administered
three weeks later, and again three months after therapy, indicated that the client
was back at work "enjoying a normal sex life and symptom free" (Clark, 1963, p.
405). Similar techniques have been used to treat other fetishes (Raymond, 1956)
and homosexuality (e.g., Freund, 1960).

Might such counterconditioning produce excessive generalization? For example, might counterconditioning a man who has a fetishistic attraction to women's
undergarments cause him to lose not only his interest in the fetish but also in
women? In one study (Marks & Gelder, 1967; Gelder & Marks, 1969) many fetish-
ists and transvestites received electric shock while they engaged in their deviant
acts either overtly or in imagination. For example, one transvestite was aversively
counterconditioned to a series of items including panties, pajamas, and a slip—one

item at a time. His excitement (measured by erectile responses) diminished only to the specifically counterconditioned items and did not generalize to untreated ones. Thus, after completion of the aversion therapy the client remained responsive to appropriate heterosexual stimuli (such as female nude photos), but his sexual arousal to the specific deviant fetish was eliminated. Human learning often is highly discriminative: the effects of conditioning depend on the specific stimuli conditioned and do not necessarily entail massively generalized changes.

Systematic counterconditioning has also been attempted with other unfortunate addictions such as alcoholism. Bandura (1969) surveyed the findings of 15 studies reporting aversion therapy for alcoholics. The studies contained from 15 to more than 4000 people and used different types of aversive stimuli. After followup, which ranged from a few months to 10 years, the percentage of complete alcohol abstinence found ranged from 23 to 96 percent. The largest study (Lemere & Voegtlin, 1950) followed 4096 cases from 1 to 10 years and found 51 percent complete abstinence. The data from these studies suggest that the long-term efficacy of aversion therapy depends on many considerations, such as the options available to the client after removal of his addiction and his persistence in the treatment.

Given that an alcoholic individual has received aversion therapy for alcohol, will he soon revert to drinking again? Figure 11-5 suggests that the answer partly depends on whether or not the person seeks and obtains supplementary conditioning sessions. Note that those who returned for four or more supplementary conditioning trials achieved 100 percent abstinence in this study. Generally, voluntary participation and strong motivation to change seem to increase the success rate of aversion therapy. For example, aversion therapy helped self-referred homosexuals to achieve heterosexual orientations much more frequently than it did homosexuals

Figure 11-5   RELATION OF ALCOHOL ABSTINENCE TO NUMBER OF SUPPLEMENTARY CONDITIONING SESSIONS

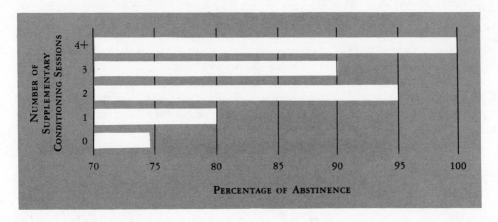

Based on Voegtlin et al. (1942).

who were reluctant to change but were coerced into therapy by relatives or legal authorities (Freund, 1960).

Psychologists often are reluctant to use treatments that inflict pain on a troubled person. However, it must be remembered that aversion therapies usually are attempted after other forms of help (such as interview therapies) have been tried unsuccessfully. In some cases aversion treatments have come as a last resort in lieu of more drastic treatments, such as long imprisonment or irreversible brain surgery (Raymond, 1956).

Aversion therapies usually are not imposed on the client: they are voluntary and the person submits himself with full knowledge and consent, except when legal authorities have charge of his case. Indeed it is this very dependence on the client's cooperation that limits the efficacy of the treatment. That is, after the initial counterconditioning trials the client often may revert to his fetish or to other deviant attractions without submitting himself voluntarily to further treatment. Since it becomes impractical to hospitalize him continuously or to remove him from exposure to the problematic stimuli, he must learn to administer aversive stimulation to himself whenever necessary. For example, he may be taught to administer electric shock to himself from a small, portable, battery-operated apparatus concealed in his clothing, or to induce aversive thoughts or imagery whenever he experiences the mildest homosexual urges (or the slightest temptation to drink, in the case of alcoholics). Thus, counterconditioning procedures ultimately provide the individual with a form of *self*-control. Whether or not he continues to practice and seek this self-control is up to him. And whether or not he practices self-control determines how effectively his new behavior will be maintained.

## CHANGING THE CONSEQUENCES OF BEHAVIOR

Many psychologists have tried to modify maladaptive behaviors by changing the consequences to which those behaviors lead. Guided to a large extent by B. F. Skinner's ideas about learning (Chapter 5), they try to withdraw reinforcement for undesired behavior and to make attention, approval, or other reinforcement contingent on the occurrence of more appropriate, advantageous behavior. Their basic procedure (discussed in the previous chapter as it bears on assessment) is well illustrated in the work of Hawkins and his colleagues (1966).

Hawkins' case was Peter, a young child of low intelligence. Peter was brought to a clinic by his mother because he was "hyperactive" and "unmanageable." Because the problems seemed to involve the relations between Peter and his mother, he was assessed and treated directly in his home. His mother served as a therapist under the guidance of the professional workers.

A first task was to specify the problematic behaviors. Direct observations of Peter in the home revealed the following problems to be among the most common and disturbing ones:

1. biting his shirt or arm
2. sticking his tongue out

3. hitting and kicking himself, other people, or objects
4. using derogatory names
5. removing his clothing or threatening to remove it.

The frequency of these and similar behaviors was carefully recorded at 10-second intervals during one-hour observation sessions in the home. After the first assessments were completed, the mother was helped to recognize the occurrence of Peter's nine most objectionable behaviors. Whenever these occurred during subsequent one-hour sessions at home she was taught to respond to them with definite steps. These steps involved signaling to Peter when his behavior became disruptive and, if a verbal warning failed, isolating him briefly in a separate, locked "time out" room devoid of toys and other attractions. Release from the room (and reinstatement of play, attention, and nurturance) was contingent on Peter's terminating the tantrum and showing more reasonable, less destructive behavior. This arrangement was opposite to the one the mother may have inadvertently used in the past, when she became increasingly solicitous, concerned, and attentive (even if distressed) as Peter became increasingly wild. Subsequent assessment revealed that the new regime was effective in minimizing Peter's outbursts. While apparently helpful to Peter's development, however, the modification of his tantrums may have been just one step toward the more extensive help he needed.

In another case, a 3-year-old girl developed "regressive" behaviors and reverted to crawling rather than walking. Naturally this regression resulted in serious problems for her and brought great concern from worried relatives. An analysis of her behavior suggested that her regressive, babyish actions were being fostered inadvertently and maintained by the attention they produced. Consequently the therapy tried to rearrange the response-reinforcement contingencies so that crawling and infantile acts were not rewarded by the attention of concerned adults. Attention and other reinforcers were made contingent on more adaptive and age-appropriate behaviors, such as jumping, running, and walking (Harris et al., 1964).

We saw this same general strategy in the case of the isolated nursery-school-child, Ann, discussed in the last chapter in the context of assessment. Recall that this strategy generally contains a series of clear stages (e.g., Bijou, 1965). Categories of problem behaviors are selected and the frequency with which they occur in a naturalistic context is recorded. Next, the assessor observes and records the reinforcing consequences that seem to maintain the behavior. Guided by this analysis, the therapist arranges for new and more advantageous response-reinforcement relations to substitute for the naturally occurring observed ones. He then repeatedly assesses the resulting changes.

For example, Lovaas (1967; Lovaas et al., 1965a) attempted to modify the speech of psychotic children. These children made bizarre word combinations and often simply echoed the words they heard. In the treatment sessions Lovaas reinforced appropriate verbal behavior (with verbal approval and sweets) and ignored psychotic talk. Figure 11-6 shows the frequency of a child's psychotic verbal and nonpsychotic verbal behavior at selected points during a series of sessions. In each session the child's speech was recorded as "psychotic" when it was senseless or odd

**Figure 11-6**   EFFECT OF REINFORCING APPROPRIATE VERBAL RESPONSES ON THE FRE-
QUENCY OF APPROPRIATE AND PSYCHOTIC VERBAL BEHAVIOR IN A CHILD

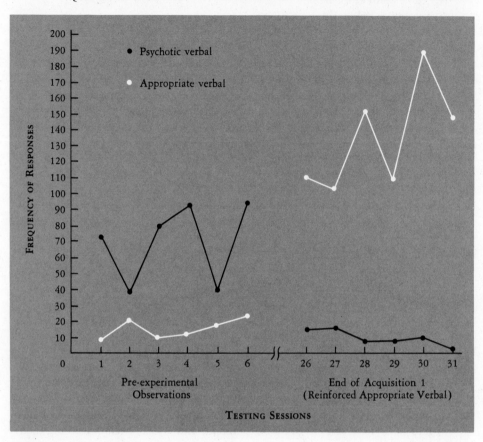

Adapted from Lovaas (1967).

("spaghetti Irene," "helicopter pillow") but was scored "appropriate" when it was
contextually meaningful ("I want a cookie," or "Let's clean up" at the end of the
session). Figure 11-6 shows the frequency of the two types of verbal behavior in the
first six pretherapeutic, observational sessions and in the last six sessions of an acquisition (learning) series in which reinforcement was contingent on appropriate
verbal behavior.

Using a combination of modeling and reinforcement procedures, Lovaas and
his co-workers (1966) also modified the deficient speech and social behaviors of severely disturbed ("autistic") children who were unable to talk. First the therapist
modeled the sounds himself. He rewarded the child only for vocalizing the modeled sounds within a specified time interval. As the child's proficiency increased the
therapist proceeded to utter more complicated verbal units so that gradually train-

ing progressed from sounds to words and phrases. As the training continued, rewards from the therapist became contingent on the child's reproducing increasingly more elaborate verbalizations more skillfully (i.e., more quickly and accurately). The combination of modeling and reinforcement procedures gradually helped the child to learn more complex meanings and complicated speech.

People often are deemed maladjusted mainly because they have not learned how to perform the behavior patterns necessary to effectively meet the social or vocational demands they encounter. They cannot behave appropriately because they lack the skills required for successful functioning. For example, the socially. deprived, economically underprivileged person may suffer because he never has acquired the response patterns and competencies needed to obtain success and avoid failure in school and in vocational and interpersonal situations. Similarly, the high school dropout in our culture does indeed carry an enduring handicap. Behavioral inadequacies, if widespread, may lead to many other problems, including severe emotional distress and avoidance patterns to escape the unhappy consequences of failure and incompetence. Using reinforcement principles, many special learning programs have been designed to teach people a variety of problem-solving strategies and cognitive skills (e.g., Bijou, 1965), to improve classroom learning (Birnbrauer et al., 1965), to help rehabilitate psychotic children (Ferster & DeMyer, 1961), and to assist families to cope with serious conduct disorders displayed by their children (Patterson, 1974).

## CONTINGENCY CONTRACTING

A move to enroll the person actively in his own behavior change program whenever possible is reflected in the increasing use of "contingency contracting" (e.g., Rimm & Masters, 1974; Thoresen & Mahoney, 1974). An example was the treatment of "Miss X" for drug abuse as described by Boudin (1972). Miss X, a heavy user of amphetamines, made a contingency contract with her therapist. She gave him $500 (all of her money) in ten signed checks of $50 each and committed him to send a check to the Ku Klux Klan (her least favorite organization) whenever she violated any step in a series of mutually agreed upon specific actions for curbing her drug use. After applying the contract for 3 months, a follow-up for a 2-year period indicated that Miss X did not return to amphetamine use. The principle of contingency contracting can be extended to a wide variety of commitments in which the client explicitly authorizes the therapist to use rewards and punishments to encourage more advantageous behaviors in ways formally agreed upon in advance.

## THERAPEUTIC COMMUNITIES (MOTIVATING ENVIRONMENTS)

There also have been efforts to modify the behavior problems of groups of people by altering the reinforcement they get in their environment. Much of this work has been conducted with hospitalized adult patients diagnosed as chronic schizophrenics (e.g., Ayllon & Azrin, 1965; Fairweather, 1964, 1967; Atthowe & Krasner, 1968). Many of the patients treated in these studies were hospitalized in the first place because of severe behavioral inadequacies. Moreover, their initial inadequacy and dependency problems usually became much worse as a result of the mental hospital regime in which they lived. The hospital routine tends to "institutionalize" the patient, discouraging individuality and fostering dependency by removal of privacy, fixed daily routines for eating, medication, and cleaning, and reinforcement (by privileges and praise) for passive, docile conformity. After being institutionalized for many years under such a regime, the patient tends to become progressively more deficient in interpersonal and vocational skills, and increasingly dependent upon the hospital. With passing years he loses whatever contacts with family and relatives he may have had in the "outside world," and his prospect of ever achieving a life beyond the institutional shelter approaches zero. Here is one comment on the typical plight of the long-term mental hospital patient:

> The great majority of patients still remain untreated. Recent statistics indicate that the median age of state mental hospital patients is approximately 65 years. This means that half of all patients in state mental hospitals are at such an advanced age that vocational opportunities are almost totally lacking and family ties have usually been broken. Even if there were nothing wrong with them, it would be difficult to discharge them into the outside world, since the outside world has no place for them. The longer these patients remain in the mental hospital, the more severe their behavioral problems seem to grow. One currently hears the phrases "hospitalism" and "institutionalization," which describe a state of apathy and lack of motivation that is acquired by a stay at a mental hospital. The hospital community is usually geared to providing the biological necessities of life, and perhaps some minimal level of recreational opportunities, but the overall relationship is a parasitic dependency in which the patient need not function in order to obtain most, if not all, of the activities or privileges that might still be of interest to him (Ayllon & Azrin, 1968, p. 3).

To help overcome this grim situation, new programs with these patients are attempting to increase their independence and to help them achieve more adequate self-care and autonomy by creating a more appropriately motivating environment. Reinforcement is made contingent on their becoming more independent, first in the simplest functions, such as grooming and self-feeding and then, gradually, in more complex and interpersonal domains such as work and social relations.

In one hospital ward long-term psychotic patients received tokens similar to money when they participated in therapeutic activities (Ayllon & Azrin, 1965). For engaging in such functions as self-care, productive work, and rehabilitative jobs, both on and off the ward, the patients received tokens that they could exchange for what they desired from a large array of alternatives (Chapter 10). It was found that the patients worked successfully at their rehabilitation jobs when the attainment of tokens depended on it. If receipt of the desired tokens was not made contingent upon adaptive behaviors, the patients quickly resumed their more usual, psychotic hospital behavior. The dependence of the patient's prosocial behavior upon contingent reinforcement is illustrated in Figure 11-7.

Some recent behavior change programs minimize the role of the professional therapeutic agent as a controller of the client's behaviors and, instead, try to transfer responsibility to the client and his peer group as rapidly as feasible. An outstanding example is the therapeutic community designed by Fairweather to rehabilitate chronic psychotics who had been hospitalized for years. This program tried to move long-term schizophrenics out of the hospital and into a specially designed patient lodge located in the larger community as rapidly as possible. Fairweather recognized that many psychotic patients who have undergone more than two years of hospitalization become "marginal men" who continue to remain in the hospital and, if discharged, are returned to the hospital within a few months (Fairweather, 1964). Therefore he tried to develop small social systems that could function in the community itself and provide these chronic psychotics with a greater measure of autonomy. He tried to organize this social system so that the members would regulate and discipline each other and share all responsibility for the step-by-step progress of their community.

**Figure 11-7**    TOTAL NUMBER OF HOURS OF ON-WARD REHABILITATIVE PERFORMANCE BY A GROUP OF 44 PATIENTS

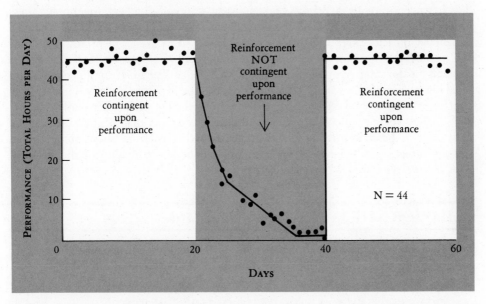

From Ayllon and Azrin (1965). For related research see T. Ayllon and N. Azrin, *The Token Economy.* New York: Appleton-Century-Crofts, 1968.

To start, a group of patients were organized in the hospital and lived and worked together in a special ward. The patients were given the greatest autonomy possible over their own behavior throughout the program. They had to make increasingly complex and difficult decisions about their collective behavior, beginning with the simplest functions (e.g., self-care, dressing). The entire group was held responsible for the behavior of all its members at each stage of the program and advanced through a carefully graded series of steps; each new step required new responsibilities but also provided more privileges (e.g., weekend passes). Reinforcement (progress to the next step) was always contingent upon success at the earlier, prerequisite step.

Soon the group moved from the hospital to the lodge, and after a month there they began to function as a basically independent, self-sufficient organization. For example, they organized and maintained a commercial and residential janitorial and yard service employing their own members, took care of their own records, arranged their transportation, and assumed responsibility for their own living, working, and health arrangements. Consultants to the lodge were gradually replaced by nonprofessional volunteers and then slowly were withdrawn completely. In time the patients themselves fully assumed such responsible roles as nurse and work manager. Within three years all external help was withdrawn, and the ex-patients then remained together freely as an autonomous, self-sufficient group in the community (Fairweather et al., 1967, 1969).

It would be naive to think that the lodge program quickly transformed these schizophrenics who had been hospitalized for years into totally new individuals. It did, however, provide a degree of competent and self-sufficient functioning to a group that previously had been considered virtually hopeless and had been utterly dependent on caretakers in a hospital, and it did so at a cost in professional time and money that was vastly cheaper than confining the patients to the custodial care of the hospital. Ex-patients living in the lodge remained in the community much longer, and were employed much more steadily, than matched patients in control groups, who were simply released from the hospital (Fairweather et al., 1969). The average cost of the community lodge was less than $5 daily, while the daily cost of hospitalizing these individuals tends to be from about three to ten times as great. The value in terms of improvement in the quality of the patients' lives outside the hospital obviously is incalculable.

## BEHAVIOR THERAPY: COMPLICATIONS

So far we have discussed examples of some of the main behavior change strategies. In clinical practice, their applications often become more complicated.

### CONVERTING THE GLOBAL TO THE SPECIFIC

Behavior therapists usually have treated specific, clearly definable behaviors, such as concrete fears, fetishes, speech problems, sexual handicaps, and motivational deficits. Many people, however, suffer from much more diffuse problems that are not as easily delineated. A person may complain, for example, of an "identity crisis," "feeling miserable," "wasting my life," or may even say "I hate my personality" or "I am lost—I just don't know what's wrong." People tend to conceptualize themselves in broad trait terms rather than in behavioral descriptions. When a person begins to describe himself he may say "I am too timid" or "I am an introvert"; he probably will not say "My heart rate seems to increase sharply and I feel dizzy and start to stutter when I have to address a group of strangers in a new situation, especially in a social setting." Thus while in some cases the treatment objectives are self-evident (as when a person is terrified of birds), in most cases it is not so easy to specify just what requires treatment and the particular behaviors that should be the goals of treatment.

In these cases the client describes his problems and objectives in vague terms with broad, global labels. The clinician's task then must be to help him elaborate and examine what he means in behavioral terms (e.g., Mischel, 1968). This may be done by written reports such as diary records, by direct discussion, or by asking the person to perform in specially structured situations in which the stimulus conditions are deliberately and systematically varied, as in an experiment.

If a person describes himself as, for example, "depressed," the clinician can explore with him just when he feels depression and when he does not. To specify examples or behavioral referents for depression, the clinician inquires into just what happens when the client feels more depressed and less depressed and the changes that occur in him and in his behavior when he experiences the depression. For example, the clinician might ask, "How do you know when you are depressed?" The purpose of these probes is to obtain behavioral examples for subjective experiences, not to validate or invalidate the truth or falseness of the client's phenomenology. The goal here is the discovery of the behaviors that are problematic for him and the conditions governing them.

Similarly, role-play situations may be used in which the meaning of the complaint is explored thoroughly. Suppose a client complains of not being sufficiently "aggressive and assertive." To understand what he means by that construct the assessor could ask him to indicate when he feels insufficiently "aggressive and assertive." Suppose he mentions "when I first meet a new person." The assessor then might suggest a role play and take the part of a person who is just being introduced to the client. In this role situation the client then has to respond as he would in real life. Afterwards the roles may be reversed and explored further. These procedures should help to clarify the construct "aggressive-assertive" and to see its relations to the client's behavior. The role plays can be quite specific—for example, first meeting with a potential employer, asking an attractive girl for a date, or having to criticize a "subordinate" at work.

An adequate assessment should make it possible to convert global problems into behavioral terms. On closer analysis, one young man's "existential neurosis," for example, translated in part to such tangibles as his current academic failures at school, his inadequate acceptance by peers in social relations, his frustrations due to the recent breakup of his engagement, and his indecision about vocational objectives. Each of these problems was treatable, and their improvement increased his sense of well-being.

## COMBINING LEARNING PRINCIPLES

In contemporary applications, behavior therapists generally combine diverse learning methods, rather than favoring only one. For example, to train highly passive persons to become more assertive there have been ingenious combinations of behavioral rehearsal, modeling, and coaching (e.g., McFall & Twentyman, 1973). Innovative treatment strategies also have been developed for social action programs and educational problems in the classroom (e.g., O'Leary & Kent, 1973), and combinations of modeling and direct reinforcement tactics have been devised for the treatment of severely disturbed (autistic) children (Lovaas et al., 1967) and for reducing cross-sex behavior (Reckers & Lovaas, 1974). In a similar vein, a number of learning-based methods have been synthesized in a step-by-step program of arousing experiences designed to increase sexual responsivity in nonorgasmic women (LoPicolo & Lobitz, 1972). The use of learning principles is also evident in the well-publicized program of Masters and Johnson (1970) for the treatment of sexual inadequacy in both sexes. The hallmark of all these programs is that they search for the most effective combinations of treatments possible and do not confine themselves to a single method, while still adhering to the general orientation of the behavioral approach.

## A CAUTION

Behavior therapies have been criticized on many grounds, often justly, often foolishly. It has been noted, for example, that some therapies that are at best loosely connected with learning theory claim to be derived from it, that the actual practice of behavior therapy may include many uncontrolled and unreported factors, and that learning theory itself often may be inadequate to deal with complex life phenomena (Breger & McGaugh, 1965). Moreover, the efficacy—and limitations—of particular forms of behavior modification for particular types of problems needs much more research (e.g., Eysenck & Beech, 1971). At present too many claims for the value of behavior change strategies still rest on case studies rather than on large scale comparisons among different methods. In addition to asking "does it work?" about each type of change strategy, one must ask "does it work better than other available alternatives?"

Critics of behavior therapies rightly note that the history of therapeutic efforts to achieve personality change is full of promising false starts and of movements whose claims and enthusiasms greatly exceeded their ultimate results. Even ardent proponents of behavior therapy now are starting to recognize that its adoption is not without danger:

There are hazards in the rapid growth of behavior therapies: that a premature orthodoxy may develop, that claims to scientific roots will not be translated into scientific appraisal and renovation, that a new generation of practitioners may be created whose lack of awareness of unresolved basic theoretical and empirical questions would create undeserved longevity for still another generation of ineffective techniques, that safeguards by society in the use of clinical behavior-control methods will not be sufficient to protect individual rights or to avoid premature social experimentation with unforeseen negative effects. However, the potential benefits, given sufficient critical evaluation and constructive research, are at least equally great (Phillips & Kanfer, 1969, p. 122).

Will a behaviorally oriented approach to the modification of complex behavior turn out to be just another false promise? Perhaps. But a behavioral orientation to personality change has one great advantage: it advances or stumbles as the science that nurtures it does. Thus its promise and its hazards are those of the science of social behavior rather than of any one man's convictions about what personality has to be or about what human nature really is.

## BEHAVIOR CHANGE AND PERSONALITY CHANGE

Critics recognize that behavior therapy may produce alterations in the individual's specific behavior, but they question the genuineness and "depth" of such behavior modification. Their doubts seem to center on several points.

### IS THERE TRANSFER?

Will beneficial effects achieved in behavior therapy *transfer* or generalize to the life situations in which the person must actually function on his own? Will a timid person who has practiced more assertive behaviors in the safety of his therapist's office really become more masterful on his job? Will he become more confident with the headwaiter who snubs him? Will a person who has learned to think calmly about taking tests during desensitization in the therapist's office also become calm when he must actually take examinations?

Generalization is enhanced to the degree that the stimulus conditions sampled in treatment are similar to those in the life situation in which the new behaviors will be used. Therefore behavior therapists try to introduce into treatment situations that closely approximate the life situations in which behavior change is desired. For example, if a person can think calmly about public speaking but becomes debilitated when he tries it, treatment might teach him to speak calmly in public rather than to think about it in private. Similarly, if a person is able to take examinations effectively but devalues and derogates his own achievements, an appropriate treatment might help him to reevaluate his performance rather than to change his test-taking skills. In other words, treatment should be directed as closely and specifically as possible to the intended terminal behaviors or objectives.

Just like the social behavior theories that guide them, behavior therapies emphasize that a person's behavior tends to be specific to particular stimulus conditions. Therefore they try to obtain close congruity between what is practiced in therapy and the behavioral objectives desired in the person's life. Consider, for example, a client who wants to improve his relations with his wife. The behavior therapist probably would focus on movement toward specific objectives in the marriage, such as improvements in sexual techniques and better forms of communication and toward specific changes in the assignment of roles and responsibilities with regard to financial decisions, recreational choices, household chores. Much lower priority would be given to more global aspects of the client's attitudes toward women in general (e.g., his feelings toward his mother). In treatment those behaviors would be encouraged and practiced that would be most similar to the ones the client wants to achieve in his daily life.

The emphasis on specificity also dictates that treatment should sample as extensively as possible the relevant stimuli or situations in which improvement is desired. Effective desensitization for snake phobia, for example, would include exposing the client to many types of snakes in many contexts; practice in assertiveness would sample many types of relationships in which assertiveness is required; training for nonpsychotic speech in autistic children would sample many aspects of language in many speaking contexts.

To facilitate generalization many therapists also believe it is best if the treatment occurs in the relevant life setting rather than in an artificial one like a laboratory or a clinic. Therefore they are bringing their treatment services into the community rather than waiting for people to be brought to mental hospitals or other institutions. For example, just as academic learning programs for children are conducted in schools so may social learning programs for youngsters with interpersonal problems be located in the school system itself. Similarly, if parent-child relations are problematic, it may be better to have consultants observe and help to modify the problems where they occur—in the home—rather than transport the family to a clinic. Moreover, in these *in vivo* settings, teachers, the parents, friends, and other nonprofessionals may be enrolled to help in the treatment process (e.g., Patterson, 1974). To help a married couple, it may be more appropriate to work with their relationship directly, treating the couple together rather than each mate in isolation. There is a trend now to engage in the treatment process the people with whom the client has important daily relations, rather than rely on repeated contacts with clinics, hospitals, special agencies, and professional personnel (Hawkins et al., 1966). Similarly, group situations often are better than treating the individual alone, especially if improving relations with other people is one of the treatment objectives. For example, Paul and Shannon (1966) found that the group provided a setting in which anxious students could spontaneously and naturally extinguish many of their social fears through their own mutually supportive interactions.

Community centers, settlement houses and clubs, civic organizations, school systems, all provide opportunities for bringing behavior change programs to the community. Considering the magnitude of the need for help, the traditional model, in which one client speaks with one expert therapist in an office several times weekly, cannot be enough.

A concern with community-oriented action programs and with "preventive health" of course has not been limited to advocates of behavior modification. In recent years an increasing number of psychologists, guided by many different theoretical orientations, have noted that effective programs to deal with the enormous problems of people in our society will have to go beyond the "patching and healing" of psychologically wrecked individuals. Just as the individual's biological health, indeed his survival, depends on the conditions around him, so does his psychological adaptation hinge on the living conditions of his personal environment. There is a psychological as well as a biological ecology, an intimate, continuous interplay of man and environment. A destructive psychological environment that submits people to excessive stress, insufficient gratification, confusing and conflicting demands, brutally chronic aggression, frustrating routines, can create havoc in human lives more quickly than any therapy can repair them. A satisfying life requires a satisfying environment. An adequate approach to psychological welfare will have to be concerned with prevention of problems before they become too difficult to handle, and with the construction of a psychological environment in which people can live without debilitatingly twisting themselves and each other.

## FEAR OF BEHAVIOR MODIFICATION

It is often said that behavioral theories and their applications to behavior modification tend to dehumanize the person. In the popular media images abound of white-coated behaviorists trying to create a society of human robots who will be controlled like puppets by conditioning and other forms of "mind control." Such fears are shared even within the profession of psychology. As the humanistic psychologist, Sidney Jourard (1974, p. 20–21) put it:

> I have always been uneasy about the behavioristic approach to man, because it appeals to the power motive in the behavior scientist. Moreover, research in behaviorism is frequently funded by agencies interested in controlling the behavior and experience of others, not necessarily with their knowledge or consent nor always with the best interest of the controllees at heart.

In part these images and accusations may be encouraged by the jargon of overzealous "behavior modifiers" who sometimes seem eager to apply the language and methods of the animal laboratory to the human condition with little sensitivity to the differences and implications. The better applications of behavior theory, however, seem increasingly alert to ethical issues and committed to actively enrolling the "subject" of behavior changes both in the choice of objectives and in the voluntary implementation of the methods for achieving them. This movement seems especially apparent in the growing emphasis on *self*-control, rather than on external control, in the modification of disadvantageous behavior (e.g., Thoresen & Mahoney, 1974).

## TOWARD SELF-MANAGEMENT

Ideally, behavior change programs are designed to increase the individual's independence and competence as rapidly as possible so that external control of his behavior by the therapeutic regime can be reduced quickly and ultimately terminated. Many techniques can help to achieve that objective (e.g., Bandura, 1969). For example, although carefully dispensed external reinforcement (like tokens or praise) may be necessary at first to help a disturbed child learn to speak, read, and write, the satisfactions deriving from these new activities, once they begin to be mastered, should help him to maintain and develop them further, even when the therapist's help is gradually withdrawn. Similarly, while a hospitalized psychiatric patient may require tokens to initiate more adaptive new behavior, such as rehabilitative work, ultimately the new behaviors themselves, if properly selected, should provide him with enough gratifying consequences so that he can maintain his new gains on his own. In other words, the new, more advantageous behaviors, which the person first practices to get "external" reinforcement, should be chosen to have reinforcing properties that gradually make them rewarding in their own right.

The foregoing examples entail the same phenomena we see in the gradual shift from external to internal control in the acquisition of new but difficult skills outside the therapeutic situation under the conditions of daily life. The young child who is learning to play the piano may at first be highly dependent on praise, attention, treats, and parental guidance to induce him to practice. However, to the extent that his learning program is structured effectively (by design or accident), his piano practice will be increasingly supported by the pleasure of the activity (e.g., the sounds he produces, and the satisfactions and "sense of competence" he starts to derive from playing). If the learning experience is successful, then in time the child "wants to play" and "loves the piano." This transition, subjectively, seems to involve a shift from performing to please others to performing to please oneself, a transition from behavior for the sake of the "extrinsic" rewards it yields to behavior for "its own sake"—that is, for "intrinsic rewards." Depending on social learning conditions, the behavior that offers the intrinsic rewards for which people strive may range from painting miniatures to racing sports cars, from playing the flute to wrestling, from climbing rocks to yoga exercises, from lifting weights to gourmet cooking. Thus whether or not an activity becomes intrinsically rewarding may have less to do with the activity than with the manner in which it was learned and the conditions influencing its performance. Often in the course of socialization the conditions of learning inadvertently are poorly arranged. We see that fact in the frequency with which activities like piano practice or schoolwork become occasions for aversive family quarrels rather than for pleasure.

Gradually there may be a shift from performing for external rewards to performing for its own sake.

To achieve relatively durable change, one needs to carefully consider the steps in the transition from control of the new behavior by external agents to self-control:

> After participants adopt new patterns of behavior on the basis of their utilitarian value, the next phase in the program may require direct training in self-reinforcement. This is achieved by gradually transferring evaluative and reinforcing functions from change agents to the individual himself. Rewards are now made contingent not only upon occurrence of desired behavior, but also accurate evaluation of one's own performances. Although at this stage the person judges when his behavior warrants reward according to the prevailing contingency structures, others still serve as the reinforcing agents. After accurate self-evaluative behavior is well established, the reinforcing function is likewise transferred so that the individual both evaluates his own behavior and reinforces himself accordingly. In addition, the artificial material rewards are gradually reduced as the person's behavior is brought increasingly under the control of self-administered and symbolic consequences. The ultimate aim of the training in self-reinforcement is to produce a level of functioning at which participants can control their own behavior with minimum external constraints and artificial inducements (Bandura, 1969, p. 620).

The transition summarized in the above paragraph may, in practice, take a long time to achieve successfully; often it remains incomplete. It would be wishful thinking to believe that we can attain major transformations in interpersonal behavior more rapidly than we can achieve competence in a musical instrument or in a sport. Moreover, just as skill at the piano depends on practice, so do new gains in social behavior depend upon the maintenance of appropriate environmental supports when the person tries out his new responses. Favorable schedules of feedback and reinforcement from others for one's newly acquired, more advantageous behaviors are essential to avoid extinction. If the patient newly discharged from a mental hospital, or the treated drug addict, returns to the same environment of stress and dissatisfaction that debilitated him in the first place, there is little hope that he will maintain any therapeutic gains for long. Treatments specifically designed to encourage self-management are starting to be developed (e.g., Homme, 1965; Thoresen & Mahoney, 1974); and they draw on the same basic concepts and methods discussed under "Self-Control" in the context of normal personality development (Chapter 19).

Efforts to improve self-management and self-regulation directly, especially in excessively impulsive individuals, are providing many different promising methods. These techniques, based mainly on learning concepts, make it possible for people to achieve much more self-directed behavior. Some good results have been found in areas that range from studying to the control of weight, smoking, and crippling fears (Watson & Tharp, 1972). A favorite technique provides the person with "controlling responses" that help him to resist the pressures of the situation and to pursue, instead, his more difficult but desired objectives. Controlling responses include various self-instructions designed to sustain the individual's continued work and effort even under difficult conditions (e.g., Kanfer & Zich, 1974; Meichenbaum & Goodman, 1971). For example, young children are helped to resist transgression if they are first given a verbalization (such as "I must not turn around and look at the toy") to repeat to themselves later when they are alone and faced by the temptation (Hartig & Kanfer, 1973). In the same vein, anxious college students may be helped to cope by learning and practicing calming, problem-solving self-instructions which they can verbalize to themselves when faced with stressful situations (e.g., Meichenbaum & Cameron, 1974). Examples of the kinds of coping statements clients are taught to make to themselves (first overtly, then silently) to handle stress and anxiety are shown in Table 11-2.

## SYMPTOM SUBSTITUTION?

It is sometimes suggested that behavior therapies neglect the causes of the person's problematic behavior and thus leave the "roots" unchanged while modifying only his "superficial" or "symptomatic" behaviors. This criticism implies that behavior therapists ignore the basic or underlying causes of problems. Advocates of behavior therapy insist that they do seek causes but that they search for *observable* causes controlling the current problem, not its historically distant antecedents nor

**TABLE 11-2  Examples of Coping Self-Statements**

Preparing for a Stressor

    What is it I have to do?

    I can develop a plan to deal with it.

    Just think about what I can do about it. That's better than getting anxious.

    No negative self-statements, just think rationally.

    Don't worry. Worry won't help anything.

    Maybe what I think is anxiety is eagerness to confront it.


Confronting and Handling a Stressor

    I can meet this challenge.

    One step at a time; I can handle the situation.

    Don't think about fear—just about what I have to do. Stay relevant.

    This anxiety is what the doctor said I would feel. It's a reminder to use my coping exercises.

    This tenseness can be an ally, a cue to cope.

    Relax; I'm in control. Take a slow, deep breath. Ah, good.


Coping with the Feeling of Being Overwhelmed

    When fear comes, just pause.

    Keep focus on the present; what is it I have to do?

    Let me label my fear from 0 to 10 and watch it change.

    I was supposed to expect my fear to rise.

    Don't try to eliminate fear totally; just keep it manageable.

    I can convince myself to do it. I can reason my fear away.

    It will be over shortly.

    It's not the worst thing that can happen.

    Just think about something else.

    Do something that will prevent me from thinking about fear.

    Just describe what is around me. That way I won't think about worrying.


Reinforcing Self-Statements

    It worked; I was able to do it.

    Wait until I tell my therapist about this.

    It wasn't as bad as I expected.

    I made more out of the fear than it was worth.

    My damn ideas—that's the problem. When I control them, I control my fear.

    It's getting better each time I use the procedures.

    I'm really pleased with the progress I'm making.

    I did it!

**From Meichenbaum and Cameron (1974).**

its hypothesized but unobservable psychodynamic mechanisms. This search for observable variables and conditions controlling the behavior of interest was demonstrated most clearly in the functional analyses discussed in the previous chapter. Traditional, insight-oriented approaches have looked, instead, for historical roots in the person's past and for theoretical mechanisms in the form of psychodynamics.

The difference between these two approaches thus is not that one looks for causes whereas the other does not: both approaches search for causes but they disagree about what those causes really are.

All analyses of behavior seek causes; the difference between social behavior and [psychodynamic] analyses is in whether current controlling causes or historically distant antecedents are invoked. Behavioral analyses seek the current variables and conditions controlling the behavior of interest. Traditional [psychodynamic] theories have looked, instead, for historical roots and developmental etiology (Mischel, 1968, p. 264).

Traditional approaches ask about their patient, "Why did he become this kind of person?" Behavioral approaches ask, "What is now causing him to behave as he does and what would have to be modified to change his behavior?"

Does a neglect in treatment of the psychodynamics hypothesized by traditional therapies produce symptom substitution? In spite of many initial fears about possible symptom substitution, behavior change programs of the kind discussed in

Instead of asking, "Why did he become this kind of person?", behavioral approaches ask, "What is *now* causing him to behave as he does?"

the preceding sections tend to be the most effective methods presently available; the changed behaviors are not automatically replaced by other problematic ones (e.g., Davison, 1968; Lang & Lazovik, 1963; Paul, 1966; Rachman, 1967). On the contrary, when people are liberated from debilitating emotional reactions and defensive avoidance patterns, they become able to function more effectively in other areas as well. After reviewing the relevant literature on symptom substitution, Grossberg (1964) notes that the overwhelming evidence is that therapy directed at elimination of maladaptive behavior is successful and the results are stable. In addition:

> Unfortunately, psychotherapists seem to have stressed the hypothetical dangers of only curing the symptoms, while ignoring the very real dangers of the harm that is done by not curing them (Grossberg, 1964, p. 83).

While fear of symptom substitution is no longer the deterrent to direct behavior modification it once appeared to be, many thorny theoretical and practical issues still remain. For example, the exact meaning of "symptom" often is not defined in theoretical discussions of symptom substitution, so that one is unsure about what might constitute a substituted symptom. How many weeks, months, or years might have to elapse before the substituted symptom can be expected to emerge? If the symptom is disguised in another form just how would we distinguish it from a problem that is wholly new? If a person whose snake phobia was removed develops problems at work or with his wife three years later, is he showing symptom substitution or new problems? In its extreme form the idea of symptom substitution may be untestable, because one cannot know what is a substituted symptom and what is a new problem.

On the other hand, some enthusiastic proponents of behavior modification overlook the complexity of the client's problems and may oversimplify his difficulties into one or two discrete phobias when in fact he may have many other difficulties. In that case, it would not be surprising to find that even after removal of his initial problem the individual still is beset with such other psychological troubles as self-doubts, feelings of worthlessness, and so on. Such a condition of course would imply that he had an incomplete treatment rather than that symptom substitution had occurred. It would be extremely naive to think that reducing Gary's public speaking anxiety, for example, would make his life free of all other problems. Whatever other difficulties he might have would still require attention in their own right.

People are especially likely to display additional disadvantageous behaviors if their treatment has consisted mainly of removing problematic behaviors without strengthening alternative adaptive patterns. Consider a former alcoholic who used to drink partly to reduce the aversiveness and frustrations that he continuously faced at work. He is likely either to drink again or to engage in other maladaptive avoidance efforts unless he also learns to cope more effectively with the stresses of his job. Or consider a child whose bizarre behaviors (hurting herself, aggressing against siblings) were maintained by the parental attention they provoked. Efforts to extinguish these maladaptive behaviors by withdrawing attention from them are unlikely to succeed in the long run unless the parents also give their child some attention when she engages in more desirable behaviors.

In sum, to avoid the emergence of disadvantageous behaviors, a comprehensive program must provide the person with more adaptive ways of achieving reinforcement; such a program may have to go beyond merely reducing his most obvious problems.

The previously noted specificity of behavior, and its dependence on the particular stimulus variables at work in each situation, also occurs in therapeutically induced behavioral changes. Behavior modification does not automatically produce generalized positive effects that remove all the person's troubles. But there is more evidence for positive generalization than there is for symptom substitution. For example, people whose phobias for snakes were removed by behavior change techniques also reported a reduction in the number and intensity of fears of other animals (Bandura, Blanchard & Ritter, 1969). They showed more positive attitudes toward other animals and became less concerned about the possibility of being harmed physically.

## BEHAVIOR CHANGE AND SELF-CONCEPT CHANGE

Often we may expect that improvements in competence will be accompanied by appropriate changes in self-reactions. Self-concepts generally reflect the individual's actual competencies: self-perceptions to a large extent reflect the information that we get about the adequacy of our own behaviors (Chapter 20). Thus the individual who learns to perform more competently and thereby achieves more gratification is also likely to develop more positive attitudes toward himself or herself. As a result of being able to overcome fears and anxieties one should also become more confident. Reducing Gary's fears of public speaking would not be a cure-all, but it might certainly help him to feel more positively about himself and would open alternatives (e.g., in his career opportunities) otherwise closed to him. But while this is often true, it does not always happen. Indeed critics of behavior therapy note that people may suffer not because their behavior is inadequate but because they evaluate it improperly. That is, some people have problems with distorted self-concepts more than with performance.

Behavior theorists consider such self-concept problems to be just as much behavior problems as any other difficulties; in these cases, the behaviors are self-evaluation and self-labeling. Often a person labels himself and reacts to his own behaviors very differently than do the people around him and the rest of society. A successful Mafia leader, for example, may experience few immediate aversive personal consequences although his activities lead to severe distress for others. On the other hand, an esteemed financier may receive the rewards and praise of society while he is privately unhappy enough to contemplate suicide. Or a popular college student who is the football hero of his school might have secret doubts about his sexual adequacy and masculinity and might be torturing himself with these fears.

Thus many human problems entail inappropriate self-evaluations and self-reactions. In these cases the difficulty often may be the person's appraisal of his performances and attributes rather than their actual quality and competence level. For example, a student may react self-punitively to his scholastic achievements even when their objective quality is high. The student who is badly upset with himself for an occasional "low A" may need help with self-assessment rather than with school work. From the viewpoint of behavior theory such problems should be amenable to modification by the same learning principles used to change any other type of behavior. In practice, however, behavior therapies still have paid relatively little attention to self-assessments; the mechanisms involved in both the genesis and treatment of self-evaluative problems require much more research.

### AM I WHAT I DO?

What happens when the conditions of reinforcement change stably in a person's life? What happens, for example, to the mother-dependent little boy when he finds that his school peers begin to have less tolerance for his "babyish" attention-getting bids and instead esteem assertiveness and self-confident independence? Usually the child's behavior will change in accord with the new contingencies. If the contingencies remain stable, so does the child's new pattern, if the contingencies shift, so does the behavior. Then what has happened to the child's dependency trait?

Many theorists, as we saw throughout Part 1, would argue that the basic personality structure remains and that merely its overt manifestation has altered. But is this just a "symptom" change that does not really affect the personality structure that generated it and the psychological life space in which it occurs? Advocates of social behavior theory contend that to treat the person as truly active and dynamic, we must recognize that he changes as his behaviors do. A behavioral view sees behavior change in an individual not as a merely superficial overlay. Consistent with the existentialist view of human nature, behavior theory insists that to find out what a person *is* we need to know what he *does;* and if his actions change then so does he.

Behavior theorists emphasize that discontinuities—real ones and not merely superficial or trivial surface changes—are part of the genuine phenomena of personality (Mischel, 1973a). They believe that an adequate conceptualization of personality has to recognize that people change as the conditions of their lives change. In that view an adequate account of human personality must have as much room for human discrimination as for generalization, as much place for personality change as for stability, and as much concern for man's self-regulation as for his victimization by either enduring intrapsychic forces or by momentary environmental constraints.

# SUMMARY

1. Behavior therapies attempt to modify disadvantageous behavior directly by planned relearning experiences and by rearranging stimulus conditions.

2. Systematic desensitization is used to help people overcome fears or anxieties. In this procedure, the individual is exposed cognitively (i.e., in imagination) to increasingly severe samples of aversive or fear-arousing stimuli; simultaneously he is helped to make responses incompatible with anxiety, such as muscle relaxation. Gradually the anxiety evoked by the aversive stimulus is reduced and the stimulus is neutralized.

3. Just as strong emotional reactions may be acquired by observing the reactions of models, so may they be modified by observing models who display more appropriate reactions. In addition to modeling fearless behavior, the model also may guide the phobic person directly to behave more bravely when faced with the anxiety-producing stimulus.

4. Inappropriate, disadvantageous positive emotional reactions to stimuli may be seen in fetishism and homosexuality. In these behaviors counterconditioning treatments may help the individual to overcome his deviant attractions. It is possible to neutralize a positive arousing stimulus (e.g., a fetishistic object) by repeatedly pairing it with one that is very aversive (e.g., shock). Periodic follow-up treatments help to sustain the new emotional reactions.

5. Maladaptive behaviors also may be modified by changing the consequences to which they lead. The basic procedure is to withdraw attention, approval, or other positive consequences from the maladaptive behavior and to make rewards contingent instead on the occurrence of more advantageous behavior. First the naturally occurring response-reinforcement contingencies are identified; then new and more advantageous response-reinforcement relations are instituted.

6. In some of the newest behavior change programs, responsibility is transferred as quickly as possible from the therapist to the client and his peer group. In one therapeutic community, chronic psychotics who had been hospitalized for many years were organized on a special ward. Their autonomy was gradually increased, and their rewards were made contingent on their increasingly responsible self-management as a group.

7. People often describe their problems and their objectives in broad terms so that it is difficult to specify the particular behaviors that need to be changed. In these cases a first step may be to help the client to elaborate his difficulties as precisely as possible in behavioral terms.

8. In everyday life, as well as in psychotherapy, several different forms of behavior therapy may occur simultaneously. Current behavior therapies often combine several learning strategies, such as modeling, desensitization, direct reward, rather than confining themselves to one.

9. There is much controversy with regard to the depth and endurance of behavior change. Some of the most important questions concern transfer of gains to life situations, the capacity of the individual for self-control independent of the therapeutic regime, the possibility of symptom substitution, and the adequacy of behavior change techniques to deal with a person's self-concepts. Basically, these questions ask, does behavior change entail genuine, durable change—that is, basic personality change—or is it restricted to relatively minor, specific behaviors that have limited applicability to major life problems?

10. To facilitate transfer from treatment to life, one introduces into treatment stimulus conditions that are as similar as possible to the life situations in which the new behaviors will be used. In treatment one samples as extensively as possible the relevant stimuli or situations and tries to conduct the treatment in the same life setting in which improvement is desired.

11. By achieving greater competence and gratifications from his new, more adequate behaviors, the individual should become able to function increasingly without external reinforcement and support. New behavior change methods are being developed to encourage self-management so that the individual may gain relative independence and control of his own behavior as rapidly as possible.

12. Many learning programs directed at the elimination of maladaptive behaviors have shown promising results. The modified behaviors are not automatically replaced by other problematic ones, and there is more evidence for positive generalization than for symptom substitution, although the theoretical issues are complex.

13. Often people suffer because they evaluate their behavior improperly. Behavior theorists believe they can modify problems stemming from inappropriate self-assessments by the same learning principles used to change other types of maladaptive behavior.

14. Social behavior theories contend that a person is what he does. Thus they see behavior change as the prerequisite for any alteration in personality. In that view, there is no personality change apart from behavior change, although the behaviors involved often may be covert and subtle, as in thoughts and self-evaluations, and therefore difficult to measure.

# CHAPTER 12
# PHENOMENOLOGICAL THEORIES Applications

The phenomenological orientation discussed in Chapter 6 has many significant applications for both personality assessment and change. As we saw, the main feature of the phenomenological orientation is its emphasis on the person's experience as he perceives it. In Kelly's phrase, if a man's private domain is ignored "it becomes necessary to explain him as an inert object wafted about in a public domain by external forces, or as a solitary datum sitting on its own continuum" (1955, p. 39). On the other hand, if different individuals are to be construed within the same general system of laws, then common denominators and higher levels of abstraction also must be discovered. To study the individual's experiences within the framework of scientific rules, methods have to be found to reach those private experiences and to bring them into the public domain.

## THE PERSON AS HIS OWN EXPERT

Phenomenologists like Rogers and Kelly seek to go beyond introspection and to anchor their theories to objective and scientific methods. In Rogers' view, for example, the therapist enters the internal world of the client's perceptions not by introspection but by observation and inference (1947). A concern with objectivity is reflected in Rogers' extensive efforts to study persons empirically, and these efforts are what place his work in the domain of psychology rather than philosophy. The same concern with objective measurement of subjective experience has characterized Kelly's approach to assessment. This chapter considers some of the main efforts that have been made by phenomenologically oriented psychologists to study experience objectively and to provide strategies to facilitate personal growth and awareness.

## GARY W.'S SELF-CONCEPTUALIZATION

The starting point of phenomenological study is the viewpoint of the person himself. To approach that viewpoint one may begin with the individual's self-presentation, as expressed in the way he depicts and describes himself. Some of the raw data of phenomenology are illustrated in the following self-description recorded by Gary W. when he was asked to describe himself as a person.

*Excerpts from Gary's Self-Description:*

I'm twenty-five years old, and a college graduate. I'm in business school working toward an MBA.

I'm an introspective sort of person—not very outgoing. Not particularly good in social situations. Though I'm not a good leader and I wouldn't be a good politician, I'm shrewd enough that I'll be a good businessman. Right now I'm being considered for an important job that means a lot to me and I'm sweating it. I know the powers at the office have their doubts about me but I'm sure I could make it—I'm positive. I can think ahead and no one will take advantage of me. I know how to work toward a goal and stick with whatever I start to the end—bitter or not!

The only thing that really gets me is speaking in a large group. Talking in front of a lot of people. I don't know what it is, but sometimes I get so nervous and confused I literally can't talk! I feel my heart is going to thump itself to death. I guess I'm afraid that they're all criticizing me. Like they're almost *hoping* I'll get caught with my pants down. Maybe I shouldn't care so much what other people think of me—but it does get to me, and it hurts—and I wind up sweating buckets and with my foot in my mouth.

I'm pretty good with women, but I've never found one that I want to spend the rest of my life with. Meanwhile I'm enjoying the freewheelin' life. I hope someday to find a girl who is both attractive and level-headed. A girl who is warm and good but not dominating and who'll be faithful but still lead a life of her own. Not depend on me for every little thing.

My childhood was fairly typical middle-class, uptight. I have an older brother. We used to fight with each other a lot, you know, the way kids do. Now we're not so competitive. We've grown up and made peace with each other—maybe it's just an armistice, but I think it may be a real peace—if peace ever really exists. I guess it was his accident that was the turning point. He got pretty smashed up in a car crash and I guess I thought, "There but for the grace of God . . . ." I count a lot on being physically up to par.

Dad wasn't around much when we were growing up. He was having business troubles and worried a lot. He and mother seemed to get along in a low-key sort of way. But I guess there must have been some friction because they're splitting now—getting divorced. I guess it doesn't matter now—I mean my brother and I have been on our own for some time. Still, I feel sorry for my Dad—his life looks like a waste and he is a wreck. A walking tragedy.

My strengths are my persistence and my stamina and guts—you need them in this world. Shrewdness. My weaknesses are my feeling that when it comes to the crunch you can't really trust anybody or anything. You never know who's going to put you down or what accident of fate lies around the corner. You try and try—and in the end it's probably all in the cards.

Well, I guess that's about it. I mean, is there anything else you want to know?

## CAN PEOPLE ASSESS THEMSELVES ACCURATELY?

How can we begin to interpret Gary's self-portrait? It is possible to proceed in terms of one's favorite theory, construing Gary's statements as reflections of his traits, or as signs of his dynamics, or as indicative of his social learning history, or as clues to the social forces that are molding him. But can one also make Gary's comments a bridge for understanding his private viewpoint, for glimpsing his own personality theory and for seeing his self-conceptions?

Because each of us is intimately familiar with his own conscious, perceived reality, it may seem deceptively simple to reach out and see another person's subjective world. In fact, we of course cannot "crawl into another person's skin and peer out at the world through his eyes," but we can "start by making inferences based primarily upon what we see him doing rather than upon what we have seen other people doing" (Kelly, 1955, p. 42). That is, we can try to attend to him rather than to our stereotypes and theoretical constructs.

A most direct way to inquire about another person's experience is to ask him, just as Gary was asked, to depict himself. Virtually all approaches to personality have asked people for self-reports. In most orientations these reports have served primarily as cues from which to infer the individual's underlying personality structure and dynamics. Perhaps because of the assumption that people engage in extensive unconscious distortion, the subject's own reports generally have been used as a basis for the clinician (or the test) to generate inferences and predictions about him, rather than as a means of conveying the subject's view of himself.

Can people be "experts" about themselves? Can they assess themselves? Can their reports serve as reliable and valid indices of their behavior? For example, in his self-appraisal Gary predicts that he can succeed in the job for which he is being considered. Is this self-assessment accurate, or is it a defensive hope, or an opportunistic ploy, or a belated effort at self-persuasion?

Some studies have tried to examine whether people can assess and predict their own behavior adequately. If they cannot, then the value of phenomenological inquiries would be limited severely; if they can, then it may be not only interesting but also useful to listen to their self-assessments most seriously. To establish the utility of a person's direct report about himself, you must compare it with the predictions about him that can be made from other data sources. For example, you must compare the individual's self-reports with the statements drawn from sophisticated psychometric tests or from well-trained clinical judges who use such techniques as the interview and the projective test to infer the subject's attributes.

It has been a surprise for many psychologists to learn that simple self-reports may be as valid as, and sometimes better predictors than, more sophisticated, complex, and indirect tests designed to disclose underlying personality. Thus, Marks, Stauffacher and Lyle (1963) tried to predict future adjustment for schizophrenic patients. They found that simple self-reports on attitude scales (like the California F Scale, discussed in Chapter 7) may yield better predictions than did psychometrically more sophisticated scales. Simple attitude statements (on the California F Scale) have also been one of the best predictors of success in the Peace Corps; they have been more accurate than far more costly personality inferences. Interviews and pooled global ratings from experts did not prove nearly as accurate as self-reports were (Mischel, 1965). Another study found that two extremely simple self-ratings (one on "adjustment" and one on "introversion-extraversion") may be as stable and useful as are inferences from factor scores based on sophisticated personality-rating schedules (Peterson, 1965). Three studies designed to test the same personality characteristics both by direct and indirect measures generally found the direct measures to be better (Scott & Johnson, 1972).

In another study the TAT stories of college students were scored for 10 "signs" of aggression (Lindzey & Tejessy, 1956). These signs were correlated with diverse criteria of aggression, including diagnostic council ratings based on observation and interview, scores on a projective picture frustration test, and self-ratings of aggressiveness. The self-ratings were associated with significantly more signs of aggression than were any of the other predictors. Similarly, students' self-rankings of achievement needs predicted their actual long-term achievements (grades) better than did experts who inferred the students' achievement motivation from the TAT (Holmes & Tyler, 1968).

Hostility, somatic concerns, achievement concerns, and religious concerns were studied by several methods in a sophisticated investigation (Wallace & Sechrest, 1963). The methods for measuring these traits included self-reports (in the form of self-descriptions), reputation rating by peers, projective techniques (incomplete sentences, Rorschach, and TAT), and behavioral indices such as scholastic average and number of visits to health services. The self-descriptions were as valid as any other source. Self-descriptions and peer ratings consistently gave better correlations than any other combination of methods.

Another study showed that individuals' self-ratings were the best predictors of peers' ratings of them (Hase & Goldberg, 1967). The self-ratings were better than the predictions based on *any* of several scales, including the best statistical equations based on the best scale combinations.

In still another study, the self-reports (on the MMPI) of psychiatric patients experiencing different crises (such as depression, anxiety, severe marital problems) were compared to other sources of information about them (Koss & Butcher, 1973). What the patients said about themselves (the item content) was analyzed carefully. The results indicated that generally they were "both willing and able to reveal truthful information about themselves" (p. 234) and to correctly identify significant aspects of their crisis situation. In a striking number of cases, what the individuals directly revealed was corroborated by other sources of information about them. These and related findings (e.g., Payne & Wiggins, 1972) further document the ability of people to volunteer correct self-statements. For example, endorsing statements such as "Most of the time I feel blue," or "I don't care what happens to me" or "Most of the time I wish I were dead" tends to accurately reflect the individual's depressive and suicidal condition. Similarly, assaultive individuals tended to be quite candid about reporting that they were said to be hotheads and sometimes had to smash things or behave in shocking or harmful ways.

At first glance evidence for the value of direct self-reports might seem more relevant to the trait approaches discussed in Chapters 7 and 8 (since many trait measures rely on self-reports) than to phenomenology. In fact, the evidence in this section does not speak to the question of the existence and nature of generalized personality traits; it merely shows that people can report directly about their own behavior with as much or better accuracy than we can get from other more indirect inferences and information about them (Mischel, 1972).

In sum, useful information about a person may be obtained most directly by simply asking him. The predictions made in simple, direct self-ratings and self-reports generally have not been exceeded by those obtained from more psychometrically sophisticated personality tests, from combined test batteries, from indirect measures and clinical judges, and from complex statistical analyses (Mischel, 1968, 1972). These conclusions seem to hold for such diverse content areas as college achievement, job and professional success, treatment outcomes in psychotherapy, rehospitalization for psychiatric patients, and parole violations for delinquent children.

# TECHNIQUES FOR STUDYING SUBJECTIVE EXPERIENCE

Thus it seems under some conditions people may be able to report and predict their own behavior at least as accurately as experts can make inferences about them through less direct techniques. Consequently, it often is reasonable to ask the person directly how he will behave, and in many instances the self-statements obtained may be as accurate as, or better than, any other data sources. These conclusions do not imply that people can always predict their own behavior accurately. There may be many circumstances in which the individual lacks either the information or the motivation to foretell his own behavior. Even if a criminal plans to steal again we cannot expect him to say so to the examining prosecutor at his trial. Moreover, many future behaviors may be determined by variables not in the person's control (e.g., other people, accidents). The obtained findings do suggest that techniques designed to obtain direct self-estimates and self-predictions merit serious attention. Some of these techniques will be reviewed in this chapter. One especially useful technique for obtaining reports about the self is the Q-technique or Q-sort.

## THE Q-SORT TECHNIQUE

The Q-sort consists of a large number of cards, each containing a printed statement (e.g., Block, 1961). The cards may contain such statements as "I am a submissive person," "I am likable," and "I am an impulsive person." Or the items might be "is a thoughtful person," "gets anxious easily," "works efficiently."

The Q-sort may be used for self-description, for describing the ideal self, or even to describe a relationship. For a self-sort, the client would be instructed to sort the cards to describe himself as he sees himself currently, placing cards in separate piles according to their applicability, ranging from those attributes which are least like him to those which are most like him. For example, the terms that Gary W. had indicated as most self-descriptive were: "haughty, determined, ambitious, critical, logical, moody, uncertain."

For an ideal sort, the subject would be instructed to use the cards to describe the person he would most like to be—his ideal person. To describe a relationship, he would sort the cards into piles ranging from those that are most characteristic of the relationship to those least characteristic. Research-oriented Rogerians have made especially extensive use of the Q-sort to study changes in the perceived self in the course of therapy.

As these examples indicate, a chief feature of the method is that the subject is instructed to sort the cards into a prearranged or "forced" distribution along a continuum from items that are least characteristic (or descriptive) to those that are most characteristic of what he is describing. The forced distribution is usually approximately normal (see Figure 12-1). To achieve a normal distribution the subject must place relatively few items in the "most characteristic" and "least characteristic" piles, and must sort most of the statements into categories near the center of the distribution. The forced distribution makes it easier to deal with the results statistically in research. It also may control response sets, such as the tendencies to stick to the "average" ratings or to give extreme ratings. On the other hand, the forced distribution has been criticized for forcing subjects into molds that they feel do not accurately reflect their perceptions. A person might feel that most of the statements do not belong in the middle category, yet he is forced by the instructions to sort them into it. For example, in a self-sort one individual might feel that the majority of the statements are highly characteristic, while another person might believe that most of the statements do not apply to him at all.

The items for a Q-sort may come from a variety of sources. They may stem from a particular theory of personality (Stephenson, 1953), from therapeutic protocols (Butler & Haigh, 1954), or from personality inventories (Block, 1961). To establish empirically the validity of Q-sort reports, one has to proceed exactly as was discussed in the context of trait measurement. That is, one has to examine the correlations between the Q-sorts and other data of interest. For many phenomenologically oriented psychologists, however, the self-statements may be of central interest in themselves, and their value as predictors or as valid indices of anything else may be irrelevant. In that case, the subject's self-reports are of intrinsic interest, apart from their possible relations to other information about him.

**Figure 12-1   A FORCED Q-SORT DISTRIBUTION OF DESCRIPTIVE STATEMENTS**

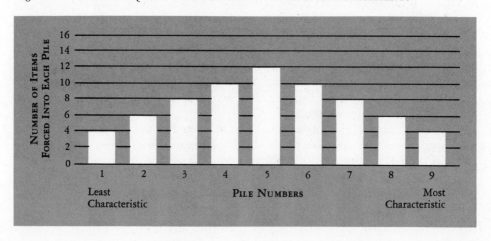

## INTERVIEWS

Most modern phenomenologists have recognized that self-reports may not reveal everything important about behavior and may not give a complete picture of personality. A person may be conscious of the reasons for his behavior but be unable or unwilling to report them. Or he may not be conscious of all his experiences, in which case he cannot communicate them no matter how hard he tries. In spite of these limitations, such phenomenologists as Rogers prefer the client's frame of reference as the vantage point for understanding. The psychologist's task, in Rogers' view, is to provide conditions that are conducive to growth and that facilitate free exploration of feelings and self.

One cannot expect people to be honest about themselves when they fear that their statements may incriminate them or lead to negative decisions about their future. In order for a person to reveal his private feelings, he needs a nonthreatening atmosphere that allays anxieties, reduces inhibitions, and fosters self-disclosure (Jourard, 1967). Phenomenologically-oriented psychologists therefore pay much attention to creating conditions of acceptance, warmth, and empathy in which the individual may feel more at ease to explore himself openly. These conditions of acceptance are illustrated vividly in "client-centered" (Rogerian) therapy, discussed later in this chapter. Rogerians have not only tried to create conditions conducive to personal growth; they also have studied those conditions in the interview.

In their earliest efforts the approach was informal. They selected excerpts from recorded interviews in client-centered therapy mainly to document how the client's verbalizations reflect his self-picture, and how this picture changes in the course of therapy (e.g., Rogers, 1942; Rogers & Dymond, 1954). Since these early beginnings, the content analysis of interview protocols has become a systematic research method. Going far beyond the mere tape recording of interviews, researchers have devised theory-relevant categories for reliably scoring the client's expressions. For example, many investigators have scored changes in self-references on various dimensions during therapy. They have grouped these self-references into such categories as positive or approving self-references, negative or disapproving self-references, ambivalent self-references, and ambiguous self-references. The scores obtained could then be correlated with other aspects of the therapy, such as the point in the relationship at which they occurred, or the association among diverse types of changes as therapy progressed. For example, it has been possible to try to test propositions such as the idea that increasing acceptance of self leads to increasing acceptance of others. Research in this vein has been vigorous and extensive (e.g., Chordokoff, 1954; Marsden, 1971; Truax & Mitchell, 1971).

Rogerians have not been the only ones to attempt content analysis of verbal behavior in interviews. The technique of scoring content has been favored in descriptive studies of all sorts of psychotherapy and not just in phenomenological approaches. A typical question in psychodynamically oriented therapy, for example, might trace changes in types of conflict expressed in various phases in psychotherapy. To illustrate, Figure 12-2 depicts the percentage of total statements

Figure 12-2   GENERAL HOSTILITY CONFLICT AND SEX CONFLICT STATEMENTS

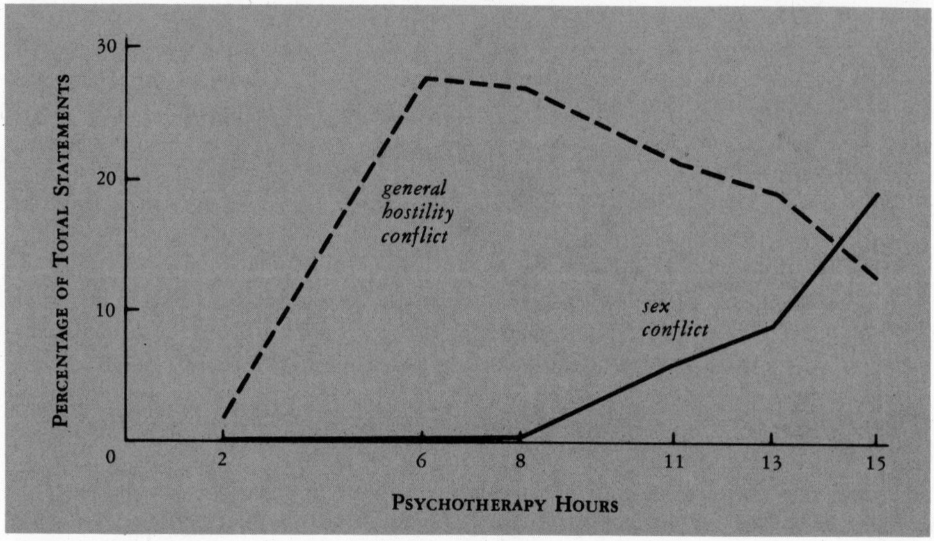

General hostility conflict statements about husband, and sex conflict statements about husband, in six random selected therapy hours with one client. (From Murray, Auld & White, 1954.)

judged to deal with general hostility conflict as opposed to sex conflict in the course of the first 15 psychotherapy hours (Murray, Auld & White, 1954). As the figure suggests, sexual conflicts began to be expressed increasingly in later sessions, whereas more general conflicts were readily verbalized in earlier phases of the relationship. These content analyses, of course, depend on the clinician's inferences about the underlying meaning of the client's statements; they do not reflect the subject's phenomenology directly.

As these studies indicate, phenomenological data from the interview have been objectified and investigated with diverse research strategies guided by many different theoretical viewpoints. Thus while the interview is a favorite tool for the phenomenologist, the data from the interview can be analyzed in many different ways. In general, the interview continues to be, for most of the major theoretical orientations, a source of data for personality assessments. Its popularity probably reflects its great flexibility and the vast range of topics that it can cover rapidly.

The validity of the interview is the subject of extensive research. When it is used to infer personality dynamics and to predict behavior from those inferences, its validity is usually not impressive (e.g., Fisher, Epstein & Harris, 1967). On the other hand, many phenomenologically oriented psychologists use the interview to observe how the individual interprets himself and describes his experiences. They employ the interview as a direct sample of the person's self-description (the ways he sees and presents himself) regardless of the validity of the data he provides as "signs" of his nontest behaviors or of his psychodynamics. They seek to create an atmosphere conducive to honest self-disclosure, an atmosphere in which self-revelation is actively encouraged (e.g., Jourard, 1974).

## THE SEMANTIC DIFFERENTIAL

Another route for phenomenologically oriented assessment has been developed to study meanings. This technique, the "semantic differential," yields ratings of the meaning of the persons, events, or concepts the investigator wants to study.

On the semantic differential test the meanings of diverse words, phrases, and concepts are rated on many scales (Osgood, Suci & Tannenbaum, 1957). The rater (or subject) is supplied with a stimulus word like "feather," or "me," or "my father," or with a phrase like "my ideal self," and is asked to rate each stimulus on a graphic, 7-point, bipolar scale. Polar adjectives like "rough-smooth" or "fair-unfair" are the extremes of each scale. The rater is instructed to mark the point that most nearly indicates the meaning of the stimulus concept for him. For example, he must rate "my ideal self" on scales like those shown in Table 12-1. The technique is both objective and flexible, and it permits investigation of the meanings of words and concepts of all sorts, as well as of changes in these meanings as a result of special experiences or procedures (for example, psychotherapy).

A great deal of factor-analytic research has repeatedly indicated three main, dichotomous, semantic factors. A primary *evaluative* (good-bad) factor seems to be most important. Two other major factors are *potency*, represented by scale items like hard-soft, masculine-feminine, strong-weak, and *activity*, tapped by scales like active-passive, excitable-calm, and hot-cold. Mulaik (1964) and Vernon (1964) have pointed out that these three semantic factors from studies of concept meanings are

**TABLE 12-1    Examples of Concepts and Rating Scales from the Semantic Differential**

Concepts whose meanings the subject is asked to rate

    MY ACTUAL SELF

    MY IDEAL SELF

    MASCULINITY

    FOREIGNER

    MOTHER

Scales for rating the meaning of concepts

| | |
|---|---|
| strong ___ : ___ : ___ : ___ : ___ : ___ : ___ | weak |
| pleasant ___ : ___ : ___ : ___ : ___ : ___ : ___ | unpleasant |
| hard ___ : ___ : ___ : ___ : ___ : ___ : ___ | soft |
| safe ___ : ___ : ___ : ___ : ___ : ___ : ___ | dangerous |
| fair ___ : ___ : ___ : ___ : ___ : ___ : ___ | unfair |
| active ___ : ___ : ___ : ___ : ___ : ___ : ___ | passive |

Based on Osgood, Suci and Tannenbaum (1957).

similar to the factors found in trait ratings. Thus trait factors from ratings of persons are often close to the meaning factors found in semantic differential studies of words and concepts.

## THE REP TEST AND THE ELABORATION OF PERSONAL CONSTRUCTS

Recall that George Kelly (1955) emphasized that different people may construe the same event differently and that every event can be construed in alternative ways. Suppose, for example, that you see a person quietly letting himself be abused by someone else. You might conclude that the person is "submissive." Yet the same behavior might be construed by other observers as sensitive, cautious, intelligent, tactful, or polite.

The personal construct is the central unit of George Kelly's theory. Kelly's (1955) definition of a construct is the way in which two things are seen as alike and as different from a third. A construct is a category that contains at least two events and excludes at least one other.

Kelly's operation for measuring a construct is best seen in his Role Construct Repertory Test or "Rep" test. On the Rep test the subject may list many people or things that are important to him (e.g., self, mother, brother). After he lists these items (or the assessor lists them for him), he considers them in groups of three. In each triad he has to indicate how two items are similar to each other and different from the third. In this way the subjective dimensions of similarity among events, and the subjective opposites of those dimensions, may be evoked systematically (Table 12-2). It is also possible to study the characteristics of the person's construct system—for example, the number of different constructs he has in his construct repertory.

Like the semantic differential, the Rep test is a flexible instrument that can be adapted for many different purposes, and it provides a convenient and fairly simple way to begin the exploration of personal constructs. Some examples, taken from

**TABLE 12-2   Elaboration of Personal Constructs: Examples from Gary W.**

1. List the three most important people in your life:
    *me     my brother     my father*
    How are any two of these alike and different from the third?
    *My brother and I both know how to be tough and succeed, no matter what—my father is soft, knocked out, defeated by life.*
2. Think of yourself now, five years ago, and five years from now. How are any two of these alike and different from the third?
    *Five years ago I was warmer, more open and responsive to others than I am now. Now I'm mostly a scheming brain. Five years from now I hope to have recaptured some of that feeling and to be more like I was five years ago.*

the study of Gary W., are shown in Table 12-2 (which illustrates the general type of procedure that may be used to elaborate personal constructs).

Research on the temporal stability of personal constructs evoked by Kelly's Rep test indicates a good deal of consistency over time (Bonarius, 1965). For example, a high retest correlation (.79) was found for constructs after a two-week interval (Landfield, Stern & Fjeld, 1961), and factor analyses of the Rep test suggest that its main factor is stable (Pedersen, 1958), and thus that an individual's main constructs may be relatively permanent.

According to Kelly, the individual's personal constructs gradually become elaborated through his answers on the Rep test, and through his behaviors in the interview and on other tests (such as the TAT). To illustrate some features of the assessment of personal constructs, here is an analysis of our case based on how Gary spontaneously elaborates and contrasts the constructs with which he views the world. What follows are excerpts from an attempt by an assessor to summarize some of Gary's main conceptions.

### A Personal Construct Conceptualization of Gary W.

*Rationality-Emotionality* is a construct dimension that seems to be of considerable importance for Gary. This construct is elaborated most clearly when he is discussing his interpersonal relationships. A sexual relationship with a woman is described in such terms as "spiritual," "instinctive," "sublime," and "beyond rationality." It is characterized by intense feeling and the primacy of emotions, and it is based on physical attraction. Real friendships, in contrast, are based upon verbalizable grounds—rational bases such as interests and ways of thinking that are common to both parties.

The distinction between the rational and the emotional is echoed when Gary describes his worries in terms of those that are "rational" versus those that are "immediate and threatening." In discussing anger, he says that he has learned to cover up his feelings, but that his emotions sometimes "surface." He no longer gets violently angry, as he did when he was a child, but is "controlled," "stony," and "devious." He gives the most positive evaluation to reason, and contrasts what is reasonable with what is "worthless."

Transposed onto a time line, his distinction between reason and emotion forms part of the contrast between adults and children. After he was about 12 years old, Gary "psyched out" his father, so the latter was no longer his "enemy" but instead became his "friendly, rational adviser." He also describes shifts in his relations with his mother and with his brother which apparently involve handling his feelings toward them in a less explosive way.

*Power and control versus dependence and weakness* seems to be a major dimension on which adults and children differ. Adults are the enemies of children. In several of his TAT stories, as well as in his interview descriptions of his childhood experiences, what parental figures require of a child is typically the opposite of what the child wants. Gary describes life as a child as involving "denial, helplessness, nothing and nobody on my side." It was a time when he "couldn't control events," when he was being "manipulated" and "shamed." Gary contrasts foresight, and events that he can plan and control, with accidents, terror, and the unpredictable.

*Defeat-Success* is a closely related dimension around which a number of constructs are clustered. Defeat is defined in terms of lack of money, passivity, compliance, dependence, frustration, undermined masculinity, and physical pain. Success means money, activity, freedom, independence, control, and being a "real" man.

*Security-Liberty* is another major dimension for Gary. In describing jobs, acquaintances, and life styles, he talks in terms of "the ordinary 9 to 5 job complete with wife, kids, and mortgage," versus the "free and easy life." "Blind obedience" is contrasted to "judging the issues for oneself." Gary describes himself as being "uncertain," and contrasts being free-wheeling with plodding determination. He sees himself as being currently without "acceptance" and "success" and he feels "cut off." His own "procrastination" hinders his "drive," but he hopes his "ambition will win out" and gain him both security and liberty.

As far as *role conceptions* are concerned, Gary now sees his father as "emasculated" and "knocked out," although once he saw him as "a giant" and as his "enemy." The father seems to have moved along the conceptual continuum from "power and control" to a point where he is seen as inadequate and as being competition no longer. He dislikes his father for the middle-class values that he feels he represents and for his passivity. There is also the implication that he resents his father for not comparing favorably with his mother. The turning point in Gary's feelings for his brother, whom he disliked for sharing many of their father's qualities, came when his brother was smashed up in a car crash. He now sees him as less conventional, more humorous and self-examining.

Gary sees his mother, and ideal women in general, as "independent partners" rather than "devouring" sources of affection. Instead of making their families central in importance, they achieve success and recognition in work outside their home. They keep the male "alive" by providing stimulation through their competence, which extends even to athletics, rather than being dependent and "clinging." Gary sees himself as similar to his mother and says he loves her best, next to himself. On the more negative side, he sees his mother as frigid and incapable of expressing affection. However, in view of his own evaluation of emotionality, this criticism is a highly qualified one. He sees his mother as having in many ways been the cause of his father's defeat, but constantly adds that she did not intend this result and feels bad about it, that it was a by-product of other admirable qualities she possesses.

His relationship with his mother is characterized by control of expression of both anger and love. He sees her dominating tendencies as dangerous, as evidenced by his childhood conception of her as omniscient and omnipotent. This fear seems to have generalized to his grandmother and to other women, as evidenced by his TAT stories.

In his relationships with women there seems to be a general distinction between sex objects and companions. In describing a sexual relationship that he felt had no potentialities for friendship, Gary says, "If we hadn't been able to 'make it' we would have stopped seeing each other." He generally prefers women who are stimulating and challenging, though he fears all forms of domination, through either authority or emotional ties.

In his relationships with men outside his family, Gary prefers distance and respect and finds that closeness leads to friction, as with his present roommate. At school he found two older men whom he could look up to: a teacher to whom he was grateful for not being "wishy-washy" and another person whom he describes as being a "real man."

## BEHAVIORAL REFERENTS FOR PERSONAL CONSTRUCTS

The foregoing descriptions indicate some of Gary's main constructs and role conceptions. These emerged from his self-descriptions and verbalizations. When a person starts to express his constructs, he usually begins with very diffuse, over-simplified, global terms. For example, Gary called himself "shrewd," "too shy," "too sharp." He also said he wanted to "feel more real," to "adjust better," and to "be happier."

What can the construct assessor do with these trait verbalizations? As we have seen in earlier chapters, psychodynamically oriented clinicians rely chiefly on their intuitive inferences about the symbolic and dynamic meanings of verbal behavior. Trait-oriented psychometric assessments either investigate the accuracy of the person's statements as indices of his nontest behavior, or treat his verbalizations as signs of his position on a personality dimension. A personal construct analysis of language, on the other hand, is completely different. The main aim of such an analysis is to decipher the content of what is being conveyed and to discover its behavioral referents and consequences; its aim is not to translate what is said into signs of underlying motives, of unconscious processes, or of personality dimensions.

Often it is hard to find appropriate words for deeply subjective states. Talk about private experiences, including thoughts and feelings, tends to be ambiguous. For example, statements of the kind commonly presented in clinical contexts, like "I feel so lost," generally are not clear. Instead of inquiring into *why* the person feels "lost," personal construct assessments try to discover referents for just *what* the statement means. An adequate personal construct assessment of what people say involves the analysis of what they mean. For this purpose the assessor's initial task is like the one faced whenever behavioral referents and operational definitions are sought for unclear theoretical constructs. Just as the psychologist interested in such concepts as extraversion, identity, or anxiety must find public referents to help specify what he means, so must the client find public referents for his private concepts, difficulties, and aspirations.

In sum, Kelly urges a specific and elaborate inquiry into personal constructs by obtaining numerous behavioral examples as referents for them. Kelly has described in detail many techniques to explore the conditions under which the individual's particular constructions about his emotional reactions may change (1955).

## NONVERBAL COMMUNICATION

Techniques like the semantic differential and the Rep test sample what the person *says*—that is, his verbal behavior. But significant communication among people is often nonverbal—it can involve facial expressions, movements, and gestures. Nonverbal expressions have intrigued psychologists of many theoretical orientations who are interested in the subject's perceptions and inner states. Research has begun to explore the possible meanings and effects of such nonverbal expressions as eye contact and the stare.

It has been found, for example, that when an interviewer evaluates subjects positively they increase eye contact with him; when he evaluates them negatively, they decrease eye contact with him (Exline & Winters, 1965). The effects of eye contact seem to interact with the verbal content conveyed in the relationship. One study varied whether an interviewer looked at the subject frequently or hardly at all, and whether the conversation was positive or threatening (Ellsworth & Carlsmith, 1968). When the verbal content was positive, more frequent eye contact produced more positive evaluations of the interviewer. In contrast, when the verbal content was negative more frequent eye contact produced more negative evaluation.

Although much is still unknown about nonverbal communication, many results have been encouraging. It has been shown, for instance, that "when people look at the faces of other people, they can obtain information about happiness, surprise, fear, anger, disgust/contempt, interest, and sadness . . . Such information can be interpreted, without any special training, by those who see the face . . ." (Ekman, Friesen & Ellsworth, 1972, pp. 176–177).

# ADAPTATION, DEVIANCE, AND CHANGE

The phenomenological orientation also has had profound influences on applied approaches to psychological "health," to problematic behavior, and to personality change.

## THE HEALTHY PERSONALITY

The phenomenological orientation implies a "humanistic" view of adaptation and deviance. There are many variations, but in general personal genuineness, honesty about one's own feelings, self-awareness, and self-acceptance are positively valued; "self-realization," the ultimate in fulfillment, involves a continuous quest to know oneself and to actualize one's potentialities for full awareness and growth as a human being. Denouncing "adjustment" to society and to other people's values as the road to dehumanization, the quest is to know oneself deeply and to be true to one's own feelings without disguise, to be oneself in the "here and now." Conversely, human problems are seen as rooted in distortions of one's own perceptions and experiences in the service of furthering the expectations of society, including the dictates of one's own self-concept with its needs for "positive regard" (Chapter 6).

One especially articulate description of the "healthy" personality from a humanistic viewpoint is provided by Maslow (1968). His characterization of the qualities of "self-actualizing" people is summarized in Table 12-3. Slightly different, but overlapping, perspectives come from other humanistic spokesmen (e.g., Jourard, 1974).

In sum, in spite of its many different versions, the phenomenological-humanistic orientation tends to view the "healthy person" as one who:

1. becomes aware of himself, his feelings, and his limits; accepts himself, his life, and what he makes of his life as his own responsibility; has "the courage to be."
2. experiences the "here-and-now;" is not trapped to live in the past or to dwell in the future through anxious expectations and distorted defenses.
3. realizes his potentialities; has autonomy and is not trapped by his own self-concept or the expectations of others and society.

To help achieve these ideals, several avenues for constructive personality change have been favored by advocates of the phenomenological approach, as discussed next.

## CLIENT-CENTERED PSYCHOTHERAPY

One of the most influential applications of the phenomenological approach was the "client-centered" therapy developed by Carl Rogers (Chapter 6). Rogers

**TABLE 12-3    Some Qualities of Maslow's "Self-Actualizing" People**

1. Able to perceive reality accurately and efficiently.
2. Accepting of self, of others, and of the world.
3. Spontaneous and natural, particularly in thought and emotion.
4. Problem-centered: concerned with problems outside themselves and capable of retaining a broad perspective.
5. Need and desire solitude and privacy; can rely on their own potentialities and resources.
6. Autonomous: relatively independent of extrinsic satisfactions, for example, acceptance or popularity.
7. Capable of a continued freshness of appreciation of even the simplest, most commonplace experiences (for example, a sunset, a flower, or another person).
8. Experience "mystic" or "oceanic" feelings in which they feel out of time and place and at one with nature.
9. Have a sense of identification with mankind as a whole.
10. Form their deepest ties with relatively few others.
11. Truly democratic; unprejudiced and respectful of all others.
12. Ethical, able to discriminate between means and ends.
13. Thoughtful, philosophical, unhostile sense of humor; laugh at the human condition, not at a particular individual.
14. Creative and inventive, not necessarily possessing great talents, but a naive and unspoiled freshness of approach.
15. Capable of some detachment from the culture in which they live, recognizing the necessity for change and improvement.

**Based on Maslow (1968).**

rejected most of Freud's concepts regarding the nature of psychodynamics and psychosexual development. He also avoided all diagnostic terms, refusing to put his labels on the client. He maintained, however, the interview format for psychotherapy (using a face-to-face arrangement rather than the orthodox psychoanalyst's couch for the client). Rogers and his students focused on the client-clinician relationship. Usually they required many fewer sessions than did psychoanalytic therapy, and they dealt more with current than with historical concerns in the client's life.

For Rogers (1959) the therapist's main task is to provide an atmosphere in which the client can be more fully open to his own "organismic" experience. To achieve a growth-conducive atmosphere, the clinician must view the client as intrinsically good and capable of self-development. The clinician's function is to be nonevaluative and to convey a sense of unconditional acceptance and regard for the client. To reach the client effectively the clinician must himself be "genuine" and "congruent"—an open, trustworthy, warm person without a facade. The congruent therapist, according to Rogers, feels free to "be himself" and to accept himself and the client fully and immediately in the therapeutic encounter, and he conveys this openness to the client by simply being himself. When a genuinely accepting, unconditional relationship is established, the client will become less afraid to face and accept his own feelings and experiences. Becoming open to the experience of himself as he is, he can reorganize his self-structure. Now, hopefully, he will accept experiences that he had previously denied or distorted (because they did not fit his self-concept) and thus achieve greater internal congruity and self-actualization.

Rogers thus advocated an empathetic, interview-based relationship therapy. He renounced the Freudian focus on psychodynamics and transference. Instead, he wanted to provide the client an unconditionally accepting relationship—an atmosphere conducive to "growth" (self-actualization). In this relationship the focus is on empathetic understanding and acceptance of feelings rather than interpretation, although the latter is not excluded. The clinician is relatively "nondirective"; the objective is to let the client direct the interview while the clinician attempts to accurately reflect and clarify the feelings that emerge.

In client-centered therapy, permissiveness and unqualified acceptance on the part of the therapist provide an atmosphere favorable to personal honesty. The psychologist is urged to abandon his "objective" measurement orientation and his concern with tests. Instead, he should try to learn from the client how he thinks, understands, and feels. "The best vantage point for understanding behavior is from the internal frame of reference of the individual himself" (Rogers, 1951, p. 494). Although their focus is on empathy, the Rogerians have not neglected objective research into the relationship, as was noted earlier in this chapter in the context of interview research. As a result, Rogerians have helped to illuminate some of the processes that occur during client-centered therapy and also have provided considerable evidence concerning its effectiveness (e.g., Truax & Mitchell, 1971).

Client-centered psychotherapy has been shown to produce some significant alterations. An extensive review of outcome research indicated that some clients may improve significantly (on measures of self-concept change), while others deteriorate significantly during treatment (Bergin, 1966). Bergin's review concluded that some forms of Rogerian psychotherapy may cause clients to become either significantly better or worse than untreated controls. For example, Gendlin (1962) reported detrimental effects from client-centered relationship therapy for some people, especially those diagnosed schizophrenic. Consequently, some current therapy research is trying to identify the characteristics of clients, clinicians, and client-clinician combinations that might predispose particular forms of therapy to success or failure (e.g., Bergin, 1971). If these attributes can be isolated it might be possible to offer particular forms of client-centered therapy only to those who can benefit from them. Research in the same vein is also aimed at trying to isolate the conditions under which certain interpersonal skills of the therapist, such as "empathy, warmth and genuineness" may be especially helpful (Truax & Mitchell, 1971).

## SIMILARITIES AND DIFFERENCES AMONG APPROACHES

It is evident that Rogers' client-centered psychotherapy differs in many ways from Freudian psychotherapy. Indeed, when Rogers first proposed his techniques they were considered revolutionary. Sometimes his approach to psychotherapy is even described as the polar opposite of Freud's. While there are major differences between Freudian and Rogerian approaches to psychotherapy, on closer inspection there also are some fundamental similarities. Both approaches retain a verbal, interview format for psychotherapy; both focus on the client-clinician relationship; both are primarily concerned with feelings; both emphasize the importance of unconscious processes (defense, repression); both consider increased awareness and acceptance of unconscious feelings to be major goals of psychotherapy. To be sure, the two approaches differ in the specific content that they believe is repressed (e.g., id impulses versus organismic experiences), in the motives they consider most important (e.g., sex and aggression versus self-realization), and in the specific insights they hope will be achieved by the client who has been successful in psychotherapy (the unconscious becomes conscious and conflict is resolved versus organismic experience is accepted and the self becomes congruent with it). But these differences should not obscure the fact that both approaches are forms of relationship treatment that emphasize awareness of hypothesized unconscious feelings and the need for the client to accept those feelings. As such, both approaches differ from the direct focus on behavior in assessment and treatment which is the fundamental feature of the behavioral approaches discussed in the preceding two chapters.

Yet there also is some commonality (often unexpected) between certain qualities of the behavioral approach and that of Rogers and other phenomenologists. Specifically, diagnostic labels and psychiatric analogies in dealing with human problems are avoided by Rogerians (and many other phenomenologists) as much as by behaviorally-oriented psychologists. Rogerians have consistently rejected trait tests and many of the constructs that guided them.

## PHENOMENOLOGICALLY ORIENTED GROUPS

As part of the search for growth and expanded awareness, in recent years a variety of group treatments have become popular. These group experiences go beyond the verbal exchange of the traditional client-clinician interview and seek to achieve better communication and contact among a group of people as well as to increase each individual's insight and self-awareness. This trend toward group experiences is found in diverse forms, especially in encounter groups and marathons like those developed at the Esalen Institute in California (Schutz, 1967) and in the "Gestalt therapy" of Fritz Perls (1969).

Encounter groups have many different labels, such as human-relations training group (T-group), sensitivity training group, personal growth group, and include many varieties of experiences, but in this discussion the focus is on their common qualities.

Schutz (1967) in his book *Joy* notes that encounter group methods involve *doing* something, not just talking. The aim is to help people to experience, to feel, to make life more vital. In this quest he advocates a host of group methods that include body exercises, wordless meetings, group fantasy, and physical "games." These games range from gentle face and body explorations by mutual touching and holding to physically aggressive encounters involving shoving, pushing, and hitting. In many activities the group leaders and group members interpret the meaning of the members' behaviors as their encounters occur.

Elliot Aronson (1972, p. 238) describes what is learned in group experiences this way: ". . . in a psychology course I learn how people behave; in a T-group I learn how *I* behave. But I learn much more than that: I also learn how others see me, how my behavior affects them, and how I am affected by other people." Referring to the process through which such learning occurs, Aronson (p. 239) emphasizes learning-by-doing; ". . . people learn by trying things out, by getting in touch with their feelings and by expressing those feelings to other people, either verbally or nonverbally." Such a process requires an atmosphere of trust so that members learn not how they are "supposed" to behave but rather what they really feel and how others view them.

---

Proponents of encounter groups emphasize their value for enhancing contact and communication among many people, not just those with severe problems.

At a theoretical level, the encounter group movement seems to involve a complex synthesis of both Freudian and Rogerian concepts with a focus on nonverbal experiences and self-discovery. The psychodynamic motivational framework is largely retained and is used in many of the interpretations, but it is implemented by direct "acting-out" procedures for expressing feelings through action in the group, by body contact designed to increase awareness of body feelings, and by games to encourage the expression of affection and aggression. Thus many of Freud's and Rogers' ideas have been transferred from the consulting room to the group encounter, and from verbal expression to body awareness and physical expression. Indeed in recent years Carl Rogers (1970) has extended many of his theoretical concepts to the encounter experience and has become one of its leading advocates. Rather than talking about his impulses, feelings, and fantasies, the individual is encouraged to act them out in the group. For example, rather than talk about repressed feelings of anger toward his father the individual enacts his feelings, pummelling a pillow while screaming "I hate you Dad, I hate you."

Many of these therapies are phenomenologically oriented and seem to emphasize the achievement of greater consciousness and personal integration. The aim is to help individuals to gain awareness, self-acceptance, and spontaneity and ultimately to achieve fulfillment and joy. The objective seems to include a feeling of wholeness and of independence and autonomy. Such a concern with "doing your own thing" and achieving self-acceptance characterizes the "Gestalt therapy" advocated by Fritz Perls (1969). The philosophy of that position is summarized in the "prayer" of Gestalt therapy (Perls, 1969, p. 4):

> I do my thing, and you do your thing
> I am not in this world to live up
>                   to your expectations
> And you are not in this world to
>                   live up to mine.
> You are you and I am I
> And if by chance we find each
>                   other, it's beautiful.
> If not, it can't be helped.

## EFFECTS OF ENCOUNTER GROUPS

Subjective reports of positive changes as a result of group experiences abound, as illustrated in this testimonial cited by Rogers (1970, p. 129):

I still can't believe the experience that I had during the workshop. I have come to see myself in a completely new perspective. Before I was "the handsome" but cold person insofar as personal relationships go. People wanted to approach me but I was afraid to let them come close as it might endanger me and I would have to give a little of myself. Since the institute

I have not been afraid to be *human*. I express myself quite well and also am likeable and also can love. I go out now and use these emotions as part of me.

While such reports are encouraging they of course are not firm evidence, and they are offset in part by reports of negative experiences and "bad trips" (e.g., Lieberman et al., 1973). Some behavior changes do seem to emerge, but their interpretation is beset by many methodological difficulties (Campbell & Dunnette, 1968). When careful control groups are used some doubt is raised if the gains from encounter experience reflect more than the enthusiastic expectancies of the group members. For example, people in weekend encounter groups showed more rated improvement than did those who remained in an at-home control group: but improvement in the encounter groups did not differ from that found in an on-site control group whose participants believed they were in an encounter group although they only had recreational activities (McCardel & Murray, 1974).

Nevertheless, a number of experimental studies indicate specific changes that may occur in some types of groups. These changes include a decrease in ethnic prejudice (Rubin, 1967), an increase in empathy (Dunnette, 1969) and in susceptibility to being hypnotized (Tart, 1970), and an increased belief by subjects that their behavior is under their own control (Diamond & Shapiro, 1973). This evidence is accompanied by a greater awareness on the part of encounter group enthusiasts that not all groups are for all people, that bad as well as good experiences may occur, and that coerciveness in groups is a real hazard that needs to be avoided (Aronson, 1972).

## DRUG-INDUCED CHANGES IN EXPERIENCES

As another route to greater awareness, some psychologists have hoped to explore the effects of drug-induced changes in mental states. The most notable examples were the efforts to "expand consciousness" and explore subjective states by means of "psychedelic" or consciousness-altering drugs such as LSD-25 (e.g., London, 1969; Solomon, 1967).

As noted previously (Chapter 6), efforts to expand consciousness and emotional experiences by means of psychedelic drugs provide the most controversial examples of the search for deeper feelings and awareness. Psychedelic drugs, first advocated by Aldous Huxley and then by Timothy Leary and Richard Alpert, became widely used in the 1960s. According to some participants these drug experiences are profoundly meaningful. For example, according to one testimonial (Leary, Litwin & Metzner, 1963, p. 570), a female graduate student, after ingesting psilocybin in the company of a supportive group of close friends reported that she:

> . . . was delighted to see that my skin was dissolving in tiny particles and floating away. I felt as though my outer shell was disintegrating, and the 'essence' of me being liberated to join the 'essence' of everything else about

me. . . . All of this time I was drifting about in a wonderously beautiful heaven of visual imagery and music.

Another student wrote:

Then, I began a series of growth or learning experiences. I felt that under-standing about oneself and about all human beings was part of the secret. The ability to communicate (on a deep level) was very important, as was the growth of competence and control over oneself and one's world. . . . One of the most disturbing insights was the fact that science was just a small game with its own set of rules. . . . It was even more circumscribed than the game of life in the Euro-American tradition. . . . Part of my successive growth and learning experience included the sensation of trying to incorporate everybody within myself. This I saw very strongly as one of the main causes of human suffering—how alone we all were. . . . Another part was that of accepting one's own defects, the parts of oneself one usually keeps hidden—physical desires, areas of incompetency, antisocial desires (Leary, Litwin & Metzner, 1963, p. 570).

Skeptics may question how novel these insights really are, and wonder about their meaning. There also have been reports of intense terror and distress reactions during drug-induced experiences. According to these reports, such "unsuccessful trips" sometimes have resulted in severe personality disorganization and psychotic episodes. As often happens when topics become explosive social controversies, it is difficult to arrive at a comprehensive and sober evaluation of the phenomenon that produced the agitation. Understandably, widespread drug use and abuse has created great public concern. As was noted in Chapter 6, the amount of research on the therapeutic effects of drugs like LSD is limited (e.g., Leary, Litwin & Metzner, 1963; Savage and his associates, 1964), and the dangers from such drugs are con-siderable.

Much of the research on the effects of psychedelic drugs has been informal and based mainly on personal testimonials from people who have taken LSD-25 or other consciousness-altering drugs. There also have been some more formal efforts both to study such drugs and to use them as a method for observing cognitive changes. A study by Honigfeld (1965) provides a simple example of how drug-induced cognitive changes may be assessed objectively in an experimental frame-work. A small group of male adult volunteers were studied individually following injections with either LSD-25 or epinephrine. The investigators were interested in the temporal effects of these drugs on language. For this reason they asked each subject to describe his drug experience verbally, as introspectively as possible, by tape recording his reactions at fixed intervals while alone. The resulting recordings were later scored objectively to assess the intelligibility of the spontaneous speech. The results are depicted in Figure 12-3, which shows the mean intelligibility scores

Figure 12-3    CHANGES IN THE INTELLIGIBILITY OF SPEECH AFTER DRUGS

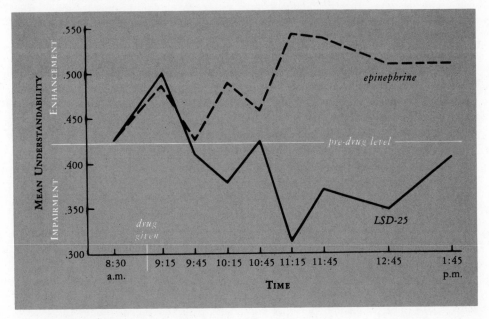

From Honigfeld (1965).

obtained by subjects in each of the two drug conditions at various times after receiving the drugs.

Concern with the possible dangers of some of the exceedingly potent drugs used in the explorations of drug-induced changes in experience has restricted much of the experimental research on the psychological effects of these chemicals. On the other hand, some ingenious efforts have been successfully conducted to explore the interaction of emotionally arousing drugs and cognitive states (e.g., Schachter & Singer, 1962, see Chapter 20). In another direction, there are growing efforts to explore and expand the nature of human awareness by use of meditation and other "consciousness-raising" methods without recourse to drugs (e.g., Ornstein, 1972; Ornstein & Naranjo, 1971).

## THE PERSON'S EXPERIENCE AND HIS UNCONSCIOUS

For many years most psychologists slighted people's perceptions and constructs and did not consider them as phenomena of interest in their own right. They preferred, instead, to infer what dispositions and motives might underlie the person's phenomenology and behavior.

The historical neglect of the subject's viewpoint probably has many reasons.

One was the belief that because of unconscious distortions and defenses, people's self-appraisals were biased and inaccurate. Some psychologists thus refrained from studying the perceptions, concepts, and reasons of the individual because they felt these data were not really scientific. But it is entirely legitimate philosophically and logically to take account of the individual's reported subjective perceptions—the rules he uses and the reasons he gives to explain his own actions (T. Mischel, 1964). It is not legitimate, however, to assume that these rules and reasons are useful bases for predicting what the individual will do—his behavior—in other situations. The links between the person's reported feelings and beliefs and his other behaviors must be demonstrated empirically.

Another reason for neglecting the subject's viewpoint in personality study was the difficulty of finding objective methods of studying private experiences. But while such experiences are obviously difficult to study, they demand attention. Indeed it has become evident in recent years that the person's conceptual dimensions and perceptions play a key part in most of the phenomena of personality psychology. The importance of the individual's concepts and categories has been shown in areas that range from the perception of persons on through the phenomena of learning itself, as later chapters discuss.

Objecting to the neglect of the "subject's" private experience in psychology, the phenomenological orientation in the last few decades has sought to explore the individual's perceptions and personal constructs. This movement, under the leadership of such theorists as Rogers and Kelly, has had a major impact on the study of personality.

Although the phenomenological orientation focuses on the subject's viewpoint, in some of its variations it also seeks to infer his unconscious characteristics and conflicts. For example, Carl Rogers in some of his formulations (e.g., 1963), has emphasized integration, unity, and man's achieving congruence with his "inner organismic processes." Rogers thought that these organismic processes were often unconscious. As a result of unfortunate socialization procedures in our culture persons often become dissociated, "consciously behaving in terms of static constructs and abstractions and unconsciously behaving in terms of the actualizing tendency" (Rogers, 1963, p. 20).

Encounter groups (Schutz, 1967) also pay considerable attention to unconscious processes. In this sense they also depend, just as psychodynamic theorists do, on clinical inferences about the person's behaviors as signs whose meaning the individual himself does not know consciously. The emphasis on interpretation of underlying meanings is evident in this excerpt from a typical introduction to an encounter session provided by the "trainer" (leader):

> . . . you, not me, decide what to do in here, such as the topic you want to talk about or the activities you try . . . but I can be counted on to ask, "What's going on?" The idea is to try to understand not only what we do or say—the content level—but also the feelings underneath, the processes going on (Lakin, 1972, p. 20).

Except for the fact that the setting is a group in which the members will be active and participate in the interpretation, this orientation may not be very different from the type supplied in more traditional psychotherapy. As such, the problems of reliability and validity found in connection with clinical judgment (Chapter 9) apply here just as strongly. It of course may be argued that each group member is always entirely free to reject any interpretations he feels do not fit him. But given the susceptibility of humans even to subtle group pressures, such "resistance" may require more independence than can be expected realistically. To try to guard against poor group practices, many advocates of encounter experiences note the importance of the leader's competence and experience and urge that prospective members choose their groups with the greatest care, cautioning "Let the buyer beware!"

To the extent that the psychologist accepts the idea that unconscious processes are key determinants, and relies on clinical judgement to infer them, he faces all the dilemmas previously discussed in the context of clinical judgment. That is true whether he intends to infer unconscious processes in the service of the actualizing tendency and personal growth, or in the service of id impulses of sex and aggression, or in the service of underlying source traits. Regardless of the hypothesized nature of the unconscious mechanisms, it is incumbent upon the psychologist to demonstrate his ability to make his inferences about them validly, reliably, and usefully. But no methodological difficulties should deter psychologists from listening more closely to what their "subjects" can tell them.

## SUMMARY

1. The assessment techniques discussed in this chapter represent attempts to study the person's subjective experience within the framework of scientific rules. Most phenomenologically oriented personality psychologists try to bring the individual's private experiences into the public domain by studying subjective experiences with objective techniques. This chapter has shown that the phenomenological orientation to personality has available a variety of methods for studying personal meanings and experiences objectively. The phenomenological approach hence is not merely a point of view about personality; it also offers distinctive techniques for studying persons.

2. Gary W.'s self-conceptualization serves as an example of the raw data of phenomenology. In the phenomenological view, the person may be his own best assessor. Research indicates that self-assessment has yielded predictions as accurate as those from more sophisticated personality tests, from combinations of tests, from clinical judgments, and from complex statistical analyses. Thus the person himself may be a good predictor of

his own behavior for such diverse outcomes as success in college, in jobs, and in psychotherapy.

3. One especially useful technique for obtaining a person's self-appraisal is the Q-sort. In this measure the person takes a large number of cards, each containing a descriptive statement, and sorts them into categories in a forced distribution. These Q-sorts may be used for self-description, to describe the ideal self, or to describe a relationship. The information yielded by a Q-sort may be of intrinsic interest, or it may yield correlations with other data of interest.

4. The interview has been favored by phenomenologically oriented psychologists. Through empathy the interviewer tries to explore the person's feelings and self-concepts and to see the world from his framework and viewpoint. Content analysis has been used by Carl Rogers and others in research on processes in the interview.

5. The "semantic differential" is a rating technique that permits the objective assessment of the meaning of the rater's words and concepts. Research with these scales reveals an evaluative, a potency, and an activity factor. These three factors are similar to those found often in trait ratings of persons.

6. The Role Construct Repertory (Rep) Test was devised by George Kelly to systematically study personal constructs. The test tries to explore the subjective dimensions of similarity among events (people or things) and the subjective opposites of those dimensions as the individual construes them. Interviews and other techniques (such as the TAT) also may be used to elaborate personal constructs more fully. A personal construct conceptualization of Gary W. illustrates some of the main features of the personal construct approach to phenomenology.

7. Recently attention has also been given to the importance of nonverbal expressions, movements, and gestures.

8. The phenomenological orientation also has influenced views of what constitutes healthy personality and it has significant practical applications for personality change. Most influential have been Rogers' client-centered therapy and a variety of encounter group experiences. These methods offer potential gains for some people but may be hazardous under certain conditions.

9. In other directions, efforts have been made to explore the use of psychedelic drugs and of meditation to change consciousness and to increase personal awareness.

10. Although phenomenological analyses tend to focus on experience and perceptions, sometimes extensive inferences are made about hypothesized unconscious problems and conflicts beyond the individual's awareness. In those cases the psychologist faces all the problems encountered in psychodynamic efforts to make clinical inferences. It is necessary to demonstrate the reliability and validity of the clinician's inferences, regardless of his particular theoretical orientation.

The previous sections provided broad overviews of major approaches to personality and of the main ideas and applications associated with each. In this section the focus will shift from frameworks and strategies for conceptualizing individuals and changing behavior to the basic processes involved in personality. Our central concerns here will be the development and causes of the overt and covert behavior patterns that have been studied by personality psychologists. Therefore we will consider some of the main findings that have come from personality research.

Investigators of personality have been guided by each of the major theoretical orientations and, most often, by a theoretical mixture that draws on some ideas from many conceptualizations. Hence in practice it becomes difficult to separate the contributions of various theories. Nevertheless, wherever possible, we shall point out major controversial issues so that some of the most important differences

# PART 3

PERSONALITY
DEVELOPMENT
AND BASIC
PROCESSES

between orientations will become more evident. We also will be alert to the implications of the research evidence for the status of central theoretical constructs.

The first chapter of this part introduces the topic of socialization and personality development. Later chapters will focus on the findings of research on diverse topics relevant to basic personality processes. These topics include the nature and formation of sexual identity, the development of psychological differences between the sexes, and such phenomena as frustration, aggression, conflict, and anxiety. Subsequent chapters in this part will examine the nature of psychological defense and the ways in which people can learn to achieve self-control. Then we will examine how the individual forms concepts about himself and becomes his own assessor. Finally, we will return to one of the most enduring and central issues in psychology: how can we conceptualize the interaction of the person and the conditions of his life?

# CHAPTER 13
# EARLY PERSONALITY DEVELOPMENT

## PATTERNS OF DEVELOPMENT

Personality development is such a vast topic that one has to find ways of simplifying it and slicing it conceptually into more manageable, smaller units. One approach does that by focusing on the major events or milestones that characterize personality development at various points in the life cycle. Numerous conditions and events throughout development provide special challenges and seem to be dominant concerns or themes for most people at various points in their lives. At least in our own culture many of these events tend to be roughly sequential, reflecting a patterning dictated both by biological maturation and by social practice.

### MATURATION AND LEARNING

The orderly development of the human organism begins in the mother's womb long before the baby's birth. The development of the fetus progresses in accord with a relatively fixed time schedule, dictated largely by genetic determinants but dependent also upon the biological environment. In that sense, embryological development is the prototype of maturation: its timing and patterning proceed in accord with the organism's genetic nature and unfold relatively independently of experience as long as a proper environment is provided.

After birth, maturation of structure and of some functions continues in an orderly pattern similar to the sequencing seen in prenatal growth. Maturation has a part in such developmental patterns as standing and crawling, walking, progressively skillful use of hands and fingers, and talking. In these functions, maturation and learning play a collaborative role. The almost inextricable interaction of maturation and learning is seen clearly in the acquisition of language. The child's receptivity to language learning, his readiness to learn, depends on his age and biological development. Yet the language he acquires and ultimately speaks depends on what he hears and on learning processes.

## BIOLOGICAL BASES OF PERSONALITY

Debates about the importance of maturation *versus* learning tend to be as fruitless as the ones that raged for many years about the role of heredity versus environment. Man is both a biological and a social organism, and the effects of heredity, maturation, learning, and environment are impressive and interactive in their impact on the total organism. The role of genetic and maturational processes is seen most clearly when one examines embryological development and the structural features of human growth.

Beyond physical development, inheritance certainly contributes to intelligence. Research with twins raised in various environments (either together or apart) suggests that when environments are similar, measured intelligence tends to be increasingly similar to the degree that the individuals have an increasing proportion of genes in common (e.g., Cartwright, 1974; Vandenberg, 1971). Consistent with these results, it is often suggested that a person's genetic endowment sets an upper limit or ceiling on the degree to which his or her intelligence can be developed (e.g., Royce, 1973); the environment may help or hinder achievement of that ceiling. Even some personality characteristics, such as emotional expressiveness (including sociability and extraversion measured on personality questionnaires like the MMPI) may involve a genetic component to some extent (e.g., Gottesman, 1963, 1966). Some psychological disorders, most notably schizophrenia, also may involve at least a small degree of heritability (e.g., Gottesman & Shields, 1969; Mosher, 1970; Rosenthal, 1971), and certain kinds of mental deficiency reflect a specific genetic influence (Vandenberg, 1971).

Humans are physical creatures, and biology provides the foundations on which all social forces impinge. Although at present neither the magnitude nor the mechanisms of the genetic and hormonal contribution to personality and social development are clear, they are receiving increasing attention in research. Biochemistry and genetics will surely help our future understanding of behavior, but currently most psychologists still focus on psychological rather than biological conditions in their research on personality.

While recognizing the importance of genes and glands, to grasp the dramatic role of social learning imagine the enormous differences that would be found in the personalities of twins with identical genetic endowments if they were raised apart in two different families—or, even more striking, in two totally different cultures. Through social learning, vast differences develop among people in their reactions to most of the stimuli encountered in daily life. As a result of social learning processes, stimuli that terrify one person may delight the next and leave a third indifferent. We see, for example, an adolescent who seems angered or bored by the same goals his parents pursue avidly, and parents, in turn, who are horrified by the activities and values their son seems to treasure.

The fact that learning experiences have obviously massive effects on personality throughout life in no way denies the role of genetic and constitutional factors. Indeed some individual differences in behavior seem to characterize even the young infant. Thus young babies appear to differ from each other in such patterns as the vigor of their activity, their irritability and how easily they cry, the rate at which they become satiated by stimuli, and their threshold for shifting attention (e.g., Korner, 1971). These initial patterns are quickly acted upon by parents and other important persons in the baby's environment and affect the attitudes and behaviors of these caretakers in their relations with him in a continuous interaction.

## STAGES IN PSYCHOLOGICAL DEVELOPMENT

Some theories hypothesize definite, distinct sequences in personality and cognitive development. A search for critical or central happenings at different times in life is most characteristic of *stage theories*. We saw such a theory in Freud's conception of psychosexual development from the oral to the anal, phallic, and genital stages. Freud emphasized the importance of biological events (changes in erogenous zones) as foci for conflict in personality development. Others have stressed key themes in psychosocial development, as we saw, for example, in Erikson's (1950) view of phases and crises in interpersonal development (Chapter 3). Still other theorists have hypothesized stages in cognitive development (Piaget, 1960) and in moral development (Kohlberg, 1969).

Stage theories suggest that there are distinct qualitative differences in personality and cognitive processes at different ages. For example, the "cognitive-developmental" stage theory hypothesizes that people have "cognitive structures" or "rules" for processing information (as in thinking), and that these structures are fundamentally different at different points in development. Kohlberg (1969) believes that these cognitive structures serve to change "stimulus inputs" (information from the environment) and that, in turn, the structures are changed by the inputs. The hypothesis that makes this a stage theory is that such structures undergo basic transformations during development and thus become qualitatively different. The *sequence* of transformations, according to a stage theory, is definite and fixed, but the *rate* of development may be changed by experience.

Are there definite stages? There is disagreement about the validity of stage theories. Some psychologists see personality and cognitive development as a continuous process in which learning experiences may accumulate in a variety of sequences, depending on the specific learning opportunities the child happens to be exposed to. Others emphasize that certain functions and skills—such as walking or talking, for example—develop most rapidly and dramatically at certain "critical periods." They suggest that some psychological functions develop best only at particular phases of development. Many are convinced that at least cognitive development entails distinct levels or stages of organization.

While there is controversy about the need to construe discrete stages in psychological development, it is widely recognized that socialization is not a haphazard accumulation of bits of behavior but entails, instead, some orderly development. That is true at least to the degree that some complex social behavior patterns are sequential. They require the preexistence of other earlier learning. Some things usually are learned much more readily after other things have been acquired. Likewise, the absence of certain behaviors and skills makes the development of behaviors that depend on them less likely although not necessarily impossible.

It also is generally recognized that the content and organization of personality may be radically different at different points in development. Obviously the ideas, beliefs, values, skills, and interests of the three-year-old are not those of the same person at 40. The child is father to the man, but what a person does and is changes with development. Hence it is often intriguing to examine lives at different points in time, when different events and crises are salient, and to assess the nature of the stability and of the change found over the years (e.g., Block, 1971).

# EARLY CHILDHOOD

## THE INFANT'S DEPENDENCY

Perhaps the most universally recognized condition of the human being is his helplessness and passive dependency in early infancy. The infant emerges from the uterus as a highly perishable creature whose survival depends on prolonged care from others. The baby can do almost nothing to fulfill his own needs, and depends on those around him to provide gratifications and to reduce discomforts. Although the infant cannot take care of his needs, a set of responses is available to him: he scans his environment, cries, sucks, smiles, thrashes about, and vocalizes. Some of these responses can exert considerable effects on the environment, as seen in the control over their mothers that some babies rapidly achieve by active crying. Thus while the baby cannot satisfy his needs directly, he can and does learn to summon and influence his caretakers, and the relationship is a transaction rather than a one-way affair.

## *THE FEEDING SITUATION*

Throughout life the human organism engages perpetually in transactions with the environment, and in this exchange each continuously alters the other. The remarkable plasticity of behavior, and the organism's magnificent sensitivity to crucial environmental changes, can be seen even in the baby's feeding activities if they are analyzed closely.

Usually the mother is the person who provides the child with fulfillment of his biological needs during infancy. She feeds him, comforts him, rocks and cuddles him, diapers him, and talks to him. Some theorists consider the relationship that develops between mother and child during this period as the prototype for the child's sense of "basic trust" (Erikson, 1950) and the foundation for later development. As we saw in Freud's "oral stage," psychoanalytic theory attributes the greatest importance to the role of the lips, tongue, and mouth as erogenous zones and to the secondary pleasure of sucking and swallowing in connection with feeding. There is disagreement about the nature and consequences of these pleasures, but there is no question that feeding and the experiences around it are major events of early infancy.

**The relationship between the child and its caretakers is a transaction, not a one-way affair.**

The mouth and the activity of feeding figure prominently in many personality theories, yet until recently such activities as sucking have been objects for speculation rather than for direct observation. As happens often in science, conjecture precedes experimental research, and experimental research awaits a methodology for studying the phenomena of interest.

A good example of harnessing a vital phenomenon so that it can be studied thoroughly is reported by Bruner (1967). To study sucking in the infant, an apparatus was devised that records changes in sucking pressure. The apparatus consists of an ordinary baby's nursing bottle except that the bottle is connected electrically to a polygraph.

The baby's sucking is not only registered on the polygraph: it is also monitored by a programming device that can be adjusted to activate milk delivery to the baby through a milk-pulsing system. The program of milk delivery can be set so that it occurs only when the baby sucks in a specified way, or at fixed intervals after each suck, or after every other suck, and so on. Thus it becomes possible to examine the precise relationships between changes in reinforcement (milk delivery) and changes in particular characteristics of the sucking response.

Results from research of this type reveal the surprising flexibility even of nutritional sucking. Using changes in sucking activity as the dependent variable and manipulating a variety of stimulus changes experimentally, investigators have found many indications of highly sensitive learning during the first few months of life. Bruner (1967, p. 16) reports, for example, that during a 15-minute session "suctioning will virtually drop out if mouthing alone produces milk." Thus even babies show subtle discrimination and responsiveness to changes in the outcomes they receive.

## VISUAL ATTENTION

Although the feeding situation is a critical phase of early development, it is only one component of the total relationship between the growing organism and the world, and contributes only one important part of the experience and stimulation available to him. Thus the baby is more than an "oral" creature. He responds to stimulation of the mouth, lips, and tongue, but in addition, he sees, hears, and feels, obtaining stimulation visually, aurally, and from being handled.

One project that was devoted to the ideal of cultivating optimal development studied physically normal but institutionalized infants. Convinced that in spite of an abundance of theories developmental psychology has much too little real data, Professor Burton L. White of Harvard University began by carefully observing infants as they lay in their cribs in the wardrooms of the institution. He and his colleagues recorded the quantity and quality of visual-motor activity to study the babies' attention. On the basis of these observations they plotted the development of the infants' tendency to explore the visual surroundings, as depicted in Figure 13-1. Some of the findings surprised the investigators.

**Figure 13-1**  THE DEVELOPMENT OF THE TENDENCY TO EXPLORE THE SURROUND (CONTROL GROUP)

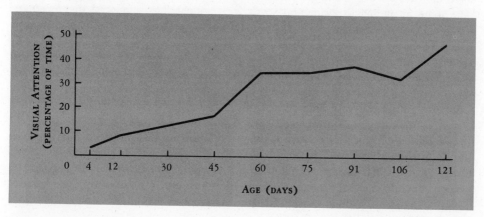

Adapted from B. L. White and R. Held, Plasticity of sensorimotor development in the human infant, in J. F. Rosenblith and Allinsmith, eds., *The causes of behavior II*, pp. 60–70; copyright 1966 by Allyn and Bacon, Inc., Boston.

One important revelation for me which resulted from these weekly observations was that, contrary to my academically bred expectations, infants weren't really very oral during the first months of life. In fact, between two and six months, a far more appropriate description would be that they are visual-prehensory creatures. We observed subject after subject spend dozens of hours watching first his fists, then his fingers, and then the interactions between hands and fingers. Thumb-sucking and mouthing were rarely observed except for brief periods when the infant was either noticeably upset or unusually hungry (White, 1967, p. 207).

These observations point up how much more we need to know about the details of the infant's activities before we can reach conclusions about what events characterize early development. It may be, as this investigator's comments imply, that the "oral" infant will turn out to be much more attentive and active, and less oral and passive, than was believed in early formulations.

## STIMULATION AND DEPRIVATION

In recent years there has been a growing recognition in our society that an alarmingly large number of people fall tragically short of their human potential. In most parts of the world, including the United States, major segments of the population live in underprivileged and deprived environments that stifle their potential development. In spite of the magnitude of this problem, we are just beginning to study and understand how a child's world may be structured so that experience can have the best effects on his growth and development.

Some intriguing experimental work with animals has suggested that postnatal handling and other forms of early stimulation may have major effects on subsequent development (e.g., Dennenberg, 1964; Levine, 1957, 1962). Animals like mice, cats, and dogs grow up to be superior on many tests if they are handled or stimulated with relative frequency early in development. For example, some rats were raised in a dimly lit, quiet room with no opportunity to contact or see other animals. "Enriched" rats, in contrast, were raised in groups of 10 animals, had "toys" in their cages, and received special learning and "play opportunities." The stimulated, "educated" rats were shown to differ from the deprived ones even in the brain chemistry of their cortexes and in the weight of their brains (Bennett and his associates, 1964; Rosenzweig and collaborators, 1960). Early handling and stimulation may also be important for human development (e.g., Casler, 1961; Yarrow, 1961). Conversely, growing up in a stimulus-impoverished environment may have negative effects on development.

## EFFECTS OF SOCIAL ISOLATION

To study the consequences of depriving an infant of social stimulation would require exposing him to prolonged total isolation. Such experiments with humans are out of the question for obvious ethical reasons, and under natural conditions babies fortunately are not submitted to total social deprivation. In experimental research, however, monkeys have been raised in isolation (without any social contacts); they have been kept alone in a cage for the first six months of life (Harlow & Harlow, 1966). When later removed from isolation these monkeys showed extreme social abnormalities. The typical animal crouched and seemed fearful, avoiding all social contact. If the isolation period was less than 6 months, the animal generally recovered and showed normal behavior; if it extended from 6 to 12 months the consequences tended to be grave and irreversible—the animal tended to become extremely fearful, and his social and sexual behavior remained abnormal.

Taken collectively, the studies in this and preceding sections suggest that early stimulation is an important condition for proper development, and that a severe, prolonged absence of minimal stimulation may have pronounced negative consequences.

According to some investigations, early deprivation of the kind found in orphanages may impede cognitive and emotional development (e.g., Goldfarb, 1944, 1945). Institutionalized infants often tend to be different from family-reared babies, and the differences are evident after about four months. In general the institutionalized baby is more likely to show many deficits. He smiles less, cries less, vocalizes little, does no cooing, and by about eight months seems uninterested, detached, and apathetic. Some observers say the institutionalized youngsters gradually seem more and more lifeless and apathetically miserable, looking and acting "as if the spark of life had gone out of them" (Provence & Lipton, 1962). Such reports are dramatic, but the findings certainly cannot be generalized to all institutions.

Moreover, it is hard to interpret the deficiencies reported for institutionalized children. First, it is possible that some institutionalized infants were atypical before being institutionalized. Second, any negative effects produced by prolonged institutionalization may be due to any one or more of a large number of uncontrolled features of institutional life. These features include the absence of the child's mother as well as the generally impoverished environment that characterizes many understaffed institutions. Often the institutionalized child grows up not only without a mother but also in an atmosphere that includes an everchanging, overworked staff, a monotonous sensory environment, and a host of other specific differences that range from lack of toys to possible dietary deficiencies. Experimental studies are needed to separate out the trivial from the really crucial variables that may exert negative influences on early development.

## EFFECTS OF ENRICHING THE ENVIRONMENT

In the previously mentioned studies of visual attention in institutionalized babies, B. L. White and his colleagues extended their careful observations to various indices of visual attention (such as visually directed reaching). Gradually the investigators began to explore experimentally how changes in rearing conditions might enhance visual attention and hence lead to more adequate development. The environment of a group of institutionalized infants was enriched in several ways—for example, by increased handling and by massively enriching the visual surroundings through the addition of colorful visual stimuli (see Figure 13-2). To assess their visual-motor development, weekly tests were made of the infants' activities (e.g., hand regard, prehension, and visual attention). Some selected results from one study are summarized in Figure 13-3. The overall results from several studies of this type indicated that aspects of early visual-motor development are extremely pliable, although "neither the limits of this plasticity nor the range of visual-motor functions" that can be modified substantially is known at this time (White, 1967, p. 223).

An earlier study on the effects of special stimulation provided institutionalized babies with extra nurturance and "mothering" (Rheingold, 1956). The investigator selected 18 six-month-old infants who were being cared for by volunteers in the institution. The investigator assigned half the children to an experimental group in which she personally mothered them for an eight-week period, eight hours daily for five days of each week. She diapered them, played with them, smiled at them, and tried to provide nurturant mothering during this period. The other eight babies served as a control group and simply continued to receive the more typical routine institutional care provided by several women caretakers. Thus the experimental children received more caretaking—from one person—during the eight weeks. All the infants were tested weekly on a variety of tests.

The specially nurtured children became much more socially responsive to the experimenter than did the control babies. When the experimenter smiled or talked to them, they were much more likely to smile back and respond facially. Again the children's behavior was highly discriminative. The improvement of the experimental children was limited to their *social* responsiveness; the two groups of children remained similar in their *motor* development. Moreover, there was some generalization of increased social responsiveness from the experimenter to a relative stranger (the examiner), but this effect was much less pronounced and not stable. Research on this type of social behavior has called attention to the reciprocal relation between caretaker and infant (e.g., Rheingold, Gewirtz & Ross, 1959). Social stimulation (smiles, pats) tends to enhance or reinforce social responsiveness. The baby's facial reactions, smiles, and vocalizations in turn increase the likelihood of eliciting smiles and responsive sounds from the mother, and hence the two mutually influence and strengthen the developing attachment.

Figure 13-2   A, THE TYPICAL NURSERY WARD FACILITY FOR CONTROL INFANTS 1 TO 4 MONTHS OF AGE. B, MASSIVE ENRICHMENT CONDITION FEATURING MANY BRIGHTLY COLORED OBJECTS AROUND THE INFANT AT DISTANCES OF 5 TO 36 INCHES

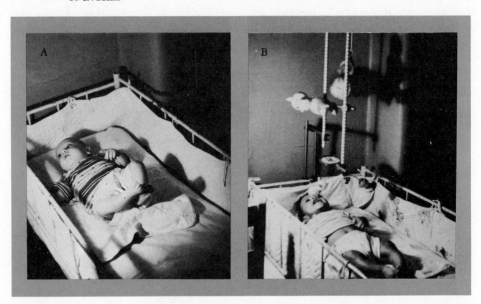

From B. L. White and R. Held, Plasticity of sensorimotor development in the human infant, in J. F. Rosenblith and Allinsmith, eds., *The causes of behavior II*, pp. 60–70; copyright 1966 by Allyn and Bacon, Inc., Boston.

**Figure 13-3**  COMPARISON OF VISUAL ATTENTION AMONG CONTROL INFANTS AND THOSE
WHO RECEIVED MASSIVE ENVIRONMENTAL ENRICHMENT

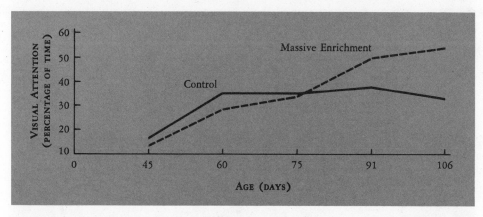

Adapted from B. L. White and R. Held, Plasticity of sensorimotor development in the human infant,
in J. F. Rosenblith and Allinsmith, eds., *The causes of behavior II*, pp. 60–70; copyright 1966 by Allyn
and Bacon, Inc., Boston.

## SOCIAL ATTACHMENT

Around the middle of his first year of life the home-reared infant normally
begins to show signs of specific attachment to the mother and to other people, especially the father. Although there are individual differences in this development,
most children start to manifest attachment in about the seventh month. The
strength of this attachment may be inferred from the amount of the child's protest
when he is separated momentarily from a person with whom he was comfortable
and close. Usually approximately a month after the first signs of attachment begin,
the child also starts to show fear when confronted by strangers (Shaffer & Emerson, 1964). Thus it is during the second part of the first year that he forms clear
discriminations between familiar and strange people. In contrast, during the first six
months of life (especially from 2 to 6 months), the infant seems to seek stimulation
more diffusely, and to smile at strange faces as well as familiar ones.

Social attachment, according to some theorists, may have its roots in the close
association between the caretaker (usually the mother) and reduction of the infant's
bodily tensions through feeding. Because of her close association with the biological tension-reduction produced by food, the mother thus becomes a satisfying and
sought-after object for the child. In turn, other people also become objects for the
child's attachments on the basis of generalization as well as for the reinforcement
they supply in their own right (Dollard & Miller, 1950).

To test this idea of the link between feeding and attachment, one would have

Social attachment develops early in life.

to separate the mother's feeding function from her other maternal attributes. This separation, practically impossible in the human situation, was achieved simply and ingeniously in experiments with monkeys (Harlow & Zimmerman, 1959). In these studies young monkeys were reared in isolation from their true mothers and were supplied with two artificial and inanimate "laboratory mothers." Neither laboratory mother really looked like a monkey. One was composed of wire mesh and, although she was hardly "soft and cuddly," could be clung to by the young monkey. The other "mother" was a similar shape but was covered with a towel-like terry cloth and hence was much more "cuddly."

The main question studied was: Would the young monkeys always cling to the mother-figure that supplied food? Accordingly food was made available from a bottle attached to the chest of one or the other mother during each monkey's development. In test trials the monkeys then were free to go to either mother. Regardless of which mother was the source of food, the young monkeys generally chose the cuddly terry-cloth mother and spent more time clinging to her. Moreover, contact with the cuddly mother seemed to be a source of security for the infant: he explored strange objects more freely when holding on to her hand, and he seemed less fearful in new environments if he could make contact with the cloth mother. The behavior of the monkeys who had been fed by the wire-mesh mother was highly discriminative. They ran to her for food when hungry but then returned to the soft-contact mother for clinging and spent most of the day with her.

The results suggest that attachment behaviors may arise independent of the food source and hunger reduction. This is perhaps most evident in animal species such as ducklings, which feed themselves from birth on but nevertheless exhibit close attachment to their mother, following her around much of the time. Association with feeding and the comfort of tension reduction often do enhance attachment, but they may not be either its main or only cause.

# LATER DEVELOPMENT

## *TOILET TRAINING*

Development involves a gradual transition from helplessness and dependency to active mastery, independence, competence, and autonomy. In the study of this transition, psychodynamic theorists have devoted considerable attention to toilet training as a prime instance of conflict between the child's impulsive pleasure-seeking and the constraining demands of socializing agents. Their interest in toilet training stems partly from the fact that learning to inhibit and control bowel and bladder functions is a universal feature of socialization. Even more important, the strong interest in toilet training reflects the psychoanalytic emphasis on the "anal stage" as the second critical phase of personality development (Chapter 3).

Undoubtedly if parents have learned to feel disgust and shame in connection with defecation and toilet habits, they may easily convey some of their anxieties when training their children. Toilet training probably was a more difficult problem when attitudes regarding body functions were more squeamish, as in Victorian society; or when nursemaids terrified youngsters with horror stories about the dire consequences of toilet accidents. Some problems also may arise if toilet training is forced when the child is very immature and has difficulty understanding just what he is supposed to do. Under such conditions, an unfortunate and unnecessary battle can arise between mother and child. Except in unusual conditions, however, it should be possible to achieve toilet training in a sufficiently mature child without undue upsets by proper instructions and the appropriate use of social approval to reinforce the desired responses. Of course if parents express bizarre attitudes regarding body functions, display anxiety, and are severely punitive, they may easily generate correspondingly disturbed behaviors and distorted feelings in the child.

A great deal of research has been conducted on toilet training. Many studies report some relationship between severity of toilet training and later maladjustment. Unfortunately most of these studies involve methodological problems that make it impossible to interpret them clearly. That is because mothers who report that they are extremely severe in toilet training may also be harsh in other areas of training; alternatively, children who were maladjusted initially or hard to care for may have provoked their mothers into toilet training them more severely. Thus we cannot know whether severe toilet training by a mother was a cause of her child's later maladjustment, or was just one part of a larger pattern of poor child-rearing practices, or was itself caused by the child's previous maladjustment.

## SEX AND AGGRESSION

As the child matures biologically and achieves better motor and cognitive skills he gains many new possibilities for self-assertion and active mastery. For example, with crawling and walking comes a new mobility that permits the youngster to manipulate his environment more actively and to explore the world more fully. Many of these exploratory behaviors delight the parents, but others may be extremely upsetting, as when the child explores the medicine cabinet or the electrical outlets rather than his toys.

Two patterns of behavior that are especially problem-producing in our culture are *aggression* and *sex*. "Aggression" is behavior aimed at inflicting injury or harm on others; it always has a victim. When the child bangs his pegboard with his hammer the parents approve, but when he bangs his siblings and playmates the social environment quickly reacts against him and the battles start.

Sex is the second behavior pattern about which socializing agents are likely to become disturbed. The child's investigations of the environment include exploration of his own body. He notices genitals and especially the fact that some people have a penis and others do not. He expresses interest in these biological facts and in his own body, and may enjoy touching himself and others.

Just as with toilet training, the child's experiences regarding aggression and sex can become a basis for anxiety and extreme inhibition. Alternatively, these experiences, like other aspects of his developing personality, may be managed without undue trauma. Threats about castration, and feelings that sexual and aggressive activities are bad, can easily be conveyed through both the attitudes displayed by socializing agents and the things they say and do directly to the child when he engages in sexual or aggressive behaviors or tries them out tentatively. Conversely, a failure to learn to control aggression and sex in socially approved ways may be as detrimental to development as are excessive anxiety and inhibition. The diffusely aggressive youngster who has not learned when and what he *cannot* hit and hurt is likely to have as many problems as the youngster who is distressed at any expression of aggressiveness. These comments about aggression apply equally to the socialization of sex.

## CURIOSITY AND INFORMATION SEEKING

While early psychological theorists stressed biological drives and simple rewards and punishments in their analyses of human motivation, more recent formulations have recognized the role of information and cognitive variables. These formulations emphasize that the informational qualities of stimuli affect their impact (e.g., Berlyne, 1966). Such attributes as novelty, complexity, and surprise, for example, influence the child's attention.

Children as well as adults seem to seek moderate amounts of uncertainty or predictable change. The desire for some surprise is seen, for example, in many types of play and recreational activity, such as the "fun houses" and grotesque distorting mirrors of amusement parks. When the environment is utterly unchanging for prolonged time periods, people become unbearably bored and perceptual and intellectual functions may be hampered. Yet extreme surprise and novelty may provoke anxiety and distress. For example, when chimpanzees are exposed to harmless but surprising sights (such as a model of a chimpanzee's head without the body) they may become terrified. Strong fear has also been reported in children in response to strange or novel sights and sounds. Similarly, while adults enjoy things that are unexpected, the borderline between pleasant surprise and unpleasant shock is often thin.

In general, novel and complex stimuli attract more attention than do completely familiar and simple events. For example, such features of the environment as irregularity of arrangement, and incongruity all enhance the observer's alertness and general arousal (Berlyne, 1966; Nunnally & Lemond, 1973). On the other extreme, an ever-changing, totally unpredictable environment is chaotic and anxiety-producing; it leaves the individual overwhelmed rather than alert. The specific ways in which the structure of the child's world best encourages his curiosity without distressing him deserve extensive research.

## COGNITIVE DEVELOPMENT AND COMPETENCE

Psychodynamic theorists originally emphasized instincts of sex and aggression and the importance of resolving conflicts with oral, anal, and Oedipal problems in development. More recently psychologists have recognized that the acquisition of competence is also a vital component of adequate adaptation (White, 1959). In every society, but especially in those that stress achievement, a failure to develop at least minimal skills and areas of adequacy dooms the individual to a life filled with dissatisfactions.

Personality development thus is not rigidly separated from cognitive and intellectual development and from the growth of competence and skills (Kohlberg, 1969; Mischel, 1973a). Adequate functioning in our society, and the individual's conception of his own worth, depend on his ability to cope with problems and on his self-evaluation of his achievements. As later chapters will emphasize, the person's concepts about himself, and the manner in which he assesses his own accomplishments and failures, are critical aspects of personality development. Experiences and self-assessments connected with competence and mastery probably begin in earliest childhood, but they do not stop there. Throughout life competencies develop and self-evaluations are made in areas that range from one's work to one's

**Figure 13-4** COGNITIVE DEVELOPMENT IS REFLECTED IN THESE DRAWINGS BY A GIRL AT THREE POINTS IN CHILDHOOD. EACH TIME THE CHILD WAS ASKED TO "DRAW A PICTURE OF A GIRL."

Age 4                              Age 5½                              Age 7½

sexuality and one's total self. Indeed, excessively harsh self-evaluations may become the grounds for painful self-tortures, just as excessively lenient self-appraisals, especially when accompanied by grossly inadequate performances, may lead to their own set of reality problems.

The exploratory behaviors, the curiosity- and mastery-oriented activities displayed by the young child, are boosted incalculably by cognitive development (Figure 13-4) and by the acquisition of language. As he becomes verbal the child begins to label things, including himself, and to form increasingly complex discriminations. These discriminations are based not only on physical attributes but also on semantic features—on what things are called. Gradually the individual's increasingly explicit awareness of himself as an entity differentiated from the rest of the world comes to include a more delineated concept of himself as a distinct person construed to have stable attributes (Chapter 20).

### ACHIEVEMENT

Closely related to the desire for competence is the individual's tendency to strive for achievement. The desire to "do well" and the achievement of competence in intellectual and social behavior have received much attention in current approaches to personality. For example, research on achievement-related motives and behaviors shows that they have some generality across situations. Even by nursery school age, children display some consistency in their achievement strivings. Children who seek approval from their mothers for achievement tend to behave similarly toward their nursery school teachers (Crandall, Preston & Rabson,

1960). Children who often initiate achievement efforts at home display similar behaviors during free play in nursery school. Consistency in achievement striving is
greatest across similar activities. For example, the intellectual striving of elementary school children was substantially correlated with their striving on mechanical
tasks: however, strivings for intellectual and mechanical achievement were not related to achievement striving in athletics (Moss & Kagan, 1961).

Achievement behavior, especially in the form of intellectual striving, may be
one of the more stable aspects of personality, showing some consistency over long
periods of time. The preschool child who strives to master cognitive and intellectual skills tends to maintain this motivation during high school and early adulthood
(Moss & Kagan, 1961). Boys and girls who start school with strong motivation to
do well and to achieve recognition thus may tend to develop into young adults
who are concerned with intellectual accomplishments and achievement, although
there are many exceptions.

The individual's degree of achievement striving tends to be related to his intelligence and level of general ability. For example, ratings of the degree to which
children strive for achievement and recognition are related positively to the children's scores on intelligence tests. That is, brighter children are more oriented toward achievement. Moreover, these positive relationships between achievement
strivings and intelligence seem to be maintained throughout childhood and in early
adulthood (Kagan & Moss, 1962). The positive relationship between ability and
achievement striving is not surprising. The more intelligent, competent, skillful
children can more readily achieve satisfaction for their achievement efforts because
they are more likely to do well. Hence their motivation to strive for excellence
becomes strengthened by the reinforcement of success.

The child's degree of achievement striving is also influenced by the reactions
of other people to his achievement efforts. For example, children who often displayed strong achievement efforts outside the home tended to be those whose
mothers frequently and spontaneously rewarded their efforts to achieve, even when
the youngsters were not seeking approval (Crandall, 1963). The mothers of children
who became high in achievement strivings seemed to foster independence early in
their children's development. They generally ignored their child's requests for help
and, instead, encouraged his tentative efforts to gain mastery and achieve solutions
by himself (Winterbottom, 1958). Mothers who rewarded early accomplishments in
their children seemed to facilitate their children's intellectual strivings and their
desire to do well in school and to learn new skills. Likewise, the encouragement of
mastery of basic skills—such as walking and talking—early in childhood, tends to
facilitate subsequent school achievement (Mussen, Conger & Kagan, 1974).

Conversely, the child who grows up in a home or subculture in which adequate stimulation is absent and intellectual achievement is not recognized is much
less likely to develop the achievement orientation, skills, and academic striving
necessary for success in school work. An environment that provides the young
child with good opportunities to observe and practice verbal and intellectual skills
may enhance substantially the chances for high intellectual achievements and competence (Wolf, 1966). Thus the child's intellectual abilities (as measured by IQ

tests) and the stimulation, encouragement, and support that the environment provides for achievements jointly influence actual accomplishments.

# SOCIAL LEARNING IN PERSONALITY DEVELOPMENT

Descriptions of what is learned, and from whom, where, and when it is learned, throughout development are often informative and intriguing. To understand personality development adequately, however, one must go beyond culture-bound descriptions to analyze how the child acquires his personality—that is, the mechanisms of his personality development. An emphasis on *process*, on the variables that regulate social learning and cognitive and emotional development, should help us to understand the general rules of personality development regardless of the particular models or settings that are most influential at specific points in the person's life. We have already considered the role of early stimulation and experience. Now we will review the principles of social learning in personality development.

## DIRECT MECHANISMS

Some of the basic processes involved in social learning were discussed in Chapters 4 and 5. Recall that the valence or value of neutral stimuli may be changed through contiguous association with emotion-evoking stimuli, as seen in *classical conditioning*. This mechanism operates throughout personality development. For example, as we saw, the child's attitudes toward defecation and body functions are affected by the emotional events closely connected with them. If toilet functions and fear-producing experiences (such as harsh punishment) become regularly associated, anxiety may become linked with various components of the eliminative functions. For example, the untrained child who is made to feel a failure for soiling himself may become anxious about going to the toilet and refuse to go. Likewise, because of the closeness of the urethra, anus, and external genitals, it may be especially easy for the child to generalize his reactions from toilet functions to sexual activity. Conversely, positive attitudes may be developed by an appropriate association among neutral and positive stimuli. As a result of their temporally contiguous association with highly affective stimuli, other stimuli thus may become either aversive or positively valued in their own right. The effects of such conditioning may be seen clearly when previously neutral stimuli start to elicit fears (phobias) because of their association with fear-provoking events.

Remember also that even seemingly deeply ingrained behavior patterns, including many severe social deviations, may be changed when new response-reinforcement relations are established, as is demonstrated in *operant conditioning*. The outcomes that the child obtains when he tries behaviors influence his future readiness to try similar behavior. For example, if whining and a temper tantrum attract the attention of a busy mother, the outburst is more likely to be repeated than if it were left unattended. Likewise if the baby easily gets help from mother even for the most trivial problems as soon as he gets into difficulty, he is more likely to develop strong dependency habits involving her.

Opportunities to practice new behavior and to experience its positive consequences facilitate the future occurrence of similar behavior, but it is also easy to use "rewards" unwisely in socialization. A major purpose of socialization is to wean the individual from external controls and rewards so that behavior will become increasingly guided and supported by "intrinsic" gratifications, i.e., it will be done for its own sake. Therefore it is essential to use incentives wisely and only to the extent necessary to initiate and sustain desired behavior. External incentives may be important in order to encourage a person to try activities that have not yet become attractive for him. For example, approval and praise from parents for trying to play a violin may be helpful first steps in encouraging the child's earliest musical interests. But when the youngster begins to experience activity-generated satisfactions (e.g., from playing the music itself) it becomes important to avoid excessive external rewards. The latter would be unnecessary and possibly detrimental, leading the child to play for the "wrong reasons" and to easily extinguish his interests when external rewards become sparse or are removed altogether. The same considerations would apply in the socialization of such activities as concern for fairness, empathy, helpfulness, and attention to the longterm consequences of behavior. While such sensitivities would initially be encouraged by external response consequences (rewards), ultimately they should become sustained by the gratifications generated by the activities themselves.

Thus it should be clear that "overjustification" of an activity by excessive external reward may interfere with the satisfactions (intrinsic interests) that would otherwise be generated by the activity itself (e.g., Lepper, Greene & Nisbett, 1973). Excessive external rewards may even have boomerang effects and lead the recipient to devalue and resist the rewarded activity. For example, a child who enjoys books may lose interest in them if bribed with money to keep on reading. Such resistance is especially likely in a culture whose members value a sense of autonomy and freedom. Under such conditions, any seemingly undue or exaggerated external rewards may be interpreted as pressures and coercions, which may lead to intense resistance either overtly or covertly (e.g., Brehm, 1966), as in the "rebelliousness" of adolescents.

## OBSERVATIONAL LEARNING AND COGNITION

While learning studies with animals have emphasized direct reward or reinforcement, people learn through observation and symbolic processes, as well as by more direct methods. In this regard, a distinction has been made between *acquisition*, or learning, and *performance* (Chapter 5). We noted that what a person knows and can do depends in part on cognitive and observational processes. Indeed as was discussed earlier in this chapter, even the young baby under normal conditions soon becomes visually attentive and responsive to what he observes in his environment. On the basis of observational and cognitive processes, the developing organism gradually learns a vast repertoire of potential response patterns—of things he *can* do.

Information about the probable consequences of particular behavior patterns can be acquired vicariously, by observing other people and the outcomes they receive. Observing the outcomes other people get for aggressiveness, for example, influences the observer's tendency to perform similar behavior (e.g., Bandura & Walters, 1963). Performance thus often may be determined by vicarious and inferred response consequences rather than by direct "trial and error" learning. For example, a young adolescent does not have to be laughed at by his peers in order to learn the consequences of trying "sissyish" behavior. Observing positive consequences, such as attention or praise, for a response pattern tends to increase the probability that he will engage in similar activities. Conversely, when social models are punished severely for their actions, people who watch them will later tend to show greater inhibition of similar behavior (Bandura, 1965).

Any information that changes the person's anticipations about the probable outcomes of a behavior should modify the likelihood that he will perform similar behavior. For example, a boy learns about the things his parents are likely to reward and those they will probably punish not just from what the parents do to him but also from what he sees them do to his siblings. He also learns about adult roles by observing his parents and the outcomes or "payoffs" they get for various behavior patterns. Through observation children may learn a variety of complex general rules (Zimmerman & Rosenthal, 1974) that can apply to everything from conduct to language and problem-solving.

Even without actually observing the model's behavior, attitudes and preferences may be changed as a result of either reading or hearing about the relevant behavior of others (e.g., Bandura & Mischel, 1965). These symbolically produced effects are sometimes surprisingly large. In one study (Duncker, 1938) preschool children were told an exciting, vivid story in which the hero, Eaglefeather, violently abhorred a pleasant-tasting food and supposedly relished a more noxious one. After listening to the exploits and emotional reactions of the hero, the children changed their food preferences to conform with Eaglefeather's and maintained their new preferences fairly stably over time. Television, movies, books, stories, and other symbolic media play an important part in the transmission of information about the probable response consequences of diverse behaviors and may influence people's preferences, values, and choices to a considerable degree.

## GENERALIZATION AND DISCRIMINATION

Considerable *generalization* occurs if a response pattern is uniformly rewarded under many conditions or in many settings. If, for example, the child is encouraged to behave aggressively with older people as well as with peers, and when visiting other families as well as at home, he is likely to develop some generalized aggressive patterns.

Similarity among stimulus situations increases generalization effects. Generalization occurs not only to physically similar stimuli, but also to those that are contextually and semantically related in terms of meaning (Lang, Geer & Hnatiow, 1963). For example, when subjects receive an electric shock during exposure to rural words like "barn" or "cow," they may later show emotional reactions to other words connected with farming like "hay" or "horse" (Diven, 1937; Lacey & Smith, 1954). The mechanisms of higher-order generalization are complex and incompletely understood (e.g., Braine, 1963; Feather, 1965). The effects depend on the exact circumstances of the individual's history with the particular stimuli and on the details of the eliciting situation, but the processes still are not completely clear.

*Discrimination* occurs when a response pattern is reinforced in the presence of one stimulus attribute and nonreinforced, or extinguished, in the presence of other stimulus properties. This happens, for example, when physical aggression is encouraged toward peers at school but not when the principal is watching. When behavior is reinforced in the presence of some stimuli but not of others, discrimination results and the individual displays the behavior in some situations (those in which it will probably be reinforced) but not in others.

We already have seen examples of the sharpness of human discrimination in many contexts. Recall the fact that Gary W.'s anxieties were confined mainly to public speaking in evaluative group situations; the psychotic and self-destructive girl (described in Chapter 10) hurt herself consistently only when people withdrew attention from behaviors that they had previously reinforced; and the babies in Bruner's sucking research quickly learned to change their sucking and mouth movements in accord with the particular reinforcement schedule employed by the milk-dispensing program as noted earlier in this chapter.

Discrimination training is a major part of the socialization process. In almost all cultures, for example, children learn within the first few years to control their bowel and bladder functions. They learn to regulate themselves so that they defecate and urinate only under some conditions and in some places and not under other circumstances. Similarly the toddler soon learns that while active exploration in the sandbox is permitted and encouraged, similar play near the stove or in the living room leads to quite different outcomes. As a result, he quickly learns extremely subtle discriminations, and his behavior begins to depend on the exact conditions in which he happens to be. As these examples suggest, consistencies in behavior from one situation to another can only be expected when behavior yields similar consequences across the situations. The concepts of discrimination and generalization suggest that broad consistency in behavior patterns may be found only to the degree that the patterns are uniformly reinforced across many stimulus conditions. Throughout his development the child learns a seemingly endless variety of roles and thus becomes increasingly discriminating in his behavior.

## THE PATTERNING OF OUTCOMES

The patterning or sequencing ("scheduling") of reinforcement affects the future occurrence and strength of the reinforced behavior (e.g., Ferster & Skinner,

1957). Sometimes the scheduling of reinforcement may be even more important than the nature of the reinforcer (Morse & Kelleher, 1966). Continuous reinforcement usually increases the speed with which responses are learned. Intermittent reinforcement tends to produce more stable behavior that is more persistently maintained when reinforcement stops. For example, rewarding temper tantrums intermittently (by occasionally attending to them in an irregular pattern) may make them very durable. Since many potentially maladaptive behaviors, such as physical aggression and immature dependency, are rewarded intermittently, they can become very hard to eliminate.

## ANXIETY AND PUNISHMENT IN SOCIALIZATION

Some learning theorists focus on the role of rewards, but punishment or "aversive stimulation" is also important in socialization. In laboratory studies of anxiety the unconditioned stimulus is usually a painful electric shock and the stimulus to be conditioned is a discrete event such as a distinctive neutral tone or a buzzer. Generally human life is not that simple and neat. Often "aversive stimuli" involve punishments that are administered in less obvious and less controlled ways. These punishments may be conveyed subtly, by facial expressions and words rather than by brute force, and in extremely complicated patterns, by the same individuals who also nurture the child and give him love and other positive reinforcement. Moreover, the events that are punished often involve more than specific responses; they sometimes entail long sequences of overt and covert behavior.

The effects of punishment are especially complicated because the punitive parents not only punish the child but, in so doing, they model aggression (Bandura, 1962; Gelfand et al., 1974). The resulting effects can seem quite paradoxical. Consider, for example, the father who tries to suppress aggression in his son by punishing him physically. Later, in the father's absence, the boy may imitate the very aggressiveness that the father modeled while punishing him.

The behaviors that are considered inappropriate and punishable depend on such variables as the child's age and sex as well as the situation. Obviously the helplessness and passivity that are acceptable in a young child may be maladaptive in an older one, and the traits valued in a girl may be laughed at in a boy. While the mother may deliberately encourage her son's dependency and discourage his aggressiveness, his school peers may do the reverse, ridiculing dependency at school and modeling and rewarding aggression and self-assertion. Given this multiplicity of variables, the influence of punishment on personality development is, not surprisingly, both important and complex (e.g., Aronfreed, 1968).

A careful review of research on the effects of punishment upon children's behavior concludes, in part, that:

> aversive stimulation, if well timed, consistent, and sufficiently intense, may create conditions that accelerate the socialization process, provided that the socialization agents also provide information concerning alternative prosocial

behavior and positively reinforce any such behavior that occurs (Walters & Parke, 1967, p. 218).

Even if parents and other socialization agents attempt to be sensitive and judicious in their use of punishments it may be neither possible nor desirable to shield a child from all aversive stimulation, expecially if "aversive" includes psychological as well as physical pain. The concept of "punishment" includes more than the administration of aversive stimulation, as in a hard spanking. It may also involve social criticism and disapproval, as well as withdrawal of material rewards (such as privileges and treats) or of nurturance and affectional responses. Learning to fear potentially dangerous stimuli and to inhibit a host of behaviors, such as extreme antisocial aggression, is an integral part of personality development. Punishment may have negative effects, however, when it is administered in ways that, intentionally or unwittingly, lead to massive behavioral inhibition or to debilitating anxieties (Chapters 17 and 18).

## CHILD-REARING PRACTICES AND REINFORCEMENT

Laboratory demonstrations of learning are impressive, but they do not illuminate the socialization patterns and reinforcement practices that occur under naturalistic conditions. Results relevant to socialization practices obtained from field studies of families tend to be much more complex and more difficult to interpret. There are many reasons for these complexities.

Under naturalistic conditions any particular behavior pattern may be subjected to extremely complex outcomes. It is often rewarded on some occasions by some people (but not by others) in highly irregular ways. For example, peers may reinforce a child for behaviors that teachers and parents react to with disapproval. Even the same person—say a teacher—may praise a child for a behavior in one setting but not in another, rewarding aggression, for example, at play but not in the classroom. Finally, the child may see others rewarded for behavior that is not condoned for him. The slum-dwelling child sees the neighborhood gangster with cars, nice clothes, and girl friends, and even the middle-class child sees televised heroes getting gratifying pay-offs for violence and aggression.

Such vicarious reinforcement may counteract and undermine the effects of direct reinforcement. This conflict happens, for example, when parents, in full view of their children, enact, enjoy, and receive ample rewards for the very practices that they deny their children and even punish them for.

The effects of reinforcement under naturalistic conditions are especially complicated because socializing agents such as the mother and father always have a multiple role. These agents of the culture not only encourage and discourage or "shape" the child's behavior through direct tuition, but they also model relevant behavior. The information conveyed to the child through these diverse modes is often inconsistent.

Many puzzles in the relationships between child-training practices and the child's subsequent behavior may reflect lack of attention to the discrepancies between the behaviors the child observes used by powerful and successful models and those that he is taught directly. One should expect, for example, that if a father tries to train his child to become "open and sincere" while he himself behaves deceitfully, he may well rear a child who develops conflicts about honest self-expression. To understand socialization properly it is thus important to take account of both modeling and direct training influences (e.g., Mischel & Liebert, 1966, discussed in Chapter 19).

## CHILD-REARING DIMENSIONS

To understand personality development many psychologists have explored the possible links between various types of child-rearing practices employed by parents and the personality that emerges in their children. For this purpose ratings were made of how parents say they treat their children on many dimensions. Because of the tremendous complexity of parent-child interactions, these ratings are not easy to make reliably. Usually the "dimensions" that emerge are based on factor analysis of many ratings of parents during interviews in which the parent (usually the mother) discusses how she tends to raise and discipline her children (e.g., Sears, Maccoby & Levin, 1957). The interviewer then rates the mother's reports on various scales, and the results are analyzed into clusters or factors.

At least two dimensions emerge repeatedly (e.g., Schaefer, 1959). The first is "warmth-hostility." The "warm" mother is characterized as accepting, affectionate, and approving; she is understanding; she explains things to her child and uses "reason" in discipline; she refrains from physical punishment and uses praise of the child as part of her discipline. In contrast, the parent who is at the "hostility" or "cold" end of this dimension is described by the opposite of these characteristics.

A second dimension that often appears is called "control-autonomy." In addition, it has been suggested that the control-autonomy dimension may have two distinguishable aspects: restrictiveness vs. permissiveness and anxious-emotional involvement vs. calm-detachment (Becker, 1964). Thus it is possible for a mother to be restrictive (or permissive) and also emotionally involved (or calmly detached).

The relationships between various patterns of parental behavior and the ultimate personality of children have been studied thoroughly. For example, the warm, permissive parent may raise somewhat different children than does the warm, restrictive parent. Likewise the children of the hostile, restrictive parent may develop differently from those of the hostile, permissive parent (e.g., Becker, 1964).

To illustrate, a child raised by a cold, hostile, restrictive mother may be more likely to develop neurotic patterns and to despise himself; the child of the restrictive but warm parent may be relatively obedient, dependent, neat, and inhibited; the youngster from a warm but permissive home may be more self-assertive, aggressive, and active; the child from a cold, hostile, but permissive home may become a delinquent or a conduct problem because of his noncompliance and aggressiveness.

Generally, however, the relations between rated child-rearing dimensions and the child's personality tend to be not very strong, and there are many exceptions in obtained patterns. The fact that the relations that have been found are limited is understandable because of the grossness of the ratings of parent behavior and because the youngster's ultimate behavior depends on many social learning variables other than his mother's remembered disciplinary practices in childhood. Consequently in recent years many psychologists have attempted a more precise analysis of the conditions influencing personality development and have searched for more specific processes rather than for broad attributes of the parent-child relationship.

## AGENTS OF SOCIALIZATION
## AND SOURCES OF LEARNING

Beginning in infancy, the child's commerce with the world involves relations with significant social agents who, deliberately or inadvertently, transmit the culture to which they belong. Just as one approach to socialization focuses on critical events in development, another popular approach concentrates on the *agents* of socialization who are most salient at different points in the child's life, and on the influences that they exert on him during development. One may analyze, for example, the different types of social behaviors modeled and encouraged by the mother, the father, siblings, school peers, teachers, and so on in the many settings of the child's life at each age period. Obviously, each of these models and settings is responsible for much of what the child learns and becomes, and each may contribute to the development of different content in the total personality.

The parents, for example, play the greatest role in the development of attitudes about the home and family. Peers, in contrast, become the sources of many of the child's attitudes and interpersonal behaviors at school and at play, influencing the youngster's concepts about his interpersonal competencies and deficits. The type of roles and attitudes encouraged or disapproved by each of these sources depends on such variables as the child's age, sex, and socioeconomic position within the particular culture.

In addition to individual socialization agents, one must also consider the role of social institutions as an influence on personality development. In the broadest sense the culture into which the child happens to be born dictates many of the social forms and behavioral possibilities available to him. The rules, values, prohibitions, and sanctions of the culture, as well as its accumulated knowledge, are transmitted actively by the schools and by the many other social organizations in which the individual participates. The mass media in technically sophisticated societies permit and influence the rapid transmission of changing norms and values.

## LEARNING IN ADOLESCENCE
## AND ADULTHOOD

Although it has been fashionable in psychology to focus on the events of early childhood, socialization does not stop at age five. The child's early school experiences, his increasing involvements with activities and relationships beyond his family, his sexual urges at puberty, his cognitive growth and intellectual successes and failures at school, his interpersonal adventures—all these events contribute to shape the person that he continues to become, and each of these milestones can be construed as an especially intriguing phase of total development.

Early psychoanalytic theories of development focused attention on the first few years of life, but more recent formulations have recognized that the challenges and crises of adaptation extend throughout life. One sign of the popular recognition of this fact is the widespread concern with the "identity crises" of puberty and adolescence that may leave the individual confused about what adult life roles to make his own (Erikson, 1950, 1968).

Socialization does not end with the individual's ultimate exodus from his parental home. Now his adoption of various new adult roles—social, marital, economic—all involve him in new relationships that require different resources and yield new outcomes that in turn change him. In time the child becomes the parent, and he who was the object of socialization becomes its agent, transmitting to his children the values and behavior patterns that have become his own. The re-

Significant experiences in the child's life may have far-reaching effects.

sponsibilities, challenges, and crises of middle life gradually shift into those of advanced age, and with that shift again come new dilemmas, crises, and experiences that alter the person further. And so it goes, a continuous interaction between person and events that mutually modify each other until the very end of life.

While events such as the ones discussed in this chapter tend to be normative landmarks for most people, many other events can be turning points in the lives of particular individuals. A serious illness, a tragic accident, a chance meeting, a religious conversion, a new political commitment in college—any of these can become extremely significant. The impact of such events depends on what has happened to the individual throughout his previous history; in turn, the consequences of these events may permeate far into his future.

We are saying that a multiplicity of events throughout development may exert critical influences on the person and hence partly determine what he becomes and does at any later point in his life. That is, behavior is multiply determined by many happenings. All these conditions influence the person and, in turn, interact with variables in the current situation as determinants of behavior.

## SUMMARY

1. Maturation and learning *both* are important in the development of the human organism. Genetic and maturational processes predominate in embryological development and structural features of human growth. The importance of learning for personality development does not preclude the possibility that genetic and constitutional factors may influence social behavior in many complex ways. Language acquisition is an example of the close interaction of maturation and learning.

2. Freud's psychosexual theory, Erickson's theory of interpersonal phases and crises, and Piaget's stages of cognitive development are examples of stage theories of development. It is uncertain whether or not it is necessary to construe development as occurring in discrete stages. It is widely agreed, however, that some patterns—such as language development—are sequential.

3. Feeding, and the child's experience around it—generally with the mother—is a major event in early infancy. In spite of the dependency and relative helplessness of the infant, research has shown that even babies are sensitive to environmental changes and may by their responses in turn affect the environment. For example, by crying the child may quickly come to exert some influence on his caretakers. Thus the social transactions between the human organism and its environment begin at birth.

4. Even very early in life, stimulation from many sources affects the child. Early formulations that characterized the infant as mainly passive, dependent, and oral thus have to be modified to take account of the greater activity and attentiveness found in recent studies that have closely observed how young babies actually spend their time. The baby sees, hears, and feels as well as feeds, and all these experiences affect his relationship to the world.

5. Early stimulation and deprivation may have major effects on subsequent development. Social stimulation increases social responsiveness on the part of the infant. In contrast, organisms reared in total social isolation may suffer grave and irreversible consequences in their social and sexual behavior.

6. Some research with animals indicates that social or attachment behaviors may develop quite independent of feeding.

7. Toilet training has been viewed as an important event in the transition from infancy to later development. This universal feature of socialization is seen by many psychologists as a prime instance of conflict between the child's impulsive pleasure-seeking and the constraining demands of society in the "anal stage" postulated by psychoanalytic theory. Research that reports a relationship between toilet training practices in infancy and later adjustment is difficult to interpret. For example, mothers who are severe in toilet training may create other types of situations that result in later maladjustment.

8. Sex and aggression are two patterns of behavior especially likely to produce problems in our culture because they generate anxiety and conflict for many people. The child's experiences in these areas may become a basis for later problems. Proper development is enhanced if the child learns to successfully discriminate the appropriate occasions for the expression of these behaviors and for their inhibition.

9. Although early psychodynamic theories stressed the role of sex and aggression, more recently psychologists have recognized that the development of curiosity, of competence, and of adequate achievement is necessary for self-esteem and effective coping. Cognitive and intellectual development and the experiences and self-assessments connected with these functions are integral parts of personality development.

10. Achievement strivings and behaviors are among the more consistent aspects of personality. Even young children show some consistency across situations in their strivings for intellectual achievement and recognition.

These strivings also may show considerable stability over time. Achievement behaviors tend to be related to the child's ability and to the stimulation and encouragement for achievement available in his environment.

11. The basic mechanisms of social learning are important in understanding personality development. Two direct learning mechanisms are classical and operant conditioning. In *classical conditioning* contiguous association between a neutral and an arousing stimulus may change the value of the neutral stimulus. Such a mechanism may influence positive and negative attitudes and feelings in many contexts. In *operant conditioning* behavior patterns may be modified by changing the consequences (reinforcements) to which they lead.

12. In addition to these direct learning mechanisms, the child learns through observational and cognitive processes. Through observation he learns a vast number of skills and potential behaviors. He also acquires information about the probable consequences of these behaviors by seeing the outcomes that other people get. Television, movies, books, and other media may all provide information about possible behaviors and their consequences, thus influencing preferences and choices.

13. Discrimination learning is a fundamental aspect of the socialization process. In almost every culture, growing up requires learning numerous behaviors that are acceptable and expected under some circumstances but prohibited or punished under others, producing many discriminations. When behavior yields similar consequences under many conditions, generalization occurs and the individual may display similar behavior patterns across diverse settings. Similarity in meaning as well as in physical characteristics results in increased generalization.

14. The patterning or sequencing of the outcomes produced by a particular behavior can be even more important than the type of outcome itself. While continuous reward or reinforcement for behavior may result in faster learning, irregular or intermittent reinforcement often produces more stable behavior that persists even when reinforcement is withdrawn. In life situations many potentially maladaptive behaviors are rewarded irregularly and may therefore become very resistant to change.

15. Under the complicated conditions of life, the effects of direct and vicarious reinforcement are not as simple and easy to interpret as they are in laboratory demonstrations. During socialization some of the child's behaviors may be encouraged or condoned in highly irregular ways. For example, one parent may approve of a certain type of behavior while the other disapproves. Likewise, peers may applaud behavior that adults discourage.

16. The influence of punishment on personality development is complex and depends on many conditions, such as its timing. Unlike conditions in laboratory studies of punishment, in the child's life punishment is often subtle and indirect. Punishment in socialization depends on many contingencies, such as the child's age and sex as well as the type of behavior and the setting.

17. Efforts have been made to rate the child-rearing practices of parents. Several rating dimensions, such as warmth-hostility and control-autonomy have emerged. Some links have been found between these dimensions of parent behavior and the child's personality.

18. The child learns from many sources. The various agents of socialization (e.g., parents, siblings, schoolmates, and teachers) may exert their influence at different age periods and in different situations. Personality development and change do not end in early childhood but continues throughout life. The events of young adulthood, middle life, and advanced age bring their own responsibilities, challenges, and crises.

# CHAPTER 14

# SEX-TYPING
# AND
# PERSONALITY
# DEVELOPMENT

In this chapter we will examine some of the socialization processes through which boys and girls gradually become psychological males or females. A study of these processes will illustrate more specifically many of the most important features of personality development and socialization. This analysis will focus on the development of sex differences in social behavior rather than on the physiology and biology of sexual behavior itself. While it will deal mostly with the development of psychological sex differences, the discussion will also bring up many issues that are relevant to socialization in general.

This chapter thus is concerned with the nature of psychological sex differences in social behavior and also with how these personality differences develop. Instead of discussing many dimensions of personality superficially, it concentrates on one in depth. The development of psychological sex differences serves as an illustration of the development of personality differences in general, but it is also fascinating in its own right.

Almost universally an individual's gender is one of the most powerful determinants of how other people treat him or her. Gender also influences the views the individual develops about himself or herself. Established invariantly at birth, biological sex soon begins to direct much of one's psychological and social development, identity, and roles and values. Moreover, it continues to exert a dominant influence throughout life. Probably no other categorization is more important psychologically than the one that sorts people into male and female and their characteristics into masculine and feminine. And in recent years probably no other categorization has become more controversial. The controversy is based on many challenges to conventional, rigid sex roles and stereotypes about what it means to be a man or a woman.

Some of the issues raised by these challenges to traditional notions about sexual identity will be discussed later in this chapter. But first we will consider some of the personality differences found between the sexes. Then we will examine their causes and consequences. This analysis is intended to give the reader a deeper understanding of the complex processes through which social behavior and personality develop. Since "masculinity" and "femininity" are often defined in terms of such other traits as aggressiveness and dependency, the study of sex differences takes us into research on many other related domains.

## PSYCHOLOGICAL SEX DIFFERENCES

In some respects the differences between the sexes, not only biologically but psychologically, may seem self-evident. On closer examination, however, the nature of the psychological differences between the sexes is not nearly as simple as it may seem.

### PERCEIVED SEX DIFFERENCES: EXAMPLES

Before examining formal studies on sex typing, it is informative to consider the subjective sex differences given by a young woman—call her "Amy Wilson"— when asked, during the course of her development, about sex differences and sex roles. Here are excerpts from Amy's comments at four ages.

At age 3½ Amy's concepts about sex differences were still vague and primarily limited to trying to distinguish the roles of mother and father:

Q. How are boys and girls different?

A. They're good (both boys and girls)—and they fight a little bit. They laugh sometimes.

Q. What do boys do that girls don't do? And what do girls do that boys don't?

A. They play outside with their daddies. They play outside with their selves and they swing around on the glider—they play outside with their mother.

Q. And when they grow up?

A. Boys be daddies. Girls be mommies, and have babies in their tummies. Mommies feed children and babies and daddies.

Q. And what do daddies do?

A. They wash the dishes.

Q. They do?

A. Well, sometimes.

When interviewed 18 months later at age 5, Amy made a more differentiated analysis, recognizing biological and role differences and focusing mainly on sex differences in aggressive behavior:

Q. How are boys and girls different?

A. Boys have penises and girls have vaginas.

Q. How else?

A. Boys make money to buy food. Girls want their children not to make too much noise. Boys work—sometimes help the mother, sometimes play with their children. Mothers—they try not to scream. Boys can grow up to be a gardener and girls want their children to be very, very quiet and good.

Q. What are the girl-things you do?

A. I play on swings and slides; I paint and make good art pictures. Boys play on slides and do the things girls do too; when they grow up they work and don't do the things girls do any more.

Q. Do you want to be a girl or boy?

A. A girl! I don't want to be a boy because they fight, hit girls, say I wanna kill you, fight their teachers, and get spanked—that's why I don't want to be a boy.

Q. Why do you do the girl-things you do?

A. Because I'm a girl—that's why I don't fight.

Q. Why don't you fight?

A. Because I don't want to—because it isn't nice—because then I would get punishment.

Q. Do boys get punished for fighting?

A. Yes, but they don't think they will—they're not so scared.

The analysis of role differentiation becomes increasingly sophisticated with age, as Amy's comments at age 7½ reveal:

Q. How are boys and girls different?

A. Men are much stronger than women. Boys grow up to be daddies, girls grow up to be mommies, and mothers have babies.

Q. How else?

A. Girls have more feelings. Boys have more strength.

Q. What are some of the girl-things you do?

A. Play handball—that's what girls and boys do, play two square, go on the slide. Sing, dance, spell. You mean what are the girl-things I do with no boys included? I don't play baseball, I don't play stick ball, I don't play hot box.

Q. Do you want to be a girl or boy?

A. A girl. Well, sometimes I wish I were a boy and sometimes I wish I weren't.

Q. Why?

A. Being a boy I could do scary things. For girls I would wear fancy dresses and be rich—live in a fancy mansion.

Q. Why do you do the girl-things you do?

A. Because I want to—I just do—I like the sport of it.

Q. What would happen if you did boy-things?

A. Oh I do boy-things sometimes, but there's nothing wrong with it.

Q. How come you don't like fighting?

A. Because girls don't fight—I guess they're too dainty. If you fight you can get in trouble. I guess boys are rougher, have more strength, don't tell on each other so much and so don't get into trouble so much.

As a mature woman, interviewed again at age 26, Amy Wilson now gave this subtle picture of sex roles and personality:

Q. How are man and women different psychologically?

A. Men are supposed to be more aggressive, stronger, more opinionated—more domineering—also have a stronger sex drive, I guess.

Q. What do men do that women don't do?

A. Things like car-racing, mountain-climbing—dangerous things—fight in wars, hunt, and kill—and make important decisions, like being president. They're also expected to provide for families. Women are supposed to create peace and harmony, care for children, be compliant, warm and giving—dependent.

Q. Do they have those qualities?

A. Not all of them. Some women are aggressive, wasteful, and self-aggrandizing.

Q. Would you rather be a man or woman?

A. I'd rather be a woman. I don't think I have the self-discipline to be a successful man—in terms of career—but I do have the qualities to be a successful, fulfilled, complete woman.

Q. How do you mean?

A. I'm attractive, competent, I love my children and am a good mother to them. I'm not selfish and I'm sexually responsive.

Q. What are some of the things you like most?

A. I like to dress nicely—I like pretty clothes.

Q. Why?

A. I like to dress nicely at home because it pleases my husband. When we go out it makes me feel good that he is proud of me—and I think it reflects well on him also. When I go shopping I like to look as elegant as possible because it makes the salespeople attend much better to me—they just get nicer then. My most feminine qualities? I am unassuming—I don't brag or boast.

Q. Why is that?

A. Because it's feminine.

Q. How would you be most different in personality if you were a man?

A. I'd put my work before my family. I would not allow myself to be so emotional—to react so strongly to things. I also wouldn't be able to get as much rest; I'd have to drive myself a lot harder.

Q. Why do you put your family before your work?

A. I put my family before my work because that's my responsibility—it's my job.

As Amy's comments indicate, from her viewpoint her feminine behavior reflects her subjective expectations about femininity, her cognitions about what it is to be female and the role responsibilities expected of an adequate woman. Her subjective viewpoint parallels to a large degree the objective conditions that have generated her feminine qualities and that serve to maintain them. Her expectations about the positive consequences of dressing attractively, for example, reflect her direct and vicarious reinforcement history in this regard; her cognitions about her role responsibilities presumably reflect the sanctions, rule system, and social structure of the environment in which she matured. The specifics of this socialization process will be discussed throughout this chapter. We will begin by surveying some of the main psychological sex differences revealed by research. The reader will note that these results support many of Amy's perceptions.

To discover personality differences between the sexes systematically, many researchers have tried to measure differences in the frequency or in the amount of particular behavior patterns typically displayed by males and females. In our culture the two behavior patterns with regard to which sex differences have received most research attention are behaviors aimed at inflicting injury on others (*aggression*) and at eliciting attention and help from others (*dependency*). Some of the main sex differences found for aggression and dependency respectively are reviewed briefly in the following sections and are summarized in Table 14-1.

## AGGRESSION

Aggression is one of the key variables defining masculine and feminine behavior (Sears, 1963, 1965). Sex differences in aggression have been found as early as the age of three years. Boys are physically more aggressive and show more "negativistic" behavior; negative attention getting, antisocial aggression, and physical aggression are more characteristic of boys than of girls. Boys also participate in

**TABLE 14-1   Some Representative Psychological Sex Differences**

| BEHAVIOR | GREATER IN | SOURCE |
|---|---|---|
| Physical and anti-social aggression (e.g., physical quarrels, fights, hyperaggressiveness) | Boys | Dawe, 1934; McCandless et al., 1961; Mischel & Mischel, 1971. |
| Rated Aggressiveness | Boys | Hattwick, 1937; Beller & Neubauer, 1963; Beller, 1962. |
| Self-rated Aggressiveness | Boys | Rothaus & Worchel, 1964; Wyer et al., 1965. |
| Dependency, Passivity | Girls (sometimes but not always: generally inconclusive) | Hovland & Janis, 1959; Kagan & Moss, 1962; Maccoby & Jacklin, 1974b; Mehrabian, 1970; Sears et al., 1953; Siegel et al., 1959. |
| Verbal Ability | Girls (beginning at age 11 years) | Maccoby & Jacklin, 1974a. |

more physical quarrels in nursery school, have more aggressive contact with their peers, initiate more fights and conflicts, and tend to resist attack more often. These results (Table 14-1) appear to have considerable generality across cultures (Whiting & Whiting, 1962). Rating studies provide similar findings, judges rating boys as more negativistic and as generally more aggressive than girls.

The sexes also differ in their self-concepts with regard to aggression. Self-ratings indicate that boys see themselves as more directly and overtly aggressive, especially after their hostility has been aroused experimentally. Greater self-reported overt aggressiveness by males holds for a wide age range, having been found for people aged from 15 to 64 (Bennett & Cohen, 1959). Projective tests also indicate more direct aggression and hostility expressed by males (e.g., Gordon & Smith, 1965).

## DEPENDENCY

Sex differences in dependency have also been studied thoroughly. In nursery school children, not many major differences have been found between the sexes on most dependency measures. At later ages (teens and college), however, girls sometimes seem to be more dependent, passive, and conforming than males (see Table 14-1), although the differences are often weak and inconclusive. Most of the findings are based on self-reports and trait ratings of dependency. Therefore it is difficult to separate the degree to which they reflect widely shared stereotypes that women are supposed to be more dependent from differences in the degree of actual dependency displayed by women versus men. Some evidence suggests that females may conform more than males, but certain factors may reverse this difference (e.g., Sampson & Hancock, 1967). For example, Iscoe and his colleagues (1964) report a significant race-by-sex interaction in conformity behavior. In this study, white females conformed more than white males, while black males were more conforming than black females. On the whole, girls are not more "suggestible" or susceptible to social pressure than boys (Maccoby & Jacklin, 1974a).

Although most research on sex differences has concentrated on aggression and dependency, other areas have not been ignored. In addition to studying differences on numerous personality variables, researchers have also explored sex differences in cognitive and intellectual functioning and in other domains (e.g., Maccoby & Jacklin, 1974b).

## INTELLECTUAL-COGNITIVE FUNCTIONS

Studies of American youngsters indicate, in general, that girls tend to do better than boys on tests of verbal ability. Girls, for example, tend to speak sooner and to be better in verbal articulation, word fluency, vocabulary, grammar, and spelling (e.g., Gesell et al., 1940; Irwin & Chen, 1946). Once one moves out of the American white middle-class group, however, the general superiority of girls to boys in verbal intellectual skills becomes more complex. Anastasi and D'Angelo (1952), for example, compared black and white preschool children in language development and found a significant sex-by-race interaction. That is, white girls were superior to white boys, while black boys were superior to black girls in length and maturity of verbal responses in a standard test situation. Still another study of children in Bristol, England, suggested that the verbal superiority often found in females may be culture-bound (Dunsdon & Frazier-Roberts, 1957). A random sample of all the schoolchildren showed boys to be superior on four oral vocabulary tests. But in spite of exceptions, females generally tend to be superior on tests of verbal ability, beginning at about age 11 years and extending at least through the high school years and perhaps beyond them (Maccoby & Jacklin, 1974a).

Sex differences are less clear on verbal reasoning tests, such as analogies. Sometimes boys do better on these tests (Klausmeier & Wiersma, 1964, 1965; McNemar, 1942), sometimes girls (Lee, 1965); and sometimes there is no difference (Bennett et al., 1959). Girls do learn to read sooner than boys (Balow, 1963; Anderson et al., 1957). Other studies show, however, that boys catch up by about the age of 10.

In general, the finding of some cultural variations indicated above limits conclusions, as does the fact that although girls may be superior to boys at an early age, boys may catch up or even excel later. Moreover, even though some sex differences in intellectual abilities have been found reliably, many of these differences tend to be small. This means that a child's sex may be a relatively minor factor in determining his mental ability in a particular area. In any classroom some boys probably will be superior to girls in vocabulary, and some girls will excel in spatial ability.

Sex differences have also been reported in a cognitive style described as "analytic" or field-independent as opposed to global or field-dependent (Witkin et al., 1962). The two measures most frequently employed in research on these styles are the Embedded Figures Test and the Rod and Frame Test. In the first, subjects have to find a simple hidden figure embedded in a more complex stimulus array. In the Rod and Frame Test a rod within a frame is projected on the wall of a darkened room, and the subject has to adjust the rod to the vertical as the frame is tilted. Boys and men tend to perform better and faster on these tasks than girls and women do, although sex differences are not found before the early school years (Maccoby, 1966). Witkin and his co-workers reported consistent sex differences only at age 17 and after, and once again the variations within each sex were greater than the consistent differences between the sexes.

In spite of some reported sex differences in cognitive styles, a close analysis of the total research on this topic indicates that the conclusions must be highly qualified. After an exhaustive review, Maccoby and Jacklin (1974a, p. 110) conclude that the belief that boys are more "analytic" than girls is one of many myths about sex differences. In fact, on cognitive style tests: "Boys are superior only on problems that require visual discrimination or manipulation of objects set in a larger context; this superiority seems to be accounted for by spatial ability . . . and does not imply a general analytic superiority (p. 110)." Thus, boys tend to excel in visual-spatial ability but not in more general analytic skills. This difference seems to begin in early adolescence.

In sum, a variety of sex differences have been found, especially on indices of physical aggression and on certain aspects of cognitive functioning. These average differences are important. However, within each of these domains there is considerable variability in the behavior of the same individual across situations. An individual's sex-typed behaviors may be relatively specific rather than highly generalized. A young boy may, for example, be good at baseball and still love painting, and he may like to tinker with tools and play with soldiers. The same child may also be extremely dependent on his mother's attention, may even like to dress his sister's dolls, may cry easily if he is hurt, but also may fight aggressively when peers provoke him.

## SEX-ROLE STEREOTYPES
## AND IDENTITY

We all share global stereotypes about masculine and feminine traits based on average differences between the sexes. A "real" boy in the United States is supposed to do such things as climb trees, dirty his knees, and disdain girls, while a "real" girl plays with dolls, jumps rope, and loves hopscotch (Brown, 1965). These stereotypes serve as bases for judging others. Sex-role stereotypes may also function as standards by which people evaluate themselves.

Sex-role stereotypes are widely shared within a particular culture and to some extent across cultures (e.g., D'Andrade, 1966). Even within a relatively homogenous subculture, however, individuals may vary in the degree to which they adopt sanctioned sex-role standards. For example, children, especially girls, from homes and schools that stressed individualized development departed more from conventional sex-role standards than did children from more traditional backgrounds (Minuchin, 1965).

*Sex-role identity* refers to the "degree to which an individual regards himself as masculine or feminine" (Kagan, 1964, p. 144). Kagan's formulation of sex-role identity stresses the person's global concept of his own overall masculinity or femininity. As he puts it (1964, p. 144):

> The degree of match or mismatch between the sex-role standards of the culture and the individual's assessment of his own overt and covert attributes provides him with a partial answer to the question, "How masculine (or feminine) am I?"

In the years since this simple conception of sex-role identity was proposed, it has become plain that the matter is more complex. An increasing number of people are unwilling to either ask or answer the traditional question "How masculine (or feminine) am I?" in the conventional ways. Some of the many controversies that surround the topic of sex-role identity are discussed later in this chapter.

## THE DEVELOPMENT OF SEX-TYPING

In order to understand psychological sex differences properly one has to consider their development. Often the extensive investigations on the development of sex roles are grouped under the heading of "sex typing." *Sex typing* is the process whereby the individual comes to acquire, to value, and to practice (perform) sex-typed behavior patterns—that is, patterns that are considered appropriate for his sex but not for the opposite sex. What are the causes of sex-typed behavior?

### BIOLOGICAL DETERMINANTS

The biological differences between the sexes are important in the development of psychological characteristics. For example, the fact that women bear children whereas men do not dictates many other differences in life roles. Beyond differences in the physical characteristics of the sexes, however, the biological or physiological approach has emphasized the possible effects of sex hormones on the development of psychological differences in nonsexual human behavior.

This biological emphasis is seen in the work of such researchers as Broverman and his associates (1968). These investigators suggest that sex differences in cognitive abilities reflect complex sex differences in biochemistry. They suggest that the relationships involved can be understood best by studying changes in people's cognitive processes induced by such organismic changes as variations in hormone levels and the administration of drugs. They speculate that "the sex differences in performances of simple perceptual-motor and inhibitory restructuring tasks are related, in part at least, to the differential effects of the 'sex' steroid hormones on activation and inhibition neural processes" (p. 42). The work of Broverman and his associates seems provocative, but for obvious ethical and practical reasons there has been little systematic experimentation with people on the possible role of sex hormones in the development of psychological sex differences.

Almost always the newborn's external sex organs match his internal biological sexuality, and his sex is identified unambiguously at birth. In some rare cases that is not true. "Hermaphrodites" are those unusual newborns who have sexual organs of both sexes. For example, they may have external male genitalia but internal female sex organs, and in this case, genetically they are females (in chromosome tests). Because these persons have both male and female sex organs, it is sometimes not clear whether they should be considered male or female. Clinical studies have investigated some of these individuals whose assignment to one sex or the other on the basis of their external genitalia was either incorrect or ambiguous. Hampson (1965) studied 19 hermaphroditic patients who were assigned and reared in a sex contrary to their true biological or chromosomal sex (established by biochemical tests of the chromatin pattern, for example through a skin biopsy). "Without a single exception it was found that the gender role and orientation as man or woman, boy or girl, was in accordance with the assigned sex and rearing rather than in accord with the chromosomal sex" (p. 113).

Likewise, Money (1965a,b) reported that genetic males with internal male genitalia who had been reared as females in accord with their external genitalia maintained a feminine psychosexual and gender role throughout life. The implication is that a person with male hormones who has been raised as a girl will dress and behave like a girl and probably will marry a man. These studies vividly illustrate the importance of the psychological gender role assigned to the child early in its life (Money & Ehrhardt, 1972).

Both Hampson and Money suggest that psychological variables are crucial in the establishment of sexual gender role. On the other hand, experimental research with lower animals suggests some possible interrelations between hormonal conditions, brain functions, and behavior (e.g., Hamburg & Lunde, 1966). The finding of greater aggression in males than in females (throughout human societies and among animal species closest to man) also strengthens the belief that sex differences in aggression have biological roots (Maccoby & Jacklin, 1974b). It is premature to draw any final conclusions on this topic. However, even if hormonal and genetic variables prove to contribute significantly to psychological sex differences, the enormous importance of social learning in the development of sex roles seems evident. It seems most likely that a person's gender role involves the close interaction of both biological and psychological variables.

Some researchers have concentrated on sex differences in newborns in order to study possible innate sex differences before socialization practices exert their effects massively. Human neonatal behavior indicates some sex differences in activity level and in reactivity to a variety of stimuli. For example, sex differences occur in infants' responses to facial stimuli during the first year of life (Lewis, 1969). Girls vocalized and smiled more and showed greater differential expression to the facial stimuli, although boys looked longer. At age 2 to 3 months, girls are more sensitive to skin exposure than boys (Wolff, 1965). Newborn females seem to react more to the removal of a covering blanket, and show lower thresholds to air-jet stimulation of the abdomen (Bell & Costello, 1964). Newborn boys raise their heads higher than newborn girls do (Bell & Darling, 1965), and there are also sex differences in infant play behavior (Goldberg & Lewis, 1969).

The interpretation sometimes drawn from these early sex differences in response to stimulation is that they are innate. But as in other domains of personality, nature and nurture—heredity and environment—tend to be deeply and often inextricably entwined:

> the sex-typed attributes of personality and temperament . . . are the product of the interweaving of differential social demands with certain biological determinants that help produce or augment differential culture demands upon the two sexes. The biological underpinnings . . . set modal tendencies for cultural demands, and set limits to the range of variation of these demands from one cultural setting to another. Still within these limits considerable variation does occur between families, between cultures, and in the nature of the behavior that a social group stereotypes as "feminine" or "masculine" (Maccoby, 1966, p. 50).

While biological limits and constraints have been recognized and acknowledged, most psychologists have emphasized socialization and cognitive processes as the causes of psychological sex-role characteristics.

## COGNITION AND LEARNING

In the course of development the young child soon recognizes his sexual identity or gender. He rapidly develops a conception of his permanent sexual identity through the same observational and cognitive processes that permit him to understand the invariable identity of physical objects in the environment (Kohlberg, 1966). These concepts seem to occur early in development, generally before the age of five years. By the time children reach school age they clearly have learned the concepts "male" and "female" (Hartup & Zook, 1960; Kagan, Hosken & Watson, 1961). Early during the course of socialization they also rapidly learn the stereotypes about masculinity and femininity prevalent in their subculture.

Sex-role concepts and stereotypes probably arise in part from children's observations of sex differences in bodily structure and capacities. When they reach the age of four or five years, children become distinctly aware of adult sex differences in size and strength. These perceived differences in turn may be associated with concepts about sex differences in power.

Some theorists emphasize the importance of cognitive strivings for consistency, and view consistency motivation as the crux of sex-role development. According to Lawrence Kohlberg, cognitive self-categorizations as "boy" or "girl" are made as reality judgments early in the child's development. Once formed, these judgments tend to be fairly irreversible, being maintained by the physical reality of one's sex: a person is male or female forever. Kohlberg's cognitive-developmental formulation gives this direct self-categorization of gender central importance as the fundamental organizer of sex-role attitudes and values:

> Basic self-categorizations determine basic valuings. Once the boy has stably categorized himself as male he then values positively those objects and acts consistent with his gender identity (1966, p. 89).

Kohlberg also says:

> The child's sexual identity is maintained by a motivated adaptation to physical social reality and by the need to preserve a stable and positive self-image (1966, p. 88).

Kohlberg's theorizing assumes that strong tendencies or strivings toward cognitive consistency lead the person to acquire values consistent with his cognitive judgments about himself (as discussed in Chapter 6). Granting the existence of such powerful strivings for cognitive consistency, just what are the processes through which the individual adopts his specific values and behaviors from among the many possibilities that could be consistent with his gender?

Kohlberg hypothesizes that after the child has categorized himself as male or female he then values positively whatever is consistent with his gender identity. That hypothesis is provocative. However, one has to explain how the boy learns and selects the particular sets of sex-typed behaviors that he adopts from the vast array that could be "consistent with his gender." There are many different appropriate ways of being a boy or a girl, and even more diverse ways of being a man or a woman, in any given culture. Boys and girls are exposed to a great variety of potentially appropriate sex-typed behaviors by same-sex models. From this diverse array of gender-consistent possibilities, they select and choose discriminatively. To understand sex typing fully we must account for individual differences in sex-typed behavior *within* each sex and not just for modal differences between the sexes. It is therefore necessary to go beyond cognitive self-categorization and consistency strivings to consider social learning.

Social learning theorists find it helpful to distinguish between the mechanisms through which the individual learns sex-typed behaviors and those that regulate his selection of particular sex-typed behaviors from the repertoire that is already available to him. As we have stressed before, people obviously do not perform all the behaviors that they have learned and could enact, and members of each sex know a great deal about the role behaviors of both sexes. In our culture both men and women know, for example, how to fight aggressively, and how to use cosmetics, although they differ in the frequency with which they perform these activities.

The acquisitional (learning) phases of sex typing involve cognitive and observational processes through which concepts and potential behaviors are learned. On the other hand, the individual's choice or selection of sex-typed behaviors from the available array that he already has mastered and knows how to execute depends on motivational and situational considerations. This distinction between acquisition and response selection is not limited to sex typing; it has also been made for all other aspects of social behavior by most current social learning theories. We are referring here to the previously discussed view that the acquisition of novel responses is regulated by sensory, attentional, and cognitive processes, but that direct and vicarious reinforcement is the important regulator of response selection in *performance*.

Boys and girls discover quickly that the consequences for many of the things that they try are affected by their sex. Indeed, that is exactly the meaning of "sex-typed" behaviors: their appropriateness depends on the sex of the person who displays them. Sex-typed behaviors are those that are typically more expected and approved for one sex than for the other and that lead to different outcomes or consequences when performed by males as opposed to females in the particular community. Because they yield differential consequences for males and females,

**The performance of sex-typed behavior depends on the expected consequences.**

these sex-typed behaviors come to be performed with different frequency by the sexes and to have different value for them. Thus a person's sex influences the consequences he gets for many of the things he does and affects how people relate to him as well as how he reacts to himself.

Consider, for example, the sex-typed domain of dependency. Under many conditions dependency is an effective way for getting help when it is displayed by females but not by males. In an experiment with college students, women who were dependent received the most help, while dependent men were not helped more often than independent ones (Gruder & Cook, 1971). But the greater dependency that women may develop because it "works" for them in our culture also exerts a toll. For example, college women thinking about their distant future anticipated more dependency than men, and also expressed more concern and anxiety about it, probably realistically (Kalish, 1971).

## CHILD-REARING PRACTICES AND SEX-TYPING

Parents, teachers, and other significant social agents tend to reward sex-appropriate behaviors and to punish or ignore sex-inappropriate responses. Even young children soon learn that their parents expect boys and girls to behave differently. For example, a group of five-year-olds were shown a series of paired pictures illustrating masculine and feminine activities (Fauls & Smith, 1956). The children were asked which activity Mother and Father would prefer for boys and girls (e.g., "Which does Mother want the boy to do?"). Children of both sexes indicated that parents wanted the child to perform sex-appropriate activities more often than sex-inappropriate activities.

Starting with different names, clothes, and color schemes for the nursery, parents seem to treat boys and girls differently, and children soon perceive important sex differences between their parents as well. In one study, seventh-grade boys and girls rated their mothers and fathers separately on a number of rearing variables (Droppleman & Schaefer, 1961). The results show that "girls as contrasted to boys report both mother and father to be more affectionate and as less rejecting, hostile and ignoring" (1961, p. 5). The authors conclude (1961, p. 5): "Females report that they received more affection as children than do males, and both sexes report that the female parent gives more affection than does the male parent."

In the strongly sex-typed behavior areas of aggression and dependency, we would expect the greatest differential treatment of boys and girls by their parents. Careful investigations of attitudes and training practices have been conducted for these two areas of special interest.

Parents tend to rear boys and girls most differently in the area of *aggression* (Sears, Maccoby & Levin, 1957). Boys were given greater freedom in the expression of aggression toward the parents and toward other children. Girls were more often praised for "good" behavior and more often subjected to withdrawal of love for "bad" behavior. These reported differences are not strong, but they are consistent with the cultural sanction of physical aggression in males. "Prosocial" aggressions (verbalizations about the goodness or badness of behavior and verbal threats) are more acceptable for girls but are considered "sissyish" for boys. These results are consistent with the sex differences discussed earlier showing that boys are more frequently physically aggressive, while girls display more prosocial and verbal aggression.

Although parents tend to sanction physical aggression for boys more than for girls, they are not indiscriminate. They obviously do not condone aggression for boys regardless of circumstances and setting. This fact is illustrated in the finding that boys who were aggressive at school had parents who encouraged aggression toward peers; many of these boys, however, were nonaggressive at home, and their parents indeed punished aggression at home (Bandura, 1960).

Females probably are allowed to display greater *dependency* than males in our culture. Laboratory studies have demonstrated that permissiveness for dependency, and reward for dependency, increased children's dependency behavior. Heathers (1953), for example, found that children who accepted help from the experimenter in a difficult situation tended to have parents who encouraged them to depend on others rather than to be independent.

A positive relation between the demonstrativeness and warmth of parents and the dependency of their children has also been found. Mothers who are affectionately demonstrative respond positively to their children's dependent behavior and describe their children as high in dependency (Sears, Maccoby & Levin, 1957). Similarly, a field study by Bandura (1960) indicated, among other results, that parents who reward dependency have children who tend to display a high degree of dependency behavior.

An experimental study by Goldberg and Lewis (1969) is especially important because it gives information on differentiation of sex-appropriate behavior in infancy. A free-play situation was used to observe sex differences in behavior toward the mother, toys, and a frustration situation at 13 months of age. Information on the children in the study at age 6 months was also available.

Boys and girls at 13 months showed clear differences in their behavior toward their mothers. Girls were more reluctant than boys to leave their mothers and returned to them more quickly and more often than did boys. The girls also touched their mothers more frequently and for a longer time period, and they played closer to their mothers than did boys. In the frustration situation, girls cried and motioned for help consistently more than boys.

When the children were 6 months old the mothers touched, talked to, and handled their daughters more than their sons. The mothers' greater attention to daughters at the early age may have been one of the causes of the finding that at age 13 months girls touched and talked to their mothers more than did boys.

## SOCIAL STRUCTURE

Sex typing also is affected by influences outside the immediate family. To understand socialization and especially the development of psychological sex differences fully, we must recognize the role of the social system in which the individual lives. The emphasis on the person in psychology must not obscure the intimate dependence of personality on environment—and the vital role of social forces, institutions, and groups in molding that environment throughout the person's development.

Even within any one broad culture there are important differences among the component subcultures. For example, the extent to which children develop traditional sex-role concepts and sex typing depends on the degree to which they participate in a subculture that shares, models, and encourages those traditional attitudes and values (Minuchin, 1965).

On the other hand, some sex differences in socialization are found cross-culturally, as revealed in a survey of ethnographic reports (Barry, Bacon & Child, 1957). Two competent judges rated the socialization data from 110 cultures, a majority of which were nonliterate. They judged sex differences in socialization on five variables: nurturance, obedience, responsibility, achievement, and self-reliance. The differences they found in childhood socialization pressures on these five variables are summarized in Table 14-2.

As Table 14-2 indicates, not only in our society but also in many other cultures, girls are socialized to become nurturant, obedient, and responsible, whereas boys are socialized toward greater self-reliance and achievement striving. These relations were not invariant, however, and there were exceptions. Since there were some reversals, and since many cultures showed no detectable sex differences on these dimensions, the evidence favors the role of socially learned rather than biologically established determinants. Nevertheless, it is likely that many of the sex differences in social behavior obtained cross-culturally partly reflect the widespread adaptation of cultures to universal biological variables such as child-bearing. The authors commented on the differences they obtained as follows:

> The observed differences in the socialization of boys and girls are consistent with certain universal tendencies in the differentiation of adult sex role. In

**TABLE 14-2    Ratings of Cultures for Sex Differences in Childhood
Socialization Pressure on Five Variables**

| VARIABLE | NUMBER OF CULTURES | BOTH JUDGES RATE SOCIALIZATION PRESSURE HIGHER FOR | |
|---|---|---|---|
| | | GIRLS | BOYS |
| Nurturance | 33 | 17 | 0 |
| Obedience | 69 | 6 | 0 |
| Responsibility | 84 | 25 | 2 |
| Achievement | 31 | 0 | 17 |
| Self-reliance | 82 | 0 | 64 |

Adapted from Barry, Bacon and Child (1957).

the economic sphere, men are more frequently allotted tasks that involve leaving home and engaging in activities where a high level of skill yields important returns; hunting is a prime example. Emphasis on training in self-reliance and achievement for boys would function as preparation for such an economic role. Women, on the other hand, are more frequently allotted tasks at or near home that minister most immediately to the needs of others (such as cooking and water carrying); these activities have a nurturant character, and in their pursuit a responsible carrying out of established routines is likely to be more important than the development of an especially high order of skill. Thus training in nurturance, responsibility, and, less clearly, obedience, may contribute to preparation for this economic role. These consistencies with adult role go beyond the economic sphere, of course. Participation in warfare, as a male prerogative, calls for self-reliance and a high order of skill where survival or death is the immediate issue. The childbearing which is biologically assigned to women, and the child care which is socially assigned primarily to them, lead to nurturant behavior and often call for a more continuous responsibility than do the tasks carried out by men. Most of these distinctions in adult role are not inevitable, but the biological differences between the sexes strongly predispose the distinction of role, if made, to be in a uniform direction (Barry, Bacon & Child, 1957, pp. 328–329).

## MODERATOR VARIABLES IN SEX-TYPING

Although the consequences produced by a person's behavior depend in part on his sex, they also hinge on numerous other considerations. The type of behavior, the situation in which it occurs, the individual's age, status, and other characteristics, are some of the many variables that interact with his sex to determine how people will react to him. The many variables that moderate the exact effects of the child's sex become evident from careful studies of child-rearing practices.

These practices depend not only on the sex of the child but also on the sex of the parent. For example, Rothbart and Maccoby (1966) found complex interactions between sex of parent and sex of child. Parents of preschool children listened to tape-recorded statements of a child's voice and indicated what they would say or do to their own sons or daughters in response to each statement. Mothers' reactions showed almost no overall average difference from fathers' reactions, but sex of parent did interact with sex of child. Mothers tended to be more permissive toward sons than toward daughters, whereas fathers tended to be more attentive and permissive toward their daughters than their sons. This interaction was most pronounced when the child expressed pain (complaining that the baby had stepped on its hand) but it did not affect many other behaviors strongly and it appeared for only one form of aggression (expression of direct anger at the parent).

Rothbart and Maccoby concluded that inconsistency between parents with regard to sex-typed behavior seems to be the rule and also that a parent's reactions could vary from one behavior area to another. The exact form of a behavior, the child's sex, and the sex of the parent reacting to it are all important variables in determining the consequences of the behavior. If parental reactions hinge on numerous situational variables, then global concepts like "permissiveness" (construed as primarily stimulus-free attributes of the parent) may be of only limited value in understanding the development of children's behavior.

An experiment by Taylor and Epstein (1967) illustrates how complexly sex roles influence behavior; at the same time it shows the discriminations people make as a function of moderating conditions. They exposed male and female college students to fictitious male and female opponents in a competitive situation. The aggressiveness of the students was assessed by having them set the amount of electric shock they wanted their opponent to receive after each trial. The fictitious opponent administered increasing amounts of shock to the students.

In accord with the cultural sanctions against physical aggressiveness toward women, both sexes administered less shock to the opponent believed to be a female, even when she herself administered increasingly higher shocks. When the highly aggressive opponent was thought to be male, however, it was the females who ultimately became most aggressive; now the females doubled the initial intensity of the electric shocks against their male antagonists. Thus even for a specific type of aggression, such as physical punishment, sex differences are moderated by such situational variables as the sex of the victim and the sex of the aggressor.

The behavior patterns that are appropriate for males as opposed to females also change as a function of the individual's age. Different forms of dependency, for example, may be broadly acceptable for both sexes when they are young but not in later phases of their development. When dependency is manifested by older boys it may be unacceptable, whereas similar dependent behaviors may be condoned for girls who are equally old.

Within any given society the particular clusters of behavior that are sex typed, the consequences for appropriate and inappropriate sex typing, the sex-role models that are valued and those that are disapproved, change significantly and repeatedly in the course of the individual's development. Most psychological studies of the development of personality in general and of sex typing in particular have been conducted with young children (usually under age seven) as the subjects. Yet some of the most important aspects of personality, and of distinctively male and female behavior, emerge at later ages—at and after puberty. It is at these later times that the individual practices adult sex-role behavior, not during the child's dress-up play in his parent's shoes, but in actuality and in his own right.

In early adulthood, rather than in childhood, sex-typed expectations become relevant for a host of new interpersonal and sexual behaviors. During adolescence, for example, sex differences in character, in the cultivation of skills, and in the expression of sexual feelings, become most apparent (Douvan & Kaye, 1957; Harris, 1959). It is also during adolescence that critical interactions between physical sexual maturation and psychological socialization may take place. For example, during adolescence boys whose physical development is retarded are more likely to develop personality difficulties, presumably because they cannot engage as successfully in many prestigious sex-typed activities, such as athletics (Mussen & Jones, 1957, 1958).

Some of the dramatic differences in sex-typed behaviors that commence in adolescence do not end there and continue to influence the individual for many years. Throughout their lives the role expectations and the role behaviors of the sexes differ in numerous critical respects. These patterns continue to change dynamically. They come under new influences as appropriate role demands and role models vary, and as the consequences for particular forms of sex-typed behavior shift, in accord with changes throughout the individual's life and in the larger culture.

In sum, sex-typed response patterns often are affected by the situation in which they are made and by such variables as the individual's age and the sex of the other persons in the situation. In research many interactions occur between the experimenter's sex and the sex of the subject. As the examples in this section indicate, the reinforcing consequences produced by behavior depend not only on the performer's sex and on the content of the behavior, but also on his age and the particular circumstances. Individuals learn to discriminate sharply in their behaviors, moderating their actions in the light of the probable consequences they may produce. Again we see that many conditions may combine to determine what the individual does.

## THE CORRELATES OF SEX-TYPING

There are enormous individual differences in masculinity-femininity. As with most other dimensions of personality, research has revealed extensive correlations between masculinity-femininity indices and other personality measures. For example, one set of investigations has studied the relations between indices of personality adjustment and sex typing. It was found that adolescent boys who had highly masculine interests (on the Strong Vocational Interest Test) when compared to those with highly feminine interests, had more positive self-concepts and more self-confidence on the TAT (Mussen, 1961). The children with more masculine interests were also rated by peers as more masculine.

The adolescents in Mussen's studies were reexamined to assess their adjustment when they reached their late thirties. Using many personality measures, Mussen compared the men who as adolescents had expressed more traditionally masculine interests with those who had reported more feminine interests.

Comparison of the ratings assigned to the two groups showed that in adulthood, as during adolescence, those who had relatively feminine interest patterns manifested more of the "emotional-expressive" role characteristics—e.g., they were rated as more dependent but more social in orientation. In contrast, those with highly masculine adolescent interest patterns possessed, in their late teens and in their late thirties, more active, "instrumental" characteristics: greater self-sufficiency, less social orientation and, in adulthood, less introspectiveness. There was little congruence between the adolescent and adult statuses of the two groups with respect to several other characteristics, however. During adolescence, highly masculine subjects possessed more self-confidence and greater feelings of adequacy than the other group, but as adults, they were relatively lacking in qualities of leadership, dominance, self-confidence, and self-acceptance (Mussen, 1962, p. 440).

Thus sex-appropriate identification in adolescence is not a fixed sign of an overall enduring adjustment pattern. Adolescents who have stereotyped masculine interests may adjust more happily during adolescence and are rated more positively at that time. Middle-class adolescents who profess stereotypically masculine interests, attitudes, and values probably would fare better, especially with their peers, than would boys who express strongly feminine interests. These adolescent sex-typed preferences, however, do not guarantee a generalized pattern of adjustment for life. Indeed, Mussen (1962, p. 440) pointed out that:

In general there seems to have been a shift in the self-concepts of the two groups in adulthood, the originally highly masculine boys apparently feeling less positive about themselves after adolescence, and, correlatively, the less masculine groups changing in a favorable direction.

The correlates of sex-typing have also been studied in experimental situations. For example, the relationships between sex-role preferences and the youngsters' susceptibility to verbal conditioning conducted by a male or female adult have been explored. In one experiment (Epstein & Liverant, 1963) boys between the ages of five and seven were divided according to whether they were very high or very low in masculinity (judged by their preferences on a scale). They were then exposed to a male or female adult who verbally approved whenever they answered "mother" (in one condition) or "father" (in another condition) to many questions. The masculine boys tended to be more readily conditioned by a male than by a female. This finding suggested that adult men had acquired greater reinforcement value for these youngsters. All the boys, regardless of masculinity scores, tended to condition more readily when the verbally approved response was "father" than when it was "mother."

The component of sex typing whose correlates have been studied most thoroughly is dependency. The findings indicate that dependency may have quite different meanings—and hence correlates—for girls than it has for boys. Sears (1963) found that for preschool girls dependency is correlated with indices of maternal permissiveness for dependency. The mother who approves of dependency and encourages intimacy with her daughter often has a daughter who engages in "positive attention seeking." For boys various forms of dependent behavior seem to be associated with "coldness in the mother, slackness of standards, and a rejection of intimacy by the father" (Sears, 1963, p. 60). The parents of these boys were described as "an inhibited and ineffectual mother—and to some extent father, too—who provides little freedom for the boy, and little incentive for maturing" (p. 62).

The different antecedents of dependency will seem more understandable if you consider the different consequences produced by dependency behaviors when displayed by boys and by girls. Dependency by girls more often gets approval from parents, teachers, and peers. It would be expected, therefore, that dependency in girls would be correlated with indices of parental warmth and satisfaction and with general adjustment and other signs of age-appropriate behavior. Dependency behavior in a boy, on the other hand, may reflect that he is not adequately performing sanctioned, age-appropriate, independent behavior. The dependent, clinging boy is more likely to be the one who shows poor adjustment on other indices and who is upsetting to adults.

## STABILITY OF SEX-TYPED BEHAVIORS

There are sex differences in the durability of various sex-typed behavior patterns. In the Fels Longitudinal Study, Kagan and Moss (1962) found some significant consistency between childhood and early adulthood ratings of achievement behavior, sex-typed activity and spontaneity for both sexes. Certain other variables, like dependency and aggression, were stable for one sex but not for the other. In particular, childhood dependency and passivity were related to adult dependency and passivity for women, but not for men. Conversely, "the developmental consistency for aggression was noticeably greater for males" (p. 95). They suggested that these sex-linked differences in the continuity of behaviors may reflect differences in their "congruence with traditional standards for sex-role characteristics" (p. 268).

## CHANGING STEREOTYPES AND SEX-ROLE BIAS

Although some aspects of an individual's sex-typed behaviors may be relatively stable, others may change, even in adulthood, especially when alterations occur in the social structures that support them. In recent years there have been some dramatic challenges to conventional sex roles in our culture, as exemplified in the Women's Movement. Some of these influences may be reflected in Amy Wilson's changing concepts of sex differences and sex roles when she was interviewed again four years later.

Amy Wilson revisited at age 30; a rising consciousness?

Q. How are men and women different psychologically?
A. The psychological differences are greatest in self-concept. Men feel dominant, important. Women are the "other." They are sort of what's left . . . unfortunately.

Q. What do men do that women don't do?

A. Men have more privileges in our society. They are better paid for the same work, have more legal rights, etc. They are seldom allowed to be passive, dependent, and nurturant—whereas these qualities are almost demanded of women.

Q. Would you rather be a man or a woman?

A. I'm proud and happy to be a woman—but I'll be a lot happier when society makes some of the fundamental changes necessary to ensure the maximum individual development of all individuals, men and women.

Q. What are some of the things you like most?

A. I like to feel I'm really stretching myself. That whatever I do, I'm using all my abilities to the fullest. I get no real satisfaction out of routine jobs just as much as I resent such tasks at home. I love being with my kids when we're exploring places or talking about ideas—I hate being forced into the role of chauffeur or—worse—nag.

Q. How would you be most different in personality if you were a man?

A. If I were a man I think I'd have a better self-concept without having to fight for it. I'd be less unassuming and as a consequence I'd probably do better in all my roles as well. I think in many ways I, as a female, have been brought up to be self-defeating. I too easily get distracted, too easily do the 'helpful' thing because I've been conditioned that way . . . and that's wrong.

At this juncture in her life, Amy seems to have a new consciousness of the role society has played in determining her behavior. She is far more aware now of the conditions which generated and serve to maintain the psychological differences she perceives and experiences between men and women. New in Amy's response is her conception of alternatives to the status quo and her desire to break down some of the existing inequalities and stereotypes. This reexamination and new consciousness reflect not only new information and a new emphasis on the nature of sex differences conveyed by the media and by the Women's Movement, but also Amy's personal experiences in her new career as a free lance writer.

## SEX-ROLE BIAS IN SOCIETY

There has been a growing recognition in psychology, as well as in the Women's Movement, that psychologists, teachers, and parents should not unquestioningly perpetuate stereotyped sex roles (Bardwick, 1972). To automatically encourage boys and girls to accept the stereotyped roles society expects them to play may prevent each person from realizing his or her full potential. The sex role ideology, explicit or implicit, prevalent in the United States has been accused of producing an unfortunate "homogenization" of American women (Bem & Bem, 1972). It has been pointed out that there is widespread acceptance in America of an "un-

Sex-role stereotypes should not prevent each person from realizing his or her full potential.

conscious ideology" about women. This ideology is reflected in the fact that the majority of American women end up in virtually the *same* role, that of home-maker, often combined with a dead-end job (e.g., sales clerk, secretary, factory worker). In contrast, a male is more likely to become whatever his talents and interests permit him to be, with great diversity in his occupational potential. But a woman often is consigned to her role on the basis of sex, without regard to her unique abilities and capacities. The American ideology regarding the female sex tends to close options to women and constrict ". . . the emerging self-image of the female child and the nature of her aspirations from the very beginning . . ." (Bem & Bem, 1972, p. 7).

The same authors contend further that the American male also may be disadvantaged by the prevailing ideology; for example, he may be discouraged from developing such desirable traits as tenderness and sensitivity on the grounds that those qualities are "unmanly." Further, the relationship between males and females may suffer from the inequities in current sex-role stereotypes. Once we become conscious of this pernicious ideology, changes may be necessary: (1) to prevent discrimination (at the legal and economic levels); (2) to avoid constrictive, personally debilitating sex-role socialization; and (3) to encourage institutions and ideologies that will nullify the presumed incompatibility of family and career for women in our society.

Many statements have been made about the constricted and inequitable nature of the traditional female sex roles and some of these assertions have been seen as unfounded propaganda by critics (e.g., Dechter, 1972). Although polemics have been abundant on all sides of this heated social issue, some sound work has been done on several aspects of bias due to sex roles. For example, it has been asserted widely that clear sex-role stereotypes which prevent the full expression of individuality in interests and abilities are imparted early to children. A recent study of elementary school reading textbooks examined the treatment of males and females in the stories to which school children are routinely exposed (C. Jacklin and H. Mischel, 1973). The results were quite clear. Female characters in the children's reading texts were consistently underrepresented and were rarely main figures in the stories. Males were the heroes, carried the action, and experienced more positive consequences as a result of their own efforts and initiative. In contrast, females were passive, and whatever positive consequences they received came from the situation (e.g., from what others did for them, from luck) rather than from their own actions and initiative. These inequitable portraits of males and females became even stronger as the series of books progressed from kindergarten through third grade.

## SEX-ROLE STEREOTYPING IN PSYCHOLOGY

Sex-role stereotyping has been laid squarely at the door of psychology itself in a study by Broverman, et. al. (1970). Clinically trained psychologists, psychiatrists, and social workers were asked to describe a healthy, mature, socially competent a. man, b. woman, c. adult, sex unspecified. Judgments of what characterized mentally healthy males and females differed in a way congruent with stereotypic sex-role differences (see Table 14-3 for examples). The qualities used to define mental health

**TABLE 14-3    Examples of Traits Attributed by Clinicians to "Healthy" Women Compared to "Healthy" Men**

| "HEALTHY" WOMEN ARE LESS | "HEALTHY" WOMEN ARE MORE |
|---|---|
| independent | submissive |
| adventurous | easily influenced |
| aggressive | excitable in minor crises |
| competitive | conceited about their appearance |

Based on data from Broverman et al. (1970).

for an ideal adult (of unspecified sex) closely resembled those attributes judged healthy for men but differed significantly from those considered to be healthy for women. For example, the healthy adult of unspecified sex was described as dominant, independent, adventurous, aggressive, and competitive. These adjectives were also used to describe the healthy adult male. In contrast, the healthy adult female was described as more submissive, less independent, less adventurous, less aggressive, less competitive, more easily influenced, more excitable in minor crises, and more conceited about her appearance. As the authors noted (p. 5), "this constellation seems a most unusual way of describing any mature, healthy individual." Moreover, this negative assessment of women was shared equally by the women professionals and by the men.

The implication is that a woman who is assertive and independent, or who is aggressive and adventurous, is likely to be judged maladjusted, while the same qualities in a male (or in a person of unspecified sex) are considered assets. In addition, stereotypic masculine traits (such as "very aggressive," "very worldly," "very logical") were seen twice as often as more desirable than were stereotypic feminine traits. Among the few feminine traits seen as desirable were "very talkative," "very tactful" and "very gentle." In sum, the overall results suggest that not only is "healthy male" synonymous with "healthy adult" and antithetical to "healthy female," but masculine traits are the ones that tend to be seen as desirable, while most feminine traits are seen as undesirable, even in the eyes of well-trained psychologists, psychiatrists, and social workers.

## CONSEQUENCES OF SEX-ROLE STEREOTYPES

Sexual stereotypes have many painful effects. One of these negative consequences was pointed out by Matina Horner (1969, 1972) who suggested that in our culture women develop a "motive to avoid success." According to Horner, for men success is perceived as compatible with their sense of masculinity. But for women success often is a conflict-producing, mixed blessing, because professional success may imply failure in the personal sphere, and the qualities demanded for success at work may conflict with those required for success as a woman. Other researchers have disputed whether or not women really have a distinct motive to avoid success. But there tends to be agreement that in many instances in our culture success and failure have very different implications and consequences for men and women. For example, when a woman does succeed on a task considered "masculine," her performance is as likely to be attributed to her luck as to her skill (Deaux & Emswiller, 1974; see Figure 14-1).

Especially discouraging is the finding that when more women enter a high-status profession, its perceived prestige declines. Male and female college students were led to believe that certain high-status professions (e.g., college professor and physician) would have an influx of women. They rated the fields as less prestigeful and desirable than a control group informed that the proportions of women in

**Figure 14-1**   WHAT IS SKILL FOR THE MALE MAY BE LUCK FOR THE FEMALE

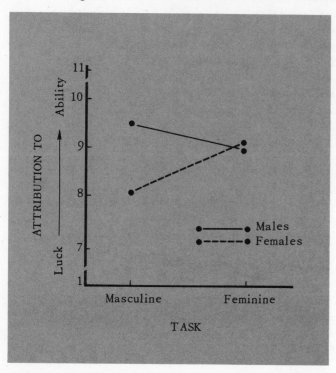

Graph showing that when females were able to find hidden pictures of such items as tire jacks and wrenches (masculine tasks) in a larger picture, their success was attributed partly to their luck, whereas the performance of males on this task was credited more to their skill. When the task was to discover hidden pictures of mops and double boilers (feminine tasks) the performance of both sexes was judged to be due to their ability to the same degree. (Adapted from Deaux & Emswiller, 1974, p. 82)

these fields would remain stable and low. This devaluation was expressed equally by women and by men (Touhey, 1974).

Also unjust and frustrating is the fact that some professional work may be judged less favorably when it is done by women than by men, even when the work is identical (Goldberg, 1967). In this line of research, subjects were asked to judge a series of professional articles. The identical articles were shown as authored by either males or females simply by varying the name on them (e.g., John Simpson or Joan Simpson). Goldberg's results suggested that when U.S. college women were the judges they devalued the achievements of other women and they did so even in fields which are traditionally associated with women, such as dietetics and primary education.

A group of later studies, conducted in both the U.S. and Israel with both males and females, questions the existence of a generalized preference for male expertise (H. Mischel, 1974). Using the same method as Goldberg, this study found that professional sex bias in the U.S. depended on the particular field in which work was judged. Judges of both sexes preferred authors whose sex was the same as that normative for (or stereotypically associated with) the professional field in which the article was written. For example, bias was in favor of a female author in primary education but in favor of a male author in law. Israeli subjects subscribed to the same stereotypes as the U.S. subjects regarding the sex association of the diverse fields, but did not show the evaluative biases found in the U.S. These results highlight the complexity and specificity of existing sex biases, and show that they are double-edged, with discrimination against men (when they are in stereotypically female fields) as well as against women (when they venture into male-dominated fields).

## TOWARD ANDROGYNY?

Alert to the negative effects of rigid traditional sex-role stereotypes, Sandra Bem (1975) questioned the very notion of "masculinity" and "femininity" as two opposite ends of a single dimension. She reasoned that this bipolar dimension has obscured the possibility that individuals might be "androgynous," i.e., *both* masculine *and* feminine, as those terms are usually defined. Moreover, traditionally narrow sex-role concepts might inhibit persons from behaving flexibly across situations that threaten their stereotypes about sex-appropriate behavior. In this research, androgynous persons were defined as those who are not rigidly sex-typed but instead endorse masculine and feminine attributes equally. The results provide some evidence that androgynous people (of both sexes) may display greater sex-role flexibility (for example, by resisting social pressure on an influence task). These findings are provocative. Although much more research is needed before firm conclusions can be reached, Bem (p. 643) speculates that the sex-role flexibility of androgynous people "enables them to engage in situationally effective behavior without regard for its stereotype as masculine or feminine. Accordingly, it may well be—as the Women's Liberation Movement has urged—that the androgynous individual will someday come to define a new and more human standard of psychological health."

Results of the type reviewed in this section should sensitize psychologists against inadvertently perpetuating traditional stereotypic conceptions of masculinity and femininity. Most psychologists would probably agree that concepts like "sex-appropriate behavior" (used throughout this chapter) merely describe the existing norms and practices of the culture and would insist that they do not necessarily endorse those norms. Yet we have seen that psychologists—just like most other people—may inadvertently perpetuate sex-role stereotypes. Fortunately, there appears to be a growing recognition that the conventional practices of society—which often may constrict human potentialities for both sexes—must not be confused with the ideals toward which its members should strive.

## SUMMARY

1. Psychological sex differences and the sex-typing processes through which they develop are crucial aspects of personality. The subtlety and complex-

ity of sex typing is illustrated by self-reports about perceived sex differences at different ages, from childhood to maturity, in the life of one person.

2. Aggressive behavior is one of the main dimensions on which sex differences have been consistently found. Boys show more physical aggression and antisocial aggression than girls as early as age three years. These differences appear cross-culturally and are found in rating studies, self-ratings, and projective tests.

3. Sex differences in dependency, another thoroughly studied variable, are not so clear-cut as those in aggression. At nursery school age few major differences in dependency are found. Later on, females are sometimes more conforming than males, but situational factors and socioeconomic demographic variables may reverse this difference.

4. Some sex differences have been found in intellectual functioning. Beginning early in adolescence boys tend to excel in visual-spatial ability; girls tend to have greater verbal ability.

5. Sex-role stereotypes are widely shared ideas about what is masculine and what is feminine, on the basis of average differences between the sexes within the culture. These stereotypes may serve as standards for judging and evaluating one's own behavior as well as for judging others. There are great individual differences in the degree to which people adopt particular sex-role standards.

6. Sex typing is the development of patterns of behavior considered appropriate for one sex but not the other. The development of sex roles and sex typing involves biological determinants as well as learning and cognitive processes.

7. The biological or physiological approach emphasizes the possible effect of sex hormones on the development of differences even in nonsexual human behavior. Research with lower animals suggests interrelations between hormonal conditions, brain functions, and behavior. Studies with hermaphrodites dramatize the importance of the psychological gender role assigned to the child. Research with newborns suggests some sex differences in activity and sensitivity to a variety of stimuli.

8. Cognitive-developmental theory emphasizes the striving for cognitive consistency as a determinant of sex roles. According to this theory, once the cognitive self-categorization of "boy" or "girl" is made, then positive valuation of objects and behaviors consistent with this gender identity follows.

9. Social learning theories stress that children within every culture learn quite early about sex differences in behavior. Through observational learning children of both sexes know about, and are capable of performing, many role behaviors from both sexes. The sexes differ, however, in the frequency with which they perform these activities and in how they value them. Thus observational and cognitive processes, as well as direct experiences and motivational differences, are involved in the development of sex typing.

10. In the social learning view, because sex-typed behaviors yield different consequences when displayed by males and by females they rapidly become valued and practiced differentially by boys and by girls. A person's sex is an important determinant of how other people react to his behavior and of how he reacts to himself.

11. Parents and other significant social agents encourage the child's sex-appropriate behavior and ignore or punish sex-inappropriate behaviors in the course of development. Aggression is the area in which boys and girls probably are reared most differently. Parents permit more physical aggression in boys than in girls. This sanction is not indiscriminate, however. Parents teach their children to discriminate in the expression of aggression with regard to circumstances and setting.

12. Social forces, institutions, and groups have a vital role in the development of psychological sex differences throughout the life cycle. Cultures differ in their sex-role standards, and even within a given culture there may be important subcultural differences. However, some cross-cultural differences in sex-role socialization have been found repeatedly. Many of the cross-culturally obtained sex differences in social behavior may partly reflect the widespread adaptation of cultures to universal sex differences in biological variables such as child-bearing.

13. Not only the child's sex, but also the sex of the people who react to him, can be important "moderators" determining some of the consequences he receives for his sex-typed behavior. There are many interactions, for example, between the sex of the parent and the sex of the child with respect to particular behaviors and situations. Thus in addition to the child's own sex, such other variables as his age, the sex of other people in the situation, and the type of behavior also interact to influence the consequences he gets for engaging in such sex-typed behaviors as aggression and dependency.

14. Within any society the role expectations and role behaviors of the sexes change significantly and repeatedly in the course of the individual's development. Some of the most important aspects of personality and of dis-

tinctively male and female behavior may emerge at and after puberty. Dramatic differences in sex-typed behaviors begin in adolescence and continue to influence the individual throughout his life. Sex-typed behavior changes as important role models change and new role demands are experienced. Changes in role standards in the larger culture also can influence sex-typed behavior substantially.

15. Many correlations exist between masculinity-femininity indices and other personality measures. For example, relations have been found between sex-typing and such indices of personality adjustment as positive self-concepts and self-confidence. Often these correlations are complex. Thus dependency in girls seems to be associated with different rearing patterns than dependency in boys. The durability of various sex-typed behaviors also differs for the two sexes.

16. Traditional sex-role stereotypes and sex-typing practices are being questioned and challenged increasingly. Sex-role biases are prevalent in society, including education and the mental health fields, and narrow sex-role stereotypes undoubtedly have negative, constrictive consequences that limit the human potentiality of both sexes. As part of the growing recognition of sex bias and the constriction produced by stereotypic sex-roles, there has been a move to measure—and perhaps encourage—increasing "androgyny" so that both sexes may achieve greater sex-role flexibility.

# CHAPTER
# 15

# IDENTIFICATION
# AND
# OBSERVATIONAL
# LEARNING

Some of the most striking features of personality often seem to develop independently of direct reinforcement. For example:

> A pervasive quality such as masculinity (or femininity) receives at least some intentional reinforcement by parents and peers, of course, but the training task required for creating this kind of role conformity seems too great to permit an explanation in terms of the direct reinforcement of each of the behavioral components that compose the roles (Sears, Rau & Alpert, 1965, p. 2).

To understand the development of personality with concepts other than direct reinforcement, many researchers have invoked the process of "identification." In their view, the developing child acquires a broadly integrated pattern of basic attitudes and values that encompass his sense of sexual identity as well as his conscience and his standards of moral judgment and conduct. This set of basic dispositions, they believe, may be facilitated by some of the processes discussed in the last chapter, but these theorists stress that additional concepts are required. The present chapter deals with those concepts.

# IDENTIFICATION

Identification has been the favorite theoretical mechanism to explain how children develop broad attributes and generalized behavior patterns similar to those of their parents and of the other significant social models in their lives. The theorizing of Sigmund Freud has had an enduring impact on formulations about identification, but the concept of identification has had at least three distinct meanings in Freudian thinking and in the extensions provided by most of his followers.

## DEFINING IDENTIFICATION

First (according to Bronfenbrenner's 1960 analysis), identification refers to *behavior,* as when one person acts or feels like another person (called the "model"). Behavioral similarity between two people, however, does not necessarily mean that one person has identified with the other. It may be caused by different variables that independently produced the same effects in both persons. A father and son may both, for example, be unhappy at the same time, but each independently and for completely different reasons.

Second, identification also refers to a *motive,* in the form of a generalized disposition to act or to be like another. This motive usually refers to the tendency to emulate the idealized standards and behaviors of the parent. Many definitions of identification stress that the child must have a motive to be like the model and to want to possess some of his attributes (Mussen, Conger & Kagan, 1974). It is quite likely that most children subjectively experience a strong motive or wish to become more like their parents. Such a wish is illustrated in the following dialogue between a 6½-year-old girl and her father:

> DAUGHTER: I love you. . . . I want to be just like you.
> FATHER: In what ways?
> DAUGHTER: In all ways.
> FATHER: Why?
> DAUGHTER: Because I love you.
> FATHER: And why do you want to be just like me?
> DAUGHTER: 'Cause then I could do all the things you do—
> FATHER: And?
> DAUGHTER: And that would be fun.

This young girl certainly seems to be expressing a motive to become like her father. A scientifically satisfying account of what causes her to take on some of the parental characteristics, however, would be incomplete if it simply noted her motive to be like the parent. A more complete analysis has to consider the causes of the motive itself. We are back again with the need to consider the conditions that control or regulate experiences as well as the subjective or perceived features of the experience itself. A closer examination of the child's expressed wish hints at some of the reasons for it. The girl is saying she wants to be like her father because she loves him and because if she were more like him she could do all the "fun" things he does. A great deal of research has been devoted to understanding the processes implied by this girl's comments, as later sections discuss.

Finally, a third meaning of the term identification refers to the *process* or mechanisms through which the child comes to emulate a model and to be like him. Concepts regarding such mechanisms have been posited by different theorists, beginning with Freud (Chapter 3). These concepts have been created to understand how the child "internalizes" parental and societal standards for appropriate sex-role behavior and moral conduct, and how he "incorporates" (or makes part of himself) many of the attributes and characteristics of his parents, especially his same-sex parent.

## THE ROLE OF THE PARENT AND FATHER-ABSENCE

Most studies of identification have emphasized the child's immediate family, and especially the parents, as models. Identification theories have focused on the father as the main model for the development of appropriate sex typing in boys. In the Freudian view, for example, if the father is absent the boy tends to remain mother-identified and is more likely to develop latent or even overt homosexual tendencies and feminine attributes (e.g., Fenichel, 1945). Guided by psychodynamic theory, much research has been devoted to the effects of father-absence on personality development. Studies on this question indicate that father-absent boys generally tend to show less appropriate sex-typing (e.g., Bach, 1946; Lynn & Sawrey, 1959).

Children whose fathers are absent may be less adequately socialized than comparable father-present children, not just in sex-linked attributes but also in non-sex-typed behaviors. For example, there is a significant relation between father-absence and preference for immediate gratification for children aged 8 to 9 years (Mischel, 1958, 1961c). The father-absent youngsters were less willing to wait for delayed rewards than were children from father-present homes. This relationship held *regardless of the child's sex*, and it was replicated consistently. It suggests that father-absence may be a sign of an inadequate home environment that is not conducive to trust, to voluntary delay of reward, or to other characteristics of appropriate socialization for children of both sexes.

The relationship between father-absence and preference for immediate gratification was found for young children but not for older ones (Mischel, 1961c). It may be that as children gain more experiences outside the limits of their immediate families they become increasingly influenced by extrafamilial sources. They then become less dependent upon the expectations and response patterns modeled and supported in the home, and their behaviors become more influenced by social reinforcement from peers (e.g., Patterson & Anderson, 1964) and by sociological variables.

The relationship between prolonged father-absence and direct measures of sex-typed behavior in adolescent delinquent boys has also been studied (Greenstein, 1966). Contrary to the expectations of most identification theories, the father-absent boys did not differ from those from father-present homes on any measures of overt or covert sex-typing. An intriguing feature of this study was that it included a direct measure of homosexuality. This measure involved the youngster's answers under sodium amytal medication ("truth serum") to carefully structured questions about homosexual encounters. There were no differences in homosexual behavior between father-present and father-absent boys. These results seem consistent with the previously mentioned finding that father-absence seems to have less effect (or even no effect) when children are older because their behavior then may be more influenced by variables outside the home.

In Greenstein's (1966) study, social workers also rated the dominance of the father in the home and his closeness to his son in the sample of adolescents who came from father-present homes. The relations between rated father-dominance and son's sex-typing were not significant. Surprisingly, the ratings of father-closeness indicated *more* overt homosexuality in sons whose fathers were rated as "close" to them.

This finding is hard to interpret. It may be that the fathers who were rated as closer to their sons had greater homosexual propensities. Or it may be that these fathers had more tolerance for homosexual tendencies in their sons, and perhaps even provoked them. On the basis of case histories, Greenstein favors the latter interpretation and thinks that the fathers who were rated closer to their sons may have been more seductive toward them. His reports indicate that some of the fathers rated as closest to their sons may have encouraged and reinforced homosexual tendencies in them. Alternatively, if these "warmer" fathers were themselves more homosexually inclined, then the greater homosexuality of their sons may be a sign of closer father-son identification. Thus under some conditions paternal nurturance may enhance the son's identification with the father but may also result in a more homosexual son.

It is sometimes assumed that the development of sex-appropriate social behaviors in the boy depends on his adopting the characteristics of his father. For the girl, normative sex-typing and socialization supposedly hinges on her adopting behaviors modeled by her mother. These assumptions seem plausible only for sex-role stereotypes, according to which fathers embody masculinity and mothers are the personification of femininity. If we transcend these stereotypes and examine individual lives more closely, some greater complexities become apparent.

Obviously enormous individual differences exist among fathers in their "masculinity" (no matter how it is defined), just as among millions of mothers vast differences exist in "femininity." Consequently, a boy who closely emulates his father actually may through this identification acquire "feminine" characteristics, to the degree that his father displays feminine attributes. Similarly, the girl who identifies closely with a "masculine" and dominating mother would herself become correspondingly masculine. Given these considerations, one cannot assume that the extent to which a child shows socially normative behaviors—such as appropriate sex-typing or conformity to social standards of honesty and self-control—serves as a reliable index of his identification.

For example, would the son of a hardened criminal show more identification if, unlike his father, he became a pillar of society, or would he be more strongly identified if he followed closely in his father's path? The belief that the amount of normative behavior (in sex roles, conscience, self-control, or other hypothesized products of identification) shown by the child is an index of the degree to which he has identified with the parents seems to be rooted in the idea that the parents are the sources of the superego and the transmitters of social rules, norms, and restrictions. When the parents themselves violate social norms, however, their ability to fulfill roles as superego models transmitting societal standards becomes highly questionable.

# OBSERVATIONAL LEARNING IN PERSONALITY DEVELOPMENT

In the past, identification has been singled out as a special process that required concepts different from those needed to account for other forms of social learning. According to some more recent formulations, however, the development of the diverse components of personality may be described by the basic principles of social learning.

## SOCIAL LEARNING THROUGH IDENTIFICATION OR OBSERVATION?

Bandura and Walters (1963) pointed out that although numerous distinctions have been proposed between observational learning and identification, the same phenomena are encompassed by both terms. Both imitation and identification refer to the tendency for a person to produce the actions, attitudes, or emotional responses exhibited by real-life or symbolized models. Consequently, Bandura argues that, for the sake of clarity and parsimony, the terms "identification," "imitation," and "observational learning" may be used interchangeably to refer to behavioral modifications produced by exposure to modeling stimuli (1969).

Unlike some earlier behavior theories, current social learning theories no

Complex behaviors may be learned rapidly through observation without having to be reinforced.

longer depend on the concept of specific reinforcement for discrete acts, and on the tedious "shaping" or "training" of each minuscule role component by external reinforcements administered by the parent or other socialization agents. Indeed, it now has been shown often that children may rapidly learn large and complex sequences through cognitive-perceptual processes that require their observing events rather than being reinforced for performing acts (Zimmerman & Rosenthal, 1974).

## PROCESSES IN OBSERVATIONAL LEARNING

It is necessary now to consider briefly the basic processes that occur in observational learning. These processes have four components: attention, retention, reproduction, and motivation (Bandura, 1971).

To learn from observation it is obviously essential to *attend* to the distinctive features of the modeled behavior. Models would have little longterm impact if we did not *remember* (retain) their behavior after watching it. Consequently, organizing and rehearsing what was observed are important ingredients of learning from models. Especially when the behavior involves complex motor activities (as in swimming, driving, or tennis), the observer also must be able to put together physically the components of the action. Such *motor reproduction* requires accurate self-observation and feedback during rehearsal. For example, it is essential to observe the consequences of particular movements on the steering wheel, and on the gas and brake pedals of the car, when learning to park. Finally, to go from knowledge to performance the observer must have the *motivation* (reinforcement) to enact the behaviors that he or she has learned.

## EXPOSURE TO DIVERSE MODELS

The developing child synthesizes and adopts components from many models. He observes diverse models play many roles and thus starts to learn some of the behaviors relevant to the roles that he himself will assume at different points in his life. For example, by watching his parents he begins to learn about how to be a parent; by observing his teachers he learns how to be a teacher; by observing his playmates he learns various role relationships with peers. The potential roles acquired in this fashion may then be utilized at the appropriate times in his own life, when he has to face situations that require them. Thus when the child becomes a parent he may find himself, to his own surprise (and sometimes chagrin), acting remarkably as his parents did twenty years earlier.

Thus under normal life conditions, children are exposed to many models, and they adopt in varying degrees the behavior of many of these models rather than simply copying one. The child's behavior reflects a synthesis and a creative, novel recombination and integration of elements; it is not a mechanical replica of a single model (Bandura, Ross & Ross, 1963a). For example, all the models in a family, including the siblings, and the sex constellation of the entire family, affect the sex-role learning of all its members (Rosenberg & Sutton-Smith, 1968). Children's social behavior patterns and preferences therefore are not just a child-sized version of those exhibited by the same-sex parent.

# MODEL AND CHILD CHARACTERISTICS INFLUENCING OBSERVATIONAL LEARNING

Parents are the most potent models in the child's life for several reasons. First, the parents usually are the earliest models in the child's development; second, they are the most enduring models, usually being present longer than any other social agents; third, the child's parents are by far the most powerful people in his life. They provide nurturance and control his resources, and in his early life, his very survival depends on them. Consequently the parents become prime models for the child, much of whose observational learning is based on watching mother and father.

Although the child's parents are his earliest and most important models, he is exposed to many other models—for example, siblings, grandparents, televised baseball heros. Yet obviously children do not emulate the behaviors of everyone they see, and they do not imitate in equal degrees all the people they know. Therefore it is important to understand the variables that determine the extent to which the child takes on for himself the attributes and behaviors displayed by the different models he observes throughout his development.

Many recent studies have tried to clarify how the characteristics of a model influence the extent to which observers imitate him. The results are directly relevant to theories of identification because in these theories several different hypotheses have been advanced about the conditions that enhance modeling. The results also help us to understand how children may acquire the behavioral repertoires that gradually make up their personalities.

The young girl who wished to be like her parent (cited at the start of this chapter) hinted at two of the main variables that determine the likelihood that an observer will emulate a model. She mentioned wanting to be like her father because she loved him and, second, because then she could do all the fun things that he does. As the following researches indicate, her intuitive reasons seem to be largely correct. Many studies have analyzed what characteristics of the model influence observers to adopt aspects of the modeled behavior. The most important of these characteristics include: (1) the model's nurturance or rewardingness, (2) his power, and (3) his similarity to the observer.

## NURTURANCE (REWARDINGNESS)

Extensions of Freud's identification theory have emphasized "anaclitic identification," based on the loving, nurturant, and rewarding qualities of the model (e.g., Mowrer, 1960). For example, the extremely influential conceptualizations of Robert Sears emphasized the nurturant relationship between the care-taking mother and her child as the roots for identification. Sears (1957) suggested that the mother becomes valuable for the child through her nurturance and care-taking. As a result, early in his life the child develops strong dependency needs for her. Later in development, when he is frustrated because his mother is unavailable (as when she is too busy to attend to his needs), he can imitate her in play by enacting her role, or fantasize about her in imagination, in order to mentally recapture and enjoy her nurturant acts and rewarding qualities.

There is much evidence that the model's nurturance and rewardingness do in fact facilitate the tendency of observers to emulate him. Mussen (1961) investigated adolescent boys who were either highly masculine or highly feminine in their vocational interests, as measured by their masculinity-femininity scores on the Strong Vocational Interest Blank. These boys also took personality tests (such as the TAT and inventories), and in addition, their behavior was rated by others. The results suggested that boys with more masculine interests tended to portray their relationships with their fathers (inferred from TAT stories) as more positive and rewarding. Moreover, they less often told TAT stories in which fathers were punitive or restrictive toward their sons. Boys whose fathers were affectionate and warm also were more similar to their fathers on a personality inventory (Payne & Mussen, 1956). Likewise, young boys whose fathers were nurturant tended to assume the father role more often in doll play (P. S. Sears, 1953) and showed greater preference for the male role (Mussen & Distler, 1959).

Experimental studies have also shown that a model's nurturance facilitates the observer's tendency to emulate him. Bandura and Huston (1961), for example, engaged nursery-school-children in a highly nurturant and rewarding play relationship with a female adult model. A second group of children saw the same model for the same period of time, but her behavior toward them was distant and nonnurturant. Instead of playing warmly with the child, the model ignored him. After these interactions, each youngster saw the model display a series of novel aggressive (e.g., hitting a doll) and nonaggressive (e.g., saying "a stickeroo" while pasting decals) behaviors during the course of a game. Most children readily imitated the aggressive responses regardless of their initial relationship with the model. The model's nonaggressive behaviors, however, were much more frequently adopted by children toward whom she had been more rewarding than by those toward whom she had been aloof. The authors concluded that nurturance may enhance the tendency to emulate a model but is not an essential prerequisite for the occurrence of imitation.

## POWER (CONTROL OVER RESOURCES)

Until now the discussion has focused on the model's rewardingness. Other theorists have attached great importance to the parent's power over important outcomes in the child's life (e.g., Maccoby, 1959). These formulations emphasize the model's control over the child, in the form of both rewards and punishments, as determinants of the youngster's tendency to adopt the model's behaviors and to be influenced by him.

Whiting (1959, 1960) is one of the few theorists who has expanded Freud's concept of "defensive identification" or "identification with the aggressor." Freud's concept was that the boy defensively became like his father in order to reduce the threat of being castrated by him during their rivalry for the mother in the Oedipal conflict. Whiting, however, focused on the more general rivalry between child and parent. He considered this competition not merely in the sexual context of the Oedipal situation, but more broadly as unsuccessful rivalry over all sorts of valuable resources (such as the parents' food, care, affection, attention). Whiting assumed that the child envies the status and the resources of his parents, yet cannot compete for them directly but only through fantasy and identification with the parent (for example, by pretending to be the parent). His identification thus may be motivated by his envy of the parents' status and his desire to have and to consume their resources. But is the child motivated by the desire to get and to *consume* the valued resources or, instead, by the wish to *control* those resources?

Bandura, Ross, and Ross (1963b) conducted an experiment relevant to this question. Each nursery school boy or girl participated with one male and one female adult in a three-person relationship. This three-person group was designed as analogous to the family, and each one contained the child plus an adult who controlled resources and another adult who either consumed them or was an ignored onlooker. The sex of the controller, the consumer, and the onlooker was varied systematically so that both a male and a female adult served in each role in different groups. Thus in one condition an adult male controlled the group's positive resources and an adult female received and consumed them while the child watched. Specifically, the adult who "controlled" the resources offered the "consumer" a variety of attractive games and treats (e.g., toy TV sets, a juice dispenser) that he controlled, and he participated in play with the consumer for 20 minutes. Meantime the child was ignored as a passive onlooker. In another condition, the child was the consumer of the valued resources while one adult was the controller who dispensed them to him and the second adult was the powerless, ignored onlooker. In this group the adult "controller" dispensed his treats to the child and played with him while the other adult looked on and was neglected. Other conditions varied the other combinations of the controller-consumer-onlooker relationship. After these relationships were established, the children were assessed for their tendency to imitate each of the adult models in the course of another special game. Each adult in this game now engaged in many distinctive verbalizations, gestures, and mannerisms (hands on hips while saying "ready," for example), and the child was scored for the degree to which he imitated each model's behaviors.

In general, the children imitated the controller of the rewards much more than they imitated the other adult who received and consumed the rewards (Table 15-1). The results therefore suggest that power (control of resources) is the more important determinant of imitation.

While the powerful adult was generally greatly preferred to the noncontrolling adult, there were some important exceptions. When the boy was the recipient of the rewards (i.e., the "consumer") but the adult male was the onlooker and the female the controller, there was a tendency for the boy to prefer the noncontrolling male and to reject the powerful female (bottom row, last column in Table 15-1). This tendency may have reflected the strong stereotype shared by many children that only a male can control potent resources. For example (p. 533): "He's the man and it's all his because he's a daddy. Mommy never really has things belong to her." A closer assessment revealed that several of the youngsters indeed had attributed rewarding power to the ignored male adult in spite of the efforts to render him powerless in the experiment. Thus sex-role relationships and stereotypes may influence the effectiveness of social models.

Studies in which the real parents are the models also show the model's power and dominance to be important determinants of identification. Parental dominance facilitates imitation in both boys and girls (Hetherington, 1965). In families in

**TABLE 15-1  Mean Number of Imitative Responses Performed by Subgroups of Children Exposed to Different Pairs of Adult Models**

| SUBJECTS | ADULT MODELS IMITATED | | | |
|---|---|---|---|---|
| | MALE CONTROLLER | FEMALE CONSUMER | FEMALE CONTROLLER | MALE CONSUMER |
| Girls | 29 | 10 | 26 | 10 |
| Boys | 30 | 19 | 22 | 16 |
| | MALE CONTROLLER | FEMALE ONLOOKER | FEMALE CONTROLLER | MALE ONLOOKER |
| Girls | 22 | 16 | 32 | 22 |
| Boys | 29 | 17 | 27 | 34 |

Adapted from Bandura, Ross and Ross (1963b). All means are rounded to nearest digit.

which the mother was the dominant figure, boys developed somewhat less appropriate sex-role preferences. Under these conditions, boys also tended to be rated as less similar to their fathers. As expected, girls in mother-dominant homes identified much more with mother than with father. In father-dominant homes, girls seemed more similar to their fathers than they were in mother-dominant homes. Paternal dominance seems to be especially important for appropriate identification in boys, but the mother's warmth seems to encourage girls to imitate her most (Hetherington & Frankie, 1967).

It often has been noted that people rehearse and transmit to others behaviors that had aversive consequences for them. Parents say, for example, that they unwittingly repeat acts toward their children that produced pain for themselves when their own parents performed them. The variables that govern reproduction of a model's behaviors that were painful to the individual in his prior interactions with that model have remained unclear and puzzling. For example, why does a child say "no, no" to himself and scold his own behavior? And why does he spank his dolls? Several theories (e.g., Maccoby, 1959; Sears, 1957; Whiting & Child, 1953) including the theory of "identification with the aggressor" or defensive identification (Bettelheim, 1943; A. Freud, 1946), have been invoked to account for this reproduction and transmission of social punishments. Information on this issue has been primarily anecdotal and informal. Even the existence of the phenomenon has rarely been demonstrated.

Mischel and Grusec (1966) therefore studied how the characteristics of a model influence the reproduction of social punishments, such as imposed frustrations and criticisms, which the child not only observed but also received directly from the model. Preschool children were exposed to an adult female model. The first phase of the experiment varied the model's nurturance and future control over the child. To manipulate nurturance or "rewardingness," the investigators varied the degree to which the model provided the child with both material and social noncontingent reward (such as attention, games, treats, praise) in a preexperimental interaction. For example, in the highly nurturant or rewarding interaction the adult played warmly with the child and shared attractive toys with him. In the low nurturance condition the adult busied herself with her own work in one corner of the room, leaving the youngster to play alone with a few unattractive objects.

Power or control over both rewards and punishments was manipulated cognitively by varying the model's role. Specifically, in the low future control condition the model was introduced to the children as a visiting out-of-town teacher who would never reappear; in the high control condition she was introduced as the child's new schoolteacher.

In the next phase, all the children participated with the model in a "special game" that involved a cash register and other toys in a playstore setting. During this game, the model was aversive to the child in novel ways ("aversive" behaviors), and she also exhibited novel behaviors that had no direct consequences for the child ("neutral" behaviors).

After the child played the game with the model he was left alone briefly and was observed through a one-way mirror. Any of the model's neutral or aversive behaviors reproduced by the child, either in the model's presence or while alone, were scored as "rehearsals." In the last phase the child's task was to show another person (a confederate of the experimenter dressed as a clown) how to play the game in the model's absence. The transmission of the modeled neutral and aversive behaviors to the "clown" in the model's absence was also measured.

The model's attributes had highly specific effects. For example, more children *rehearsed* both the model's aversive and neutral behaviors when the model both was highly rewarding and had future control than when her rewardingness and control were low (Figure 15-1). The model's rewardingness, but *not* her control, also led to greater *transmission* of her aversive behaviors to the clown. Children thus imposed upon the clown the painful behaviors that had been inflicted on them initially by rewarding models, rather than by models with high control. This finding seems to contradict the expectations of the theory of "defensive identification" or "identification with the aggressor." According to that theory, the punitive behaviors of potentially threatening models (high future control) should be transmitted most (e.g., Bettelheim, 1943). In fact, exposure to a warm, permissive, nurturant model, rather than to an aloof but powerful and potentially threatening one, seemed to encourage the children most to punish others with the behaviors that their model used.

The overall findings showed that the model's rewardingness and his power may determine in part the extent to which his behavior is adopted. However, these two variables have different effects that depend on the type of behavior (neutral or aversive) shown by the model and on the stimulus situation in which the subject reproduces it (rehearsal or transmission). These findings once more highlight the specificity of the determinants controlling behavior. They demonstrate that the

Figure 15-1   EFFECTS OF A MODEL'S CHARACTERISTICS ON OBSERVERS' TENDENCY TO
REHEARSE HER NEUTRAL AND AVERSIVE BEHAVIORS

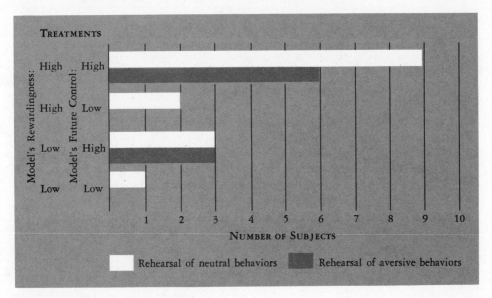

Adapted from Mischel and Grusec (1966).

effects of the model's attributes depend on the particular behavior and situation
involved, rather than having a unitary generalized influence.

## SIMILARITY BETWEEN MODEL
## AND OBSERVER

Similarity between the observer and the model also may enhance imitation.
One especially important dimension of observer-model similarity is their sex.
Maccoby and Wilson (1957) examined how similarity between the observer and the
model influences observational learning. In their study seventh-grade students
watched films that displayed different interpersonal behaviors. One film featured an
adolescent boy and an adolescent girl as the primary characters. A week after they
had observed the film each sample of children was assessed. The investigators now
measured how well the children had learned (that is, could recall) the behaviors
displayed. The children also were questioned about the attractiveness of the characters. They were asked, for example, to indicate which character was most like
them and which one they would wish to be like in real life. Their answers to these
questions were summed into an "identification index."

Viewers did identify themselves more with the same-sex leading character.
Most interesting, the children tended to recall somewhat better the actions and
verbalizations of the model of their own sex. This tendency to learn more closely

the behaviors of the same-sex model was highly discriminative and depended on the sex-typed nature of the behavior being modeled.

> For boy viewers, aggressive content appears to be particularly relevant, for they remember aggressive content better than girls, *provided* its agent is the boy hero. For girls, boy-girl interactive content appears most relevant, and they remember this content better than boys whenever the girl heroine is the agent of the action (Maccoby and Wilson, 1957, p. 86).

In another film in the Maccoby and Wilson study, similarity was not found to be a determinant of modeling. This film showed two boys, one obviously from an upper-middle-class background and the other from a low socioeconomic class, displaying various behaviors. The observing children tended to prefer and to recall more clearly the model whose social class matched the one to which he aspired (as assessed independently) rather than the one of the class he currently belonged to.

Thus the results for social class similarity and the ones for sex similarity were different. In part this difference may reflect the obvious fact that people can change their social class identity much more readily than their sexual gender. For many children a major discrepancy exists between the social class to which they aspire and their actual socioeconomic level. In contrast, children generally report overwhelmingly that they prefer adults of their own sex (e.g., Stevenson et al., 1967) and that they do not want to change their sex, whether it be male or female (e.g., Hartley & Hardesty, 1964).

The finding in the Maccoby and Wilson study that children tended to recall better the behaviors of the same-sex model (especially when he was displaying appropriately sex-typed behaviors) supports the hypothesis that people often attend more closely to same-sex models. In a later study, Maccoby and her colleagues measured the eye movements of young adults while they were viewing an entertainment film. The men spent more time looking at the male lead and the women spent proportionately more time watching the female lead (Maccoby, Wilson & Burton, 1958). Hetherington and Frankie (1967) also found greater observational learning from same-sex models. Boys tended to imitate their fathers more than their mothers, while girls imitated their mothers more than their fathers.

The greater attentiveness to same-sex models, especially when they are displaying appropriately sex-typed behavior, may mean that people have been reinforced more for learning the sex-typed behaviors of same-sex models than those of cross-sex models. That is, children probably are much more frequently rewarded for observing and imitating models of their own sex, especially when the models display sex-typed behaviors. Boys do not learn football by watching girls and girls don't learn about cooking from observing boys.

Same-sex models also may have the power to encourage stereotypically "sex-inappropriate" behaviors. In an experiment within a naturalistic setting (a YMCA summer camp), children were exposed individually to a peer model who played with a toy that was sex-inappropriate for the observing child (Wolf, 1973). As expected, children played alone with the sex-inappropriate toy more after they had seen a same-sex model compared to an opposite-sex model (or to a no-model control group) play with it first. Specifically, if a young boy watches another boy play with a sex-inappropriate object (like a stove) he will later tend to engage in similar play by himself more uninhibitedly than if he had observed a girl in the same activity. Conversely, a girl who watches another girl play with a sex-inappropriate object (like a toy truck) will later tend to do so more freely herself than if she had watched a boy playing the same way. These findings document the view that sex-role stereotypes in behavior may be overcome more readily when the models for disinhibition are of one's own sex.

In general, people tend to match the behavior of another person more when they think the other person is more similar, rather than dissimilar, to them. For example, if individuals are led to believe that they have musical preferences similar to those of a confederate they match his choice of nonsense syllables more than if they believe his tastes are dissimilar to their own (Stotland, Zander & Natsoulas, 1961). People also tend to like others who are similar to themselves and to find less similar individuals less attractive (Byrne, 1969). An observer is usually more influenced by a model's actions when he perceives himself to be similar, as opposed to dissimilar, to the hero (Rosekrans, 1967; Tannenbaum & Gaer, 1965). But matters are not that simple: The effects of perceived similarity are not uniform and there are interactions with other variables. For example, when people perceive themselves as similar rather than dissimilar to a model they imitate him more when he is competent but *less* when he is incompetent or unsuccessful (Baron, 1970).

## EFFECTS OF THE OBSERVER'S CHARACTERISTICS

So far the discussion has focused on the characteristics of the models, but the observer's (or "subject's") characteristics also influence which models he will attend to and the ways in which he may be affected by them (Akamatsu & Thelen, 1974).

Sex is one of the person's many important attributes that moderate his observational learning. For example, boys tend to imitate physically aggressive models more than do girls. In one experiment, adult models displayed aggressive behavior toward a Bobo doll, pummeling and kicking the doll vigorously, while nursery school children observed (Bandura, Ross & Ross, 1961). After a short delay the child was put in a new setting in which toys and another Bobo doll were available. The child was left to play freely, and the frequency of his physical and verbal aggressiveness, as observed through a one-way mirror, was recorded. Children who had observed an aggressive model showed more aggressiveness than did those exposed to a nonaggressive model, but boys imitated the model's physical aggressiveness more than did girls.

Apart from sex differences in susceptibility to social models, various personality characteristics and situational factors may predispose individuals to be influenced more by particular modeling stimuli. For example, more dependent children may show more imitative behavior (D. Ross, 1966). Imitation is also enhanced by a history of failure, especially punishment for independence (Gelfand, 1962), and by social deprivation experiences (Rosenblith, 1961). The characteristics of the observer may be especially important when the cues about appropriate behavior in the situation remain ambiguous (e.g., Akamatsu & Thelen, 1974).

## SUMMARY

Conceptions of the identification process that were influenced most by Freud's ideas have regarded it as a special phenomenon requiring special concepts. Some more recent formulations consider identification as basically similar to any interpersonal modeling through which observers learn and adopt the attributes, attitudes, and actions of other people. Viewed in this perspective, the study of identification becomes part of the investigation of observational learning. Extensive research has explored many of the conditions that enhance observational learning. It has been found that such attributes as the model's noncontingent rewardingness or nurturance, his power and control over resources, and his perceived similarity to the observer may facilitate the observer's tendency to emulate him.

These model attributes often increase imitation, but they are not essential for observational learning, at least in the older children usually studied. The characteristics of the model that exert the most potent influences depend, in part, on the type of behavior that is modeled and on the conditions in which the observer repeats the behavior; that is, whether he rehearses or transmits it. Modeling effects also depend on characteristics of the observer—for example, his sex and age.

We all adopt components from the behaviors of many models and synthesize these components into unique new patterns. Indeed, identificatory processes are not confined to the child's imitation of his parents, but involve observational learning from many sources and models throughout life. While observational processes affect what the individual knows and can do, reinforcement and motivational conditions regulate his performance of the behaviors available to him.

## PRODUCTS OF IDENTIFICATION

So far we have considered some of the conditions that may enhance identification and observational learning. According to some theorists, a vital feature of identification is that it leads the child to acquire or "internalize" a broad pattern or syndrome of personality traits. According to Sears and other theorists, the product of the identification process is a pattern of closely interrelated traits, somewhat similar to the components of the superego in Freudian theory. Specifically, Sears and his associates hypothesized that this pattern includes "sex typing, adult role formation, self-control, self-recrimination, prosocial forms of aggression, guilt feelings, and other expressions of conscience" (Sears, Rau & Alpert, 1965, p. 1). That is, a broad group of socialized behaviors, ranging from appropriate sex roles through adult-like behavior and conscience, were seen as the products of the child's identification. These behaviors seem to be referents for even broader concepts, such as Freud's construct of superego and ego-ideal (Freud, 1959). Sears and his associates hypothesized:

> If our presumptions are correct, and if there is a single mediating process governing the various hypothesized behavioral products of identification, there should be some unity among them. . . . In other words, within a group of young children there should be high positive correlations among the measures of the several so-called identification behaviors (Sears, Rau & Alpert, 1965, p. 2).

Are people, in fact, highly consistent in their sex-role behaviors, and in other indices, such as conscience, that are assumed to be the products of identification? Are there close relations among the behaviors and traits hypothesized to result from identification? Sears tried to answer these questions, and the answers have profound significance for personality theory.

One of the hypothesized products of identification that interested the Sears group most was the child's sexual identification—that is, his "sex typing." As the last chapter indicated, sex typing refers to the child's adoption of the behaviors and attributes (values, interests, attitudes) appropriate to his own sex. But how do we study sex typing? How do we find behavioral referents for "masculinity" and "femininity"? The Sears group reasoned that they could start empirically by examining the social behaviors on which the sexes seem to differ most.

*Dependency* and *aggression*, as the last chapter showed, are the two dimensions on which the sexes are often thought to differ most. Consequently these two dispositions were selected to serve as key referents for sex typing. That is, the appropriately sex-typed, "masculine" boy was defined as the one who is more aggressive and less dependent, whereas "femininity" was conceptualized as involving less aggression and more dependency. The Sears group looked for consistency on these dimensions of aggression and dependency to assess whether the hypothesized identification process really produces generalized traits. Their question here was: Does identification yield generalized traits that characterize the individual in many situations? For example, is the child who is "feminine" (dependent, nonaggressive) in some situations also feminine in other settings in a consistent fashion?

To answer such questions, Sears and his colleagues studied the consistency of identification-mediated behaviors such as dependency and aggression in preschool girls and boys. Recognizing the kinds of methodological problems that complicate the meaning of broad, global trait ratings (as we discussed in Chapter 8) the researchers carefully included objective and detailed observational measures of the child's actual behavior in clearly defined situations.

Sears (1963) studied five categories of dependency behavior. His categories were: negative attention seeking, for example, by disruption or aggressive activity;

positive attention seeking, as in seeking praise; nonaggressive touching or holding; being near (for example, following a child or teacher); and seeking reassurance. The children were observed carefully at nursery school, and their behavior was sampled at different times and was scored reliably. Each child was observed in free play for many hours. Contrary to expectations, the children were not consistently dependent. The intercorrelations among the five dependency categories reached statistical significance in only one of the 20 consistency coefficients that were computed. A child's dependency in one setting thus was unrelated to his dependency in other settings. Reviewing their own data, Sears, Rau & Alpert (1965) concluded that a unitary concept of dependency was not justified.

Other studies of dependency, summarized by Maccoby and Masters (1970), also indicate little consistency in observational studies when dependency is sampled in closely related situations. Mann (1959) obtained ratings of many two-minute observations of nursery children in free play on six kinds of dependency behavior. Only one of 15 intercorrelations among these components was significant. Likewise, observations of nursery school children revealed no relation between the frequencies of their "affection seeking" and "approval seeking" (Heathers, 1953).

Dependency seems to be much more consistent, however, when raters make broad, global judgments rather than observe specific behaviors. High correlations have been found among teachers' ratings of five dependency components in nursery school children (Beller, 1955). The correlations from such broad trait ratings often are impressively large. Unfortunately the presence of rating biases and stereotyped impressions in such trait judgments makes them hard to interpret (e.g., Mischel, 1968). If there is no consistency when boys and girls are measured on specific and objectively defined dependency behaviors, but there *is* consistency in broad, global ratings of their dependency, then the consistency may reside in the judges' biased concepts and not in the children's behavior.

Sears, Rau, and Alpert (1965) also investigated the consistency of aggression in their sample of nursery school children. Their results suggested some clustering of aggressive behaviors, especially in boys. But considering the large number of coefficients computed, and the generally modest magnitude of even those relations that reached statistical significance, there was no strong evidence for a broadly consistent aggressive trait.

The relations among other measures of sex role also were studied carefully by the Sears group. Their tests included several in which children chose among objects, toys, and activities that differed in their sex appropriateness. For example, the youngsters indicated whether they preferred a picture showing a child walking a doll in a buggy or a child playing cowboy. Other measures included the children's preferences for various real and symbolic play areas and activities. Adult observers then rated each child on a five-point scale of "sex typing," or the degree to which he behaved in accord with expectations for his sex. In addition, the children's doll play was scored for sex typing. Their willingness to adopt the opposite sex role in a game while interacting with their mother was also recorded. Agreement among raters was adequate and the scoring was done reliably.

Of main interest were the correlations among the sex-role measures themselves. There was some consistency among the measures for girls; for boys there was almost no consistency. The overall relations for both sexes were modest and complex. For example, while girls were somewhat consistent on certain sex-typed preference measures and boys were not, in their doll play these trends were reversed. In doll play the girls were not consistent in their tendencies to perform male or female adult work, while there was a trend toward such consistency for boys. Thus even within a fairly narrow subset of gender role measures, such as different aspects of doll play, the youngsters' behavior was far from consistent.

The relationships obtained by the Sears group are fairly representative of those found by other researchers on the same topic (e.g., Mischel, 1966, 1968; Borstelmann, 1961; Hetherington, 1965). In sum, although substantial correlations may be found among masculinity-femininity self-reports and global ratings, consistency among indices of sex typing (such as dependency or aggression) tends to be limited when more direct and more diverse observational measures of behavior are used. This general conclusion is congruent with results on the relative specificity of other identification-relevant personality dimensions, such as indices of conscience and impulse control in adults as well as in children, as discussed in later chapters.

To summarize, some theorists have assumed that many broad personality traits—such as sex typing, conscience, and adult-role-taking in the child—are the closely intercorrelated products of the child's identification with his parents, especially the parent of the same sex. Some consistency has been found in the hypothesized products of identification, but the empirical results generally do not strongly support identification as a unitary process that leads to widely generalized behavioral products. Rather than comprising broadly generalized traits that are interrelated closely, many of the hypothesized products of identification seem to be relatively specific patterns that may be independent of each other. In the light of these findings, some researchers prefer to construe identification not as a special, unitary process but, instead, as part of observational learning or modeling.

## IMPLICATIONS

The specificity (discriminativeness) found in sex typing—and in other personality traits hypothesized to be the products of identification—is *not* so great that we cannot recognize continuity in people. It is also not so great that we have to treat each new behavior from a person as if we never saw anything like it from him before. But the obtained specificity does suggest that the degree and subtlety of discrimination shown in human behavior appear to be as impressive as the variety and extensiveness of generalization. What people do in any situation may be altered radically even by seemingly minor variations in their prior experiences or slight alterations in the specific characteristics of the evoking situation.

This state of affairs—namely, the enormously subtle discriminations that people continuously make and, consequently, the flexibility of behavior—is congruent with the findings on discrimination training throughout socialization discussed in the last chapter. The relative specificity of behavior and its dependence on environmental conditions is an understandable result of complex discrimination learning and subtle cognitive differentiation. When the evoking and maintaining conditions for behavior change—as they generally do across settings—then behavior changes also. When maintaining conditions remain stable—as they often do for the same behavior pattern in the same setting at different times—then behavioral stability may be expected and found (Mischel, 1973a).

When the probable consequences for such sex-typed behaviors as aggressiveness differ widely across situations depending on the particular task and circumstances, impressive generality will not be found. For example, a middle-class American adolescent boy may find it reinforcing to occasionally fight with his peers at home, but he is less likely to find the same behavior rewarded in the classroom. To the extent that aggressiveness is sanctioned in one context but not in the other, cross-situational consistency should not occur.

In accord with the principles of stimulus generalization and discrimination, behaviors become widely generalized only when they are reinforced uniformly across many stimulus conditions. Since the bulk of social behaviors yield positive outcomes in some contexts but negative consequences in other situations, the behaviors tend to become remarkably specific. As a result, poor associations among response patterns even in seemingly similar situations are found often as noted earlier (Chapter 8); many traits thus tend to be relatively specific rather than highly generalized (Mischel, 1968; Peterson, 1968; Vernon, 1964). It is sometimes believed that specificity in behavior implies randomness or chaos. But it may also be seen as evidence of the adaptiveness and flexibility of personality and of people's resilient responsiveness to even subtle changes in conditions.

The discussion of personality development in this chapter and the previous one has emphasized sex typing and the phenomena of identification. It may be, however, that all social behavior can be understood by fundamentally similar causal principles—such as observational learning, reinforcement, cognitive consistency strivings, and so on.

The particular principles favored as the best explanations for the phenomena of personality are still controversial and sure to change. It would be surprising, however, if different basic laws were required ultimately to understand sex-typed behaviors and non-sex-typed behaviors, or if a different set of theoretical rules were needed for every possible trait or dimension of personality, such as dependency, aggression, self-control, altruism, and so on. For example, if reinforcement processes are important determinants of behavior, one would expect them to function in basically similar ways regardless of what is being reinforced. While the specific events that constitute reinforcers would differ, the principles of learning would be the same. Likewise, if observational learning is an important cause of behavior, one would expect modeling processes to be similar regardless of the particular behavior being modeled. Obviously the specific behaviors modeled by a "feminine" mother, for example, would differ from those shown by a less "feminine" parent, but the variables that control a child's adoption of the modeled behavior should be fundamentally similar. Moreover, if observational learning is an important determinant of behavior, one would expect the same principles to apply, regardless of whether the modeling occurs in school or in the home. As the principles of personality development become increasingly clear, they may permit us to elucidate the causes of socialized behavior regardless of its particular content.

## SUMMARY

1. Some of the most impressive features of a child's personality seem to develop independently of direct training by the parents. Many psychologists have invoked the theoretical mechanism of identification to explain the development of broad attributes and generalized behavior patterns similar to those of the parents and other significant social models.

2. Definitions of identification have three aspects: similarity in behavior (including feelings and attitudes) between a child and the model with whom he is identifying; the child's motive or desire to be like a model; and the process through which the child takes on the attributes of the model.

3. Studies of identification have investigated the effects of father-absence on personality development. Father-absent children generally tend to show less appropriate sex typing. However, children whose fathers are absent also may be less adequately socialized in various non-sex-typed behaviors. Father-absence thus may be one index of an inadequate home environment that has a debilitating influence on children of both sexes.

4. Some theorists suggest that identification is not a unitary process but rather that it involves observational learning and requires no special constructs. In their view, through observational processes children learn large and complex sequences of behavior. The developing child observes, synthesizes, and adopts components from many models. He acquires potential behaviors that may be utilized at appropriate times and in situations that require them. The process of observational learning includes four components: attention, retention, motor reproduction, and motivation.

5. Children are exposed to many models, and obviously they do not imitate all of them in similar degree. The characteristics of the model affect the observer's tendency to adopt his behavior. The model's nurturance, his power, and his similarity to the observer are especially important attributes that influence his impact on those who observe him. The effects of these model attributes depend on many conditions. For example, nurturance often enhances a child's tendency to emulate a parent or other social model, but nurturance may not be an essential prerequisite for the occurrence of imitation.

6. Some theoretical formulations focus on the model's power and control over the child's resources as a determinant of imitation. Relevant research has tried to elucidate the concept of "defensive identification." Naturalistic studies suggest that paternal dominance may be especially important for appropriate identification in boys, while maternal nurturance may be most helpful for appropriate sex-role development of girls.

7. Similarity between the observer and the model often enhances imitative tendencies and facilitates observational learning. Thus children tend to recall better the actions and verbalizations of an adolescent model of their own sex. However this tendency may be highly discriminative, and it also depends on such variables as the sex-typed nature of the behavior that is modeled, the child's aspirations and desired attributes, and the model's perceived competence.

8. In addition to the model's attributes, the observer's characteristics influence the models to which he attends and the ways in which he may be affected by them. Sex is one important attribute determining the individual's susceptibility to influence from a social model.

9. Some psychologists postulated a unitary mechanism of identification through which the child internalizes a broad cluster of related traits and behaviors. This hypothesized cluster was believed to include appropriate sex roles, adult-like behavior, and conscience. To support this hypothesis, researchers have tried to show that people really develop the consistent, interrelated traits assumed to be the products of identification. Most of the findings, however, indicate that the personality dimensions included as effects of identification (such as masculinity-femininity, conscience, and impulse control) may be relatively specific and not closely related.

10. The specificity often found in various aspects of personality may be indicative of the subtle discriminations and flexibility shown in human behavior. People learn to discriminate sensitively between situations in which a particular behavior pattern (e.g., aggression) is appropriate and those in which it is not, and hence their behavior may not be broadly generalized across situations.

# CHAPTER 16
# FRUSTRATION AND AGGRESSION

Some contemporary behavior theorists are more interested in analyzing and facilitating the learning process than in describing what is learned. Their interest is understandable since they view all social phenomena as explicable by the same basic principles of learning (as was seen in the last chapter). Other personality psychologists, however, have been most interested in certain specific aspects of personality—such as the ways in which people deal with aggressive and sexual impulses and their vicissitudes, especially as manifested in the lives of disturbed individuals. Indeed, personality psychology began in large measure with the study of disturbed people, and especially through the impact of Freud's work, much of the field has concentrated on pathological phenomena. Freud and his followers worked mostly with emotional maladjustment and focused on the traumatic aspects of human experience, on maladaptive reactions, on distress and anxiety. Consequently the "negative" or painful emotions of life, and the external and internal stresses that might produce these deeply unhappy feelings, have become dominant topics of the field.

Personality psychologists often focus on frustration and aggression, on stress and anxiety, on painful experiences and defenses against them. This focus reflects, above all, the Freudian conception of personality dynamics, according to which, you will recall, man is engaged in a perpetual conflict between impulses seeking release and external frustrations and barriers that inhibit the expression of those impulses. For Freud and for many other theorists the experiences of frustration and anxiety, and the way in which the individual defends himself and deals with his frustrated motives and conflicts, is at the very core of personality. Therefore these topics—frustration and aggression, anxiety, and defense—will be the subject matter of this and the following two chapters. We will examine each of these topics and the concepts necessary to understand them.

This chapter deals with reactions to frustration. The main questions here are: What happens when goal-directed behavior is thwarted? How do people cope with the problems that may arise when their ways of achieving satisfaction become blocked or interrupted?

## DEFINING FRUSTRATION

### FRUSTRATING SITUATIONS

Frustration occurs almost everywhere. Frustration results when there is an interruption in a sequence of organized or goal-directed behavior so that its completion and the goals or rewards associated with it are blocked or delayed (Figure 16-1). Frustration occurs, for example, when an infant's bottle is suddenly withdrawn, when the house key gets stuck in its lock, when the dog arrives for his feeding but finds his food bowl is empty, or when a friend fails to keep his date with you. A fundamental common denominator of these situations is that all involve an imposed interruption or delay of expected goal attainment.

Frustrations may be especially painful when they are caused by the person's own condition and when they are persistent. For example, the child with a new but enduring physical handicap—such as blindness after an accident—faces a world filled with frustration. Less obvious but also painful are the effects of the individ-

Figure 16-1

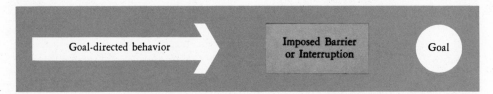

Goal-directed behavior → Imposed Barrier or Interruption    Goal

Frustration occurs when goal-directed behavior is blocked or interrupted before its completion. It is greatest when the blocked behavior pattern has often led to the expected outcome in the past.

ual's own failures or incompetence—the flunked examination, the muffed job interview, the inept social encounter that leads to rejection.

Probably the most dramatic instances of prolonged frustration are those in which the person's control over his own life is interrupted and he is placed in enforced captivity (e.g., Biderman, 1967). The slave or the political prisoner, and even the involuntary military conscript, provide vivid examples of adaptation to total interruption of a life resulting in a massive disorganization of habitual behavior patterns.

## VIOLATIONS OF EXPECTANCY

In common-sense terms, frustration is most bitter when the person has built up high hopes and then is prevented from realizing them. The disgruntlement of severely disadvantaged minority groups, for example, seems to become most apparent and painful only after they have started to build hopes and expectations for a better life. Frustration seems to be most keen when it involves the thwarting of a built-up hope or expectancy for important goal attainment. As was noted many years ago by de Tocqueville: "Patiently endured so long as it seemed beyond redress, a grievance comes to appear intolerable once the possibility of removing it crosses men's minds" (cited in Rubin, 1968). Indeed, as history attests, political dictators sometimes have shared de Tocqueville's insight and have proceeded to "treat" the disappointments of their people by systematically eliminating their hopes.

Thus the experience of frustration involves a thwarting of expected goal attainment. These expectations of gratification are the result of the individual's learning experiences. That is, the actions that we expect to execute smoothly and without interruption are those that have been "overlearned" or repeatedly practiced successfully on past occasions (Mandler, 1964). The more overlearned the sequence, the more arousing its disruption tends to be and the more aversive is the delay of expected gratification or goal attainment. Furthermore, the closer one gets to completion of the goal-directed activity, the more intense is the reaction to being interrupted and prevented from finishing (e.g., Haner & Brown, 1955).

## EMOTIONAL AROUSAL

Intense frustration leads to a state of emotional arousal. Numerous bodily changes occur during high states of arousal and involve a variety of "autonomic" events (physiological changes mediated by the autonomic nervous system). These bodily changes may include an increase in heart rate and blood pressure, sweating, and vasoconstriction in the fingers (Elliott, 1974). We saw how some of these bodily changes may be measured in Chapter 10.

The emotional arousal produced by frustration is often manifested by an increase in the vigor or amplitude of behavior (Amsel & Roussel, 1952). Increased vigor produced by frustration has been found, for example, in the form of more energetic plunger-pulling or lever-pushing by children after frustration in experimental game situations (e.g., Haner & Brown, 1955; Holton, 1961). Similarly, frustrated rats have been shown to display dramatic increases in energetic behavior. It is not clear whether increased vigor of responses after thwarting is an intrinsic effect of frustration or a well-learned common reaction to it.

### PERSISTENCE

Usually a first reaction to the interruption of behavior is to attempt to persist with the blocked sequence (Mandler, 1964). The cliché, "If at first you don't succeed, try again," fits the repetitive behavior typically found in first reactions to an imposed delay—as when one vainly repeats jiggling the stuck key in the lock, usually more and more vigorously, or when the toddler whose mother disappears behind the kitchen door starts pushing against it more and more forcefully, with increasing distress.

## DOES FRUSTRATION HAVE UNITARY EFFECTS?

Early theorizing speculated that frustration has unitary effects on behavior. One hypothesis, consistent with psychodynamic theory, was that extreme frustration (for example in psychosexual development) would lead the child to regress to earlier, more primitive forms of adaptation. This view suggests that frustration may adversely affect adaptation and may lead to more childish, regressive attempts that undermine the quality of the individual's behavior.

### FRUSTRATION AND REGRESSION

How does frustration affect the quality of performance? To try to answer this question, one study observed the behavior of 30 nursery school children, first under normal free-play conditions and then after frustration (Barker, Dembo & Lewin, 1941). In the free-play situation, each child was left alone to play with a set of standard play materials for a half-hour period. Observers recorded and scored the constructiveness of the child's play on a seven-point scale. Low scores were given for such unproductive behavior as superficially examining the toys, and high constructiveness scores were given for originality and creativeness in play (for example, elaborate games and stories).

In the next phase of the study the frustration experience was induced. The child was again exposed to the standard toys, but now they were intermixed with some much more attractive ones. After the child became deeply engrossed in his play the experimenter removed the attractive toys, placed them in a tantalizing play setting in another part of the room in the child's full view, and lowered and locked a wire screen wall to separate the child from the desirable toys. Thus the frustrated youngster and the standard materials were left on one side while the excitingly attractive toys were placed on the other side, in his view but inaccessible to him, for a period of 30 minutes.

Comparisons of the children's behavior in the free-play and frustration periods revealed dramatic differences. When frustrated and unhappy, children played much less creatively and tried in a variety of ways to overcome the barrier. Sometimes they pleaded with the experimenter, sometimes they aggressed against the experimenter or the barrier, and sometimes they became apathetic, talking about things outside the room and generally showing less interest and constructiveness in their play with the standard toys.

This experiment has been widely cited as showing that frustration leads to regression because the children's postfrustration play with the standard toys seemed less mature than their prefrustration play with the same toys. But it is not clear that this ingenious study really supports the psychoanalytic concept of regression as a response to frustration (e.g., Child & Waterhouse, 1952). From the children's viewpoint the experimenter's behavior must have seemed deliberately cruel, irrational, and unjustified. It could be argued that the observed aggression against the experimenter and the barrier, and the accompanying decline of interest in the unattractive "standard" toys, may have been a more mature reaction than sheepish continuation of play with the standard toys. Obviously to the extent that a child was preoccupied with the barrier and trying to overcome it, he could not engage in creative play, and hence his constructiveness scores declined.

Frustration sometimes may impair the quality of the interrupted performance (as it did in the above study), but under other conditions it may have different effects. In one study (Wright, 1942), for example, pairs of children were exposed to the frustration situation from the Barker, Dembo, and Lewin experiment just described. Some of the pairs were close friends while others were casual acquaintances. Pairs of close friends showed less decrement in the constructiveness of their play after frustration than did pairs of acquaintances. Thus the availability of a close peer helped to minimize the impact of frustration. Moreover, under some frustrating circumstances, there may even be an increase in the cooperativeness of play among close friends compared with casual friends (Wright, 1943); close friends became less hostile toward each other and more collectively aggressive against the frustrating experimenter. Observation of the children's reactions also revealed extensive differences in their modes of coping with frustration.

## THE FRUSTRATION-AGGRESSION HYPOTHESIS

A second hypothesis concerning the unitary effects of frustration suggests an association between frustration and aggression. A link between frustration as a stimulus and aggression as a response has been noted for years in many theoretical formulations. The strongest version of this idea was the classical "frustration-aggression hypothesis" (Dollard and associates, 1939). The essence of the original frustration-aggression hypothesis was that:

1. all frustrations increase the probability of an aggressive reaction and
2. all aggression presupposes the existence of prior frustration.

The hypothesis of an unlearned, invariable association between frustration and aggression is most compelling if aggression is conceptualized as an unlearned drive or instinct, and that indeed is how it was viewed by proponents of the frustration-aggression hypothesis.

If it is assumed that people (and other animals) have an instinct to inflict harm or injury on others, it seems plausible also to hypothesize that this instinct will function to enhance the organism's survival. The most adaptive function of aggression in the course of evolution might be as a way of coping with frustrations, especially those that threaten the organism's survival. In their evolutionary history perhaps organisms may have to develop "killer instincts" if they are to survive in their competition with others for the limited essential resources available to them. If nature supplies more organisms than resources for their maintenance, a struggle for survival readily develops and the aggressive animal may be more likely to win.

# AGGRESSION AS A DRIVE RESPONSE TO FRUSTRATION

It became clear some time ago that the frustration-aggression hypothesis, as originally formulated, was oversimplified and required modification (e.g., Bandura &

Does frustration always increase the probability of an aggressive reaction?

Walters, 1963; Berkowitz, 1969). Changes have had to be made for two main reasons:

1. While aggression often may follow frustration, it is by no means the only possible response; there are vast differences among individuals and groups in their reactions to frustration. There also are major differences in any one individual's reaction to particular frustrations, depending on many variables specific to the situation.

2. It has been shown that aggressive reactions can occur without prior frustration. For example, unfrustrated preschool children observed an adult model physically aggress against a Bobo doll. Later these children readily imitated the model's aggressiveness and violently attacked the Bobo doll after the model had left the room (Bandura, 1965).

The modified frustration-aggression hypothesis recognizes that many conditions may affect the specific link between frustration and aggression. This modified hypothesis takes special account of the learned inhibitions that people may acquire during socialization and that may block the direct expression of aggression. Nevertheless, the modified hypothesis still implies that aggression is the natural or prepotent, unlearned drive response to frustration.

## IS AGGRESSION AN INSTINCT?

There is disagreement about the instinctual nature of aggression. The concept of aggressive instincts—of aggression as an innate drive or impulse—was seen most clearly in Freud's view that aggression and sex are fundamental instincts. A similar position is taken by some current observers of animal behavior in natural settings ("ethologists"). Most notably, the ethologist Konrad Lorenz (1966) believes aggression is a fighting instinct, in animals and man, directed against members of the same species. Although Dollard and Miller (1950) emphasize the importance of learning in the socialization and channeling of aggressive impulses, they also see aggression as a basic drive that demands expression either directly or indirectly. Guided by this idea, many researchers have studied the conditions that may either enhance or inhibit the expression of aggression in response to frustration. Some of those conditions are discussed next.

## FEAR OF RETALIATION AND INHIBITION OF AGGRESSION

The direct expression of aggression is inhibited most obviously by the prospects of counterattack or retaliation. The belief that the fear of retaliation is a deterrent to aggression is starkly evident in the "balance of terror" that characterizes the international nuclear arms race. Guided by the conviction that an aggressor will restrain himself if he faces a potentially destructive counterattack, military defense policies urge an awesome deterrent as an essential prerequisite for inhibiting the aggression of enemies.

In the interpersonal sphere, deterrents involve social punishments rather than atomic weapons, but the principles seem to be similar. Thus interpersonal cues suggesting that aggressiveness will be rewarded rather than punished tend to encourage observers to behave aggressively (Bandura & Walters, 1963). Children who watched models receiving rewards for aggressiveness tended to become more aggressive than did those who saw a model punished for aggression.

Human inhibitions about direct aggression also depend on subtler cues concerning the potential victim's power. For example, and not surprisingly, when military personnel are insulted by someone of higher rank they communicate little aggression, while a great deal of aggression is expressed when the insultor is of lower rank (Thibaut & Riecken, 1955).

Another variable that decreases the likelihood of retaliation and punishment is the aggressor's anonymity, as when personal identity remains disguised and the individual can hide behind his bandit's mask, or Ku Klux Klan hood, or military uniform. When persons are thus "deindividuated" they may become more boldly aggressive, impulsive, and punitive (Zimbardo, 1969).

The aggressor's proximity to the victim and the nature of the pain cues that he can observe also affect his willingness to be physically aggressive. For example, bombardiers in wartime often report feeling immune about dropping their missiles on areas that are so far below them that they cannot really witness the damage they are inflicting. When the victim is closer and his pain is more evident, the aggressor may become more sensitized and hence more reluctant to administer severe punishments.

In some experiments on obedience, adults were hired to give electric shocks to another person ostensibly as part of a research project on human learning (Milgram, 1965, 1974). In fact the wires were disconnected, but the victim convincingly feigned the appearance of being hurt by the shocks. Many subjects "carried out their orders" and dutifully administered shocks at levels that they thought were torturous for the victim, supporting the notion that a surprisingly large number of people are capable of behaving like the Nazis who "simply did their job" and followed orders to murder their helpless victims (Fig. 16-2).

Of main interest to the present discussion was the finding that resistance to

**Figure 16-2** MILGRAM'S "OBEDIENCE" SITUATION
Subjects deliver "shock" to another person under various conditions of proximity.
(From Milgram, 1974)

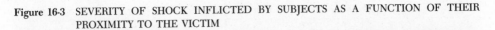

Figure 16-3    SEVERITY OF SHOCK INFLICTED BY SUBJECTS AS A FUNCTION OF THEIR PROXIMITY TO THE VICTIM

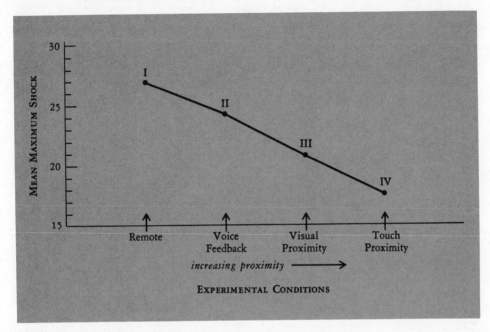

In Condition I the subject neither sees nor hears his victim; in II he hears his victim's protests; in III he also sees his victim close up; in IV he must touch his victim, placing his hand on the shock apparatus. Adapted from Milgram (1965).

carrying out the punitive orders increased as the aggressor was placed nearer to the victim and observed his suffering more closely. Figure 16-3 summarizes the effects of the aggressor's proximity to the victim on the average amount of shock he administered.

While observing the victim's pain may inhibit aggression under some conditions, under other circumstances it may enhance and reinforce it. Thus, when a person is angered it may be reinforcing for him to see the individual who angered him being hurt (Feshbach, Stiles & Bitter, 1967). That is, pain cues may serve as reinforcers under conditions of anger arousal. Since the aggressor often is angry he may find his victim's pain satisfying. On the other hand, if the aggressor is not experiencing anger, then seeing pain in the victim may inhibit him (as in the case of the bombardiers).

In sum, conditions that make aggression more rewarding for the aggressor tend to enhance the occurrence of aggressive behavior; conversely, aggression generally is less likely when it probably will be punished or nonrewarded. Some of the conditions that may enhance the probability of aggression are summarized in Table 16-1.

**Table 16-1    Examples of Conditions That Enhance Aggression**

| AGGRESSION IS INCREASED BY | RESEARCH SOURCE |
| --- | --- |
| Being attacked (insulted) by a non-powerful aggressor (rather than by a powerful one) | Thibaut & Riecken (1955) |
| Watching aggressive models rewarded | Bandura, Ross & Ross (1963) |
| Anonymity | Zimbardo (1969) |
| Distance from victim | Milgram (1965, 1974) |

## INHIBITION AND ANXIETY

Dollard and Miller (1950), like Freud, believed many socialization practices really teach the child to fear his own angry feelings. They say (1950, p. 148): "We assume . . . that anger responses are produced by the innumerable and unavoidable frustration situations of child life. . . . Society takes a special stand toward such anger responses, generally inhibiting them and allowing them reign only in a few circumstances (self-defense, war, etc.)."

Again like Freud, Dollard and Miller believed that problems in development to a large extent are caused by punishment for aggression, which leads the person to become anxious about his own angry feelings. They comment (1950, p. 148): "Parents intuitively resent and fear the anger and rage of a child, and they have the support of the culture in suppressing its anger." Guided by the psychodynamic belief that unacceptable angry feelings are repressed but may return in disguised form as symptoms, they wrote (1950, p. 148): "Lift the veil of repression covering the childhood mental life of a neurotic person and you come at once upon the smoking responses of anger."

## CONFLICT AND INDIRECT AGGRESSION

What happens to aggression when its expression is prevented? The answer partly depends on whether aggression is conceptualized as a drive-like natural impulse provoked by frustration or as a learned but not inevitable response. First, consider aggression as a basic impulse or drive, as conceptualized both by psychodynamic theory and the behavioral version of that theory developed by Dollard and Miller.

Dollard and Miller hypothesized that frustration triggers the aggressive drive. They believed that aggression is the prepotent drive response to frustration. Often, however, the aggressive drive cannot be expressed directly against the perceived source of frustration. Blocking or inhibition may be caused either by objective danger (such as realistic fear of retaliation) or by anxiety about the expression of aggression (due to prior punishment for aggressiveness). As a result, the individual becomes conflicted. He experiences an approach-avoidance conflict between wanting to vent his aggression and anxiety about the consequences of his aggressiveness. To reduce this conflict, he may try to inhibit his aggressive impulses.

Although the expression of aggressiveness may be inhibited, the impulse to aggress remains and presses for discharge in one form or another. According to psychodynamic theory, unexpressed impulses become "pent up" and must be released. Freud thought that impulses that are not discharged may gradually "build up" to the point where they lead to an explosive outburst. When direct expression and discharge are blocked, the drive may manifest itself indirectly in many forms.

Figure 16-4 shows some of these theoretical possibilities schematically. This scheme is suggested both by Freud's ideas on the nature of impulses and their transformation, and by Dollard and Miller's concepts concerning frustration-aggression. As the figure shows, aggressive impulses are triggered by frustration. When their direct discharge is blocked, they may be released indirectly through *displacement* to less threatening objects or by *catharsis*.

## DISPLACEMENT

Consider this example of displacement from Dollard and Miller (1950, pp. 432–433). George, a 14-year-old boy, had an arrangement with another boy for a Saturday outing to the country and planned the holiday carefully. On the morning of the trip the friend's mother called to say her son had a cold and could not go. Deeply disappointed, George pretended to his friend's mother that he accepted the

**Figure 16-4**  THE FRUSTRATION-AGGRESSION HYPOTHESIS AND ITS ELABORATIONS

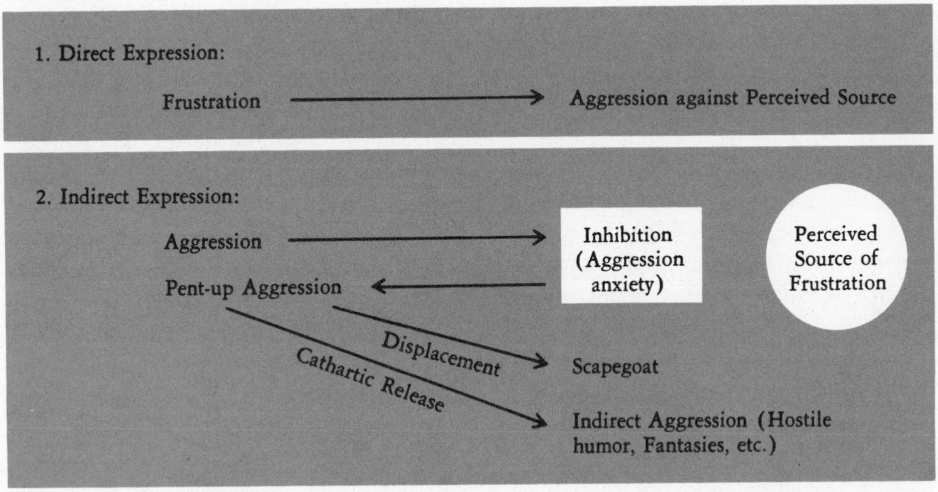

Frustration produces aggression: The aggressive impulse then is expressed directly or indirectly (e.g., through displacement). The form of expression depends on learned inhibitions and defenses.

circumstances and "he suppressed his anger since he had learned it was no use fighting the inevitable (p. 433)."

Later George started to play in his backyard where he happened to meet his 12-year-old sister. As usual, she teased him a little, but this time George flared up, struck her, and the two wound up in an intense quarrel that their mother had to terminate. Dollard and Miller interpret this case as an example of how anger and aggression are called forth as prepotent responses to frustration but are quickly suppressed because of prior inhibition learning. But, in their view, the aggressive drive is not eliminated but merely suppressed and rechanneled, and it emerges in displaced form in the boy's attack on his younger sister.

According to Dollard and Miller, displacement of aggression depends on several factors, including similarity between the cause of frustration and the available targets for aggression. Their drive theory of aggression suggests that aggression may be displaced from the real target to safer, less threatening "scapegoats" (such as subordinates at work).

## CATHARSIS

To help release pent-up aggressive impulses in nondestructive ways, some theorists have encouraged therapeutic expression or "catharsis" of angry feelings by direct or vicarious participation in midly aggressive enactments (e.g., violent plays). In its most extreme form, this position may suggest that frustrated people supposedly must cathart or vent their aggressive impulses gradually, or civilization faces the prospect of extreme violent outbursts of war and killing when the pent-up impulses burst forth uncontrollably. Critics attack this theory as a "drainage" or "pus" view of aggression. They suggest that catharisis, rather than draining off aggressiveness, much as pus is drained out of a festering wound, actually may lead to more aggressive behavior (Bandura, 1973; Berkowitz, 1970).

Does the expression of aggressiveness in a permissive setting indeed have the cathartic effect of reducing the person's subsequent level of aggression? The issue is still not fully settled. Several studies, however, suggest that the performance of aggressive responses in a permissive context maintains the original level of aggression or even enhances further aggression (Feshbach, 1956; Mallick & McCandless, 1966). For example, after play sessions with aggressive toys, children seemed to become more inappropriately aggressive than after play sessions with neutral toys (Feshbach, 1956). Rather than "draining" pent-up aggressive impulses, aggressive play and fantasy thus may actually increase the likelihood of open aggression.

These findings do not mean that aggressive fantasy must always increase violence. Under some conditions of high arousal fantasy might reduce violence, for example by distracting the person long enough to help him inhibit himself effectively before acting (Berkowitz, 1969).

In a related vein, are there cathartic effects from observation of aggressive models and vicarious participation in aggression (such as watching filmed violence)? Some interpretations of Aristotle's ideas concerning vicarious participation in theatrical dramas predict a cathartic drainage or "emotional purge" after watching aggressiveness. While participation in emotional enactments may have many valuable effects, most research suggests that the probability of behaving aggressively generally increases after exposure to live, filmed, or televised violence (Bandura, 1973).

For example, Hartmann (1969) studied adolescent delinquents. In his experiment some of the delinquents were deliberately aroused to anger and some were not. Thereafter all the adolescents were exposed either to a film depicting aggressive behavior or to a film with nonaggresive content. The young delinquents became more aggressive after the aggressive film than after the nonaggressive film. Moreover, the aroused viewers generally were more aggressive after the aggressive film than were the nonangered ones. This finding contradicted the idea that catharsis might occur for angry subjects even if it did not happen for nonaroused viewers. Hartmann therefore concluded that instead of draining the aggressive impulses of the viewers, exposure to the filmed aggression increased their own likelihood of behaving aggressively, and did so especially if they had been aroused. Thus aggression seems to beget aggression.

## LEARNED RESPONSES TO FRUSTRATION

The previous sections have considered research and theory that conceptualize aggression as the natural, prepotent, drive-like reaction to frustration. These formulations recognize the importance of learning in the expression of aggression, but they view aggression as a basic drive that builds up and hence requires release either directly or indirectly. In contrast, several current learning theorists generally conceptualize aggression as learned response patterns and do not assume either instinctual or drive-like properties for them (Bandura, 1973; Berkowitz, 1970).

### SOCIAL LEARNING VIEW OF FRUSTRATION AND AGGRESSION

A social learning view of aggression distinguishes between the acquisition of aggressive responses or capabilities and their performance. A repertoire of extensive aggressive skills may be acquired under emotionally neutral, nonfrustrating conditions:

> . . . military recruits acquire and perfect combat skills through many hours of target practice and simulated skirmishes; boxers develop hurtful pummeling abilities by using punching bags and sparring partners whom they do not necessarily intend to hurt; and huntsmen acquire the basic rudiments of hunting by shooting at inanimate targets before they go out in search of game. Indeed if aggressive repertoires were taught only while individuals were hos-

tilely aroused and entertained injurious designs, many of the tutors and learn-ers would probably be maimed during the acquisition phase (Bandura, 1969, p. 378).

During the course of socialization children are exposed to almost endless in-formation relevant to the acquisition of elaborate aggressive skills. Through obser-vation of filmed and televised violence at home, at school, and in the larger com-munity, the child in our culture soon learns a set of potential aggressive behaviors. These potentially aggressive responses may range from angry verbal abuse and ex-pressions of sarcastic annoyance and hostility to skills in the sophisticated use of knives, guns, karate blows and other murderous techniques for assaulting, hurting, and killing people.

Although through observational and cognitive processes the person soon pos-sesses an awesome repertoire for violence, his choice of aggressive or nonaggressive behaviors in any situation depends on numerous determinants. In the social learn-ing view, a person may be more likely to react aggressively after frustration and emotional arousal because strong reactions are likely to work and thus to be rein-forced under those circumstances. However, the relationship between frustration and aggression is not inevitable. Instead, aggressive behaviors are considered to be governed by the same principles as other socially learned response patterns: their occurrence depends on the person's prior experiences in related situations and on his current expectancies concerning the probable outcomes of the response alterna-tives available to him. Thus any experiences that change the probable conse-quences of aggressive behavior, or that permit a reconceptualization of the mean-ing of the frustrating situation, should affect the nature of the person's response to frustration. This social learning view is schematized in Figure 16-5.

## REWARDS FOR AGGRESSIVE REACTIONS TO FRUSTRATION

The increased vigor or response amplitude so often seen in reactions to frus-tration may indicate that such strong reactions probably have helped the organism

Figure 16-5  SOCIAL LEARNING VIEW OF FRUSTRATION AND ITS CONSEQUENCES

Frustration ⟶ Emotional arousal and disruption of overlearned response-reinforcement sequence

New Response = f (Available alternatives and their probable reinforcement consequences)

Reaction to frustration is a function of the alternative responses available to the person and their probable reinforcement consequences in the situation. Whether or not the selected new response will be aggressive depends on prior learning history and current expectancies.

to cope with delay of gratification in the past. One of the most direct and effective ways of overcoming barriers and achieving blocked goals is to pursue them more forcefully. When a door that one needs to enter is stuck, a swift kick will often dislodge it; when a child's pursuit of a desired gratification is blocked by an interfering younger sibling, a hard punch will often successfully remove the competition.

Aggressive behavior often "gets results" most effectively. Assertive, forceful, dominating behavior is widely attended and often rewarded throughout our society. While passive protests may be politely acknowledged and then ignored, aggressiveness gets action and recognition. Through aggressiveness the ambitious executive pushes his way to the top, the lonely child gets attention, the social protestor achieves his confrontations, the underprivileged ghetto resident instantaneously dramatizes his condition, and the nagging housewife controls her husband. Aggression demands attention. It often also removes barriers and achieves substantial redress of grievances. The prevalence throughout history of political dictators who achieved power through aggression attests to the potency of aggression as a route to personal gain. Given all these direct and vicarious rewards for aggression, the pervasiveness of violence as a response to frustration in our society should not be surprising. Too often in our culture, as one psychologist put it most simply, "aggression pays" (Buss, 1971).

## NONAGGRESSIVE REACTIONS TO FRUSTRATION

Although aggressiveness is often the response to frustration, nonaggressive reactions occur if the person has been appropriately rewarded for them in the past.

Davitz (1952), working with 10 small groups of children, rewarded half the groups with praise and approval for making aggressive and competitive responses during a series of brief training sessions. The remaining groups were rewarded for cooperative and constructive behavior during the training periods. Thereafter all the children were frustrated by exposure to a film that was interrupted just as it approached its climax. At this point the children also were forced to return a candy that had been given to them earlier. Their reactions to these frustrations were recorded immediately on motion picture film in a free play situation. Analyses of the filmed behavior showed that children who had been rewarded previously for constructiveness responded more constructively to the frustration. On the other hand, children who had been rewarded for aggression in competitive games during training now reacted more aggressively to the frustrating experience.

As this study illustrates, responses to frustration depend on the person's social learning history. They also depend on modeling cues and other variables that affect expectancies about the probable consequences of behaviors and the meaning of the situation.

The social learning view recognizes that frustration is often followed by persistent emotional arousal. Such arousal, however, is not taken as a sign of pent-up aggressive impulses that press for release. Rather, as Bandura (1969) has suggested, the frustrated person may repeatedly revivify the upsetting event by thinking about it and thus re-arouse his intense emotions even after the frustrating incident has passed. If that is true, distracting oneself after frustration, or reinterpreting the event cognitively to render it less aversive, should reduce arousal. In contrast, thinking about the anger-inducing qualities of the frustration (e.g., the injustice of it) should enhance one's arousal.

Often a cognitive reinterpretation which is designed to excuse the frustration does seem to make it less anger-arousing. Frustrations and punishments are probably resented much less when they are not imposed arbitrarily but, instead, are explained reasonably (Pastore, 1952). For example, in one study children lost a cash prize because of another child's clumsiness (Mallick & McCandless, 1966). Children who heard the frustrating clumsiness reinterpreted (by explanations that the other child was "sleepy and upset") subsequently showed less aggression against their frustrator than did other children.

If a person's particular social learning history and cognitions critically affect aggressive reactions to frustration, then vast differences may be expected among individuals in how they deal with frustration—and indeed such differences are found.

## SEX DIFFERENCES IN AGGRESSIVE RESPONSES TO FRUSTRATION

Differences between the sexes in aggression as a response to frustration have been especially striking. Such sex differences occur in both children and adults. For example, after they are frustrated (by a brief period of social isolation), nursery school boys were more aggressive in doll play than were girls (Hartup & Himeno, 1959). Boys also were more physically aggressive after frustration, as evidenced by such behaviors as hitting a punch toy (Moore & Updergraff, 1964).

In one experiment, college students were told to administer shock to another student to guide him in a learning task. The students' own rewards depended on the performance of their alleged partner, who was actually nonexistent. The students were deliberately frustrated by being led to believe that their bogus partner supposedly learned too slowly to earn the rewards. Under these conditions men used more shock than did women, and they shocked male partners more than female partners (Buss, 1963).

The average sex differences usually found in aggressive reactions to frustration seem entirely consistent with cultural differences in tolerance for aggression displayed by males and females. It is also possible, however, that sex differences in physical aggression in response to frustration partly reflect physiological or genetic sex differences in the propensity toward physical aggression.

While females may on the average react less aggressively to frustration than do males, they are capable of severely aggressive reactions to frustration when properly provoked. College students were led to believe that the electric shocks they were receiving with increasing intensity on a competitive task were being delivered by males. In this condition females reacted more aggressively than males did, reciprocating against their ostensible male opponents with electric shock levels averaging twice their initial intensity (Taylor & Epstein, 1967).

## DISPLACEMENT OR DISCRIMINATION?

Although verbal and physical aggression are liberally rewarded in our culture, this is by no means indiscriminately true. Reinforcement for aggressiveness is highly discriminative and depends on the exact details of the situation, as well as on the aggressor and the type of aggression. According to current social learning theories, such discriminativeness is at the root of the phenomena of aggressive "displacement" and scapegoating. In the social learning view, the phenomenon of bigoted "discrimination" may be understandable by the psychological principle of the same name—discrimination learning—without requiring the concept of drive or energy displacement. Moreover, if aggression against minority groups or "outgroup" individuals is modeled and highly rewarded in its own right, then its meaning as a "displacement" becomes questionable. The idea of displacement might be supported if one could show a *decrease* in overall level of aggression after aggression against scapegoats. That does not seem to be the case if, as previously cited studies have suggested, aggressive expressions and vicarious participation, rather than draining off aggression, actually make violence more likely.

## REDUCING AROUSAL

Physiological studies help to clarify the conditions that may reduce emotional arousal in response to frustration and aggression. In one set of investigations, the measures of arousal reduction were based on changes in vasoconstriction in the blood volume of the finger (measured by plethysmographic recording; Stone & Hokanson, 1969). The investigators wanted to see if a reduction in emotional arousal in response to frustration and attack really depended on an aggressive counterresponse or whether, instead, the victim could regain his tranquility by non-aggressive means. That is, does the angered person have to "act out" his angry feelings, or can he effectively handle and reduce his emotional upset in other ways?

College students were frustrated by having a "fellow subject" (actually a confederate of the experimenter) aggress against them with painful electric shocks (Hokanson et al., 1968). This experiment was designed so that only friendly responses by the subject successfully reduced the attacks. The physiological measures revealed that under these circumstances reductions in emotional arousal gradually occurred only when subjects made *friendly* counterresponses to aggression.

In a similarly designed experiment, self-punitive behavior (self-administered shock) was made the response through which subjects could avoid receiving even more severe shocks from their aggressive frustrator. Under these conditions, reduction in emotional arousal was obtained by self-punitive behavior (Stone & Hokanson, 1969).

These studies most clearly indicate that cathartic-like emotional relief and tension reduction are not contingent on an aggressive counterresponse against the source of frustration. Instead, given the appropriate conditions and history, virtually any response to frustration and pain can lead to reduction of the arousal state. Hokanson and his colleagues thus suggest that *any* response to frustration may have arousal-reducing effects *if* that response has previously been effective in terminating aversive or painful stimulation. Hence we must question the view that frustration produces a distinct form of emotional arousal and angry feelings that can only be reduced by direct or vicarious aggression.

## AGGRESSION WITHOUT FRUSTRATION: THE CASE AGAINST TV VIOLENCE

Before leaving the topic of the frustration-aggression relationship, it is important to emphasize that aggression often may occur even when there has been no noticeable frustration to provoke it. Emotional arousal and anger are not necessary prerequisites for aggression. As Bandura (1973, p. 59) noted: "A culture can produce highly aggressive people, while keeping frustration at a low level, by valuing aggressive accomplishments, furnishing successful aggressive models, and ensuring that aggressive actions secure rewarding effects."

The occurrence and contagion of aggression, regardless of frustration, is evident in studies on the effects of viewing aggression on television. Although the television networks have taken pains to deny it, exposure to televised violence can have unmistakably negative effects even on viewers who are not especially aroused or frustrated (Liebert, 1972; Murray, 1973). For example, after watching aggressive film segments (from *The Untouchables*), children demonstrated a greater willingness to hurt others than they did after watching a neutral program that featured a track race (Liebert & Baron, 1972). And after watching violent cartoons for a specified time daily, children became more assaultive toward their peers (compared to other children who had watched nonviolent cartoons for the same amount of time; Steuer, Applefield & Smith, 1971). Televised aggression also sensitizes the viewers so that they perceive greater violence around them, and become more favorable to aggression as a mode of resolving conflicts (Greenberg & Gordon, 1972).

The foregoing research indicates that observers may imitate aggressive models even if they have not been especially frustrated. But this tendency may be increased if the observer is in a frustrated state (Hanratty, O'Neal & Sulzer, 1972). Given the prevalence of frustrations in everyday life, the potential harm produced by filmed aggression becomes highly disturbing. The contagion of aggression is increased further when the models are shown reaping great rewards for their violence.

## EFFECTS OF FRUSTRATION ON THE VALUE OF THE BLOCKED GOAL

This chapter has explored the nature of frustration and focused on its complex link with aggression. Another aspect of frustration has nothing to do with aggression but concerns an important theoretical question: How does frustration affect the way we subjectively value the "blocked" or frustrated goal?

The experience of frustration usually seems aversive, but sometimes people, objects, goals, and situations that frustrate us seem to become more attractive. Curiously, the frustrated and difficult outcome often may appear the most desirable. "Forbidden fruit" may be the most tempting, and people sometimes seem to want most exactly those things that they cannot have. As many sportsmen boast, frustrations and delay of gratification, including the risk of not achieving desired outcomes, enhance the thrill and value of the activity. The relationship between the expectation of obtaining an outcome and its subjective value thus can be quite complex.

What is the relationship between the expectancy for attaining a blocked or delayed reward and the value attributed to that reward? In one experiment, children were subjected to a frustration, in the form of an externally produced delay of reward (Mischel & Masters, 1966). The experimental treatments involved variations in the probability that the frustration would be terminated and the blocked reward attained. More specifically, elementary schoolchildren viewed an exciting motion picture that was interrupted near the climax on the pretext of a damaged electrical fuse. The probability that the fuse could be repaired and the film resumed was presented either as a certainty, a 50–50 chance, or a virtual impossibility.

The results showed that the value of a blocked or delayed reward can be affected by the expectancy of its ultimate attainment (Figure 16-6). When the probability of seeing the interrupted film was stated as virtually zero, its rated value increased most dramatically. The findings indicated that in our culture un-

**Figure 16-6**   EFFECTS OF FRUSTRATION ON VALUE OF THE BLOCKED GOAL: MEAN INCREASES IN RATED VALUE OF FILM IMMEDIATELY AFTER ITS INTERRUPTION IN EACH EXPECTANCY CONDITION

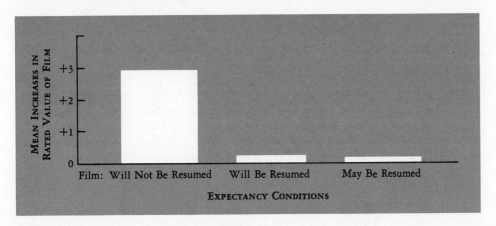

Based on data from Mischel and Masters (1966).

attainable positive outcomes may be more valued than those that are attainable, and that the unavailability of a positive outcome may enhance its perceived desirability. People may value most what they think they cannot have. It is even intrinsic to our economy that attractive things are valued to the degree that they are scarce: the lower the supply of goods, the higher their price.

Time may be a critical determinant of the relationship between expectancy and value. The initial response to an unattainable goal may be to overevaluate it (as in the Mischel and Masters study) but, after a period of time, justification processes may commence and the value of the reward may become minimized. In accord with Festinger's (1957) dissonance theory, for example, the person may devaluate what he cannot have and may persuade himself he didn't really like it.

## FRUSTRATION IS NOT A UNITARY PHENOMENON

When researchers first began to study frustration they thought it might be a homogeneous variable that leads to uniform effects, such as predominantly aggressive or regressive reactions. In fact, as happens with most other phenomena when they are examined closely, "frustration" turns out to be more complex than it at first seemed to be. Indeed "frustration" is not a unitary phenomenon (Lawson, 1965). As we have seen, frustration may be induced by diverse operations, and it can lead to many different behavioral consequences.

## SUMMARY

1. Frustrating situations involve an interruption or delay in the attainment of an expected goal. An individual's learning experiences determine the particular behavioral sequences that he expects will lead to gratification and also the strength of that expectation. The more successful a person has been in achieving a goal in the past, the more frustrating it is to have it blocked. Also, the closer one is to completion of the goal-directed activity, the more intense is the reaction to being thwarted.

2. Often the first reaction to interruption and delay of gratification is an attempt to persist with the behavior. Typically there is emotional arousal that may result in an increase in the strength of the behavior.

3. The hypothesis that frustration leads to regression to earlier more primitive forms of behavior is consistent with psychoanalytic theory. While frustration may sometimes lower the quality of the behavior that was interrupted, it also may have other effects. There are vast individual differences in modes of coping with frustration.

4. The frustration-aggression hypothesis suggests that there is an unlearned and invariable association between frustration and aggression. This hypothesis is most compelling if aggression is conceptualized as an instinct or innate drive or impulse that seeks expression in direct release.

5. The direct expression of aggressive impulses in response to frustration is often blocked or punished. Hence the individual learns to fear retaliation and may become inhibited about expressing aggression directly.

6. Watching the suffering of the victim of an aggressive act may be a deterrent to physical aggression under some circumstances. However, under other circumstances (for example, when the aggressor is angry), the pain of the victim may actually enhance aggression.

7. Aggression is construed as a basic impulse or drive provoked by frustration in Dollard and Miller's behavioral version of psychodynamic theory. They posit that if inhibition of aggression occurs because of possible danger or anxiety, conflict results. The person seeks release of his aggressive impulses but simultaneously becomes anxious about them. Attempts to inhibit the expression of aggressiveness do not remove the impulse, and the drive may manifest itself indirectly, as in "displacement" to a safer target.

8. Current social learning theories do not assume that aggression is an instinct or a drive, but rather view it as learned response patterns. These positions distinguish the acquisition of aggressive responses from the performance of aggression. Even in emotionally neutral, nonfrustrating conditions aggressive skills may be acquired. That is, through observational and cognitive processes during the course of socialization the child in our culture soon learns a set of potentially aggressive behaviors. He uses these behaviors when the motivational conditions are appropriate.

9. In the social learning view, the relation between frustration and aggression is not inevitable. Thus, while frustration and emotional arousal often are more likely to produce aggressive reactions, aggressive behaviors are believed to be governed by the same principles as other socially learned response patterns.

10. Aggressiveness is an effective attention-getter. A vigorous, aggressive response may remove a barrier, alleviate the frustration by satisfying the thwarted desire, and in other ways prove rewarding for the aggressor. In our culture aggressiveness is often the most profitable response to frustration, and hence it may be a frequent one.

11. Nonaggressive reactions to frustration are possible, and they occur if they have proved effective in the individual's past. They are also more likely if nonaggressive reactions have been modeled by others and if the person believes that nonaggression will be the best course of action in the particular situation. Changes in cognitions and interpretations about the meaning of the frustration (e.g., its intentionality and arbitrariness) also may affect an individual's manner of coping with it.

12. Males usually react more aggressively to frustration than do females. This difference may be partly due to physiological or genetic differences between the sexes. It is also consistent with the differential tolerance of aggression by males and females in our culture. Experimental studies indicate that under some circumstances females are capable of severely aggressive reactions to frustration.

13. "Scapegoating" is interpreted by social learning theorists not as a displacement of aggression but as a form of discrimination learning in which aggression against certain groups is modeled and highly rewarded. Under conditions of emotional arousal (such as frustration), individuals may strike out at scapegoats. This kind of aggression usually does not seem to lower the overall level of aggression. Furthermore, experimental studies of physiological reactions to frustration and aggression suggest that even such responses to frustration as friendliness and self-punitive behavior may reduce arousal if they have previously been effective in terminating aversive circumstances.

14. Aggression also may happen in the absence of any noticeable frustration if it is modeled, encouraged, and effective. An example of the routine transmission of aggression is televised violence; watching aggression may increase both the occurrence and the acceptance of violence.

15. One nonaggressive effect of frustration is that the people, objects, goals, and situations that are frustrating may become more attractive (or, under other circumstances, less attractive).

16. The causes, effects, and consequences of frustration may be diverse and vary according to the situation. Frustration does not seem to be a unitary phenomenon with uniform effects.

# CHAPTER 17
# ANXIETY

The emotion that has received the most attention in personality theory is anxiety. Indeed anxiety is a main concept in many of the theoretical orientations discussed in previous chapters.

## CONCEPTUALIZING ANXIETY

Anxiety is most simply defined as an acquired (learned) fear; for the moment we will employ the terms *anxiety* and *fear* interchangeably, although they are often used in somewhat different ways. Examples of anxiety are all around us: the student who is anxious about taking examinations, the businessman with anxiety about his financial future, the teen-age girl who is anxious about her appearance and sex appeal, and the child who wakes up anxious from a nightmare.

## THE EXPERIENCE OF ANXIETY:
## AN EXAMPLE

Before we discuss anxiety abstractly, try to consider the experience of anxiety itself. Here is a description of the subjective feeling of anxiety, as reported by an adult male seeking psychological help:

> That evening as we walked under the skyscrapers it seemed to me I could feel the giant buildings start to sway. Although I knew my fear was prepos- terous the imagined collapse of these huge giants was utterly terrifying. I was convinced that the towers would split and crash down on me and could al- ready picture the people and traffic crushed under them. The strength sapped out of my legs and they became so weak I felt I could not take a step. It became hard to breathe, and not to choke I had to gasp for air with my mouth wide open. I felt my vision darkening and a splitting pressure filled my chest. I was afraid the buildings would really crash and at the same time I was afraid my son would notice my panic.

As this man's description indicates, the experience of anxiety involves an in- tense feeling of fear or dread of impending danger, accompanied by a state of au- tonomic physiological arousal. When the danger is objective, this kind of emotional reaction seems appropriate. In the example, if the buildings were really in danger of falling, as in an earthquake, the reaction would be understandable as reality- based fear. It is harder to comprehend when it seems objectively unjustified, or when the exact conditions causing the fear are difficult to identify. For example, anxiety may seem "irrational" when it is a response to dangers that are already past, or that are expected in the future but have not yet occurred, or that seem idiosyncratic or unusual. The distinction between an objectively justified fear and an irrational one is a matter of degree only and it depends on many considerations. For example, if the man who feared that the buildings would fall down had lost his wife and home in an earthquake two weeks earlier, his present anxiety would seem less irrational.

## CHARACTERISTICS OF ANXIETY REACTIONS

Although different individuals manifest intense anxiety reactions in different ways, the following three components often are found (Maher, 1966):

1. A conscious feeling of fear and anticipated danger, without the ability to identify immediate objective threats that could account for these feelings of appre- hension.

2. A pattern of physiological arousal and bodily distress that may include mis- cellaneous physical changes and complaints. Common examples include *cardiovascu- lar* symptoms (heart palpitations, faintness, increased blood pressure, pulse changes); *respiratory* complaints (breathlessness, feeling of suffocation); and *gastro- intestinal* symptoms (diarrhea, nausea, vomiting). If the anxiety persists, the pro- longed physical reactions to it may have chronic effects on each of these bodily

systems. In addition the person's agitation may be reflected in sleeplessness, frequent urination, perspiration, muscular tensions, fatigue, and other signs of upset and distress.

3. A disruption or disorganization of effective problem-solving and cognitive control, including difficulty in thinking clearly and coping effectively with environmental demands.

## FROM TRAUMA TO ANXIETY

Probably the clearest examples of anxiety reactions are found after the individual has experienced a life-threatening danger or trauma. A near-fatal automobile accident, an almost catastrophic combat experience, an airplane crash—these and similarly intense episodes of stress are often followed by a prolonged aftermath of anxiety. The emotional upset produced by actual dangers may be activated, after they have passed, by stimuli that remind the individual of those dangers, or by signs that lead him to expect new dangers. That is, stressful episodes generate anxiety that may persist or recur after the trauma is over.

After severe trauma, the victim is more likely to respond anxiously to other stress stimuli that occur later in his life (Archibald & Tuddenham, 1965). Surviving victims of Nazi concentration camps, for example, sometimes continued for years to be hypersensitive to threat stimuli and to react to stress readily with anxiety and sleep disturbances (Chodoff, 1963). These observations support the idea that anxiety involves a learned fear reaction that is highly resistant to extinction and that may be evoked by diverse stimuli similar to those that originally were traumatic. That is, the fear evoked by the traumatic stimuli may be reactivated and also may *generalize* to stimuli associated with the traumatic episode. For example, after a child has been attacked and bitten by a dog, his fear reaction may generalize to other dogs, animals, fur, places similar to the one in which the attack occurred, and so on (Figure 17-1). Moreover, if the generalization stimuli are very remote from the original traumatic stimulus, the person may be unable to see the connection between the two and the anxiety may appear (even to him) particularly irrational. Suppose, for example, that the child becomes afraid of the room in which the dog bit him and of similar rooms. If the connection between his new fear of rooms and the dog's attack is not recognized, the fear of rooms now may seem especially bizarre.

From a learning point of view, anxieties after traumas, like other learned fears, may be interpreted in accord with conditioning principles. If neutral stimuli have been associated directly or vicariously with aversive events or outcomes (such as traumatic pain or danger), then they also may come to elicit anxiety in their own right. Such aversively conditioned emotional reactions may also generalize extensively to new stimuli (Figure 17-1). These generalizations may be based on dimensions of semantic as well as physical stimulus similarity, as was noted earlier. Clinical examples of aversive arousal and avoidance include many phobic and anxious reactions to objects, people, and social and interpersonal situations. Not only external events, but also their symbolic representations in the form of words or of

Figure 17-1   FROM TRAUMA TO ANXIETY

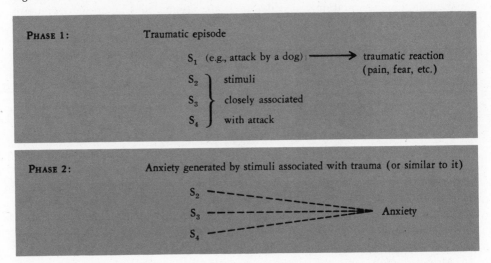

PHASE 1:           Traumatic episode

$S_1$ (e.g., attack by a dog) ⟶ traumatic reaction (pain, fear, etc.)

$S_2$ ⎫
$S_3$ ⎬ stimuli closely associated with attack
$S_4$ ⎭

PHASE 2:           Anxiety generated by stimuli associated with trauma (or similar to it)

$S_2$
$S_3$ ⟶ Anxiety
$S_4$

thoughts and fantasies, may engender painful emotions. In our example of the child traumatized by the dog, even thinking about the incident, or the room in which it occurred, or similar rooms may terrify the youngster.

Stimuli closer or more relevant to those associated with emotional arousal tend to elicit stronger affective reactions. In one study, novice sports parachutists and control subjects were administered a specially constructed word association test (Epstein & Fenz, 1962; Fenz, 1964). The words contained four levels of relevance to parachuting. Throughout the word association tests, subjects' physiological reactions (GSR) were recorded to measure their emotional arousal in response to the various stimulus words. This procedure was followed on three days: one testing occurred two weeks before the scheduled jump, another testing was done the day before the jump, and a final test was administered on the day of the parachute jump.

The results showed more arousal in parachutists for parachute-relevant words. The effect was greatest for the words most relevant to parachuting, and the gradient of arousal was highest and steepest when the testing time was closer to the emotion-arousing parachute jump itself.

While traumas often may lead to anxiety, many other effects are also possible if the prevailing social conditions encourage them. One study examined differences between children in Israeli settlements subjected to frequent artillery shellings during Arab-Israeli conflicts and those from comparable settlements that were not shelled (Ziv, Kruglanski & Shulman, 1974). The children in the shelled settlements appeared to cope actively with the stress and did so in ways that were supported by the social norms in their community. Specifically, they developed greater patriotism for the settlement in which they resided, showed more externally-oriented aggressiveness, and became more appreciative of courage as a personality trait.

## THEORETICAL VIEWS OF ANXIETY

As was discussed in Part 1 of this book, each of the major theoretical orientations has conceptualized anxiety somewhat differently, in accord with its own views of what constitutes grave danger or threat for people. Thus Freudian formulations emphasize the breakthrough into consciousness of unacceptable impulses, learning theories focus on association with painful or aversive stimulation, and phenomenological-existential theories stress the perception of a basic threat to the self or to the individual's very existence as a personality (e.g., May, 1950). Still other formulations of anxiety construe it mainly as a state of distress and helplessness in which the organism has no alternatives (Mandler & Watson, 1966) or as a "disease of overarousal" (Malmo, 1957). Taken together these definitions provide a glimpse of the great variety of events that may constitute subjective danger for any particular individual and that may make him anxious.

There is no reason to restrict the meaning of anxiety to any single conception. Indeed it seems plausible that each individual has a somewhat different, personal set of threats that engender greatest anxiety for him. Because each person can conceptualize arousal states in somewhat different ways, the experiences that can be subsumed under the label "anxiety" may be almost endless, and they range from birth traumas to death fears. Therefore rather than seek a universally acceptable definition of anxiety, it may be more fruitful to examine how anxiety can be measured and to consider its antecedents, consequences, and correlates.

## TRAIT ANXIETY

A distinction has been made between *state* and *trait* anxiety (Spielberger, 1966). State anxiety is conceptualized as a person's momentary or situational anxiety and it varies in intensity over time and across settings. Trait anxiety, in contrast, refers to his more stable, characteristic overall level of anxiety. Usually trait anxiety is measured by the subject's self-report on questionnaires as discussed next.

### SELF-REPORTED ANXIETY

Anxiety inventories require the individual to report the extent to which various anxiety responses generally characterize him. The MMPI is the forerunner and model for most anxiety questionnaires. For example, the most popular anxiety test, the Manifest Anxiety Scale or MAS (Taylor, 1953) borrowed from the pool of MMPI items. Construction of the scale started with selection of 200 items from the MMPI. These items were given to five clinical psychologists with instructions to identify those that seemed to tap manifest anxiety. To facilitate judgment, the clinicians were given a lengthy description of chronic anxiety reaction. Gradually the best items were selected and the meaning of the resulting scale was elaborated through extensive construct validity research. The items on anxiety scales like the

MAS deal with various forms of anxiety such as feeling uneasy, worrying, perspiring, and experiencing unhappiness and discomfort (see Table 17-1).

## RELATIONS AMONG ANXIETY MEASURES

Are people who feel anxious in some situations likely to feel anxious in many other situations? For instance, are people who are anxious about taking tests also likely to worry more about their health and their family? The basic question is: Does "anxiety" constitute a broadly generalized trait? To study this question, investigators assess the correlations among people's anxiety responses on diverse measures.

Substantial correlations are often found among different self-report anxiety questionnaires that deal with topics like "test anxiety" (anxiety about taking tests) or more "general anxiety" reactions (e.g., Sarason et al., 1960; Ruebush, 1963). For example, the correlation between scores on the Test Anxiety Scale for Children and the General Anxiety Scale for Children tends to be highly significant. The associations become low or negligible, however, when anxiety is measured by diverse methods involving response modes and formats other than questionnaires—for example, measures of physiological (autonomic) arousal and actual avoidance behavior. The relations between self-reports of anxiety and physiological arousal are especially unreliable. Generally, physiological measures of anxiety tend to be unrelated to anxiety measured by self-report inventories (e.g., Katkin, 1965; Martin, 1961).

Sometimes, however, significant correlations are found across response systems. For example, Geer (1965) administered a fear survey schedule to undergraduates in order to select a "high-fear" and a "low-fear" group for spider phobia. Equal numbers of high- and low-fear subjects were then assigned to an experimental and a control condition. In the experimental condition subjects were shown pictures of a spider; in the control condition they saw pictures of a snake. For all subjects, measures of autonomic arousal were taken physiologically (in the form of GSR re-

**Table 17-1    Items Similar to Those on the Manifest Anxiety Scale**

| ITEM | HIGH ANXIETY RESPONSE |
|---|---|
| I rarely get really tired. | False |
| I am not a worrier. | False |
| I cannot keep my mind focused on anything. | True |
| I almost never blush. | False |
| Often I cannot keep from crying. | True |
| It's hard for me to attend to a job. | True |
| Often I think I am no good. | True |

The subject must respond "true" or "false."

sponses through finger electrodes). When they were presented with pictures of spiders, people who had reported high spider fear on the inventory showed significantly greater arousal than did the other subjects. Moreover, this increased arousal was found only in response to directly relevant fear stimuli: when students with high fear of spiders were shown pictures of snakes, their arousal did not increase.

The relationships typically obtained between self-report measures of subjective arousal and physiological measures may be summarized this way:

> It is possible to obtain fairly reliable estimates as to what extent people notice or discriminate their internal visceral events. Such ratings show remarkable individual differences, varying from people who rarely if ever notice their guts acting up to others who report that their insides appear to be in a constant state of turmoil. When these reports about habitual perceptions of visceral events are compared with actual levels of physiological reaction in a stress situation, we find that at the extreme ends (that is, people who report very little or very much of such goings-on) there are rather striking differences in overall physiological activity. However, when the full range of individual differences is taken into account the relation between report and measured activity is positive but of rather small magnitude (Mandler, 1962, p. 317; Mandler, Mandler, and Uviller, 1958; Mandler and Kremen, 1958).

## INTERACTION OF TRAIT ANXIETY AND THE SITUATION

Just as with most other personality traits, research has revealed that anxiety is not situation-free. Instead, anxiety reactions depend on the exact stimulus conditions and response mode as well as on the individual (Endler & Hunt, 1966, 1969). To make this point, Endler and Hunt devised a series of self-report anxiety inventories. On these questionnaires they varied both the type of threat situation and the mode of response to it.

The questionnaire sampled many situations, ranging from such innocuous events as "You are starting on a long automobile trip" and "You are undressing for bed" to more typically threatening situations, such as "You are on a ledge high upon a mountainside" (Endler & Hunt, 1969, p. 4). The response modes were systematically varied to include a wide range of possible reactions. They sampled the subject's perception of his physiological reaction ("hands trembling," "fluttering feeling in stomach") as well as his self-reported feelings of anxiety (e.g., "can't concentrate").

The questionnaires were given to many different groups of students in many schools in order to sample a wide range of individual differences. The answers were submitted to sophisticated statistical analyses that provided separate estimates of the relative effects of hypothetical stimulus situations, response modes, and persons as determinants of test responses. The analyses consistently revealed that the most potent effects by far were the interactions of person, situation, and response mode. Taken alone, neither individual differences (persons) nor situations accounted for more than a trivial fraction of the test results. These findings suggest that anxiety is not a stimulus-free characteristic of the person, nor is it intrinsic to stimuli alone. Anxiety reactions depend jointly on stimulus, person, and response mode: that is, they depend on the individual, on the particular stimulus confronting him (e.g., "underessing for bed"), and on the specific mode of response measured (e.g., "hands trembling," "heart racing").

## ANXIETY AND PERFORMANCE

Many studies have examined how trait anxiety interacts with other variables to affect performance. Some researchers have conceptualized trait anxiety in motivational terms as an arousal state similar to a physiological drive and have studied its relation to performance. For example, people who differ in self-reported trait anxiety have been tested under various anxiety-arousing instructions to see who does best on different learning tasks. These tasks range from simple conditioning situations to measures of complex performance. One popular performance task in these studies is the pursuit rotor (Figure 17-2).

More than 60 years ago Yerkes and Dodson (1908) suggested that the relationship between arousal and performance could be depicted as an inverted U (Figure 17-3). Figure 17-3 shows that when arousal is low or absent, the individual is unmotivated and his performance is likely to be poor. When arousal is extremely

**Figure 17-2**

The "pursuit rotor" has often been used to study the effects of drive on performance. The subject must try to keep his stylus on the target (small disc), which is mounted on a rapidly revolving turntable.

**Figure 17-3**  THE HYPOTHESIZED U RELATION BETWEEN AROUSAL AND PERFORMANCE

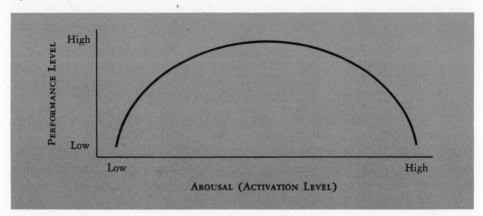

high, stimulation becomes excessive and performance deteriorates because the individual becomes overwhelmed and disorganized. Thus performance was believed to be of highest quality when anxiety or arousal was at a moderate level: under these conditions the person is attentive and alert, but not swamped.

More recent research indicates that while the relationship between arousal level (or anxiety) and performance quality sometimes is curvilinear, the exact effects depend on many interacting variables, both in the person and in the specific situation. For instance, they depend on the person's self-reported "test anxiety" as well as on the difficulty of the task. Examples of some of these relations are given in the following sections.

## ANXIETY AND TASK DIFFICULTY

The efficiency of learning may involve an interaction between test anxiety and task difficulty. People who are highly anxious (on self-report measures) tend to learn a simple conditioned response faster than do subjects low in anxiety, but this relationship is reversed when the learning task is complex (e.g., Spence & Spence, 1964).

These results lead to interesting theoretical interpretations. For example, if anxiety is conceptualized as a drive (like hunger or thirst), high anxiety (i.e., higher drive level or arousal) should lead to greater performance output (Spence & Spence, 1964). This greater output would facilitate simple conditioning by producing the conditioned response more readily (for example, the eyeblink in eyeblink conditioning to an air puff).

In contrast, when the learning task is more complex, adequate learning requires correct discriminations from among a number of competing responses (as in memorizing a list of paired words). Enhanced drive level then would increase the strength of the *wrong* response as well as of the right one, and thus the highly anxious (high-drive) subjects do not learn as efficiently. To understand how drive level or arousal affects performance, one therefore may have to consider both the subject's general arousal or drive level and the difficulty of the task (Eysenck, 1965).

## ANXIETY AND ACHIEVEMENT-ORIENTED INSTRUCTIONS

In our achievement-oriented society, great pressure is exerted on people to strive to compete and excel. Competition is actively encouraged, and the child soon learns to make continuous comparisons between his accomplishments and those of others. This achievement-oriented and evaluative set is seen in grading throughout the school system and in the obvious competitiveness of sports and many activities of the business and professional worlds.

Does a competitive achievement orientation really improve the quality of human performance? Does a deliberate stress on "doing well" spur people to do better, to solve problems efficiently and to learn more effectively? Or, perhaps, might such an orientation have a boomerang effect on anxious individuals that interferes with effective problem-solving and creativity?

To study this problem researchers have examined the excellence of performance when students work under different orienting sets. Some subjects get threatening or achievement-oriented instructions that present the learning task as a "test" on which they will be evaluated; other students have to do the same tasks under neutral or relaxed instructions. Who does better?

The effects of achievement orientation on performance may depend on the person's overall level of self-reported test anxiety. That is, individuals who differ greatly in test anxiety also may react quite differently to achievement-oriented instructions and to other anxiety-arousing cues. Specifically, when tasks are made more "test-like" and evaluative, people who are low in self-reported test anxiety often perform somewhat better than they do under neutral conditions. On the other hand, highly anxious persons tend to do less well when the motivating instructions emphasize the test-like, threatening features of the task (Sarason, 1966). An example of this interaction between threatening instructions and the subject's level of test anxiety is depicted in Figure 17-4.

## ANXIETY AND INTELLIGENCE

Anxiety and intelligence also may interact as determinants of the quality of complex performance. The effects of anxiety level on meaningful, nonlaboratory measures of performance, such as college grades, seem to depend importantly on the student's intelligence. In one study, students were categorized into five ability levels on the basis of tests of scholastic aptitude as depicted in Figure 17-5. Highly anxious subjects achieved lower average grades than students low in self-reported anxiety. At the extreme ends of the ability range, however, anxiety level did not

The possible impact of anxiety on performance depends both on the person and the situation.

influence grades and the students' college performance depended mainly on their ability regardless of their anxiety.

The relationship between anxiety and intelligence is also moderated by age. For example, in early childhood, brighter preschool children tend to have more fears than do less intelligent youngsters. The types of fears displayed by children also tend to change with age in the course of development (Mussen, Conger & Kagan, 1974). As children grow older, the correlations between their self-reported

Figure 17-4   THE INTERACTING EFFECTS OF TRAIT (TEST) ANXIETY AND THREAT IN-
STRUCTIONS ON SOLUTION OF A DIFFICULT TASK

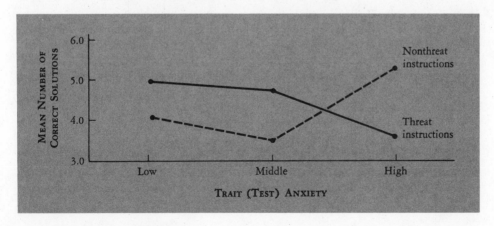

Drawn from data in Sarason (1961).

Figure 17-5  MEAN GRADE POINT AVERAGES FOR HIGH AND LOW ANXIETY COLLEGE
STUDENTS AT FIVE LEVELS OF SCHOLASTIC ABILITY

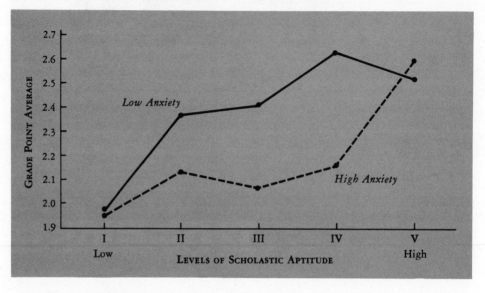

Adapted from Spielberger (1962).

anxiety and their intellectual and academic achievements tend to become increasingly negative (Hill & Sarason, 1966).

## SUMMARY

In sum, the individual's anxiety is related to his performance, but the relationship depends on many variables. Some of these variables are instructions, task difficulty, and intelligence. These are only a few of the relevant variables. We have not even mentioned many others, such as the individual's achievement motivation (e.g., Atkinson, 1964). Considering the large number of variables and conditions that may influence behavior, it is not surprising that correlations between performance and anxiety measures tend to be of modest strength and depend on many "moderating" conditions.

The associations between measures of trait anxiety and performance are moderated by, or dependent upon, such other variables as the subject's age, sex, and intelligence, the specific testing situation and instructions, the experimenter, and other situational cues. Because of the many variables that moderate the relations between self-report measures of anxiety and other nonquestionnaire variables, the correlations, while extensive, tend to be of low magnitude and unstable (e.g., Sarason, 1969).

# ANXIETY AS A REACTION TO STRESS

Another approach to anxiety has examined the consequences of stress. "Stress" has been the label used to classify a host of potentially unpleasant or dangerous events that include unavoidable pain, excessive noise and fatigue under strenuous work conditions, and traumatic dangers. The main question here has been: What are the conditions that affect the degree to which stress will elicit anxiety?

## THE EFFECTS OF DEGREE OF STRESS

Obviously individuals differ in the events that they perceive as most anxiety-provoking. In general, however, the more objectively intense the stress, the greater and more upsetting the person's reaction to it. For example, during the bombing air raids of World War II in England the occurrence of traumatic aftermaths (in the form of intense or neurotic anxiety reactions) depended on the degree to which the individual had been victimized by the air raids. Among uninjured survivors of bombing attacks, for example, anxiety occurred much more often if the victim had suffered severe personal loss. Victims who had a relative killed in the air raid or whose homes were destroyed developed acute anxiety reactions much more often than did those who were less personally victimized or who were physically more remote from the center of the attack (Fraser, Leslie & Phelps, 1943).

Similar conclusions emerge from studies of other traumatic episodes under combat conditions: the intensity of subsequent anxiety is directly related to the proximity of danger and to the objective probability of being killed or injured. Thus insomnia, gastrointestinal disturbance, feelings of nervousness, tremors, and similar signs of anxiety occur more often among front-line soldiers in active combat than among those in safer areas more distant from the main fighting zone (Star, 1949). Similarly, the incidence of anxiety in members of air crews depended partly on the number of combat missions they had participated in (Janis, 1949). Moreover, among combat pilots, "clinical neuroses" increase as their assignments become more dangerous (Tompkins, 1959).

In sum, while anxiety is a subjective experience it also is directly related to the severity and duration of external stress and danger.

## COGNITIVE APPRAISAL OF STRESS

A series of studies (e.g., Lazarus & Alfert, 1964) attempted to demonstrate that a person's "cognitive appraisal" of a potential stressful event affects his emotional reactions to it. Subjects viewed a film that depicted some gruesome shop accidents. Not surprisingly, they reacted with arousal not just to the actual scenes but also to instructions that led them to anticipate the gory scenes before they saw them. A person's reactions thus depend on what he *believes* is happening or about to happen, regardless of the objective foundation of his belief. For example, if a man is told his children are in danger he will react with great arousal, even if he is being told a lie. One's specific cognitive appraisal of the total emotion-producing situation influences how one copes with it (Lazarus & Averill, 1972). A variety of strategies can be used to help one cope with stress effectively, as will be discussed in the context of self-control (Chapter 19).

## THE EFFECTS OF WARNINGS

Does it help to be forewarned of future stress and danger? Sometimes a person may be less likely to develop acute distress if he is given adequate warning and information about impending pain and stress than if he is uninformed and hence surprised by the traumatic event (Janis, 1958, 1971). That is, forewarnings may help the person to brace himself psychologically for the trauma and to rehearse for it so that he can cope with it better when it occurs. This process, sometimes called "emotional innoculation," may involve either defensive self-desensitization or other forms of rehearsal that help to undermine the emotional upset of the trauma when it finally does occur. However, while some people may benefit from forewarnings, others may become debilitated by anticipatory anxiety. Moreover, many people may find it difficult to imagine traumatic experiences before they occur, especially if they have not had relevant past experiences with similar dangers.

In the military, for example, in spite of ample information and objective forewarnings, novices on combat missions reported that they felt only a sort of detached interest in flak bursts when they first encountered them. They did not feel the awesomeness of the situation personally until they actually saw a nearby plane hit or observed a friend injured or killed by shrapnel (Grinker & Spiegel, 1945). The same feeling of emotional detachment and subjective disbelief was reported by many Jews in Nazi Germany before they personally saw or experienced persecution.

Perhaps without prior experience the person often cannot bring himself to visualize clearly the horror of the disaster and does not believe that it will really happen to him. Likewise, the vast majority of the people who respond to flood warnings by actually attempting to flee tend to be those who previously experienced floods (Danzig et al., 1958). Thus the impact of warnings about danger may depend on prior experience with similar danger.

In many life situations forewarnings have great value because they permit the person to avoid the danger or somehow to guard or prepare against it. But what of situations in which the impending danger is inescapable or unavoidable and the person can do nothing to prevent the aversive situation?

To study an analogy to this type of stressful anticipatory situation some researchers have led adult volunteer subjects to believe that they might have to experience an unavoidable pain (usually in the form of an electric shock). While waiting, the subject is attached to equipment that monitors changes in his emotional arousal (as evidenced by sweating or heart rate changes, for example). This arrangement permits study of how various conditions affect emotional activity during the waiting period as the person anticipates the unavoidable shock.

## THE EFFECTS OF UNCERTAINTY

How does uncertainty about the nature and advent of an anticipated unavoidable stress affect reactions to it? Is anxiety greater when the person knows the details of the expected painful event, or when he is uncertain about what to expect?

In one study, college students were led to believe that an electric shock would be forthcoming. The experiment manipulated the information given to the students about the shock (Elliott, 1966). In one group the students were first given a "mild" shock as a sample of the forthcoming shock; subjects in a second group were given a sample shock of considerable strength and were led to believe that the forthcoming shock would be of similar intensity; in a third group the subjects waited for an unknown shock—they received no sample of the shock but were told that one would be forthcoming. Thereafter the students waited for the shock, and their reactions to it were measured. Self-reports indicated that anxiety was greatest for those in the group waiting for the unknown shock; these subjects, who had not sampled the shock, dreaded it most. This group also experienced the greatest rise in heart rate (relative to rest) while waiting, averaging an acceleration of about 20 beats per minute as compared with approximately 4 beats per minute in the other groups.

Even when persons cannot influence an aversive future outcome (for example, by escaping from it), they often prefer knowledge of it (Lanzetta & Driscoll, 1966) and will work to get such knowledge (Jones, Bentler & Petry, 1966). People also tend to be less tense and aroused while waiting for a painful event when they know what to expect (Deane, 1961; Elliott, 1966) and when they expect that it probably will occur rather than that it may occur but is less likely (Epstein & Roupenian, 1970). Most normal adults also greatly prefer immediate aversive outcomes to unavoidable delayed ones of comparable magnitude (Hare, 1966; Mischel & Grusec, 1967).

In another study, college females were exposed to stress in the form of aversive noise (Glass, Singer & Friedman, 1969). The noise occurred either at predictable or at unpredictable times. The investigators assessed the effects of these stresses on subsequent tolerance for frustration (persistence at a difficult task) and performance efficiency.

When the noise was predictable it did not adversely affect later tolerance of frustration or performance, but when it was unpredictable it did produce adverse consequences. These adverse effects could be reduced substantially if, during the stress period, subjects believed that they could control the termination of the noise. Thus, it is most difficult to cope with unpredictable and seemingly uncontrollable aversive stimuli; people tend to be less upset and debilitated when they must cope with aversive events of the same magnitude if they think they can predict and control them (Staub, Tursky & Schwartz, 1971).

Even physiological reactions may be different when a person can cope with situations actively (by initiating and anticipating responses) and when he cannot. One provocative series of studies, for example, tentatively suggests that heart rate acceleration may be most "sensitive to situations in which responses can be anticipated and initiated, and are worth making" (Elliott, 1969, p. 221). For example, heart rate was high in subjects during a series of shocks that they could act to terminate, but actually lower during a series that only the experimenter could terminate.

It thus seems that the nature of anxiety reactions may partly depend on the alternatives available to the individual for coping effectively with the stress. Most people seem to react differently to stressful events that they think they can control and those that they believe are out of their control, although the specific relationships often are very complex and depend on the situation as well as on the person (Averill, 1973).

## ANXIETY AND AVOIDANCE

Guided by Freud's theory, many personality psychologists have been most concerned with the effects of anxiety on avoidance behavior. The relationship between anxiety and avoidance is crucial for psychodynamic theory; it forms the basis for the Freudian conception of defense mechanisms.

### AVOIDANCE BEHAVIOR

Because anxiety is aversive we quickly try to reduce or avoid it. When the dangerous event is external—like an attacker—anxiety may be reduced by physical escape from the threatening situation or by other forms of problem-solving (such as calling for help). The reduction of the anxiety state in turn reinforces the behaviors that led to the relief. Consequently the person's successful escape or avoidance behaviors become strengthened.

The strengthening of successful escape behaviors may be adaptive to the extent that the organism can then more readily avoid similar future dangers. On the other hand, because the escape pattern was reinforced, the person may continue to avoid similar situations in the future when in fact they are no longer dangerous. That is, his previously reinforced quick escape and avoidance maneuvers may prevent him from learning that the danger he fears is no longer there or that he can master its aversive effects. In that case the fearful person continues to defensively avoid similar or related situations instead of unlearning his fear of them. Hence avoidance reactions may be highly persistent (Seligman, 1975).

Reinforced escape and avoidance patterns, if widely generalized, may have debilitating consequences. As an example, consider the case of a little girl who has been sexually molested by an intruder at home. As a result of this traumatic experience the child may acquire a phobic reaction, not just to the painful encounter and the man who terrified her, but also to other men and to many aspects of sexual experience and intimacy. Her subsequent refusal of dates and her generalized avoidance of closeness with men would make it increasingly difficult for her to overcome her anxieties and to develop satisfying heterosexual relationships.

In the early stages of avoidance learning the person's avoidance reactions seem to depend on his physiological (autonomic) arousal state. However, avoidance learning can also occur without emotional arousal. For example, dogs can learn to avoid stimuli connected with electric shock even when their autonomic responsiveness (ability to become emotionally aroused) is impaired deliberately by surgery or drugs (Wynne & Solomon, 1955). Emotional arousal seems to facilitate avoidance learning, but it is not essential, especially after the avoidance pattern is well established (Bandura, 1969). The important implication is that a person may continue to avoid stimuli even when they no longer elicit autonomic arousal states in him. We may run away from cues connected with previously frightening events even when they no longer induce strong arousal states in us. Sometimes the result may be a tragic "learned helplessness" in which the individual develops the expectation that he cannot exert control over his environment and consequently may become its passive, hopeless, depressed victim (Seligman, 1975).

## CONFLICT AND ANXIETY

Avoidance reactions may become most problematic when the threat stimuli are persistent and cannot be escaped by moving away from them physically. Often an individual cannot escape from the sources of possible anxiety around him by simply avoiding them. This is true when he is dependent upon and loves the very people who threaten him.

In the course of socialization the same significant persons who nurture the child and care for him, and to whom he becomes most deeply attached, are also the ones who discipline and punish him. For example, the same mother who reinforces the child with her attention and social approval may cause him pain and anxiety. Thus the same social stimulus—the mother, in this example—that has been associated with positive rewards and gratification is also connected with pain because of the punishments she dispenses and the rewards that she withholds from the child. The phenomena of "ambivalence" and "conflict" may result whenever the same persons or objects who evoke positive feelings and approach tendencies are also the sources for negative emotions and avoidance reactions. This duality is common in life and it does not end with childhood. In an adult's life, for example, the same spouse who gives love may also be the source of many bitter frustrations. Hence, mixed feelings develop.

Just how the individual will feel and react in relation to these ambivalence-producing stimuli depends on many considerations. For example, a child may be harshly punished by his father when he is physically aggressive to his baby sister, but may be warmly praised by his father when he is physically self-assertive with peers. If that happens consistently he soon may learn to expect positive gratification from his father in one context but punishment and aversive consequences in the other context. Thus in one situation he will expect praise and love from the same father who is the source of his anxiety in the second situation. These situations will be discriminated clearly, and anxiety associated with uncertainty and conflict therefore will probably be minimal.

Anxiety may be much higher, however, when the child is uncertain about the behaviors that will lead to punishment and those that will not, and when he does not feel that he can control the important aversive outcomes in his life. It may be especially difficult for a child to cope adequately if punishment from the parent (and other important people) is unpredictable and inconsistent so that he is unsure of what to expect. In that case the child may experience a more generalized dread, because threat and punishment are possible at almost any time and place.

Because people are capable of thought and symbolic representations, they also can generate anxiety in themselves with their own ideas and memories. Thoughts about masturbation or infidelity, for example, as well as the sexual acts themselves, may evoke anxiety in a person for whom these events have become threatening. Similarly, a child may feel anxious if he thinks hostile thoughts about his mother, for example, or if he starts to experience prohibited sexual fantasies. When his own thoughts and feelings are dangerous, the individual may try to avoid them cognitively through various psychological maneuvers, as the next chapter discusses.

## SUMMARY

1. Anxiety may be defined as an acquired (learned) fear. The experience of anxiety involves an intense feeling of fear or dread of impending danger accompanied by a state of autonomic physiological arousal. Often anxiety leads to difficulty in thinking clearly and coping effectively with environmental demands.

2. Each major personality theory has conceptualized anxiety in somewhat different ways. Thus Freudian formulations, for example, emphasize the breakthrough into consciousness of unacceptable impulses; learning theories focus on association with painful or aversive stimulation; and phenomenological-existential theories stress the perception of a basic threat to the self.

3. Life-threatening dangers or "traumas" result in the clearest examples of intense anxiety reactions. Moreover, a person's traumatic fear may generalize so that events and cognitions closely associated with the original traumatic experiences may later evoke anxiety reactions even after the objective danger is gone. If the anxiety spreads to stimuli remote from

the traumatic stimulus, the connection may not be apparent and the anxiety may seem particularly irrational. Under some conditions, however, traumas may lead to active coping rather than to generalized anxiety.

4. Individual differences in trait anxiety usually are measured by a psychometric self-report inventory on which subjects indicate the extent to which various fears characterize them. Anxiety is not a situation-free personality trait. Anxiety reactions depend on the exact stimulus conditions and response mode measured, as well as on the individual. It is the interaction of all three of these sources that determines the anxiety reaction.

5. A person's anxiety affects the quality of his performance. The exact effect of arousal level on performance depends on many variables, both in the person and in the specific situation. For example, if the response to be learned is a simple conditioned response (such as an eye blink), then anxious people may learn faster; on more difficult tasks, however, the best performance may be achieved by people with less anxiety. Many other personality and situational variables may also interact to affect the quality of the person's performance.

6. The effects of anxiety on meaningful, nonlaboratory measures of performance (such as college grades) also depend on intelligence. For example, while students high in self-reported anxiety had lower grade averages than low-anxiety students, at the extreme ends of the ability range anxiety level did not influence college grades.

7. Usually the intensity of anxiety reactions is directly related to the objective intensity and duration of the experienced stress. The particular events or stimuli that are stressful for an individual depend on his interpretation of them.

8. Uncertainty about the possibility of occurrence and the details of an expected painful event may cause greatest tension and arousal. Most normal adults also prefer an unavoidable painful event to occur immediately rather than after a delay. People generally prefer to be able to predict and control inevitable stressful events. Adequate warning and information about impending stress may make the development of acute anxiety less likely. On the other hand, some people may become debilitated by anticipatory anxiety when they are forewarned. The value of warnings may depend on the individual's prior experience with similar danger.

9. Avoidance or escape behaviors performed in a state of anxiety become strengthened when they are successful in reducing the anxiety state.

Avoidance reactions that are highly persistent and widely generalized may have debilitating consequences. Escape and avoidance maneuvers may prevent a person from learning that the danger he fears is no longer there.

10. Ambivalence and conflict may result when the same persons (or events) are associated with both positive and aversive experience, as happens commonly in life. The very people the child loves and depends upon also may threaten and punish him. Because he cannot simply leave them he may, instead, resort to various psychological avoidance mechanisms.

# CHAPTER 18
# DEFENSE

An outstanding characteristic of the human being is that he can create great anxiety in himself even when he is not in any immediate external danger. A man may be seated comfortably in front of his hearth, adequately fed and luxuriously sheltered, seemingly safe from outside threats, and yet torture himself with anxiety-provoking memories of old events, with terrifying thoughts, or with expectations of imagined dangers in years to come. He also can cognitively, within his own mind, eliminate such internally cued anxiety without altering his external environment, simply by avoiding or changing his painful thoughts or memories.

Conceptually, "defense mechanisms" are attempts to cope cognitively with internal anxiety-arousing cues. Usually it has also been assumed, in accordance with Freudian theory, that these cognitive efforts to deal with internal anxiety-producing stimuli are at least partly unconscious—that is, they occur without the person's awareness. Many defense mechanisms have been hypothesized, mainly in the framework of Freudian theory. These hypothesized defenses have been called "repression," "projection," "denial," "sublimation," "reaction formation," and so on, as previously discussed (Chapter 3). Each of these terms refers to a different way of reducing or eliminating anxiety.

# REPRESSION

Greatest attention has been devoted to repression, probably because of the theoretical importance of that concept in Freudian psychology and psychoanalysis. Because most theoretical issues and research studies have focused on repression, it will be the defense that this chapter will emphasize. Rather than dealing with many defenses superficially, we will concentrate on this important one in depth.

## THE CONCEPT OF REPRESSION

Most people sometimes feel that they actively try to avoid painful memories and ideas and struggle to "put out of mind" thoughts that are aversive to them. Common examples are trying not to think about a forthcoming threatening surgical operation, and trying to shunt attention away from the unknown results of an important test. Psychologists often call such efforts to avoid painful thoughts "cognitive avoidance."

The existence of cognitive avoidance is widely recognized, and few psychologists doubt that thoughts may be inhibited. However, the mechanisms underlying cognitive avoidance have been controversial and have been interpreted in different ways. The crux of the controversy is whether or not cognitive avoidance includes an unconscious defense mechanism of "repression" that forces unacceptable material into an unconscious region without the person's awareness.

The psychoanalytic concept of repression as a defense mechanism is closely linked to the Freudian idea of an unconscious mind. The unconscious mind was construed by early Freudians as a supersensitive entity whose perceptual alertness and memory bank surpassed the same properties of the conscious mind (e.g., Blum, 1955). A chief function of the unconscious mind was to screen and monitor memories and perceptual inputs. This screening served to inhibit the breakthrough of anxiety-arousing stimuli from the unconscious mind to the conscious, or from the outside world to consciousness. Just as the conscious mind was believed capable of deliberately (consciously) inhibiting events by *suppression,* so the unconscious was considered capable of inhibition or cognitive avoidance at the unconscious level by *repression.*

Suppression occurs when one voluntarily and consciously withholds a response or turns attention away from it deliberately. Unconscious repression, in contrast, may function as an automatic guardian against anxiety, a safety mechanism that prevents threatening material from entering consciousness. Psychoanalysts offered clinical evidence for the existence of repression in the form of cases in which slips of the tongue ("parapraxes"), jokes, dreams, or free associations seemed to momentarily bypass the defenses and betray the person, revealing a brief glimpse of his repressed unconscious impulses.

Recall that Freud based his ideas concerning repression and defense on his clinical observations of hysterical women at the turn of this century. He noted that some of these patients seemed to develop physical symptoms that did not make sense neurologically, such as hysterical difficulties with vision, or cases of "glove anesthesia," in which the patient showed an inability to feel in the hands—a symptom that is impossible neurologically. In their 1895 studies of hysteria Freud and his associate Breuer hypnotized some of the patients and found, to their great surprise, that when the origins and meanings of hysterical symptoms were talked about under hypnosis, the symptoms tended to disappear. This finding proved beyond any doubt that the symptoms were not caused by organic damage or physical defects.

Partly to understand hysteria, Freud developed his theory of unconscious conflict and defense. In his view, such symptoms as hysterical blindness and hysterical anesthesias reflected defensive attempts to avoid painful thoughts and feelings by diversionary preoccupation with apparently physical symptoms. Freud thought that the key mechanism in this blocking was unconsciously motivated repression. Through repression the basic impulses that are unacceptable to the person are rendered unconscious and thereby less frightening. Because such diversionary measures are inherently ineffective ways of dealing with anxiety-provoking impulses, the impulses persist and press for release in disguised and distorted forms that are called "symptoms."

## RESEARCH ON REPRESSION

Repression has remained a central concept for most psychoanalysts, and it has been the subject of a great deal of research for many years. In general, many of the early efforts to assess whether or not particular findings demonstrated the truth of Freud's concepts created more controversy than clarity. In more recent years it has been recognized that well-designed experiments on the topic of cognitive avoidance can provide useful information about cognitive processes and personality regardless of their direct relevance to the Freudian theory of repression.

Early experimental research on repression studied the differential recall of pleasant and unpleasant experiences (e.g., Jersild, 1931; Meltzer, 1930). These investigators seemed to assume that repression manifested itself in a tendency to selectively forget negative or unpleasant experiences rather than positive ones. It was soon pointed out, however, that the Freudian theory of repression does not imply that experiences associated with unpleasant affective tone are repressed (Rosenzweig & Mason, 1934; Sears, 1936). Freudian repression, instead, was believed to depend on the presence of an "ego threat" (for example, a basic threat to self-esteem) and not on mere unpleasantness.

Later it also was recognized that an adequate paradigm for studying repression should be able to demonstrate that when the cause of the repression (the ego threat) is removed, the repressed material is restored to consciousness (Zeller, 1950a). This assumption was consistent with the psychoanalytic belief that when the cause of a repression is discovered by insight in psychotherapy the repressed material rapidly emerges into the patient's consciousness. In other words, if the threat is eliminated it becomes safe for the repressed material to return to awareness. Reports by psychoanalysts often have cited cases in which a sudden insight supposedly lifted a long-standing amnesia (memory loss).

In an empirical study, Zeller (1950b) tried to take these considerations into account. Experimental and control subjects first were administered a paired-associate learning task (i.e., associating nonsense syllables like ZIK and DEM). Three days later the subjects participated in a relearning task for the same material, and the two groups were shown to perform similarly. As soon as the relearning task was over, the subjects took a "block tapping" test that ostensibly measured their abilities. On this test the experimental subjects were "ego-threatened" by being led to believe that they had failed badly. Subjects in the control group were carefully convinced that they had done well. Immediately thereafter all the subjects were again presented with the paired-associate learning task. On measures of retention and relearning of this material, the ego-threatened (experimental) group now performed less well than the control group. This finding was interpreted as due to repression resulting from the ego threat that had been created in the experimental subjects.

After a delay of three days all the subjects were again administered the paired-associate learning task and, as expected, the experimental subjects still performed less well. Next, to undo the ego threat and thereby lift the repression, all subjects were readministered the block-tapping test, but now the people in the experimental group as well as those in the control group were led to believe that they had succeeded on it. When the paired-associate learning task was administered again, there were no retention or relearning differences between the groups. Seemingly, lifting the repression had caused recall to be restored.

Were Zeller's findings really due to repression? To answer this question, one must consider the possible effects of the failure experience. In other research severe failure experiences have been shown to impair performance, including speed of relearning (Weiner, 1966). Zeller's results therefore may not reflect repression, but only poorer learning under the conditions of emotional upset and disorganization experienced by the failure group. Moreover, whenever a measure of retention of material is inferred from the speed with which it is relearned, it becomes impossible to separate the role of original learning from that of remembering. Differential recall of material has been shown to stem from differences in initial learning and covert rehearsal of the material, at least under some conditions (e.g., Caron & Wallach, 1957). Thus Zeller's failure subjects, rather than repressing more, may simply have learned less after failure by becoming disorganized or unmotivated.

In view of these considerations, in the Zeller study how can we account for the improvement in relearning and recall found after the "repression" was lifted—that is, after the failure subjects experienced success? The simplest explanation might be that after the students were relieved of their distress they devoted themselves more efficiently to the recall and relearning task and hence performed better.

More than 10 years later D'Zurilla (1965) used a different strategy to study defensive changes in memory due to stress. In his experiment, control and experimental subjects (college students) first were shown 20 words and tested for recall of the words to establish that there were no preexperimental group differences. Next the subjects were exposed to a series of ten slides. Each slide contained one Holtzman inkblot (a modification of the Rorschach) and two of the words that had been shown to them previously. For each slide the subjects had to indicate the word that best described the inkblot. The experimental group was told that this was a test designed to detect latent homosexual tendencies. They were told that one of the two words on each slide was a response that homosexuals tend to give but the other word was given by normal people. The control group, was told only that it was taking part in the development of a new psychological inkblot test.

After responding to all of the cards the students in both groups were given another recall test. Again there were no group differences. Now threat was induced in the experimental subjects. They were told that they had picked nine of the 10 "homosexual" words, whereas the control group subjects were told that they had done very well. After five minutes all the subjects took another recall test. The people in the control group improved from their prior recall performance, but, as expected, subjects in the experimental group did less well than they had before. The investigator then tried to remove the repression effect by revealing the deception to the subjects and explaining that the inkblot test did not measure homosexual tendencies. Finally, the last recall test was administered: on this test, as predicted, now that the threat had been removed, the two groups recalled equally well.

You might conclude that the concept of repression was supported by D'Zurilla's results. Some doubt is cast on this conclusion, however, by findings from interviews after the experiment in which the students were asked to describe what they had thought about during the poststress retention interval. Contrary to expectations from repression theory, most of the experimental subjects had thought about things related to the threatening task, while only a few control subjects had thought about the task at all. During the retention period the experimental subjects said they had thought about the inkblots, past memories, their "homosexual tendencies," and many other events. As the investigator noted, these cognitions could have reduced the efficiency of recall by competing with the responses to be recalled and interfering with them.

Holmes and Schallow (1969) recognized that the threatened subjects may have spent the poststress retention interval thinking about their problems and that these competing cognitions could have disrupted their efforts to recall the words. Therefore they decided to study the role of response competition and interference in the repression paradigm. In their study, Holmes and Schallow included an ego-threat-ened group and a control group. They also added a group that was not ego-threat-ened but that was distracted during the retention interval by exposure to irrelevant neutral stimuli.

After the threat, the ego-threatened group recalled less well than the control group, replicating the effect previously attributed to repression. However, recall in the interference group was below that of the control group and quite similar to that of the ego-threatened group. The investigators therefore concluded that re-sponse interference, rather than repression, may have caused the differential per-formance of the threatened and control groups. Their interpretation is plausible, but it does not completely rule out the possibility of a repression effect. A more recent laboratory study (using recall for successes versus failures) found no support whatsoever for repression effects (Tudor & Holmes, 1973). Likewise, an extensive review of experimental research on repression, after surveying many studies, led the reviewer to conclude that "there is no evidence to support the predictions gen-erated by the theory of repression" (Holmes, 1974, p. 651).

## PERCEPTUAL DEFENSE

The studies described in the last section tried to investigate repression as a defense that blocks the memory for material connected with an ego threat. If unconscious repression is a mechanism that guards against painful intrusions into consciousness, one might also expect it to screen and block threatening perceptual inputs to the eyes and to monitor auditory messages to the ears. Indeed, clinical reports from Freudian psychoanalysts suggest that in some cases of "hysteria" massive repression may prevent the individual from perceiving or consciously registering threatening stimuli such as sexual scenes or symbols.

One very severe instance of this hypothesized syndrome would be "hysterical blindness," in which the individual seems to lose his vision although no physical damage to the eyes or to his perceptual system can be detected. Case reports have suggested that such psychological failures to see might be linked to traumatic sex-ual experiences with resulting repression of stimuli that might unleash anxiety. Clinical case reports such as those on hysteria often may provide suggestive evi-dence, but they are never conclusive.

To go beyond clinical impressions, experimentally oriented researchers have tried to study repressive perceptual defenses by examining possible anxiety-reduc-ing distortions in perception. Since it was obviously both unfeasible and unethical to induce sexual traumas in human subjects, considerable ingenuity was needed to find even a rough experimental analog for perceptual defense.

### RESEARCH STRATEGY

In the 1940s and 1950s a general research strategy was devised to explore per-ceptual defenses, guided by the then prevalent faith in projective devices as methods for revealing conflictful areas of personality. Specifically, proponents of projective methods believed that persons who did *not* give sexual or aggressive responses to ambiguous stimuli must be inhibiting or defending against this type of ideation, especially if the same stimuli generally elicited many such responses from most normal people. Consequently one could use the failure to identify potentially threatening percepts, such as anxiety-arousing sexual words or threatening scenes, as signs of perceptual inhibition or defense.

To accomplish this objective, one would have to present these threatening perceptual stimuli in decreasing degrees of ambiguity from a point at which subjects could reasonably interpret them in many ways to a point of definiteness that permitted only one clearly correct interpretation. A helpful device for this purpose was the tachistoscope, a machine through which potentially threatening words (e.g., "bitch," "penis, "whore") and neutral words (e.g., "house," "flowers") could be flashed at varying speeds. These stimulus words were presented on a screen very rapidly at first and then gradually exposed for increasingly long durations. The length of time required before each subject correctly recognized the stimulus served as his "defensiveness" score; the longer the time required to recognize threatening stimuli the greater the subject's defensive avoidance tendencies were assumed to be.

In one study college students viewed tachistoscopically presented words that were either emotional or neutral in meaning (McGinnies, 1949). Each student was requested to state the word he had seen after each exposure. If his answer was wrong the same word was presented again at a slightly longer exposure time, and the subject again tried to recognize it.

The emotional and neutral words used, and the mean recognition thresholds associated with them, are shown in Figure 18-1. It was predicted that such "taboo" words as "penis" or "raped" would be anxiety-laden and therefore more readily

**Figure 18-1**   MEAN   THRESHOLDS   OF   RECOGNITION   OF   NEUTRAL   AND   EMOTION-CHARGED WORDS

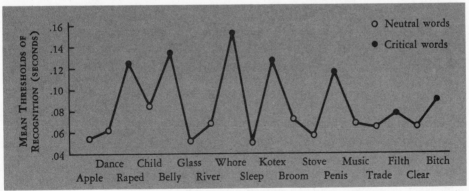

From McGinnies (1949).

inhibited than neutral words such as "apple." As Figure 18-1 illustrates, the results confirmed this prediction, showing greater "perceptual defense" (longer recognition times) for taboo words than for neutral words.

## METHODOLOGICAL PROBLEMS

An extremely serious methodological problem in perceptual defense research was pointed out by Howes and Solomon (1951), who called attention to the fact that the critical or taboo words used in perceptual defense experiments (e.g., McGinnies, 1949) were much less familiar to the subjects because they occurred much less frequently in the English language than did the "neutral" words. Hence it would not be surprising that people took longer to recognize them when they were ambiguously presented by the tachistoscope! Longer recognition time for taboo words could easily reflect unfamiliarity with the words rather than unconscious defense against their threatening meanings. Their data demonstrated a direct relation between infrequency of use and recognition time, so that a subject would show "defense" against such unusual words as "flume," "chaise," or "rapt."

Howes and Solomon also noted that the perceptual recognition situation placed the subject in an embarrassing predicament. In the typical procedure, an undergraduate is brought to the laboratory by a professor or his assistant and is then exposed to brief and unclear stimulus presentations by the tachistoscope. His task is essentially a guessing game in which he tries to discern the correct word from fleeting fragments. On the first trial of a word he may, for example, see something like an "r" and a "p" and guess "rope." On the next trial he may say to himself "good grief, that looked like 'rape'!" But rather than hazard such a guess to a professor or his assistant in the academic atmosphere of the scientific laboratory, he may deliberately suppress the response. Instead of saying what he thinks he sees, he offers "rope" again and withholds the taboo word until he is absolutely sure that his perception is correct.

## SELECTIVE PERCEPTION

Under ambiguous conditions individuals may be somewhat more ready to interpret and construe unclear events in accord with their expectations and momentary states. Consequently if people have just failed they more readily perceive failure words (tachistoscopically presented); if they have just succeeded they may perceive success words at shorter exposures (Postman & Brown, 1952). Potentially need-satisfying stimuli also may be perceived somewhat more readily and may be accentuated and made more salient. The observer may even endow these need-relevant valued stimuli with more striking characteristics, such as greater size and brightness (e.g., Bruner & Goodman, 1947).

The tendency to interpret ambiguities in the environment in accord with one's momentary drive state has been studied extensively. For example, moderately hungry subjects tend to produce somewhat more food-related responses than satiated subjects when they try to identify briefly exposed ambiguous stimuli (e.g., Levine, Chein & Murphy, 1942; McClelland & Atkinson, 1948). This tendency, however, seems weak and is not correlated with the degree of hunger induced in the subjects. Indeed, under conditions of more intense deprivation people may become *less* likely to ideate about drive-related themes (Lazarus, Yousem & Arenberg, 1953; Murray, 1959).

While there is no doubt that individuals interpret their environment subjectively, the intrusion of their subjective states and needs into their actual *perceptions* of the environment is a far more complex matter. The possible distortions of perception by unconscious needs have been of special interest to Freudian psychologists. If the unconscious system is as powerful as Freud's theory assumed, then it should produce distortions of perceptual and learning processes without the individual's awareness. One approach to this critically important topic has taken the form of experiments on "subception" (unconscious perception).

## SUBCEPTION AND THE UNCONSCIOUS

Public interest in subception has been great because of its evident moral and social implications for subtly molding people's behavior without their awareness. What if stimuli—such as propaganda messages or advertisements presented below the threshold of perceptual awareness—could really shape people's beliefs and actions? During a movie, for example, if advertisements were secretly included and flashed too indistinctly for the victim's conscious awareness could his behavior be unconsciously influenced by the message? The potentialities—and the horrors—of "mind control" might be staggering; they are reminiscent of George Orwell's nightmarish *1984* and Huxley's *Brave New World*.

An experiment by Lazarus and McCleary (1951) attracted great attention because it seemed to demonstrate that subception does occur. In the first phase of their study, subjects watched as 10 nonsense syllables were projected on a screen supraliminally (above awareness thresholds) in random order. In the next phase the presentation of half the syllables was paired with electric shock to the subject, so that these "shock syllables" became the conditioned emotional stimuli eliciting the galvanic skin response (GSR). In the third phase of the study, the shock and non-shock syllables were again projected in random order, but now subliminally (at speeds too fast for clear awareness).

The two measures obtained from the subjects were their "conscious" recognition through verbal reports of the subliminal shock stimuli, and an "unconscious" index of recognition inferred from the emotional activity reflected in their GSR. It was assumed that if a subject does not report recognizing the shock-associated syllables, but the GSR measure shows that he is responding to them, then he must be recognizing them unconsciously. The investigators believed that they had found subception because when the self-report predicted the shock syllables poorly, the GSR predicted them relatively well. They interpreted these data as demonstrating that people can make unconscious discriminations of events that they cannot report recognizing consciously.

## METHODOLOGICAL PROBLEMS AGAIN?

The foregoing conclusion of a subception effect is most exciting, but it has been seriously challenged. Some critics have interpreted the evidence for subception as reflecting nothing more than a methodological problem. Thus C. W. Eriksen (1958, 1960) argued cogently that the seeming subception effect may be due to artifacts. The exact methodological problems are extremely complex, and the specific details need not concern us here. In general, the methodological difficulty arises from the way in which the verbal and GSR measures were used and compared. There are many methodological reasons why the GSR may *seem* more sensitive than the verbal measure even if it is not.

One problem is that verbal reports are more susceptible to conscious inhibitions than are physiological measures like the GSR. Subjects who are unsure can give a cautious verbal report, but they have less direct influence over their physiological (GSR) responses. Further, the experimental procedures may have made it more difficult to respond correctly in one mode than in another. For example, in the Lazarus and McCleary study, subjects had to recognize accurately any one of 10 possible verbal responses, but their GSR responses were scored only as high (recognition) or low (nonrecognition). This scoring procedure increases the probability that GSR responses will seem more accurate than verbal ones.

When such artifacts are avoided, how do physiological, autonomic responses (like the GSR) compare with the person's verbal reports as indices of his having recognized (discriminated) an event? According to Eriksen, when the sensitivity of these two types of responses is compared, people have not been shown to be more sensitive in their autonomic reactions than in their verbal reports. On the basis of much research it seems that "a verbal report is as sensitive an indicator of perception as any other response that has been studied" (Eriksen, 1960, p. 298).

## CONSCIOUS RESPONSE SUPPRESSION OR UNCONSCIOUS REPRESSION?

The conclusions that may be drawn from research on subception hence remain controversial and open to different interpretations. We are left with these fundamental questions: Do cognitive avoidance and selective perception merely involve suppression of responses so that they are less likely to become verbalized? Or are people driven by impulses whose meanings they unconsciously disguise beyond their own recognition? Can they thus be victimized unconsciously by their own psychic apparatus? Or can the phenomena of cognitive avoidance and "misperception" be understood as learned inhibitions without requiring a special concept of the unconscious as a psychic entity? Most critical, just what is the status of the unconscious as a force in psychic functioning? The problem is a complicated one

Does "cognitive avoidance" involve more than conscious suppression?

that resists easy answers because it entails serious methodological difficulties in defining and determining whether another person is or is not consciously aware of a given event.

The term "consciousness" may be confusing because it has many meanings. "Awareness" is the most common synonym for consciousness in psychological usage. Conversely, the "unconscious" tends to be equated with lack of awareness. But how do you know whether or not another person is aware or unaware of something? A means of judging awareness that has been favored by many clinicians involves highly indirect inferences about the person's insight into his motivations, his internal states, his feelings, and his dynamics. Such a clinical strategy depends most heavily on the clinical judge and his tools (for example, projective tests), and its limitations are serious, as we have seen (Chapter 9).

The more obvious and direct way to study another person's awareness of an event is to ask him, and to get his own verbal report of whether or not he has recognized its occurrence. In research on perceptual defense, for example, as we have seen, subjects are exposed to various stimuli (such as taboo words) and asked to report their perceptions. As was noted, however, the subject's report may not fully reflect his private awareness.

There may be many reasons why a person's awareness and his verbalizations about it can be discrepant. He may not want to publicly acknowledge an event although he is aware of it (for example, because it is embarrassing or threatening). As pointed out before, students are unlikely to report seeing words like "penis" to their professor unless they are completely sure their perception is correct. Even if a person is motivated to report accurately, words may not be capable of correctly describing his subjective awareness. Consider, for instance, how difficult it would be to verbally describe the image of a face. Even a detailed verbal description of a stranger's face might still not permit one to recognize him in a crowd. The labels of language often are too gross to capture the nuances of the events to which they are applied, especially when the events keep changing rapidly.

The value of verbal self-reports about awareness depends on the adequacy of the interrogation method. The phenomenon of awareness involves many subtleties, and proper questioning techniques to help the subject verbalize his experience have to be suitably thorough and ingenious. Otherwise we might conclude that someone is unaware of an event when, instead, we merely have not asked him well enough about what he knows.

Can people learn discriminations without awareness or consciousness? It would certainly be impressive evidence for the unconscious if important learning and discriminations were shown to occur in people without their awareness. Thus the role of awareness in the learning process is one of the most important theoretical issues. Eriksen (1960) undertook an extensive survey and analysis of research on human learning without awareness. The results led him to conclude that the existence of discrimination learning at levels not available to conscious awareness (equated with verbal report) has not been shown adequately. Although some simple human conditioned responses may be learned without awareness, in most forms of human learning awareness seems to play a major role (e.g., Dulany, 1962; Spielberger & De Nike, 1966) and facilitates the learning process dramatically.

These findings cast doubt on the unconscious as a powerful force in human discrimination and learning, and they have led some researchers to suggest abandoning the concept of the unconscious as a psychic entity:

> A science of personality is not furthered by the frequent tendency of psychologists to discuss the "unconscious" with all the ambiguity and reverence that religions accord to the soul. There is great need to spell out explicitly the assumed characteristics of the unconscious and to search for explanations of so-called unconscious phenomena in terms of more commonplace psychological variables. To do so may destroy the titillating mystery that the unconscious seems to hold but then that is the business of science (Eriksen, 1960, p. 298).

Reviewing developments more recently, Eriksen (1966, p. 354) concluded that "the possibility must be seriously entertained that the concept of repression is only a very well-learned or overlearned response suppression."

Eriksen (1966) suggests that unpleasant or painful material may at first be consciously suppressed (rather than unconsciously repressed) and that response suppression, after sufficient rehearsal, becomes automatic. But it also seems possible that even without a deliberate suppression mechanism, painful thoughts and memories are less likely to be evoked and covertly rehearsed because they are aversive and less reinforcing than competing, potentially available cognitions. In the social learning view, just as the probability for the occurrence of overt behaviors depends on their probable reinforcing consequences, so the presence of cognitions, images, and other covert events hinges on the internal and external effects they produce for the person. In that view, an individual will not make "unpleasant" covert responses unless they in fact have become positively reinforcing (for example, by having stopped him in the past from thinking about even more negative things).

The foregoing does not imply that people are aware of all the discriminations that they make. As personal experience attests, while during new learning we usually feel aware and even "self-conscious," once a behavior is mastered and over-learned it often seems to flow smoothly and automatically without any subjective awareness whatsoever. We usually stay safely clear of hot stoves, cross busy streets only when the traffic lights are appropriate, and drive our cars for miles without self-conscious awareness of every step and discrimination made along the route. While learning to park a car may at first require great awareness and self-conscious attention to subtle positional cues, thousands of trials later one is likely to be unaware of the procedure (unless startled by a sudden bump). Moreover, obvious methodological problems prevent us from knowing much about the awareness of organisms that cannot provide verbal reports, such as young children and animals. Yet these essentially mute organisms certainly learn, and even lowly forms of life may be conditioned, although their state of consciousness is unknown to us.

Understandably discouraged by experiments on unconscious processes, psychoanalytically oriented critics have been quite skeptical of the relevance of many of these experimental studies for their theory. They argue that it is confusing and misleading to study single processes (such as repression) in isolation as lone variables outside the context of the person's total psychic functioning. Such critics believe that these experimental studies at best have value as independent and suggestive, but clinically irrelevant, analogs, and they doubt that long-term psychodynamic processes can be studied under the artificial conditions of the typical laboratory experiment. They attribute the discouraging findings to the artificiality of the measures typically used in such research and to the hazards of generalizing from college sophomores in a laboratory (or even from rats in a maze) to clinical populations and clinical problems. They assert that the mild anxiety induced by experimental threats to cognitively mature college students may have little relevance for understanding the traumas experienced by the young child trying to cope with Oedipal fantasies, or the severely disturbed patient in the clinic.

For example, studies like the previously discussed experiment on repression by Zeller (1950) provide only a remote analog of the motivational aspects of clinical repression. In Freud's theory (Madison, 1960), repression (or more broadly speaking, any defense) involved motives that were associated with traumatic childhood experiences for a particular individual. Suppose that failure on such tasks as Zeller's block-tapping was not preceded by similar childhood failures and hence did not arouse those residual childhood emotional patterns. Then there would be no reason for the adult to repress rather than to cope with Zeller's ego insults in other learned ways of dealing with threat. While studies like Zeller's provide interesting information about the effects of failure, they may not really inform us about the nature of repression.

Thus, many psychoanalytically oriented critics maintain that evidence obtained from controlled experimental research conducted outside the clinical setting (such as the studies reviewed in the preceding sections) is largely irrelevant. On the other hand, as we have seen (Chapter 9), the clinician's judgments and intuitive procedures for inferring unconscious dynamics cannot be relied upon safely either. Consequently one has to seriously question not merely the methods of studying the unconscious but also the nature of the phenomenon itself, while remaining fully open to the possibility that better methods and studies will bring new understanding.

One promising but still unproven new direction is suggested by reformulating the issue of "perceptual defense" in information-processing terms. Such a reformulation treats "perceptual defense" as just one instance of the selectivity that occurs throughout cognition. Selectivity (or bias) occurs in our choice of the things to which we attend, the manner in which we organize and rehearse the flood of information that enters the sense receptors, and the response that we ultimately generate (Erdelyi, 1974). Hopefully, repression and perceptual defense will be studied more fruitfully when they are placed in the larger context of selective information processing, but a final verdict awaits new data as well as new ideas.

## SUMMARY

While need-relevant distortions in the subjective *interpretation* of the environment have often been found, in general any effects on *perception* tend to be fragile, momentary, and trivial. The weakness of need-related distortions should not be surprising when one realizes that reasonably accurate perceptions are essential for adaptive behavior and survival. For example, while the thirsty man may need to become oriented to water in order to satisfy his need, it could be fatal for him to start perceiving all fluids as if they were water.

Expectations, needs, and other states often do, however, increase attention, influence interpretations, provide direction for behavior, and change the stimuli to which one attends. And attentional shifts may occasionally be accompanied by distortions in perception; but perhaps the more remarkable feature of human perception is how accurate it manages to be even when the organism is confronted by an incredibly complex and shifting environment, as is usually the case (Bruner, 1957; Eriksen & Eriksen, 1972).

Although the research is extremely difficult to evaluate conclusively, at present there is little firm evidence to show unconscious repression either in memory or in perception. Awareness certainly enhances human learning if, indeed, it is not a precondition for most of it. Usually the person's self-reports of his subjective experiences constitute the best evidence as to whether or not he has discriminated an event. Verbal self-report evidence generally is not surpassed by physiological indicators of autonomic emotional arousal. Because of the inadequacies of language, however, and the ease with which accurate self-reports can be inhibited, one has to use careful interrogation techniques to get a proper account of a person's awareness of whether or not an event has occurred. When awareness is assessed carefully, it seems that persons generally are aware of what they are discriminating, learning, and perceiving, although some provocative exceptions of conditioning without awareness have been reported (e.g., Martin et al., 1974). In spite of the importance of awareness for most human learning, after overlearning has occurred or after deliberate suppression has been practiced repeatedly, the rehearsed behavioral sequences may seem to flow almost automatically and without awareness.

Some of the early studies on repression and perceptual defense were beset with methodological problems that did not seem obvious at the time. In retrospect it may be difficult to understand why researchers should have thought that college students would be profoundly disturbed by lists of taboo words such as "Kotex," "bitch," or "belly." Their belief assumed, dubiously, that all sexually connected words would provoke anxiety, and in addition ignored individual differences in reaction to anxiety-arousing cues. It erroneously supposed that all people would defend against the perception of anxiety cues by repressing them. More recent research has explored individual differences in coping with stress and anxiety-arousing cues, as discussed in the following sections.

# PATTERNS OF DEFENSE AND THEIR DETERMINANTS

In the course of research it became evident that while some people might react to anxiety-arousing cues by avoiding them cognitively, other people do not. Beginning with some of the earliest studies on the role of needs as determinants of perception, individual differences in "defensive" patterns were found (e.g., Bruner & Postman, 1947).

## INDIVIDUAL DIFFERENCES IN COGNITIVE AVOIDANCE: REPRESSION-SENSITIZATION

The dimension on which these differences seemed to fall was a continuum of behaviors ranging from avoiding the anxiety-arousing stimuli to approaching them more readily and being extravigilant or supersensitized to them. The former end of the continuum included behaviors similar to the defensive mechanisms that psychoanalysts called denial and repression; the latter pattern—vigilance or sensitization to anxiety-provoking cues—seemed more like the intellectual ruminations subsumed under such mechanisms as intellectualization and obsessive worrying. This dimension now has become known as the *repression-sensitization* continuum. Repression-sensitization became the focus of much research both as a dynamic process and as a personality dimension on which individuals might show consistent patterns.

There is some individual consistency in defensive behavior across various learning, memory, and perceptual tasks (e.g., Eriksen, 1966). For example (Eriksen, 1952a), college students were given an ego-involving intellectual task on which they were led to feel that they were failing. As part of the procedure they were asked, under the guise of an intelligence test, to complete a series of sentences half of which actually could not be logically completed. Subsequently they took a memory test for recall of the sentences. On the basis of their test scores, subjects were categorized according to whether they remembered more of their successes relative to their failures (i.e., more completed sentences than incompleted sentences) or the reverse. The "repressing" reaction was attributed to the subjects who recalled more successes than failures; the "sensitizing" defense to the opposite pattern.

The 10 most extreme repressors and the 10 subjects with the strongest sensitizing pattern were then selected for a paired-associate learning task. On that task some of the word associates were highly affective (had long association times) and others were affectively neutral (had short association times) for the particular subject. It was found that the repressors (of the incompleted sentences) tended to learn and relearn the affective words more slowly than the neutral words. Thus individuals who displayed extreme cognitive avoidance in the recall of their failures also tended to require more time to learn affectively arousing words. In contrast, the sensitizers (subjects who previously recalled more failures than successes) showed no such tendency.

In general, individuals show some consistency in their cognitive avoidance of symbolic, anxiety-provoking cues such as threatening words (e.g., Eriksen, 1952b; Eriksen & Kuethe, 1956). Consistency evidence usually has been strongest when extreme groups are preselected. Reaction time and other measures of avoidance in the auditory recognition of poorly audible sentences with sexual and aggressive content were significantly related to indicators of avoidance of sexual and aggressive sentence stems in a sentence completion test (Lazarus, Eriksen & Fonda, 1951). People who more readily recalled stimuli associated with a painful shock also tended to recall their failures; those who forgot one were more likely to forget the other (Lazarus & Longo, 1953).

There also have been some failures to find consistency in cognitive avoidance patterns. Kurland (1954) reported a lack of generality in avoidance mechanisms. In his study psychiatric patients were judged as using either predominantly repressive or sensitizing ("obsessive-compulsive") defense mechanisms for handling anxiety. The judgments were made by psychiatrists who saw the patients in intensive psychotherapy three times weekly. The rated defense mechanisms obtained were unrelated to auditory recognition thresholds for emotional words.

In studies of the generality of defense, perceptual recognition thresholds for threatening words have been a critical index of avoidance behavior. Byrne and Holcomb (1962) studied the consistency or reliability of recognition thresholds for threatening versus neutral words. To the investigators' surprise, the resulting coefficient of internal consistency was .00. While judges agreed about the nature of the threatening and nonthreatening stimuli, and about the scoring of responses, the subjects' scores were entirely unreliable: there was no consistency in their perceptual defense (differential response thresholds) across supposedly similar hostile stimuli.

Another study investigated the consistency of defensive responses by college students to threatening stimuli (Palmer, 1968). Each subject was tested on six measures of "vigilance-defense behavior." The results provided 15 correlations; of these only two indicated a degree of consistency greater than chance:

> In general, then, the overall consistency observed is so low, and the correlations between individual tests so uneven, as to cast serious doubt on the hypothesis of a strong unitary process underlying all vigilance-defense behavior. These results offer relatively little support for a simple individual-centered theory of defense consistency. They suggest, rather, that a full understanding of vigilant and defensive styles of response to threat may require a much greater attention to the identification and conceptualization of task variables specific to each test situation (Palmer, 1968, p. 33).

In sum, sometimes there is some significant consistency in approach versus avoidance responses to threatening stimuli of various kinds, but generally the degree of consistency is not very strong. A tendency for some consistency in cognitive avoidance may exist at least when extremely high and low groups are selected (Eriksen, 1966). Correlations between cognitive avoidance on experimental tasks and various other measures of repression-sensitization also imply some consistency (e.g., Byrne, 1964; Markowitz, 1969). However, like most other dispositions, cognitive avoidance is not a stimulus-free trait: it depends on the situation as well as on the person's learning history.

## SUBJECTIVE CONTROL, AVOIDANCE, AND VIGILANCE

Regardless of how consistent or inconsistent individuals are in their cognitive avoidance patterns, it is important to find the determinants of these behaviors. Research on this topic has important implications for the current theoretical status of defense mechanisms as concepts.

Whether you react to potentially painful stimuli by trying to avoid them cognitively or by becoming vigilantly alert to them may depend in part on what you can do to control the threat. Consider first the situation in which a person receives aversive stimulation but cannot control its occurrence. That is, the individual can do nothing to change the objective circumstances to render the aversive or negative stimuli less painful through his own problem-solving actions. Examples of this frustrating dilemma would include most experimentally induced stress experiments in which the researcher administers painful but unavoidable electric shocks to the subject, confronts him with embarrassing words or pictures, provides him with insoluble problems, or deprives him of food or sleep for long periods of time.

Under all these conditions the aversive stimulation is essentially inescapable (unless the subject terminates the situation altogether by abandoning the experiment). If the subject can have no control over the painful stimuli by means of his own instrumental actions such as problem-solving, it may be most adaptive for him to avoid them cognitively and thus not think about them or attend to them. On the other hand, if escape from the noxious or distressing stimulation is possible and depends on the person's ability to find a solution (cognitively or physically), then vigilance or sensitization to the anxiety-arousing cues would be adaptive and often even essential for survival.

The foregoing speculations (similar to some of the ideas discussed by Jones & Gerard, 1967) have received some experimental support. Reece (1954) tested subjects' recognition thresholds for various nonsense syllables in the first phase of his experiment. Thereafter, the subjects underwent a training period during which some of the syllables were paired with electric shock. In the final phase of the study the subjects' recognition thresholds after training were assessed again. Post-training recognition thresholds for the syllables were longer if during training the syllable-shock combinations were inescapable (i.e., subjects could do nothing to prevent them). In contrast, if subjects could escape shock during training by verbalizing the syllable as soon as it was presented then the syllables were later recognized as rapidly as in a control group that received no shock. Similar evidence comes from a study by Rosen (1954), who controlled for the effect of the electric shock itself.

Under experimental conditions of prolonged sleep deprivation (over which subjects have no control), fewer sleep-related ideas and themes are found in projective material (Murray, 1959). Similarly, food ideation is less when subjects are severely deprived of food than when they are not hungry (Lazarus, Yousem & Arenberg, 1953). Thus whether or not persons react to negative stimuli by avoiding them "defensively" in their cognitions and perceptions may depend on whether or not they believe that they can somehow cope with them by problem-solving and action. If adaptive action seems impossible, cognitive suppressive attempts may be more likely, but if the painful cues can be controlled by the person's actions then greater attention and vigilance to them may occur.

## AVOIDANCE LEARNING OF DEFENSES

The previous section suggested that whether a person becomes cognitively vigilant or avoidant to anxiety-arousing cues may depend on whether or not he believes he can control the onset of danger. This conclusion refers to the person's subjective state, his personal beliefs about his ability to cope with threat through his own action. The subjective feeling that one can control the occurrence of dangerous outcomes is not achieved arbitrarily—it reflects, instead, the person's previous experiences and current condition. Depending on the exact learning history and the structure of the particular situation, he might react to anxiety cues either with vigilance or with avoidance.

Some of the conditions under which perceptual defense and perceptual vigilance may be learned have been carefully investigated (Dulany, 1957). Dulany noted that it is difficult to interpret the meaning of studies on defensive behavior whenever the subjects' learning history with the threatening stimulus is unknown and uncontrolled. To know the exact significance for the subject of particular threatening stimuli one has to create the relevant learning history in the experiment. Dulany therefore directly investigated the mechanisms through which perceptual defense and vigilance might be learned by creating the necessary conditions in a laboratory study.

He exposed people to pictures of four geometrical figures presented simultaneously below the threshold for clear awareness. Their task over a series of trials was to report the figure that was most easily recognizable, the placement of the figures in the array being varied from trial to trial. A particular figure from the four was arbitrarily chosen to become the "critical stimulus." Half the subjects received "defense training," designed to encourage nonrecognition of a threatening stimulus. These subjects received a painful electric shock whenever they selected the critical figure as more recognizable. Moreover, they avoided the shock whenever they selected one of the other three geometrical figures. The remaining subjects were given "vigilance training." Whenever these subjects selected the critical figure they avoided the electric shock: conversely selection of any of the other three figures produced shock for them. Thus during vigilance training, recognition of the critical stimulus was instrumental for shock avoidance.

The crucial assessments occurred after these training procedures were completed. Now the shock apparatus was disconnected and the subjects were assured that there would be no more shock. The same sets of four figures were presented for 64 more trials, and on each trial each subject had to indicate the one figure that was most recognizable. The results for the training series and the final assessment series are summarized in Figure 18-2.

Learning of perceptual defense and vigilance occurred as predicted. When the perceptual response to the threatening stimulus was punished during training and nonrecognition was instrumental for shock avoidance (analogous to anxiety reduction), defense was learned. Conversely, when recognition of the threatening stimulus was anxiety reducing (shock avoidance), and competing perceptual responses were punished during training, the subjects became increasingly vigilant. These findings occurred even though subjects seemed unable to verbalize the rules regulating the occurrence of the shock. (The interrogation, however, may not have been sufficiently sensitive to detect awareness.) Dulany's overall results indicate that the phenomena of "defense" can be produced by manipulating learning conditions without invoking any special unconscious mechanisms or unique processes.

Covert responses such as thoughts and associations may be modified by punishment in the same fashion as overt responses (e.g., Eriksen & Kuethe, 1956). If a thought or association elicited by a stimulus is punished, then it tends to be inhibited and a new association becomes more likely. The recall or retrieval of memories may be hampered when the person expects punishment for recalling the material (Weiner, 1968). According to learning theory, if behaviors such as sexual and

**Figure 18-2** EFFECTS OF DEFENSE AND VIGILANCE TRAINING ON PERCEPTUAL RECOG-
NITION

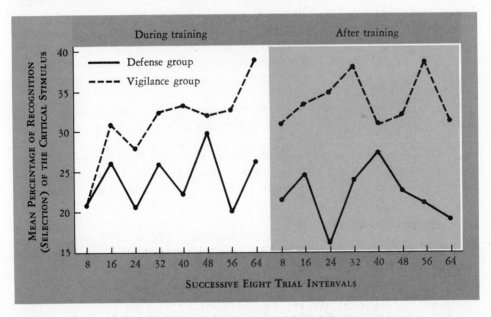

During training, in the defense group recognition of the critical stimulus produces shock and nonrecognition avoids it; in the vigilance group, conversely, nonrecognition produces shock and recognition avoids it. As a result, subjects became either defensive or vigilant toward the critical stimulus,
even after training ended. (Adapted from Dulany, 1957.)

aggressive responses have been punished, they are more likely to become inhibited
and to be replaced by other responses that, on the basis of prior learning, are less
likely to produce painful consequences.

In sum, the phenomena of cognitive avoidance may become less mysterious
when they are seen as learned functional responses. Such learning involves suppression of thoughts, images, percepts, associations, or other cognitive events that have
been punished. In turn, competing unpunished responses will become more likely.

## THE MEANING OF INCONSISTENCY

The belief in a special unconscious mechanism of repression is sometimes bolstered by the observation that people often seem to behave inconsistently. For example, in his self-reports a man may depict himself as well controlled, orderly, and
unaggressive, but his stories on the TAT projective test may be full of murder and
violence. Such discrepancies across response modes may seem intuitively to provide
support for unconscious repressive mechanisms. These defensive mechanisms might

inhibit the individual's motives in some contexts but permit repressed materials to slip through defenses under other, less guarded circumstances, such as in jokes or in fantasy expressions.

An alternative interpretation of the same phenomenon emphasizes the fact that the response mode in which behavior occurs influences the consequences to which the behavior leads. The consequences for similar content expressed in different response modes usually are drastically different. For example, an individual's thoughts, stories, self-reports, jokes, daydreams, and other responses all dealing with the same theme—such as aggressiveness—do not lead to similar consequences. A person whose projective test stories abound with violent themes might be diagnosed as having a healthy, active fantasy life. But the same individual probably would be institutionalized if he enacted similar content in his interpersonal relations or if he expressed similar themes in his self-reports and self-descriptions. Because the consequences the individual receives for the same response pattern across different response modes are radically different he learns to discriminate sharply among them, and therefore his behavior across them becomes different (Mischel, 1968). For example, if sexual fantasies are gratifying and acceptable but sexual orgies are not, the individual may be expected to engage in the former rather than in the latter.

But who does the punishing and the permitting when the "unacceptable" responses are primarily covert events such as thoughts and images? Obviously in the course of socialization persons somehow become regulators of their own behavior, punishing and rewarding themselves and judging their own actions, feelings, and ideas. The development of these self-regulatory mechanisms constitutes one of the most important topics in personality, and the details of this process are discussed in the next chapter.

## SUMMARY

1. People can cognitively avoid internal anxiety-generating cues such as threatening thoughts. While the phenomenon of "cognitive avoidance" is widely recognized, a controversial issue is whether or not it involves a mechanism of unconscious repression.

2. The Freudian concept of defense mechanisms refers to attempts to cope cognitively with internal anxiety-arousing cues without awareness—that is, unconsciously. Freud thought that the key mechanism of defense entailed unconsciously motivated repression of unacceptable (anxiety-arousing) material. According to his theory, repressed impulses are not eliminated but are only camouflaged; hence, they may ultimately return in disguised and distorted forms, such as "slips" of the tongue or symptoms.

3. The concept of repression has been the subject of extensive research for many years. Although several empirical studies have been interpreted as supporting the concept of repression, alternative interpretations are possible (such as poorer learning under conditions of emotional upset and response interference due to stress).

4. Repressive "perceptual defenses" might produce anxiety-reducing distortions and avoidance in perception. Some researchers reasoned that if certain stimuli generally elicited many sexual or aggressive responses, then the *failure* to give such responses meant that the person must be inhibiting or defending against this type of ideation. Often a tachistoscope was used to present stimuli briefly, and the length of time required to recognize threatening stimuli (such as taboo words) was the measure of defensive avoidance.

5. Methodological problems left the conclusions uncertain. For example, the threatening words used in perceptual defense experiments occur less frequently in the English language than the neutral words. Thus longer recognition time could result from unfamiliarity rather than from unconscious defense. Another difficulty lies in the problem of distinguishing between the subject's *report* and his *perception*. The subject in a perceptual recognition situation may see the taboo stimulus but may deliberately suppress his response because he is embarrassed about saying or admitting it. Other experiments on unconscious defense have been limited by many similar methodological dilemmas.

6. Evidence from controlled experimental research on unconscious defense and need-distorted perception is often negative. Many psychoanalytically oriented critics, however, maintain that most of this evidence is irrelevant. They point to the artificiality of the measures usually employed and to the hazards of generalizing from laboratory subjects to clinical populations and problems. Alternatively, the clinician's judgments and the intuitive procedures used for inferring the phenomena of unconscious dynamics have been questioned most seriously.

7. A major effort to assess the role of the unconscious has investigated learning and discrimination processes to see if they can occur without awareness or consciousness. In general, while some simple conditioned responses may be learned without awareness, awareness plays a major role in most forms of human learning. Yet, although most learning may require awareness, once behavior is mastered it often seems to proceed without subjective awareness. Similarly, painful or unpleasant material at first may be deliberately suppressed and this response suppression may gradually become automatic. Thus the phenomenon of "repression" may reduce to overlearned response suppression.

8. Individual differences in coping with stress and anxiety-arousing cues seem to fall on a continuum from avoidance behaviors to supersensitive and vigilant ones. This "repression-sensitization" continuum, as it has come to be known, has been the focus of much research, both as a dynamic process and as a personality dimension.

9. Whether a person reacts to a painful stimulus by trying cognitively to avoid it or by becoming vigilantly alert to it may depend partly upon what he can do to control the threat. If adaptive action seems impossible, cognitive suppression may be more likely. If, however, the potentially painful events can be controlled by the person's actions, then greater attention and vigilance to them may be found.

10. Experimental research has explored the mechanisms through which perceptual defense and vigilance can be learned. In one experiment, for example, if recognition of painful stimuli was punished and nonrecognition was necessary to avoid punishment, avoidance defense was learned. In contrast, subjects became increasingly vigilant if they could avoid punishment by recognizing the threatening stimuli.

11. The inconsistent behavior of a person in different response modes (such as thoughts, self-reports, daydreams, and overt behavior) is often construed as evidence for unconscious repression. The defensive mechanisms are seen as inhibiting the individual's basic motives in some contexts but as permitting repressed materials to slip through in less guarded circumstances. The same phenomenon of inconsistency, however, may reflect the fact that consequences for expressing similar content in different response modes usually are drastically different. This difference leads a person to discriminate sharply among different response modes.

# CHAPTER 19
# SELF-CONTROL

Defensive reactions to frustration and anxiety are by no means the only forms of self-regulation. This chapter examines some other important ways through which people solve problems and control their own behavior. These mechanisms have been called "ego controls," "internalization," and "processes of self-control." Regardless of the labels, the phenomena discussed encompass the ways in which individuals solve problems and evaluate and control their own behavior.

## FRUSTRATION TOLERANCE
## AND VOLUNTARY DELAY

Man's ability to control his personal world has intrigued not only philosophers and psychologists but most laymen as well. This concern is reflected in such diverse concepts as "will power," "mastery," and "competence," and in their psychological opposites, such as "helplessness" and "hopelessness." All of these concepts involve the idea of volition ("will") and deal with the ability of the individual to affect his own outcomes and to influence his personal environment. Sometimes this influence is judged to be for the social good, and therefore prosocial or "moral"; often it is not. Always it entails the individual's efforts to modify conditions in the light of particular goals.

One especially striking characteristic of human "will" is that people frequently impose barriers on themselves, interrupting their own behavior and delaying available gratification. When a delay of gratification is imposed on an individual by external conditions or forces we talk about "frustration" (Chapter 16); when the delay is self-imposed we call it "self-control."

## DELAY OF GRATIFICATION

The ability to voluntarily refuse immediate gratification, to tolerate self-imposed delays of reward, is at the core of most philosophical concepts of "will power" and their parallel psychological concept of "ego strength." It is hard to imagine socialization, or indeed civilization, without such self-imposed delays. Learning to wait for desired outcomes and to behave in the light of expected future consequences is essential for the successful achievement of long-term, distant goals. Even the simplest, most primitive steps in socialization require learning to defer one's impulses and to express them only under special conditions of time and place, as seen in toilet training. Similarly, enormously complex chains of deferred gratification are required for people to achieve the delayed rewards provided by our culture's social system and institutions.

Consider, for example, the self-imposed deferrals of pleasure required to achieve occupational objectives such as careers in medicine or science. The route leading to such a goal involves a continuous series of delays of gratification, as seen in the progression from one grade to the next, and from one temporal barrier to another in the long course from occupational choice to occupational success. In social relationships the culture also requires delays, as seen in the expectation that people should postpone sexual relations, marriage, and children until they are "ready for them." Although judgments of what constitutes such readiness differ greatly across cultures and among different people, some norms concerning appropriate timing are found in every society.

The importance of self-control patterns that require delay of gratification has been widely recognized by theorists from Freud to the present. The concept of voluntary postponement of gratifications for the sake of more distant, long-term gains is fundamental for many conceptualizations of complex human behavior.

## SHOULD GRATIFICATION BE DELAYED?

The cultural norm of impulse delay is expressed most clearly in the so-called "Protestant Ethic," with its puritanical demands for self-restraint and its negative attitude toward pleasure. Understandably there are many strong reactions against such extremes of self-denial. Some thoughtful people question the wisdom of building a society on endless chains of deferred gratification. Others have experimented with more utopian communal societies, seeking simpler forms for the creation of a more satisfying community. The goals that people struggle toward in our society and the barriers that both they and the society impose need to be questioned. But although the particular goals and frustrations may change, it is difficult to conceive of organized life without some temporal delays and barriers. Even the simplest agricultural or folk community needs both delay and planning. The issue therefore is not delay of gratification in itself, but when, how, and for what one should delay.

## LEARNING TO CHOOSE DELAYED GRATIFICATIONS

The extreme self-imposed delay symbolized by the ethics of puritanism contrasts sharply with the inadequate voluntary delay and the deficiencies in self-control that seem to characterize many people in our society. Inadequate delay patterns often are partial causes of antisocial and criminal behavior (including violence and physical aggression) and of failure to achieve reasonable work and interpersonal satisfactions (Mowrer & Ullmann, 1945). Thus while some personal and social problems stem from excessive frustration, others result from the failure of individuals to learn and practice appropriate patterns of delay and restraint. Indeed, deficiencies in voluntary delay may become a prime source of frustration and may victimize the individual by guaranteeing him an endless chain of failure experiences in our culture. Consider, for example, the "high school dropout" who leaves school because he cannot tolerate postponing pleasures and working for more distant goals. His school failure in turn may sentence him to future vocational hardships and prevent him from achieving durable satisfactions. Given the magnitude of the social problems associated with the inability to delay rewards, it becomes important to understand the causes of voluntary delay behavior in detail.

To explore the cognitive and social learning variables controlling self-imposed delay of reward, one research program has studied delay of reward and self-control with direct behavioral measures (Mischel, 1966b, 1974). In this research subjects usually have to choose among actual alternatives that vary in delay time and value (e.g., immediate smaller versus delayed larger rewards) in realistic situations, as was discussed in Chapter 8. For example, preschool children are given a choice between getting a less valuable but immediate reward or a more attractive reward for which they must wait. This type of choice situation is depicted in Figure 19-1.

The figure shows the "clown box" with two windows displaying the two items in the choice (Mischel, 1970). The window in front of the smaller reward can be opened at once, whereas the window displaying the larger reward remains sealed for a predetermined time period. By depositing a token in the appropriate slot (in the clown's hands) the child may choose whether he wants to open the window in front of the smaller reward now or wait for the other window to spring open after

**Figure 19-1**    A SET OF PAIRED REWARDS IN PLACE IN THE MAGIC CLOWN SURPRISE BOX

From Mischel (1970).

a specified delay time. Basically similar choices involving age-appropriate outcomes have been presented to older children and adults by means of questionnaires that describe the choices verbally.

To a considerable degree a person's willingness to defer gratification depends on the outcomes that he expects from his choice (Mischel, 1966b, 1968). Of particular importance are the individual's expectations that future (delayed) rewards for which he would have to work and wait would actually materialize, and their relative value for him. Such expectations or feelings of trust depend, in turn, on the person's history of prior promise-keeping and on past reinforcement for waiting behavior and for other forms of planful, goal-directed self-control. When the attainment of delayed gratification requires the person to reach particular achievement levels, then his willingness to work and wait for these future outcomes also hinges on his expectations that he can adequately fulfill the necessary contingencies (Mischel & Staub, 1965). These expectations depend not only on his direct personal experiences, but also on his observation of the behavior of social models, such as peers, parents, and teachers.

## EFFECTS OF WATCHING IMPULSIVE VERSUS FUTURE-ORIENTED MODELS

Laboratory experiments have investigated most precisely the determinants of preferences for immediate, less valuable as opposed to more desirable but delayed outcomes and similar forms of self-control. To illustrate this type of experiment, here is one example in some detail.

The transmission of delay behavior through modeling without any direct reinforcement was studied by Bandura and Mischel (1965). They hypothesized that self-imposed delay of reward would be determined in part by the delay patterns displayed by social models. The study also compared the relative magnitude and stability of changes in delay-of-reward behavior as a function of exposure to real-life and symbolic (written) modeling cues.

In the initial phase of this experiment many children were administered a series of paired rewards. In each of these pairs they were asked to select either a small reward that could be obtained immediately, or a more valued item contingent on a delay period ranging from one to four weeks. For example, children chose between a smaller, immediately available candy bar and a larger one that required waiting. From the total pool of subjects those falling in the extreme upper and lower 25 percent of scores were selected for the succeeding phases of the experiment.

Children from each of these extreme groups (who exhibited predominantly either delayed-reward or immediate-reward patterns of behavior) were then assigned to treatment conditions. In one treatment children observed a live adult model who exhibited delay-of-reward responses counter to their own self-gratification pattern. For example, if the child was initially high in delay preferences, the adult model consistently chose immediate rewards. (He selected, for instance, a cheaper set of plastic chess figures immediately instead of a more attractive set available a week later.) The model also made explanatory statements about his choices. For example, he said: "Chess figures are chess figures. I can get much use out of the plastic ones right away." Or he commented: "You probably have noticed that I am a person who likes things now. One can spend so much time in life waiting that one never gets around to really living. . . ." Conversely, children who initially displayed strong immediate reward preferences were exposed to models who chose delayed, costlier rewards. In other treatment groups children were similarily exposed to a model displaying delay-of-reward behavior opposite to their own, with the exception that the model's responses were presented only in written form rather than "live." In a final condition children had no exposure to any models.

Immediately following the experimental procedure the children's delay-of-reward responses were measured. In order to test the generality and stability of changes in delay behavior, they were reassessed by a different experimenter in a different social setting approximately one month later. The overall results revealed strong effects. Figure 19-2, for example, shows the mean percentage of immediate-reward responses produced by the high-delay children in each of the test periods as a function of treatment conditions. Children who had shown a predominantly delayed-reward pattern displayed an increased preference for immediate and less valuable rewards as a function of observing models favoring immediate gratification; conversely, those who had exhibited a marked preference for immediate rewards increased and maintained their willingness to wait for more valuable but delayed reinforcers following exposure to models displaying high-delay behavior. The effects of seeing the model's written responses were similar to those of watching live models, although less pronounced and less generalized.

**Figure 19-2**  EFFECTS OF MODELING ON DELAY OF GRATIFICATION

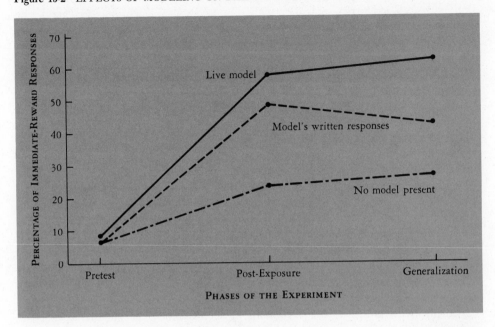

Mean percentage of immediate-reward responses by high-delay children on each of three test periods for each of three experimental conditions. (Adapted from Bandura & Mischel, 1965.)

Conclusions from this study were strengthened by the finding of similar effects when similar procedures were extended to a population of young prison inmates. Specifically, exposure to high-delay peer models substantially increased delay of gratification in 18- to 20-year-old inmates who initially had displayed an extreme preference for immediate rewards (Stumphauzer, 1972). The effects showed some generalization and were maintained in a follow-up one month later.

## MECHANISMS DURING SELF-IMPOSED DELAY OF GRATIFICATION

Although choice preferences for immediate or delayed rewards are beginning to be understood, the psychological mechanisms during the delay period remain remarkably unstudied. Given that one has chosen to wait for a larger deferred gratification, how can the delay period be managed?

### THEORETICAL PREDICTIONS

Freud (1911) provided one of the few theoretical treatments of how delay of gratification may be bridged. According to the psychoanalytic formulation, ideation arises initially when there is a block or delay in the process of direct gratification (Rapaport, 1967). During such externally imposed delay, according to Freud, the child constructs a "hallucinatory image" of the physically absent, need-satisfying object. This mental image provides fantasy satisfactions (e.g., Freud, 1911; Singer, 1955). But in spite of much psychoanalytic theorizing and speculation about the role of the mental representation of blocked gratifications in the development of delaying capacity, the exact process remains far from clear.

In their theoretical discussion of impulse control, Jones and Gerard (1967) hypothesized that "time-binding" (the capacity to bridge delay of gratification) probably hinges on self-instructional processes through which the individual increases the salience or dominance of the delayed consequences or outcomes of his action. In their view, any factors (situational or within the individual) that make delayed consequences more salient should enhance impulse control and voluntary delay. Their position also implies covert "self-reinforcement" processes through which the person may reinforce his own waiting behavior by vividly anticipating some of the positive consequences to which it will lead.

A cognitive-developmental view might lead one to expect that cognitively immature young children may more readily forget the delayed outcomes for which they are waiting, and hence cease to wait unless they are reminded of the relevant contingencies and rewards involved in the delay-of-gratification paradigm.

In line with the foregoing arguments, it seems most plausible that conditions that help the individual to attend mentally to the delayed reward for which he is waiting should sustain his ability to wait for it (e.g., Jones & Gerard, 1967). In that case, any cues that make the delayed gratification more salient—that help the person to make deferred consequences psychologically more vivid or immediate (e.g., by letting him look at them, by visualizing them in imagination, or by reminding him of the object for which he is waiting)—should facilitate waiting behavior.

Such expectations seem congruent with the results of earlier work on choice of immediate, smaller versus delayed but larger rewards (Mahrer, 1956; Mischel & Staub, 1965; Mischel, 1966b, 1974). These earlier studies showed that an important determinant of preference for delayed rewards is the individual's expectation or "trust" that he will actually get the delayed (but more valuable) outcome. Consequently, conditions that increase the salience or visibility of the delayed gratification may enhance the person's willingness to wait by increasing his subjective confidence that the delayed outcome will materialize and be available after the waiting time ends.

Therefore one might expect that voluntary delay behavior is easier when the person converts, as it were, the deferred or delayed object into more tangible form by making it psychologically more immediate, as by providing himself with symbolic representations or physical cues about it. The most direct way to focus attention on the deferred outcomes would be to have them physically present and facing the subject so that he can attend to them readily and vividly. To investigate how attention to delayed and immediate outcomes influences waiting for them, one study manipulated the availability of those outcomes for attention during the delay time (Mischel & Ebbesen, 1970).

## A METHOD FOR OBSERVING
## WAITING BEHAVIOR

To study this problem a paradigm was constructed in which very young (pre-school) children would be willing to remain in an experimental room, waiting entirely alone for at least a short time without becoming upset and debilitatingly anxious. After the usual play periods for building rapport, each child was taught a "game" in which he could immediately summon the experimenter by a simple signal. This step was practiced repeatedly, until the child clearly understood that he could immediately terminate his waiting period in the room simply by signaling for the experimenter, who regularly returned from outside as soon as the child signaled. Next, the child was introduced to the relevant contingency.

He was shown two objects (e.g., food treats), one of which he clearly preferred (as determined by pretesting). To attain the preferred object he had to wait for it until the experimenter returned "by himself." The child was, however, entirely free throughout the waiting period to signal at any time for the experimenter to return; if he signaled he could have the less preferred object at once but had to forego the more desirable one.

## THE VALUE OF NOT THINKING

To manipulate the extent to which children could attend to the reward objects while they were waiting, the rewards were removed from the experimental room in all combinations, creating four conditions with respect to the objects available for attention. Examples are shown in Figure 19-3. In one condition, the children waited with both the immediate (less preferred) and the delayed (more preferred) reward facing them in the experimental room so that they could attend to both outcomes. In another group neither reward was available for the subject's attention, both having been removed from sight. In the remaining two groups either the delayed reward only or the immediate reward only was available for attention

**Figure 19-3**   WAITING FOR DELAYED GRATIFICATION

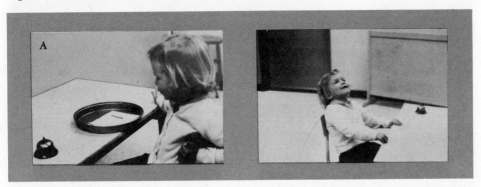

From Mischel, Ebbesen, and Raskoff (1971).

while the child waited. The measure was the length of time before each child voluntarily stopped waiting.

The initial theorizing about delay behavior led to predictions of results that were the direct opposite of the obtained findings (shown in Figure 19-4). It was predicted that attention to the outcomes available in the choice situation while waiting would enhance delay behavior; instead it sharply reduced delay of gratification. The children waited longest when no rewards were available for attention.

One of the most striking delay strategies used by some youngsters was exceedingly simple and effective. These children seemed to manage to wait for the preferred reward for long periods apparently by converting the aversive waiting situation into a more pleasant, nonwaiting one. They seemed to do this by elaborate self-distraction techniques through which they spent their time psychologically doing something (almost anything) other than waiting. Rather than focusing prolonged attention on the objects for which they were waiting, they avoided looking at them. Some of these children covered their eyes with their hands, rested their heads on their arms, or found other similar techniques for averting their eyes from the reward objects. Moreover, subjects seemed to try to reduce the frustration of delay of reward by generating their own diversions: they talked to themselves, sang, invented games with their hands and feet, and when all other distractions seemed exhausted, even tried to fall asleep during the waiting situation—as one child successfully did.

These observations suggest that diverting yourself from attention to the delayed reward stimulus (while maintaining behavior directed toward its ultimate at-

**Figure 19-4**  EFFECTS OF ATTENTION ON DELAY OF GRATIFICATION

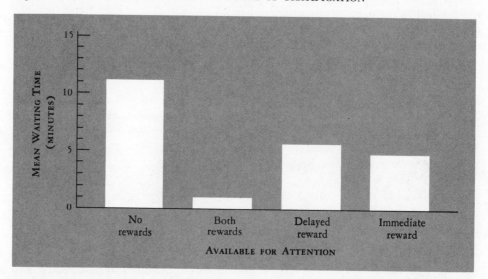

Based on data from Mischel and Ebbesen (1970).

tainment) may be a key step in bridging temporal delay of reward. That is, learning *not* to think about what you are awaiting may enhance effective delay of gratification much more than does ideating about the outcomes.

These observations seem consistent with theoretical considerations that focus on the aversiveness of frustration and delayed rewards. If wanting something but not being able to have it is actively aversive, it seems likely that cues that enhance the salience of the desired but still unavailable (delayed) reward should increase the aversiveness of the delay period. In that case, the greater and more vivid the anticipation of reward, the greater the frustration generated by its delay. When hungry, for example, it is easier to wait for supper if one is not confronted with the sight and smell of food.

This line of reasoning would suggest that conditions that decrease a person's attention to the blocked reward—and that distract him by internal or overt activity from the frustrative delay of reward—would make it less aversive for him to continue his goal-directed waiting and hence permit him to wait longer for gratifications. In other words, just as cognitive avoidance may facilitate coping with anxiety (as noted in the last chapter) so may it help the individual to cope with other aversive stimuli, such as the frustration of waiting and wanting something that he cannot have yet.

## SELF-DISTRACTION IN RESPONSE TO FRUSTRATION

If these ideas are correct then delay of gratification and frustration tolerance should be enhanced when the person can readily transform the aversive waiting period into a more pleasant, nonwaiting situation. He might do that by converting his attention and thoughts away from the frustrative components of delay of gratification and thinking instead about other things. Such distractions can be achieved if he can engage in activities, overtly or mentally, during the delay period that help him to suppress or decrease cognitively the aversiveness of waiting for the delayed but preferred outcome.

If that is true then voluntary delay of reward should be aided by any overt or covert activities that serve as distractors from the rewards and thus from the aversiveness of wanting them but not having them. Through such distraction the individual should be able to convert the frustrative delay-of-reward situation into a psychologically less aversive condition. Therefore motoric activities and internal cognitions and fantasy that can distract the individual from the rewards potentially available in the situation should increase the length of time that he will delay gratification for the sake of the more valuable reward.

Follow-up studies support this reasoning (Mischel, Ebbesen & Zeiss, 1972). Children waited much longer for a preferred reward when they were distracted cognitively from the goal objects than when they directly attended to them. Another experiment demonstrated that only certain cognitive events (thinking "fun things") served as effective ideational distractors. Thinking "sad thoughts" produced short delay times similar to thinking about the rewards themselves. In a final experiment the delayed rewards were physically not available for direct attention during the delay period. The children's attention to the absent rewards was manipulated cognitively by prior instructions.

It was found that cognitions directed toward the rewards while the children waited greatly reduced, rather than enhanced, the length of time that the children were able to delay gratification. Thus attentional and cognitive mechanisms that enhance the salience of the rewards substantially shortened the length of voluntary delay of gratification. In contrast, distractions from the rewards, overtly or cognitively, facilitated waiting for preferred but delayed reinforcement.

The data from these experiments seem to contradict the notion that "will power" requires one to bear up and force oneself to maintain directed attention to things that are aversive, difficult, or boring. Rather than trying to maintain aversive activities such as delay of reward through "acts of will" and focused attention, effective self-control may hinge on *transforming* the difficult into the easy, the aversive into the pleasant, the boring into the interesting, while still maintaining the task-required (reward-contingent) activity.

Such transformations may occur either by engaging in the appropriate overt distracting activity or changing one's own mental content and ideation. A good way to master the difficult or aversive thus may be to think or do something pleasant while performing the necessary, task-relevant response (e.g., waiting, working). Rather than "willing" oneself to heroic bravery one needs to perform the necessary "difficult" response while engaging in another one cognitively.

## COGNITIVE TRANSFORMATIONS AND DELAY

If the young child is left during the waiting period with the actual reward objects (e.g., pretzels or marshmallows) in front of him, through instructions he can cognitively transform them in many ways that enable him to wait for long time periods (e.g., Mischel & Baker, 1975). If he cognitively transforms the reward stimulus, for example, by thinking about the pretzel sticks in front of him as little brown logs, or by thinking about the marshmallows as round white clouds or as cotton balls, he may wait long and patiently. Conversely, if the child has been instructed to focus cognitively on the arousing (consummatory) qualities of the reward objects, such as the pretzel's crunchy, salty taste or the chewy, sweet, soft taste of the marshmallows, he tends to be able to wait only a short time. Similarly, through instruction the children can easily transform the real objects (present in front of them) into a "color picture in your head," or they can transform the picture of the objects (presented on a slide projected on a screen in front of them) into the "real" objects by pretending in imagination that they are actually there on a plate in front of them (Moore et al., 1975).

Thus what is in the children's heads—not what is physically in front of them—determines their ability to delay. Regardless of the stimulus in their visual field, if they imagine the real objects as present they cannot wait long for them. But if they imagine pictures (abstract representations) of the objects they can wait for long time periods (and even longer than when they are simply distracting themselves with abstract representations of objects that are comparable but not relevant to the rewards for which they are waiting). Through instructions about what to imagine during the delay period, it is possible to completely alter (even to reverse) the effects of the physically present reward stimuli in the situation, and to cognitively control delay behavior. But while in experiments the experimenter provides instructions (which the subject often obligingly follows) about how to construe the stimulus situation, in life the "subject" supplies his own instructions and may transform the situation in many alternative ways.

## SUMMARY

Taken collectively, research on delay-of-gratification and tolerance for self-imposed frustration suggests a two-part process. First, consider the determinants of the *choice* to undergo frustrative delay for the sake of preferred delayed outcomes. This choice is influenced mainly by expectations concerning the probable consequences of the choice. These consequences include the relative subjective values of the immediate and delayed outcomes themselves as well as other probable reinforcing outcomes associated with each alternative. Expectancies relevant to these outcomes depend on direct and vicarious past experiences and trust relationships, modeling cues, the specific contingencies in the choice, and so on (e.g., Mischel, 1966b).

Second, once the choice to self-impose delay of gratification has been made, effective delay depends on cognitive and overt self-distractions to reduce the aversiveness of the self-imposed frustration. For this purpose, the person needs to avoid the goal objects, generating his own distractions while maintaining the necessary behavior on which goal-attainment is contingent. An effective way of coping with the frustrations imposed by delay in many life situations is to transform the aversive delay period cognitively into a more positive or interesting experience. This can be achieved by doing something else, overtly or internally, while continuing to wait for the desired goal, or by cognitively transforming the desired goal objects to reduce their excessively arousing qualities.

## COGNITIVE TRANSFORMATIONS AND STRESS REDUCTION

The discussion in this section has focused on voluntary delay of gratification, but the findings fit those from many other areas of self-control. For example, not surprisingly it helps to distract oneself when trying to endure various kinds of pain and stress (e.g., Kanfer & Seidner, 1973). Likewise, people feel better if they use cognitive transformations to redefine stressful situations in more positive ways (Holmes & Houston, 1974). When stress and pain are inevitable (as in patients awaiting major surgery), the adage to look for the silver lining and to "accentuate the positive" may be wise. In one study, surgical patients were helped to recon-strue their threatening ordeal (Langer, Janis & Wolfer, 1975). For example, they were encouraged to focus on the hospital experience as an escape from pressure and a "vacation" with a chance to relax, and were given other similar techniques for emphasizing the positive side. These patients tended to cope better with their traumas, seeming to experience less stress and requesting fewer pain relievers and sedatives.

## SELF-REACTIONS AND SELF-REGULATION

People judge and evaluate their own behavior and reward and punish themselves. In the typical animal laboratory the organism performs, and the experimenter or his apparatus reinforces him at predetermined points. Unlike the animals in the researcher's laboratory, people exert considerable control over the rewarding and punishing resources available to them. They congratulate themselves for their own characteristics and actions; they praise or abuse their own achievements; and they self-administer social and material rewards and punishments from the enormous array freely available to them.

A critical aspect of self-regulation thus stems from the fact that people assess and monitor themselves. Self-praise and censure, self-imposed treats and punish-ments, self-indulgence and self-laceration are manifestations of this pervasive human tendency to congratulate and condemn oneself. Learning research with ani-mals generally has focused on the effects of environmentally or externally adminis-tered reinforcers. Much less is known about the processes through which persons learn to set their own performance standards and to make their own self-reward contingent upon their achieving these self-prescribed criteria. To adequately under-stand human social behavior, we must know how the person self-administers and regulates rewards and punishments that are in his own control (e.g., Masters & Mokros, 1974).

### SELF-REINFORCEMENT METHODOLOGY

To investigate self-reward and self-punishment, a method has been developed in which subjects (usually grade school children) work on a performance task that seemingly requires skill (e.g., Bandura & Kupers, 1964). They have free access to a large supply of rewards (e.g., assorted candies, tokens exchangeable for prizes, small toys, and desirable trinkets). The experiments are designed so that the child's information about his level or quality of performance can be manipulated readily. For example, many of these studies use a realistic looking electronic bowling game on which the child bowls and receives feedback in the form of scores automatically illuminated on a display panel. The scores may be programmed by the experi-menter so that the child gets fixed, predetermined feedback although he thinks the scores reflect his real performance.

## *MODELING EFFECTS*

One study, for example, tested the hypothesis that patterns of self-reinforcement are acquired imitatively (Bandura & Kupers, 1964). Children in one group observed either peer or adult models who adopted a high criterion for self-reinforcement during a bowling game like the one described. In this condition the model praised and rewarded his performance (by helping himself to freely available treats) only when his bowling scores were high. When the model's scores were low he refrained from self-reward. In a second group children were exposed to models who exhibited a similar pattern of self-reward and self-disapproval except that these models adopted a relatively low criterion. Children in a control group observed no models. Tests of self-reward after exposure to the models revealed that the children's reinforcement patterns closely matched those of the model they had observed.

Figure 19-5 shows the children's self-reward when they achieved low, moderate, and high performance levels for bowling in each condition. Note that the children who initially were exposed to high-standard adults are the ones who later made their own self-reinforcement almost always contingent on high levels of performance. In contrast, children who had observed low-standard models, or no models, were relatively more casual and lenient in their self-reinforcement; they treated themselves generously even after moderate or mediocre achievements. An-

**Figure 19-5**  SELF-REINFORCEMENT AT EACH PERFORMANCE LEVEL BY CONTROL CHILDREN AND THOSE EXPOSED TO ADULTS MODELING HIGH AND LOW STANDARDS FOR SELF-REWARD

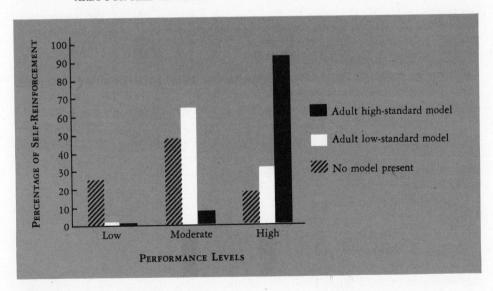

Adapted from Bandura and Kupers (1964).

other part of the same study showed that adults generally served as more powerful models than peers in the transmission of self-reinforcing patterns.

In this and similar studies each child's self-reward behavior was observed after exposure to the experimental treatments under conditions that led him to think he was all alone. In fact, the child was watched through a one-way mirror while he performed alone. The reason for providing the subject with ostensible privacy is to assure that his performance does not merely reflect social pressure and "demands" from the experimenter. That is, the final testing conditions must be dissociated from the experimenter and his implicit demands if the person's behavior is to be taken as an index of his "internalized" standards (e.g., Aronfreed, 1968).

Under these conditions of privacy external constraints were minimal and the children could indulge themselves freely in self-gratification. However, they did not simply help themselves to all the rewards they could get; instead, they regulated their own behavior. The manner of self-regulation depended on numerous factors and especially on immediately prior observation of the standards employed by other people. It also has been shown that the modeled standards may persist and generalize: children continue to set higher standards for themselves even in new situations several weeks after observing a high-standard model (Lepper, Sagotsky & Mailer, 1975).

## DO AS I SAY OR DO AS I DO?

How does the relationship between the standards that the socialization agent practices and those that he "preaches" to the child affect his impact on the child's subsequent self-control? Take, for example, the common case of the parent who tries to instill self-control in his child while he himself models self-indulgence. Consider the father who regularly urges his son to study hard while he himself lounges in front of the television set. When researchers refer to "consistency" in child-rearing practices they usually mean consistency in direct training techniques across different situations; almost no attention has been given to the effects of consistency or discrepancy between direct training and modeling procedures. When an adult model acts one way himself but imposes opposite demands on the child, how will the child act afterwards when he is on his own: Will he do what the model did himself or what the model asked him to do? To investigate this question, Mischel and Liebert (1966) studied the effects of discrepancies in the stringency of the self-reward standards used by an adult and the criteria she imposed on a child.

In this study children participated with a female adult model in a task (the bowling game) that seemingly required skill but on which scores were experimentally controlled. Both the model and the subject had free access to a large supply of tokens that could be exchanged later for attractive rewards and prizes. In one condition, the model rewarded herself only for high performances but guided the subject to reward himself for lower achievements; in a second condition the model rewarded herself for low performances but led the subject to reward himself only for high achievements; in the third group the model rewarded herself only for high performances and guided the child to reward himself only for equally high achievements. After exposure to these experimental procedures the children's self-reward patterns displayed in the model's absence were observed and scored through a one-way mirror.

When the observed and imposed criteria were consistent they later were adopted and maintained readily by all children. The experiment illustrated that self-reactions are affected jointly by the criteria displayed by social models and the standards directly imposed on the child. The children's self-reward patterns were determined by a predictable interaction of both observational and direct training processes. As Figure 19-6 indicates, when the modeled and imposed standards were consistently high, the children adopted them uniformly. When they were inconsistent, the children who had been allowed to be lenient (although the model was stringent) all remained lenient. Those who had been trained to be stringent by a model who herself was lenient seemed conflicted, and about half of them remained stringent and half became lenient.

Finally, in a posttest the children demonstrated the game to a younger child, still in the absence of external constraints and of the experimenter herself. It was found that the children consistently both demonstrated and imposed on their peers the same standards that they had adopted for themselves, hence transmitting their own learned self-reward criteria to others.

Figure 19-6    SELF-REWARD AND REWARD OF OTHER CHILD, AS A FUNCTION OF THE INITIAL CRITERIA EXHIBITED BY THE MODEL AND IMPOSED ON THE SUBJECT

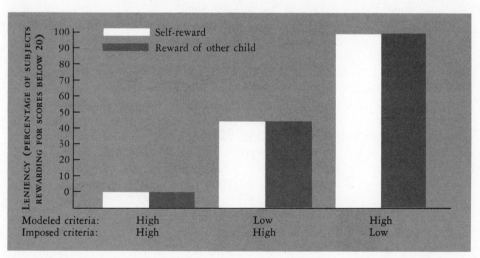

Adapted from Mischel and Liebert (1966).

## COMPENSATION AND SELF-CONGRATULATION

Often self-reward seems to be a congratulatory reaction contingent on success-ful performance or attainment of adequate achievements, as in the previously dis-cussed studies. Self-gratification also appears, however, under opposite circum-stances, namely following painful failure or stress experiences. Not uncommonly, persons seem to become more generous with themselves after failure or other un-happy experiences, and indulge themselves with extra gratifications whose primary function may be to reduce the aversiveness of the prior unpleasant experiences. Such self-indulgence seems to have a therapeutic rather than a self-congratulatory effect.

When people think that they are doing well on a task they generally reward themselves more generously than when they believe that their performance is less meritorious (e.g., Kanfer & Phillips, 1970; Kanfer & Marston, 1963a,b). As ex-pected, success on a task tends to increase self-reward on it and failure tends to lower self-reward for one's performance. But how do such success and failure ex-periences influence later, *noncontingent* self-gratification, that is, self-gratification in a domain that is objectively irrelevant to the initial success or failure?

If a person has experienced failure at work, for example, he might continue to recriminate himself later at home and self-punitively deprive himself of readily available pleasures. Or, instead, he might become more self-indulgent at home, en-gaging in self-therapeutic efforts to reduce the aversiveness of the earlier work failure. Similarly, after a successful achievement, the individual might feel more generally deserving and become more self-indulgent and generous to himself. Al-ternatively, some psychodynamically oriented theories might suggest that after suc-cess a person should have less need for gratification (and greater frustration toler-ance) and would therefore become less self-indulgent.

To study the role of these emotional experiences in the self-regulation of grati-fication, one experiment investigated how success and failure experiences in an achievement activity affect subsequent self-gratification in a new nonachievement situation (Mischel, Coates & Raskoff, 1968). In the new situation success was no issue; instead the child was able to indulge himself freely and noncontingently, as long as he wanted to do so and as generously as he wished. Specifically, grade school children were led to believe that they had either succeeded or failed re-peatedly in the bowling game. Just as in the earlier studies, the game seemed to require skill, but actually the scores were controlled electronically by the experi-menter without the children's awareness. In one group children were led to believe that their bowling achievements were excellent while another group failed and a third (control) received no scores.

The main question was how these success and failure experiences would affect self-gratification in a new situation that permitted the children to indulge them-selves freely and *noncontingently* with reinforcers. The new situation was an ex-ceedingly simple activity structured to be so easy that all children could do it readily. The reinforcers were huge supplies of tokens that could be exchanged for attractive treats and that were available noncontingently so that the children could help themselves to as many as they wished. To minimize inhibitions each child was left entirely alone, although his behavior was observed through a one-way mirror.

After failure there was no significant self-therapeutic compensating or self-consolation through greater indulgence, nor was there self-deprivation of the available resources (Figure 19-7). The children who had a failure experience seemed to be able to separate it psychologically from the new and different maze task and were not statistically different from those who had received no scores at all for performance on the bowling game. The main effect, instead, was that children who had a successful experience later tended to become more generous and indulgent with themselves, gratifying themselves more than did subjects who had failed and those who had no performance feedback. Feeling strongly positive and "glowing with success" (Isen, 1970), the youngsters seem to have celebrated by helping themselves more generously to freely available, noncontingent gratifications.

Related research has shown the importance of the person's momentary emotional state not only for his self-reactions but also for his reactions to others. Whether one feels good or bad, happy or sad, influences such diverse actions as generosity and charitability to other people as well as to oneself. Specifically, positive feelings tend to encourage greater generosity (e.g., Isen, Horn & Rosenhan, 1973) and altruism (e.g., Rosenhan, Moore & Underwood, 1975) as well as greater noncontingent self-gratification (e.g., Mischel, Coates & Raskoff, 1968; Moore, Underwood & Rosenhan, 1973).

## THE VARIETY OF SELF-REACTIONS

The work discussed so far in this chapter merely provided some selected examples from the large number of investigations that have dealt with the many as-

**Figure 19-7**  NONCONTINGENT SELF-GRATIFICATION AFTER SUCCESS AND FAILURE

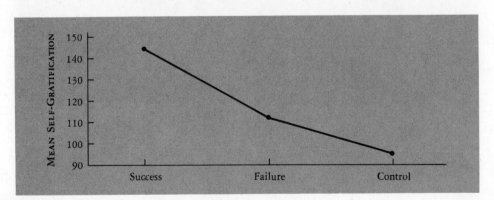

From sequential condition in Mischel, Coates, and Raskoff (1968).

pects of self-reactions and self-control. Such researches are much too numerous to be even listed here comprehensively. They included, for example, experiments on the determinants of self-criticism (e.g., Aronfreed, 1968; Grusec, 1966), resistance to temptation (e.g., Burton, Maccoby & Allinsmith, 1961; Mischel & Gilligan, 1964), and conscience and guilt after transgression (e.g., Grinder, 1964), as well as many other aspects of self-regulation (e.g., Thoresen & Mahoney, 1974).

## CONTROL OF VISCERAL AND GLANDULAR RESPONSES

Most work on personality and self-control has focused on the control of motoric and verbal behaviors—such as voluntary actions and choices. Through the application of reinforcement principles it also may be possible to achieve substantial control of autonomic responses, such as the "involuntary" glandular and visce-

**Figure 19-8**  MODIFICATION OF INTESTINAL CONTRACTION AND HEART RATE

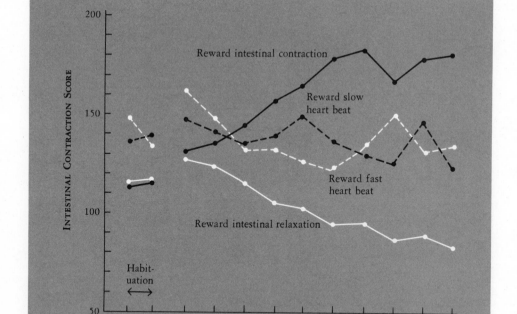

Graph showing that the intestinal contraction score is changed by rewarding either increases or decreases in intestinal contractions but is unaffected by rewarding changes in heart rate.

ral responses involved in emotion (Miller, 1969) and of the electrical waves that accompany brain activity (Stoyva & Kamiya, 1968).

Indeed, laboratory explorations with animals indicate that such supposedly involuntary bodily responses as salivation, kidney functions, stomach contractions, blood volume in the periphery of the body, heart rate, and brain waves all can be significantly affected by making reinforcement contingent upon increases or decreases in those responses. Some representative findings with animals are summarized in Figure 19-8.

As the figure shows, reward contingent on specific body changes affected those changes predictably. For example, reward for intestinal contractions increased the contractions, while reward for intestinal relaxation decreased them. The effects were highly specific, so that reward for intestinal contraction or relaxation did not affect heart rate. Conversely, heart rate was changed by rewarding increases or decreases in heart rate, but it was not influenced by rewarding changes in intestinal contractions. The implications of these findings are exciting for future forms of

**Figure 19-8** *(cont.)*

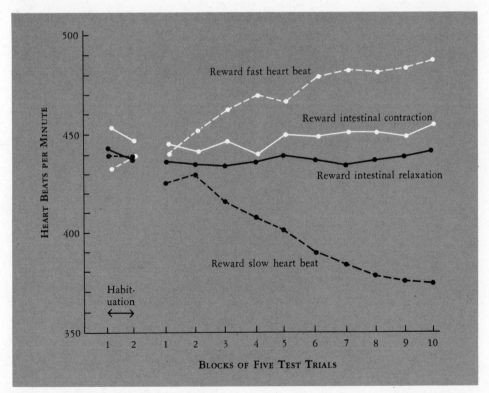

Graph showing that the heart rate is changed by rewarding either increases or decreases in heart rate but is unaffected by rewarding changes in intestinal contractions. (From Miller & Banuazizi, 1968.)

therapy directed at alleviating all sorts of emotional and psychosomatic problems. But as Miller (1969) has said, it is too early to promise any cures.

## BIOFEEDBACK AND ELECTRIC ZEN?

In some human investigations of the same phenomenon, the individual is made aware of his own bodily responses (for example, by observing an ongoing recording of his brain waves). If he gets appropriate immediate feedback about changes in these responses he may learn to control them voluntarily (Kamiya, 1967), perhaps in a manner similar to that employed by Zen masters and mystics in their practice of self-control of bodily activities. Studies of this type suggest the possibility that people may be able to achieve far greater control over themselves and their own bodily states than usually has been believed. If individuals can learn and apply appropriate self-reinforcement and feedback principles to themselves they may be able to achieve mastery over many aspects of their being, including their physiological state.

The name adopted for human laboratory applications based on the foregoing operant conditioning research is "biofeedback." In the example illustrated in Figure 19-9, the subject receives biofeedback about her brain rhythms. A tone tells her when she achieves certain distinctive brain waves (recall the discussion in Chapter 10, p. 198), such as those found in deep meditation. With increasing practice one may more easily achieve desired internal states, guided by feedback about one's physiological condition.

**Figure 19-9**  EXAMPLE OF BIOFEEDBACK

In this application, electrodes on the scalp monitor brain waves (EEG) shown on the polygraph console. The waves are filtered and converted into a tone. The subject receives continuous immediate feedback about her brain waves through the tones transmitted in the earphones.

There are some fascinating parallels between the efforts to achieve control of internal bodily responses through biofeedback (and "operant conditioning") on the one hand and, on the other hand, the attempts of mystics (including those influenced by Zen, Yoga, and other "esoteric" traditions) to get into closer contact with their bodily states and internal "signals." Both strategies involve observing (monitoring) one's own inner states and changing them through some internal, and perhaps indescribable, effort. Ornstein (1972, pp. 195–196) compares the two strategies this way:

> There are, now, two major procedures available for contacting the weak signals within. In the esoteric traditions, one tries to turn off the competing activity, to turn day into night, so that the subtle signals are perceptible. In the newly developed feedback system, the "stars" are brought to consciousness by another method. The faint signals *themselves* are amplified, to make them perceptible even in the brilliance of the daylight. In the esoteric traditions, the "noise" is lessened; in biofeedback research, the "signal" is strengthened. In both cases, when these normally unconscious processes enter consciousness, we can receive this subtle information, and can learn to control what was previously an "unconscious" or "autonomic" process.

These parallels are intriguing. But it must be emphasized that although some popular reports "have given the impression that Electric Zen is just around the corner for all, this prophecy will be fulfilled only (if at all) after years of research" (Ornstein, 1972, p. 196). Similar cautions are being sounded by many other researchers who warn that the therapeutic benefit of biofeedback is still more of a promise than a fact (e.g., Blanchard & Young, 1973; Schwartz, 1973).

## CONTROLS AS TRAITS: MORAL BEHAVIOR

So far this chapter has examined experimental research on some of the conditions that determine self-control and self-reactions. In self-regulation, as in most other forms of behavior, great differences exist among individuals. As part of the long-standing tradition of examining individual differences on personality dimensions, many psychologists have studied self-control behaviors as indices of traits. They have tried to relate the person's hypothesized position on these trait dimensions to other aspects of his behavior (using the methods of construct validity discussed in Chapter 8).

### EGO CONTROLS

Some investigators have studied individual differences in children's patterns of "ego control," that is, their ability to cope with their impulses and with environmental demands. In one study the adequacy and type of ego control were inferred

from ratings of the children's tendency to inhibit impulses as well as from oberva-
tions of their delay behavior in experimental situations (Block & Martin, 1955).
The children also were exposed to a frustration similar to the one in the classic
Barker, Dembo, and Lewin research (described in Chapter 16) in which a barrier
separated the child from desired and expected toys. The "undercontrolling" children (those who had been rated as not inhibiting their impulses) reacted more violently to the frustrating barrier than did "overcontrolling," inhibited children. The
undercontrolling youngsters also showed a greater decrement in their level of play
constructiveness after being frustrated.

Individual differences in ego control also have been inferred from indirect
measures such as responses to inkblots on the Rorschach test (e.g., Singer, 1955;
Spivack, Levine & Sprigle, 1959). Individuals who are high (rather than low) on
such indices of ego control tend to be somewhat more able to control and inhibit
their motoric activity; for example, they may be able to sit still longer or draw a
line more slowly without lifting their pencil.

## DELAY OF GRATIFICATION

The beginning of this chapter discussed the determinants of delay of gratification found in experimental research. Delay of gratification has also been conceptualized as a personality trait on which individuals differ, and the correlates of
those differences have been studied (as was discussed in Chapter 8), yielding many
relationships between preferences for immediate, smaller or delayed, larger rewards
and other theoretically relevant behaviors.

Two contrasting patterns of delay and impulsivity have been conceptualized as
extreme poles (e.g., Mischel, 1966b; 1974). On one end is the individual who predominantly chooses larger, delayed rewards or goals for which he must either wait
or work. This person is more likely to be oriented toward the future (Klineberg,
1968) and to plan carefully for distant goals. He also is apt to have high scores on
"ego control" measures, high achievement motivation, to be more trusting and socially responsible, to have a high level of aspiration, and to show less uncontrolled
impulsivity. This extreme pattern resembles what has been called the "Puritan
character structure." Socioculturally, this pattern tends to be found most often in
middle and upper (in contrast to lower) socioeconomic classes, and in highly
achievement-oriented ("Protestant Ethic") cultures. This pattern of high ego
strength is also related to a relatively high level of competence, as revealed by
higher intelligence, more mature cognitive development, and a greater capacity for
sustained attention (Grim, Kohlberg & White, 1968).

At the opposite extreme is the individual who predominantly prefers immediate gratification and declines the alternative of waiting or working for larger, delayed goals. Correlated with this is a greater concern with the immediate present
than with the future, and greater impulsivity. Socioculturally, this pattern is correlated with membership in the lower socioeconomic classes, with membership in
cultures in which the achievement orientation is low, and with indices of lesser
social and cognitive competence.

In their extreme forms, both these patterns might be "maladaptive": the former might characterize an emotionally constricted person whose gratifications are perpetually postponed, and the latter, an impulsive person who does not behave in accord with long-term goals and who is not cognizant of the ultimate consequences of his present actions. Clinically, persons diagnosed as "delinquents" and "psychopaths" are often characterized by an immediate reward choice pattern (Shybut, 1968).

The foregoing polarity of gratification patterns has some descriptive value. It is limited, however, by the fact that self-control patterns tend to be highly discriminative. For example, Trinidadian lower-class subjects rarely chose to wait for promised delayed rewards. Instead they usually preferred immediately available, albeit smaller, gratifications (Mischel, 1958, 1961a). In their past experiences promises of future rewards had often been broken, and these people had participated in a culture in which immediate gratification was modeled and rewarded extensively (Mischel, 1961b,c). Nevertheless, the same people saved money, planned elaborately, and were willing to give up competing immediate gratifications in order to plan ahead for such future rewards as annual feasts, religious events, and carnival celebrations.

Similarly, it has been found that answers on questionnaires dealing with attitudes and hypothetical matters may correlate with answers on other questionnaires but are less likely to relate to nonquestionnaire behavior (Mischel, 1962). In one study children were asked questions about whether or not they would postpone immediate, smaller rewards for the sake of larger, delayed outcomes in hypothetical situations (e.g., "If your father gave you a choice between a cheap, new bicycle now or a fancy, racing bike next month, which would you take?") Their answers here were related to their verbal responses on other questionnaires dealing with trust and a variety of verbally expressed attitudes. What they said, however, was not related to what they actually did in real delay of reward choices that went beyond questionnaires—for example, choices between things like candy and cheap toys now or more attractive objects later.

## PERCEIVED LOCUS OF CONTROL

People also differ in the degree to which they believe that they have self-control and feel personally responsible for what happens to them. According to Rotter (1966) such perceptions involve a dimension of "perceived locus of control" (also called "internal-external control of reinforcement"). *Internal control* refers to "the perception of positive and/or negative events as being a consequence of one's own actions and thereby under personal control" (Lefcourt, 1966, p. 207). Conversely, *external control* refers to the "perception of positive and/or negative events as being unrelated to one's own behaviors" (Lefcourt, 1966, p. 207) and hence beyond personal control. Individual differences on this internal-external control dimension have been measured by a questionnaire that has yielded many correlates (e.g., Phares, Ritchie & Davis, 1968; Rotter, 1966, 1975). For example, more intelligent people tend to perceive more outcomes as under their own control, presumably because they in fact can control their fate better than can less competent individuals.

People often react quite differently to situations in which the pay-offs or outcomes seem to involve luck or chance and those that, instead, appear to depend on their own skill. Many variables may affect whether or not an individual will attribute responsibility to himself for the outcomes that he encounters. For example, people attribute causality to internal sources more for success outcomes than for failure outcomes: they tend to credit success to themselves but to blame failure on external conditions (Fitch, 1970).

Internal-external control may not be a single dimension. For example, it is helpful to distinguish between perceived locus of control at the *personal* (self) and *ideological* (social system) levels (Lao, 1970). Thus among black college students in the deep South, an "internal" belief in personal control (that is, attributing responsibility for personal outcomes to the self) was positively related to general competence. However, an "external" belief in social ideology (that is, blaming the "system" rather than the self for the black's disadvantages in society) was related positively to creative, innovative behavior. As Lao noted, it is not always desirable and adaptive for the individual to believe in internal control and to blame himself. She reports that black students who can focus on "system obstacles" (societal barriers and racial discrimination) seem to be more realistic in their assessment of the situation, and they are more likely to select innovative occupational roles and social action.

Perceived locus of control may be of special theoretical importance because it seems to influence how people may react to many situations (Lefcourt, 1972; Phares, 1973). We saw that reactions to stress seem to be affected by whether or not the individual believes he can control the stress stimuli (that is, prevent or terminate pain), as was discussed in Chapter 17. Perceived control over impending aversive stimuli appears to affect whether a person will react by cognitively avoiding them or by becoming vigilantly alert to them (Chapter 18).

## MORAL BEHAVIOR AND THE SUPEREGO

Another aspect of self-control whose consistency has been carefully studied is "moral behavior." A classic investigation more than 40 years ago exposed thousands of children to a host of situations in which they could cheat, lie, and steal in many settings, including the home, party games, and athletic contests (Hartshorne & May, 1928). The children were fairly consistent in their self-reported thoughts and opinions about moral issues when they were questioned in their classrooms. The correlations among various forms of these paper-and-pencil tests also tended to be relatively high. But when different forms of the tests were administered in diverse social settings (such as lying at home, cheating in Sunday school, stealing at club meetings, being dishonest in the classroom), the correlations were much lower. The more the situation was altered the more inconsistent the youngsters' moral behavior became.

Hartshorne and May did not suggest capriciousness in behavior. They recognized beyond-chance consistencies, but they stressed the relative specificity of responses and their dependence on the exact particulars of the evoking situation.

> It may be contended of course that as a matter of fact we rarely reach a zero correlation, no matter how different may be our techniques, and that this implies some such common factor in the individual as might properly be called a trait. We would not wish to quarrel over the use of a term and are quite ready to recognize the existence of some common factors which tend to make individuals differ from one another on any one test or on any group of tests. Our contention, however, is that this common factor is not an inner entity operating independently of the situations in which the individuals are placed but is a function of the situation in the sense that an individual behaves similarly in different situations in proportion as these situations are alike, have been experienced as common occasions for honest or dishonest behavior, and are comprehended as opportunities for deception or honesty (Hartshorne & May, 1928, p. 385).

Burton (1963) reanalyzed some of the Hartshorne and May data from their most reliable tests of resistance to temptation. Often the resulting reanalysis has been cited as if it were evidence for the consistency of moral behavior. But Burton's reanalysis revealed no errors in the original work; it only reconstrued the same correlations in a way that emphasized the moderate (but statistically significant) consistencies that were found in the original study. Thus a person's moral behaviors across diverse situations are not totally unrelated (i.e., random), but they are far from consistent.

Hartshorne and May's finding of relative specificity in moral behavior foreshadowed the results of later research. Since Hartshorne and May, most research on self-control and moral behavior has focused on three areas: moral judgment and verbal standards of right and wrong (e.g., Kohlberg, 1963); resistance to temptation in the absence of external constraints (e.g., Aronfreed, 1968); and feeling guilty after transgression (e.g., Allinsmith, 1960; Sears, Maccoby & Levin, 1957). Behaviors across these three areas of morality are only minimally interrelated (e.g., Becker, 1964; Hoffman, 1963; Kohlberg, 1964). Moreover, within each subtype of morality, specificity again tends to be high, so that what a person does on one moral task is not necessarily related to what he does on another one (e.g., Aronfreed, 1961; Sears, Rau & Alpert, 1965).

In sum, the data on self-control and moral behavior do not support the existence of a unitary, intrapsychic moral agency like the superego, nor do they suggest a unitary trait of conscience or honesty. Rather than a homogeneous conscience that determines all aspects of self-control, people seem to develop subtler discriminations that depend on many conditions. Self-control patterns and moral actions as well as immoral ones are affected by the same discrimination learning that influences other forms of behavior (such as anxiety and cognitive avoidance) considered in earlier chapters. Consequently it should not be surprising that self-control and moral behavior also become relatively specific to particular situations and tend to be idiosyncratically (uniquely) patterned within each individual.

## PEOPLE AS MORAL PHILOSOPHERS

In addition to learning diverse forms of overt self-control, people also differ in their ideas and attitudes about justice, right and wrong, and the nature of conscience. Under the influence of Jean Piaget's studies of cognitive development in children, Kohlberg (1963) has studied these individual differences, focusing on the child as a "moral philosopher" who constructs theories about morality.

Influenced by Piaget's cognitive developmental stages, Kohlberg has hypothesized three levels of moral thinking (preconventional, conventional, and postconventional). He further suggests that each of the three levels contains two related stages. These six hypothesized stages of cognitive development are summarized in Table 19-1.

Kohlberg believes that these six moral stages follow a developmental progression that is a function of increasing cognitive maturation. While social experience may affect the rate of progress across stages, he believes that the nature of the sequence is fundamentally the same even in such widely different cultures as the U.S., Taiwan, Mexico, Turkey, and Yucatan. A person's stage position is inferred from the kind of reasoning displayed on a moral judgment scale that presents a number of moral dilemmas.

Kohlberg (1968) buttresses his argument for moral stages with many intriguing cases. For example, he cites the answers of a boy, Tommy, to the question, "Is it better to save the life of one important person or a lot of unimportant people?" At age 10, Tommy's answer seems to confuse the value of a human being with the value of the property that he owns. Thus he answers that he would save the many unimportant people because they might have more furniture and even more money collectively, although "it doesn't look it." At age 13, Tommy's answers start to show the characteristics of Stage 2, and gradually (at age 16) his orientation is closer to Stage 3.

A person's moral reasoning typically does not fit any one stage exclusively. As Kohlberg (1969, p. 387, Fig. 6.4) reports, on the average somewhat less than 50 percent of a subject's moral judgments fit a single stage, the remainder being distributed in the stages both above and below his most frequent one. Similarly, Bandura and McDonald (1963, p. 280) found that children from ages 5 to 11 years used different types of moral reasoning simultaneously. Among college students "not one of the subjects studied employed moral reasoning that was exclusively rated at any single level of development" (Fishkin and colleagues, 1973, p. 114).

Kohlberg's hypotheses will need much more research before final conclusions can be reached. Of special importance will be the relationship between a person's moral orientation and his moral behavior and other forms of self-control and social responsibility. Kohlberg suggests that people who "understand justice" act more

**Table 19-1    Moral Levels and Developmental Stages According to
Kohlberg (1963, 1967)**

| | |
|---|---|
| Preconventional Level | STAGE 1: Orientation toward punishment. Deference to superior power. Goodness or badness is determined by the physical consequences of action. |
| | STAGE 2: Right actions are those that satisfy needs (mainly one's own needs). People share but in a pragmatic way, not out of a sense of justice or loyalty. |
| Conventional Level | STAGE 3: "Good boy-good girl orientation." Behavior that pleases or helps others and is approved by them is good behavior. Emphasis on conformity and on being "nice" to gain approval. |
| | STAGE 4: Focus on authority, fixed rules, and the social order. Right behavior consists of maintaining the given social order for its own sake. Respect is earned by performing dutifully. |
| Postconventional Level | STAGE 5: "Social contract orientation"—legalistic, utilitarian. Standards that have been agreed upon by the whole society define right action. Emphasis upon procedural (legal) rules for reaching consensus. Awareness of the relativism of personal values. |
| | STAGE 6: Emphasis on decisions of conscience and self-chosen, abstract ethical principles that are "logical, comprehensive, universal, and consistent." These abstract ethical principles are universal principles of justice, of reciprocity and equality of human rights, and of respect for the dignity of human beings as individuals. |

justly. That point seems most reasonable in the abstract. However, the exact relations between moral thought and moral action merit much further empirical study and generally the associations that have been found are not high (Mischel & Mischel, 1975). A critical review of the total research within Kohlberg's approach and of his scale for assessing moral judgment concluded: ". . . There are *no* reported reliability estimates for the scale itself. . . . There is no clearly demonstrated connection between moral judgment, as measured by the Moral Judgment Scale, and moral action." (Kurtines & Greif, 1974, p. 468). One waits for future research to fill in some of the many gaps in our understanding of moral reasoning and its links to moral action.

How people reason about the solution of moral dilemmas is fascinating and age-related changes in this activity are especially informative. But an interest in moral reasoning does not reduce the need to understand the many other aspects and determinants of moral (and immoral) behavior. Alston (1971, p. 283), a philosopher, commenting on Kohlberg's position, puts it this way:

> . . . there is no reason to think that it [Kohlberg's moral stage assignments] will do the whole job. In fact, there is every reason to think that it will not. So long as there is any significant discrepancy between the moral judgment a person makes about a situation (or would make if the question arose) and what he actually does, there will be a need, in describing persons, for an account of what they are likely to do as well as what they are likely to think. And Kohlberg has given us no reason to suppose that there is no such significant discrepancy.

Generally, different measures of ideology, beliefs, and attitudes tend to be more closely related to each other than to what the person actually does in the same content area (Abelson, 1972; Mischel, 1968). This also seems to hold in the domain of morality, in which indices of moral ideology tend to relate well to other measures of social and political beliefs. For example, it is reassuring (but not particularly surprising) to find that a student responding to Kohlberg's moral dilemmas test with reasons involving principles of equality, the universality of all moral formulations, and concern with the issue of justice (thereby earning a Stage 6 score) would be unlikely to agree with a slogan such as "The best place for women in the [civil rights movement] is prone" (Fishkin et al., 1973). Similarly unsurprising, the same study found that individuals who dominantly justify their moral decisions in terms of law and order are less likely to endorse such slogans as "kill the pigs," "property is theft," and "turn on, tune in, and drop out." Such internal consistencies in belief statements were demonstrated by high correlations between moral reasoning that emphasizes law and order and a conservative opposition to radical violence on an ideology scale. These data provide further support for the well-established conclusion that answers to measures of political and social ideology tend to be consistent.

But while cognitive measures of beliefs and values may be both internally consistent and temporally enduring (E. L. Kelly, 1955), it is the link between them and behavior that remains tenuous (e.g., Abelson, 1972; Festinger, 1964; Kurtines & Greif, 1974). We should be alert to the fact that the same individual who espouses high moral principles also may engage in harmful, aggressive actions against others who violate his conceptions of justice. Pascal's comment, "evil is never done so thoroughly or so well as when it is done with a good conscience" is supported by the many historical and contemporary incidents in which the individuals who committed evil deeds seemed more deficient in compassion and empathy than in moral reasoning.

History is full of atrocities that were justified by invoking the highest principles and that were perpetrated upon victims who were equally convinced of their own moral principles. In the name of justice, of the common welfare, of universal ethics, and of God, millions of people have been killed and whole cultures destroyed. In recent history, concepts of universal right, equality, freedom, and national security have been used to justify every variety of crime including murder. Presidential assassinations, airplane hijackings, and massacres of Olympic athletes have been committed for allegedly selfless motives of highest morality and principle. The supreme moral self-sacrifices of the Japanese suicide pilots in World War II were perceived as moral outrages by others who did not share their perspective.

People may easily justify their own actions and commitments no matter how reprehensible they may seem to others. A wide variety of self-deceptive mechanisms may be used to facilitate and excuse the most horrendous acts. Invocation of higher principles, dehumanization of victims, diffusion and displacement of responsibility, blame attribution, and the adoption of inhumane codes for self-reinforcement all may serve to maintain extraordinarily cruel aggressions (Bandura, 1973).

## HAZARDS IN CATEGORIZING "GOOD" AND "BAD" PEOPLE

The extremely complex relations among diverse aspects of self-control within the same person, and the specific interactions between human conduct and the psychological conditions in which it occurs, prevent global generalizations about the "overall" nature and causes of moral—and immoral—actions. It is tempting but misleading to categorize people into the cross-situationally moral versus the broadly immoral. A world of good guys versus bad guys, as in the Western films in which the cowboys' white or black hats permit easy identification of the virtuous and the villainous, is seductive. More sophisticated social science versions of stratification systems that categorize people in terms of their overall level of morality, "ego strength," or "moral competence," unless carefully moderated, can lead to an elitism that is scientifically unjustified as well as socially hazardous (Mischel & Mischel, 1975). While it may be useful for some purposes to label and assess people's status on our dimensions of character and moral value, perhaps the greatest challenge to social science will be to discover the optimal conditions that can help each person realize himself in the ways he construes as best within the great range of capacities potentially open to him.

## SUMMARY

1. People learn to evaluate and control their own behavior and act in the light of future-oriented considerations. There have been many approaches to these processes. Some studies on self-control have explored the determinants of the individual's willingness to delay immediate, smaller grati-

fication for the sake of delayed but larger rewards and goals. The person's subjective expectations concerning the outcome of his choice influence his willingness to select delayed rather than immediate gratification. Will the delayed rewards for which he postpones immediate satisfaction actually materialize? Will they be worthwhile? Will he be able to earn them? A person's answers to these questions depend partly on his past history and on his observation of the behavior of social models. For example, after children were exposed to the patterns of delayed or immediate gratification displayed by social models, their own choices changed in accord with the preferences they had observed.

2. What are the psychological mechanisms through which persons can delay gratification for the sake of preferred but delayed outcomes? When young children attended to the available outcomes while waiting they were less able to wait for them. Thus under some conditions *not* thinking about the delayed outcomes seems to enhance effective delay behavior. Delay of gratification may be helped by cognitive and overt self-distractions to reduce the aversiveness of waiting.

3. Another pervasive feature of human social behavior is the self-administration and regulation of rewards and punishments. Persons learn to set their own performance standards and to make their self-reward contingent upon achievement of the self-prescribed criteria. Children's patterns of self-reward are influenced by the models whom they have observed, as well as by standards imposed on them through direct training. Self-reward patterns are also affected by the individual's immediately prior experience. For example, achieving success in one setting may influence later self-gratification in a different situation.

4. Apart from self-reward, people show other diverse forms of self-control such as self-punishment, conscience, and guilt after transgression. Even in the area of visceral and glandular responses, which are generally thought of as "involuntary," some mastery and self-control may be achieved, since these responses can be sensitively influenced by appropriate rewards or feedback. Some parallels were noted between "biofeedback" research and esoteric techniques to achieve greater contact with one's own bodily states.

5. People differ greatly in the control patterns they use. For example, one approach to individual differences in self-control has related measures of "ego control" to the person's ability to inhibit his motoric activity and impulsivity.

6. Individual differences in preference for delay of gratification also have been studied as a trait dimension and have been related to a variety of other behaviors.

7. There are great individual differences in perceived control over outcomes and perceived responsibility for the things that happen. Differences among people in perceived control have been conceptualized on a dimension of "internal-external" control of reinforcement. An individual's status on this dimension is related to many other aspects of his personality and may affect his interpretation of different situations.

8. Individuals show some consistency in their control patterns across situations. However there is much discrimination in control and self-reactions. Thus even people who often seem unable to wait for larger, delayed rewards may be able to delay gratification under the proper circumstances. Similarly, verbally expressed attitudes about delay of gratification may not be related to the actual choice behavior. The associations found among measures of moral judgment, verbal standards of right and wrong, and resistance to temptation tend to be low. Hence there is little support for the existence of a unitary concept of morality or superego, or for a unitary trait of conscience or honesty.

9. There may be some developmental regularity in the formation of children's ideas and attitudes about justice and morality. Six moral stages, fundamentally the same regardless of social experience, have been hypothesized by cognitive-developmental theory. While there is some consistency in moral reasoning, the same individual tends to use moral reasoning both above and below his most "typical" stage level. The links between moral reasoning and moral action often are complex and thin. The many hazards in trying to classify people into stable moral categories were noted.

# CHAPTER 20

# SELF-CONCEPTS AND ATTRIBUTION

In addition to being an organism that emits behavior in continuous interaction with the environment, man also perceives and interprets himself: he is "self-conscious." The individual as the perceiver and "knower" of his own behavior has been the focus of many phenomenological, cognitive, and "self" theories (Chapters 6 and 12). This chapter discusses some of man's self-perceptions and some of their relations to his actions.

## IMPRESSION FORMATION

To understand how enduring impressions about the self are formed, one may begin by seeing how impressions about other people are generated. Indeed the processes of forming self-impressions and of forming impressions of others may be identical (Bem, 1972; Kelley, 1973).

When you try to conceptualize other people you do not describe their motoric acts objectively, nor do you analyze their specific responses in relation to
particular stimuli. Instead, you form broad impressions about their characteristics
as people, evaluate their intentions, and assess their worth. To understand anyone's
actions (including one's own) the human perceiver tries to find the reasons for
them, and he does so by attributing intentions to the actor.

Heider (1958) has discussed many of the subjective or "common sense" features that people feel guide their perceptions of others and of themselves. These
features include judgments about intentions, personal causation and causal responsibility, ability, effort, and motives. For example, in daily relations, our perceptions
are affected dramatically by our assessments of whether or not an action was deliberate or accidental. Slamming a door, tossing a book, dropping a baby—the interpretation of these seemingly simple behaviors depends on inferences about the intentions and motives of the person who does them. Similarly our judgments of
ourselves and our behaviors presumably involve continuous self-assessments of our
guilt or innocence, our responsibility or immunity, our effort or laziness.

## ATTRIBUTION OF TRAITS AND MOTIVES

In forming their impressions, people thus proceed like trait theorists. On the
basis of behavioral cues they infer purposeful dispositions and motives in others
and in themselves. Moreover, they tend to infer such dispositions even when the
available cues are fragmentary and minimal.

Human observers tend to interpret even the simplest behaviors as signs of
underlying traits and motives, and they easily attribute elaborate intentions to behavioral sequences, rapidly going from observed acts to hypothesized dispositions.
They may even endow moving geometric shapes with purposes and emotions that
range from anger through fear (Michotte, 1954).

For example, when people watch a disk, a large triangle, and a smaller triangle moving about, they tend to interpret the shapes as if they were human beings
engaging in interpersonal conflicts and competitions: the larger triangle is seen as
aggressive while the smaller one may be heroic and the disk timid and feminine
(Heider & Simmel, 1944). From (1960) even suggests that what we think we see
always depends on the intentions we ascribe to others. Not that people really believe that cartoons or moving shapes possess psychological qualities; the findings
simply demonstrate how readily people can endow the agents of behavior with
trait attributes, responsibilities, and intentions, especially under ambiguous conditions.

## ORGANIZATION OF IMPRESSIONS

The impressions we form of each other are not perceived as isolated bits of
information, but rather as organized units. The nature of the organization depends

Judgments about the meaning of behavior depend on the context and judge as well as on the behavior.

on many variables, including the other cues in the situation, the sequence of observation, and the observer's concepts or categories.

Even the simplest impressions depend on the context in which the cues occur. In one study subjects gave impressions of outline drawings of three faces—one "glum," one "frowning," and one "smiling"—presented in pairs (Cline, 1956). The judgments made about each face depended in part on the face with which it was paired. When paired with the glum face, for example, the smiling face tended to be seen as dominant, vicious, gloating, and bullyish; when paired with the frowning face, however, the smiling face was interpreted as peaceful and peace-making, and as wanting to help and to be friendly.

In our impressions we easily go beyond the information given to us and infer a whole cluster of related traits on the basis of a few "central" ones. If "warmth" is attributed to a person, he is more likely to be perceived as also being generous, good natured, happy, sociable, and wise (Asch, 1946; Wishner, 1960). But if "cold" rather than "warm" is part of the stimulus configuration, observers are more likely to see the person as ungenerous, unhappy, irritable, and humorless. Many factors may influence which traits in a given constellation will have "central" influence on the rest of the traits that will be attributed to the stimulus person (Wishner, 1960).

People within a single culture often learn to make similar interpretations about the meaning of particular behaviors and attributes. "Tight" lips, "shifty" eyes, high foreheads, facial scars, are examples of the cues whose meanings as signs of personality may be identical for most members of a given culture. As a result of common learning experiences, observers may agree with each other about the meanings of such signs and may reach similar interpretations and labels from minimal cues. If a person wears glasses, for example, he will probably be perceived as intelligent (Thornton, 1944). The resulting stereotypes may be extremely efficient for many forms of casual communication because they permit us to categorize experiences without much cognitive effort. They also may be tragic, as when ethnic cues become the bases for bitter discrimination and prejudice, or physical infirmities and handicaps become cues for ridicule and abuse among children.

## CONSTRAINING EFFECTS OF FIRST IMPRESSIONS

The total image or impression that emerges in person perception tends to depend on the *sequence* of observations. For example, if we learn first that a person is sociable and later that he is also introverted, our impression of him is quite different than if the sequence is reversed (e.g., Luchins, 1957). Much research has been devoted to the mechanisms through which new information may be added to the total impression. One model, for example, suggests a *weighting* process in which every piece of information is averaged into the total impression, but later information is given a smaller weight than data already processed (e.g., Anderson, 1965, 1974). The means through which impressions are formed of oneself and others are receiving increasing theoretical attention (e.g., Bem, 1972; Kelley, 1967). In general, first impressions are especially important and are given extra weight in the total image that is formed. The earliest information seems to serve as a conceptual anchor or base that influences the interpretation or weighting of later information. This biasing effect of initial information is the "primacy effect."

The first impression or category that an observer generates about events (including other people and himself) thus influences his further observations about those events. Both sophisticated scientists and naive subjects intuitively but often erroneously interpret small samples of observations as if they were highly representative (Kahnemon & Tversky, 1973). Once an individual has categorized or grouped stimuli he may tend to retain the category he formed even when he gets contradictory evidence. Having formed his category or impression he may pay less attention to contradictory new information and may focus instead on information that confirms his hypothesis.

This constraining effect of a category has been shown in such diverse contexts as impression formation in person perception (e.g., Asch, 1946; Anderson, 1965; Wishner, 1960); hypothesis-testing in problem-solving (Davison, 1964; Wyatt & Campbell, 1951); and clinical diagnosis (e.g., Rubin & Shontz, 1960; Sines, 1959). In all these contexts people often generate impressions rapidly, even on the basis of little information, and then hold on to their hypotheses. For example, psychotherapists develop fairly stable images of their clients within the first four hours of psychotherapy. They tend to retain these categories more or less unchanged even after 24 therapy sessions (Meehl, 1960). In another study judges first formed their hypotheses about a subject by studying his biographical data and later observed him in nine role-playing situations. They employed the additional information mainly to confirm their initial conceptualizations (Soskin, 1959).

Here is an example of one experimental approach to studying the constraining effects of categories. College students were exposed to a series of decreasingly ambiguous stimuli in the form of out-of-focus slide pictures. On successive presentations, the focus became increasingly clear, and after each presentation the subject stated what he thought the picture was. The findings indicated that the hypotheses the subject formed during the early stages of inaccurate guessing constrained and retarded the development of more veridical perceptions of the stimulus (e.g., Davison, 1964; Wyatt & Campbell, 1951). Thus people tend to adhere to their concepts and to interpret new information in the light of available hypotheses.

This finding of primacy effects is based mainly on studies of short-term impression formation, usually within one brief experimental session. It is tempting to speculate that similar anchoring mechanisms and primacy effects may be involved in the enduring self-impression processes through which self-images and self-concepts are acquired during personality development. It seems likely that a person's impressions of himself also show strong primacy effects, the earliest images of ourselves probably serving to shape and selectively channel or bias the later information we get.

## THE IMPORTANCE OF THE PERCEIVER'S CATEGORIES

Our impressions about personality attributes thus depend partly on our concepts and stereotypes as well as on the attributes of the person whom we are perceiving. The important role of the observer's concepts was demonstrated in a study in which boys and girls who lived together at a camp gave free verbal descriptions of each other. Their descriptions were reliably coded into dispositional categories (Dornbusch et al., 1965). There were several conditions: either one child described two others, or two children described the same child, or two children described two different other children. The most similar (overlapping) descriptions were obtained when the same perceiver (A) rated *different* children (B and C); these descriptions overlapped more than when the same child (B) was described by different perceivers (A and C). The overall results thus revealed that the children's categories and interpersonal perceptions depended more on the perceiver than on the child who was being perceived.

Because the judges in this study were children there might have been special difficulties in obtaining accuracy. It might be expected that adults could overcome their own categories more readily and achieve ratings that primarily reflect the ratee's traits. As was previously discussed (Chapter 8), many sophisticated efforts have been made to show that adults are good raters. It may be recalled, however, that those studies also showed the importance of the observer's constructs.

Thus, the particular impressions that are formed depend on the concepts or categories available to the perceiver. Enormous informational inputs face the perceiver in the process of impression formation. These inputs about events, about people, and about oneself are simplified and restricted by the categories and the organizational limits available to the perceiver. By categorizing our perceptions into fewer and simpler dimensions and units, we place them within the limited scope of memory (e.g., Bruner, 1958). Incoming data are coded and simplified by assigning labels to them and sorting them into broader units. Without such information-processing it would be impossible to deal with the continuous flood of perceptions that impinge from the environment (Miller, 1956; Neisser, 1967). Thus the construction of stereotypes about other people, by assigning their many diverse behaviors into a few broader categories, may be highly adaptive.

The judgments that we make about traits tend to fall on a few broad categories or dimensions. Research on trait ratings (by factor analysis) has revealed three major dimensions (Chapter 8). This same set of dimensions is found for ratings of other people and for ratings of the self and of concepts and words (D'Andrade, 1965; Mulaik, 1964; Vernon, 1964). Usually a prominent good versus bad (evaluative) factor is found; this factor includes such traits as emotional stability and reliability versus instability. In addition, one often finds an extravert-introvert dimension and some variant of "active and strong" versus "passive and weak."

## SELF-CONCEPT FORMATION

Just as we form impressions of other people so also do we generate concepts about ourselves. Each normal person experiences himself as a distinct, continuous being or "object" with clear body boundaries. In the course of maturation, each individual develops attitudes toward that object and calls it names: "I" or "me" or "myself." To help make sense of man's feelings about himself, psychologists and philosophers have created such terms as the "ego" or the "self." Each of these nouns represents a way of thinking and speaking about one's experience rather than a "thing" or a psychic entity.

The discussion so far of constraints in impression formation should make it plain that the individual's self-concepts are not a simple mirror-like reflection of some absolute reality. Rather, self-concepts, like impressions of other aspects of the world, involve a synthesis and organization of a tremendous amount of information. Although self-concepts are not a mirror of reality, they are correlated with the outcomes that the person has obtained throughout his experience and that he ex-

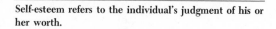
Self-esteem refers to the individual's judgment of his or her worth.

pects to obtain in the future. The same basic social learning and cognitive variables that determine the social behaviors discussed in earlier chapters also presumably influence the development of self-concepts. One of the most critical aspects of the self-concept is "self-esteem."

## SELF-ESTEEM

Self-esteem refers to the individual's personal judgment of his own worth (e.g., Coopersmith, 1967). Self-esteem is such an important aspect of the self-concept that the two terms are often used synonymously. Although "self-esteem" is sometimes discussed as if it were a single entity, it may be that a person evaluates his functioning in different areas of his life discriminatively. These self-evaluations presumably reflect in part the feedback that he continuously gets from the environment.

In one approach, self-concepts about one's adequacy may be thought of as consisting of both highly situation-specific, self-relevant performance expectancies and more generalized expectancies. According to Rotter (1954), "specific expectancies" refer to the individual's expectancies that a particular set of behaviors on his part will lead to particular outcomes (reinforcements) in the specific situation confronting him. "Generalized expectancies" refer to somewhat broader expectations regarding the probable outcomes of the person's behavior based on his past experiences and total history in similar situations. Both kinds of expectancies regarding future performance depend on information about past performance. The precise relationships between performance, performance feedback, and changes in the person's expectancies about himself have been studied extensively (e.g., Weiner, 1972).

Most studies on this topic are based on the "level-of-aspiration" situation devised by Kurt Lewin and extended by J. B. Rotter and others. In this situation, people typically are asked to verbalize their subjective expectations (sometimes their hopes or aspirations) with regard to how good their performance will be in a particular area. For example, students are requested to state their expectancies about the scores they are likely to obtain on tests of arithmetic reasoning, social competencies, interpersonal sensitivity, and so on. They are told to record their estimated scores for each of these tests on a scale (for example, 0 to 100) and are given information about norms and average scores obtained by other people who supposedly took the tests before.

Thereafter the students take parts of the tests and are given feedback about the quality of their performance. Depending on the experimental condition to which the individual is assigned, his score might be considerably above ("success") or below ("failure") his stated expectancy. All subjects are asked again to state their expectancies for the next series of performances. These new tests are described in ways designed to systematically vary their similarity to the tasks on which the person has already received feedback.

Studies of this type have shown that specific self-concepts about performance level generally tend to follow more or less directly the feedback the person receives from his experiences. For example, after repeated failure on a task, a person usually expects to fail it again. Moreover, the expectancies formed in one situation also tend to generalize to other related situations to the degree that they are perceived as similar and as likely to lead to similar outcomes or reinforcements.

While self-concept changes are related to the feedback that the individual gets about himself, the relationship may be influenced by many important variables. For example, people who are highly oriented to achievement and who are anxious to avoid failure may react quite differently to failure experiences than do people who are low in achievement striving (e.g., Atkinson & Feather, 1966; Heckhausen, 1969; Weiner, 1965, 1974). Depending on such moderating variables, the person may adopt many different strategies to cope with performance feedback. Hence self-concept changes are not a direct reflection of performance feedback; they are mediated by many other factors.

Self-concepts are related to other aspects of behavior, such as dependency, conformity, and susceptibility to influence. For example, Gelfand (1962) defined self-esteem in terms of the value an individual places on himself and reasoned that this value depends upon past success and failure experiences. Presumably, then, the high-esteem individual has had a past history of chiefly positive reinforcement for his behavior, while a low-esteem person has failed in many situations.

Gelfand attempted to alter self-concept through administration of success or failure. Her results indicated that self-ratings changed significantly in the expected direction: success increased self-esteem and failure decreased it, at least momentarily. Most interesting, people low in initial self-esteem were more easily influenced to conform (by verbal conditioning) than were those high in rated self-esteem. This was interpreted as support for an earlier finding which had suggested that high self-esteem persons were generally less dependent upon situational pressures and hence less influenced by experimental manipulations.

Gelfand also found that, regardless of initial level of self-esteem, people who experienced failure became more susceptible to subsequent manipulations than those who experienced success. Finally, subjects exposed to experiences inconsistent with their customary self-evaluations (high-esteem persons who experienced failure and low-esteem persons who experienced success) were more influenced (on the verbal conditioning task) than were those whose experiences were congruent with their initial self-opinions.

In a more naturalistic investigation, Coopersmith (1967, 1968) studied a sample of normal, middle-class urban boys from preadolescence to early adulthood. He examined their family backgrounds through interviews and exposed the children to diverse personality and ability tests. For example, he assessed how high the children set their goals in situations such as the "bean bag" study illustrated in Figure 20-1. He then analyzed the patterns that emerged.

His results suggest that children with high self-esteem tend to be those who are more esteemed and more competent; they also tend to be those who are exposed to parental models who display high self-esteem (Coopersmith, 1967, 1968). Some of the specific child-rearing practices associated with self-esteem in the boys are summarized in Figure 20-2.

Coopersmith found that if he categorized the boys into three levels or degrees of self-esteem (low, medium, and high), certain traits seemed to best fit each level. Although there were many exceptions, and the relationships generally were of only modest strength, some consistent trends emerged (see Figure 20-2). Coopersmith noted some of the trait terms that seem to best fit boys of different degrees of self-esteem; examples of these relationships are summarized in Table 20-1. As these examples suggest, the high-self-esteem youngsters seemed to be the ones who felt and behaved more competently. Presumably these qualities helped them to achieve more recognition and self-satisfaction and, in turn, their self-esteem was strengthened by their achievements.

A person's self-esteem is also related to his perceived masculinity-femininity or sex-role identity. Sex-role identity refers to the person's conceptualization of his own degree of masculinity or femininity. A vital part of self-esteem involves attitudes about sex-role adequacy. For example, the young man who feels he is "too feminine" and who believes that to be an adequate person he must somehow be more "masculine" may experience great distress. Some studies indicate that general level of self-esteem may be correlated with various indices of masculinity-femininity. Sears (1970) found that in sixth-grade children, self-reported femininity (on a questionnaire) was associated with poor self-concepts in both boys and girls. Moreover, high self-concepts in both sexes were associated with high maternal and paternal "warmth."

**Figure 20-1**   SELF-ESTEEM AND GOAL-SETTING

The more distant the target that the child selects in the "beanbag game" the higher the score that he could win but the greater the risk of failing. From Coopersmith (1968).

## SELF-ESTEEM AND SELECTIVE ATTENTION TO THE SELF

Throughout this chapter we have assumed that the self may be viewed as an object about which information is available. Given this assumption, it becomes important to ask what determines the type of information about the self to which the

**Figure 20-2**  PERCENTAGE OF CHILDREN IN EACH SELF-ESTEEM GROUP RATED NEGA-
TIVELY BY THEIR MOTHERS

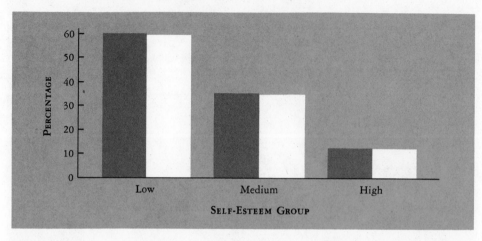

Children with lower self-esteem were appraised more often by their mothers as having marked, frequent problems (black bars) rather than limited, infrequent ones, and also as being relatively destructive (white bars) rather than nondestructive. (Based on data from Coopersmith, 1967).

individual attends. The potential information available about the self is almost
boundless. Depending on where one looks and how one searches, it is possible to
attend to widely diverse data about oneself. We can seek, and doubtless find, information to support our strengths or weaknesses, our successes or failures, almost
endlessly. Since a person's experiences are neither completely successful nor totally
negative, it is important to ask what determines selective attention to information
about the self.

**TABLE 20-1    Examples of Trait Terms Characterizing Boys
of High and Low Self-Esteem**

| SELF-ESTEEM | DESCRIPTIVE TRAIT TERMS |
|---|---|
| High | Active, expressive, successful; little childhood destructiveness and not much anxiety; self-confident, optimistic. |
| Low | Discouraged, felt depressed, unlovable, fearful of angering others, isolated from others; shrank away from being noticed. |

Based on Coopersmith (1968).

To explore this question one study attempted to experimentally alter the momentary self-esteem of college students with regard to mental abilities (Mischel, Ebbesen & Zeiss, 1973). In a second phase the study assessed how the changes affected the students' selective attention to written information about their positive as opposed to negative personality traits. People who were led to feel more positive about their abilities, it was found, spent more time attending to other positive (relative to negative) information about their personalities. Thus, "feeling good" about oneself may produce further, chain-like effects on other aspects of the person's behavior: the person who feels good about himself may selectively channel his attention and cognitions to quite different experiences than does the person whose feelings toward himself are more negative. The effects of success and failure depended both on the individual's expectancies in the situation and on his tendency to avoid threatening information. The latter tendency was inferred from scores on the Byrne (1964) "repression-sensitization" self-report scale. Thus alterations in self-esteem may produce changes in selective attention to other aspects of the self, but the effects are complex and depend both on momentary expectations and on more stable individual differences in information-seeking. Essentially similar conclusions come from much other research on the self (Gergen, 1971).

People who differ on the dimension of perceived locus of control also may react differently to information about the self (Phares, Ritchie & Davis, 1968). Groups of college students were selected who were either relatively "internal" or "external" on a self-report measure of perceived locus of control. As discussed in the last chapter, "internal" subjects are those who most often report that they control (cause and are responsible for) the reinforcements that occur in their lives; "externals," in contrast, say that these outcomes are due to luck or to other external conditions outside their control. These two groups then were administered a set of personality tests. Later they were provided reports that contained positive and negative information about their personalities. Externals recalled more of the negative material about themselves than did internals.

## THE SELF-PERCEPTION OF EMOTIONS

Another quality of the self is the subjective experience of emotions; we are aware of our own feelings and of our many different emotional states. This subjective impression—of fear, joy, anger, pride, shame—is a distinctive quality of self-perception. But how do such self-perceptions of emotion occur?

### HOW DO WE KNOW WHAT WE FEEL?

One possibility is that the different emotions we feel might involve different physiological changes. In accord with the subjective conviction that clearly different emotions exist, psychologists and physiologists for many years tried to differentiate emotional states into specific types and to discover the particular patterns of bodily activity that might accompany each of these states. The general result of a good deal of investigation appears to be that, though there are sometimes subtle differences in the patterns of physiological responses associated with different emotions (e.g., Ax, 1953), what they have in common is far more striking. A diffuse state of general physiological arousal seems to characterize different emotional experiences.

Nevertheless, we all have the subjective impression of experiencing distinctly different feelings such as anger and euphoria. How can one account for these subjectively different experiences if the bodily arousal underlying them is the same? Discriminations among emotions are based mainly on situational cues rather than on distinctive visceral changes. On the basis of situational cues, the individual labels his state cognitively, assigning a name to his arousal. Thus emotions involve at least two components: a state of general physiological arousal and a cognitive appraisal of the situation (Schachter, 1964).

Often the source of emotional arousal is easy to identify. When faced by an attacking dangerous animal, or by an impending car crash, or by imminent loss of a loved person, the source of excitement is self-evident. The label attached to the experience in these cases depends on the source—the stimulus producing the arousal. Thus the emotional response to an attacking animal is probably *fear*, identified by the fact that a dangerous animal is approaching. Identification of the emotion also depends on the person's goal-directed or instrumental response when confronted by the stimulus. For example, attempted escape from the animal also leads to calling the emotion fear. As another example, suppose that the arousal source is an insult. The resulting emotion is probably "anger," especially if the insulted person responds aggressively; but it might be "fear," if the insulted person appraises the insult as a prelude to greater attack. These examples illustrate that the label for the emotion depends in part on the *source* of arousal and in part on the *response* to it.

The emotional meaning attributed to arousing stimuli and response patterns depends on social learning and cognition. This point becomes most evident from anthropological reports of differences among cultures in the ways in which feelings are expressed. A visitor to a strange culture would make many mistakes if he tried to assess the meaning of emotional expressions in terms of his own social learning history. A Masai warrior honors a young man who looks promising by spitting in his face, an Andaman Islander greets a visitor by sitting down on his lap and sobbing his salutation tearfully, a scolded Chinese schoolboy takes a reprimand with cheerful grinning as a sign of his respect, and to show anger Navajo and Apache Indians lower the voice instead of raising it (Opler, 1967).

Within each culture people reach good agreement about the meaning of emotional cues. Sometimes, however, persons cannot correctly identify the source of their own arousal and are uncertain about their response to it. Under these ambiguous conditions cognitive and social variables play an especially dominant part in determining the experience. Depending on the cognitive label assigned, the context, and social cues from other people, the individual might experience the same physiological arousal pattern as anything from joy to hate.

## COGNITION AND PHYSIOLOGICAL AROUSAL

Stanley Schachter (1964), whose experiments on the way we label emotions were crucial, has discussed his theory in relation to the controversial effects of smoking marihuana. He notes that, according to pharmacological reports, marihuana usually causes an increase in pulse rate, some rise in blood pressure, elevation in blood sugar and metabolic rate, and so on. Given these symptoms the smoker could consider himself either as "high" or as "sick." The smoker has to decide whether his feelings of dizziness, misjudgments of time and distance, and so on are "pleasant" or not, and his decision involves cognitive judgments that depend on social learning cues.

Schachter extended his provocative theorizing to the topic of obesity. He noted that hunger, although a primary motive, also may require cognitive identification. Attaching the label "hunger" to the physiological changes accompanying food deprivation is a learned cognitive act. The obese person, he speculated, may not have learned to attach the right label to his feelings and may not be discriminating properly between hunger and other intense emotional states.

Support for Schachter's ideas concerning the effects of cognition on the experience of emotions comes from several experiments. For example, Schachter and Singer (1962) submitted college students to drug-induced autonomic arousal (through injections of epinephrine, a sympathetic stimulant). Some subjects were informed of the side effects of the drug while others were not, and subjects in a control group received a placebo injection (of saline solution). Thereafter all subjects were exposed to a confederate who was supposedly just another subject. The confederate modeled extensive verbal aggression and displayed anger toward the experimental procedure. The subjects who had been given the physiologically arousing drug without information about its effects were most susceptible to the angry model and became most angry themselves. Another part of the experiment established that subjects exposed to a euphoric confederate became most euphoric when they were physiologically aroused but not informed or misinformed concerning the side effects of the drug.

The total findings supported the hypothesis that if a person is in an aroused physiological state that he cannot explain, he will label his state in accord with the environmental cues determining his cognitions. On the other hand, if the person can explain his state rationally ("I'm experiencing these feelings because of the drug injection") then his evaluative self-labels will be less dependent on momentary situational cues. Momentary environmental cues were most influential when the subject was physiologically aroused by the epinephrine injection but misinformed about its effects and, secondly, when he was aroused but uninformed. The interacting effects of arousal and cognition are also shown in the cartoon in Figure 20-3. As the cartoon shows, physiologically aroused subjects interpreted their state

**Figure 20-3   THE SCHACHTER EXPERIMENTS**

From Mandler (1962).

in accord with the available modeling cues (the stooge's behavior) when they were misinformed about the nature of their arousal (lower portion of cartoon) but not when they had an appropriate explanation of the visceral arousal they felt (upper portion of cartoon).

In sum, an aroused individual's behavior may depend on his cognitive interpretation and labeling of the arousal. His interpretation, in turn, depends on the cues available to him in the situation and on the meaning that these stimuli have acquired as a result of his prior learning and development. The subjective, phenomenal experience of emotion often seems to be labeled from contextual cues, and we know what we feel partly by seeing where we are and what is happening. To understand another person's emotional experiences fully we have to consider the person in his context and the complex relations between the contextual variations and subjective experience; to understand our own feelings, we have to do the same.

## CAUSAL ATTRIBUTIONS AND EMOTIONS

The close links between cognition and emotion are also seen if we examine how "causal attributions" influence our emotional responses. Causal attributions refer to the perception of the causes of behavior (e.g., Kelley, 1973). For example, we may see the same event—say getting an A on an exam—as due to internal causes (such as high ability or hard work) or as due to external causes (such as the ease of the task or good luck). How we feel about the grade depends on whether we see it as due to internal or external causes. Generally, "pride and shame are maximized when achievement outcomes are ascribed internally, and minimized when success and failure are attributed to external causes" (Weiner, 1974, p. 11). In other words, a success that is perceived to be the result of one's ability or effort (internal causes) produces more positive feelings about oneself than does the same success when it is viewed as merely reflecting luck or an easy task (external causes). Conversely, we feel worse (e.g., experience "shame") when we perceive our failure as reflecting low ability or insufficient effort than when it is seen as due to bad luck or the difficulty of the particular task. For example, being fired from a job for one's incompetence has a different emotional impact than does being fired because the firm went bankrupt.

Emotional reactions to behavior also depend on inferences about the *intentions* motivating it (i.e., its perceived causes). For example, how you react to a physical blow from someone else will depend on whether you perceive it as accidental or deliberate. Similarly, whether you react to praise and attention with a warm glow or suspicion (and a rebuff) depends on whether you perceive these compliments as sincere or as ingratiating (Jones, 1964). Thus the perceived causes of behavior influence the meanings we give them and their impact on us.

## COGNITIVE CONSISTENCY

Perhaps the most compelling quality of the private or "phenomenological" self is its perceived continuity and consistency. The experience of subjective continuity in ourselves—of basic oneness and durability in the self—seems to be a fundamental feature of personality. Indeed the loss of a feeling of consistency and identity may be a chief characteristic of personality disorganization, as is seen in schizophrenic patients who sometimes report vividly experiencing two distinct selves, one of them disembodied (Laing, 1965).

### PERCEIVED UNITY IN THE FACE OF DIVERSITY

It seems remarkable how each of us normally manages to reconcile his seemingly diverse behaviors into one self-consistent whole. A man may steal on one occasion, lie on another, donate generously to charity on a third, cheat on a fourth, and still readily construe himself as "basically honest and moral." People often seem to be able to transform their seemingly discrepant behaviors into a constructed continuity, making unified wholes out of almost anything (Mischel, 1969).

How can we reconcile our shared perception of continuity, our feeling of identity, with the equally impressive evidence, found throughout previous chapters, that on virtually all measures of personality substantial changes occur in the actual behaviors of the individual across even seemingly similar settings and situations? How can we understand the fact of the specificity of behavior in light of the equally compelling impression of basic consistency in ourselves and in the people we know? Probably many complex factors are involved (Mischel, 1969, 1973a), but part of the answer to this question may be that people tend to reduce cognitive inconsistencies and, in general, to simplify information so that they can deal with it. The overall evidence from many sources (clinical, experimental, developmental, correlational) suggests that the human mind may function like an extraordinarily effective reducing valve that creates and maintains the perception of continuity even in the face of perpetual, observed changes in actual behavior.

## COGNITIVE CONSISTENCY THEORY

Some conceptualizations of personality attach the greatest importance to cognitive strivings for consistency (e.g., Festinger, 1957; Kohlberg, 1966; Lecky, 1945). The most influential statement of this position is Festinger's "cognitive dissonance" theory.

Cognitive dissonance refers to relations between cognitions that, like the dictionary meaning of the word "dissonant," are harsh, grating, inharmonious, or contradictory (Festinger, 1957). According to Festinger, cognitive dissonance occurs if an individual knows two things that do not fit together. Consider, for example, a person who knows that he is extremely competent and intelligent, but simultaneously knows that he fails often. These two cognitions do not fit well together and hence are dissonant. Festinger further hypothesized that dissonance is an aversive, tension-producing state, and therefore that people are motivated to reduce or avoid it.

Festinger had the opportunity to observe a religious sect that was predicting a catastrophic flood. Knowledge of the flood was given to the people in the sect by direct communication from God. When the appointed day arrived, but the predicted catastrophe did not, considerable dissonance was generated in the group's members. Observation of their behavior revealed some of the ingenious ways in which people coped with dissonance. For example, at one point a message arrived from God announcing he had saved the world for the sake of the strength and light the sect had spread. After their prophecy had failed, many sect members became especially eager to hold press conferences "explaining" the reasons for the reprieve, presumably reducing their dissonance by trying to persuade others (and themselves) of the validity of their heavenly messages.

Festinger thus began his theory with the informal observation that people strive to reduce inconsistencies in their beliefs. He proposed that inconsistency among related beliefs generates cognitive dissonance and motivates the individual to do whatever is easiest to reduce dissonance and to regain cognitive consistency or consonance among his beliefs.

## CONSTRUCTING CONSISTENCY

Consistency theories would predict that people should retain important cognitions about the self fairly stably. They may achieve consistency by distorting self-inconsistent cognitions regarding discrepant behaviors so as to make them seem more consonant with previous cognitions about the self.

Guided by dissonance theory, Aronson and Carlsmith (1962) reasoned that individuals are motivated to maintain consistent self-concepts. Extending this basic idea, they predicted that even if a person develops a *negative* self-relevant performance expectancy, he will seek to maintain it. That is, the person who has learned to expect poor performances from himself will experience discomfort when his performance turns out to be much better than he expected it to be. To reduce the discomfort or dissonance he feels, he will try to deny or minimize his superior performance.

In a laboratory study, false feedback was given to subjects on a series of tests to establish either excellent or poor performance expectancies (Aronson & Carlsmith, 1962). On a subsequent test the subjects performed again and were given false scores that either confirmed or disconfirmed their high or low performance expectancies. Under the guise of elaborate instructions the subjects were surreptitiously allowed to perform again and hence to alter their task responses on this retest. The conditions and results are summarized in Table 20-2.

As the table shows, people who had been given information inconsistent with their expectancies changed more of their responses than did those who had obtained consistent information. As predicted, subjects who had expected to do badly but who performed well seemed to exhibit more discomfort with their performance (as inferred from their changing more responses) than did those whose negative expectations had been confirmed by a poor performance.

In a similar vein, male college students were provided with plausible but false positive or negative information about their personalities to momentarily raise or lower their self-esteem (Bramel, 1962). Thereafter these subjects were led to discover a piece of negative information about themselves (specifically, that they had unconscious homosexual tendencies). Individuals with experimentally produced low self-esteem were more willing to accept the negative information than were those who experienced high self-esteem.

Similarly, experimentally induced increases in self-esteem may somewhat de-

**Table 20-2   Number of Responses Altered on Retest**

| EXPECTED PERFORMANCE ON TEST | OBTAINED PERFORMANCE ON TEST | |
|---|---|---|
| | HIGH | LOW |
| High | 3.9 | 11.1 |
| Low | 10.2 | 6.7 |

Adapted from Aronson and Carlsmith (1962).

crease an individual's tendency to cheat. This finding was interpreted as reflecting the unacceptable self-concept inconsistency that would be produced in high self-esteem subjects if they were to engage in dishonest behavior while experiencing high self-esteem (Aronson & Mettee, 1968). To avoid such dissonance they may have cheated somewhat less. It must be noted, however, that this finding was not strong.

The foregoing studies are just a few examples of many experiments on cognitive incongruity that have shown in general that persons tend to reduce inconsistencies between incompatible cognitions (e.g., Glass, 1968). People do minimize and avoid discrepant cognitions about themselves and others and reconstrue discrepant events to impose compatibility upon them.

Specific feedback about one's performance, such as arithmetic skill in the previously discussed level-of-aspiration design, is hard for most persons to deny and to distort. In life, however, most feedback about the self tends to be much more ambiguous and to involve vague qualitative appraisals of broad dispositions rather than concrete scores on specific performances. Under these more ambiguous conditions it is much easier to distort and to attend to information about the self selectively.

Some psychological constructs about ourselves have such broad and ambiguous semantic meanings that they are virtually impossible to disconfirm definitively. For example, the construct that a particular woman is "very feminine," or that she is "basically hostile," may be potentially supported by almost any kind of evidence about her behavior. Since the construct about what constitutes "real" femininity, or "real" hostility, may be modified and progressively elaborated as new evidence becomes available, it can be stretched so that diverse behaviors are taken as confirmation of behavioral consistency. Almost any data can be made to fit such broad hypotheses about personality; hence the hypotheses may be stably retained.

An excessive "stretching" of constructs may produce difficulties, for example, in the form of hostile efforts to coerce the data of our observations into patterns that match our preconceived categories (Kelly, 1955). Sometimes such stretching violates the data so that the fit between observation and construct is poor.

Nevertheless we may try to squeeze our observations into the constructs available to us, even when the match is poor. According to George Kelly's personal construct theory, coercing round data into square categories often may produce serious problems for us, both as persons and as scientists.

On the other hand, the adaptiveness with which constructs may be extended helps us to encompass and unify the diverse and seemingly inconsistent components of our lives and of our own behavior. This conceptual breadth and flexibility of concepts helps us to achieve the sense of integration, of continuity and oneness, of wholeness that characterizes the normal subjective perception of oneself.

## STABILITY OF TRAIT ATTRIBUTIONS

Consistency over time seems to be high for the self-concepts and for the attitudes and values that individuals attribute to themselves on trait-rating scales. E. L.

Kelly (1955) compared trait self-descriptions obtained on questionnaires answered almost 20 years apart. During the years 1935 to 1938 several personality questionnaires were administered to 300 engaged couples. Most of these people were retested with the same measures in 1954. The questionnaires included the Allport-Vernon values test, the Bernreuter personality questionnaire, and the Strong Vocational Interest Blank, among others. Self-reports of attitudes about marriage were highly unstable. However, the consistency found for such self-concept ratings as self-confidence and sociability, and for self-descriptions of interests and of economic and political values, was remarkably high.

In general, the self-concepts reported on many personality questionnaires seem to show a good deal of stability (Byrne, 1966; Gough, 1957; Mischel, 1968). As previously discussed (Chapter 6), personal constructs as measured by Kelly's Role Construct Repertory Test (Reptest) also show much consistency over time (Bonarius, 1965). Thus there is a great deal of evidence that our cognitive constructions about ourselves and the world—our personal theories about ourselves and those around us—tend to be extremely stable and highly resistant to change. Data from many sources document this point. Studies of the self-concept, of impression formation in person perception and in clinical judgment, of attitudes, of cognitive sets guiding selective attention—all these phenomena and many more reveal the consistency and tenacious continuity of many human construction systems (Mischel, 1968, 1969). Often these construction systems are built quickly and on the basis of little information (e.g., Bruner, Olver & Greenfield, 1966). But, once established, these systems, whether generated by "subjects" or by psychologists, become exceedingly difficult to disconfirm.

It may be that the dispositional labels people attribute to themselves and others and the self-concepts that they form are relatively permanent; they probably are more enduring than the behaviors to which they refer. Thus while what people *do* tends to be relatively situation-specific, they categorize and conceptualize themselves fairly stably with dispositional terms and motives that go far beyond the information directly available from observation of behavior.

Presumably the tendency to perceive and interpret oneself consistently reflects frequent reinforcement of such consistency and the likelihood that perceived inconsistency will lead to unfortunate consequences. Perceived consistency increases our feeling that we can predict other people and ourselves, and helps our world to seem more orderly and less chaotic. It might be distressing to believe that our most trusted friends are capable of disloyalty, or that those on whom we rely profoundly might be dishonest at times, or that those whom we love might change in unexpected ways that we really cannot predict.

Thus consistency is often reinforced and reinforcing. But that is not always true: "surprise" and novelty also are valued under some conditions, at least within limits (Berlyne, 1966).

The over-attribution of consistency may be something people do unto others even more than to themselves. Jones and Nisbett (1971) note that when explaining *other* people's behavior we invoke their consistent personality dispositions: Steve is the sort of person who puts bumper stickers on his car; Jill tripped because she's clumsy. But when asked to explain our *own* behavior we are more likely to consider specific conditions: "AAA sent me this catchy bumper sticker in the mail" or "I tripped because it was dark." Thus Jones and Nisbett (1971, p. 58) theorize that "actors tend to attribute the causes of their behavior to stimuli inherent in the situation while observers tend to attribute behavior to stable dispositions of the actor." Jones and Nisbett analyze many possible reasons for this seemingly paradoxical state of affairs, including the tendency to treat every sample of behavior we observe from another person as if it were typical for him. It thus seems as if traits may be the consistent attributes that *other* people have. When describing other people, we seem to act more like trait theorists but when we attempt to understand ourselves we may function more like social behaviorists. If that is true it may be because we have more information about ourselves and the variety and complexity of the situations we encounter in our own lives, whereas we know others in only limited contexts and therefore tend to overgeneralize from their behavior in those instances.

## COGNITION AND BEHAVIOR

The relations between cognitive consistency strivings and behavior are not simple. Our tendencies to reduce cognitive dissonance do not necessarily control our actions. The complexity of the causal relations between cognitions and actions becomes most apparent, as Festinger (1964) has pointed out, in research on the effects of cognitive or attitudinal changes upon behavior changes. Festinger noted, in his review of the literature on this issue, that there is unexpectedly little evidence that alterations in attitudes or beliefs produce changes in relevant behavior. But there does seem to be much data to suggest that cognitive and value changes may follow after new behaviors have been performed. Rather than being the antecedents or prerequisites for new actions, cognitions may come after behavior changes and may be used to justify them (e.g., Brehm & Cohen, 1962).

Rather than causing our actions, consistency strivings thus often may serve to justify our behavior, while the behavior itself changes and adapts to the needs of the moment and the situation. Although Festinger noted that evidence showing that attitudinal changes lead to behavior change is limited, such effects can and do occur, even if not inevitably. For example, when false feedback about their heart rates led men to *think* that women had aroused them sexually they became more attracted to them (Valins, 1966). But while a person's attitudes and his cognitions are a critical part of the chain of behavior, they do not necessarily have singular unidirectional causal powers. Alterations in what a person does can lead to cognitive reorganization, just as cognitive changes can facilitate behavior modification. Many conditions jointly determine the degree of consistency—or of inconsistency— that is achieved among cognitions, feelings, and actions (e.g., Fishbein & Ajzen, 1974; Insko & Schopler, 1967).

The links between attitudes and cognitions about the self on the one hand and overt behavior on the other are often indirect. Some significant association between attitudes and measures of the relevant overt behavior are found, but the correlations often are small (e.g., Becker, 1960; Wicker, 1969). The total results on the relations between cognition and action suggest that while people may easily construe diverse behaviors as congruent, the bridge between their constructed cognitive consistencies and other relevant aspects of their behavior may be quite complex.

## SUMMARY

1. The processes through which we form our impressions of other people are similar to those through which we develop impressions about the self. Thus the study of how we perceive others may inform our understanding of self-perceptions. Impressions of the self, like impressions of other people and events, involve a complex synthesis and organization of a great deal of information. This information comes from observed behavior, but the perceiver goes beyond observation and seeks motives and dispositions to explain the behavior he sees.

2. During impression formation isolated bits of information are quickly organized into units. The organization depends on such things as context and sequence. Context is very important even in simple impressions. The same stimulus may be judged differently in different contexts. Moreover, any one attribute may lead us to infer a cluster of related traits.

3. The first impressions generated about others and about oneself may have a constraining effect by decreasing the attention paid to contradictory new information. Selective channeling or biasing of new information may be adaptive in coping with enormous informational inputs because it simplifies them.

4. The person's existing construct system influences his new impressions. Even when people know each other well, the impressions each forms of the other may depend more on his own categories than on the attributes of the other person. Regardless of what is being rated, the judgments we make tend to fall on a few dimensions of meaning, such as "good-bad."

5. Self-concepts develop as a result of the outcomes a person has obtained in the past and expects to obtain in the future. Self-esteem is an important aspect of the self-concept. Concepts of adequacy or ability with regard to particular performance areas have been studied extensively. Specific self-concepts about performance level tend to depend on the feedback the person received from his past performance. These expectancies may generalize to other situations to the degree that the situations

are perceived as similar. Changes in self-esteem also may be mediated by factors other than performance feedback, for example, by the person's achievement orientation.

6. Self-esteem level has been related to other aspects of personality. Children with high self-esteem are those who are more esteemed by others and more competent; and their parents also display high self-esteem. Self-esteem also appears to be related to one's evaluation of his sex-role adequacy and to perceived responsibility and control.

7. A person must attend selectively to the immense amount of information available about himself. Determinants of selective attention include momentary self-esteem and more stable personality differences in information-seeking and perceived control.

8. In the perception of feelings, although we may subjectively experience distinct emotions, corresponding distinct patterns of physiological responses generally have not been found. Instead, a diffuse state of general physiological arousal characterizes the various emotional experiences. The discriminations that we make among emotions seem primarily to be based on cognitions and situational cues. The source of the arousal and the person's response to it affect the cognitive appraisal of that arousal and the label that the individual attaches to it. The meaning of arousal stimuli and response patterns depends in turn upon social learning and cognition.

9. When you cannot easily identify the source of your own arousal and are uncertain about your response to it, cognitive and social variables may enter most strongly to determine your experience. If a person is in an aroused physiological state that he cannot explain plausibly, he tends to label his state in accord with the environmental cues and his cognitions about them so as to explain his state reasonably.

10. Emotional reactions to an event also depend on its perceived causes. For example, a success that is seen as due to one's own ability or efforts (internal causes) produces more feelings of pride than does the same event when it is seen as due to luck or the easiness of the task (external causes).

11. We tend to perceive people as basically consistent even in the face of seemingly contradictory evidence from behavior. Consistency theories, such as Festinger's cognitive dissonance theory, view people as actively striving to reduce cognitive dissonance and to maintain cognitive consistency, especially about important concepts like the self. People often minimize and avoid discrepant cognitions about themselves, and they may reconstrue events to render them compatible.

12. Self-concepts, attitudes, and values may show remarkable stability. Indeed the dispositional labels people apply to themselves and use in the formation of their self-concepts may be more enduring and situation-free than the actual behaviors to which they refer.

13. The relations between cognitions, attitudes, and behavior often are indirect and complex. Attitudes and cognitions are not always the causes of action. Sometimes changes in cognitions may come after changes in behavior and may be used to justify them. Many conditions jointly determine the degree of consistency among cognitions, feelings, and action.

# CHAPTER 21

# THE INTERACTION OF PERSON AND SITUATION

As the end of this survey approaches, the reader may still be feeling somewhat uncertain about the view of man to which contemporary personality psychology leads, puzzled about the interplay of the individual's characteristics with the conditions of his or her life, and looking for a more cohesive perspective for understanding people. If so, this book has succeeded in conveying a sense of the field as it exists; a deep concern with how to best conceptualize the person in personality psychology is widely shared within the discipline. The purpose of this final chapter is to examine more closely some of the bases of these concerns and to try to point, even if only tentatively and with no guarantee of success, toward hopefully promising future directions from the author's perspective (developed more fully in Mischel, 1973a). This perspective is offered not as the "final word" in the field; indeed, one of the few things that may be assumed with certainty is that the conceptualizations favored (and required) in personality psychology will continue to evolve as the field grows and changes. The present perspective is intended only to offer one way of trying to construe and integrate some of the main current controversial issues in the field.

# SOME BASIC ISSUES IN PERSONALITY PSYCHOLOGY

One of the most challenging, persistent problems for the field of personality comes from the findings on the "specificity" of personality traits. The reader has encountered these findings throughout this volume and their implications may be leading to a crisis in the area (e.g., Fiske, 1974). It is therefore not surprising that they are highly controversial and often debated vehemently (e.g., Endler & Magnusson, 1975).

## BEHAVIORAL SPECIFICITY OR DISCRIMINATIVE FACILITY?

It is time to briefly review the meaning of the findings on "behavioral specificity." People often have been found to be consistent on measures of intelligence and on behavior patterns such as "cognitive styles" (problem-solving strategies) that are strongly correlated with intelligence (e.g., Witkin, 1965). Ratings of personality characteristics (by self and others) also show appreciable stability even over many years; moreover, self-ratings tend to agree with trait ratings by other judges (e.g., Block, 1975). Each life has a coherence and continuity that is perceived both by the person and by those who know him. But such perceived continuity coexists with the fact that people also show great discriminativeness in their behavior as they cope with changing environmental demands. Hence, it is difficult to demonstrate impressive consistencies across situations when ongoing behavior is studied objectively as it occurs, rather than rated on broad trait dimensions (Block, 1975; Mischel, 1975). A given individual's actual behavior, while certainly not haphazard, often may be fairly specific to the situation.

Relative specificity of behavior patterns was seen, for example, in the modest associations obtained among seemingly close indices of such sex-typed behaviors as dependency, and of sex-typing itself, as was discussed before (Chapters 14 and 15). Similar specificity was found for measures of self-control and moral behavior (Chapter 19), and for other personality dimensions, such as anxiety (Chapter 17) and cognitive avoidance (Chapter 18). While an individual may display some significant consistency on these traits, the degree of consistency found tends to be modest when behavior is measured objectively.

There are many ways to interpret the findings of "behavioral specificity," but there is little doubt that personality organization is very subtly differentiated. Complex behavior is regulated by interactions that depend intimately on situational variables, as well as on dispositions. Humans are capable of extraordinary adaptiveness and discrimination as they cope with a continuously changing environment.

Seen from the vantage point of traditional trait theory, the specificity often found in behavior is a problem that tends to be attributed to defects in existing methods and measurements. Thus research evidence for the specificity of traits usually has been interpreted as due mainly to the inadequacies of the tests and the studies that used them (e.g., Alker, 1972; Block, 1975).

The "specificity" so often found in studies of personality traits, however, also may be viewed as accurately reflecting man's great discriminative facility and the inadequacy of global trait theories, not merely the biases of faulty measurement. But the term "discriminative facility" (responsivity to changing conditions) seems preferable to "specificity" because it avoids the negative meanings implied by the "specificity" of behavior—the implications of inconsistency, fickleness, and unreliability in human nature.

Whereas discriminative facility is highly adaptive (Gibson, 1969), a reduced sensitivity to changing consequences (i.e., indiscriminate responding) may be characteristic of an organism adapting poorly. In fact, indiscriminate responding (i.e., extremely "consistent" behavior across situations) may be more characteristic of maladaptive, severely disturbed or less mature persons than of well-functioning ones (Moos, 1968). While relatively more indiscriminate behavior tends to be found in more immature and/or disturbed individuals, its extent should not be exaggerated. Even extremely disturbed behavior, for example, may turn out to be highly discriminative when it is examined in detail (e.g., Lovaas et al., 1965), as we saw earlier (Chapters 10, 11).

## CONSISTENCY IN SOME OF THE PEOPLE SOME OF THE TIME

Fully recognizing the discriminativeness so often displayed by most people on most of the personality dimensions studied, Bem and Allen (1974) proposed that consistency may characterize *some* people at least in *some* areas of behavior. They began by noting that traditional personality research on traits has assumed incorrectly that all traits would characterize all people. Bem and Allen suggested, instead, that while some people may be consistent on some traits, practically nobody is consistent on all traits; indeed, many traits that are studied by investigators may not even apply to many of the people who are studied. To get beyond this problem, Bem and Allen suggested looking only for those people who would be consistent on particular traits. Specifically, they tried to identify (preselect) those college students who would be consistent and those who would not be consistent on the traits of friendliness and conscientiousness. Their hypothesis was simply this: "Individuals who identify themselves as consistent on a particular trait dimension will in fact be more consistent cross-situationally than those who identify themselves as highly variable" (Bem & Allen, 1974, p. 512). The results, on the whole, supported the hypothesis; for example, students who described themselves as consistent in their level of friendliness tended to show a relatively consistent level of friendliness across a number of measures (such as ratings by their mothers, fathers, and peers, as well as direct observations of their friendliness in a small group discussion and in a waiting room). In contrast, those who described themselves as variable in their friendliness in fact tended to be less consistent.

The Bem and Allen study nicely demonstrated the point that individuals may (and do) display some consistency in some behavior patterns but not in others. For example, one person may show relatively consistent friendliness, another consistent dependency, and a third consistent honesty, but it is less likely that anyone will be consistent with regard to all of these dimensions. Consequently, when an investigator tries to compare many people on any given dimension, only some will be consistent but most people will be highly discriminative. Therefore, efforts to find cross-situational consistency in randomly selected samples of people are bound to yield poor results. It may be possible to demonstrate consistency, but, as Bem and Allen put it, only for "some of the people some of the time." Interestingly, it was the people themselves who predicted their own consistency, again providing support for the notion that each person knows his or her own behavior best (Chapter 12).

In a closely related direction, other researchers have also acknowledged the importance of situational variables for a large portion of people. But they also suggest that some people who are consistent may be identified. Hence these researchers treat "specificity-consistency" as a dimension of individual differences and attempt to discover those individuals who will be cross-situationally consistent (e.g., Campus, 1974). The degree to which this strategy will prove useful can only be determined by future research.

## THE STUDY OF ENVIRONMENTS

While some psychologists have been searching for cross-situationally consistent people, others have been focusing more and more on the social and psychological environments in which people live and function. The dramatic increase of interest in the environment as it relates to man is documented easily: from 1968 to 1972 more books appeared on the topic of man-environment relations from an ecological perspective than had been published in the prior three decades (Jordan, 1972). This new area still has not been given a final name; it is sometimes called environmental psychology and sometimes social or psychological ecology. Regardless of name, the field studies "the impact that physical and social environments have on human beings" (Moos & Insel, 1974, p. IX), and is concerned with "human problems in relation to an environment in which man is both victim and conqueror . . ." (Proshansky, et al., 1970, p. 4). The interest in the environment is a much needed corrective for an area of psychology that historically has focused on the individual as a unit, often forgetting the intimate links between the person and the conditions of his or her life.

As is true in most new fields, a first concern in the study of environments has been to try to classify them, just as trait psychologists had tried to classify traits into a taxonomy (Chapters 7 and 8). Environments, like everything else, can be classified in many ways, depending mainly on the purposes and imagination of the classifiers. One typical effort to describe some of the almost infinite dimensions of environments was proposed by Moos and is summarized in Table 21-1. The classi-

**TABLE 21-1    Some Dimensions of Human Environments**

| DIMENSIONS | EXAMPLES |
|---|---|
| 1. Ecological | Climate and geographical qualities; architectural and physical use of space and constraints (e.g., the walls of a prison) |
| 2. Behavioral settings | School, drugstore, football game, church |
| 3. Organizational | Size and type of staff in a hospital; student/teacher ratio in a school; population density |
| 4. Characteristics of inhabitants | Age, sex, abilities, status of members |
| 5. Perceived social climate (psychosocial characteristics) | Nature and intensity of personal relations |
| 6. Functional properties | Reinforcement consequences for particular behaviors in that situation |

Based on Moos (1973).

fication in Table 21-1 calls attention to the complex nature of environments and to the many variables that can characterize them. These variables include the weather, the buildings and settings, the perceived social climates, and the reinforcements obtained for behaviors in that situation—to list just a few.

The classification alerts us to a fact that has been slighted by traditional trait-oriented approaches to personality: much human behavior depends on environmental considerations, such as the setting (e.g., Barker, 1968), and even on such specific physical and psychosocial variables as how hot and crowded the setting is, or how the room and furniture are arranged, or how the people in the setting are organized (e.g., Krasner & Ullmann, 1973; Moos & Insel, 1974). Many links between characteristics of the environment and behavior have been demonstrated. For example, measures of population density (such as the number of people in each room) may be related to certain forms of aggression (even when social class and ethnicity are controlled; Galle, Gove & McPhersen, 1972). Likewise, interpersonal attraction and mood are negatively affected by extremely hot, crowded conditions (Griffitt & Veitch, 1971).

Some psychologists have tried to classify situations with characteristics ranging from gravity and the physical terrain to social norms (Sells, 1973). Focusing on the *perceptions* of observers, there also have been efforts to classify situations on the basis of their perceived similarity, emerging with such trait-like characterizations of situations as "positive," "negative," "passive," "social," and "active" (e.g., Magnusson & Ekehammer, 1973). Similarly, Moos and his associates have obtained ratings of the "perceived social climate" in such institutions as psychiatric wards, prisons, and schools (1973, 1974). These ratings are intended to measure such qualities as the perceived degree to which a given program or setting provides support (encouragement) for its members, fosters spontaneity and involvement, and helps people have autonomy in decision-making.

Depending on one's purpose, many different classifications are possible and useful. To seek any single "basic" taxonomy of situations may be as futile as searching for a final or ultimate taxonomy of traits; we can label situations in at least as many different ways as we can label people. It will be important to avoid emerging simply with a trait psychology of situations, in which events and settings, rather than people, are merely given different labels. The task of naming situations cannot substitute for the job of analyzing *how* conditions and environments interact with the people in them (as discussed in later sections).

## THE CHARGE OF "SITUATIONISM": WHERE IS THE PERSON IN PERSONALITY PSYCHOLOGY?

As noted earlier (Chapter 5), many critics feel that in recent years psychology has been overemphasizing the importance of the environment and the situation while underemphasizing—or even "losing"—the person (e.g., Bowers, 1973; Carlson, 1971). This is a serious charge; losing the person in personality psychology would be as bizarre as losing matter in physics or the elements in chemistry. The person is what personality psychology must be about; no one really disputes that. But there is disagreement about how to best study and conceptualize the person, as we saw throughout this book (especially in Parts 1 and 2).

Bowers (1973, p. 307) attacks a "situationism" that emphasizes situations as the causes of behavior while "being inattentive to the importance of the person." Situationism is defined as an explanatory bias that tends "either to ignore organismic factors or to regard them as . . . subsidiary to the primary impact of the external stimulus" (Harré & Secord, 1972, p. 27).

Closely paralleling the charge of "situationism" is the humanistic protest to the behavioral approach in general. We have considered many aspects of the humanistic (phenomenological) position in Chapters 6 and 12. The essence of the humanistic protest is that behaviorally oriented psychologists (i.e., "situationists") treat and manipulate man as if he were externally controlled rather than a free, self-determining being who is responsible for his own actions and growth. Some of these criticisms and charges may seem justified objections against the pure environmentalism of B. F. Skinner's (1974) radical behaviorism. The characteristics of the environment interact with the attributes of the people in it, and it would be foolish to ignore either side of this interaction.

The recognition that the environment is important for human behavior is a welcome (even if tardy) insight for most personality psychologists. But a psychological approach requires that we move from descriptions of the environment—of the climate, buildings, social settings, etc., in which we live—to the psychological processes through which environmental conditions and people influence each other reciprocally. For this purpose, it is necessary to consider how the environment influences behavior and how people's behavior in turn shapes the environment in an endless interaction. To understand the interaction of person and environment we must consider *person variables* as well as environmental variables, and we must analyze the nature of person-situation *interactions* psychologically. Later sections attempt to do just that.

## THE PREVALENCE AND MEANING OF INTERACTION

The new interest in environments (situations, psychological ecology) expressed by personality psychologists reflects in part increased dissatisfaction with traditional trait-oriented theories that tried to understand people without adequately considering the specific conditions of the individual's life from moment to moment. It also reflects a recognition that many important human behaviors not only fluctuate as the situation changes but also depend crucially on the mutual (reciprocal) influence of the person and the situation; that is, their "interaction." We noted repeatedly throughout this book that the effects of conditions depend on the individuals in them, and that the *interaction* of individual differences and specific conditions is usually crucial. For example, the impact of different types of classroom arrangements depends on the particular students in them; small group discussion that might be helpful for some students might be a bore or even a handicap for others.

Some researchers hoped that studies of persons, environments, and their interaction would answer the question "are persons or situations more important for predicting behavior?" But the question serves mostly to stimulate futile debates. The answer must always depend on the particular situations and the particular persons sampled. The question of whether individual differences or situations are more important is an empty one that has no general answer.

Moreover, in current debates on this topic, "situations" are often treated like entities that supposedly exert either major or only minor control over behavior, without specifying what, psychologically, they are or how they function. But while some situations may be powerful determinants of behavior, others are trivial. The relative importance of individual differences and situations will depend on the situation selected, the type of behavior assessed, the particular individual differences sampled, and the purpose of the assessment.

## THE SPECIFICITY OF SITUATIONS (TREATMENTS)

The other side of the coin of "behavioral specificity" is the realization that situations (or "treatments" in experimental and clinical contexts) also tend to produce specific rather than generalized effects, and that the effects are often weak (e.g., Sarason, Smith & Diener, 1975). As one psychologist put it, "Although it is undoubtedly true that behavior is more situation specific than trait theory acknowledged . . . situations are more person specific than is commonly recognized" (Bowers, 1973, p. 307). That is, the impact of particular situations or treatments depends on the particular people in them. A particular "enrichment" course, or social influence effort, or creativity-training session, or therapy program might work well for some individuals but be ineffective (or even harmful) for others.

There is a growing belief throughout psychology and the social sciences that "treatments" may not have broad, highly generalized, stable effects. Specificity may occur because of the large range of different ways that different people may react to the "same" treatments and reinterpret them (e.g., Cronbach, 1975; Neisser, 1974), and because the impact of most situations usually can be changed easily by other "moderating" conditions (Mischel, 1974). Thus, even a relatively simple "stimulus" or "situation" may produce a variety of often unpredictable specific (and weak) effects depending on a large number of moderating variables and the many different ways in which the particular "subjects" may view them. (Recall, for example, the many variables that may determine whether or not one chooses to delay gratification, discussed in Chapter 8.)

The recognition that behavior is always determined by many variables and that a focus on any one of them will lead to limited predictions and generalizations is not confined to the area of personality psychology. This conclusion has been reached for "treatments" as diverse as interview styles in psychotherapy, teaching practices and classroom arrangements in education, and instructions to aid recall in memory experiments. For example, after a survey of research on memory we are cautioned that: ". . . What is remembered in a given situation depends on the physical and psychological context in which the event was experienced, the knowledge and skills that the subject brings to the context, the situation in which we ask for evidence for remembering, and the relation of what the subject remembers to what the experimenter demands" (Jenkins, 1974, p. 793). The same conclusions probably apply as well to the subject matter studied in any other sub-area of psychology.

As a consequence, it may become difficult to achieve broad, sweeping generalizations about human behavior; many qualifiers (moderators) must be appended to our "laws" about cause-and-effect relations—almost without exception and perhaps with no exceptions at all (Cronbach, 1975). On the other hand, while the need to qualify generalizations about human behavior complicates life for the social scientist, it does not prevent one from studying human affairs scientifically; it only dictates a respect for the complexity of the enterprise and alerts one to the dangers of oversimplifying the nature and causes of human behavior. That danger is equally great whether one is searching for generalized (global) person-free situational effects or for generalized (global) situation-free personality variables.

## CONCEPTUALIZING THE PERSON

It has been easier to demonstrate the existence of extensive person-situation interactions than to explain them. It is now necessary to analyze the psychological bases for "interaction"; without such an analysis, an emphasis on interaction is in danger of being little more than the announcement of the obvious. Granted that both environments and individual differences are important and interact, how can the impact of situations be conceptualized in *psychological* terms? When people respond to the environment they are confronted with a potential flood of stimuli; how are these stimuli selected, perceived, processed, interpreted, and used by the individual?

To answer these questions requires the development of more adequate conceptualizations of individual differences or "person variables." In recent years a great deal of personality research has focused on the processes through which social behaviors are acquired, evoked, maintained, and modified. Throughout Part 3 the reader has seen how these processes (such as observational learning) influence a wide range of phenomena from sex-typed activities, reactions to frustration, and coping with anxiety to self-control and self-concepts. Much less attention has been given to the psychological *products* within the individual of cognitive development and social learning experiences. A focus on processes—on the psychological conditions that influence behavior—is an important advance in a field that traditionally has dwelt on the stable attributes of persons with little attention to how conditions affect what people think and feel and do. But a comprehensive psychology of personality also must attend to person variables that are the products of each individual's total history and that, in turn, regulate how new experiences affect him or her.

The person variables to be discussed in this section were proposed to provide a synthesis of seemingly promising constructs about persons developed in the areas of cognition and social learning (Mischel, 1973a); hence they are called "*cognitive social learning* person variables." The selections should be seen as only suggestive and always open to progressive revision. These variables were not expected to provide ways to accurately predict broadly cross-situational behavioral differences between persons; the discriminativeness of behavior and its unique organization within each person are facts of nature, not limitations unique to particular theories. But these variables should suggest useful ways of conceptualizing and studying specifically how the qualities of the person influence the impact of stimuli ("environments," "situations," "treatments") and how each person generates distinctive complex behavior patterns in interaction with the conditions of his or her life.

First, one must deal with the individual's *competencies* to construct (generate) diverse behaviors under appropriate conditions. Next, one must consider the individual's *encoding* and categorization of situations. A comprehensive analysis of the behaviors a person performs in particular situations also requires attention to his *expectancies* about outcomes, the *subjective values* of such outcomes, and his *self-regulatory systems and plans*. The following five sections discuss each of these person variables. While these variables obviously overlap and interact, each may provide distinctive information about the individual and each may be measured objectively and studied systematically.

## COMPETENCIES

Earlier chapters showed that through direct and observational learning each individual acquires information about the world and his or her relationship to it.

As a result of learning and cognitive development each of us develops competencies to construct (create, generate) many cognitions and behaviors. Our competencies include such knowledge as the rules that guide conduct (Chapter 19), the concepts generated about self and others (Chapter 20), and a host of interpersonal and physical skills.

The concept of "competencies" refers to the individual's abilities to transform and use information actively and to create thoughts and actions (as in problem-solving), rather than to a store of static cognitions and responses that one "has" in some mechanical storehouse. Each individual acquires the capacity to actively construct a multitude of potential behaviors with the knowledge and skills available to him. Great differences between persons exist in the range and quality of the cognitive and behavioral patterns that they can generate, as becomes obvious from even casual comparison of the different competencies, for example, of a professional weight lifter, a chemist, a retardate, an opera star, or a convicted forger.

## ENCODING STRATEGIES AND PERSONAL CONSTRUCTS

Personality psychology also must consider the ways we encode (represent, symbolize) and group information from stimulus inputs. The same "hot weather" that upsets one person may be a joy for another who views it as a chance to go to the beach. A stimulus perceived as "dangerous" or "threatening" by one person may be seen as "challenging" or "thrilling" by the one next to him. The "environment," the "situation," the "stimulus" are perceived, coded, and categorized by each person, and these cognitive operations influence the impact that they have on him.

As discussed earlier (Chapter 19), people can readily perform *cognitive transformations* on stimuli, focusing on selected aspects of the objective stimulus (e.g., the taste versus the shape of a food object); such selective attention, interpretation, and categorization change the impact the stimulus exerts on behavior (Geer, Davison & Gatchel, 1970; Holmes & Houston, 1974; Schachter, 1964). How we encode and selectively attend to observed behavioral sequences also greatly influences what we learn and subsequently can do. Clearly, different persons may group and

Different individuals may encode even the same situation in different ways.

encode the same events and behaviors in different ways (e.g., Argyle & Little, 1972) and selectively attend to different kinds of information.

Even if we focus on "behavior" we cannot avoid the fact that the definition and selection of a behavior unit for study requires grouping and categorizing. In personality research, it is the psychologist who does the categorizing; he includes and excludes events in the units he studies, depending on his interests and objectives. He chooses a category—such as "anxiety," "masculinity-femininity," or "delay of gratification," for example—and studies its behavioral referents. In the study of individuals, however, it soon becomes evident that the "subject" (like the psychologist) also groups events into categories and organizes them actively into meaningful units. The layman usually does not describe experience objectively; as the phenomenologists emphasize (Chapters 6, 12), each person groups events in terms of his or her own categories and perceptions (G. Kelly, 1955) and these may or may not overlap with those of the psychologist or of others. For example, what is "conscientiousness" for one person may have an entirely different meaning for another (Bem & Allen, 1974); a trait dimension that fits me may be quite irrelevant for you.

People abstract and infer traits and other dispositions to describe and explain their experience and themselves, just as professional psychologists do, and it would be strange if personality psychologists ignored the concepts, perceptions, and experiences of those whom they are studying. We noted before that people categorize their own personal qualities in relatively stable trait terms (e.g., on self-ratings and self-report questionnaires, as discussed in the previous chapter). These self-categorizations, while often only complexly related to nonverbal behavior, may be relatively durable and generalized (Chapter 20) and an adequate psychology of personality must take them into account.

## EXPECTANCIES

So far the person variables considered deal with what the individual *can* do and how one categorizes (codes) events. But we also must move from what we know and how we perceive (categorize) events to what we *do*, from potential behaviors to actual performance in specific situations. This move requires attention to the determinants of *performance*. For this purpose, the person variables of greatest interest are the individual's expectancies. If you cheat on the final exam and are caught, what do you expect will be the consequences? If you tell your friend what you really think of him, what will happen to your relationship? If you switch to another career plan, what will be the probable effects?

To predict specific behavior in a particular situation it is essential to consider the individual's specific expectancies about the consequences of different behavioral possibilities in that situation. These expectancies guide the person's selection (choice) of behaviors from among the many which he is capable of constructing within any situation. We generate behavior in light of our expectancies even when they are not in line with the objective conditions in the situation. If you expect to be attacked you become vigilant even if your fears later turn out to have been unjustified.

One type of expectancy concerns *behavior-outcome relations*. These *behavior-outcome expectancies* (hypotheses, contingency rules) represent the "if ___, then ___" relations between behavioral alternatives and expected probable outcomes in particular situations. In any given situation, we generate the response pattern which we expect is most likely to lead to the most subjectively valuable outcomes (consequences) in that situation (e.g., Mischel, 1973a; Rotter, 1954). In the absence of new information about the behavior-outcome expectancies in any situation, one's performance will depend on one's previous behavior-outcome expectancies in similar situations. That is, if you do not know exactly what to expect in a new situation (a first job interview, for example) you are guided by your previous expectancies based on experiences in similar past situations. This point is illustrated in a study which showed that the expectancies people brought to a situation influenced their behavior in the situation when no other relevant information was available (Mischel & Staub, 1965). But the same study also showed that new information about probable outcomes in the particular situation may quickly overcome the original expectancies. The new information produces highly specific situational expectancies that influence performance most significantly.

Adaptive performance requires the recognition and appreciation of new contingencies. To cope with the environment effectively, we must identify new contingencies as quickly as possible and reorganize behavior in the light of the new expectancies. Strongly established behavior-outcome expectancies may handicap our ability to adapt to changes in contingencies. Indeed, "defensive reactions" may be seen in part as a failure to adapt to new contingencies because one is still behaving in response to old contingencies that are no longer valid (Chapter 18). For example, if on the basis of past experiences a man overgeneralizes and becomes convinced that people will take advantage of him unless he is hostile toward everyone, his own suspicious, aggressive behavior may prevent him from ever being able to disconfirm his belief, even when people are trying to be considerate. The "maladaptive" individual is behaving in accord with expectancies that do not adequately represent the actual behavior-outcome rules in his current life situation.

A closely related second type of expectancy concerns *stimulus-outcome relations*. The outcomes we expect depend on a multitude of stimulus conditions. These stimuli ("signs") essentially "predict" for us other events that are likely to occur. More precisely, each of us learns that certain events (cues, stimuli) predict certain other events. Outside the artificial restrictions of the laboratory, in the human interactions of life, the "stimuli" that predict outcomes often are the social behaviors of others in particular contexts. The meanings attributed to those stimuli hinge on learned associations between behavioral signs and outcomes.

For example, through learning, "shifty eyes," "tight lips," "lean and hungry looks," obese body build, age, sex, eye contact, posture, gestures, and many even subtler behavioral cues (e.g., regarding the status and power of others) come to predict for us other behaviors correlated with them. If your friend nods "understandingly" when you start to talk frankly about a personal problem you will proceed differently than if he taps his foot "impatiently," gets up abruptly, or yawns. Each of these "signs" implies a very different outcome in the particular situation. Some expected stimulus-outcome associations presumably reflect the perceiver's idiosyncratic (unique) learning history, and his or her own evolving personal rules about stimulus meanings. Many of these associations, however, are likely to be widely shared by members of the same culture who have a common language for verbal and nonverbal communication.

## SUBJECTIVE VALUES

Two individuals who have similar expectancies nevertheless may act differently because the outcomes they expect have different *values* for them (e.g., Rotter, 1954, 1972). For example, if everyone in a group expects that approval from a teacher depends on saying certain things, there may be differences in how often they are said due to differences in the perceived value of obtaining the teacher's approval. Praise from the teacher may be important for one person (e.g., a youngster striving for grades), but not for another (e.g., a rebellious adolescent who rejects school). Such differences reflect the degree to which different individuals value the same expected outcome. What delights one person may repel his neighbor. Therefore it is necessary to consider still another variable: the subjective (perceived) value for the individual of particular classes of events, that is, his stimulus preferences and aversions, his likes and dislikes, his positive and negative values.

## SELF-REGULATORY SYSTEMS AND PLANS

While behavior depends to a considerable extent on externally administered consequences for actions, we also have seen that everyone regulates his own behavior by self-imposed goals (standards) and self-produced consequences (Chapter 19). Even in the absence of external constraints and social monitors, we set performance goals for ourselves and react with self-criticism or self-satisfaction to our behavior depending on how well it matches our expectations and standards. The expert sprinter who falls below his past record may condemn himself bitterly, while the same performance by a less experienced runner who has lower standards may produce self-congratulation and joy.

Another feature of self-regulatory systems is the person's adoption of *contingency rules* and *plans* that guide his behavior in the absence of, and sometimes in spite of, immediate external situational pressures. Such rules specify the kinds of behavior appropriate (expected) under particular conditions, the performance levels (standards, goals) which the behavior must achieve, and the consequences (positive and negative) of attaining or failing to reach those standards. Plans also specify the sequence and organization of behavior patterns (e.g., Miller, Gallanter & Pribram, 1960). Individuals differ with respect to each of the components of self-regulation depending on their unique earlier histories or on more recently varied instructions or other information.

Self-regulation provides a route through which we can influence our environment substantially, overcoming "stimulus control" (the power of the situation). We can actively *select* the situations to which we expose ourselves, in a sense creating our own environment, entering some settings but not others, making decisions about what to do and what not to do. Such active choice, rather than automatic responding, may be facilitated by thinking and planning and by rearranging the environment itself to make it more favorable for one's objectives. If one cannot study well in the midst of noise one may try to find a quiet place for work or attempt to soundproof one's room as much as possible. Even when the environment cannot be changed physically (by rearranging it or by leaving it altogether and entering another setting), it may be possible to *transform* it psychologically by self-instructions and ideation (Chapters 11, 19), as in mental self-distractions or, conversely, concentrated attention.

## *SUMMARY OF PERSON VARIABLES*

To summarize, individual differences in behavior may be due to differences in each of the discussed person variables (summarized in Table 21-2) and in their interactions. First, individuals differ in their *competencies*, i.e., in their ability to generate cognitions and actions. For example, because of differences in skill and earlier learning, individual differences may arise in cognitive-intellective achievements. Differences in behavior also may reflect differences in how individuals *categorize* (encode) a particular situation. That is, people differ in how they encode, group, and label events and in how they construe themselves and others. Performance differences in any situation depend on differences in *expectancies* and specifically on differences in the expected outcomes associated with particular response pat-

**TABLE 21-2   Summary of Cognitive Social Learning Person Variables**

1. COMPETENCIES: ability to construct (generate) particular cognitions and behaviors. Related to measures of IQ, social and cognitive (mental) maturity and competence, ego development, social-intellectual achievements and skills. Refers to what the person knows and *can* do.
2. ENCODING STRATEGIES AND PERSONAL CONSTRUCTS: units for categorizing events and for self-descriptions.
3. EXPECTANCIES: behavior-outcome and stimulus-outcome relations in particular situations.
4. SUBJECTIVE VALUES: motivating and arousing stimuli, incentives, and aversions.
5. SELF-REGULATORY SYSTEMS AND PLANS: rules and self-reactions for performance and for the organization of complex behavior sequences.

Mischel (1973a).

terns and stimuli. Differences in performance also may be due to differences in the subjective *values* of the expected outcomes in the situation. Finally, individual differences may reflect differences in the *self-regulatory systems and plans* that each individual brings to the situation.

It would be both easy and inappropriate to transform these person variables into generalized trait-like dispositions by endowing them with broad cross-situational consistency or removing them from the context of the specific conditions on which they depend. Consider, for example, the variable of "generalized expectancies." In fact, "generalized expectancies" tend to be generalized only within relatively narrow, restricted limits (e.g., Mischel & Staub, 1965). The generality of "locus of control" (Chapter 19), for instance, is limited, with distinct, unrelated expectancies found for different kinds of outcomes (Mischel, Zeiss & Zeiss, 1974). If the above person variables are converted into global trait-like dispositions and removed from their close interaction with situational conditions they are likely to have limited usefulness.

## TOWARD A UNIFIED IMAGE OF MAN?

Does a distinctive image of man begin to emerge from the work discussed throughout this volume and from the person variables examined in this section? Can one glimpse a more unified conception of man in the study of personality? Some psychologists (e.g., Singer & Singer, 1972), including this author, think so. In the present view, this image seems to reflect a growing synthesis of several theoretical influences in current personality psychology. It is an image that seems compatible with many qualities of both the behavioral and the cognitive phenomenological approaches to personality and yet departs from each in some respects.

This image is one of the human being as an active, aware problem-solver, capable of profiting from an enormous range of experiences and cognitive capacities, possessed of great potential for good or ill, actively constructing his or her psychological world, interpreting and processing information in potentially creative ways, influencing the world but also being influenced by it lawfully—even if the laws are difficult to discover and hard to generalize. It views the person as so complex and multi-faceted as to defy easy classifications and comparisons on any single or simple common dimensions, as multiply influenced by a host of determinants, as uniquely organized on the basis of prior experiences and future expectations, and yet as studyable by the methods of science, and continuously responsive to stimulus conditions in meaningful ways. It is an image that has moved a long way from the instinctual drive-reduction models, the static global traits, and the automatic stimulus-response bonds of earlier times (discussed at many points in Part 1). It is an image that highlights the shortcomings of all simplistic theories that view behavior as the exclusive result of any narrow set of determinants, whether these are habits, traits, drives, constructs, instincts, genes, or reinforcers. And yet it is an image that is sure to shift in still unpredictable directions as our understanding and knowledge increase.

# CONCEPTUALIZING INTERACTION

With this image as background, let us now consider more concretely how the interaction of persons and situations may work.

## *WHEN DO INDIVIDUAL DIFFERENCES MAKE A DIFFERENCE?*

The conditions or "situational variables" of the psychological environment may be conceptualized as providing the individual with information; this information influences person variables, thereby affecting how the individual thinks and acts under those conditions. "Situations" (environments) thus influence our behavior by affecting such person variables as how we encode the situation, the outcomes we expect, their subjective value for us, and our competencies.

Recognizing that the question "are persons or situations more important?" is misleading and unanswerable, one can now turn to the more interesting issue: *When* are situations most likely to exert powerful effects and, conversely, *when* are person variables likely to be most influential?

Psychological "situations" ("stimuli," "treatments") are powerful to the degree that they lead everyone to construe the particular events the same way, induce *uniform* expectancies regarding the most appropriate response pattern, provide adequate incentives for the performance of that response pattern, and require skills that everyone has to the same extent. A good example of a powerful stimulus is a red traffic light; it exerts powerful effects on the behavior of most motorists because they all know what it means, are motivated to obey it, and are capable of stopping when they see it. Therefore it would be easier to predict drivers' behavior at stop lights from knowing the color of the light than from making inferences about the "conformity," "cautiousness," or other traits of the drivers.

Conversely, situations are weak to the degree that they are not uniformly encoded, do not generate uniform expectancies concerning the desired behavior, do not offer sufficient incentives for its performance, or fail to provide the learning conditions required for successful genesis of the behavior. An extreme example of such a weak stimulus is the blank card on the TAT projective test (Chapter 9, p. 175) with the instructions to create a story about what might be happening; clearly the answers will depend more on the story-tellers than on the card.

In sum, individual differences can determine behavior in a given situation most strongly when the situation is ambiguously structured (as in projective testing) so that each person is uncertain about how to categorize it, has to structure it in his own terms, and has no clear expectations about the behaviors most likely to be appropriate (normative, reinforced) in that situation. To the degree that the situation is "unstructured" and the person expects that virtually all responses from him are equally likely to be appropriate (i.e., will lead to similar consequences), the significance of individual differences will be greatest. Conversely, when everyone expects that only *one* response will be appropriate (e.g., only one "right" answer on an achievement test, only one correct response for the driver when the traffic light turns red) and that no other responses are equally good, and all people are motivated and capable of making the appropriate response, then individual differences become minimal and situational effects dominant. To the degree that people are exposed to powerful treatments, the role of the individual differences among them will be minimized. Conversely, when treatments are weak, ambiguous, or trivial, individual differences in person variables should have the most significant effects.

So far we have considered "treatments" like those in laboratory studies or therapy programs. But the complex social settings of everyday life also vary in the degree to which they prescribe and limit the range of expected and acceptable behavior for persons in particular roles and settings and hence permit the expression of individual differences (e.g., Barker, 1968; Price, 1974). In some settings the rules and prescriptions for enacting specific role behaviors greatly limit the range of possible behaviors (e.g., in church, at school, in a theater, at a conference), while in others the range of possible behaviors is broad and often the individual can select, structure, and reorganize situations with few external constraints. Because in particular settings certain response patterns are rewarded (effective) while others are not, different settings become the occasion for particular behaviors in different degrees.

## BEHAVIORAL APPROPRIATENESS AND SITUATIONAL CONSTRAINTS

Situations can be classified according to the range and type of behaviors considered appropriate within them. In one study, college students were asked to rate the appropriateness of 15 behaviors in 15 situations (Price & Bouffard, 1974). Examples of the behaviors are *run, belch, kiss, write, eat;* examples of the situations are *in class, on a date, on a bus, at a family dinner, in a restroom.* The average appropriateness ratings were calculated for each of the many combinations of behaviors and situations. These ratings could range from 0 ("the behavior is extremely inappropriate in this situation") to 9 ("the behavior is extremely appropriate in this situation"). To illustrate, Table 21-3 summarizes the average appropriateness ratings found for five behaviors in relation to five situations.

Analyses of this kind applied to a wide range of behaviors and situations can provide useful information. High values for a behavior indicate that it is considered appropriate in many situations, low values suggest that it is generally inappropriate. Likewise, the degree of *situational constraint* for a particular situation can be indexed simply by averaging the appropriateness ratings of the behaviors in that situation (e.g., the rows of Table 21-3). The results of follow-up research also indicated that situations that have high constraint tend to be seen as potentially embarrassing, as requiring more careful self-monitoring of one's behavior, and as demanding certain behaviors rather than others.

**TABLE 21-3  Average Appropriateness Ratings for 5 Behaviors in 5 Situations**

| SITUATIONS | BEHAVIORS | | | | |
|---|---|---|---|---|---|
| | RUN | WRITE | MUMBLE | BELCH | CRY |
| Class | 2.52 | 8.17 | 3.62 | 1.77 | 2.21 |
| Family Dinner | 2.56 | 2.58 | 2.54 | 2.50 | 3.21 |
| Job Interview | 1.94 | 4.85 | 1.31 | 1.21 | 1.37 |
| Bar | 1.96 | 5.38 | 6.21 | 5.04 | 3.44 |
| Own Room | 6.15 | 8.29 | 7.67 | 6.81 | 8.00 |

Based on data from Price and Bouffard (1974).
Note: The higher the number the higher the rated appropriateness of the behavior in the situation.

It would be especially interesting to examine the degree of *variation* among individuals (not just the average level) found for particular behaviors in particular situations. The most "powerful" situations would be those that usually allow little variation; the "weakest" situations would be those in which variation among people is typically high. Individual differences would be expected to exert the greatest influence in the weak (high variation) situations and to have the smallest effect in the powerful (low variation) ones.

## PREDICTING FROM SITUATIONS AND/OR PERSONS

Person-condition interactions are never static, but environmental stabilities can be identified which help to account for continuities in behavior and permit useful predictions. While the psychology of personality cannot ignore the person, it is also true that behavior sometimes may be predicted and influenced simply from knowledge about relevant stimulus conditions, expecially when those conditions are powerful. The potency of predictions based on knowledge of stimulus conditions is seen, for example, in studies that tried to predict the posthospital adjustment of mental patients. Accurate predictions of posthospital adjustment required knowledge of the environment in which the ex-patient will be living in the community—such as the availability of jobs and family support—rather than any measures of person variables or in-hospital behavior (e.g., Fairweather, 1967; Fairweather et al., 1969).

In another domain, to predict intellectual achievement it also helps to take account of the degree to which the child's environment supports (models and reinforces) intellectual development (Wolf, 1966). Finally, when powerful treatments are developed—such as modeling and desensitization therapies for phobias—predictions about outcomes may be best when based on knowing the treatment to which the individual is assigned (e.g., Bandura, Blanchard & Ritter, 1969).

The significance of the psychological situation was vividly demonstrated in a simulated prison study conducted in the basement of a psychology department building (Haney, Banks & Zimbardo, 1973). College student volunteers were selected carefully, on the basis of extensive interviewing and diagnostic testing, to have exemplary backgrounds and no antisocial tendencies. Nevertheless, less than one week after being exposed around the clock to what the authors refer to as the "inherently pathological characteristics of the realistically simulated prison situation itself," all subjects assigned to the role of "guards" were exhibiting extreme antisocial behavior—harassing and victimizing their "prisoners" brutally. The authors concluded that few of the "guards'" reactions could be attributed to individual differences on generalized dimensions (e.g., lack of empathy, excessively rigid adherence to conventional values) existing before they began to play their assigned roles. The potency of the situation undoubtedly left some lasting effects, particularly in beliefs, as evidenced by the subjects' postexperimental statements (e.g., "I learned that people can easily forget that others are human," p. 88). But it is also most likely that once the prison experiment was over, the "guards" gave up their newly characteristic aggressive and harassing behavior and all ex-subjects soon started to respond in terms of the current contexts of their lives.

While some situations can be extremely potent, often we need to know about person variables. Information about person variables becomes essential when relevant information about situations is absent or minimal, or when predictions are needed about how different individuals will respond to the same conditions, or when situational variables are weak. And as we saw in earlier sections, such predictions may be possible at least for "some of the people some of the time."

## MUTUAL INFLUENCES BETWEEN PERSONS AND CONDITIONS

Traditionally, trait-oriented personality research has studied individual differences in response to the "same" situation. But some of the most striking differences between persons may be found not by studying how they react to the same situa-

Person variables also influence the "situations" one selects—including the people to whom one attends.

tion but by analyzing their *selection* and construction of stimulus conditions. In the conditions of life outside the laboratory the psychological "stimuli" that people encounter are neither questionnaire items, nor experimental instructions, nor inanimate events, but involve other people and reciprocal relationships (e.g., with spouse, with boss, with children). We continuously influence the "situations" of our lives as well as being affected by them in a mutual, organic interaction (e.g., Raush et al., 1974). Such interactions reflect not only our reactions to conditions but also our active selection and modification of conditions through our own choices, cognitions, and actions (Wachtel, 1973). Different people select different settings for themselves; conversely, the settings that people select to be in may provide clues about their personal qualities (Eddy & Sinnett, 1973).

The mutual interaction between person and conditions (so easily overlooked when one searches for generalized traits on paper-and-pencil tests) cannot be ignored when behavior is studied in the interpersonal contexts in which it is evoked, maintained, and modified. The analysis of complex social interactions (e.g., Patterson & Cobb, 1971) vividly illustrates how each of us continuously selects, changes, and generates conditions just as much as we are affected by them.

If you change your behavior toward another person he or she generally shows reciprocal changes in behavior toward you. In Raush's (1965, p. 492) studies of naturalistic interactions, for example, "the major determinant of an act was the immediately preceding act. Thus if you want to know what child B will do, the best single predictor is what child A did to B the moment before." Construed from the viewpoint of child A, this means that A's own behavior determines B's reactions to him; if A provokes B, B will reciprocate aggressively. In that sense, the person is generating his own conditions.

The other side of the interaction is the fact that B's behavior is always constrained by what A did the moment before. Studies of the interactions among husbands and wives illustrate this point (Raush et al., 1974). In these studies, husband-wife interactions were observed as the couples coped with such conflicts as how to celebrate their first wedding anniversary when each had made different plans. For example, Bob has arranged and paid in advance for dinner at a restaurant, but Sue has spent half the day preparing for a special dinner at home. As the couple realize their conflict and try to resolve it, their interactions continuously reveal that each antecedent act (what Sue has just said to Bob) constrains each consequent act (how Bob responds).

The meaning and impact of each act also depends on such additional considerations as the total context and situation in which it occurs as well as on the relationship and "style" that each couple develops. ". . . Situations thus 'inform' persons, selecting segments of personal experience; persons also inform situations, selecting segments to respond to" (Raush et al., 1974, p. 212). Such variables as the person's constructs, expectancies, self-regulatory rules and plans presumably guide the situations that he selects and generates, and how he interprets them; they influence the responses that he emits and that in turn shape his environment as much as he is shaped by them.

The conceptualization of behavior must be linked to the specific conditions in which it occurs. Rather than talk about "behavior," it may be more useful to tie specific patterns of behavior to the conditions in which they may be expected. Accurate descriptions require specifying as precisely as possible the response mode of the behavior as well as the conditions in which it is expected to be strong or weak. Thus rather than describe a person as "aggressive" it would be necessary to qualify the mode of aggressive behavior (e.g., verbal insults, but not physical attacks) and the specific circumstances (e.g., when criticized for poor athletic performance on the playground, but not in class). Such cumbersome, hyphenated descriptions would lack the "thumbnail sketch" appeal of global trait portraits. But they would remind us of the discriminativeness, complexity, and uniqueness of each individual's behavior, its dependence on conditions, and the risks of trying to abbreviate and oversimplify it.

In sum, an adequate approach to personality psychology must recognize the interdependence of behavior and conditions. It must recognize the human tendency to invent constructs and to adhere to them, as well as to generate subtly discriminative behaviors across settings and over time. It must be alert to the crucial role of situations (conditions) but can view them as informational inputs whose behavioral impact depends on how they are processed (interpreted) by the person. It also must consider how such information processing hinges, in turn, on person variables as well as on the prior conditions that the individual has experienced. And it has to recognize that the person selects and changes the situations of his life as well as being changed by them. "Personality psychology" does not have to be restricted to the study of differences between individuals in their consistent attributes; it must also help us understand each individual's cognitive and behavioral activities in interaction with the conditions of his or her life.

## SUMMARY

1. The sensitivity of behavior to the conditions in which it occurs may be interpreted as reflecting the adaptiveness and discrimination of which people are capable. Such discrimination facilitates the individual's attempts to cope with a continuously changing environment.

2. There are extensive individual differences in reactions to the same "stimulus" (situation, treatment) and some consistent differences in how a person behaves in particular classes of situations. To analyze and predict an individual's behavior adequately, individual differences generally must be linked to the conditions in which that behavior occurs. At least some people, however, may be consistent on some dimensions some of the time, and sensitivity to situations versus consistency across situations may itself be construed as a dimension of individual differences.

3. There has been growing interest in the environments in which the individual functions. Human environments can be classified according to many dimensions. Labeling and classifying situations, however, is only one aspect of the analysis of environments.

4. As critics of "situationism" stress, an emphasis on the environment and on the conditions in which the person acts should not lead one to lose sight of the person. People can and do change and determine their environments through their own choices and actions. The relative importance of an individual's characteristics and of the situation in determining behavior depends on the particular individual differences, the type of situation, the behavior one is analyzing, and the purpose of the analysis.

5. Just as there is considerable "behavioral specificity," so also is there much specificity in the effects of most situations and treatments. While some conditions are powerful, others exert weak, specific, and ungeneralizable effects that require many qualifiers in efforts to find general laws about cause and effect relations.

6. Person variables are the products within the individual of cognitive development and social learning history. They in turn regulate the meaning of new experiences for the individual. The person variables described in this chapter are intended as tools in the conceptualization and study of the interaction between the individual and his environment. They are an attempted synthesis based on cognitive and social learning psychology.

7. Person variables include the individual's competencies, encoding strategies, and personal constructs, expectancies about probable outcomes, subjective values, and self-regulatory systems and plans. The nature and limits of these variables were discussed.

8. A converging image of man may be arising from several directions in the study of cognition and behavior. That image is of man as an active, aware processor of information, a problem-solver who actively constructs and influences the world rather than responding to it passively. It is also an image of the individual as highly responsive to experience and situations, uniquely organized, defying simple classifications but lawfully influenced by events (even if the laws are complex and hard to discover), and studyable by the methods of science.

9. Person variables help us to analyze the interaction of the individual and situations. Situations provide information that may affect each person variable—for example, the ability to generate behavior patterns, expectancies, the values placed on certain outcomes in the situation, the way the

situation is construed. Powerful situations are those which everyone construes the same way, in which everyone agrees about the most appropriate behavior and has adequate competence and incentives to enact it. When situations are less powerful and more ambiguous, individual differences become more important. The expectancies, encoding strategies, values, and response capabilities that the person brings into the situation are especially important when the situation is unstructured and when there are few external restraints.

10. Behaviors and situations can be analyzed according to their range of appropriateness. Behaviors vary with regard to the range of situations in which they are appropriate; situations differ in the number and kinds of behaviors they allow. (Compare, for example, football games, church services, and family mealtimes.)

11. To predict behavior when situational variables are powerful, knowledge of the relevant situational variables is crucial. When situational variables are weak, when there is little known about them, or when the goal is the prediction of individual differences in response to the same situation, person variables become crucial.

12. Individual differences typically have been studied by holding the situation constant and observing the differences in the way people react to the same situation. Yet one of the most important differences between people is the way *they* select, influence, and change the situations of their lives. The interpersonal relations that comprise much of our daily lives are constantly selected and modified by us in accord with our competencies, constructs, expectancies, values, and plans. Each person generates many of the very conditions to which he or she then reacts in a series of continuous interactions between behavior and conditions.

# References

Abelson, R. Are attitudes necessary? In B. T. King & E. McGinnies (Eds.), *Attitudes, conflicts, and social change.* New York: Academic Press, 1972.

Abelson, R. P., & Rosenberg, M. J. Symbolic psycho-logic: A model of attitudinal cognition. *Behavioral Science,* 1958, *3,* 1–13.

Adinolfi, A. A. Relevance of person perception research to clinical psychology. *Journal of Consulting and Clinical Psychology,* 1971, *37,* 167–176.

Adorno, I. W., Frenkel-Brunswik, E., Levinson, D. J., & Sanford, R. N. *The authoritarian personality.* New York: Harper & Row, 1950.

Akamatsu, T. J., & Thelen, M. H. A review of the literature on observer characteristics and imitation. *Developmental Psychology,* 1974, *10,* 38–47.

Alexander, F., & French, T. M. *Psychoanalytic therapy.* New York: Ronald, 1946.

Alker, H. A. Is personality situationally specific or intrapsychically consistent? *Journal of Personality,* 1972, *40,* 1–16.

Allen, E. K., Hart, B. M., Buell, J. S., Harris, F. R., & Wolf, M. M. Effects of social reinforcement on isolate behavior of a nursery school child. *Child Development,* 1964, *35,* 511–518.

Allinsmith, W. The learning of moral standards. In D. R. Miller & G. E. Swanson (Eds.), *Inner conflict and defense.* New York: Holt, Rinehart and Winston, 1960, pp. 141–176.

Allport, G. W. *Personality: A psychological interpretation.* New York: Holt, Rinehart and Winston, 1937.

Allport, G. W. Motivation in personality: Reply to Mr. Bertocci. *Psychological Review,* 1940, *47,* 533–554.

Allport, G. W. Pattern and growth in personality. New York: Holt, Rinehart and Winston, 1961.

Allport, G. W., & Odbert, H. S. Trait-names: A psycho-lexical study. *Psychological Monographs: General and Applied,* 1936, *47* (1, Whole No. 211).

Alston, W. P. Comments on Kohlberg's "From is to ought." In T. Mischel (Ed.), *Cognitive Development and Epistemology.* New York: Academic Press, 1971.

Amsel, A., & Roussel, J. S. Motivational properties of frustration: I. Effect on a running response of the addition of frustration to the motivational complex. *Journal of Experimental Psychology,* 1952, *43,* 363–368.

American Psychological Association. *Standards for educational and psychological tests and manuals.* Washington, D.C.: APA, 1966.

Anastasi, A., & D'Angelo, R. A comparison of Negro and white preschool children in language development and Goodenough Draw-a-Man I.Q. *Journal of Genetic Psychology,* 1952, *81,* 147–165.

Anderson, H. H., & Anderson, G. L. (Eds.). *An introduction to projective techniques.* Englewood Cliffs, N.J.: Prentice-Hall, 1951.

Anderson, I. H., Hughes, B. O., & Dixon, W. R. The rate of reading development and its relation to age of learning to read, sex, and intelligence. *Journal of Educational Research,* 1957, *50,* 481–494.

515

Anderson, J. R., & Bower, G. H. *Human associative memory.* New York: Wiley, 1973.

Anderson, N. H. Primacy effects in personality impression formation using a generalized order effect paradigm. *Journal of Personality and Social Psychology,* 1965, *2,* 1-9.

Anderson, N. H. Cognitive algebra: Integration theory applied to social attribution. In L. Berkowitz (Ed.), *Advances in experimental social psychology,* 1974, *7,* 2-93.

Archibald, H. C., & Tuddenham, R. D. Persistent stress reaction after combat. *Archives of General Psychiatry,* 1965, *12,* 475-481.

Argyle, M., & Little, B. R. Do personality traits apply to social behavior? *Journal of Theory of Social Behavior,* 1972, *2,* 1-35 (Great Britain).

Aronfreed, J. The origin of self-criticism. *Psychological Review,* 1964, *71,* 193-218.

Aronfreed, J. The internalization of social control through punishment: Experimental studies of the role of conditioning and the second signal system in the development of conscience. *Proceedings of the XVIIIth International Congress of Psychology.* Moscow, USSR, August, 1966, *35,* 219-230.

Aronfreed, J. *Conduct and conscience: The socialization of internalized control over behavior.* New York: Academic Press, 1968.

Aronson, E. *The social animal.* San Francisco: Freeman, 1972.

Aronson, E., & Carlsmith, J. M. Performance expectancy as a determinant of actual performance. *Journal of Abnormal and Social Psychology,* 1962, *65,* 178-182.

Aronson, E., & Carlsmith, J. M. Effect of severity of threat on the devaluation of forbidden behavior. *Journal of Abnormal and Social Psychology,* 1963, *66,* 584-588.

Aronson, E., & Mettee, D. Dishonest behavior as a function of differential levels of induced self-esteem. *Journal of Personality and Social Psychology,* 1968, *9,* 121-127.

Asch, S. E. Forming impressions of personality. *Journal of Abnormal and Social Psychology,* 1946, *41,* 258-290.

Ash, P. The reliability of psychiatric diagnoses. *Journal of Abnormal and Social Psychology,* 1949, *44,* 272-276.

Atkinson, J. W. Motivational determinants of risk-taking behavior. *Psychological Review,* 1957, *64,* 359-372.

Atkinson, J. W. (Ed.). *Motives in fantasy, action and society.* Princeton, N.J.: Van Nostrand, 1958.

Atkinson, J. W. *An introduction to motivation.* Princeton, N.J.: Van Nostrand, 1964.

Atkinson, J. W., & Feather, N. T. *A theory of achievement motivation.* New York: Wiley, 1966.

Atthowe, J. M., Jr., & Krasner, L. A preliminary report on the application of contingent reinforcement procedures (token economy) on a "chronic" psychiatric ward. *Journal of Abnormal Psychology,* 1968, *73,* 37-43.

Averill, J. Personal control over aversive stimuli and its relationship to stress. *Psychological Bulletin,* 1973, *80,* 286-303.

Ax, A. F. The physiological differentiation between fear and anger in humans. *Psychosomatic Medicine,* 1953, *15,* 433-442.

Ayllon, T., & Azrin, N. H. The measurement and reinforcement of behavior of psychotics. *Journal of the Experimental Analysis of Behavior,* 1965, *8,* 357-383.

Ayllon, T., & Azrin, N. H. *The token economy.* New York: Appleton, 1968.

Ayllon, T., & Haughton, E. Control of the behavior of schizophrenic patients by food. *Journal of the Experimental Analysis of Behavior,* 1962, *5,* 343-352.

Ayllon, T., & Haughton, E. Modification of symptomatic verbal behaviour of mental patients. *Behaviour Research and Therapy,* 1964, *2,* 87-97.

Bach, G. R. Father-fantasies and father-typing in father-separated children. *Child Development*, 1946, *17*, 63–80.

Baldwin, A. L. A cognitive theory of socialization. In D. A. Goslin (Ed.), *Handbook of socialization theory and research*. Chicago: Rand McNally, 1969, 325–480.

Balow, I. H. Sex differences in first grade reading. *Elementary English*, 1963, *40*, 303–306.

Bandura, A. Relationship of family patterns to child behavior disorders. Progress Report, U.S.P.H. Research Grant M-1734, Stanford University, 1960.

Bandura, A. Punishment revisited. *Journal of Consulting Psychology*, 1962, *26*, 298–301.

Bandura, A. Vicarious processes: A case of no-trial learning. In L. Berkowitz (Ed.), *Advances in experimental social psychology*. Vol. II. New York: Academic Press, 1965, 1–55.

Bandura, A. *Principles of behavior modification*. New York: Holt, Rinehart and Winston, 1969.

Bandura, A. *Social learning theory*. Morristown, N. J.: General Learning Press, 1971.

Bandura, A. *Aggression: A social learning analysis*. Englewood Cliffs, N.J.: Prentice-Hall, 1973.

Bandura, A., Blanchard, E. B., & Ritter, B. Relative efficacy of desensitization and modeling approaches for inducing behavioral, affective, and attitudinal changes. *Journal of Personality and Social Psychology*, 1969, *13*, 173–199.

Bandura, A., Grusec, J. E., & Menlove, F. L. Observational learning as a function of symbolization and incentive set. *Child Development*, 1966, *37*, 499–506.

Bandura, A., Grusec, J. E., & Menlove, F. L. Vicarious extinction of avoidance behavior. *Journal of Personality and Social Psychology*, 1967, *5*, 16–23.

Bandura, A., & Huston, A. C. Identification as a process of incidental learning. *Journal of Abnormal and Social Psychology*, 1961, *63*, 311–318.

Bandura, A., & Jeffery, R. W. Role of symbolic coding and rehearsal processes in observational learning. *Journal of Personality and Social Psychology*, 1973, *26*, 122–130.

Bandura, A., & Kupers, C. J. Transmission of patterns of self-reinforcement through modeling. *Journal of Abnormal and Social Psychology*, 1964, *69*, 1-9.

Bandura, A., & McDonald, F. J. Influence of social reinforcement and the behavior of models in shaping children's moral judgments. *Journal of Abnormal Social Psychology*, 1963, *67*, 274–281.

Bandura, A., & Mischel, W. Modification of self-imposed delay of reward through exposure to live and symbolic models. *Journal of Personality and Social Psychology*, 1965, *2*, 698–705.

Bandura, A., & Rosenthal, T. L. Vicarious classical conditioning as a function of arousal level. *Journal of Personality and Social Psychology*, 1966, *3*, 54–62.

Bandura, A., Ross, D., & Ross, S. A. Transmission of aggression through imitation of aggressive models. *Journal of Abnormal and Social Psychology*, 1961, *63*, 575–582.

Bandura, A., Ross, D., & Ross, S. A. Imitation of film-mediated aggressive models. *Journal of Abnormal and Social Psychology*, 1963, *66*, 3–11. (a)

Bandura, A., Ross, D., & Ross, S. A. A comparative test of the status envy, social power, and secondary reinforcement theories of identificatory learning. *Journal of Abnormal and Social Psychology*, 1963, *67*, 527–534. (b)

Bandura, A., & Walters, R. *Social learning and personality development*. Holt, Rinehart and Winston, 1963.

Bardwick, J. *Psychology of women: A study of biocultural conflicts*. New York: Harper & Row, 1972.

Barker, R. G. *Ecological psychology.* Stanford: Stanford University Press, 1968.

Barker, R. G., Dembo, T., & Lewin, K. Frustration and regression: An experiment with young children. *University of Iowa Studies in Child Welfare,* 1941, *18,* Whole No. 386.

Barker, R. G., & Wright, H. F. *One boy's day.* New York: Harper & Row, 1951.

Baron, R. A. Attraction toward the model and model's competence as determinants of adult imitative behavior. *Journal of Personality and Social Psychology,* 1970, *14,* 345–351.

Barry, H. B., III., Bacon, M. K., & Child, I. L. A cross-cultural survey of some sex differences in socialization. *Journal of Abnormal and Social Psychology,* 1957, *55,* 327–332.

Bass, B. M. Authoritarianism or acquiescence? *Journal of Abnormal and Social Psychology,* 1955, *51,* 616–623.

Becker, W. C. The matching of behavior rating and questionnaire personality factors. *Psychological Bulletin,* 1960, *57,* 201–212.

Becker, W. C. Consequences of different kinds of parental discipline. In M. L. Hoffman and L. W. Hoffman (Eds.), *Review of Child Development Research.* Vol. I. New York: Russell Sage Foundation, 1964, pp. 169–208.

Bell, J. E. *Projective techniques.* New York: Longmans, Green, 1948.

Bell, R., & Costello, N. Three tests for sex differences in tactile sensitivity in the newborn. *Biologia Neonatorum,* 1964, *7,* 335–347.

Bell, R., & Darling, J. The prone head reaction in the human newborn: relationship with sex and tactile sensitivity. *Child Development,* 1965, *36,* 943–949.

Beller, E. K. Dependency and independence in young children. *Journal of Genetic Psychology,* 1955, *87,* 25–35.

Beller, E. K. Personality correlates of perceptual discrimination in children. Progress Report, 1962.

Beller, E. K., & Neubauer, P. B. Sex differences and symptom patterns in early childhood. *Journal of Child Psychiatry,* 1963, *2,* 414–433.

Bem, D. J. Constructing cross-situational consistencies in behavior: Some thoughts on Alker's critique of Mischel. *Journal of Personality,* 1972, *40,* 17–26.

Bem, D. J. Self-perception theory. In L. Berkowitz (Ed.), *Advances in experimental social psychology.* Vol. 6. New York: Academic Press, 1972.

Bem, D. J., & Allen, A. On predicting some of the people some of the time: The search for cross-situational consistencies in behavior. *Psychological Review,* 1974, *81,* 506–520.

Bem, S. L. Sex-role adaptability:.One consequence of psychological androgyny. *Journal of Personality and Social Psychology,* 1975, *31,* 634–643.

Bem, S. L., & Bem, D. J. Homogenizing the American woman: The power of an unconscious ideology. Unpublished manuscript. Stanford University, 1972.

Bennett, E. L., Diamond, M. C., Krech, D., & Rosenzweig, M. R. Chemical and anatomical plasticity of the brain. *Science,* 1964, *146,* 610–619.

Bennett, E. M., & Cohen, L. R. Men and women: Personality patterns and contrasts. *Genetic Psychology Monographs,* 1959, *59,* 101–155.

Bennett, G. K., et al. *Differential aptitudes tests manual,* 3rd ed. New York: Psychological Corporation, 1959.

Berger, S. M. Conditioning through vicarious instigation. *Psychological Review,* 1962, *69,* 450–466.

Bergin, A. E. Some implications of psychotherapy research for therapeutic practice. *Journal of Abnormal Psychology,* 1966, *71,* 235–246.

Bergin, A. E. The evaluation of therapeutic outcomes. In A. E. Bergin and S. I. Garfield (Eds.), *Handbook of psychotherapy and behavior change.* New York: Wiley, 1971, pp. 217–270.

Berkowitz, L. Control of aggression. In B. M. Caldwell & H. Ricciuti (Eds.), *Review of Child Development Research*, vol. 3, 1969.

Berkowitz, L. The contagion of violence: An S-R mediational analysis of some effects of observed aggression. In M. Page (Ed.), *Nebraska symposium on motivation*. Lincoln: University of Nebraska Press, 1970.

Berlyne, D. E. Conflict and arousal. *Scientific American*, 1966, *215* (2), 82–87.

Bettelheim, B. Individual and mass behavior in extreme situations. *Journal of Abnormal and Social Psychology*, 1943, *38*, 417–452.

Biderman, A. D. Life and death in extreme captivity situations. In M. H. Appley & R. Trumbull (Eds.), *Psychological stress*. New York: Appleton 1967, pp. 242–277.

Bieri, J., Atkins, A. L., Briar, S., Leaman, R. L., Miller, H., & Tripoldi, T. *Clinical and social judgment*. New York: Wiley, 1966.

Bijou, S. W. Experimental studies of child behavior, normal and deviant. In L. Krasner & L. P. Ullmann (Eds.), *Research in behavior modification*. New York: Holt, Rinehart and Winston, 1965, pp. 56–81.

Birnbrauer, J. S., Bijou, S. W., Wolf, M. M., & Kidder, J. D. Programmed instruction in the classroom. In L. Ullmann & L. Krasner (Eds.), *Case studies in behavior modification*. New York: Holt, Rinehart and Winston, 1965.

Blanchard, E. B., & Young, L. D. Self-control of cardiac function: A promise as yet unfulfilled. *Psychological Bulletin*, 1973, *79*, 145–163.

Blashfield, R. An evaluation of the DSM-II classification of schizophrenia as a nomenclature. *Journal of Abnormal Psychology*, 1973, *82*, 382–389.

Block, J. *The Q-sort method in personality assessment and psychiatric research*. Springfield, Ill.: Charles C Thomas, 1961.

Block, J. *The challenge of response sets*. New York: Appleton, 1965.

Block, J. Some reasons for the apparent inconsistency of personality. *Psychological Bulletin*, 1968, *70*, 210–212.

Block, J. *Lives through time*. Berkeley, Calif.: Bancroft, 1971.

Block, J. Recognizing the coherence of personality. Paper presented at the International Conference on Interactional Psychology, Saltsjöbaden, Sweden, 1975.

Block, J., & Martin, B. Predicting the behavior of children under frustration. *Journal of Abnormal and Social Psychology*, 1955, *51*, 281–285.

Blum, G. S. *The Blacky Pictures, Manual of instructions*. New York: Psychological Corporation, 1950.

Blum, G. S. *Psychoanalytic theories of personality*. New York: McGraw-Hill, 1953.

Blum, G. S. Perceptual defense revisited. *Journal of Abnormal and Social Psychology*, 1955, *51*, 24–29.

Bonarius, J. C. J. Research in the personal construct theory of George A. Kelly: Role construct repertory test and basic theory. In B. A. Maher (Ed.), *Progress in experimental personality research*. New York: Academic Press, 1965, pp. 1–46.

Borstelmann, L. J. Sex of experimenter and sex-typed behavior of young children. *Child Development*, 1961, *32*, 519–524.

Boudin, H. M. Contingency contracting as a therapeutic tool in the deceleration of amphetamine use. *Behavior Therapy*, 1972, *3*, 604–608.

Bower, G. H. Mental imagery and associative learning. In L. Gregg (Ed.), *Cognition in learning and memory*. New York: Wiley, 1969.

Bowers, K. Situationism in psychology: An analysis and a critique. *Psychological Review*, 1973, *80*, 307–336.

Braine, M. D. S. On learning the grammatical order of words. *Psychological Review*, 1963, *70*, 323–348.

Bramel, D. A. A dissonance theory approach to defensive projection. *Journal of Abnormal and Social Psychology*, 1962, *64*, 121–129.

Breger, L., & McGaugh, J. L. Critique and reformulation of "learning theory" approaches to psychotherapy and neurosis. *Psychological Bulletin*, 1965, *63*, 338–358.

Brehm, J. W. *A theory of psychological reactance.* New York: Academic Press, 1966.

Brehm, J. W., & Cohen, A. R. *Explorations in cognitive dissonance.* New York: Wiley, 1962.

Brill, A. A. *Basic principles of psychoanalysis.* Garden City, N.Y.: Doubleday, 1949.

Bronfenbrenner, U. Freudian theories of identification and their derivatives. *Child Development*, 1960, *31*, 15–40.

Broverman, D. M., Klaiber, E. L., Kobayashi, Y., & Vogel, W. Roles of activation and inhibition in sex differences in cognitive abilities. *Psychological Review*, 1968, *75*, 23–50.

Broverman, I. K., Broverman, D. M., Clarkson, F. E., Rosenkrantz, P. S., & Vogel, S. R. Sex-role stereotypes and clinical judgments of mental health. *Journal of Consulting and Clinical Psychology*, 1970, *34*, 1–7.

Brown, D. G. Masculinity-femininity development in children. *Journal of Consulting Psychology*, 1957, *21*, 197–202.

Brown, J. S. The generalization of approach responses as a function of stimulus intensity and strength of motivation. *Journal of Comparative Psychology*, 1942, *33*, 209–226.

Brown, J. S. Gradients of approach and avoidance responses and their relation to level of motivation. *Journal of Comparative and Physiological Psychology*, 1948, *41*, 450–465.

Brown, R. *Social psychology.* New York: Free Press, 1965.

Bruner, J. S. On perceptual readiness. *Psychological Review*, 1957, *64*, 123–152.

Bruner, J. S. Social psychology and perception. In E. E. Maccoby, T. M. Newcomb, & E. L. Hartley (Eds.), *Readings in social psychology*, 3rd ed. New York: Holt, Rinehart and Winston, 1958.

Bruner, J. S. Processes of cognitive growth in infancy. Heinz Werner Memorial Lectures, Clark University, December, 1967.

Bruner, J. S., & Goodman, C. C. Value and need as organizing factors in perception. *Journal of Abnormal and Social Psychology*, 1947, *42*, 33–44.

Bruner, J. S., Olver, R. R., & Greenfield, P. M. *Studies in cognitive growth.* New York: Wiley, 1966.

Bruner, J. S., & Postman, L. Emotional selectivity in perception and reaction. *Journal of Personality*, 1947, *16*, 69–77.

Burton, R. V. Generality of honesty reconsidered. *Psychological Review*, 1963, *70*, 481–499.

Burton, R. V., Maccoby, E. E., & Allinsmith, W. Antecedents of resistance to temptation in four-year-old children. *Child Development*, 1961, *32*, 689–710.

Buss, A. H. Physical aggression in relation to different frustrations. *Journal of Abnormal and Social Psychology*, 1963, *67*, 1–7.

Buss, A. H. Aggression pays. In J. L. Singer (Ed.), *The control of aggression and violence.* New York: Academic Press, 1971.

Butler, J. M., & Haigh, G. V. Changes in the relation between self-concepts and ideal concepts consequent upon client-centered counseling. In C. R. Rogers & R. F. Dymond (Eds.), *Psychotherapy and personality change: Co-ordinated studies in the client-centered approach.* Chicago: University of Chicago Press, 1954, p. 55–76.

Byrne, D. Repression-sensitization as a dimension of personality. In B. A. Maher (Ed.), *Progress in experimental personality research*. Vol. 1. New York: Academic Press, 1964.

Byrne, D. *An introduction to personality*. Englewood Cliffs, N.J.: Prentice-Hall, 1966.

Byrne, D. Attitudes and attraction. In L. Berkowitz (Ed.), *Advances in experimental social psychology*. Vol. 4. New York: Academic Press, 1969.

Byrne, D., & Holcomb, J. The reliability of a response measure: differential recognition-threshold scores. *Psychological Bulletin*, 1962, *59*, 70–73.


Cairns, R. B. The influence of dependency-anxiety on the effectiveness of social reinforcers. Unpublished doctoral dissertation, Stanford University, 1959.

Campbell, D. T. Recommendations for APA Test Standards regarding construct, trait, or discriminant validity. *American Psychologist*, 1960, *15*, 546–553.

Campbell, D. T., & Fiske, D. Convergent and discriminant validation. *Psychological Bulletin*, 1959, *56*, 81–105.

Campbell, D., Sanderson, R. E., & Laverty, S. G. Characteristics of a conditioned response in human subjects during extinction trials following a single traumatic conditioning trial. *Journal of Abnormal and Social Psychology*, 1964, *68*, 627–639.

Campbell, J., & Dunnette, M. Effectiveness of T-group experiences in managerial training and development. *Psychological Bulletin*, 1968, *70*, 73–104.

Campus, N. Transituational consistency as a dimension of personality. *Journal of Personality and Social Psychology*, 1974, *29*, 593–600.

Carlson, R. Where is the person in personality research? *Psychological Bulletin*, 1971, *75*, 203–219.

Caron, A. J., & Wallach, M. A. Recall of interrupted tasks under stress: A phenomenon of memory or of learning? *Journal of Abnormal and Social Psychology*, 1957, *55*, 372–381.

Cartwright, D. S. *Introduction to personality*. Chicago: Rand McNally, 1974.

Casler, L. Maternal deprivation: A critical review of the literature. *Monographs of the Society for Research in Child Development*, 1961, *26*, 1–64.

Cattell, R. B. Confirmation and clarification of primary personality factors. *Psychometrika*, 1947, *12*, 197–220.

Cattell, R. B. *Personality: A systematic theoretical and factual study*. New York: McGraw-Hill, 1950.

Cattell, R. B. *Personality and motivation structure and measurement*. Yonkers-on-Hudson: World Book, 1957.

Cattell, R. B. *The scientific analysis of personality*. Baltimore: Penguin Books, 1965.

Chapman, L. J., & Campbell, D. T. Response set in the F Scale. *Journal of Abnormal and Social Psychology*, 1957, *54*, 129–132.

Chapman, L. J., & Chapman, J. P. Illusory correlations as an obstacle to the use of valid psychodiagnostic signs. *Journal of Abnormal Psychology*, 1969, *74*, 271–280.

Child, I. L., & Waterhouse, I. K. Frustration and the quality of performance: I. A critique of the Barker, Dembo, and Lewin experiment. *Psychological Review*, 1952, *59*, 351–362.

Chodoff, P. Late effects of concentration camp syndrome. *Archives of General Psychiatry*, 1963, *8*, 323–333.

Chodorkoff, B. Self-perception, perceptual defense, and adjustment. *Journal of Abnormal and Social Psychology*, 1954, *49*, 508–512.

Chomsky, N. *Aspects of the theory of syntax.* Cambridge, Mass.: M.I.T. Press, 1965.

Clark, D. F. Fetishism treated by negative conditioning. *British Journal of Psychiatry,* 1963, *109,* 404–407.

Cline, N. G. The influence of social context on the perception of faces. *Journal of Personality,* 1956, *25,* 142–158.

Cline, V. B. Interpersonal perception. In B. A. Maher (Ed.), *Progress in experimental personality research.* Vol. 1. New York: Academic Press, 1964, pp. 221–284.

Colby, K. M. Things to come: Designing neurotic computers. In L. Krasner & L. P. Ullmann (Eds.), *Research in behavior modification.* New York: Holt, Rinehart and Winston, 1965, pp. 305–309.

Colby, K. M., & Hilf, F. D. *Multidimensional analysis in evaluating a simulation of paranoid thought.* Stanford Artificial Intelligence Laboratory Computer Science Department. Report No. CS-347, National Technical Information Service, Springfield, Va., 1973.

Coopersmith, S. *The antecedents of self-esteem.* San Francisco: Freeman, 1967.

Coopersmith, S. Studies in self-esteem. *Scientific American,* 1968, *218* (2), 96–106.

Cowen, E. L., Gardner, E. A., & Zax, M. *Emergent approaches to mental health problems.* New York: Appleton, 1967.

Crandall, V. J. Achievement. In H. W. Stevenson (Ed.), *Child psychology (Sixty-second Yearbook of the National Society for the Study of Education).* Chicago: University of Chicago Press, 1963, pp. 416–459.

Crandall, V. J., Preston, A., & Rabson, A. Maternal reactions and the development of independence and achievement behavior in young children. *Child Development,* 1960, *31,* 243–251.

Cronbach, L. J. Statistical methods applied to Rorschach scores: A review. *Psychological Bulletin,* 1949, *46,* 393–429.

Cronbach, L. J. Beyond the two disciplines of scientific psychology. *American Psychologist,* 1975, *30,* 116–127.

Crow, W. J. The effect of training upon accuracy and variability in interpersonal perception. *Journal of Abnormal and Social Psychology,* 1957, *55,* 355–359.

Crow, W. J., & Hammond, K. R. The generality of accuracy and response sets in interpersonal perception. *Journal of Abnormal and Social Psychology,* 1957, *54,* 384–390.

Crowne, D. P., & Marlowe, D. *The approval motive: Studies in evaluative dependence.* New York: Wiley, 1964.


D'Andrade, R. G. Trait psychology and componential analysis. *American Anthropologist,* 1965, *67,* 215–228.

D'Andrade, R. G. Sex differences and cultural institutions. In E. E. Maccoby (Ed.), *The development of sex differences.* Stanford: Stanford University Press, 1966, pp. 174–204.

D'Andrade, R. G. Cognitive structures and judgment. Paper prepared for T.O.B.R.E. Research Workshop on *Cognitive Organization and Psychological Processes,* Huntington Beach, Calif., August 16–21, 1970.

Danet, B. N. Prediction of mental illness in college students on the basis of "nonpsychiatric" MMPI profiles. *Journal of Consulting Psychology,* 1965, *29,* 577–580.

Danzig, E. R., Thayer, P. W., & Galanter, L. R. The effects of a threatening rumor on a disaster-stricken community. Washington, D.C.: National Academy of Sciences, National Research Council, Disaster Research Group, *Disaster Study No. 10,* 1958.

Davison, G. C. The negative effects of early exposure to suboptimal visual stimuli. *Journal of Personality*, 1964, *32*, 278–295.

Davison, G. C. Systematic desensitization as a counterconditioning process. *Journal of Abnormal Psychology*, 1968, *73*, 91–99.

Davison, G. C., & Neale, N. M. *Abnormal psychology*. New York: Wiley, 1974.

Davitz, J. R. The effects of previous training on postfrustration behavior. *Journal of Abnormal and Social Psychology*, 1952, *47*, 309–315.

Dawe, H. C. An analysis of 200 quarrels of preschool children. *Child Development*, 1934, *5*, 139–157.

Deane, G. E. Human heart rate responses during experimentally induced anxiety. *Journal of Experimental Psychology*, 1961, *61*, 489–493.

Deaux, K., & Emswiller, T. Explanation of successful performance on sex linked tasks: What is skill for the male is luck for the female. *Journal of Personality and Social Psychology*, 1974, *29*, 80–85.

Dechter, M. *The new chastity and other arguments against women's liberation*. New York: Coward McCann, 1972.

DeNike, L. D. The temporal relationship between awareness and performance in verbal conditioning. *Journal of Experimental Psychology*, 1964, *68*, 521–529.

Dennenberg, V. H. Critical periods, stimulus input and emotional reactivity: A theory of infantile stimulation. *Psychological Review*, 1964, *71*, 335–351.

Diamond, M. J., & Shapiro, J. L. Changes in locus of control as a function of encounter group experiences: A study and replication. *Journal of Abnormal Psychology*, 1973, *82*, 514–518.

Diven, K. Certain determinants of conditioning of anxiety reactions. *Journal of Psychology*, 1937, *3*, 291–308.

Dollard, J., Doob, L. W., Miller, N. E., Mowrer, O. H., & Sears, R. R. *Frustration and aggression*. New Haven: Yale University Press, 1939.

Dollard, J., & Miller, N. E. *Personality and psychotherapy: An analysis in terms of learning, thinking, and culture*. New York: McGraw-Hill, 1950.

Dornbusch, S. M., Hastorf, A. H., Richardson, S. A., Muzzy, R. E., & Vreeland, R. S. The perceiver and the perceived: Their relative influence on the categories of interpersonal cognition. *Journal of Personality and Social Psychology*, 1965, *1*, 434–440.

Douvan, E., & Kaye, C. *Adolescent girls*. Ann Arbor: Survey Research Center, University of Michigan, 1957.

Droppleman, L. F., & Schaefer, E. S. Boys' and girls' reports of maternal and paternal behavior. Paper read at American Psychological Association, August 31, 1961, New York City.

Dulany, D. E., Jr. Avoidance learning of perceptual defense and vigilance. *Journal of Abnormal and Social Psychology*, 1957, *55*, 333–338.

Dulany, D. E., Jr. The place of hypotheses and intentions: An analysis of verbal control in verbal conditioning. In C. W. Eriksen (Ed.), *Behavior and awareness*. Durham, N.C.: Duke University Press, 1962, pp. 102–129.

Duncker, K. Experimental modification of children's food preferences through social suggestion. *Journal of Abnormal Psychology*, 1938, *33*, 489–507.

Dunnette, M. D. People feeling: Joy, more joy, and the "slough of despond." *Journal of Applied Behavioral Science*, 1969, *5*, 25–44.

Dunsdon, M. I., & Fraser-Roberts, J. A. A study of the performance of 2,000 children on four vocabulary tests. *British Journal of Statistical Psychology*, 1957, *10*, 1–16.

D'Zurilla, T. Recall efficiency and mediating cognitive events in "experimental repression." *Journal of Personality and Social Psychology*, 1965, *1*, 253–257.

Eddy, G. L., & Sinnett, R. E. Behavior setting utilization by emotionally disturbed college students. *Journal of Consulting and Clinical Psychology*, 1973, *40*, 210–216.

Edwards, A. L. *The social desirability variable in personality assessment and research.* New York: Dryden, 1957.

Edwards, A. L. Social desirability and the description of others. *Journal of Abnormal and Social Psychology*, 1959, *59*, 434–436.

Edwards, A. L. Social desirability or acquiescence in the MMPI? A case study with the SD scale. *Journal of Abnormal and Social Psychology*, 1961, *63*, 351–359.

Ekman, P., Friesen, W. V. & Ellsworth, P. *Emotion in the human face.* New York: Pergamon, 1972.

Elliott, R. Effects of uncertainty about the nature and advent of a noxious stimulus (shock) upon distress. *Journal of Personality and Social Psychology*, 1966, *3*, 353–356.

Elliott, R. Tonic heart rate: Experiments on the effects of collative variables lead to a hypothesis about its motivational significance. *Journal of Personality and Social Psychology*, 1969, *12*, 211–228.

Elliott, R. The motivational significance of heart rate. In P. A. Obrist, A. H. Black, J. Brener, & L. V. D. Cara (Eds.), *Cardiovascular psychophysiology: Current issues in response mechanisms, biofeedback, and methodology.* Chicago. Aldine, 1974.

Ellsworth, P. C., & Carlsmith, M. J. Effects of eye contact and verbal content on affective response to a dyadic interaction. *Journal of Personality and Social Psychology*, 1968, *10*, 15–20.

Endler, N. S. The person versus the situation—A pseudo issue? *Journal of Personality*, 1973, *41*, 287–303.

Endler, N. S., & Hunt, J. McV. Sources of behavioral variance as measured by the S-R inventory of anxiousness. *Psychological Bulletin*, 1966, *65*, 336–346.

Endler, N. S., & Hunt, J. McV. Generalizability of contributions from sources of variance in the S-R inventories of anxiousness. *Journal of Personality*, 1969, *37*, 1–24.

Endler, N. S., & Magnusson, D. (Eds.). *Interactional psychology and personality.* Washington, D.C.: Hemisphere Publishing Corp., 1975.

Epstein, R., & Liverant, S. Verbal conditioning and sex-role identification in children. *Child Development*, 1963, *34*, 99–106.

Epstein, S. The measurement of drive and conflict in humans: Theory and experiment. In M. R. Jones (Ed.), *Nebraska symposium on motivation.* Lincoln: University of Nebraska Press, 1962, pp. 281–321.

Epstein, S. Toward a unified theory of anxiety. In B. A. Maher (Ed.), *Progress in experimental personality research.* Vol. 4. New York: Academic Press, 1967, pp. 1–89.

Epstein, S., & Fenz, W. D. Theory and experiment on the measurement of approach-avoidance conflict. *Journal of Abnormal and Social Psychology*, 1962, *64*, 97–112.

Epstein, S., & Roupenian, A. Heart rate and skin conductance during anxiety: The effect of uncertainty about receiving a noxious stimulus. *Journal of Personality and Social Psychology*, 1970, *16*, 12–19.

Erdelyi, M. H. A new look at the new look: Perceptual defense and vigilance. *Psychological Review*, 1974, *81*, 1–25.

Eriksen, C. W. Defense against ego-threat in memory and perception. *Journal of Abnormal and Social Psychology*, 1952, *47*, 230–235. (a)

Eriksen, C. W. Individual differences in defensive forgetting. *Journal of Experimental Psychology*, 1952, *44*, 442–446. (b)

Eriksen, C. W. Unconscious process. In M. R. Jones (Ed.), *Nebraska symposium on motivation*. Lincoln: University of Nebraska Press, 1958, pp. 169–227.

Eriksen, C. W. Discrimination and learning without awareness: A methodological survey and evaluation. *Psychological Review*, 1960, *67*, 279–300.

Eriksen, C. W. Cognitive responses to internally cued anxiety. In C. D. Spielberger (Ed.), *Anxiety and behavior*. New York: Academic Press, 1966, pp. 327–360.

Eriksen, B. A., & Eriksen, C. W. *Perception and personality*. Morristown, N.J.: General Learning Press, 1972.

Eriksen, C. W., & Kuethe, J. L. Avoidance conditioning of verbal behavior without awareness: A paradigm of repression. *Journal of Abnormal and Social Psychology*, 1956, *53*, 203–209.

Erikson, E. *Childhood and society*. New York: Norton, 1963.

Erikson, E. *Identity: Youth and crisis*. New York: Norton, 1968.

Exline, R., & Winters, L. C. Affective relations and mutual glances in dyads. In S. Tomkins & C. Izard (Eds.), *Affect, cognition, and personality*. New York: Springer, 1965.

Eysenck, H. J. The effects of psychotherapy: An evaluation. *Journal of Consulting Psychology*, 1952, *16*, 319–324.

Eysenck, H. J. The effects of psychotherapy. In H. J. Eysenck (Ed.), *Handbook of abnormal psychology: An experimental approach*. New York: Basic Books, 1961, pp. 697–725.

Eysenck, H. J. Extraversion and the acquisition of eyeblink and GSR conditioned responses. *Psychological Bulletin*, 1965, *63*, 258–270.

Eysenck, H. J. *The biological basis of personality*. Springfield, Ill.: Charles C Thomas, 1967.

Eysenck, H. J., & Beech, R. Counterconditioning and related methods. In A. E. Bergin & S. L. Garfield (Eds.), *Handbook of psychotherapy and behavior change*. New York: Wiley, 1971.

Eysenck, H. J., & Rachman, S. *The causes and cures of neurosis: An introduction to modern behavior therapy based on learning theory and the principles of conditioning*. San Diego: Knapp, 1965.

Fairweather, G. W. *Social psychology in treating mental illness: An experimental approach*. New York: Wiley, 1964.

Fairweather, G. W. *Methods in experimental social innovation*. New York: Wiley, 1967.

Fairweather, G. W., Sanders, D. H., Cressler, D. L., & Maynard, H. *Community life for the mentally ill: An alternative to institutional care*. Chicago: Aldine, 1969.

Farina, A. *Schizophrenia*. Morristown, N.J.: General Learning Press, 1972.

Fauls, L. B., & Smith, W. D. Sex-role learning of five-year-olds. *Journal of Genetic Psychology*, 1956, *89*, 105–117.

Feather, B. W. Semantic generalization of classically conditioned responses. *Psychological Bulletin*, 1965, *63*, 425–441.

Feather, N. T. Subjective probability and decision under uncertainty. *Psychological Review*, 1959, *66*, 150–164.

Feldman, R. B., & Werry, J. S. An unsuccessful attempt to treat a tiqueur by massed practice. *Behaviour Research and Therapy*, 1966, *4*, 111–117.

Fenichel, O. *The psychoanalytic theory of neurosis*. New York: Norton, 1945.

Fenz, W. D. Conflict and stress as related to physiological activation and sensory, perceptual and cognitive functioning. *Psychological Monographs*, 1964, *78*, No. 8, (Whole No. 585).

Ferster, C. B., & DeMyer, M. K. The development of performances in autistic children in an automatically controlled environment. *Journal of Chronic Diseases*, 1961, *13*, 312–345.

Ferster, C. B., & Skinner, B. F. *Schedules of reinforcement.* New York: Appleton, 1957.

Feshbach, S. The catharsis hypothesis and some consequences of interaction with aggressive and neutral play objects. *Journal of Personality*, 1956, *24*, 449–462.

Feshbach, S., Stiles, W. B., & Bitter, E. The reinforcing effect of witnessing aggression. *Journal of Experimental Research in Personality*, 1967, *2*, 133–139.

Festinger, L. *A theory of cognitive dissonance.* Stanford: Stanford University Press, 1957.

Festinger, L. Behavioral support for opinion change. *Public Opinion Quarterly*, 1964, *28*, 404–417.

Fishbein, M., & Ajzen, I. Attitudes toward objects as predictors of single and multiple behavioral criteria. *Psychological Review*, 1974, *81*, 59–74.

Fisher, J., Epstein, L. J., & Harris, M. R. Validity of the psychiatric interview: Predicting the effectiveness of the first Peace Corps volunteers in Ghana. *Archives of General Psychiatry*, 1967, vol. *17*, 744–750.

Fishkin, J., Keniston, K., & MacKinnon, C. Moral reasoning and political ideology. *Journal of Personality and Social Psychology*, 1973, *27*, 109–119.

Fiske, D. W. The limits of the conventional science of personality. *Journal of Personality*, 1974, *42*, 1–11.

Fitch, G. Effects of self-esteem, perceived performance, and choice on causal attribution. *Journal of Personality and Social Psychology*, 1970, *16*, 311–315.

Frank, L. K. Projective methods for the study of personality. *Journal of Psychology*, 1939, *8*, 389–413.

Fraser, R., Leslie, I., & Phelps, D. Psychiatric effects of severe personal experiences during bombing. *Proceedings of the Royal Society of Medicine*, 1943, *36*, 119–123.

Freud, A. *The ego and the mechanisms of defense.* New York: International University Press, 1946.

Freud, S. Psychopathology of everyday life. *Standard edition*, 1901, vol. 6. London: Hogarth, 1960.

Freud, S. Leonardo da Vinci: A study in psychosexuality. *Standard edition*, 1909, vol. 11. London: Hogarth, 1957.

Freud, S. Formulations regarding the two principles of mental functioning, *Collected papers*, 1911, vol. IV. New York: Basic Books, 1959.

Freud, S. Instincts and their vicissitudes. *Standard edition*, 1915, vol. 14. London: Hogarth, 1957.

Freud, S. On transformations of instinct as exemplified in anal eroticism. *Standard edition*, 1917, vol. 18. London: Hogarth, 1955.

Freud, S. *A general introduction to psychoanalysis*, 1920. New York: Boni and Liveright, 1924.

Freud, S. *New introductory lectures on psychoanalysis*, W. J. H. Sproutt (transl.). New York: Norton, 1933.

Freud, S. *An outline of psychoanalysis*, J. Strachey (transl.), 1940. New York: Norton, 1949.

Freud, S. An outline of psychoanalysis. *International Journal of Psychoanalysis*, 1940, *21*, 27–84.

Freud, S. *Collected papers*, vols. I–V. New York: Basic Books, 1959.

Freund, K. Some problems in the treatment of homosexuality. In H. J. Eysenck (Ed.), *Behaviour therapy and the neuroses.* Elmsford, N.Y.: Pergamon, 1960, pp. 312–325.

From, E. Perception of human action. In H. P. David & J. C. Brengelmann (Eds.), *Perspectives in personality research*. New York: Springer, 1960, pp. 161–174.

Fromm, E. *Escape from freedom*. New York: Holt, Rinehart and Winston, 1941.

Fromm, E. *Man for himself*. New York: Holt, Rinehart and Winston, 1947.

Galle, O. R., Gove, W. R., & McPherson, J. M. Population density and pathology: What are the relations for man? *Science*, 1972, *176*, 23–30.

Gallimore, R., Weiss, L. B., & Finney, R. Cultural differences in delay of gratification: A problem of behavior classification. *Journal of Personality and Social Psychology*, 1974, *30*, 72–80.

Geer, J. H. The development of a scale to measure fear. *Behavior Research and Therapy*, 1965, *3*, 45–53.

Geer, J. H., Davison, G. C., & Gatchel, R. I. Reduction of stress in humans through non-veridical perceived control of aversive stimulation. *Journal of Personality and Social Psychology*, 1970, *16*, 731–738.

Gelder, M. G., & Marks, I. M. Aversion treatment in transvestism and transsexualism. In R. Green (Ed.), *Transsexualism and sex reassignment*. Baltimore: Johns Hopkins Press, 1969.

Gelfand, D. M. The influence of self-esteem on rate of verbal conditioning and social matching behavior. *Journal of Abnormal and Social Psychology*, 1962, *65*, 259–265.

Gelfand, D. M., Hartmann, D. P., Lamb, A. K., Smith, C. L., Mahan, M. A., & Paul, S. C. The effects of adult models and described alternatives on children's choice of behavior management techniques. *Child Development*, 1974, *45*, 585–593.

Gendlin, E. T. client-centered developments and work with schizophrenics. *Journal of Counseling Psychology*, 1962, *9*, 205–211.

Gergen, K. J. *The concept of self*. New York: Holt, Rinehart and Winston, 1971.

Gesell, A., et al. *The first five years of life*. New York: Harper & Row, 1940.

Getzels, J. W., & Jackson, P. W. *Creativity and intelligence*. New York: Wiley, 1962.

Gibson, E. J. *Principles of perceptual learning and development*. New York: Appleton, 1969.

Gilberstadt, H., & Duker, J. *A handbook for clinical and actuarial MMPI interpretation*. Philadelphia: Saunders, 1965.

Glass, D. C. Theories of consistency and the study of personality. In E. F. Borgatta & W. W. Lambert (Eds.), *Handbook of personality theory and research*. Chicago: Rand McNally, 1968, pp. 788–854.

Glass, D. C., Singer, J. E., & Friedman, L. N. Psychic costs of adaptation to an environmental stressor. *Journal of Personality and Social Psychology*, 1969, *12*, 200–210.

Goldberg, L. R. The effectiveness of clinicians' judgments: The diagnosis of organic brain damage from the Bender-Gestalt Test. *Journal of Consulting Psychology*, 1959, *23*, 25–33.

Goldberg, L. R. Simple models or simple processes? Some research on clinical judgments. *American Psychologist*, 1968, *23*, 483–496.

Goldberg, L. R. The exploitation of the English Language for the development of a descriptive personality taxonomy. Paper delivered at the 81st Annual Convention of the American Psychological Association, Montreal, Canada, 1973.

Goldberg, L. R., & Werts, C. E. The reliability of clinician's judgments: A multitrait-multimethod approach. *Journal of Consulting Psychology*, 1966, *30*, 199–206.

Goldberg, P. A. Misogyny and the college girl. Paper presented at Eastern Psychological Association, Boston, Mass., April 1967.

Goldberg, S., & Lewis, M. Play behavior in the year-old infant: Early sex differences. *Child Development*, 1969, *40*, 21–31.

Golden, M. Some effects of combining psychological tests on clinical inferences. *Journal of Consulting Psychology*, 1964, *28*, 440–446.

Goldfarb, W. Effects of early institutional care on adolescent personality: Rorschach data. *American Journal of Orthopsychiatry*, 1944, *14*, 441–447.

Goldfarb, W. Psychological privation in infancy and subsequent adjustment. *American Journal of Orthopsychiatry*, 1945, *15*, 247–255.

Goldfried, M. R., & Sprafkin, J. N. *Behavioral personality assessment*. Morristown, N.J.: General Learning Press, 1974.

Gordon, J. E., & Smith, E. Children's aggression, parental attitudes, and the effects of an affiliation-arousing story. *Journal of Personality and Social Psychology*, 1965, *1*, 654–659.

Gormly, J., & Edelberg, W. Validation in personality trait attribution. *American Psychologist*, 1974, *29*, 189–193.

Gottesman, I. J. Heritability of personality. *Psychological Monographs*, 1963, 77, 1–21.

Gottesman, I. J. Genetic variance in adaptive personality traits. *Journal of Child Psychology and Psychiatry*, 1966, *7*, 199–208.

Gottesman, I. J., & Shields, J. Schizophrenia in twins: Sixteen years consecutive admissions to a psychiatric clinic. In M. Manosevitz, G. Lindzey, & D. D. Thiessen (Eds.), *Behavioral genetics: Method and research*, 1969. New York: Appleton, pp. 677–691.

Gough, H. G. Identifying psychological femininity. *Educational and Psychological Measurement*, 1952, *12*, 427–439.

Gough, H. G. *Manual, California Psychological Inventory*. Palo Alto: Consulting Psychologists Press, 1957.

Greenberg, B. S., & Gordon, T. F. Children's perceptions of television violence: A replication. In G. A. Comstock, E. A. Rubinstein, & J. P. Murray (Eds.), *Television and social behavior*, vol. 5. *Television's effects: Further explorations*. Washington, D.C.: GPO, 1972.

Greenstein, J. M. Father characteristics and sex typing. *Journal of Personality and Social Psychology*, 1966, *3*, 271–277.

Griffitt, W., & Guay, P. "Object" evaluation and conditioned affect. *Journal of Experimental Research in Personality*, 1969, *4*, 1–8.

Griffitt, W., & Veitch, R. Hot and crowded: Influences of population density and temperature on interpersonal affective behavior. *Journal of Personality and Social Psychology*, 1971, *17*, 92–98.

Grim, P. F., Kohlberg, L., & White, S. H. Some relationships between conscience and attentional processes. *Journal of Personality and Social Psychology*, 1968, 8, 239–252.

Grinder, R. E. Relations between behavioral and cognitive dimensions of conscience in middle childhood. *Child Development*, 1964, *35*, 881–891.

Grinker, R. R., & Spiegel, J. P. *Men under stress*. Philadelphia: Blakiston, 1945.

Grossberg, J. M. Behavior therapy: A review. *Psychological Bulletin*, 1964, *62*, 73–88.

Gruder, C. L., & Cook, T. D. Sex, dependency, and helping. *Journal of Personality and Social Psychology*, 1971, *19*, 290–294.

Grusec, J. Some antecedents of self-criticism. *Journal of Personality and Social Psychology*, 1966, *4*, 244–252.

Guilford, J. P. *Personality*. New York: McGraw-Hill, 1959.

Guthrie, E. R. *The psychology of learning*. New York: Harper & Row, 1935.

Hamburg, D. A., & Lunde, D. T. Sex hormones in the development of sex differences in human behavior. In E. E. Maccoby (Ed.), *The development of sex differences.* Stanford: Stanford University Press, 1966, pp. 1–24.

Hampson, J. L. Determinants of psychosexual orientation. In F. A. Beach (Ed.), *Sex and behavior.* New York: Wiley, 1965.

Haner, C. F. & Brown, P. A. Clarification of the instigation to action concept in the frustration-aggression hypothesis. *Journal of Abnormal and Social Psychology*, 1955, *51*, 204–206.

Haney, C., Banks, C., & Zimbardo, P. Interpersonal dynamics in a simulated prison. *International Journal of Criminology and Penology*, 1973, *1*, 69–97.

Hanratty, M. A., O'Neal, E., & Sulzer, J. L. The effect of frustration upon imitation of aggression. *Journal of Personality and Social Psychology*, 1972, *21*, 30–34.

Hare, R. D. Psychopathy and choice of immediate versus delayed punishment. *Journal of Abnormal Psychology*, 1966, *71*, 25–29.

Harlow, H. F., & Harlow, M. H. Learning to love. *American Scientist*, 1966, *54*, 244–272.

Harlow, H. F., & Zimmermann, R. R. Affectional responses in the infant monkey. *Science*, 1959, *130*, 421–432.

Harré, R., & Secord, P. F. *The explanation of social behavior.* Oxford: Blackwell, 1972.

Harris, D. B. A scale for measuring attitudes of social responsibility in children. *Journal of Abnormal and Social Psychology*, 1957, *55*, 322–326.

Harris, D. B. Sex differences in the life problems and interests of adolescents, 1935 and 1957. *Child Development*, 1959, *30*, 453–459.

Harris, F. R., Johnston, M. K., Kelley, S. C., & Wolf, M. M. Effects of positive social reinforcement on regressed crawling of a nursery school child. *Journal of Educational Psychology*, 1964, *55*, 35–41.

Hartig, M., & Kanfer, F. H. The role of verbal self-instructions in children's resistance to temptation. *Journal of Personality and Social Psychology*, 1973, *25*, 259–267.

Hartley, R. E., & Hardesty, F. P. Children's perceptions of sex roles in childhood. *Journal of Genetic Psychology*, 1964, *105*, 43–51.

Hartmann, D. Influence of symbolically modeled instrumental aggression and pain cues on aggressive behavior. *Journal of Personality and Social Psychology*, 1969, *11*, 280–288.

Hartmann, H., Kris, E., & Loewenstein, R. M. Comments on the formation of psychic structure. In A. Freud et al. (Eds.), *The psychoanalytic study of the child*, vol. 2. New York: International Universities Press, 1947, pp. 11–38.

Hartshorne, H., & May, M. A. *Studies in deceit.* New York: Macmillan, 1928.

Hartup, W. W., & Himino, Y. Social isolation vs. interaction with adults in relation to aggression in preschool children. *Journal of Abnormal and Social Psychology*, 1959, *59*, 17–22.

Hartup, W. W., & Zook, E. A. Sex role preferences in three- and four-year-old children. *Journal of Consulting Psychology*, 1960, *24*, 420–426.

Hase, H. D., & Goldberg, L. R. Comparative validity of different strategies of constructing personality inventory scales. *Psychological Bulletin*, 1967, *67*, 231–248.

Hathaway, S. R., & McKinley, J. C. A multiphasic personality schedule. (Minnesota): III. The measurement of symptomatic depression. *Journal of Psychology*, 1942, *14*, 73–84.

Hathaway, S. R., & McKinley, J. C. *MMPI Manual.* New York: Psychological Corporation, 1943.

Hattwick, L. A. Sex differences in behavior of nursery school children. *Child Development*, 1937, *8*, 343–355.

Hawkins, R. P., Peterson, R. F., Schweid, E., & Bijou, S. W. Behavior therapy in the home: Amelioration of problem parent-child relations with the parent in a therapeutic role. *Journal of Experimental Child Psychology,* 1966, *4,* 99–107.

Heathers, G. Emotional dependence and independence in a physical threat situation. *Child Development,* 1953, *24,* 169–179.

Heckhausen, H. Achievement motive research: Current problems and some contributions towards a general theory of motivation. In W. J. Arnold (Ed.), *Nebraska Symposium on Motivation,* 1968. Lincoln: Nebraska University Press, 1969, pp. 103–174.

Heider, F. *The psychology of interpersonal relations.* New York: Wiley, 1958.

Heider, F., & Simmel, M. An experimental study of apparent behavior. *American Journal of Psychology,* 1944, *57,* 243–259.

Hetherington, E. M. A developmental study of the effects of sex of the dominant parent on sex-role preference, identification, and imitation in children. *Journal of Personality and Social Psychology,* 1965, *2,* 188–194.

Hetherington, E. M., & Frankie, G. Effect of parental dominance, warmth, and conflict on imitation in children. *Journal of Personality and Social Psychology,* 1967, *6,* 119–125.

Hilgard, E. R. Experimental approaches to psychoanalysis. In E. Pumpean-Mindlin (Ed.), *Psychoanalysis as science.* Stanford: Stanford University Press, 1952, pp. 3–45.

Hill, K. T., & Sarason, S. B. The relation of test anxiety and defensiveness to test and school performance over the elementary-school years: A further longitudinal study. *Monographs of the Society for Research on Child Development,* 1966, *31,* No. 2.

Hobbs, N. Helping disturbed children: Psychological and ecological strategies. *American Psychologist,* 1966, *21,* 1105–1115.

Hoffman, M. L. Child rearing practices and moral development: Generalizations from empirical research. *Child Development,* 1963, *34,* 295–318.

Hokanson, J. E., Willers, K. R., & Koropsak, E. Modification of autonomic responses during aggressive interchange. *Journal of Personality,* 1968, *36,* 386–404.

Holmes, D. S. The conscious control of thematic projection. *Journal of Consulting and Clinical Psychology,* 1974, *42,* 323–329. (a)

Holmes, D. S. Investigations of repression: Differential recall of material experimentally or naturally associated with ego threat. *Psychological Bulletin,* 1974, *81,* 632–653. (b)

Holmes, D. S., & Houston, K. B. Effectiveness of situation redefinition and affective isolation in coping with stress. *Journal of Personality and Social Psychology,* 1974, *29,* 212–218.

Holmes, D. S., & Schallow, J. R. Reduced recall after ego threat: Repression or response competition? *Journal of Personality and Social Psychology,* 1969, *13,* 145–152.

Holmes, D. S., & Tyler, J. D. Direct versus projective measurement of achievement motivation. *Journal of Consulting and Clinical Psychology,* 1968, *32,* 712–717.

Holton, R. B. Amplitude of an instrumental response' following the withholding of reward. *Child Development,* 1961, *32,* 107–116.

Holtzman, W. H., et al. *Inkblot perception and personality: Holtzman Inkblot Technique.* Austin: University of Texas Press, 1961.

Holtzman, W. H., & Sells, S. B. Prediction of flying success by clinical analysis of test protocols. *Journal of Abnormal and Social Psychology,* 1954, *49,* 485–490.

Homme, L. Perspectives in psychology—XXIV. Control of coverants, the operants of the mind. *The Psychological Record,* 1965, *15,* 501–511.

Honigfeld, G. Temporal effects of LSD-25 and epinephrine on verbal behavior. *Journal of Abnormal Psychology,* 1965, *70,* 303–306.

Horner, M. S. Fail: Bright women. *Psychology Today,* November 1969.

Horner, M. S. Toward an understanding of achievement related conflicts in women. *Journal of Social Issues,* 1972, *28,* 157–176.

Hovland, C. I., Janis, I. J., et al. *Personality and persuasibility.* New Haven: Yale University Press, 1959.

Howard, K. I. The convergent and discriminant validation of ipsative ratings from three projective instruments. *Journal of Clinical Psychology,* 1962, *18,* 183–188.

Howes, D. H., & Solomon, R. L. Visual duration threshold as a function of word-probability. *Journal of Experimental Psychology,* 1951, *41,* 401–410.

Insko, C. A., & Schopler, J. Triadic consistency: A statement of affective-cognitive-conative consistency. *Psychological Review,* 1967, *74,* 361–376.

Irwin, O. C., & Chen, H. P. Development of speech during infancy: Curve of phonemic types. *Journal of Experimental Psychology,* 1946, *36,* 431–436.

Iscoe, I., Williams, M., & Harvey, J. Age, intelligence, and sex as variables in the conformity behavior of Negro and white children. *Child Development,* 1964, *35,* 451–460.

Isen, A. M. Success, failure, and reactions to others: The warm glow of success. *Journal of Personality and Social Psychology,* 1970, 294–301.

Isen, A., Horn, N., & Rosenhan, D. Effects of success and failure on children's generosity. *Journal of Personality and Social Psychology,* 1973, *27,* 239–247.

Ittelson, W. H., Proshansky, H. M., Rivlin, L. G., & Winkel, G. H. *An introduction to environmental psychology.* New York: Holt, Rinehart and Winston, 1974.

Jacklin, C. N., & Mischel, H. N. As the twig is bent: Sex role stereotyping in early readers. *The School Psychology Digest,* Summer 1973, pp. 30–38.

Jackson, D. N., & Messick, S. Content and style in personality assessment. *Psychological Bulletin,* 1958, *55,* 243–252.

Janis, I. L. Objective factors related to morale attitudes in the aerial combat situation. In S. Stouffer, A. A. Lumsdaine, R. Williams, M. B. Smith, I. L. Janis, S. A. Stas, & L. Cottrell, Jr., *The American soldier, vol. 2. Combat and its aftermath.* Princeton: Princeton University Press, 1949. pp. 362–410.

Janis, I. L. *Psychological stress.* New York: Wiley, 1958.

Janis, I. L. *Stress and frustration.* New York: Harcourt, 1971.

Jasper, H. H. Electroencephalography. In W. Penfield & T. Erickson (Eds.), *Epilepsy and cerebral localization.* Springfield, Ill.: Charles C Thomas, 1941, pp. 380–454.

Jenkins, J. J. Remember that old theory of memory? Well, forget it! *American Psychologist,* 1974, *29,* 785–795.

Jersild, A. Memory for the pleasant as compared with the unpleasant. *Journal of Experimental Psychology,* 1931, *14,* 284–288.

Jones, A. Information deprivation in humans. In B. A. Maher (Ed.), *Progress in experimental personality research,* vol. 3. New York: Academic Press, 1966, pp. 241–307.

Jones, A., Bentler, P. M., & Petry, G. The reduction of uncertainty during future pain. *Journal of Abnormal Psychology,* 1966, *71,* 87–94.

Jones, E. E. *Ingratiation: A social psychological analysis.* New York: Appleton, 1964.

Jones, E., & Gerard, H. B. *Foundations of social psychology.* New York: Wiley, 1967.

Jones, E. E., & Nisbett, R. E. The actor and the observer: Divergent perceptions of the causes of behavior. In E. E. Jones, et al. (Eds.), *Attribution: Perceiving the causes of behavior.* Morristown, N.J.: General Learning Press, 1971.

Jordan, P. A real predicament. *Science,* 1972, *175,* 977–978.

Jourard, S. M. Experimenter-subject dialogue: A paradigm for a humanistic science of psychology. In J. Bugental (Ed.), *Challenges of humanistic psychology.* New York: McGraw-Hill, 1967, pp. 109–116.

Jourard, S. M. *Healthy personality: An approach from the viewpoint of humanistic psychology.* New York: Macmillan, 1974.

Jung, C. G. *Memories, dreams, reflections.* New York: Pantheon, 1963.

Jung, C. G. *Man and his symbols.* Garden City, N.Y.: Doubleday, 1964.

Kagan, J. The acquisition and significance of sex typing and sex role identity. In M. Hoffman & L. Hoffman (Eds.), *Review of child development research,* vol. 1. New York: Russell Sage, 1964.

Kagan, J. Continuity in development. Paper presented at the meeting of the Society for Research in Child Development, March 27, 1969, Santa Monica, Calif.

Kagan, J., Hosken, B., & Watson, S. The child's symbolic conceptualization of the parents. *Child Development,* 1961, *32,* 625–636.

Kagan, J., & Moss, H. A. *Birth to maturity: A study in psychological development.* New York: Wiley, 1962.

Kahneman, D., & Tversky, A. On the psychology of prediction. *Psychological Review,* 1973, *80,* 237–251.

Kalish, R. Sex and marital role differences in anticipation of age-produced dependency. *Journal of Genetic Psychology,* 1971, *119,* 53–62.

Kamiya, J. Conditioned introspection. Paper read at the Institute of Personality Assessment and Research, University of California, Berkeley, 1967.

Kanfer, F. H., & Marston, A. R. Determinants of self-reinforcement in human learning. *Journal of Experimental Psychology,* 1963, *66,* 245–254. (a)

Kanfer, F. H., & Marston, A. R. Conditioning of self-reinforcing responses: An analogue to self-confidence training. *Psychological Reports,* 1963, *13,* 63–70. (b)

Kanfer, F. H., & Phillips, J. S. *Learning foundations of behavior therapy.* New York: Wiley, 1970.

Kanfer, F. H., & Seidner, M. L. Self-control: Factors enhancing tolerance of noxious stimulation. *Journal of Personality and Social Psychology,* 1973, *25,* 381–389.

Kanfer, F. H., & Zich, J. Self-control training: The effects of external control on children's resistance to temptation. *Developmental Psychology,* 1974, *10,* 108–115.

Katkin, E. S. Relationship between manifest anxiety and two indices of autonomic response to stress. *Journal of Personality and Social Psychology,* 1965, *2,* 324–333.

Kelley, H. H. Attribution theory in social psychology. In D. Levine (Ed.), *Nebraska symposium on motivation.* Lincoln: University of Nebraska Press, 1967, pp. 192–238.

Kelley, H. H. The processes of causal attribution. *American Psychologist,* 1973, *28,* 107–128.

Kelly, E. L. Consistency of the adult personality. *American Psychologist,* 1955, *10,* 659–681.

Kelly, E. L., & Fiske, D. W. *The prediction of performance in clinical psychology.* Ann Arbor: University of Michigan Press, 1951.

Kelly, G. A. *The psychology of personal constructs,* vols. 1 & 2. New York: Norton, 1955.

Kelly, G. A. Man's construction of his alternatives. In G. Lindzey (Ed.), *Assessment of human motives.* New York: Holt, Rinehart and Winston, 1958, pp. 33–64.

Kelly, G. A. Training for professional obsolescence. Unpublished manuscript, Brandeis University, 1965.

Kiesler, D. J. Some myths of psychotherapy research and the search for a paradigm. *Psychological Bulletin,* 1966, *65,* 110–136.

Klausmeier, H. J., & Wiersma, W. Relationship of sex, grade level, and locale to perform-ance of high IQ students on divergent thinking tests. *Journal of Educational Psychol-ogy,* 1964, *55,* 114–119.

Klausmeier, H. J., & Wiersma, W. The effects of IQ level and sex on divergent thinking of seventh grade pupils of low, average, and high IQ. *Journal of Educational Research,* 1965, *58,* 300–302.

Klineberg, S. L. Future time perspective and the preference for delayed reward. *Journal of Personality and Social Psychology,* 1968, *8,* 253–257.

Kogan, N., & Wallach, M. A. *Risk taking: A study in cognition and personality.* New York: Holt, Rinehart and Winston, 1964.

Kohlberg, L. The development of children's orientations toward a moral order: 1. Sequence in the development of moral thought. *Vita Humana,* 1963, *6,* 11–33.

Kohlberg, L. Development of moral character and moral ideology. In M. L. Hoffman & L. W. Hoffman (Eds.), *Review of child development,* vol. 1. New York: Russell Sage Foundation, 1964, pp. 383–431.

Kohlberg, L. A Cognitive-developmental analysis of children's sex-role concepts and atti-tudes. In E. E. Maccoby (Ed.), *The development of sex differences.* Stanford: Stanford University Press, 1966, pp. 82–173.

Kohlberg, L. Moral and religious education and the public schools: A developmental view. In T. Sizer (Ed.), *Religion and public education.* Boston: Houghton Mifflin, 1967.

Kohlberg, L. The child as a moral philosopher. *Psychology Today,* 1968, 25–30.

Kohlberg, L. Stage and sequence: The cognitive-developmental approach to socialization. In D. A. Goslin (Ed.), *Handbook of socialization theory and research.* Chicago: Rand McNally, 1969, pp. 347–480.

Kohlberg, L. From is to ought: How to commit the naturalistic fallacy and get away with it in the study of moral development. In T. Mischel (Ed.), *Cognitive development and epistemology.* New York: Academic Press, 1971, pp. 151–235.

Korner, A. F. Individual differences at birth: Implications for early experience and later development. *American Journal of Orthopsychiatry,* 1971, *41* (4).

Koss, M. P., & Butcher, J. N. A comparison of psychiatric patients' self-reports with other sources of clinical information. *Journal of Research in Personality,* 1973, *7,* 225–236.

Kostlan, A. A method for the empirical study of psychodiagnosis. *Journal of Consulting Psychology,* 1954, *18,* 83–88.

Krasner, L., & Ullmann, L. P. *Behavior influence and personality: The social matrix of human action.* New York: Holt, Rinehart and Winston, 1973.

Kremers, J. *Scientific psychology and naive psychology.* Groningen, Netherlands: Nordhoff, 1960.

Krech, K., Crutchfield, R., & Ballachey, E. *Individual in society.* New York: McGraw-Hill, 1962.

Kurland, S. H. The lack of generality in defense mechanisms as indicated in auditory per-ception. *Journal of Abnormal and Social Psychology,* 1954, *49,* 173–177.

Kurtines, W., & Greif, E. B. The development of moral thought: Review and evaluation of Kohlberg's approach. *Psychological Bulletin,* 1974, *81,* 453–470.


Lacey, J. I. Somatic response patterning and stress: Some revisions of activation theory. In M. H. Appley & R. Trumbull (Eds.), *Psychological stress.* New York: Appleton, 1967.

Lacey, J. I., & Smith, R. L. Conditioning and generalization of unconscious anxiety. *Sci-ence,* 1954, *120,* 1045–1052.

Laing, R. D. *The divided self.* Middlesex, England: Penguin, 1965.

Lakin, M. *Experiential groups: The uses of interpersonal encounter, psychotherapy groups, and sensitivity training.* Morristown, N.J.: General Learning Press, 1972.

Landfield, A. W., Stern, M., & Fjeld, S. Social conceptual processes and change in students undergoing psychotherapy. *Psychological Reports,* 1961, *8,* 63–68.

Lang, P. J., Geer, J., & Hnatiow, M. Semantic generalization of conditioned autonomic responses. *Journal of Experimental Psychology,* 1963, *65,* 552–558.

Lang, P. J., & Lazovik, A. D. Experimental desensitization of a phobia. *Journal of Abnormal and Social Psychology,* 1963, *66,* 519–525.

Lang, P. J., Lazovik, A. D., & Reynolds, D. J. Desensitization, suggestibility, and pseudotherapy. *Journal of Abnormal Psychology,* 1965, *70,* 395–402.

Langer, E. J., Janis, I. L., & Wolfer, J. A. Reduction of psychological stress in surgical patients. Unpublished manuscript, Yale University, 1975.

Lanzetta, J. T., & Driscoll, J. M. Preference for information about an uncertain but unavoidable outcome. *Journal of Personality and Social Psychology,* 1966, *3,* 96–102.

Lao, R. C. Internal-external control and competent and innovative behavior among Negro college students. *Journal of Personality and Social Psychology,* 1970, *14,* 263–270.

Lawrence, D. H. The nature of a stimulus: Some relationships between learning and perception. In S. Koch (Ed.), *Psychology: A study of a science.* New York: McGraw-Hill, 1959, pp. 179–212.

Lawson, R. *Frustration: The development of a scientific concept.* New York: Macmillan, 1965.

Lay, C. H., & Jackson, D. N. Analysis of the generality of trait-interferential relationships. *Journal of Personality and Social Psychology,* 1969, *12,* 12–21.

Lazarus, A. A. Group therapy of phobic disorders by systematic desensitization. *Journal of Abnormal and Social Psychology,* 1961, *63,* 504–510.

Lazarus, A. A. The treatment of chronic frigidity by systematic desensitization. *Journal of Nervous and Mental Diseases,* 1963, *136,* 272–278.

Lazarus, R. S., & Alfert, E. The short circuiting of threat by experimentally altering cognitive appraisal. *Journal of Abnormal and Social Psychology,* 1964, *69,* 195–205.

Lazarus, R. S., & Averill, J. R. Emotion and cognition: With special reference to anxiety. In C. D. Spielberger (Ed.), *Anxiety: Current trends in theory and research,* vol. II. New York: Academic Press, 1972.

Lazarus, R. S., Eriksen, C. W., & Fonda, C. P. Personality dynamics and auditory perceptual recognition. *Journal of Personality,* 1951, *58,* 113–122.

Lazarus, R. S., & Longo, N. The consistency of psychological defense against threat. *Journal of Abnormal and Social Psychology,* 1953, *48,* 495–499.

Lazarus, R. S., & McCleary, R. A. Autonomic discrimination without awareness: A study of subception. *Psychological Review,* 1951, *58,* 113–122.

Lazarus, R. S., Yousem, H., & Arenberg, D. Hunger and perception. *Journal of Personality,* 1953, *21,* 312–328.

Leary, T., Litwin, G. H., & Metzner, R. Reactions to psilocybin administered in a supportive environment. *Journal of Nervous and Mental Diseases,* 1963, *137,* 561–573.

Lecky, P. *Self-consistency.* New York: Island Press, 1945.

Lee, L. C. Concept utilization in preschool children. *Child Development,* 1965, *36,* 221–227.

Lefcourt, H. M. Internal versus external control of reinforcement: A review. *Psychological Bulletin,* 1966, *65,* 206–220.

Lefcourt, H. M. Recent developments in the study of locus of control. In B. A. Maher (Ed.), *Progress in experimental personality research,* vol. 6. New York: Academic Press, 1972.

Lemere, F., & Voegtlin, W. L. An evaluation of the aversion treatment of alcoholism. *Quarterly Journal of Studies on Alcohol*, 1950, *11*, 199–204.

Lepper, M., Greene, D., & Nisbett, R. E. Undermining children's intrinsic interest with extrinsic reward: A test of the "overjustification" hypothesis. *Journal of Personality and Social Psychology*, 1973, *28*, 129–137.

Lepper, M. R., Sagotsky, G., & Mailer, J. Generalization and persistence of effects of exposure to self-reinforcement models. *Child Development*, 1975, *46*, 618–630.

Leventhal, H., Jacobs, R. L., & Kudirka, N. Z. Authoritarianism, ideology, and political candidate choice. *Journal of Abnormal and Social Psychology*, 1964, *69*, 539–549.

Levine, R., Chein, I., & Murphy, G. The relation of the intensity of a need to the amount of perceptual distortion: A preliminary report. *Journal of Psychology*, 1942, *13*, 283–292.

Levine, S. J. Infantile experience and resistance to physiological stress. *Science*, 1957, *126*, 405.

Levine, S. J. Psychophysiological effects of infantile stimulation. In E. L. Bliss (Ed.), *Roots of behavior*. New York: Hoeber, 1962.

Lewin, K. *A dynamic theory of personality*. New York: McGraw-Hill, 1935.

Lewin, K. *Principles of topological psychology*. New York: McGraw-Hill, 1936.

Lewin, K. *Field theory in social science; selected theoretical papers*, D. Cartwright (Ed.), New York: Harper & Row, 1951.

Lewis, M. Infants' responses to facial stimuli during the first year of life. *Developmental Psychology*, 1969, *1*, 75–86.

Lieberman, M. A., Yalom, I. D., & Miles, M. B. *Encounter groups: First facts*. New York: Basic Books, 1973.

Liebert, R. M. Television and social learning: Some relationships between viewing violence and behaving aggressively. In J. P. Murray, E. A. Rubinstein, & G. A. Comstock (Eds.), *Television and social behavior*, vol. 2. *Television and social learning*. Washington, D.C.: GPO, 1972, pp. 1–34.

Liebert, R. M., & Allen, K. M. The effects of rule structure and reward magnitude on the acquisition and adoption of self-reward criteria. Unpublished manuscript, Vanderbilt University, 1967.

Liebert, R. M., & Baron, R. A. Some immediate effects of televised violence on children's behavior. *Developmental Psychology*, 1972, *6*, 469–475.

Lindzey, G., & Tejessy, C. Thematic Apperception Test: Indices of aggression in relation to measures of overt and covert behavior. *American Journal of Orthopsychiatry*, 1956, *26*, 567–576.

Little, K. B., & Shneidman, E. S. Congruencies among interpretations of psychological test and anamnestic data. *Psychological Monographs*, 1959, *73*, No. 6 (Whole No. 476).

Loehlin, J. C. *Computer models of personality*. New York: Random House, 1968.

Loevinger, J. Objective tests as instruments of psychological theory. *Psychological Reports Monographs*, No. 9. Southern University Press, 1957.

London, P. *Behavior control*. New York: Harper & Row, 1969.

LoPicolo, J., & Lobitz, W. C. The role of masturbation in the treatment of orgasmic dysfunction. *Archives of Sexual Behavior*, 1972, *2*, 163–171.

Lorenz, K. Z. *On aggression*. New York: Harcourt, 1966.

Lorr, M., Bishop, P. F., & McNair, D. M. Interpersonal types among psychiatric patients. *Journal of Abnormal Psychology*, 1965, *70*, 468–472.

Lott, A. J., & Lott, B. E. A learning theory approach to interpersonal attitudes. In A. G. Greenwald, T. C. Brock, and T. M. Ostrom (Eds.), *Psychological foundations of attitudes*. New York: Academic Press, 1968.

Lovaas, O. I. A behavior therapy approach to the treatment of childhood schizophrenia. In J. P. Hill (Ed.), *Minnesota symposia on child psychology*, vol. 1. Minneapolis: University of Minnesota Press, 1967, pp. 108–159.

Lovaas, O. I., Freitag, G., Gold, V. J., & Kassorla, I. C. Experimental studies in childhood schizophrenia: I. Analysis of self-destructive behavior. *Journal of Experimental Child Psychology*, 1965, *2*, 67–84. (a)

Lovaas, O. I., Freitag, G., Gold, V. J., & Kassorla, I. C. Recording apparatus for observation of behaviors of children in free play settings. *Journal of Experimental Child Psychology*. 1965, *2*, 108–120. (b)

Lovaas, O. I., Freitag, L., Nelson, K., & Whalen, C. The establishment of imitation and its use for the development of complex behavior in schizophrenic children. *Behavior Research and Therapy*, 1967, *5*, 171–181.

Luborsky, L., & Spence, D. P. Quantitative research on psychoanalytic therapy. In A. Bergin and S. Garfield (Eds.), *Handbook of psychotherapy and behavior change*. New York: Wiley, 1971.

Luchins, A. S. Experimental attempts to minimize the impact of first impressions. In C. Hovland (Ed.), *The order of presentation in persuasion*. New Haven: Yale University Press, 1957, pp. 63–75.

Luft, J. Differences in prediction based on hearing versus reading verbatim clinical interviews. *Journal of Consulting Psychology*. 1951, *15*, 115–119.

Lynn, D. B., & Sawrey, W. L. The effects of father-absence on Norwegian boys and girls. *Journal of Abnormal and Social Psychology*. 1959, *59*, 258–262.

McCandless, B. R., Bilous, B., & Bennett, H. L. Peer popularity and dependence on adults in preschool age socialization. *Child Development*, 1961, *32*, 511–518.

McCardell, J., & Murray, E. J. Nonspecific factors in weekend encounter groups. *Journal of Consulting and Clinical Psychology*, 1974, *42*, 337–345.

McClelland, D. C. *Personality*. New York: Holt, Rinehart and Winston, 1951.

McClelland, D. C. Longitudinal trends in the relation of thought to action. *Journal of Consulting Psychology*, 1966, *30*, 479–483.

McClelland, D. C., & Atkinson, J. W. The projective expression of needs: I. The effects of different intensities of the hunger drive on perception. *Journal of Psychology*, 1948, *25*, 205–222.

McClelland, D. C., Atkinson, J. W., Clark, R. A., & Lowell, E. L. *The achievement motive*. New York: Appleton, 1953.

McFall, R. M., & Twentyman, C. T. Four experiments on the relative contributions of rehearsal, modeling, and coaching on assertive training. *Journal of Abnormal Psychology*, 1973, *81*, 199–218.

McGinnies, E. Emotionality and perceptual defense. *Psychological Review*, 1949, *56*, 244–251.

McNemar, Q. *The revision of the Stanford-Binet Scale: An analysis of the standardization data*. Boston: Houghton Mifflin, 1942.

Maccoby, E. E. Role-taking in childhood and its consequences for social learning. *Child Development*, 1959, *30*, 239–252.

Maccoby, E. E. Sex differences in intellectual functioning. In E. E. Maccoby (Ed.), *The development of sex differences*. Stanford: Stanford University Press, 1966, pp. 25–55.

Maccoby, E. E., & Jacklin, C. N. What we know and don't know about sex differences. *Psychology Today*, December 1974, 109–112. (a)

Maccoby, E. E., & Jacklin, C. N. *The psychology of sex differences*. Stanford: Stanford University Press, 1974. (b)

Maccoby, E. E., & Masters, J. C. Attachment. In P. H. Mussen (Ed.), *Carmichael's manual of child psychology*, rev. ed. New York: Wiley, 1970.

Maccoby, E. E., & Wilson, W. C. Identification and observational learning from films. *Journal of Abnormal and Social Psychology*, 1957, *55*, 76–87.

Maccoby, E. E., Wilson, W. C., & Burton, R. V. Differential movie-viewing behavior of male and female viewers. *Journal of Personality*, 1958, *26*, 259–267.

MacFarlane, J. W., & Tuddenham, R. D. Problems in the validation of projective techniques. In H. H. Anderson and G. L. Anderson (Eds.), *Projective techniques*. New York: Prentice-Hall, 1951, pp. 26–54.

Madison, P. *Freud's concept of repression and defense: Its theoretical and observational language*. Minneapolis: University of Minnesota Press, 1960.

Magnusson, D., & Ekehammar, B. An analysis of situational dimensions: A replication. *Multivariate Behavioral Research*, 1973, *8*, 331–339.

Maher, B. A. *Principles of psychotherapy: An experimental approach*. New York: McGraw-Hill, 1966.

Mahoney, M., & Thoresen, C. (Eds.), *Self-control: Power to the person*. Monterey, Calif.: Brooks/Cole, 1974.

Mahrer, A. R. The role of expectancy in delayed reinforcement. *Journal of Experimental Psychology*, 1956, *52*, 101–105.

Mallick, S. K., & McCandless, B. R. A study of catharsis of aggression. *Journal of Personality and Social Psychology*, 1966, *4*, 591–596.

Malmo, R. B. Anxiety and behavioral arousal. *Psychological Review*, 1957, *64*, 276–287.

Malmo, R. B. Activation: A neuropsychological dimension. *Psychological Review*, 1959, *66*, 367–386.

Mandler, G. Emotion. In E. Galanter (Ed.), *New directions in psychology I*. New York: Holt, Rinehart and Winston, 1962, pp. 267–343.

Mandler, G. The interruption of behavior. In D. Levin (Ed.), *Nebraska symposium on motivation*. Lincoln; University of Nebraska Press, 1964, pp. 163–219.

Mandler, G. & Kremen, I. Autonomic feedback: A correlational study. *Journal of Personality*, 1958, *26*, 388–399.

Mandler, G., Mandler, M., & Uviller, T. Autonomic feedback: The perception of autonomic activity, *Journal of Abnormal and Social Psychology*, 1958, *56*, 367–373.

Mandler, G., & Watson, D. L. Anxiety and the interruption of behavior. In C. D. Spielberger (Ed.), *Anxiety and behavior*. New York: Academic Press, 1966, pp. 263–288.

Mann, R. D. A review of the relationships between personality and performance in small groups. *Psychological Bulletin*, 1959, *56*, 241–270.

Markowitz, A. Influence of the repression-sensitization dimension, affect value, and ego threat on incidental learning. *Journal of Personality and Social Psychology*, 1969, *11*, 374–380.

Marks, I. M., & Gelder, M. G. Transvestism and fetishism: clinical and psychological changes during faradic aversion. *British Journal of Psychiatry*, 1967, *113*, 711–729.

Marks, J., Stauffacher, J. C., & Lyle, C. Predicting outcome in schizophrenia. *Journal of Abnormal and Social Psychology*, 1963, *66*, 117–127.

Marks, P. A., & Seeman, W. *Actuarial description of abnormal personality*. Baltimore: Williams & Wilkins, 1963.

Marsden, G. Content analysis studies of psychotherapy: 1954 through 1968. In A. E. Bergin & S. L. Garfield (Eds.), *Handbook of psychotherapy and behavior change*. New York: Wiley, 1971.

Martin, B. The assessment of anxiety by physiological behavioral measures. *Psychological Bulletin*, 1961, *58*, 234–255.

Martin, D. G., Hawryluk, G. A., & Guse, L. L. Experimental study of unconscious influences: Ultrasound as a stimulus. *Journal of Abnormal Psychology*, 1974, *83*, 589–608.

Marx, M. H. Some relations between frustration and drive. In M. R. Jones (Ed.), *Nebraska symposium on motivation*. Lincoln: University of Nebraska Press, 1956.

Masling, J. M. The effects of warm and cold interaction on the administration and scoring of an intelligence test. *Journal of Consulting Psychology*, 1959, *23*, 336–341.

Masling, J. M. The influence of situational and interpersonal variables in projective testing. *Psychological Bulletin*, 1960, *57*, 65–85.

Maslow, A. H. Some basic propositions of a growth and self-actualization psychology. In G. Lindzey & C. Hall (Eds.), *Theories of personality: Primary sources and research*. New York: Wiley, 1965, pp. 307–316.

Maslow, A. H. *Toward a psychology of being*, 2nd edition. New York: Van Nostrand, 1968.

Maslow, A. H. *The farther reaches of human nature*. New York: Viking, 1971.

Masserman, J. H. Experimental approaches to psychoanalytic concepts. *Samiksa*, 1952, *6*, 243–261.

Masters, J. C., & Mokros, J. R. Self-reinforcement processes in children. In H. Reese (Ed.), *Advances in child development and behavior*, vol. 9. New York: Academic Press, 1974.

Masters, W. H., & Johnson, V. *Human sexual inadequacy*. Boston: Little, Brown, 1970.

May, R. *The meaning of anxiety*. New York: Ronald, 1950.

May, R. Existential psychology. In R. May (Ed.), *Existential psychology*. New York: Random House, 1961, pp. 11–51.

May, R. (Ed.). *Existential psychology*. New York: Random House, 1961.

Meehl, P. E. The dynamics of "structured" personality tests. *Journal of Clinical Psychology*, 1945, *1*, 296–303.

Meehl, P. E. *Clinical versus statistical prediction*. Minneapolis: University of Minnesota Press, 1954.

Meehl, P. E. The cognitive activity of the clinician. *American Psychologist*, 1960, *15*, 19–27.

Mehrabian, A. The development and validation of measures of affiliative tendency and sensitivity to rejection. *Educational and Psychological Measurement*, 1970, *30*, 417–428.

Meichenbaum, D. H., & Cameron, R. The clinical potential of modifying what clients say to themselves. In M. J. Mahoney & C. E. Thoresen (Eds.), *Self-control: Power to the person*. Monterey, Calif.: Brooks-Cole, 1974.

Meichenbaum, D. H., & Goodman, J. Training impulsive children to talk to themselves: A means of developing self-control. *Journal of Abnormal Psychology*, 1971, *77*, 115–126.

Melikian, L. Preference for delayed reinforcement: An experimental study among Palestinian Arab refugee children. *Journal of Social Psychology*, 1959, *50*, 81–86.

Meltzer, H. The present status of experimental studies of the relation of feeling to memory. *Psychological Review*, 1930, *37*, 124–139.

Messick, S., & Jackson, D. N. Acquiescence and the factorial interpretation of the MMPI. *Psychological Bulletin*, 1961, *58*, 299–304.

Metcalfe, M. Demonstration of a psychosomatic relationship. *British Journal of Medical Psychology*, 1956, *29*, 63–66.

Michotte, A. *La perception de la causalite*, 2nd ed. Louvain: Publications universitaires de Louvain, 1954.

Milgram, S. Some conditions of obedience and disobedience to authority. *Human Relations*. 1965, *18*, 57–76.

Milgram, S. *Obedience to authority*. New York: Harper & Row, 1974.

Miller, G. A. The magical number seven, plus or minus two: Some limits on capacity for processing information. *Psychological Review*, 1956, *63*, 81–97.

Miller, G. A., Galanter, E., & Pribram, K. H. *Plans and the structure of behavior*. New York: Holt, Rinehart and Winston, 1960.

Miller, N. E. Theory and experiment relating psychoanalytic displacement to stimulus response generalization. *Journal of Abnormal and Social Psychology*, 1948, *43*, 155–178.

Miller, N. E. Liberalization of basic S-R concepts: extensions to conflict behavior, motivation, and social learning. In S. Koch (Ed.), *Psychology: A study of a science*, vol. 2. New York: McGraw-Hill, 1959, pp. 196–292.

Miller, N. E. Some reflections on the law of effect produce a new alternative to drive reduction. In M. R. Jones (Ed.), *Nebraska symposium on motivation*. Lincoln: University of Nebraska, 1963.

Miller, N. E. Learning of visceral and glandular responses. *Science, 163* (3866), 1969, 434–445.

Miller, N. E., & Banuazizi, A. Instrumental learning by curarized rats of a specific visceral response, intestinal or cardiac. *Journal of Comparative and Physiological Psychology*, 1968, *65*, 1–7.

Miller, N. E., & Dollard, J. *Social learning and imitation*. New Haven: Yale University Press, 1941.

Minuchin, P. Sex-role concepts and sex typing in childhood as a function of school and home environments. *Child Development*, 1965, *36*, 1033–1048.

Mischel, H. Sex bias in the evaluation of professional achievements. *Journal of Educational Psychology*, 1974, *66*, 157–166.

Mischel, T. Personal constructs, rules, and the logic of clinical activity. *Psychological Review*, 1964, *71*, 180–192.

Mischel, W. Preference for delayed reinforcement: An experimental study of a cultural observation. *Journal of Abnormal and Social Psychology*, 1958, *56*, 57–61.

Mischel, W. Preference for delayed reinforcement and social responsibility. *Journal of Abnormal and Social Psychology*, 1961, *62*, 1–7. (a)

Mischel, W. Delay of gratification, need for achievement, and acquiescence in another culture. *Journal of Abnormal and Social Psychology*, 1961, *62*, 543–552. (b)

Mischel, W. Father absence and delay of gratification: Cross-cultural comparisons. *Journal of Abnormal and Social Psychology*, 1961, *63*, 116–124. (c)

Mischel, W. Delay of gratification in choice situations. NIMH Progress Report (mimeo), Stanford University, 1962.

Mischel, W. Predicting the success of Peace Corps Volunteers in Nigeria. *Journal of Personality and Social Psychology*, 1965, *1*, 510–517.

Mischel, W. A social learning view of sex differences in behavior. In E. E. Maccoby (Ed.), *The development of sex differences*. Stanford: Stanford University Press, 1966, pp. 56–81. (a)

Mischel, W. Theory and research on the antecedents of self-imposed delay of reward. In B. A. Maher (Ed.), *Progress in experimental personality research*, vol. 3. New York: Academic Press, 1966, pp. 85–132. (b)

Mischel, W. *Personality and assessment*. New York: Wiley, 1968.

Mischel, W. Continuity and change in personality. *American Psychologist*, 1969, *24*, 1012–1018.

Mischel, W. Sex typing and socialization. In P. H. Mussen (Ed.), *Carmichael's manual of child psychology* rev. ed. New York: Wiley, 1970.

Mischel, W. Direct versus indirect personality assessment: Evidence and implications. *Journal of Consulting and Clinical Psychology*, 1972, *38*, 319–324.

Mischel, W. Toward a cognitive social learning reconceptualization of personality. *Psychological Review*, 1973, *80*, 252–283. (a)

Mischel, W. On the empirical dilemmas of psychodynamic approaches: Issues and alternatives: *Journal of Abnormal Psychology*, 1973, *82*, 335–344. (b)

Mischel, W. Processes in delay of gratification. In L. Berkowitz (Ed.), *Advances in experimental social psychology*, vol. 7. New York: Academic Press, 1974.

Mischel, W. The interaction of person and situation. Paper presented at International Conference on Interactional Psychology, Saltsjöbaden, Sweden, 1975.

Mischel, W. & Baker, N. Cognitive transformations of reward objects through instructions. *Journal of Personality and Social Psychology*, 1975, *31*, 254–261.

Mischel, W., Coates, B., & Raskoff, A. Effects of success and failure on self-gratification. *Journal of Personality and Social Psychology*, 1968, *10*, 381–390.

Mischel, W., & Ebbesen, E. Attention in delay of gratification. *Journal of Personality and Social Psychology*, 1970, *16*, 329–337.

Mischel, W., Ebbesen, E. B., & Zeiss, A. R. Cognitive and attentional mechanisms in delay of gratification. *Journal of Personality and Social Psychology*, 1972, *21*, 204–218.

Mischel, W., Ebbesen, E., & Zeiss, A. R. Selective attention to the self: Situational and dispositional determinants. *Journal of Personality and Social Psychology*, 1973, *27*, 129–142.

Mischel, W., & Gilligan, C. Delay of gratification, motivation for the prohibited gratification, and responses to temptation. *Journal of Abnormal and Social Psychology*, 1964, *69*, 411–417.

Mischel, W., & Grusec, J. Determinants of the rehearsal and transmission of neutral and aversive behaviors. *Journal of Personality and Social Psychology*, 1966, *3*, 197–205.

Mischel, W., & Grusec, J. Waiting for rewards and punishments: Effects of time and probability on choice. *Journal of Personality and Social Psychology*, 1967, *5*, 24–31.

Mischel, W., Jeffery, K. M., & Patterson, C. J. The layman's use of trait and behavioral information to predict behavior. *Journal of Research in Personality*, 1974, *8*, 231–242.

Mischel, W., & Liebert, R. M. Effects of discrepancies between observed and imposed reward criteria on their acquisition and transmission. *Journal of Personality and Social Psychology*, 1966, *3*, 45–53.

Mischel, W., & Masters, J. C. Effects of probability of reward attainment on responses to frustration. *Journal of Personality and Social Psychology*, 1966, *3*, 390–396.

Mischel, W., & Metzner, R. Preference for delayed reward as a function of age, intelligence, and length of delay interval. *Journal of Abnormal and Social Psychology*, 1962, *64*, 425–431.

Mischel, W., & Mischel, H. The nature and development of psychological sex differences. In G. Lesser (Ed.), *Psychology and educational practice*. Glenview, Ill.: Scott, Foresman, 1971.

Mischel, W., & Mischel, H. N. A cognitive social learning approach to morality and self-regulation. In T. Lickona (Ed.), *Moral development and behavior: Theory, research, and social issues*. New York: Holt, Rinehart and Winston, 1976.

Mischel, W., & Moore, B. Effects of attention to symbolically presented rewards upon self-control. *Journal of Personality and Social Psychology*, 1973, *28*, 172–179.

Mischel, W., & Schopler, J. Authoritarianism and reactions to "sputniks." *Journal of Abnormal and Social Psychology*, 1959, *59*, 142–145.

Mischel, W., & Staub, E. Effects of expectancy on working and waiting for larger rewards. *Journal of Personality and Social Psychology*, 1965, *2*, 625–633.

Mischel, W., Zeiss, R., & Zeiss, A. R. Internal-external control and persistence: Validation and implications of the Stanford Preschool Internal-External Scale. *Journal of Personality and Social Psychology*, 1974, *29*, 265–278.

Money, J. Influence of hormones on sexual behavior. *Annual Review of Medicine*, 1965, *16*, 67–82. (a)

Money, J. Psychosexual differentiation. In J. Money (Ed.), *Sex research, new developments*. New York: Holt, Rinehart and Winston, 1965. (b)

Money, J., & Ehrhardt, A. *Man and woman: Boy and girl*. Baltimore: Johns Hopkins University Press, 1972.

Moore, B., Underwood, B., & Rosenhan, D. L. Affect and altruism. *Developmental Psychology*, 1973, *27*, 129–142.

Moore, B., Mischel, W., Zeiss, A., & Mailer, J. Cognitive factors in delay of gratification. Paper presented at SRCD meetings, Denver, Colo., April 1975.

Moore, S., & Updergraff, R. Sociometric status of pre-school children related to age, sex, nurturance-giving and dependency. *Child Development*, 1964, *35*, 519–524.

Moos, R. H. Situational analysis of a therapeutic community milieu. *Journal of Abnormal Psychology*, 1968, *73*, 49–61.

Moos, R. H. Sources of variance in responses to questionnaires and in behavior. *Journal of Abnormal Psychology*, 1969, *74*, 405–412.

Moos, R. H. Conceptualizations of human environments. *American Psychologist*, 1973, *28*, 652–665.

Moos, R. H. Systems for the assessment and classification of human environments. In R. H. Moos, & P. M. Insel (Eds.), *Issues in social ecology*. Palo Alto, Calif.: National Press Books, 1974.

Moos, R. H., & Insel, P. M. (Eds.), *Issues in social ecology*. Palo Alto, Calif.: National Press Books, 1974.

Morse, W. H., & Kelleher, R. T. Schedules using noxious stimuli I. Multiple fixed-ratio and fixed-interval termination of schedule complexes. *Journal of the Experimental Analysis of Behavior*, 1966, *9*, 267–290.

Mosher, L. R., Feinsilver, D., Katz, M. M., & Wienckowski, L. A. *Special report on schizophrenia*. Bethesda, Md.: U.S. Department of Health, Education, and Welfare, National Institute of Mental Health, April 1970.

Moss, H. A., & Kagan, J. The stability of achievement and recognition seeking behavior from childhood to adulthood. *Journal of Abnormal and Social Psychology*, 1961, *62*, 543–552.

Mowrer, O. H. *Learning theory and behavior*. New York: Wiley, 1960.

Mowrer, O. H., & Ullmann, A. D. Time as a determinant in integrative learning. *Psychological Review*, 1945, *52*, 61–90.

Mulaik, S. A. Are personality factors raters' conceptual factors? *Journal of Consulting Psychology*, 1964, *28*, 506–511.

Murray, E. J. Conflict and repression during sleep deprivation. *Journal of Abnormal and Social Psychology*, 1959, *59*, 95–101.

Murray, E. J., Auld, F., Jr., & White, A. M. A psychotherapy case showing progress but no decrease in the discomfort-relief quotient. *Journal of Consulting Psychology*, 1954, *18*, 349–353.

Murray, H. A. Foreword *An introduction to projective techniques*, H. H. Anderson & G. L. Anderson (Eds.), Englewood Cliffs, N.J.: Prentice-Hall, 1951, pp. XI-XIV.

Murray, H. A. (and collaborators). *Explorations in personality.* New York: Oxford, 1938.

Murray, J. Television and violence: Implications of the surgeon general's research program. *American Psychologist,* 1973, *28,* 472–478.

Murstein, B. I. *Theory and research in projective techniques.* New York: Wiley, 1963.

Mussen, P. H. Some antecedents and consequents of masculine sex-typing in adolescent boys. *Psychological Monographs,* 1961, *75,* No. 2 (Whole No. 506).

Mussen, P. H. Long-term consequents of masculinity of interests in adolescence. *Journal of Consulting Psychology,* 1962, *26,* 435–440.

Mussen, P. H., Conger, J. J., & Kagan, J. *Child development and personality.* New York: Harper & Row, 1974.

Mussen, P. H., & Distler, L. Masculinity, identification and father-son relationship. *Journal of Abnormal and Social Psychology,* 1959, *59,* 350–356.

Mussen, P. H., & Jones, M. C. Self-conceptions, motivations, and interpersonal attitudes of late- and early-maturing boys. *Child Development,* 1957, *28,* 243–256.

Mussen, P. H., & Jones, M. C. The behavior-inferred motivations of late-and early-maturing boys. *Child Development,* 1958, *29,* 61–67.

Mussen, P. H., & Naylor, H. K. The relationship between overt and fantasy aggression. *Journal of Abnormal and Social Psychology,* 1954, *49,* 235–240.


Neisser, U. *Cognitive psychology.* New York: Appleton, 1967.

Neisser, U. Review of "Visual information processing". *Science,* 1974, *183,* 402–403.

Norman, W. T. Development of self-report tests to measure personality factors identified from peer nominations. *USAF ASK Technical Note,* 1961, No. 61–44.

Norman, W. T. Toward an adequate taxonomy of personality attributes: Replicated factor structure in peer nomination personality ratings. *Journal of Abnormal and Social Psychology,* 1963, *66,* 574–583.

Norman, W. T. Convergent and discriminant validation of personality factor measurements. Unpublished manuscript, University of Michigan, 1966.

Norman, W. T. To see ourselves as others see us!: Relations among self-perceptions, peer-perceptions, and expected peer-perceptions of personality attributes. *Multivariate Behavioral Research,* 1969, *4,* 417–443.

Nunnally, J. C., & Lemond, L. C. Exploratory behavior and human development. In H. W. Reese (Ed.), *Advances in child development and behavior,* vol. 8. New York: Academic Press, 1973.


Office of Strategic Services Assessment Staff. *Assessment of men.* New York: Holt, Rinehart and Winston, 1948.

O'Leary, K. D., & Kent, R. N. Behavior modification for social action: Research tactics and problems. In L. Hamerlynck et al. (Eds.), *Critical issues in research and practice.* New York: Research Press, 1973.

Opler, M. K. Cultural induction of stress. In M. H. Appley & R. Trumbull (Eds.), *Psychological stress.* New York: Appleton, 1967, pp. 209-241.

Ornstein, R. E. *The psychology of consciousness.* San Francisco, Calif.: Freeman, 1972.

Ornstein, R. E., & Naranjo, C. *On the psychology of meditation.* New York: Viking, 1971.

Osgood, C. E., Suci, G. J., & Tannenbaum, P. H. *The measurement of meaning.* Urbana, Ill.: The University of Illinois Press, 1957.

Oskamp, S. Overconfidence in case-study judgments. *Journal of Consulting Psychology,* 1965, *29,* 261–265.

Overall, J. Note on the scientific status of factors. *Psychological Bulletin,* 1964, *61,* 270–276.

Palmer, R. D. Patterns of defensive response to threatening stimuli: Antecedents and consistency. *Journal of Abnormal Psychology*, 1968, *73*, 30–36.

Passini, F. T., & Norman, W. T. A universal conception of personality structure? *Journal of Personality and Social Psychology*, 1966, *4*, 44–49.

Pastore, N. The role of arbitrariness in the frustration-aggression hypothesis. *Journal of Abnormal and Social Psychology*, 1952, *47*, 728–731.

Patterson, G. R. Interventions for boys with conduct problems: Multiple settings, treatments, and criteria. *Journal of Consulting and Clinical Psychology*, 1974, *42*, 471–481.

Patterson, G. R., & Anderson, D. Peers as social reinforcers. *Child Development*, 1964, *35*, 951–960.

Patterson, G. R., & Cobb, J. A. Stimulus control for classes of noxious behaviors. In J. F. Knutson (Ed.), *The control of aggression: Implications from basic research*. Aldine, 1971.

Paul, G. L. *Insight vs. desensitization in psychotherapy*. Stanford: Stanford University, 1966.

Paul, G. L. Insight versus desensitization in psychotherapy two years after termination. *Journal of Consulting Psychology*, 1967, *31*, 333–348.

Paul, G. L., & Shannon, D. T. Treatment of anxiety through systematic desensitization in therapy groups. *Journal of Abnormal Psychology*, 1966, *71*, 124–135.

Payne, D. E., & Mussen, P. H. Parent-child relations and father identification among adolescent boys. *Journal of Abnormal and Social Psychology*, 1956, *52*, 358–362.

Payne, F. D., & Wiggins, J. S. MMPI profile types and the self-report of psychiatric patients. *Journal of Abnormal Psychology*, 1972, *79*, 1–8.

Pedersen, F. A. Consistency data on the role construct repertory test. Unpublished manuscript, Ohio State University, Columbus, 1958.

Perls, F. S. *Gestalt therapy verbatim*. Lafayette, Calif.: Real People Press, 1969.

Peterson, D. R. Scope and generality of verbally defined personality factors. *Psychological Review*, 1965, *72*, 48–59.

Peterson, D. R. *The clinical study of social behavior*. New York: Appleton, 1968.

Phares, E. J. *Locus of control: A personality determinant of behavior*. Morristown, N.J.: General Learning Press, 1973.

Phares, E. J., Ritchie, E. D., & Davis, W. L. Internal-external control and reaction to threat. *Journal of Personality and Social Psychology*, 1968, *10*, 402–405.

Phillips, J. S., & Kanfer, F. H. The viability and vicissitudes of behavior therapy. *International Psychiatry Clinics*, 1969, *6*, 75–131.

Phillips, L. Case-history data and prognosis in schizophrenia. *Journal of Nervous and Mental Diseases*, 1953, *117*, 515–525.

Phillips, L., & Rabinovitch, M. S. Social role and patterns of symptomatic behaviors. *Journal of Abnormal and Social Psychology*, 1958, *57*, 181–186.

Piaget, J. The general problems of the psychobiological development of the child. In J. M. Tanner & B. Inhelder (Eds.), *Discussions on child development: Proceedings of the World Health Organization study group on the psychobiological development of the child*, vol. IV. New York: International Universities Press, 1960, pp. 3–27.

Piaget, J. Piaget's theory. In P. H. Mussen (Ed.), *Carmichael's manual of child psychology*. New York: Wiley, 1970.

Postman, L., & Brown, D. R. The perceptual consequences of success and failure. *Journal of Abnormal and Social Psychology*, 1952, *47*, 213–221.

Premack, D. Reinforcement theory. In D. Levine (Ed.), *Nebraska symposium on motivation*. Lincoln: University of Nebraska Press, 1965, pp. 123–180.

Price, R. H. The taxonomic classification of behaviors and situations and the problem of behavior-environment congruence. *Human Relations*, 1974.

Price, R. H., & Bouffard, D. L. Behavioral appropriateness and situational constraint as dimensions of social behavior. *Journal of Personality and Social Psychology*, 1974, *30*, 579–586.

Proshansky, H., Ittelson, W., & Rivlin, L. G. (Eds.), *Environmental psychology*. New York: Holt, Rinehart and Winston, 1970.

Provence, S., & Lipton, R. *Infants in institutions*. New York: International Universities Press, 1962.

Rachman, S. Systematic desensitization. *Psychological Bulletin*, 1967, *67*, 93–103.

Rapaport, D. The autonomy of the ego. *Bulletin of the Menninger Clinic*, 1951, *15*, 113–123.

Rapaport, D. On the psychoanalytic theory of thinking. In M. M. Gill (Ed.), *The collected papers of David Rapaport*. New York: Basic Books, 1967.

Raush, H. L. Interaction sequences. *Journal of Personality and Social Psychology*, 1965, *2*, 487–499.

Raush, H. L., Barry, W. A., Hertel, R. K., & Swain, M. A. *Communication conflict and marriage*. San Francisco: Jossey-Bass, 1974.

Raymond, M. S. Case of fetishism treated by aversion therapy. *British Medical Journal*, 1956, *2*, 854–857.

Reece, M. M. The effect of shock on recognition thresholds. *Journal of Abnormal and Social Psychology*, 1954, *49*, 165–172.

Rekers, G. A., & Lovaas, O. I. Behavioral treatment of deviant sex-role behaviors in a male child. *Journal of Applied Behavior Analysis*, 1974, *7*, 173–190.

Renner, K. E. Conflict resolution and the process of temporal integration. *Psychological Reports*, 1964, *15*, 423–438. Monograph Supplement 15–2.

Renner, K. E. Temporal integration: An incentive approach to conflict resolution. In B. A. Maher (Ed.), *Progress in experimental personality research*, vol. 4. New York: Academic Press, 1967.

Reynolds, G. S. Contrast, generalization, and the process of discrimination. *Journal of the Experimental Analysis of Behavior*, 1961, *4*, 289–294.

Rheingold, H. L. The modification of social responsiveness in institutional babies. *Monographs of the Society for Research on Child Development*, 1956, *21*, No. 2 (Whole No. 63).

Rheingold, H. L., Gewirtz, J. L., & Ross, H. Social conditioning of vocalization in the infant. *Journal of Comparative and Physiological Psychology*, 1959, *52*, 68–73.

Rimm, D. C., & Masters, J. C. *Behavior therapy: Techniques and empirical findings*. New York: Academic Press, 1974.

Rogers, C. R. *Counseling and psychotherapy: Newer concepts in practice*. Boston: Houghton Mifflin, 1942.

Rogers, C. R. Some observations on the organization of personality. *American Psychologist*, 1947, *2*, 358–368.

Rogers, C. R. *Client-centered therapy: Its current practice, implications and theory*. Boston: Houghton Mifflin, 1951.

Rogers, C. R. Persons or science? A philosophical question. *American Psychologist*, 1955, *10*, 267–278.

Rogers, C. R. A theory of therapy, personality and interpersonal relationships, as developed in the client-centered framework. In S. Koch (Ed.), *Psychology: A study of a science*, vol. 3. New York: McGraw-Hill, 1959, pp. 184–256.

Rogers, C. R. The actualizing tendency in relation to "motives" and to consciousness. In M. R. Jones (Ed.), *Nebraska symposium on motivation.* Lincoln: University of Nebraska Press, 1963, pp. 1-24.

Rogers, C. R. *Carl Rogers on encounter groups.* New York: Harper & Row, 1970.

Rogers, C. R. In retrospect: Forty-six years. *American Psychologist,* 1974, *29,* 115–123.

Rogers, C. R., & Dymond, R. F. (Eds.), *Psychotherapy and personality change; co-ordinated studies in the client-centered approach.* Chicago: University of Chicago Press, 1954.

Rorer, L. G. The great response-style myth. *Psychological Bulletin,* 1965, *63,* 129–156.

Rosekrans, M. A. Imitation in children as a function of perceived similarity to a social model and vicarious reinforcement. *Journal of Personality and Social Psychology,* 1967, *7,* 307–315.

Rosen, A. C. Change in perceptual threshold as a protective function of the organism. *Journal of Personality,* 1954, *23,* 182–195.

Rosenberg, B. G., & Sutton-Smith, B. Family interaction effects on masculinity-femininity. *Journal of Personality and Social Psychology,* 1968, *8,* 117–120.

Rosenblith, J. F. Imitative color choices in kindergarten children. *Child Development,* 1961, *32,* 211–223.

Rosenhan, D. L. On being sane in insane places. *Science,* 1973, *179,* 250–258.

Rosenhan, D. L., Moore, B., & Underwood, B. The social psychology of moral behavior. In T. Lickona (Ed.), *Moral development and behavior: Theory, research, and social issues.* New York: Holt, Rinehart and Winston, 1976.

Rosenthal, D. *Genetics of psychopathology.* New York: McGraw-Hill, 1971.

Rosenzweig, M. R., Krech, D., & Bennett, E. L. A search for relations between brain chemistry and behavior. *Psychological Bulletin,* 1960, *57,* 476–492.

Rosenzweig, S. A trans-valuation of psychotherapy: A reply to Hans Eysenck. *Journal of Abnormal and Social Psychology,* 1954, *49,* 298–304.

Rosenzweig, S., & Mason, G. An experimental study of memory in relation to the theory of repression. *British Journal of Psychology,* 1934, *24,* 247–265.

Ross, D. Relationship between dependency, intentional learning, and incidental learning in preschool children. *Journal of Personality and Social Psychology,* 1966, *4,* 374–381.

Rothaus, P., & Worchel, P. Ego-support, communication, catharsis, and hostility. *Journal of Personality,* 1964, *32,* 296–312.

Rothbart, M. K., & Maccoby, E. E. Parents' differential reactions to sons and daughters. *Journal of Personality and Social Psychology,* 1966, *4,* 237–243.

Rotter, J. B. *Social learning and clinical psychology.* Englewood Cliffs, N.J.: Prentice-Hall, 1954.

Rotter, J. B. Generalized expectancies for internal versus external control of reinforcement. *Psychological Monographs,* 1966, *80* (Whole No. 609).

Rotter, J. B. Beliefs, social attitudes, and behavior: A social learning analysis. In J. B. Rotter, J. E. Chance, & E. J. Phares (Eds.), *Applications of a social learning theory of personality.* New York: Holt, Rinehart and Winston, 1972.

Rotter, J. B. Some problems and misconceptions related to the construct of internal versus external control of reinforcement. *Journal of Clinical and Consulting Psychology,* 1975, *43,* 56–67.

Rotter, J. B., Chance, J. E., & Phares, E. J. (Eds.). *Applications of a social learning theory of personality.* New York: Holt, Rinehart and Winston, 1972.

Royce, J. E. Does person or self imply dualism? *American Psychologist,* 1973, *28,* 833–866.

Rubin, I. The reduction of prejudice through laboratory training. *Journal of Applied Behavioral Science,* 3, 1967, 29–50.

Rubin, I. J. Analyzing Detroit's riot: The causes and responses. *The Reporter*, Feb. 22, 1968, 34–35.

Rubin, M., & Shontz, F. C. Diagnostic prototypes and diagnostic processes of clinical psychologists. *Journal of Consulting Psychology*, 1960, *24*, 234–239.

Ruebush, B. E. Anxiety. In H. A. Stevenson, et al. (Eds.), *Child psychology. The sixty-second yearbook of the National Society for the Study of Education.* Chicago: University of Chicago Press, 1963, pp. 460–516.


Sampson, E. E., & Hancock, T. An examination of the relationship between ordinal position, personality, and conformity: An extension, replication, and partial verification. *Journal of Personality and Social Psychology*, 1967, *5*, 398–407.

Sandifer, M. G., Jr., Pettus, C., & Quade, D. A study of psychiatric diagnosis. *Journal of Nervous and Mental Diseases*, 1964, *139*, 350–356.

Sarason, I. G. The effects of anxiety and threat on the solution of a difficult task. *Journal of Abnormal and Social Psychology*, 1961, *62*, 165–168.

Sarason, I. G. *Personality: An objective approach.* New York: Wiley, 1966.

Sarason, I. G. Birth order, test anxiety, and learning. *Journal of Personality*, 1969, *37*, 171–177.

Sarason, I. G., Smith, R. E., & Diener, E. Personality research: Components of variance attributable to the person and the situation. *Journal of Personality and Social Psychology*, 1975, *32*, 199–204.

Sarason, S. B., Davidson, K. S., Lighthall, F. F., Waite, R. R., & Ruebush, B. K. *Anxiety in elementary school children.* New York: Wiley, 1960.

Sartre, J. P. Existentialism. In W. Kaufmann (Ed.), *Existentialism from Dostoevsky to Sartre.* New York: Meridian, 1956, pp. 222–311.

Sartre, J. P. *Existentialism and humanism.* (tr. by Mairet.) London: Methuen, 1965.

Satir, V. *Conjoint family therapy.* Palo Alto, Calif.: Science and Behavior Books, 1967.

Savage, C., Savage, E., Fadiman, J., & Harman, W. LSD: Therapeutic effects of psychedelic experience. *Psychological Reports*, 1964, *14*, 111–120.

Schachter, S. The interaction of cognitive and physiological determinants of emotional state. In L. Berkowitz (Ed.), *Advances in experimental social psychology*, vol. 1. New York: Academic Press, 1964, pp. 49–80.

Schachter, S., & Singer, J. E. Cognitive, social and physiological determinants of emotional state. *Psychological Review*, 1962, *69*, 379–399.

Schaefer, E. S. A circumplex model for maternal behavior. *Journal of Abnormal and Social Psychology*, 1959, *59*, 226–235.

Schmidt, H. O., & Fonda, C. P. The reliability of psychiatric diagnosis: A new look. *Journal of Abnormal and Social Psychology*, 1956, *52*, 262–267.

Schneider, D. J. Implicit personality theory: A review. *Psychological Bulletin*, 1973, *73*, 294–309.

Schutz, W. C. *Joy: Expanding human awareness.* New York: Grove, 1967.

Schwartz, G. E. Biofeedback as therapy. *American Psychologist*, 1973, *28*, 666–673.

Scott, W. A., & Johnson, R. C. Comparative validities of direct and indirect personality tests. *Journal of Consulting and Clinical Psychology*, 1972, *38*, 301–318.

Sears, P. S. Child-rearing factors related to playing of sex-typed roles. *American Psychologist*, 1953, *8*, 431. (Abstract)

Sears, R. R. Functional abnormalities of memory with special reference to amnesia. *Psychological Bulletin*, 1936, *33*, 229–274.

Sears, R. R. Survey of objective studies of psychoanalytic concepts. *Social Science Research Council Bulletin*, 1943, No. 51.

Sears, R. R. Experimental analyses of psychoanalytic phenomena. In J. McV. Hunt (Ed.), *Personality and the behavior disorders*, vol. 1. New York: Ronald, 1944, pp. 306–332.

Sears, R. R. Identification as a form of behavior development. In P. B. Harris (Ed.), *The concept of development*. Minneapolis: University of Minnesota Press, 1957, pp. 149–161.

Sears, R. R. Dependency motivation. In M. R. Jones (Ed.), *Nebraska symposium on motivation*. Lincoln: University of Nebraska Press, 1963, pp. 25–64.

Sears, R. R. Development of gender role. In F. A. Beach (Ed.), *Sex and behavior*. New York: Wiley, 1965, pp. 133–163.

Sears, R. R. Relation of early socialization experiences to self-concepts and gender roles in middle childhood. *Child Development*, 1970, *41*, 267–289.

Sears, R. R., Maccoby, E. E., & Levin, H. *Patterns of child rearing*. New York: Harper & Row, 1957.

Sears, R. R., Rau, L., & Alpert, R. *Identification and child rearing*. Stanford: Stanford University Press, 1965.

Sears, R. R., Whiting, J., Nowlis, V., & Sears, P. Some child rearing antecedents of aggression and dependency in young children. *Genetic Psychology Monographs*, 1953, *47*, 135–234.

Sechrest, L., Gallimore, R., & Hersch, P. D. Feedback and accuracy of clinical prediction. *Journal of Consulting Psychology*, 1967, *31*, 1–11.

Seligman, M. E. P. *Helplessness—On depression, development, and death*. San Francisco: Freeman, 1975.

Sells, S. B. A multivariate model of personality. In J. R. Royce (Ed.), *Contributions of multivariate analysis and psychological theory*. New York: Academic Press, 1973.

Shaffer, H. R., & Emerson, P. E. The development of social attachment in infancy. *Monograph of The Society for Research in Child Development*, 1964, *29*, No. 3.

Sheldon, W. H. (with the collaboration of S. S. Stevens). *The varieties of temperament: A psychology of constitutional differences*. New York: Harper & Row, 1942.

Shure, G. H., & Rogers, M. S. Note of caution on the factor analysis of the MMPI. *Psychological Bulletin*, 1965, *63*, 14–18.

Sherwood, J. J. Self-report and projective measures of achievement and affiliation. *Journal of Consulting Psychology*, 1966, *30*, 329–337.

Shybut, J. Delay of gratification and severity of psychological disturbance among hospitalized psychiatric patients. *Journal of Consulting and Clinical Psychology*, 1968, *32*, 462–468.

Siegel, A. E., Stolz, L. M., Hitchcock, E. A., & Adamson, J. Children of working mothers and their controls. *Child Development*, 1959, *30*, 533–546.

Sines, L. K. The relative contribution of four kinds of data to accuracy in personality assessment. *Journal of Consulting Psychology*, 1959, *23*, 483–492.

Singer, J. L. Delayed gratification and ego development: Implications for clinical and experimental research. *Journal of Consulting Psychology*, 1955, *19*, 259–266.

Singer, J. L., & Antrobus, J. S. Dimensions of day-dreaming: A factor analysis of imaginal processes and personality scales. In P. Sheehan (Ed.), *The adaptive function of imagery*. New York: Academic Press, 1972.

Singer, J. L., & Singer, D. G. Personality. In P. Mussen and M. Rosenzweig (Eds.), *Annual Review of Psychology*, vol 23. Palo Alto, Calif.: Annual Reviews, Inc., 1972.

Skinner, B. F. *Science and human behavior*. New York: Macmillan, 1953.

Skinner, B. F. Behaviorism at fifty. In T. W. Wann (Ed.), *Behaviorism and phenomenology.* Chicago: University of Chicago Press, 1964, pp. 79–108.

Skinner, B. F. *About behaviorism.* New York: Knopf, 1974.

Skolnick, A. Motivational imagery and behavior over twenty years. *Journal of Consulting Psychology,* 1966, *30,* 463–478.

Smith, M. B. The phenomenological approach in personality theory: Some critical remarks. *Journal of Abnormal and Social Psychology,* 1950, *45,* 516–522.

Snyder, S. H., Banerjee, S. P., Yamomura, H. I., & Greenberg, D. Drugs, neurotransmitters, and schizophrenia. *Science,* 1974, *184,* 1243–1253.

Snygg, D., & Combs, C. W. *Individual behavior.* New York: Harper & Row, 1949.

Solomon, D. (Ed.) *LSD: The consciousness-expanding drug.* New York: Berkeley, 1967.

Soskin, W. F. Bias in postdiction from projective tests. *Journal of Abnormal and Social Psychology,* 1954, *49,* 69–74.

Soskin, W. F. Influence of four types of data on diagnostic conceptualization in psychological testing. *Journal of Abnormal and Social Psychology,* 1959, *58,* 69–78.

Spence, K. W., & Spence, J. T. Relation of eyelid conditioning to manifest anxiety, extraversion, and rigidity. *Journal of Abnormal and Social Psychology,* 1964, *68,* 144–149.

Spielberger, C. D. The effects of manifest anxiety on the academic achievement of college students. *Mental Hygiene,* 1962, *46,* 420–426.

Spielberger, C. D. The effects of anxiety on complex learning and academic achievement. In C. D. Spielberger (Ed.), *Anxiety and behavior.* New York: Academic Press, 1966, pp. 361–398.

Spielberger, C. D., & DeNike, L. D. Descriptive behaviorism versus cognitive theory in verbal operant conditioning. *Psychological Review,* 1966, *73,* 306–326.

Spivack, G., Levine, M., & Sprigle, H. Intelligence test performance and the delay function of the ego. *Journal of Consulting Psychology,* 1959, *23,* 428–431.

Star, S. A. Psychoneurotic symptoms in the Army. In S. Stouffer et al., *The American soldier.* (Vol. 2) *Combat and its aftermath.* Princeton: Princeton University Press, 1949, pp. 411–455.

Staub, E., Tursky, B., & Schwartz, G. E. Self-control and predictability: Their effects on reactions to aversive stimulation. *Journal of Personality and Social Psychology,* 1971, *18,* 157–162.

Stelmachers, Z. T., & McHugh, R. B. Contribution of stereotyped and individualized information to predictive accuracy. *Journal of Consulting Psychology,* 1964, *28,* 234–242.

Stephenson, W. *The study of behavior.* Chicago: University of Chicago Press, 1953.

Stevenson, H. W., Hale, G. A., Hill, K. T., & Moely, B. E. Determinants of children's preferences for adults. *Child Development,* 1967, *38,* 1–14.

Steuer, F. B., Applefield, J. M., & Smith, R. Televised aggression and the interpersonal aggression of preschool children. *Journal of Experimental Child Psychology,* 1971, *11,* 442–447.

Stone, L. J., & Hokanson, J. E. Arousal reduction via self-punitive behavior. *Journal of Personality and Social Psychology,* 1969, *12,* 72–79.

Stotland, E., Zander, A., & Natsoulas, T. The generalization of interpersonal similarity. *Journal of Abnormal and Social Psychology,* 1961, *62,* 250–256.

Stoyva, J., & Kamiya, J. Electro-physiological studies of dreaming as the prototype of a new strategy in the study of consciousness. *Psychological Review,* 1968, *75,* 192–205.

Stumphauzer, J. S. Increased delay of gratification in young prison inmates through imitation of high delay peer models, *Journal of Personality and Social Psychology*, 1972, *21*, 10–17.

Szasz, T. S. The myth of mental illness. *American Psychologist*, 1960, *15*, 113–118.

Taft, R. The ability to judge people. *Psychological Bulletin*, 1955, *52*, 1–28.

Tannenbaum, P. H., & Gaer, E. P. Mood change as a function of stress of protagonist and degree of identification in a film-viewing situation. *Journal of Personality and Social Psychology*, 1965, *2*, 612–616.

Tart, C. Increases in hypnotizability resulting from a prolonged program for enhancing personal growth. *Journal of Abnormal Psychology*, 1970, *75*, 260–266.

Taylor, J. A personality scale of manifest anxiety. *Journal of Abnormal and Social Psychology*, 1953, *48*, 285–290.

Taylor, S. P., & Epstein, S. Aggression as a function of the interaction of the sex of the aggressor and the sex of the victim. *Journal of Personality*, 1967, *35*, 474–486.

Terman, L. M., & Miles, C. C. *Sex and personality: Studies in masculinity and femininity.* New York: McGraw-Hill, 1936.

Thibaut, J., & Riecken, H. Authoritarianism, status, and the communication of aggression. *Human Relations.* 1955, *8*, 95–120.

Thoresen, C., & Mahoney, M. *Self-control.* New York: Holt, Rinehart and Winston, 1974.

Thornton, G. R. The effect of wearing glasses upon judgments of personality traits of persons seen briefly. *Journal of Applied Psychology*, 1944, *28*, 203–207.

Titus, H. E., & Hollander, E. P. The California F scale in psychological research: 1950–1955. *Psychological Bulletin*, 1957, *54*, 47–64.

Tompkins, V. H. Stress in aviation. In J. Hambling (Ed.), *The nature of stress disorder.* Springfield, Ill.: Charles C Thomas, 1959.

Touhey, J. Effects of additional women professionals on ratings of occupational prestige and desirability. *Journal of Personality and Social Psychology*, 1974, *29*, 86–89.

Truax, C. B., & Mitchell, K. M. Research on certain therapist interpersonal skills in relation to process and outcome. In A. E. Bergin & S. I. Garfield (Eds.), *Handbook of psychotherapy and behavior change.* New York: Wiley, 1971, pp. 299–344.

Tudor, T. G., & Holmes, D. S. Differential recall of successes and failures: Its relationship to defensiveness, achievement motivation, and anxiety. *Journal of Research in Personality*, 1973, *7*, 208–224.

Tupes, E. C., & Christal, R. E. Stability of personality trait rating factors obtained under diverse conditions. *USAF WADC Technical Note*, 1958, no. 58–61.

Tupes, E. C., & Christal, R. E. Recurrent personality factors based on trait ratings. *USAF ASD Technical Report*, 1961, no. 61–67.

Tyler, L. E. *The psychology of human differences.* New York: Appleton, 1956.

Ullmann, L. F., & Krasner, L. *A psychological approach to abnormal behavior.* Englewood Cliffs, N.J.: Prentice-Hall, 1969.

Ulrich, R. E., Stachnik, T. J., & Stainton, N. R. Student acceptance of generalized personality interpretations. *Psychological Reports*, 1963, *13*, 831–834.

Valins, S. Cognitive effects of false heart-rate feedback. *Journal of Personality and Social Psychology*, 1966, *4*, 400–408.

Vandenberg, S. G. What do we know today about the inheritance of intelligence and how do we know it? In R. Cancro (Ed.), *Intelligence: Genetic and environmental influences.* New York: Grune & Stratton, 1971, 182–218.

Vernon, P. E. *Personality assessment: A critical survey.* New York: Wiley, 1964.

Voegtlin, W. L., Lemere, F., Broz, W. R., & O'Hollaren, P. Conditioned reflex therapy of chronic alcoholism. IV. A preliminary report on the value of reinforcement. *Quarterly Journal of Studies on Alcohol,* 1942, 2, 505–511.

Wachtel, P. Psychodynamics, behavior therapy, and the implacable experimenter: An inquiry into the consistency of personality. *Journal of Abnormal Psychology,* 1973, 82, 323–334.

Wahler, R. G., Winkel, G. H., Peterson, R. F., & Morrison, D. C. Mothers as behavior therapists for their own children. *Behavior Research and Therapy,* 1965, 3, 113–124.

Wallace, J., & Sechrest, L. Frequency hypothesis and content analysis of projective techniques. *Journal of Consulting Psychology,* 1963, 27, 387–393.

Wallach, M. A. Commentary: Active-analytical vs. passive-global cognitive functioning. In S. Messick & J. Ross (Eds.), *Measurement in personality and cognition.* New York: Wiley, 1962, pp. 199–215.

Wallach, M. A., & Leggett, M. I. Testing the hypothesis that a person will be consistent: Stylistic consistency versus situational specificity in size of children's drawings. *Journal of Personality,* 1972, 40, 309–330.

Walters, R. H., & Parke, R. D. The influence of punishment and related disciplinary techniques on the social behavior of children: Theory and empirical findings. In B. A. Maher (Ed.), *Progress in experimental personality research,* vol. 4. New York: Academic Press, 1967, pp. 179–228.

Watson, D. L., & Tharp, R. G. *Self-directed behavior: Self-modification for personal adjustment.* Belmont Calif.: Wadsworth, 1972.

Watson, J. B. *Behaviorism.* New York: Norton, 1925.

Watson, J. B., & Rayner, R. Conditioned emotional reactions. *Journal of Experimental Psychology,* 1920, 3, 1–14.

Watson, R. I. Historical review of objective personality testing: The search for objectivity. In B. M. Bass & I. A. Berg (Eds.), *Objective approaches to personality assessment.* Princeton: Van Nostrand, 1959, pp. 1–23.

Weiner, B. Need achievement and the resumption of incompleted tasks. *Journal of Personality and Social Psychology,* 1965, 1, 165–168.

Weiner, B. Effects of motivation on the availability and retrieval of memory traces. *Psychological Bulletin,* 1966, 65, 24–37.

Weiner, B. Motivated forgetting and the study of repression. *Journal of Personality,* 1968, 36, 213–234.

Weiner, B. *Theories of motivation: From mechanism to cognition.* Chicago: Markham, 1972.

Weiner, B. *An attributional interpretation of expectancy value theory.* Paper presented at the AAAS Meetings, February 1974, San Francisco, Calif.

Weir, M. W. Children's behavior in a two-choice task as a function of patterned reinforcement following forced-choice trials. *Journal of Experimental Child Psychology,* 1965, 2, 85–91.

White, B. L. An experimental approach to the effects of experience on early human behavior. In J. P. Hill (Ed.), *Minnesota symposia on child psychology,* vol. 1. Minneapolis: University of Minnesota Press, 1967, pp. 201–226.

White, B. L., & Held, R. Plasticity of sensorimotor development in the human infant. In J. F. Rosenblith & W. Allinsmith (Eds.), *The causes of behavior II*. Boston: Allyn & Bacon, 1966, pp. 60–70.

White, R. W. *Lives in progress*. New York: Dryden, 1952.

White, R. W. Motivation reconsidered: The concept of competence. *Psychological Review*, 1959, *66*, 297–333.

White, R. W. *The abnormal personality*. New York: Ronald, 1964.

Whiting, J. W. M. Sorcery, sin, and the superego. A cross-cultural study of some mechanisms of social control. In M. R. Jones (Ed.), *Nebraska symposium on motivation*. Lincoln: University of Nebraska Press, 1959, pp. 174–195.

Whiting, J. W. M. Resource mediation and learning by identification. In I. Iscoe & H. W. Stevenson (Eds.), *Personality development in children*. Austin, University of Texas Press, 1960, pp. 112–126.

Whiting, J. W. M., & Child, I. L. *Child training and personality*. New Haven: Yale University Press, 1953.

Whiting, J. W. M., & Whiting, B. Personal communication on a current research project, 1962. Reported in Oetzel, R. Annotated bibliography in E. E. Maccoby (Ed.), *The development of sex differences*. Stanford: Stanford University Press, 1966.

Wicker, A. W. Attitudes vs. actions: The relationship of verbal and overt behavioral responses to attitude objects. *Journal of Social Issues*, 1969, *25*, 41–78.

Wiggins, J. S. *Personality and prediction: Principles of personality assessment*. Reading, Mass.: Addison-Wesley, 1973.

Winder, C. L., & Wiggins, J. S. Social reputation and social behavior: A further validation of the peer nomination inventory. *Journal of Abnormal and Social Psychology*, 1964, *68*, 681–685.

Winterbottom, M. R. The relation of need for achievement to learning experiences in independence and mastery. In J. W. Atkinson (Ed.), *Motives in fantasy, action, and society*. Princeton, N.J.: Van Nostrand, 1958, pp. 453–478.

Wishner, J. Reanalysis of "impressions of personality." *Psychological Review*, 1960, *67*, 96–112.

Wissler, C. The correlation of mental and physical tests. *Psychological Review Monograph Supplement*, 1901, *3*, No. 16.

Witkin, H. A. Psychological differentiation and forms of pathology. *Journal of Abnormal Psychology*, 1965, *70*, 317–336.

Witkin, H. A., Dyk, R. B., Faterson, H. F., Goodenough, D. R., & Karp, S. A. *Psychological differentiation*. New York: Wiley, 1962.

Wolf, R. The measurement of environments. In A. Anastasi (Ed.), *Testing problems in perspective*. Washington, D.C.: American Council on Education, 1966, pp. 491–503.

Wolf, T. M. Effects of live modeled sex-inappropriate play behavior in a naturalistic setting. *Developmental Psychology*, 1973, *9*, 120–124.

Wolff, P. Unpublished paper presented at the Tavistock Conference on Determinants of Infant Behavior, London, September, 1965. (Cited in Hamburg, D. A., & Lunde, D. T. Sex hormones in the development of sex differences in human behavior. In E. E. Maccoby (Ed.), *The development of sex differences*. Stanford: Stanford University Press, 1966, pp. 1–24.)

Wolpe, J. *Psychotherapy by reciprocal inhibition*. Stanford: Stanford University Press, 1958.

Wolpe, J. Behavior therapy in complex neurotic states. *British Journal of Psychiatry*, 1963, *110*, 28–34.

Wolpe, J., & Lang, P. J. A fear survey schedule for use in behavior therapy. *Behavior Research Therapy*, 1964, *2*, 27–30.

Wolpe, J., & Lazarus, A. A. *Behavior therapy techniques: A guide to the treatment of neuroses*. Oxford: Pergamon, 1966.

Wright, M. E. Constructiveness of play as affected by group organization and frustration. *Character and Personality*, 1942, *11*, 40–49.

Wright, M. E. The influence of frustration upon the social relations of young children. *Character and Personality*, 1943, *12*, 111–122.

Wyatt, D. F., & Campbell, D. T. On the liability of stereotype or hypothesis. *Journal of Abnormal and Social Psychology*, 1951, *46*, 495–500.

Wyer, R. S., Weatherley, D. A., & Terrell, G. Social role, aggression, and academic achievement. *Journal of Personality and Social Psychology*, 1965, *1*, 645–649.

Wynne, L. C., & Solomon, R. L. Traumatic avoidance learning: Acquisition and extinction in dogs deprived of normal peripheral autonomic functions. *Genetic Psychology Monographs*, 1955, *52*, 241–284.

Yarrow, L. J. Maternal deprivation: Toward an empirical and conceptual re-evaluation. *Psychological Bulletin*, 1961, *58*, 459–490.

Yerkes, R. M., & Dodson, J. D. The relation of strength of stimulus to rapidity of habit-formation. *Journal of Comparative Neurological Psychology*, 1908, *18*, 459–482.

Zeller, A. An experimental analogue of repression. I. Historical summary. *Psychological Bulletin*, 1950, *47*, 39–51. (a)

Zeller, A. An experimental analogue of repression. II. The effect of individual failure and success on memory measured by relearning. *Journal of Experimental Psychology*, 1950, *40*, 411–422. (b)

Zigler, E., & Phillips. L. Psychiatric diagnosis and symptomatology. *Journal of Abnormal and Social Psychology*, 1961, *63*, 69–75.

Zimbardo, P. The human choice: Individuation, reason, and order versus de-individuation, impulse, and chaos. In W. J. Arnold and D. Levine (Eds.), *Nebraska symposium on motivation*. Lincoln: University of Nebraska Press, 1969, pp. 237–307.

Zimmerman, B. J., & Rosenthal, T. L. Observational learning of rule-governed behavior by children. *Psychological Bulletin*, 1974, *81*, 29–42.

Ziv, A., Kruglanski, A. W., & Shulman, S. Children's psychological reactions to war-time stress. *Journal of Personality and Social Psychology*, 1974, *30*, 24–30.

Zubin, J., Eron, L. D., & Schumer, F. *An experimental approach to projective techniques*. New York: Wiley, 1965.

# Author Index

# Subject Index